SOUTHAMPTON ON
SHIPPING LAW

**Related titles:**

*Maritime Law*
6th edition
Christopher Hill
(2004)

*Laytime and Demurrage*
5th edition
John Schofield
(2005)

*General Average: Law and Practice*
2nd edition
Francis Rose
(2005)

*Dictionary of Shipping Terms*
5th edition
Peter Brodie
(2007)

*Liability Regimes in Contemporary Maritime Law*
D. Rhidian Thomas
(2007)

*Shipping Law Handbook*
4th edition
Michael Bundock
(2007)

*Voyage Charters*
3rd edition
Cooke et al
(2007)

*Legal Issues Relating to Time Charterparties*
D. Rhidian Thomas
(2008)

*Introduction to Marine Cargo Management*
Mark J. Rowbotham
(2008)

*Time Charters*
6th edition
Coghlin et al
(2008)

# Southampton on Shipping Law

INSTITUTE OF MARITIME LAW

informa
LONDON
2008

Informa Law
Mortimer House
37–41 Mortimer Street
London W1T 3JH
*law.enquiries@informa.com*

an Informa business

First published 2008



*British Library Cataloguing in Publication Data*
A catalogue record for this book
is available from the
British Library

ISBN 978-1-84311-755-1



Text set in 9.5/11.5pt Century Schoolbook by Tony Lansbury, Tonbridge, Kent
Printed in Great Britain by MPG Books, Bodmin, Cornwall
Printed on paper sourced from sustainable sources

# Preface

Shipping law has a long history at the University of Southampton. Optional subjects like Admiralty, Carriage of Goods by Sea, International Trade and Marine Insurance have been offered to undergraduate and graduate students for almost 40 years. The annual three-week Maritime Law Short Course grew out of those optional subjects into a highly regarded course attracting legal practitioners and members of the shipping industries to Southampton for the last 34 years. In 1982, our interests in shipping law led to the creation of the Institute of Maritime Law, which celebrated its 25th Anniversary last year with its Quartercentenary Donald O'May Lecture delivered in the City of London by The Rt. Hon. The Master of the Rolls, Sir Anthony Clarke.

The Institute now numbers no fewer than 13 shipping lawyers, comprising full-time members of the School of Law, Visiting Research Fellows and research assistants. The School's LLM, which offers 26 optional subjects across a wide range of interests, now attracts almost 100 graduate students annually from all around the world, a heavy proportion of whom choose to take one or more of the maritime law subjects. Many of our LLM graduates go on to practise maritime law within the legal professions or the shipping industry in the City or abroad. For its part, the Institute of Maritime Law now constitutes the largest concentration of maritime lawyers in any UK university.

With so many maritime lawyers under one roof, combining practical and academic experience, it is not surprising that we have been asked many times why we did not have our own text covering as wide a gamut as possible of the many areas which make up shipping law. *Southampton on Shipping Law* is the result.

Our purpose in this book was to produce a readable but authoritative work introducing the newcomer to the fascination of the subject which has kept us in, and attracted so many students to, Southampton. Maritime law is a subject which combines the intellectual challenge of the basic principles of contract, tort and property with the fundamentals of the shipping and commodity markets. It is also a subject which cuts across traditional boundaries of private and public law. We have been able to put together a team of 10 contributors to this volume, covering a wide area of what most people would class under the title "Shipping Law".

*Southampton on Shipping Law* is targeted explicitly at solicitors and barristers about to start their practice in maritime law; at claims handlers in P&I Clubs and commodity houses; at professionals in the shipping industry who want a broad but reliable introduction to the basic structure of the subject; and last (but not least, because so many of the former groups emerge from this one), at LLM students taking courses in the way English law regulates international shipping and maritime business.

The book went from design to production in a little over a year – a considerable feat, given the collaboration needed for a crew of 10 writers all of whom have many other academic and professional commitments. My first thanks as Director of the Institute must therefore rightly go to my co-contributors, all of whom have worked to very tight deadlines. I must also thank Vicky Ophield and Laura Brown of Informa Publishing, both of whom have had an infectious enthusiasm for this project. All of us as contributors owe a special debt of gratitude to Ainhoa Campas Velasco, an LLM graduate who returned to Southampton after some 10 years' legal practice in Spain. Ainhoa has provided invaluable research assistance for each contributor, encouraging us gently but firmly to avoid repetition, hesitation and deviation. My greatest personal word of thanks must, however, go to my colleague Professor Yvonne Baatz, who kindly and generously agreed to manage the project and who did so from start to finish with her customary tact and efficiency.

We all hope now that you, the reader, enjoy this book. We have written it to entice you to want to become a shipping lawyer, if you are completely new to the area; or to confirm your best instincts if you have recently become one. We very much hope that you do enjoy the book – and that it may, perhaps, provide an opportunity for contact with members of the School of Law and of the Institute of Maritime Law, here at Southampton.

The law is stated as at 1 May 2008.

CHARLES DEBATTISTA
*Professor of Commercial Law*
*Director of the Institute of Maritime Law*
*May 2008*

# Contents at a glance

*Preface by Professor Charles Debattista* ........ v
*About the authors* ........ xix
*Table of Cases* ........ xxi
*Table of Legislation, Conventions and Rules* ........ xxxix

CHAPTER 1: The Conflict of Laws ........ 1
*Professor Yvonne Baatz*

CHAPTER 2: Charterparties ........ 45
*Professor Yvonne Baatz*

CHAPTER 3: Cargo claims and Bills of Lading ........ 93
*Professor Charles Debattista*

CHAPTER 4: International Trade and Shipping Documents ........ 125
*Filippo Lorenzon*

CHAPTER 5: Carriage of Passengers ........ 147
*Richard Shaw*

CHAPTER 6: The Liabilities of the Vessel ........ 155
*Richard Shaw and Dr Michael Tsimplis*

CHAPTER 7: International Regulations for Ship Operators, their Verification and Enforcement ........ 227
*Richard Pilley and Filippo Lorenzon*

CHAPTER 8: Marine Pollution from Shipping Activities ........ 251
*Dr Michael Tsimplis*

CHAPTER 9: Public International Law Aspects of Shipping Regulation ........ 297
*Andrew Serdy*

CHAPTER 10: Marine Insurance ........ 327
*Professor Robert Merkin, Richard Shaw, Richard Pilley and Johanna Hjalmarsson*

CHAPTER 11: Procedures for Enforcement ........ 349
*Dr Michael Tsimplis*

CHAPTER 12: The Application of the EC Competition Rules to the Maritime Sector ........ 371
*Andrea Lista*

*Bibliography* ........ 399
*Index* ........ 403

# Detailed Table of Contents

*Preface by Professor Charles Debattista* ........ v
*About the authors* ........ xix
*Table of Cases* ........ xxi
*Table of Legislation, Conventions and Rules* ........ xxxix

CHAPTER 1: THE CONFLICT OF LAWS
*Professor Yvonne Baatz*

1. Introduction ........ 1
2. Arbitration ........ 3
3. Court jurisdiction ........ 4
   (a) The EC Jurisdiction Regulation ........ 5
      (i) A jurisdiction clause – Article 23 of the EC Jurisdiction Regulation 6
      (ii) Multiple proceedings ........ 8
      (iii) Related actions ........ 12
      (iv) No jurisdiction clause ........ 13
      (v) Contract claims – Article 5(1) ........ 14
      (vi) Tort claims – Article 5(3) ........ 16
      (vii) Agency – Article 5(5) ........ 19
      (viii) Remuneration for salvage of cargo or freight – Article 5(7) ........ 19
      (ix) Multiple defendants – Article 6(1) ........ 19
      (x) Third party proceedings – Article 6(2) ........ 20
      (xi) Limitation – Article 7 ........ 21
      (xii) Other international conventions ........ 21
   (b) Common law ........ 23
      (i) *Forum non conveniens* ........ 24
      (ii) Jurisdiction agreement ........ 25
      (iii) Tonnage limitation ........ 28
   (c) Anti-suit injunctions ........ 30
   (d) Damages for breach of a jurisdiction agreement ........ 31
4. Governing law ........ 32
   (a) The scope of the Rome Convention ........ 33
   (b) Freedom of choice ........ 35
   (c) Limits on party choice ........ 39
   (d) No choice ........ 41

CHAPTER 2: CHARTERPARTIES
*Professor Yvonne Baatz*

1. Introduction ........ 45

2. Shipbrokers ..... 46
3. The Hague, Hague-Visby and Hamburg Rules ..... 47
4. Seaworthiness ..... 51
5. Remedies for owner's breach ..... 55
6. Reasonable despatch ..... 59
7. Deviation ..... 60
8. Safe ports ..... 61
9. Frustration ..... 63
10. Timing at the beginning of the charterparty ..... 66
11. Time charterparties ..... 69
(a) For how long does the time charterer have the use of the ship? ..... 69
(i) Early redelivery ..... 70
(ii) Late redelivery ..... 71
(b) The charterer's obligation to pay hire ..... 73
(c) Withdrawal ..... 74
(d) Off hire ..... 76
(e) Deductions from hire ..... 77
12. Voyage charterparties ..... 78
(a) Freight ..... 79
(b) When does laytime start? ..... 80
(i) Arrived ship ..... 80
(ii) Notice of readiness ..... 82
(iii) Readiness ..... 83
(c) The calculation of laytime ..... 85
(d) The calculation of demurrage ..... 86
(e) The distinction between demurrage and damages for detention ..... 87
(f) Termination for non-payment ..... 87
13. Liens ..... 88
(a) On cargo ..... 88
(b) On sub-freight ..... 90

CHAPTER 3: CARGO CLAIMS AND BILLS OF LADING
*Professor Charles Debattista*

1. Cargo claims – the general picture ..... 93
2. The claimant's title to sue ..... 95
(a) Who cares about title to sue? ..... 95
(b) Where there is no doubt about title to sue ..... 96
(c) Where problems with title to sue arise ..... 97
The privity problem ..... 97
The Carriage of Goods by Sea Act 1992 ..... 98
(d) Where problems with title to sue are not solved by the 1992 Act ..... 102
The *Brandt v Liverpool* contract ..... 102
The party with title to sue claiming for the benefit of another ..... 103
The f.o.b. seller and title to sue ..... 103
3. The identity of the carrier ..... 104
(a) Is this a problem? ..... 104
(b) Where the claimant is a charterer ..... 105
(c) Where the claimant is not a charterer ..... 105
(d) Claiming against the "actual" carrier ..... 106
4. Do the Hague-Visby Rules apply? ..... 107

5. Proving the claimant's loss ..... 109
(a) Notice of loss at discharge ..... 109
(b) Where the shipper claims: a *prima facie* presumption ..... 109
(c) Where a third party claims: conclusive evidence ..... 110
(d) Why the estoppel is weaker than it seems ..... 111
(e) Clausing bills ..... 111
(f) "Weight and quantity unknown" clauses ..... 113
6. Proving the carrier's breach ..... 114
(a) Where are the terms of the contract of carriage? ..... 114
(i) The contract itself ..... 114
(ii) The bill of lading ..... 116
(iii) A charterparty ..... 116
(iv) A bill of lading incorporating charterparty terms ..... 117
(b) Breach of which term in the contract of carriage? ..... 118
7. Excluding or limiting the carrier's liability ..... 120
(a) The one year time-bar ..... 120
(b) Exceptions to liability ..... 121
(c) Quantification and limitation of loss ..... 121
(d) Breaking limitation ..... 122
8. The claimant's potential liability towards the carrier ..... 123

CHAPTER 4: INTERNATIONAL TRADE AND SHIPPING DOCUMENTS
*Filippo Lorenzon*

1. Introduction: shipping and international trade ..... 125
2. International commercial sales on shipment terms ..... 125
(a) The contract and its terms ..... 126
(b) C.i.f. and f.o.b. contracts and carriage arrangements ..... 127
(i) The risk of market fluctuations ..... 128
(ii) The parties to the contract of carriage ..... 128
3. The passing of risk and property in the goods ..... 129
(a) Risk passes on or as from shipment ..... 129
(b) The exceptions to the rule ..... 131
(i) Contractual exceptions ..... 131
(ii) Legal exceptions ..... 128
(c) Property passes when intended to pass ..... 132
4. Performance of the contract ..... 132
(a) The seller's physical duties ..... 133
(i) Shipping contractual goods ... ..... 133
(ii) ... as agreed in the sale contract ..... 135
(b) The seller's documentary duties ..... 137
(i) To the buyer under the sale contract in cash against documents transactions ..... 138
(ii) To the bank under the letter of credit ..... 139
5. Rejection: The buyer's remedy and the seller's right to cure ..... 143
(a) Rejection of goods and documents by the buyer ..... 144
(i) Documentary final evidence of physical performance ..... 144
(ii) Acceptance of documents evidencing a physical repudaitory breach 144
(b) Rejection of documents by the bank ..... 145
(c) The seller's right to cure a defective tender ..... 146

CHAPTER 5: CARRIAGE OF PASSENGERS
*Richard Shaw*

1. Introduction .......... 147
2. The Athens Convention 1974 relating to the Carriage of Passengers and their Luggage by Sea .......... 147
(a) Basis of liability .......... 148
(b) Limit of liability .......... 148
3. The 2002 Protocol to the Athens Convention .......... 148
4. Interaction between the Athens Convention amd the 1976 and 1996 Conventions on Limitation of Liability for Maritime Claims .......... 149
5. The real world .......... 150
6. Quantum of damages for death and injury .......... 150
7. Forum shopping .......... 151
8. The EU Package Travel Directive .......... 151

CHAPTER 6: THE LIABILITIES OF THE VESSEL
*Richard Shaw and Dr Michael Tsimplis*

1. Introduction .......... 155
2. Collisions .......... 155
(a) Introduction .......... 155
(b) Insurance interest concerned .......... 156
(c) Surveys .......... 156
(d) Security .......... 156
(e) Investigation of a collision .......... 157
(f) Independent evidence .......... 157
(g) Choice of jurisdiction .......... 157
(h) Principles of liability for collision .......... 158
(i) The 1910 Collision Convention .......... 158
(ii) The International Regulations for Preventing Collisions at Sea .......... 159
(iii) Claims by the owners of cargo damaged or delayed by collision .......... 159
(i) The "Innocent Cargo" Rule in the USA .......... 160
(j) Remoteness and causation .......... 160
(k) Collision litigation in the Admiralty Court .......... 160
3. Salvage .......... 161
(a) Introduction .......... 161
(b) The Salvage Convention .......... 163
(c) The salvage reward .......... 166
(d) Who can claim a salvage reward? .......... 168
(e) Financial security .......... 169
(f) Apportionment of the salvage reward .......... 170
(g) Time bar and limitation of liability .......... 170
(h) Salvage contracts under the Salvage Convention 1989 .......... 171
(i) Dismissal of salvors .......... 172
(j) The Lloyd's Open Form – "No Cure–No Pay" .......... 172
(k) Public law issues of salvage .......... 175
(l) The control of the salvage operation by the coastal State .......... 175
(m) Responder immunity .......... 176
4. Towage .......... 177
(a) Introduction .......... 177
(b) The contract of towage .......... 177

(c) Standard forms of towage ..... 179
(i) UK Standard Towing Conditions 1986 ..... 180
(ii) TOWHIRE 1985 ..... 182
(iii) TOWCON ..... 185
(d) Salvage and towage law ..... 185
(e) Towage and carriage of goods by sea ..... 188
(f) Collisions during the towage operation ..... 188
5. Wreck removal ..... 189
(a) Introduction ..... 189
(b) The Nairobi Wreck Removal Convention 2007 ..... 190
(c) Historic wrecks ..... 192
(d) International conventions ..... 193
6. Ports and harbours ..... 193
(a) Introduction ..... 193
(b) Port safety management ..... 193
(c) Limitation of liability ..... 194
(d) Claims by port authorities ..... 194
(e) Port State control ..... 194
(f) Places of refuge ..... 195
7. Pilotage ..... 196
(a) Introduction ..... 196
(b) Statutory provisions ..... 197
(c) Liability for the faults of ships under pilotage ..... 198
(i) Liability of the pilot ..... 198
(ii) Liability of the harbour authority ..... 198
(iii) Shipowner's vicarious liability ..... 200
8. Limitation of liability ..... 201
(a) Introduction ..... 201
(b) Who is entitled to limit liability ..... 202
(c) Can owners limit liability against each other? ..... 204
(d) Which ships are subject to limitation of liability? ..... 205
(e) Claims subject to limitation of liability ..... 206
(f) Claims excluded from limitation ..... 210
(g) When is the privilege to limited liability lost? ..... 211
(h) The limits of liability ..... 216
(i) Limits of liability for property damage ..... 216
(ii) Limits of liability for loss of life or personal injury ..... 216
(i) Multiplicity of defendants and counterclaims ..... 218
(j) Constitution of the limitation fund and priority of claims ..... 219
(k) Which claims are paid out of the limitation fund ..... 221
(l) Consequences of the constitution of the limitation fund ..... 222
(m) Limitation of liability without the constitution of the fund ..... 223
(n) Jurisdictional issues ..... 224

CHAPTER 7: INTERNATIONAL REGULATIONS FOR SHIP OPERATORS, THEIR VERIFICATION AND ENFORCEMENT
*Richard Pilley and Filippo Lorenzon*

1. Introduction ..... 227
2. The International Convention for the Safety of Life at Sea (SOLAS) 1974 ..... 227
3. The International Safety Management (ISM) Code ..... 228

(a) Certification, verification and control ........ 228
(b) The designated person ........ 229
(c) Impact on litigation ........ 229
(i) Disclosure of documents ........ 229
(ii) Cargo claims and unseaworthiness ........ 230
(iii) Limitation of liability ........ 230
(iv) Insurance cover ........ 231
(d) Criminal proceedings ........ 231
(e) Conclusion ........ 231
4. The IMO International Ship & Port Facility Security (ISPS) Code ........ 232
(a) Ship modifications (SOLAS amendments) ........ 232
(b) Some ISPS Code provisions ........ 232
(c) Continuous synopsis record ........ 233
(d) Ships entering port ........ 234
(e) Declaration of security ........ 234
(f) Control measures ........ 234
(g) Obligations of contracting governments ........ 235
(h) Requirements for ports ........ 235
(i) Commercial and insurance implications of ISPS ........ 235
(j) Summary and comments ........ 236
5. The International Convention on Standards of Training, Certification and Watch-Keeping as amended in 1995 (STCW95) ........ 236
(a) Responsibilities of shipowners ........ 237
Documentation ........ 237
Certification ........ 237
Manning ........ 238
Record-keeping ........ 238
Ship-specific familiarisation ........ 238
Crew coordination ........ 238
Minimum rest periods ........ 238
Basic safety familiarisation for all seafarers ........ 238
Basic safety training ........ 239
Responsibility ........ 239
(b) Flag administrations ........ 239
(c) Non-compliance and the legal consequences ........ 240
6. The Maritime Labour Convention 2006 ........ 240
(a) Entry into force ........ 241
(b) Fundamental rights and principles ........ 241
7. The European Maritime Safety Agency ........ 243
8. Classification societies and their liability under Directive 94/57/EC ........ 245

CHAPTER 8: MARINE POLLUTION FROM SHIPPING ACTIVITIES
*Dr Michael Tsimplis*

1. Introduction ........ 251
2. Ship standards in construction, operation and manning ........ 252
3. Liability for oil pollution from ships ........ 254
(a) Civil liability from oil pollution ........ 254
(b) The 1992 Civil Liability Convention ........ 255
(c) Imposition of liability ........ 257
(i) What types of vessel are covered? ........ 257

(ii) Who is liable? ..... 257
(iii) When liability may arise ..... 257
(iv) Exclusion of liability ..... 259
(v) Time bar ..... 259
(d) Limitation of liability ..... 260
(i) Application of the limitation regime ..... 260
(ii) Who may limit liability? ..... 261
(iii) What types of vessel may be subject to limitation ..... 261
(iv) The limitation amounts ..... 261
(e) When does the shipowner lose the right to limit liability ..... 262
(f) The shipowner's limitation fund ..... 262
(g) Jurisdictional issues ..... 263
(h) The role of the IOPC Fund ..... 264
(i) Liability for the IOPC Fund ..... 264
(ii) Time bar ..... 265
(iii) Limitation of liability for the IOPC Fund ..... 266
(iv) Jurisdiction for actions under the 1992 IOPC Fund Convention ..... 267
(i) The 2003 Supplementary Fund ..... 267
(j) STOPIA 2006 and TOPIA 2006 ..... 268
4. Bunker and lubricating oils: the 2001 Bunker Pollution Convention ..... 268
(a) The scope and definitions of the Convention ..... 269
(b) Liability for bunker oil pollution ..... 270
(c) Time bar ..... 271
(d) Limitation of liability ..... 271
(e) Direct action against the insurer ..... 272
(f) Jurisdiction and enforcements of judgments ..... 272
5. Other liabilities for oil pollution ..... 273
(a) Liability under section 154 of the 1995 Merchant Shipping Act ..... 273
(b) Oil pollution damage under EC Directive 2004/35 and other EC provisions ..... 275
(c) Non-persistent oils ..... 276
6. Liability for pollution from hazardous and noxious substances ..... 276
(a) Scope of application ..... 277
(b) Which ships are subject to the 1996 HNS? ..... 278
(c) Damages covered ..... 278
(d) Where does the 1996 HNS apply? ..... 279
(e) Who is liable ..... 280
(f) Type of liability imposed ..... 280
(g) Insurance issues ..... 280
(h) Limitation of liability ..... 280
(i) The applicable limits ..... 281
(ii) Conduct causing loss of the right to limit liability ..... 282
(iii) Establishment and distribution of the limitation fund ..... 283
(i) Time bars ..... 283
(j) Jurisdictional issues ..... 284
7. The 1996 HNS Fund ..... 285
(a) Time bar ..... 286
(b) Jurisdictional issues ..... 286
8. The obstacles to the ratification of the 1996 HNS ..... 287
(a) The HNS accounts ..... 287

(b) The definition of "receiver" .......... 288
(c) Reporting obligations .......... 288
(d) The draft Protocol to the 1996 HNS Convention .......... 289
9. Pollution from radioactive substances .......... 290
10. Liability arising from carriage of hazardous wastes .......... 291
(a) General legal framework .......... 291
(b) Carrier's liability .......... 292
(c) Scrapping of ships .......... 293
(d) The fate of old ships and pollution issues .......... 294

CHAPTER 9: PUBLIC INTERNATIONAL LAW ASPECTS OF SHIPPING REGULATION
*Andrew Serdy*

1. Introduction .......... 297
2. Sources of international law .......... 298
(a) "International custom, as evidence of a general practice accepted as law" .......... 299
(b) Treaties .......... 300
(c) General principles of law recognised by civilised nations .......... 301
(d) Judicial decisions and academic writings .......... 301
3. Maritime zones relevant to shipping .......... 301
(a) The two "traditional" maritime zones .......... 302
(b) New maritime zones in the modern law of the sea .......... 303
4. Coastal and flag State rights over shipping in the main maritime zones .......... 305
(a) Internal waters (including ports) .......... 305
(b) The territorial sea .......... 306
(c) The high seas and the nationality of ships .......... 308
(d) Exceptions to exclusivity of flag State jurisdiction on the high seas .......... 310
5. The IMO and its Conventions .......... 312
(a) Role of the IMO .......... 312
(b) Structure of the IMO .......... 314
(c) IMO Conventions as multilateral treaties .......... 317
(d) Becoming party to IMO Conventions – "final clauses" .......... 317
(e) IMO as the "competent international organization" in UNCLOS .......... 321
6. The UNCLOS Article 292 prompt release procedures .......... 323

CHAPTER 10: MARINE INSURANCE
*Professor Robert Merkin, Richard Shaw, Richard Pilley and Johanna Hjalmarsson*

1. Introduction .......... 327
2. Introduction to marine insurance law .......... 327
(a) Background .......... 327
(b) Policies within the 1906 Act .......... 327
(c) Formation of marine policies .......... 328
(d) Content of the policy .......... 330
(e) Marine insurance losses and claims .......... 331
3. Hull and machinery insurance .......... 332
4. Cargo insurance .......... 333
5. General average .......... 333
(a) What is general average? .......... 333
(b) Typical examples of general average sacrifices or expenditure .......... 334

(c) The York-Antwerp Rules ..... 334
(d) General average on an unseaworthy ship ..... 335
(e) How general average works ..... 335
(f) Recent developments ..... 336
1990 ..... 336
1994 ..... 336
2004 ..... 337
(g) The future? ..... 337
6. Protection and indemnity insurance: P&I Clubs ..... 337
(a) Introduction ..... 337
(b) The risks covered ..... 338
(c) Structure of the clubs ..... 338
(d) Conditions and exceptions ..... 339
(e) The International Group of P&I Clubs ..... 340
(f) The managers' agents: underwriting and claims handling; calls ..... 341
(g) Technical advice and support ..... 342
(h) "Pay to be paid" rule: direct action ..... 342
(i) Claims settlement: disputes ..... 343
(j) Freight, demurrage and defence cover ..... 343
(k) Conclusion ..... 343
7. Letters of undertaking ..... 344
(a) Purpose of a letter of undertaking ..... 344
(b) Construction of a letter of undertaking ..... 345
(c) The effect of a letter of undertaking ..... 346

CHAPTER 11: PROCEDURES FOR ENFORCEMENT
*Dr Michael Tsimplis*

1. Enforcement of maritime claims ..... 349
(a) Introduction ..... 349
(b) The Admiralty Jurisdiction of the High Court ..... 350
(c) Enforcement ..... 351
(i) Action *in rem* in respect of claims to the possession or ownership of a ship ..... 352
(ii) Action *in rem* arising from maritime liens ..... 352
(iii) Action *in rem* in respect of other claims ..... 353
(d) Procedure for claims *in rem* ..... 355
(e) Action *in rem* in respect of collisions ..... 356
(f) Arrest ..... 356
(i) Consequences of the arrest of the ship ..... 357
(ii) Release of the ship under arrest ..... 358
(iii) Judical sale ..... 358
(iv) Caution against arrest and caution against the release of the ship .. 358
(v) Damages for wrongful arrest ..... 358
(g) Priority of claims ..... 360
(h) Limitiation actions ..... 361
2. Maritime liens ..... 362
3. Freezing injunctions ..... 364
(a) When can the English courts issue a freezing injunction? ..... 365
(b) When will the English courts issues a freezing injunction? ..... 365
(c) Consequences of the freezing injunction on the defendant ..... 367

(d) Consequences of the freezing injunction on third parties ........ 368
(e) Worldwide freezing injunctions ........ 369
(f) Assets subject to the freezing injunction ........ 369

CHAPTER 12: THE APPLICATION OF THE EC COMPETITION RULES TO THE MARITIME SECTOR
*Andrea Lista*

1. The meaning of competition law – the general picture ........ 371
2. Article 81 of the Treaty and the control of collusive behaviours ........ 372
(a) The application of Article 81 EC to the shipping industry ........ 373
(b) The past regime: Regulation 4056/86 and the block exemption for liner conferences ........ 373
(c) The repeal of Regulation 4056/86 ........ 375
(d) The current scenario for liner conferences ........ 375
Possibility of individual exemption under Article 81(3) ........ 376
(e) Article 81 and the tramp shipping and cabotage sectors ........ 378
(f) General consequences in case of non-compliance with Article 81 EC ........ 379
3. Article 82 EC: Abuses of dominant position by one or more undertakings: meaning and issues ........ 380
(a) The application of Article 82 EC to the shipping sector ........ 381
The identification of the relevant geographic market in the maritime sector ........ 381
The identification of the relevant product market in the maritime sector ........ 382
The assessment of dominance in the maritime sector ........ 383
Examples of abuse of dominant position in the maritime industry ........ 384
Impact on trade between Member States ........ 386
4. State aid ........ 387
State aid and the shipping sector ........ 389
5. The EC Merger Regulation framework ........ 390
The application of the Merger Regulation to the shipping industry ........ 392
6. Concluding remarks ........ 394
(a) Compliance with Article 81 EC ........ 394
(b) Compliance with Article 82 EC ........ 396
(c) State aid ........ 397
(d) Merger Regulation of the shipping industry ........ 397

*Bibliography* ........ 399
*Index* ........ 403

# About the authors

PROFESSOR YVONNE BAATZ qualified as a solicitor in 1981. She practised with two leading firms of solicitors in the City of London, specialising in shipping litigation. Since 1991 she has been a lecturer in the School of Law at the University of Southampton and was made a professor in 2007.

PROFESSOR CHARLES DEBATTISTA is the director of the Institute of Maritime Law. He is also an active arbitrator in international commercial disputes and an associate member and arbitrator at Stone Chambers, London. He is a registered European lawyer with the Bar of England and Wales and a member of the Middle Temple. He is also a member of the Chartered Institute of Arbitrators, of GAFTA and of FOSFA, and a supporting member of the London Maritime Law Association. He is also vice chairman of the Commission for Commercial Law and Practice of the International Chamber of Commerce; he chaired the Drafting Group for Incoterms 2000 and was a member of the International Consulting Group for the UCP600.

JOHANNA HJALMARSSON (JUR KAND Stockholm 1995, LLM Soton 2004) joined the Institute of Maritime Law in 2004, having served as a junior judge in Sweden, a legal advisor with the UN in Vienna and a deputy head of unit with the Office of the High Representative in Bosnia and Herzegovina.

ANDREA LISTA (DOTT. GIUR. LLD (Italy), LLM (Soton)) has notably worked as legal advisor and company secretary to a multinational enterprise leading in underwater technology, and has been a consultant to the European Parliament. He is currently teaching European law and company law at University of Southampton and is a visiting lecturer in company law at Queen Mary College, University of London.

FILIPPO LORENZON (LLD (Italy), LLM (Soton), FCIL, Avvocato (Italy) and solicitor in England and Wales (n.p.)) is a lecturer in the School of Law at the University of Southampton and a member of the Institute of Maritime Law, a solicitor admitted in England and Wales and an advocate in Venice (Italy). Filippo has taught and consulted in the areas of international trade and maritime law, with particular emphasis on sale of commodities, chartering and cargo claims. He has also written extensively in the same areas.

ROB MERKIN is consultant to Barlow Lyde & Gilbert LLP. He is the author of a number of texts on insurance, reinsurance and arbitration law. His works have been cited in numerous decisions in England and in decisions in a number of jurisdictions overseas including the High Court of Australia and the US Supreme Court. Rob sits on the Presidential Council of AIDA (International Association of Insurance Law), is secretary to AIDA's Reinsurance Working Party, is a trustee of the British Insurance Law Association and acts as consultant to the English and Scottish Law Commissions for their review of insurance law.

CAPTAIN RICHARD PILLEY, after a career at sea, joined Thos Miller & Co, managers of the UK P&I Club, in 1982, where he became a claims syndicate manager and later set up the UK Club ship inspection programme. He is now a senior research fellow at the University of Southampton and is a Younger Brother of Trinity House.

ANDREW SERDY lectures at the School of Law in public international law and the international law of the sea, in which he previously practised from 1995 to 2005 for the Australian Government. Since 2004 he has also been a visiting fellow in the Faculty of Law at the University of Wollongong (NSW).

DR MICHAEL TSIMPLIS is a senior lecturer in law and ocean sciences, jointly appointed by the School of Law and the National Oceanography Centre. He is a contributing author to the fourth IPCC report and participates to the activities of various national and international scientific bodies.

# Table of Cases


A v B [2006] EWHC 2006 (Comm); [2007 1 Lloyd's Rep 237 .... 31, 35
A v B (No 2) [2007] EWHC 54 (Comm); [2007] 1 Lloyd's Rep 358 .... 32, 35
A Meredith Jones & Co Ltd v Vangemar Shipping Co Ltd (The Apostolis) (No 2) [1999] 2 Lloyd's Rep 292 .... 86
ABCI v Banque Franco Tunisienne [2003] [2003] 2 Lloyd's Rep 146 .... 18
Aboukir, The, [1905] 21 TLR 200 .... 178
Acrux, The, (No 2) [1962] 1 Lloyd's Rep 405 .... 358
Action Navigation Inc v Bottigliere di Navigatione SpA (The Kitsa) [2005] EWHC 177; [2005] 1 Lloyd's Rep 432; LMLN 660 .... 76
Actis Co Ltd v The Sanko Steamship Co Ltd (The Aquacharm) [1982] 1 Lloyd's Rep 7 .... 54, 76
Adamastos Shipping Co v Anglo-Saxon Petroleum Co (The Saxon Star) [1959] AC 133 .... 49, 50, 52
Adler v Dickinson and Another (The Himalaya) [1954] 2 Lloyd's Rep 267 (CA) .... 203
Aegean Sea, The, [1998] 2 Lloyd's Rep 39 .... 203, 205, 207, 208
Aegnoussiotis Shipping Corp v A/S Kristian Jebsens Rederi (The Aegnoussiotis) [1977] 1 Lloyd's Rep 268 .... 89
Affreteurs, Les, Réunis v Walford [1919] AC 801 .... 47
Afovos, The, [1983] 1 Lloyd's Rep 335 .... 75
Afromar Inc v Greek Atlantic Cod Fishing Co (The Penelope II) [1980] 2 Lloyd's Rep 17 .... 219
Agios Giorgis, The, [1976] 2 Lloyd's Rep 192 .... 89
Agios Lazaros, The, [1976] 2 Lloyd's Rep 47 .... 51
Agnew v Lansforsakringsbolagens AB [2000] 1 Lloyd's Rep 317 (HL); [1997] 4 All ER 937 (CA); [1996] 4 All ER 978 .... 15
AIC Ltd v Marine Pilot Ltd (The Archimidis) [2008] EWCA Civ 175 .... 62, 79
AIG Group (UK) Ltd v The Ethniki [2000] 1 Lloyd's Rep 343 .... 16
Akai Pty Ltd v People's Insurance Co [1998] 1 Lloyd's Rep 90 .... 26
Al Bida, The, [1987] 1 Lloyd's Rep 124 .... 78
Al Wahab, The, [1983] 2 Lloyd's Rep 365 .... 35
Albionic, The, (1942) 72 Ll L Rep 91 .... 168
Aldebaran Compania Maritima SA v Aussenhandel AG (The Darrah) [1977] AC 157 .... 82
Alegrete Shipping Co Inc v Int'l Oil Pollution Compensation Fund 1971 (The Sea Empress) [2003] 1 Lloyd's Rep 327 .... 258, 259
Aliakmon Maritime Corp v Transocean Continental Shipping Ltd and Frank Truman Export Ltd (The Aliakmon Progress) [1978] 2 Lloyd's Rep 499 .... 54
Ally, The, [1952] 2 Lloyd's Rep 427 .... 361
Alma Shipping Corp of Monrovia v Mantovani (The Dine) [1975] 1 Lloyd's Rep 115 (CA) .... 69
Almatrans SA v Steamship Mutual Underwriting Association [2007] 1 Lloyd's Rep 104 .... 345
Andrew Frederick Parker v CS Structured Credit Fund Ltd, Elegant Hotels Ltd [2003] EWHC 391 .... 364
Alpha, The, [1991] 2 Lloyd's Rep 515 .... 336
Alphapoint Shipping Ltd v Rotem Amfert Negev Ltd (The Agios Dimitrios) [2005] 1 Lloyd's Rep 23 .... 84
Aluflet SA v Vinave Empresa de Navegaçao Maritima LDA (The Faial) [2000] 1 Lloyd's Rep 473 .... 354
American Motorists Insurance Co v Cellstar Corp Welex [2003] EWCA Civ 206; [2003] Lloyd's Rep IR 295 (CA); EWHC 421 (Comm); [2002] 2 Lloyd's Rep 216 .... 42
Anderson & Ors v Int'l Oil Pollution Compensation Fund [2001] Scottish Court of Session 34 (14 Sept 2001) .... 263

Angelo Perotti v Kenneth Corbett and Others [2002] EWCA Civ 1993 (CA) .......................... 367
Anglo Northern Trading Co Ltd v Emlyn Jones & Williams [1917] 2 KB 78 .......................... 64
Anna H, The, [1995] 1 Lloyd's Rep 11 .......................... 22, 350, 355, 359
Antclizo, The, (No 2) [1992] 1 Lloyd's Rep 558 .......................... 84
Anton Durbeck GmbH v Den Norske Bank ASA (The Tropical Reefer) [2002] EWHC 1173; [2002] All ER (D) 67 .......................... 19
Antares, The, [1987] 1 Lloyd's Rep 424 .......................... 60, 61
Apollo, The, [1987] 1 Lloyd's Rep 200 .......................... 76
Arcos Ltd v EA Ronaasen & Son (1933) 45 Ll L Rep 33; [1933] AC 470 .......................... 135
Arena Corp Ltd v Peter Schroeder [2003] EWHC 108 .......................... 366
Aries, The, [1977] 1 Lloyd's Rep 334 .......................... 80
Aries v Total Transport [1977] 1 All ER 3998 .......................... 78
Arnhold Karberg & Co v Blythe, Green, Jourdain & Co [1916] 1 KB 495 (CA) .......................... 132
Arta, The, [1985] 1 Lloyd's Rep 534 .......................... 47, 55
Arta Shipping Co Ltd v Thai Europe Tapioca Shipping Service Ltd (The Johnny) [1977] 2 Lloyd's Rep 1 (CA) .......................... 69
Arthur Guinness Son & Co (Dublin) Ltd v Owners of the Motor Vessel Freshfield (The Lady Gwendolen) [1965] 1 Lloyd's Rep 335; [1965] P 294 (CA) .......................... 213
Assuranceforeningen Skuld v Int'l Oil Pollution Compensation Fund (No 1) [2000] SLT 1333 .......................... 263
Atlantic Container Line AB and Others v Commission, Joined Cases T-191/98 to 214/98; [2003] ECR II-3275 (TACA) .......................... 384
Atlantic Star, Owners of, v Owners of the Bona Spes (The Atlantic Star and The Bona Spes) [p1973] 2 Lloyd's Rep 197 (HL) .......................... 158
Atlas Shipping Agency (UK) Ltd v Suisse Atlantique Société D'Armement Maritime SA (The Gulf Grain and El Amaan) [1995] 2 Lloyd's Rep 188 .......................... 16

B & I Line plc v Sealink Harbours Ltd and Sealink Stena Ltd, Case IV/34.174; [1992] 5 CMLR 255 .......................... 382, 385
Babanaft Int'l Co SA v Avant Petroleum Inc (The Oltenia) [1982] 2 Lloyd's Rep 99 (CA); [1982] 1 Lloyd's Rep 448 .......................... 54, 87
Babanaft Int'l Co SA v Bassatne and another [1990] Ch 13; [1988] 2 Lloyd's Rep 435 ........ 223, 369, 370
Baghlaf Al Zafer Factory Co v Pakistan National Shipping Co [1998] 2 Lloyd's Rep 229 ........ 28
Baleares, The, [1993] 1 Lloyd's Rep 215 .......................... 68
Baltic Shipping Co v Owners of Cargo on the Mekhanik Evgrafov (The Mekhanik Egrafov and the Ivan Derbenev) [1988] 1 Lloyd's Rep 330; [1988] 1 FTLR 235; 1988 WL 622963 .... 226
Banco Nacional de Comercio Exterior SNC v Empresa de Telecommunicaciones de Cuba SA, British Telecommunications plc (intervening) [2007] 2 Lloyd's Rep 484 (CA) .......... 365, 367
Bank Line Ltd v Arthur Capel & Co [1919] AC 435 .......................... 64
Bank Mellat v Nikpour [1985] FSR 87 .......................... 365
Bank of Baroda v Vysya Bank Ltd [1994] 2 Lloyd's Rep 87 .......................... 42, 43, 139
Bank of Boston Connecticut (formerly Colonial Bank) v European Grain & Shipping Ltd (The Dominique) [1989] 1 Lloyd's Rep 431 (HL) .......................... 78, 80
Bank of China v NBM LLC and Others [2002] 1 Lloyd's Rep 1; [2002] 1 Lloyd's Rep 506 (CA) .... 369
Bank of Nova Scotia v Hellenic War Risks Assoc Ltd (Bermuda) Ltd, The Good Luck [1991] 3 All ER 1 .......................... 330
Bank of Tokyo-Mitsubishi Ltd c. Baskan Gida Sanayi Ve Pazarlama [1002] EWHC 945 (CH); [2004] 2 Lloyd's Rep 395 .......................... 9, 10
Bankers Trust International plc v RCS Editori SpA [1996] CLC 899 .......................... 39
Bankers Trust Int'l Ltd v Todd Shipyards Corp (The Halcyon Isle) [1980] 2 Lloyd's Rep 325; [1981] AC 221 .......................... 364
Banque de l'Indochine et de Suez SA v JH Rayner (Mincing Lane) [1983] 1 All ER 1137; [1983] 1 Lloyd's Rep 228 .......................... 145
Barclays Bank v Glasgow City Council [1994] 4 All ER 865 .......................... 15, 17
Barton v Golden Sun Holdings Ltd [2007] I L Pr 57 .......................... 21
Base Metal Trading v Shamurin [2002] CLC 322 .......................... 33
Bayoil SA v Seawind Tankers Corp (The Leonidas) [2001] 1 Lloyd's Rep 533 .................. 54, 126
Behn v Burness (1863) 3 B & S 751 .......................... 67
Benarty, The, [1984] 2 Lloyd's Rep 244 .......................... 28
Benatti v WPP Holdings Italy SRL [2007] EWCA Civ 263; [2007] I L Pr 33 .......................... 20

Bergen, The, [1997] 1 Lloyd's Rep 380 .......... 22
Bergen, The, (No 2) [1997] 2 Lloyd's Rep 710 .......... 25
Bergerco USA v Vegoil Ltd [1984] 1 Lloyd's Rep 440 .......... 138
Besix, Case C-256/00 [2002] ECR I-1699 .......... 16
Bier v Mines de Potasse d'Alsace, Case 21/76 [1976] ECR 1735 .......... 17
Bhatia Shipping v Alcobex [2004] EWHC 2323 (Com); [2005] 2 Lloyd's Rep 336 .......... 9, 39
Bisso v Inland Waterways [1955] AMC 899 .......... 179
Blitz, The, [1992] 2 Lloyd's Rep 441 .......... 360
Blue Nile Shipping Co Ltd and Another v Iguana Shipping and Finance Inc and Others (The Darfur) [2004] 2 Lloyd's Rep 469 .......... 207–208
Bocimar NV v Mira Oil Resources of Tortola (The Obo Venture) [1999] CLC 819; [1999] 2 Lloyd's Rep 101 .......... 87
Bold Buccleugh, The, (1851) 7 Moo PC 267 .......... 169, 352, 363
Bols Distilleries v Superior Yacht Services Ltd [2006] UKPC 45; [2000] WLR 12 .......... 7, 20
Borgship Tankers Inc v Product Transport Corp Ltd (The Casco) [2005] EWHC 273 (Comm); [2005] 1 Lloyd's Rep 565 .......... 54
Borvigilant, Owners of the, v Owners of the Romina G (The Borvigilant and Romina G) [2003] 2 Lloyd's Rep 520 .......... 180
Boss Group Ltd v Boss France SA [1996] 4 All ER 970 .......... 9
Bottigliere di Navigatione SpA v Cosco Qingado Ocean Shipping Co (The Bunga Saga Lima) [2005] EWHC 244; [2005] 2 Lloyd's Rep 1; LMLN 661 .......... 76
Boucher v Lawson (1734) Cas Temp Hardw. 85 .......... 201
Bouygues Offshore SA v Caspian Shipping Co [1998] 2 Lloyd's Rep 461 .......... 26, 29, 30
Bouygues Offshore SA v Caspian Shipping Co (No 3) [1997] 2 Lloyd's Rep 493; [1997] CLC 1443; 1997 WL 1102415 .......... 179
Bow Spring, Owners of, v Owners of the Manzanillo II (The Bow Spring and The Manzanillo II) [2005] 1 Lloyd's Rep 1 .......... 161
Bowbelle, The, [1990] 1 Lloyd's Rep 532 .......... 215
Bowes v Shand (1876–77) LR 2 App Cas 455 (HL) .......... 135
BP Exploration Operating Co Ltd v Chevron Shipping [2002] 1 Lloyd's Rep 77 .......... 194
BP Exploration v Hunt [1982] 1 All ER 925 .......... 66
Bramley Moore, The, [1964] P 200; [1964] 2 WLR 259; [1964] 1 All ER 105; [1963] 2 Lloyd's Rep 429; (1963) 107 SJ 980; 1963 WL 21234 .......... 188, 189
Brandt v Liverpool & River Plate Steam Navigation Co Ltd [1924] 1 KB 175; [1923] All ER Rep 656 .......... 24, 102–103
Breydon Merchant, The, [1992] 1 Lloyd's Rep 373 .......... 207, 210
Bridgestone Maru No 3 [1985] 2 Lloyd's Rep 62 .......... 76
Bristow Helicopters Ltd v Sikorsky Aircraft Corporation [2004] EWHC 401 (Comm); [2004] 2 Lloyd's Rep 150 .......... 9
British Airways v Commission, Case T-219/99; [2003] ECR II-5917 .......... 386
British Crane Hire Corp Ltd v Ipswich Plant Hire Ltd [1975] 1 QB 303 .......... 180
British Transport Docks Board v "Apollon" [1971] 1 Lloyd's Rep 476 .......... 181
British Transport Docks Board v Owners of the Proceeds of Sale of the Charger, Probe, Vigia, Dideki, Surveyor, Constellation, Errol and Regency (The Charger) (No 2) [1966] 1 Lloyd's Rep 670; [1966] 3 All ER 117 .......... 360
Brown Jenkinson & Co Ltd v Percy Dalton (London) Ltd [1957] 2 Lloyd's Rep 1 .......... 112
BS & N Ltd (BVI) v Micado Shipping Ltd (Malta) (The Seaflower) [2001] 1 Lloyd's Rep 341 .......... 57, 133
BTP Tioxide Ltd v Pioneer Shipping Ltd and Armada Marine SpA (The Nema) (No 2) [1981] 2 Lloyd's Rep 239 (HL) .......... 65
Buckman v Levi (1813) 3 Camp 414 .......... 139
Bunge Corp v Tradax Export SA [1981] 1 WLR 711; [1981] 2 Lloyd's Rep 1 .......... 57

C & CJ Northcote v The Owners of the Heinrich BJ RN (The Heinrich Bjorn) (1886) 11 App Cas 270 .......... 362
C v D [2007] EWHC 1541 (Comm); [2007] Civ 1282; [2008] 1 Lloyd's Rep 239; [2007] 2 All ER (Comm) 557 .......... 31, 32, 34
C Groom Ltd v Barber [1915] 1 KB 316 .......... 130
C Inc plc v Mrs L and Mr L [2001] 2 Lloyd's Rep 459; [2001] 151 NLJ 535 .......... 364
C Itoh & Co v Companhia de Navegaçao Lloyd Brasileiro (No 2) [1999] 1 Lloyd's Rep 115 .......... 346
C Sharpe & Co Ltd v Nosawa & Co [1917] 2 KB 814 .......... 139

Caledonia Subsea Ltd v Micoperi SRL [2003] SC 70 .......... 43
Caltex Singapore Pte Ltd v BP Shipping Ltd [1996] 1 Lloyd's Rep 286 .......... 24, 225
Camouco, The, (Panama v France), ITLOS Reports 2000, 10 .......... 324
Canada Trust Co v Stolzenberg & Co KG (No 2) [2002] 1 AC 1 .......... 20
Canmer International Inc v UK Mutual Steamship Assurance Association (Bermuda) Ltd [2005] 2 Lloyd's Rep 479 .......... 345
Carbonnade, Owners of the, v Owners of the Ruta (The Ruta) [2000] 1 WLR 2068; [2001] 1 All ER 450; [2000] 1 All ER (Comm) 847; [2000] 1 Lloyd's Rep 359; [2000] CLC 784; [2000] ICR 1024; (2000) 97 (12) LSG 39; (2000) 144 SJLB 135; The Times 21 March 2000; 2000 WL 191231 .......... 169, 359, 361
Cargill Int'l SA v CPN Tankers (Bermuda) Ltd (The Ot Sonja) [1993] 2 Lloyd's Rep 435 .......... 54
Carlson v Rio Tinto plc [1999] CLC 551 .......... 25
Caspian Basin Specialised Emergency Salvage Administration and Another v Bouygues Offshore SA and Others (The Caspian Basin) [1997] 2 Lloyd's Rep 507 .......... 207
Castle Insurance Co Ltd v Hong Kong Islands Shipping Co Ltd [1983] 2 Lloyd's Rep 376 .... 346
Castor, The .......... 176
Cathiship SA v Allanasons Ltd (The Catherine Helen) [1998] 2 Lloyd's Rep 511 .......... 87
Centrax Ltd v Citibank NA [1999] 1 All ER (Comm) 557 (CA) .......... 38
Centro Latino Americano de Commercio Exterior SA v Owners of the Ship "Kommunar" (The Kommunar) (No 2) [1997] 1 Lloyd's Rep 8 .......... 345, 359
Cero Navigation Corp v Jean Lion & Cie (The Solon) [2000] 1 Lloyd's Rep 292 .......... 85
Cerro Colorado, The, [1993] 1 Lloyd's Rep 58 .......... 358
Ceval Alimentos SA v Agrimpex Trading Co Ltd (The Northern Progress) (No 2) [1996] 2 Lloyd's Rep 319 .......... 126, 137
Channel Tunnel Group Ltd v Balfour Beatty Construction Ltd [1993] 1 Lloyd's Rep 291; [1993] AC 334 (HL) .......... 365
Charles Robert Leader and Henrietta Ada Leader v George F Duffey and Amyatt Edmond Ray (1888) LR 13 App Cas 293 (HL) .......... 126
Charlotte v Theory and Others (The Charlotte) (1921) 9 Ll L Rep 341 .......... 213
Cheikh Boutros Selim El-Khoury and others v Ceylon Shipping Lines Ltd (The Madeleine) [1967] 2 Lloyd's Rep 224 .......... 68
Chikuma, The, [1981] 1 Lloyd's Rep 371 .......... 74
China Offshore Oil (Singapore) Int'l Pte Ltd v Giant Shipping Ltd (The Posidon) [2001] 1 Lloyd's Rep 697 .......... 79
Citi-March Ltd v Neptune Orient Lines Ltd [1996] 2 All ER 545; [1997] 1 Lloyd's Rep 72 .... 26, 27
Clan Colquhoun, The, [1936] 54 Ll L Rep 221 .......... 179
Clark (Inspector of Taxes) v Perks [2001] EWCA Civ 1228 .......... 205
Clea Shipping Corp v Bulk Oil Int'l Ltd (The Alaskan Trader) [1983] 1 Lloyd's Rep 315 .......... 59
CMA CGM SA v Classica Shippng Co Ltd (The CMA Djakarta) [2003] 2 Lloyd's Rep 50; [2004] 1 Lloyd's Rep 460 .......... 203, 205, 207, 208
Cobelfret NV v Cyclades Shipping Co Ltd (The Linardos) [1994] 1 Lloyd's Rep 28 .......... 84–85
Collins v Lamport (1864) 4 De G J & Sim 500; 46 ER 1012 .......... 203
Color Drack GmbH v Lexx International Vertribs GmbH, Case C-386/05; [2007] I L Pr 35 .... 5, 16
Comandate Marine Corp v Pan Australia Pty Ltd (The Comandate) [2006] FCAFC 192; [2008] 1 Lloyd's Rep 119 .......... 351
Commissioners of Customs & Excise v Barclays Bank plc [2004] EWHC 122; [2005] 1 Lloyd's Rep 1659 (CA) .......... 368
Commune de Mesquer v Total France SA and Total Int'l Ltd, Case C-188/07 .......... 276
Compagnie D'Armement Maritime SA v Compagnie Tunisienne de Navigation SAE [1971] AC 572 .......... 35
Compagnie Maritime Belge Transport and Others v Commission, Joined Cases T-24/93 to T26/93 and T-28/93; [1996] ECR II-12-1 (CEWAL I) .......... 384
Compania de Naviera Nedelka v Tradex Int'l (The Tres Flores) [1973] 2 Lloyd's Rep 247 .... 83, 84
Compania Maritima San Basilio SA v Oceanus Mutual Underwriting Ass (Bermuda) Ltd (The Eurysthenes) [1976] 2 Lloyd's Rep 171 (CA) .......... 339
Compania Sud Americana De Vapores v Shipmair BV (The Teno) [1977] 2 Lloyd's Rep 289 .... 78
Connolly v RTZ Corp plc [1997] CLC 1357 .......... 25

Continental Pacific Shipping Ltd v Deemand Shipping Co Ltd (The Lendoudis Evangelos II) [1997] 1 Lloyd's Rep 404 .......... 69
Cooperative Centrale Raiffeisen-Boernenleenbank BA v Sumitomo Bank (The Royan, The Abukirk, The Bretagne, The Auvergne) [1988] 2 Lloyd's Rep 250 (CA) .......... 145
Coreck Maritime GmbH v Handelsveem BV, Case 387/98; [2000] ECR I-09337 .......... 7, 8
Corsica Ferries Italia Srl v Corpo dei Piloti del Porto de Genova, Case C-18/93; [1994] ECR I-1783 .......... 384
Court Line v Cant & Russell (1939) 44 Com Cas 345 .......... 76
Credit Agricole Indosuez v Generale Bank and Seco Steel Trading Inc and Considar Inc (No 2) [2000] 1 Lloyd's Rep 123 .......... 145
Crédit Lyonnais v New Hampshire Insurance Co [1997] 2 Lloyd's Rep 1 .......... 42, 43
Crédit Suisse Fides Trust v Cuoghi [1998] QB 818 (CA) .......... 367
Cretanor Maritime Co Ltd v Irish Marine Management Ltd ( The Cretan Harmony) [1978] 1 Lloyd's Rep 425 .......... 223, 364
Curtis v Wild [1991] 4 All ER 172 .......... 205

Dadourian Group Int Inc & Others v Paul Francis Simms and Others [2005] 2 All ER 651 .......... 369
Daewoo Heavy Industries Ltd v Klipriver Shipping Ltd (The Kapitan Petko Voivoda) [2003] EWCA Civ 451; [2003] 2 Lloyd's Rep 1 .......... 61
Dairy Containers Ltd v Tasman Orient Line CV (The Tasman Discoverer) [2004] UKPC 22; [2004] 2 Lloyd's Rep 647 .......... 51
Daval Acier d'Usinor et de Sacilor v Armare Srl (The Nerano) [1996] 1 Lloyd's Rep 1 .......... 4, 37, 49
David Agmashenebeli, Owners of cargo lately laden on board the, v Owners of the David Agmashenebeli (The David Agmashenebeli [2003] 1 Lloyd's Rep 92 .......... 113
Davies Contractors Ltd v Fareham Urban District Council [1956] AC 696 .......... 64, 65
Definitely Maybe (Touring) Ltd v Marek Lieberberg Konzertagentur GmbH [2001] 2 All ER (Comm) 1 .......... 43
Deforche (Société) v Tomacrau (Société) [2007] I L Pr 25 .......... 20
Deichland, The, [1989] 2 All ER 1066 .......... 22
Delos, The, [2001] 1 Lloyd's Rep 703 .......... 4
Denise, The, Unreported, 3 December 2004 .......... 224
Derby & Co and Others v Weldon and Others (Nos 3 and 4) [1990] Ch 65 (CA) .......... 223, 364, 369
Devonshire, Owners of the SS, v Owners of the Barge Leslie and Others (The Devonshire) [1912] AC 634 (HL) .......... 188
Dias Compania Naviera SA v Louis Dreyfus [1978] 1 All ER 724 .......... 86
Dictator, The, [1892] P 304 .......... 352
Domicrest Ltd v Swiss Bank Corp [1998] 3 All ER 578 .......... 16, 17, 18
Donald Johnson and Others v John Alexander Black (The Two Ellens) (1871–73) LR 4 PC 161; 17 ER 361 .......... 360
Donoghue v Stevenson [1932] AC 562 .......... 155
Donohue v Armco Inc [2001] UKHL 64; [2002] 1 Lloyd's Rep 425 .......... 25, 26, 30, 31
Dornoch Ltd v The Mauritius Union Assurance Co Ltd [2006] EWCA Civ 389; [2006] 2 Lloyd's Rep 475 .......... 42
Douglas v Ownrs of Yacht St George (The St George) (1926) 25 Ll L Rep 482 .......... 352
Dresser UK v Falcongate Ltd [1992] 1 QB 502 .......... 8
Dresser UK v Falcongate Freight Management Ltd (The Duke of Yare) [1992] 2 All ER 450 .... 9, 10
Druot Assurances SA v Consolidated Metallurgical Industries [1998] All ER (EC) 483 .......... 12

Ease Faith Ltd v Leonis Marine Management Ltd, Cloudfree Ship Management Ltd [2006] 1 Lloyd's Rep 673 .......... 179, 183, 184, 185
Edinburgh Castle [1999] 2 Lloyd's Rep 362 .......... 354
Edwinton Commercial Corp v Tsavliris Russ (Worldwide Salvage & Towage) Ltd (The Sea Angel) [2007] EWCA Civ 547; [2007] 2 Lloyd's Rep 517 .......... 64
Effort Shipping Co Ltd v Linden Management SA (The Giannis NK) [1998] AC 605; [1998] 1 Lloyd's Rep 337 .......... 209
Eglantine, Credo and Inez [1990] 2 Lloyd's Rep 390 .......... 160
Egon Oldendorff v Libera Corp [1996] 1 Lloyd's Rep 380 .......... 36, 37
El Amria, The, [1981] 2 Lloyd's Rep 119 .......... 25

Eleftheria, The, [1970] P 94 .... 25
Ellis Shipping Corp v Voest Alpine Intertrading (The Lefthero) [1992] 2 Lloyd's Rep 109 .... 82, 86
Elof Hansson v Hamel and Horley [1922] 2 AC 36; (1922) 10 Lloyd's Rep 507 .... 137
Ennstone Building Products Ltd v Stanger Ltd [2002] EWCA Civ 916; [2002] 2 All ER (Comm) 479 .... 43
Enrico Furst & Co v WE Fischer Ltd [1960] 2 Lloyd's Rep 340 .... 140
Environment Agency v Milford Haven Port Authority (The Sea Empress) [2000] JPL 943 .... 194, 200
Epsilon Rosa, The, [2003] EWCA Civ 938; [2003] 2 Lloyd's Rep 509 .... 4
Equitable Trust Co of New York v Dawson Partners Ltd (1926) 25 Ll L Rep 90 .... 141
Erich Gasser GmbH v MISAT Srl, Case C-116/02; [2003] ECR I-14693; [2005] QB 1 .... 10, 25, 30
Eridania SpA v Rudolf A Oetker (The Fjord Wind) [2000] 2 Lloyd's Rep 191; [1999] 1 Lloyd's Rep 207 .... 53, 65
Erika, The .... 260
Erkowit, Owners of cargo laden on board the MV, v Owners of the Eschersheim (The Eschersheim, The Jade and the Erkowit) [1976] 1 WLR 1 All ER 920; [1976] 2 Lloyd's Rep 1 (1976) 120 SJ 315; 1976 WL 46782 (HL) .... 352
Esso Petroleulm Co Ltd v Hall Russell & Co Ltd (The Esso Bernicia) [1989] AC 643; [1989] 1 Lloyd's Rep 8 .... 199, 204
Ets A de Bloos SPRL v Société en Commandite par actions Bouyer, Case 14/76; [1996] ECR 1497 .... 16
Europeanballage Corp and Continental Can Co Inc v Commission, Case 6/72; [1973] 215 .... 380
Ever Success, Crew members of the, v Owners of the Ever Success (The Ever Success) [1999] 1 Lloyd's Rep 824; 1998 WL 1045100 .... 363
Evergos Naftiki Eteria v Cargill plc (The Voltaz) [1997] 1 Lloyd's Rep 35 .... 87
Evpo Agnic, The, [1988] 2 Lloyd's Rep 411 (CA) .... 355

Fanti, The, and Padre Island [1989] 1 Lloyd's Rep 239 .... 190
Feasey v Sun Alliance Life Assurance Corp [2003] Lloyd's Rep IR 640 .... 328
Federal Commerce and Navigation Ltd v Molena Alpha Inc (The Nanfri, Benfri and Lorfri) [1978] 2 Lloyd's Rep 132 .... 78
Fercometal Sarl v MSC Mediterranean Shipping Co SA (The Simmona) [1988] 2 All ER 742; [1988] 2 Lloyd's Rep 199 (HL) .... 68
Ferguson Shipbuilders v Voith Hydro GmbH and Co KG [2000] SLT 229 .... 43
Festival Holdings Ltd v The Demise Charterers of the Ship Ocean Glory 1 (The Ocean Glory 1) [2002] 1 Lloyd's Rep 679; 2001 WL 1560842 .... 361
Fibrosa v Fairbairn [1943 AC 32 .... 66
Ficom SA v Sociedad Cadex Ltda [1980] 2 Lloyd's Rep 118 .... 140
Finagra (UK) Ltd v OT Africa Line Ltd [1998] 2 Lloyd's Rep 622 .... 51
Fiona Trust & Holding Corp v Privalov [2008] 1 Lloyd's Rep 254 .... 34
Firma C-Trade SA Respondents v Newcastle Protection and Indemnity Association (The Fanti) [1990] 3 WLR 78; [1990] 2 Lloyd's Rep 191 (HL) .... 204, 342
Fjord Wind, The, [2000] 2 Lloyd's Rep 191; [1999] 1 Lloyd's Rep 207 .... 53, 65
FKI Engineering Ltd v Dewind Holdings Ltd [2008] EWCA Civ 316 .... 20
Fonderie Officine Meccaniche Tacconi SpA v Heinrich Wagner Sinto Maschinenfabrik GmbH, Case C-334/00; [2002] ECR I-7357 .... 15
Fort Kipp, The, [1985] 2 Lloyd's Rep 168 .... 90
Fraser & White Ltd v Vernon [1951] 2 Lloyd's Rep 175 .... 178
Freccia del Nord, The, [1989] 1 Lloyd's Rep 388 .... 9
Freeport plc v Olle Arnoldsson Case C-98/06 [2007] WLR (D) 252 .... 20

Galaxia Mineralimportexport (The Eleftherios) [1982] 1 WLR 539; [1982] 1 Lloyd's Rep 351 .... 368
Galaxy Energy Int'l Ltd and Corona Trading Associates SA v Assuranceforeningen Skuld (Ejensidie) (The Oakwell) [1999] 1 Lloyd's Rep 249 .... 346, 354
Galaxy Energy Int'l Ltd v Novorossiysk Shipping Co (The Petr Schmidt) [1998] 2 Lloyd's Rep 1 .... 83
Gan Insurance Co Ltd v Tai Ping Insurance Co Ltd [1999] CLC 1270 .... 37, 43
Gangway Ltd v Caledonian Park Investments (Jersey) Ltd [2001] 2 Lloyd's Rep 715 .... 364, 368
Gantner Electronic GmbH v Basch Exploitatie Maatshcappij BV, Case C-111/01; [2003] ECR I-4207 .... 9

Garden City, The, (No 1) [1982] 2 Lloyd's Rep 382 .......... 213
Gatoil International Inc v Arkwright-Boston Manufacturers Mutual Insurance Co and Others (The Sandrina) [1985] 1 Lloyd's Rep 181 (HL) .......... 354
Gatoil Int'l Inc v Tradox Petroleum Ltd (The Rio Sun) [1985] 1 Lloyd's Rep 350 .......... 131, 137
Gaupen, The (1925) 22 Ll L Rep 57 .......... 361
Genie, The, [1979] 2 Lloyd's Rep 184 .......... 223
Georgian Maritime Corp plc v Sealand Industries (Bermuda) Ltd (The North Sea) [1999] 1 Lloyd's Rep 21 .......... 68
GIE Groupe Concorde v The Master of the vessel Suhadiwarno Panjan, Case C-440/97; [1999] CLC 1976 .......... 16
Gill & Duffus SA v Berger & Co Inc [1984] AC 382; [1984] 1 Lloyd's Rep 227 (HL) .......... 144
Gill & Others v Flighwise Travel Service Ltd & Another [2003] EWHC 3082 .......... 366
Glenaffaric, The, (1948–49) 81 Ll L Rep; [1949] 1 All ER 245 .......... 181
Glencore Grain Ltd v Flacker Shipping Ltd (The Happy Day) [2002] 2 Lloyd's Rep 487 .......... 79, 82, 84
Glencore Grain Rotterdam v Lebanese Organisation for Int'l Commerce (The Lorico) [1997] 4 All ER 514; [1997] 2 Lloyd's Rep 386 (CA) .......... 140
Global Marine Drilling v Triton Holdings (The Sovereign Explorer) (No 2) [2001] 1 Lloyd's Rep 60 .......... 358
Global Mariner, Owners of, v Owners of the Atlantic Crusader (The Global Mariner and Atlantic Crusader) [2005] 1 Lloyd's Rep 699 .......... 160
Glynn v Margetson [1893] AC 351 .......... 60
Golden Fleece Maritime Inc v ST Shipping & Transport Inc (The Ellie and the Frixos) [2007] EWHC 1890 (Comm); [2008] 1 Lloyd's Rep 262 .......... 53
Golden Light, The, [1861] Lush 355 .......... 178
Golden Strait Corp v Nippon Yusen Kubishka Kaisha (The Golden Victory) [2007] UKHL 12; [2007] 2 Lloyd's Rep 164 .......... 70
Goldman v Thai Airways Int'l Ltd [1983] 1 WLR 1186 (CA .......... 214, 215
Goshawk Dedicated Ltd v Roo Inc [2006] EWHC 1730; [2006] Lloyd's Rep IR 711 .......... 30
Goulandris Bros Ltd v B Goldman and Sons Ltd [1957] 2 Lloyd's Rep 207 .......... 54
Grand Prince, The (Belize v France), ITLOS Reports 2001, 17 .......... 325
Gray and Another v The Braer Corporation and Others and Int'l Oil Pollution Compensation Fund [1999] 2 Lloyd's Rep 541 .......... 259
Greenmar Navigation v Owners of Ships Bazias 3 and Bazias 4 and Sally Line (The Bazias 3 and The Bazias 4) [1993] QB 673; [1993] 2 All ER 964; [1993] 1 Lloyd's Rep 101 .......... 355
Gregos, The, [1995] 1 Lloyd's Rep 1 .......... 71–72
Grimaldi Compagnia di Navigazione Spa v Sekihyo Lines Ltd (The Seki Rolette) [1998] 2 Lloyd's Rep 638 .......... 50, 54
Groupement D'Intérêt Economique (GIE) Réunion Européenne v Zurich España, Case C-77/04 [2005] I L Pr 456 .......... 21
Gubisch Mashinenfabrik KG v Giulio Palumbo, Case 144/86; [1987] ECR 4861 .......... 9
Gunter and Others v Beaton and Others [1993] 2 Lloyd's Rep 369 .......... 214

Hain Steamship Co Ltd v Tate & Lyle Ltd [1936] 2 All ER 597 .......... 60
Halki Shipping Corp v Sopex Oils Ltd [1998] 1 Lloyd's Rep 465 .......... 4
Hamtun, Owners of the, v Owners of the St John (The Hamtun and the St John) [1999] 1 Lloyd's Rep 883 .......... 164
Happy Day, The, [2002] 2 Lloyd's Rep 487 .......... 79, 82, 84
Happy Fellow, The, [1998] 1 Lloyd's Rep 13 (CA); [1997] 1 Lloyd's Rep 130 .......... 10, 12–13, 225
Happy Ranger, The, [2002] 2 Lloyd's Rep 357 .......... 40, 50, 51
Harlow, The, (1922) 10 Ll L Rep 311 .......... 218
Hedley Byrne v Heller [1964] AC 465 .......... 56
Heidberg, The, [1994] 2 Lloyd's Rep 287 .......... 31
Hellenic Dolphin, The, [1978] 2 Lloyd's 336 .......... 53
Hellenic Steel Co v Svolamar Shipping Co Ltd (The Komninos S) [1991] 1 Lloyd's Rep 370 .......... 23, 35, 40
Henderson v Henderson (1843) 3 Hare 100 .......... 226
Henderson v Merrett [1994] 3 All ER 506 .......... 46
Herceg Novi, Owners of, v Owners of the Ming Galaxy (The Herceg Novi and the Ming Galaxy) [1998] 2 Lloyd's Rep 454 .......... 2, 24, 29, 225

HIB Ltd v Guardian Insurance Co Inc [1997] 1 Lloyd's Rep 412 .............................................. 43
HIH Casualty and General Insurance Ltd v Chase Manhattan Bank [2003] 2 Lloyd's Rep 61; [2003] Lloyd's Rep IR 230 .............................................. 56, 329
Homburg Houtimport BV v Agrosin Private Ltd (The Starsin) [2003] 1 Lloyd's Rep 571 ...... 106
Hong Kong Fir Shipping Co Ltd v Kawasaki Kisen Kaisha Ltd [1962] 2 QB 26; [1961] 2 Lloyd's Rep 478 .............................................. 51, 57–59, 77
Horn Linie GmbH & Co v Panamericana Formas E Impresos SA, Ace Seguros SA (The Hornbay) [2006] EWHC 373 (Comm); [2006] 2 Lloyd's Rep 44 .............................................. 27, 30, 31, 38
Houda, The, [1994] 2 Lloyd's Rep 541 .............................................. 76
Howard Marine & Dredging Co Ltd v Ogden & Sons (Excavations) Ltd [1978] QB 574 .... 54, 56
Hyundai Merchant Marine Co Ltd v Furness Withy (Australia) Pty (The Doric Pride) [2006] EWCA Civ 599; [2006] 2 Lloyd's Rep 175 .............................................. 77
Hyundai Merchant Marine Co Ltd v Gesuri Chartering Co Ltd (The Peonia) [1991] 1 Lloyd's Rep 100 .............................................. 72–73
Hyundai Merchant Marine Co Ltd v Karander Maritime Inc (The Niizuru) [1996] 2 Lloyd's Rep 66 .............................................. 67

ICI v Commission, Case C-48/69 [1972] ECR 619 .............................................. 385
ICL Shipping Ltd, Steamship Mutual Underwriting Association (Bermuda) Ltd v Chin Tai Stele Enterprise Co Ltd and Others (The ICL Vikraman) [2004] 1 Lloyd's Rep 21 .......... 219, 224
Indian Oil Corp v Vanol Inc [1991] 2 Lloyd's Rep 634 .............................................. 126
Independent Petroleum Group v Seacarriers (The Count) [2006] EWHC 3173 ...................... 61
Industrie Chemiche Italia Centrale SpA v Alexander G Tsavliris & Sons Maritime Co (The Choko Star) [1996] 1 WLR 774; [1996] 1 All ER 1214; [1995] 2 Lloyd's Rep 608; [1995] CLC 1461; The Times, 8 Aug 1995; The Independent, 4 Sept 1995 (CS); 1995 WL 1081833 .... 171
Industrie Chemiche Italia Centrale SpA v Nea Ninemia Shipping Co SA (The Emmanuel C) [1983] 1 Lloyd's Rep 310 .............................................. 54
Ingmar GB Ltd v Eaton Leonard Technologies Inc [1999] ECC 49 (CA) .............................. 39
Interbulk Ltd v Ponte dei Sospiri Shipping Co (The Standard Ardour) [1988] 2 Lloyd's Rep 159 .............................................. 54
International Association of Independent Tanker Owners and Others, Case C-308/06 (ECJ) .............................................. 254
International Bulk Carriers (Beirut) SARL v Evlogia Shipping Co SA, and Marathon Shipping Co Ltd (The Mihalios Xilas) [1978] 2 Lloyd's Rep 186 .............................................. 74, 90
International Transportation Service Inc v Owners and/or Demise Charterers of the Ship Convenience Container [2006] 2 Lloyd's Rep 556 .............................................. 354
Internationale Nederlanden Aviation Lease BV v The Civil Aviation Authority [1997] CLC 43 .............................................. 9
Investors Compensation Scheme v West Bromwich Building Society [1998] 1 All ER 98 ...... 345
Ira, The, [1995] 1 Lloyd's Rep 103 .............................................. 76
Iran Continental Shelf Oil Co v IRI International Corp [2002] EWCA Civ 1024; [2004] 2 CLC 696 .............................................. 42, 43
Irina Zharkikh, The, and The Ksenia Zharkikh [2001] 2 Lloyd's Rep 319; 2001 WL 949854 .... 370
Irish Continental Group plc v Chambre de Commerce et Industries de Morlaix [1995] 4 CMLR 177 .............................................. 381
Isabelle, The, [1984] 1 Lloyd's Rep 366 (CA); [1982] 2 Lloyd's Rep 81 .............................. 81
ISS Machinery Services Ltd v Aeolian Shipping SA (The Aeolian) [2001] 2 Lloyd's Rep 641 .... 43
Itex Itagrani Export SA v Care Shipping Corp (The Cebu) (No 2) [1990] 2 Lloyd's Rep 316 .... 90

James Finlay & Co Ltd v Kwik Hoo Tong Handel Maatschappij [1929] 1 KB 500; (1928) 32 Ll L Rep 245 .............................................. 143
JI MacWilliam Co Inc v Mediterranean Shipping Co SA (The Rafaela S) [2005] UKHL 11; [2005] 1 Lloyd's Rep 347 .............................................. 49, 108
Jindal Iron & Steel Ltd v Islamic Solidarity Shipping Co (The Jordan II) [2004] UKHL 49; [2005] 1 Lloyd's Rep 57 .............................................. 60, 120, 137
Jogoo, The, [1981] 1 Lloyd's Rep 513 .............................................. 355
Johanna Oldendorff, The, [1973] 2 Lloyd's Rep 285 .............................................. 81
Johnson v Agnew [1980] AC 369 .............................................. 59
Johnson Control Systems Ltd v Techi-Track Europa Ltd (In Administrative Receivership) [2003] EWCA Civ 1126 (CA) .............................................. 368

JP Morgan Europe Ltd v Primacom AG [2005] EWHC 508; [2008] 2 Lloyd's Rep 665 ........ 9, 10
Julia, The, [1861] Lush 224 .......... 178
Juno Trader, The, (St Vincent and the Grenadines v Guinea-Bissau), ITLOS Reports 204, 17 .......... 325
Juntha Rajprueck, The, [2003] 2 Lloyd's Rep 107 .......... 344

K/S Arnt J Moerland v Kuwait Petroleum Corp (The Fjordaas) [1988] 1 Lloyd's Rep 336 ........ 81
K/S Merc-Skandia XXXXII v Lloyd's Underwriters, The Mercandian Continent [2001] Lloyd's Rep IR 802 .......... 329
K/S Penta Shipping A/S v Ethiopian Shipping Lines Corp (The Saga Cob) [1992] 2 Lloyd's Rep 545 .......... 62
Kalfelis v Bankhaus Schroder, Munchmeyer, Hengst & Co, Case 189/97; [1988] ECR 5565 ...... 14, 16, 17, 20
Kallang Shipping SA v Axa Assurance Senegal (The Kallang) [2006] EWHC 2825; [2007] 1 Lloyd's Rep 160 .......... 31
Kastner v Jason [2005] 1 Lloyd's Rep 397 .......... 364, 365
Keighley Maxted & Co and Bryan Durant & Co, Re, [1893] 1 QB 405; (1894) 7 Asp MLC 418 .......... 135, 139
Kenburn Waste Management Ltd v Bergmann [2002] EWCA Civ 98; [2002] CLC 644 .......... 43
Ketchum Int'l plc v Groupo Public Relations [1997] 1 WLR 4 .......... 223, 366
KH Enterprise, Owners of cargo lately laden on board the, v Owners of the Pioneer Container (The Pioneer Container, The KH Enterprise) [1994] 1 Lloyd's Rep 593; [1994] 2 AC 324 (PC) .......... 107, 188
Khian Sea, The, [1979 1 Lloyd's Rep 545 .......... 62
Kish v Taylor [1912] AC 604 .......... 60
Kissavos Shipping Co SA v Empresa Cubana de Fletes (The Agathon) [1982] 2 Lloyd's Rep 211 (CA) .......... 64
Kleinwort Benson Ltd v Glasgow City Council [1998] 4 All ER 641 (HL); [1996] 2 All ER 257 (CA) .......... 15
Kodros Shipping Corp v Empresa Cubana de Fletes (The Evia) (No 2) [1982] 2 Lloyd's Rep 307 .......... 62, 64
Kolden Holdings Ltd v Rochette Commerce Ltd [2008] EWCA Civ 10; [2008] 1 L Pr 20 .......... 12
Kominos S, The, [1991] 1 Lloyd's Rep 370 .......... 23, 35, 40
Kongress Agentur Hagen GmbH v Zeehaghe BV, Case C-365/88 [1990] ECR I-1845 .......... 21
Konkola Copper Mines plc v Coromin [2006] EWCA Civ 5; [2006] 1 Lloyd's Rep 410 .......... 26
Kriti Akti, The, [2004] EWCA Civ 116; [2004] 1 Lloyd's Rep 712 .......... 59, 70, 73, 77
Kwei Tek Chao & Others v British Traders and Shippers Ltd [1954] 2 QB 459; [1954] 1 Lloyd's Rep 16 .......... 132, 143, 144
Kyrgyz Mobil v Fellowes International [2005] EWHC 1314 (Comm) .......... 32

Laconia, The, [1977] 1 Lloyd's Rep 315 .......... 74
Laconian Confidence, The, [1997] 1 Lloyd's Rep 139 .......... 76
Landcatch Ltd v International Oil Pollution Compensation Fund [1999] 2 Lloyd's Rep 316 .... 255, 257, 258, 259
Las Mercedes (Owners of) v Owners of the Abidin Daver (The Abidin Daver) [1984] 1 Lloyd's Rep 339 (HL) .......... 158
Lauritzen Reefers v Ocean Reef Transport Ltd SA (The Bukhta Russkaya) [1997] 2 Lloyd's Rep 744 .......... 51
Leathertex Divisione Sintetici SpA, Case C-420/97; [1999] CLC 1983 .......... 16
Lee and Another v Airtours Holidays Ltd and Another [2004] 1 Lloyd's Rep 683 .......... 152–153
Leeds Shipping Co v Société Française Bunge (The Eastern City) [1958] 2 Lloyd's Rep 127 ....61
Lefthero, The, [1992] 2 Lloyd's Rep 109 .......... 82, 86
Leigh & Sullivan Ltd v Aliakmon Shipping Co Ltd (The Aliakmon) [1986] AC 785; [1986] 2 Lloyd's Rep 1 (HL) .......... 132
Lennard's Carrying Co Ltd v Asiatic Petroleum Co Ltd [1915] AC 705 (HL) .......... 211, 213, 262
Leoborg, The, (No 2) [1964] 1 Lloyd's Rep 380 .......... 360, 363
Leon Blum, The, [1915] P 90; [1915] P 290 (CA) .......... 187
Leon Corp v Atlantic Lines and Navigation Co Inc (The Leon) [1985] 2 Lloyd's Rep 470 ........ 78
Leyland Shipping v Norwich Union Fire Insurance Society [1918] AC 350 .......... 330
Li Hai, The, [2005] EWHC 735; [2005] 2 Lloyd's Rep 389 .......... 75, 78
Linea Nsaviera Paramaconi SA v Abnormal Load Engineering Ltd [2001] 1 Lloyd's Rep 763 ...... 54

Lister v Stubbs (1890) 45 ChD 1 ........ 349, 364–365
Lloyd Instruments Ltd v Northern Star Insurance Co Ltd, The Miss Jay Jay [1987] 1 Lloyd's Rep 32 ........ 330
London Helicopters Ltd v Heliportugal LDA-INAC [2006] EWHC 108 ........ 18
Lubbe v Cape plc [2000] 1 Lloyd's Rep 139 ........ 25
Lucullite, Owners of the, v Owners of the R Mackay (The Lucullite) (1929) 33 Ll L Rep 186 ........ 218
Lukoil-Kaliningradmorneft plc v Tata Ltd and Global Marine Inc [1999] 1 Lloyd's Rep 356; [1999] 2 Lloyd's Rep 129 (CA) ........ 180, 184, 188
Lutetian, The, [1982] 2 Lloyd's Rep 140 ........ 78
Lyric Shipping Inc v Intermetals Ltd (The Al Taha) [2990] 2 Lloyd's Rep 117 ........ 60
Lyrma, The, (No 2) [1978] 2 Lloyd's Rep 30 ........ 361

M Godoletz & Co Inc v Czarnikow-Rionda Co Inc (The Galatia) [1980] 1 Lloyd's Rep 453 (CA) .... 112, 137, 139
M'Bundis v Waratah Towage LMLN [1992 343 ........ 182
Maas Logistics (UK) Ltd v CDR Trucking BV [1999] 2 Lloyd's Rep 179 ........ 9
MC Pearl, The, [1997] 1 Lloyd's Rep 566 ........ 26
Maciej Rataj, The, Case C 406/92; [1994] ECR I-5439; [1995] 1 Lloyd's Rep 302 ........ 9, 12, 22, 273, 285, 287, 351
Maersk Olie & Gas A/S v Firma M de Haan en W de Boer, Case C-39/02; [2004] ECR I-9657; [2005] 1 Lloyd's Rep 210 ........ 9, 10, 225
Maersk/PONL, Case Compo/M.3829 ........ 393
Maersk/Safmarine, Case IV/M.1474 ........ 393
Maersk/Sea-land, Case IV/M.165 ........ 393
Mainschiffahrts-Genossenschaft eG v Les Gravieres Rhenanes (MSG), Case C-106/95; [1997] All ER (EC) 385 ........ 7, 15, 16
Manbre Saccharine Co Ltd v Corn Products Co Ltd [1919] 1 KB 198 ........ 130
Manifest Shipping Co Ltd v Uni-Polaris Insurance Co Ltd (The Star Sea) [1995] 1 Lloyd's Rep 651 ........ 52, 329
Maratha Envoy, The, [1977] 2 Lloyd's Rep 301 ........ 81
Marc Rich & Co AG and Others v Bishop Rock Marine Co Ltd and Nippon Kaiji Kyokai (The Nicholas H) [1996] AC 211; [1995] 2 Lloyd's Rep 299 (HL) ........ 204, 248
Marc Rich & Co AG v Societa Italiana PA (The Atlantic Emperor), Case C-190/89; [1993] 1 Lloyd's Rep 342 ........ 31
Marconi v PT Pan Indonesia Bank Ltd TBK [2004] 1 Lloyd's Rep 594 ........ 38
Maréchal Suchet, The [1911] P 1 ........ 178
Maredelanto Compania Naviera SA v Bergbau-Handel GmbH (The Mihalis Angelos) [1970] 2 Lloyd's Rep 43 ........ 67, 68
Mareva Compania Naviera SA v International Bulkcarriers SA (The Mareva) [1975] 2 Lloyd's Rep 509 (CA) ........ 349, 364
Mareva Navigation Co v Canaria Armadora SA (The Mareva AS) [1977] 1 Lloyd's Rep 368 .... 69
Margaronis Navigation Agency Ltd v Henry W Peabody & Co of London Ltd [1965] 2 QB 430 ........ 85
Margolle and Another v Delta Maritime Co Ltd and Others (The Saint Jacques II and Gudermes) (CA) [2002] EWHC 2452; [2003] 1 All ER (Comm) 102; [2003] 1 Lloyd's Rep 203; [2002] WL 31599631 (QB) (Admlty) ........ 215
Maria, The, (1869) 1 W Rob 95 ........ 199, 200
Maridive VII, Maridive XIII, Maridive 85 and Maridive 94, owners of, v Owners and Demise Charterers of the Key Singapore [2004] EWHC 2227; [2005] 1 All ER (Comm) 99; [2005] 1 Lloyd's Rep 91; 2004 WL 2458650 ........ 163, 164, 168, 186
Marifortuna Naviera v Government of Ceylon (The Mariasmi) [1970] 1 Lloyd's Rep 247 ........ 51
Marika M, The, [1981] 2 Lloyd's Rep 622 ........ 76
Marimpex Mineraloe-Handelsgesellschaft GmbH & Co KB v Compagnie de Gestion et d'exploitation Ltd (The Ambor and the Once) [2001] 1 All ER (Comm) 182 ........ 73
Marion, The, [1982] 2 Lloyd's Rep 52 ........ 213
Markappa Inc v NW Spratt & Son Ltd (The Arta) [1985] 1 Lloyd's Rep 534 ........ 47, 55
Markel International Co Ltd v Craft (The Norseman) [2006] EWHC 3150 (Comm); [2007] Lloyd's Rep IR 403 ........ 31
Mash & Murrell Ltd v Joseph I Emanuel Ltd [1961] 2 Lloyd's Rep 326 (CA) ........ 132, 134
Mass Glory, The, [2002] 2 Lloyd's Rep 244 ........ 84
Mastro Georgis, The, [1983] 2 Lloyd's Rep 66 ........ 76

Maurice Federation v Stewart (The West Bay III) [1969] 1 Lloyd's Rep 158 .......................... 185
Mauritius Oil Refineries Ltd v Stolt-Nielsen Nederlands BV (The Stolt Sydness) [1997] 1 Lloyd's Rep 273 .......... 1, 41, 51
Mediterranean Shipping Co SA v Polish Ocean Lines (The Tychy) [1999] 2 Lloyd's Rep 11 ...... 203, 353
Merak, The, [1964] 2 Lloyd's Rep 527 .......... 41
Mercedes Benz AG v Herbert Heinz Horst Leiduck [1995] 2 Lloyd's Rep 417; [1996] AC 284 (PC) .......... 366
Merci Convenzionali Porto de Genova SpA v Siderurgica Gabrielli SpA, OJ 1997 L301/27; [1998] 4 CMLR 91 .......... 387
Merci Convenzionali Porto de Genova SpA v Siderurgica Gabrielli SpA, Case C-179/90; [1991] ECR I-5889; [1994] 4 CMR 422 .......... 387
Merdeka, The, [1982] 1 Lloyd's Rep 401 .......... 355
Meridian Global Funds Management Asia Ltd v Securities Commissioner [1995] 2 AC 500 ...... 212, 213, 231, 262
Messier Dowty Ltd v Sabena SA [2000] 1 Lloyd's Rep 428 .......... 9
Midas Merchant Bank plc v Senator Musa Bello, Aisha Musa Bello [2002] EWCA Civ 1496 ...... 366
Mihalios Xilas, The, [1978] 2 Lloyd's Rep 186 .......... 74, 90
Mihalis Angelos, The, [1970] 2 Lloyd's Rep 43 .......... 67, 68
Ministry of Defence and Support of the Armed Forces for Iran v Faz Aviation Ltd [2007] EWHC 1042 (Com); [2007] I L Pr 42 .......... 6
Minnehaha [1861] Lush 335; (1861) 15 Moo PC 133 .......... 178, 186, 187
Miramar Maritime Corp v Holborn Oil Trading Ltd (The Miramar) [1984] 2 Lloyd's Rep 129 .... 49, 89
Miranos International Trading Inc v Voc Steel Services BV [2005] EWHC 1812 (Comm) ...... 71
Monte Confurco, The, (Seychelles v France) ITLOS Reports 2000, 118 .......... 324
Moran, Galloway & Co v Uzielli [1905] 2 KB 555
More OG Romsdal Fylkesbatar AS v The demise charterers of the Ship Jotunheim [2005] 1 Lloyd's Rep 181 .......... 74–75
Morviken, The, [1983] 1 AC 565 .......... 23, 28, 40, 107–108
Moschanthy, The, [1971] Lloyd's Rep 37 .......... 358
Motor Oil Hellas Refineries SA v Shipping Corp of India (The Kanchenjunga) [1990] 1 Lloyd's Rep 391 .......... 63
Motorola Credit Corp v Cem Gengiz Uzan, Aysegul Akay [2003] EWCA Civ 752; [2004] EWHC 3169 (Comm) .......... 367
Mozart, The, [1985] 1 Lloyd's Rep 239 .......... 86
MSC Mediterranean Shipping Co SA v Delumar BVBA (The MSC Rosa M) [2000] 2 Lloyd's Rep 399 .......... 215
Myrto, The, [1978] 1 Lloyd's Rep 11; 1978 WL 57210 (CA) .......... 358

Nanfri, The, [1979] Lloyd's Rep 201 .......... 89
National Carriers Ltd v Panalpina (Northern) Ltd [1981] AC 675 .......... 63
National Westminster Bank v Rabobank Nederland RV [2007] EWHC (Comm) .......... 32
Navigation Maritime Bugare v Rustal Trading Ltd (The Ivan Zagubanski) [2002] 1 Lloyd's Rep 106 .......... 31
Nea Agrex SA v Baltic Shipping Co Ltd (The Agios Lazaros) [1976] 2 Lloyd's Rep 47 .......... 51
Nerano, The, [1996] 1 Lloyd's Rep 1 .......... 4, 37, 49
Nereide SpA di Navigazione v Bulk Oil Int'l (The Laura Prima) [1982] 1 Lloyd's Rep 1 .. 81, 85
Neste Chemicals SA v DK Line SA (The Sargasso) [1994] 2 Lloyd's Rep 6 .......... 9
Newsat Holdings Ltd v Zani [2006] 1 Lloyd's Rep 707 .......... 18
Nima SARL v Deves Insurance plc [2002] Lloyd's Rep IR 752 .......... 330
Ninemia Maritime Corp v Trave Schiffahrtsgesellschaft mbH (The Niedersachsen) [1984] 1 All ER 398 .......... 223, 366
Niobe, The, [1888] LR 13 PD 55; [1888] 59 LT 257; [1891] AC 401 .......... 189
Nippon Yusen v Karageorgis [1975] 2 Lloyd's Rep 137; [1975] 1 WLR 1093 (CA) .......... 349, 364
Nippon Yusen Kaisha v Marocaine de L'Industrie du Raffinage (The Tsukuba Maru) [1979] 1 Lloyd's Rep 459 .......... 86
Nippon Yusen Kaisha Ltd v Scindia Steam Navigation Co Ltd (The Jalagouri) [2000] 1 Lloyd's Rep 515 .......... 76
Norfolk v My Travel Group plc [2004] 1 Lloyd's Rep 106 .......... 152–153
Nisshin Shipping Co Ltd v Cleaves & Co Ltd [2004] 1 Lloyd's Rep 38 .......... 47

Nitrate Corp of Chile Ltd v Pansuiza Compania de Navegacion SA (The Hermosa) [1980] 1 Lloyd's Rep 638 .......... 53
Noble Assurance Co v Gerling-Konzern General Insurance Co [2007] EWHC 3150 (Comm); [2007] 1 CLC 85 .......... 31, 34
Nolisement, Owners of the Steamship, v Bunge and Born [1916] CC 135 .......... 86
Noranda Inc v Barton (Time Charter) Ltd (The Marinor) [1996] 1 Lloyd's Rep 301 .......... 54
Novorossisk Shipping Co v Neopetro Ltd (The Ulyanovsk) [1990] 1 Lloyd's Rep 425 .......... 85
Nugent and Killick v Michael Goss Aviation Ltd and Others [2000] 2 Lloyd's Rep 222 .......... 214
NV Bureau Wijsmuller v NV Owners of the Tojo Maru (The Tojo Maru) [1971] 1 Lloyd's Rep 341 (HL) .......... 204

O'Kane v Jones, The Martin P [2005] Lloyd's Rep IR 174 .......... 329
Ocean Marine Navigation Ltd v Koch Carbon Inc (The Dynamic) [2003] 2 Lloyd's Rep 693 .... 59
Ocean Pride Maritime Ltd Partnership v Qingdao Shipping Co (The Northgate) [2007] EWHC 2796 (Comm) .......... 83, 84
Ocean Tramp Tankers Corp v V/O Sovfracht (The Eugenia) [1963[ 2 Lloyd's Rep 381 (CA) .... 65
Oceangas (Gibraltar) Ltd v Port of London Authority (The Cavendish) [1993] 2 Lloyd's Rep 292 .......... 197, 199, 201
OK Petroleum AB v Vitol Energy SA [1995] 2 Lloyd's Rep 160 .......... 126
Ophthalmic Innovations International (UK) Ltd v Ophthalmic Innovations International Inc [2004] EWHC 2948 (Ch); [2005] 1 L Pr 10 .......... 43
OT Africa Line Ltd v Magic Sportswear Corp [2005] EWCA 710; [2005] 2 Lloyd's Rep 170 .... 26, 27, 30
Overseas Transportation Co v, Mineralimportexport (The Sinoe) [1972] 1 Lloyd's Rep 201 ...... 91
Owusu v Jackson, Case C-281/02 [2005] ECR I-383; [2005] 1 Lloyd's Rep 452 .......... 5

P & O/Nedlloyd, Case IV/M.831, 19/12/1996 .......... 392
Pagnan SpA v Tradax Ocean Transportation SA [1987] 2 Lloyd's Rep 342 (CA) .......... 126
Palm Shipping Inc v Kuwait Petroleum Corp (The Sea Queen) [1988] 1 Lloyd's Rep 500 ........ 81
Pan Atlantic Insurance co Ltd v Pine Top Insurance Co Ltd [1994] 3 All ER 581 .......... 329
Panchaud Frères SA v Etablissements General Grain Co [1970] 1 Lloyd's Rep 53 .......... 144
Panos Eliades, Panix Promotions Ltd, Panix of the US Inc v Lennox Lewis [2005] EWHC 2966 .......... 368
Panoutsos v Raymond Hadley Corp of New York [1917] 2 KB 473 (CA .......... 140
Papera Traders Co Ltd and Others v Hyundai Merchant Marine Co Ltd and Another (The Eurasian Dream) (No 1) [2002] 1 Lloyd's Rep 719 .......... 228
Parsons Corp v CV Scheepvaartonderneming "Happy Ranger" (The Happy Ranger) [2002] 2 Lloyd's Rep 357 .......... 40, 50, 51
Pentonville Shipping Ltd v Transfield Shipping Inc (The Johnny K) [2006] EWHC 134 (Comm); [2006] 1 Lloyd's Rep 666 .......... 79
Perrett c. Collins and Others [1998] 2 Lloyd's Rep 255 .......... 204
Petone, The, [1917] P 198 .......... 363
Petrofina SA v AOT Ltd (The Maesk Nimrod) [1991] 1 Lloyd's Rep 269 .......... 354
Petrograde Inc v Stinnes Handel GmbH [1995] 1 Lloyd's Rep 142 .......... 135
Petroleo Brasileiro SA v Kriti Akti Shipping Co SA (The Kriti Akti) [2004] EWCA Civ 116; [2004] 1 Lloyd's Rep 712 .......... 59, 70, 73, 77
Phillips v Symes [2001] CLC 1673 .......... 9, 12
Photo Production v Securicor Transport [1980] 1 Lloyd's Rep 545; [1980] 1 All ER 856 ...... 59, 60, 123
Pioneer Shipping Ltd v BTP Tioxide Ltd (The Nema) [1982] AC 724 .......... 64
Pirelli Cables Ltd v United Thai Shipping Corp Ltd (Unreported 5 April 2000) .......... 28
PNSL Berhard v Dalrymple Marine Services Pty Ltd; PNSL Berhard v Owners of the Ship Koumala (The Kouomala) [2007] QSC 101 .......... 180, 181
Po, The, [1991] 2 Lloyd's Rep 206 .......... 22
Polish Steamship C v A J Williams (Overseas Sales) Ltd (The Suwalki) [1989] 1 Lloyd's Rep 511 .......... 46
Polish Steamship Co v Atlantic Maritime Co (The Garden City (No 2)) [1984] 2 Lloyd's Rep 37 (CA) .......... 220
Portolana Cia Nav v Vitol SA (The Afrapearl) [2004] 2 Lloyd's Rep 305 .......... 86
Poseidon Schiffahrt GmbH v Nomadic Navigation Co Ltd (The Trade Nomad) [1998] 1 Lloyd's Rep 57 .......... 77

Premium Nafta Products Ltd v Fili Shipping Co Ltd [2007] UKHL 40 .... 34
President of India v Metcalfe Shipping Ltd (The Dunelmia) [1970] 1 QB 289; [1969] 2 Lloyd's Rep 476 (CA) .... 128
President van Buren, The, [1924] 19 Ll L Rep 185; [1924] 16 Asp MLC 144 .... 179
Prestige, The, USDC (SDNY) 2 January 2008, Case No 03 Civ 3573 (LTS) (RLE) Unreported .... 176, 248, 249, 260, 326
Princess Alice, The, (1849) 3 W Rob 138 .... 177
Prinsengracht, The, [1993] 1 Lloyd's Rep 41 .... 22
Print Concept GmbH v GEW (EC) [2001] EWCA Civ 352; [2002] CLC 352; [2001] ECC 36 .... 42
Pronuptia de Paris GmbH v Irmgard Schillgalis, Case C-161/84; [1986] ECR 353 .... 374
PT Pan Indonesia Bank Ltd TBK v Marconi Communications International Ltd [2005] EWCA Civ 422; [2004] 1 Lloyd's Rep 594 .... 42
Pyrene Co Ltd v Scindia Steam Navigation Co Ltd [1954] 1 Lloyd's Rep 321 .... 104, 108, 115
Pythia, The, [1982] 2 Lloyd's Rep 160 .... 76

R v Goodwin (Mark) [2005] EWCA Crim 3184; [2006] 1 Lloyd's Rep 432 .... 159, 206
R (Intertanko and Ors) v Secretary of State for Transport, Case C-308/06 .... 307
Raffeisen Zentralbank Osterreich Aktiengesellschaft v National Bank of Greece SA [1999] 1 Lloyd's Rep 408 .... 38, 43
Reardon Smith Line v Black Sea and Baltic General Insurance [1939] AC 562 .... 60
Refrigerant, The, [1925] P 130 .... 178
Reich Montage AG v Kiesel Baumachinen Handels GmbH [2007] 1 L Pr 10 .... 20
Reino de España v American Bureau of Shipping et al, sub nom The Prestige, USDC (SDNY) 2 January 2008, Case No 03 Civ 3573 (LTS) (RLE) Unreported .... 176, 248, 249, 260, 326
Rena K, The, [1979] QB 377; [1978] 1 Lloyd's Rep 545 .... 223, 370
Renpor, The, (1883) LR 8 PD 115 (CA) .... 165
Renton v Palmyra Trading Corp [1956] 1 QB 462 .... 60
Republic of Haiti and Others v Jean-Claude Duvalier and Others [1989] 1 Lloyd's Rep 111; [1990] 1 QB 202 (CA) .... 367
Republic of India and the Government of the Republic of India (Ministry of Defence) v India Steamship Co Ltd (The Indian Grace) (No 2) [1998] 1 Lloyd's Rep 1; [1997] 4 All ER 380 .... 351, 352, 363
Réunion Européenne SA v Spliethoff's Bevrachtingskantoor BV, Case C-51/97; [1997] CLC 282 .... 14
Rewia, The, [1991] 2 Lloyd's Rep 325 (CA) .... 6, 36
Richard Abel & Sons v Manchester Ship Canal (The Stonedale No 1) [1955] 2 Lloyd's Rep 9; [1956] AC 1 .... 209
River Gurara, The, [1998] 1 Lloyd's Rep 225 (CA) .... 122
River Rima, The, [1987] 2 Lloyd's Rep 106; [1988] 2 All ER 641 .... 354
River Wear Commissioners v Adamson [1877] 2 App Cas 743 .... 194
Riverstone Meat Co v Lancashire Shipping Co (The Muncaster Castle) [1961] 1 Lloyd's Rep 57 .... 53, 119
Roche Nederland and other s [2006] ECR I-6535 .... 20
Rodocanachiu Sons & Co v Milburn Brothers (1887) LR 18 QBD 67 (CA) .... 128
Rowan Companies Inc & Ors v Lambert Eggink Offshore Transport Consultants VOF & Ors [1998] CLC 1574 (CA) .... 185
Royal Sun Alliance v MK Digital FZE [2005] EWHC 1408 (Comm); [2005] 2 Lloyd's Rep 679 .... 9
Royscot Trust Ltd v Rogerson [1991] 3 All ER 294 .... 55
RPS Prodotti Siderurgici Srl v The Owners of the Sea Maas (The Sea Maas) [1999] 2 Lloyd's Rep 281 .... 16
Rudolf Kronhofer v Marianne Maier and Others, Case C-168/02 [2004] ECR I-06009 .... 18
Ruta, The, [2000] 1 Lloyd's Rep 359 .... 346–347

Saiga, The M/V, (No 1) (Saint Vincent and the Grenadines v Guinea) ITLOS Reports 1997 323
Samcrete Egypt Engineers and Contractors SAE v Land Rover Exports Ltd [2001] EWCA Civ 2019; [2002] CLC 533 .... 43
Samick Lines Co Ltd v Owners of the Ship "Antonis P Lemos" (The Antonis P Lemos) [1985] AC 711; [1985] 1 Lloyd's Rep 283 (HL) .... 350
Samsun Logix Corp v Oceantrade Corp, Deval Denizeilik VE Ticaret AS v Oceantrade Corp, Samsun Logix Corp [2007] EWHC 2372 (Comm) .... 90

San Demetrio, The, (1941) 69 Ll L Rep 5 ... 168
San Jose v Socrates and Champion (The Socrates and The Champion) (1923) 15 Ll L Rep 196 (CA); [1923] P 162 ... 189
Santiren Shipping Ltd v Unimarine SA (The Chrysovalandou Dyo) [1981] 1 Lloyd's Rep 159 ... 89, 90
Sarrio SA v Kuwait Investment Authority [1997] 4 All ER 929 (HL); [1997] 1 Lloyd's Rep 113 (CA); [1996] 1 Lloyd's Rep 650 ... 9
Satya Kailash, The, [1982] 2 Lloyd's Rep 465; [1984] 1 Lloyd's Rep 588 ... 50, 51, 54
Sava Star, The, [1995] 2 Lloyd's Rep 13 ... 169
Saxon Star, The, [1959] AC 133 ... 49, 50, 52
Scaptrade, The, [1983] 2 Lloyd's Rep 253 ... 74
Scaramanga v Stamp (1880) 5 CPD 295 ... 60
Schelde Delta Shipping BV v Astarte Shipping Ltd (The Pamela) [1995] 2 Lloyd's Rep 249 ... 75
Schiffahrtsgesellschaft MS Merkur Sky mbH & Co KG v MS Leerort Nth Schiffahrts GmbH & Co KG (The Leerort) [2001] 2 Lloyd's Rep 291 (CA) ... 215, 216
Schmidt v Wong [2005] EWCA Civ 1506; [2006] 1 WLR 561 (CA) ... 365
Scottish & Newcastle International Ltd v Othon Ghalanos Ltd [2008] UKHL 11; [2008] 1 CLC 186 ... 16, 128, 135
Sea Containers Ltd v Stena Sealink Ports and Stena Sealink Ltd, OJL 15/8, 18/01/94; [1995] CMLR 84 ... 382
Sea Crystal, The, [1894] AC 508 ... 194
Sea Empress, The, [2003] 1 Lloyd's Rep 327 ... 258, 259
Sea Empress, The, [2000] JPL 943 ... 194, 200
Sea Success Maritime Inc v African Maritime Carriers Ltd (The Sea Success) [2005] 2 Lloyd's Rep 692; [2005] 2 All ER (Comm) 445 ... 113
Seabridge Shipping AB v AC Orssleff's EFTF's A/S (The Fjellvang) [1999] 2 Lloyd's Rep 685 ... 51
Seacrystal Shipping Ltd v Bulk Transport Group Shipping Co (The Kyzikos) [1989] 1 Lloyd's Rep 1 ... 82
Seaflower, The, [2001] 1 Lloyd's Rep 341 ... 57, 133
Seismic Shipping Inc v Total E & P UK plc (The Western Regent) [2005] 2 Lloyd's Rep 359 ... 30, 223, 225
Semco Salvage & Marine Pte Ltd v Lancer Navigation Co Ltd (The Nagasaki Spirit) [1997] AC 455; [1997] 2 WLR 298; [1997] 1 All ER 502; [1997] 1 Lloyd's Rep 323; [1997] CLC 507; [1997] 6 Re LR 305; 1997 AMC 1989; (1997) 141 SJLB 43; The Times, 10 February 1997); WL 1106227 ... 167, 187
Seven Seas Transportation Ltd v Pacifico Union Marina Corp (The Satya Kailash and Oceanic Amity) [1982] 2 Lloyd's Rep 465; 1984] 1 Lloyd's Rep 588 ... 50, 51, 54
Shamil Bank of Bahrain EC v Beximco Pharmaceuticals Ltd [2004] EWCA Civ 19; [2004] 2 Lloyd's Rep 1 ... 39
Sharp v Sphere Drake Insurance Co, The Moonacre [1992] 2 Lloyd's Rep 501 ... 329
Shenevai v Kreischer [1987] ECR 239 ... 16
Shizelle [1992] 2 Lloyd's Rep 444 ... 360
SIAT di Dal Ferro v Tradax Overseas SA [1980] 1 Lloyd's Rep 53 ... 146
Siboti K/S v BP France SA [2003] EWHC 1278; [2003] 2 Lloyd's Rep 364 ... 7
Sidhu and Others v British Airways plc, Abnett (known as Sykes) v British Airways plc [1997] 2 Lloyd's Rep 76; [1997] AC 430 (HL) ... 153
Silia, The, [1981] 2 Lloyd's Rep 534; [1981] Com LR 256; 1981 WL 186630 ... 353
Sir John Jackson Ltd v Owners of the Steamship Blanche, her Master and Crew and Others (The Hopper No 66) [1908] AC 126 ... 202–203
SK Shipping Co Ltd v BB Energy (Asia) Pte Ltd [2000] 1 All ER (Comm) 810 ... 67
Skerries Salmon Ste v Braer Corp 1999 SLT 1196 ... 258
Skips A/S Nordheim v Syrian Petroleum Co (The Varenna) [1983] 2 Lloyd's Rep 592 ... 3
SL Sethia Liners Ltd v Naviagro Maritime Corp (The Kostas Melas) [1981] 1 Lloyd's Rep 18 ... 78
Smit Int'l (Deutschland) GmbH v Josef Mobius Bau-Gesellschaft GmbH & Co) [2001] 2 All ER (Comm) 265 ... 184
Smith v Braer Corp 1999 GWD 21-1023 ... 258
Smith New Court Securities Ltd v Scrimgeour Vickers Asset Management Ltd [1997] AC 254 ... 55
Société Anonyme des Minerais v Grant Trading Inc (The Ert Stefanie) [1989] 1 Lloyd's Rep 349 ... 211, 212, 213, 262

Société Group Josi Reinsurance Co SA v Compagnie d'Assurances Universal General Insurance Co, Case C-421/98; [2000] 2 All ER (Comm) 467 ........ 5
Socony Mobil Oil Co Inc and Others v West of England Ship Owners Mutual Insurance Association Ltd (London) (The Padre Island) (No 2) [1990] 2 Lloyd's Rep 191 (HL) ........ 342
Sofial SA v Ove Skou Rederi (The Helle Skou) [1976] 2 Lloyd's Rep 205 ........ 83
Soon Hua Seng Co Ltd v Glencore Grain Ltd [1996] 1 Lloyd's Rep 398 (QBD) ........ 131, 144
Soproma SpA v Marine and Animal By-Products Corp [1966] 1 Lloyd's Rep 367 ........ 139,140
Sounion, The, [1987] 1 Lloyd's Rep 230 ........ 78
Source Ltd v TUV Rheinland Holding AG [1997] 3 WLR 365 ........ 16
Span-Terza, The, [1982] 1 Lloyd's Rep 225 (CA) ........ 203, 353
Spiliada Maritime Corp v Cansulex Ltd (The Spiliada) [1987] AC 460 ........ 24
Stag Line v Foscolo, Mango & Co [1932] AC 328 ........ 60
Standard Chartered Bank v Pakistan National Shipping Corp (No 2) [2003] 1 Lloyd's Rep 227 ........ 56
Star Sea, The, [1995] 1 Lloyd's Rep 651 ........ 52, 329
Steam Barge Trishna, Owners of the, v Owners of the Motor Tug Panther (The Panther) [1957] 1 Lloyd's Rep 57; [1957] 1 All ER 641 ........ 189
Steedman v Scofield and Another [1992] 2 Lloyd's Rep 163 ........ 159, 206
Steelwood Carriers Inc of Monrovia v Evimeria Compania Naviera SA of Panama (The Agios Giorgis) [1976] 2 Lloyd's Rep 192 ........ 89
Stellar Chartering and Brokerage Inc v Efibanca-Ente Finanziario Intercambiario SpA (The Span-Terza No 2) [1984] 1 Lloyd's Rep 119 (HL) ........ 353
Stolt Filia, The, [1980] LMLN 15 ........ 223, 370
Stolt Sydness, The, [1997] 1 Lloyd's Rep 273 ........ 1, 41, 51
Stolt Tankers Inc v Landmark Chemicals SA (The Stolt Spur) [2002] 1 Lloyd's Rep 786 ........ 86
Stora Enso Oij v Port of Dundee [2006] CSOH 40; [2006] 1 CLC 453 ........ 127
STX Pan Ocean Co Ltd v Ugland Bulk Transport AS (The Livanita) [2007] EWHC 1317 (Comm) ........ 62
Sunderland Marine Mutual Insurance Co Ltd v Wiseman (The Seaward Quest) [2007] EWHC 1460 (Comm); [2007] 2 Lloyd's Rep 308 ........ 18
Super Servant Two, The, [1990] 1 Lloyd's Rep 1 ........ 65
Swift-Fortune Ltd v Magnifica Marine SA (The Capaz Duckling) [2008] 1 Lloyd's Rep 54; [2007] EWHC 1630 (Comm) (QBD) ........ 366

TA Shipping Ltd v Comet Shipping Ltd (The Agamemnon) [1998] 1 Lloyd's Rep 675 ........ 83
TACA, Case IV/M.134 ........ 393
Targe Towing Ltd and Another v Marine Blast Ltd [2004] 1 Lloyd's Rep 721 (CA) ........ 182, 184, 188
Tasmania, The, [1888] LR 13 PD 110 ........ 180, 363
Tate & Lyle Ltd v Hain Steamship Co Ltd [1936] 2 All ER 597; (1936) 55 Ll L Rep 159 (HL) ........ 128
Tatem v Gamboa [1939] 1 KB 132; (1938) 61 Ll L Rep 149 ........ 64, 65
Tatry, The (sub nom The Maciej Rataj), Case C 406/92; [1994] ECR I-5439; [1995] 1 Lloyd's Rep 302 ........ 9, 12, 22, 273, 285, 287, 351
Tavoulareas v Tsaviliris [2005] EWHC 2140; [2006] 1 All ER (Comm) 109 ........ 9, 42
TDK Take Distributor (UK) Ltd v Videochoice Ltd and Others [1986] 1 WLR 141 ........ 367
Tergeste, The, [1903] P 26 ........ 361
Tesaba, The, [1982] 1 Lloyd's Rep 397 ........ 172, 210
Tessili v Dunlop Case 12/76 [1976] ECR 1473 ........ 16
Texaco Southampton, The, [1983] 1 Lloyd's Rep 94; 1983 WL 216285 (CA NSW) ........ 168
Texas Instruments Ltd and others v Nason (Europe) and others [1991] 1 Lloyd's Rep 146 ........ 137
Thames & Mersey Marine Insurance Co Ltd v Hamilton, Fraser & Co, The Inchmaree (1887) 12 App Cas 484 ........ 332
Thane Investments Ltd v Tomlinson (No 1) [2003] EWCA Civ 1272 (CA) ........ 366
Third Chandris Shipping Corp Western Sealane and Aggelikai Ptera Compania Maritima SA v Unimarine SA (The Genie, Pythia and Angelic Wings) [1979] 2 Lloyd's Rep 184 ........ 366
Thomas Young and Sons Ltd v Hobson and Partner (1949) 65 TLR 365 ........ 137
Thor Navigation Inc v Ingosstrakh Insurance [2005] Lloyd's Rep 490 ........ 331
Through Transport Mutual Insurance Association (Eurasia) Ltd v New India Assurance Co Ltd (The Hari Bhum) [2004] EWCA Civ 1598; [2005] 1 Lloyd's Rep 67 ........ 31

Tidebrook Maritime Corp v Vitol SA (The Front Commander) [2006] 2 Lloyd's Rep 251 (CA) .......... 82
Tilly Russ v Nova, Case 71/83; [1983] ECR 2417 .......... 7
Tjaskemolen Now Named Visvliet (No 2) [1997] 2 Lloyd's Rep 476 .......... 354
Todd and Others v Adams and Chope (t/a Trelawney Fishing Co (The Maragetha Maria) 2002 WL 498836; [2002] CLC 1050; [2002] 2 Lloyd's Rep 293; [2002] 146 SJLB 118; [2002] 2 All ER (Comm) 97; (2002) 99(21) LSG 32; The Times, 5 March 2002; [2002] EWCA Civ 509 .......... 211
Toepfer (Hamburg) v Lenerson-Poortman NV (Rotterdam) [1980] 1 Lloyd's Rep 143 .......... 139
Toepfer International GmbH v Société Cargill France [1998] 1 Lloyd's Rep 379 .......... 31
Tojo Maru, The, [1972] AC 242 .......... 165, 173
Tomimaru (Japan v Russian Federation, 6 August 2007 .......... 325
Torvald Klaveness A/S v Arni Maritime Corp (The Gregos) [1995] 1 Lloyd's Rep 1 .......... 69
Tradax Internacional SA v Goldschmidt SA [1977] 2 Lloyd's Rep 604 .......... 134
Trade Indemnity plc v Forsakringsaktiebolaget Njord [1995] 1 All ER 796 .......... 35
Tradigrain SA v King Diamond Shipping SA (The Spiros C) [2000] 2 Lloyd's Rep 319 .......... 89
Trafigura Beheer BV v Mediterranean Shipping Co SA (The MSC Amsterdam) [2007] EWCA Civ 794 .......... 23, 40, 50, 108
Transfield Shipping Inc v Mercator Shipping Inc (The Achilleas) [2007] EWCA Civ 901; [2007] 2 Lloyd's Rep 555 .......... 72–73
Transgrain Shipping BV v Global Transporte Oceanico SA (The Mexico 1) [1990] 1 Lloyd's Rep 507 CA) .......... 83
Transport and General Workers Union v Associated British Ports Ltd [2001] EWCA Civ 2032 (CA) .......... 198
Trasporti Castelletti Spedizioni Internazionali SpA v Hugo Trumpy SpA, Case C-159/97; [1999] I L Pr 492 .......... 7, 11
Travelers Casualty and Surety Co of Canada v Sun Life Assurance Co of Canada (UK) Ltd [2006] EWHC 2885 (Comm) .......... 32
Tres Flores, The, [1973] 2 Lloyd's Rep 247 .......... 83, 84
Triton Navigation Ltd v Vitol SA (The Nikmary) [2003] EWCA Civ 1715; [2004] 1 Lloyd's Rep 55 .......... 83
Troilus, Owners of cargo lately laden on board the, v Owners, Masters and Crew of the Glenogle (The Troilus and The Glenogle) [1951] AC 820; [1951] 2 All ER 40; [1951] 1 Lloyd's Rep 467; [1951] 2 TLR 22; (1951) 95 SJ 465; 1951 WL 11359 .......... 164, 165, 169
Tropwave, The, [1981] 2 Lloyd's Rep 159 .......... 91
Trygg Hansa Insurance Co Ltd v Equitas Ltd [1998] CLC 979 .......... 3
Tsakiroglou & Co Ltd v Noblee Thorl GmbH [1962] AC 93 .......... 64
Tsavliris Salvage (Int'l) Ltd v Guangdong Shantou Overseas Chinese Materials Marketing Co (The Pa Mar) [1999] 1 Lloyd's Rep 338; 1997 WL 1102429 .......... 164, 171
Tug Sea Tractor, Owners and/or Demise Charterers of the, v Owners of the Tramp (The Tramp) [2007] EWHC 31 (Admlty); [2007] 2 Lloyd's Rep 363; 2007 WL 261207; 2007 WL 261207 .......... 164
Turner v Grovit, Case C-159/02 [2004] ECR I-3565; [2005] 1 AC 101 .......... 30
Two Ellens, The, (1869–72) LR 3 A&E 345 .......... 360
Tychy, The, (No 2) [2001] 2 Lloyd's Rep 403 (CA) .......... 354

Ultisol Transport Cpontractors Ltd v Bouygues Offshore SA and Comité d'Etudes et des Services des Assureurs Maritimes et Transports de France (Tigr, Ultisol v Bouygues) [1996] 2 Lloyd's Rep 140 .......... 179
Union Discount Co v Zoller [2002] 1 WLR 1517 .......... 31
Union Transport Group plc v Continental Lines SA [1992] 1 All ER 161 .......... 16
Unique Mariner (No 2) [1979] 1 Lloyd's Rep 37 .......... 172
United Brands v Commission, Case 27/76; [1978] ECR 207 .......... 380
United City Merchants (Investments) Ltd v Royal Bank of Canada (The American Accord) [1982] 2 Lloyd's Rep 1; [1983] 1 AC 168 (HL) .......... 136
United Nations Food and Agriculture Organisation World Food Programme v Caspian Navigation Inc (The Jay Ganesh) [1994] 2 Lloyd's Rep 358 .......... 85
Universal Bulk Carriers Ltd v Andre Et Cie [2001] EWCA Civ 588; [2001] 2 Lloyd's Rep 65 (CA) .......... 67
Uranienborg, The, (1935) 53 Ll L Rep 165; [1936] P 21 .......... 181

Van Eijck & Zoon v Somerville (1906) 8 F 22 (HL) .......... 263
Van Uden Maritime BV v Kommanditgesellschaft in Firma Deco-Line, Case C-391/95; [1999] All ER (EC) 258 ECJ .......... 31, 367
Vantage Navigation Corp v Suhail and Saud Bahvan Building Materials (The Alev) [1989] 1 Lloyd's Rep 138 .......... 75
Veracruz Transportation Inc v VC Shipping Co Inc and den Norske Bank A/S (The Veracruz I) [1992] 1 Lloyd's Rep 353 (CA) .......... 366
Verity Shipping SA v NV Norexa (The Skier Star) [2008] 1 CLC 45 .......... 31
Vesta v Butcher [1988] 2 All ER 43 .......... 46, 56
Viasystems (Tyneside) Ltd v Thetmal Transfer (Northern) Ltd and Others [2006] QB 510 (CA) .......... 198
Virginia M, The, [1989] 1 Lloyd's Rep 603 .......... 84
Viskase Ltd v Paul Kiefel GmbH (1999) Comm 641 (CA) .......... 17
Vitol v Norelf (The Santa Clara) [1996] AC 800 .......... 58
Vogemann v Zanzibar (1902) 7 Com Cas 254 (CA); (1901) 6 Com Cas 253 .......... 76
Volga, The, (Russian Federation v Australia), ITLOS Reports 2002, 10 .......... 325
Volvox Hollandia, The, [1988] 2 Lloyd's Rep 361 .......... 10
Von Rocks, The, [1998] 2 Lloyd's Rep 198 .......... 205

W J Alan & Co Ltd v El Nasr Export & Import Co [1972] 2 QB 189 (CA) .......... 140
Waldwiese Stiftung v Lewis [2004] EWHC 2589 (CH); [2004] WL 2652645 (Ch) .......... 43
Wallumba, Owners of the, v Australian Coastal Shipping Commission (The Wallumba) [1964] 2 Lloyd's Rep 387; [1965] 1 Lloyd's Rep 121 .......... 180, 181
Warrior, The, (1862) Lush 476 .......... 168
Waterfront Shipping Co Ltd v Trafigura AG (The Sabrewing) [2008] 1 Lloyd's Rep 286 .......... 87
Welex AG v Rosa Maritime Ltd (The Epsilon Rosa) [2003] EWCA Civ 938; [2003] 2 Lloyd's Rep 509; [2002] EWHC 762 (Comm) .......... 38
Welex AG v Rosa Maritime Ltd (The Epsilon Rosa) (No 2) [2002] 2 Lloyd's Rep 701 .......... 38
Wells and Another (Paupers) Appellant v The Owners of the Gas Float Whitton No 2 Respondents (The Gas Float Whitton No 2) [1896] P 42 (CA); [1897] AC 337 (HL) .......... 163
West Cock, The, [1911] P 208 .......... 178
West Tankers Inc v RAS Riunione Adriatica di Sicurta (The Front Comor) [2007] UKHL 4; [2007] 1 Lloyd's Rep 391 .......... 31
Western Bulk Carriers K/S v Li Hai Maritime Inc (The Li Hai) [2005] EWHC 735; [2005] 2 Lloyd's Rep 389 .......... 75, 78
Whistler Int'l v Kawasaki Kisen Kaisha Ltd (The Hill Harmony) [2001] 1 Lloyd's Rep 147 ......50, 54, 60
Wladyslaw Lokietek, The, [1978] 2 Lloyd's Rep 520 .......... 223
Workington Harbour and Dock Board v Towerfield (Owners) (The Towerfield) [1951] AC 112 (HL) .......... 199
World Symphony, The, and the World Renown [1992] 2 Lloyd's Rep 115 (CA) .......... 73

Xenos v Aldersley (The Evangelismos) (1858) 12 Moo PC 352 .......... 359
XL Insursance Ltd v Owens Corning [2000] 2 Lloyd's Rep 500 .......... 35

Yukong Line Ltd of Korea v Rendsburg Investments Corp of Liberia [2000] WL 1881248; [2001] 2 Lloyd's Rep 113 (CA) .......... 368
Yuta Bondarovskaya, The, [1998] 2 Lloyd's Rep 357 .......... 354

Z Ltd v A–Z and AA–LL [1982] Lloyd's Rep 240; [1982] QB 558 (CA) .......... 368
Zelger v Salinitri (No 2) [1984] ECR 2397 .......... 9
Zenatia, Owners of the, v Owners of the Putbus (The Putbus) [1969] 1 Lloyd's Rep 253 (CA) .......... 222

# Table of Legislation, Conventions and Rules


**National Legislation**

Arbitration Act 1996—
ss. 5, 6 .......... 3
s. 9(4) .......... 4
ss. 9–11 .......... 4
s. 11 .......... 4
12 .......... 54, 87
30 .......... 27
ss. 30, 31 .......... 3
s. 44 .......... 4, 365
69(2), (3) .......... 3
70(2), (3) .......... 3
Bills of Lading Act 1855 .......... 97
Carriage of Goods by Sea Act 1971 .......... 39, 48, 107–108, 118
s. 1 .......... 39
(6)(b) .......... 108, 110
Carriage of Goods by Sea Act 1992 .......... 98–102, 102–103, 117
s. 1(2) .......... 98
(4) .......... 102
2 .......... 8, 24, 98
(1) .......... 103
(4) .......... 103
3 .......... 8
5.2 .......... 98
Civil Jurisdiction and Judgments Act 1982—
s. 25 .......... 365
(3) .......... 367
34 .......... 351
343 .......... 226
Sched 4 .......... 18
Contracts (Applicable Law) Act 1990 .......... 32–33, 38, 39, 107–108
s. 3(1) .......... 33
Contracts (Rights of Third Parties) Act 1999 .......... 47, 97, 182, 342–344
s. 1 .......... 47
(1) .......... 343
6(5)(a) .......... 98
Gambling Act 2005 .......... 328
Harbours Act 1964 .......... 197
Harbours Docks and Piers Clauses Act 1847 .......... 189, 194
s. 56 .......... 194
Hovercraft (Civil Liability Order) 1986 .......... 206
Law Reform (Frustrated Contracts) Act 1943 .......... 66
s. 1(2) .......... 66
Limitation Act 1980 .......... 170
Marine Insurance Act 1906 .......... 15, 259, 327 *et seq*
s. 2 .......... 328
ss. 4, 5 .......... 328
s. 6 .......... 329
15 .......... 329
16 .......... 331
ss. 17–20 .......... 327, 329
27–28 .......... 328
s. 29 .......... 328
30 .......... 330
31 .......... 328
32 .......... 329
39(5) .......... 231
ss. 33, 34, 35 .......... 330
s. 37 .......... 330
38 .......... 330
39(5) .......... 339
ss. 39–44 .......... 330
45, 46 .......... 61
50, 51 .......... 329
52–54 .......... 327
s. 55(2) .......... 339
ss. 56, 57 .......... 331
61, 62, 63 .......... 331
64–66 .......... 331
s. 66 .......... 334
ss. 67–76 .......... 331
s. 77 .......... 331
78 .......... 331
79 .......... 332
81 .......... 331
ss. 82–84 .......... 328
Marine Insurance (Gambling Policies) Act 1909 .......... 328
Marine Safety Act 2003 .......... 176
Sched 1 .......... 252
Maritime Conventions Act 1911 .......... 159, 162
Merchant Shipping Act 1894—
ss. 503, 504 .......... 202
Merchant Shipping Act 1906—
s. 71 .......... 203
Merchant Shipping Act 1995 .......... 147, 176, 350

Merchant Shipping Act 1995—*continued*
ss. 92, 93 ... 165
s. 153 ... 258, 269, 274, 356
153A ... 269
(7) ... 268
153(3), (4), (5) ... 257
(7) ... 270
154 ... 268, 273–275
(5) ... 273
155 ... 259, 274
156 ... 260
(1) ... 274
(ii) ... 264
(2) ... 274
(2A) ... 271
(2B) ... 271
157 ... 255, 261
(1) ... 261
(3) ... 262
158 ... 272
(4) ... 263
(8) ... 263
ss. 159, 160 ... 358
s. 162 ... 259, 263, 271, 274
163A(2) ... 268
(1) ... 261
164(4) ... 264
165(1A) ... 268, 272
(2) ... 259
(3), (4) ... 261
166 ... 273
(2) ... 356
(4) ... 273
167(2) ... 260
(3) ... 271
168 ... 269, 272
169 ... 259
170 ... 257
(1) ... 256, 258, 270, 273
(2) ... 257
173(10) ... 266
174 ... 266
175 ... 264
(1)(b) ... 265
(c) ... 265
(5), (6), (7) ... 265
176 ... 266
(5) ... 266
177 ... 267
178(1) ... 265
185 ... 209
(4) ... 211
ss. 185–186 ... 10, 202
s. 187 ... 158, 189
188 ... 159
190 ... 159
191 ... 194, 204
192 ... 206
ss. 193–223 ... 193
s. 252 ... 209
ss. 252–254 ... 189

Merchant Shipping Act 1995—*continued*
s. 255(1) ... 190
Sched 1, ss. 7–14 ... 361
3A ... 176
5, Part I ... 266
5A ... 277
6 ... 147
7 ... 165
Part I, Art 4 ... 272
Part II ... 224, 274
4(1) ... 277
5 ... 206
9 ... 222
Art 13 ... 358
11 ... 210
11, Part II, s. 2 ... 205
Merchant Shipping and Maritime Security Act 1997 ... 192, 194, 276
Merchant Shipping (Liability of Shipowners and Others) Act 1900 ... 194
Merchant Shipping (Salvage and Pollution) Act 1994 ... 162
Sched 2 (6) ... 172
Misrepresentation Act 1967 ... 55
s. 2(1) ... 55
(2) ... 55
Nuclear Act 1991 ... 211
Nuclear Installations Act 1965 ... 290
ss. 7–11 ... 290
Pilotage Act 1913 ... 199
Pilotage Act 1987—
s. 2 ... 197
4 ... 197
7 ... 197
9 ... 197
16 ... 199, 200, 201
21(1) ... 198
(2) ... 198
(7) ... 201
22 ... 194, 204
(3) ... 200
(4) ... 200
(6) ... 200
(8) ... 198
23 ... 196, 200
31(1) ... 196
Art 2 ... 197
3 ... 197
Ports Act 1991 ... 193
Private International Law (Miscellaneous Provisions) Act 1995 ... 33
Protection of Military Remains Act 1986 .. 192
Protection of Wrecks Act 1973 ... 192
Sale of Goods Act 1979—
s. 13 ... 134, 135
14 ... 134, 135
15 ... 134, 135
17(1) ... 132
(2) ... 132
18 ... 132
20 ... 129

Sale of Goods Act 1979—*continued*
s. 20(2) .... 131
(3) .... 131
30(5) .... 135
32(1) .... 135
(2) .... 132, 136–137
(3) .... 132
Supply of Goods and Services Act 1982 .... 178, 188
ss. 13, 14 .... 178
Supreme Court Act 1981 .... 350
s. 20 .... 352
(1)(b) .... 350
(2) .... 197, 350, 351, 352, 353, 354
(3) .... 350, 351
(5) .... 351
ss. 20–24 .... 350
s. 21 .... 356, 360
(2) .... 352, 363
(3) .... 352, 354, 362
(4) .... 353, 354, 355, 356, 363
(7) .... 350
22 .... 351
37 .... 30
37(3) .... 365
Third Parties (Rights Against Insurers) Act 1930 .... 342
s. 1 .... 204
(3) .... 342
Unfair Contract Terms Act 1977 .... 177, 179
Water Resources Act 1991 .... 200

### Statutory Instruments

Carriage of Passengers and their Luggage by Sea (Domestic Carriage) Order 1987, SI 1987/670 .... 147
Merchant Shipping (Convention on Limitation of Liability for Maritime Claims) (Amendment) Order 1998, SI 1998/1258 .... 208, 218
Merchant Shipping (Oil Pollution) (Bunkers Convention) Regulations 2006, SI 2006/1244 .... 255, 256, 257, 268, 269, 270, 271, 274
Merchant Shipping (Oil Pollution) (Supplementary Fund Protocol) Order 2006, SI 2006/ 1265 .... 267
Merchant Shipping (Oil Pollution Compensation Limits) Order 2003, SI 2003/2559 .... 261, 266
Package Travel, Package Holidays and Package Tours Regulations 1992, SI 1992/3288 .... 151
Protection of Wrecks (RMS Titanic) Order 2003, SI 2003/2496 .... 192

CANADA

Marine Liability Act 2001—
s. 46(1)(b), (c) .... 26

SOUTH AFRICA

Carriage of Goods by Sea Act 1986 .... 40

UNITED STATES

Carriage of Goods by Sea Act 1936 (COGSA) ... 41, 48–50, 52, 130
s. 2(1)(b) .... 128
3(6) .... 41
Harter Act 1893 .... 48
Oil Pollution Act 1990 .... 342

### European Directives and Regulations

Directive 75/442/EEC (Waste Framework Directive) .... 276
Directive 94/57/EC (on rules and standards for ship inspection etc) .... 245 *et seq*
Art 3(2) .... 247
4(1) .... 247
6(2)(b) .... 248
Directive 2004/35 (Environmental Liability Directive) .... 275 *et seq*
Preamble, (2) .... 275
Art 1 .... 275
4(2) .... 275
4(3) .... 275
Annex IV(a–d) .... 275
V(e) .... 275
Directive 2005/35/EC (Ship Source Pollution Directive) .... 176, 253, 307
Art 3 .... 254
4 .... 253
EC Jurisdiction Convention .... 5, 6, 351
Art 17 .... 8, 22
Arts 21–23 .... 8
Art 27(3) .... 8
57 .... 21
EC Jurisdiction Regulation (Council Reg (EC) No 44/2001 of 22 Dec 2000) .... 5, 365
s. 2 .... 13
Art 1 .... 5
2 .... 5, 248, 275
4 .... 5, 23, 25
5 .... 14
(1) .... 14–16, 24, 33
(3) .... 16–19, 248
(5) .... 19, 24
(7) .... 19
6(1) .... 19–20
(2) .... 20–21, 249
7 .... 21, 225
13(5) .... 5
22 .... 5
23 .... 5, 6, 20, 22, 24
Arts 27–30 .... 8, 9, 12
Art 31 .... 367
32 .... 285
33(1) .... 285
34(3) .... 8
34 .... 285
36 .... 285

EC Jurisdiction Regulation (Council Reg (EC) No 44/2001 of 22 Dec 2000)—*continued*
Art 37 ... 365
47(2), (3) ... 365
59 ... 248
60(1) ... 249
71 ... 21, 23
73 ... 11
Recital 14 ... 5
28 ... 11
EC Regulations on Unfair Terms in Consumer Contracts 1999 ... 15
EC Second Directive on Non Life Insurance ... 35, 43
EC Treaty—
Arts 81, 82, 87 ... 371
Art 81 ... 372 *et seq*, 394 *et seq*
82 ... 380 *et seq*, 396 *et seq*
87 ... 388 *et seq*, 397
EU Package Travel Directive ... 151
Arts 4, 5, 7, 8 ... 152
Regulation (EEC) 4056/86 ... 373, 375, 376
Art 3 ... 374
4 ... 374
Regulation 259/93/EEC on Supervision and Control of Shipments of Waste within, into and out of the European Community ... 294
Regulation (EC) No 44/2001. *See* EC Jurisdiction Regulation
Regulation 1406/2002 (establishing Marine Safety Agency) ... 243
Regulation (EC) 1/2003 ... 377
Regulation (EC) 139/2004 (EC Merger Regulation) ... 390 *et seq*
Art 1 ... 390, 391
2 ... 391
(1) ... 392
(3) ... 391
3 ... 391
5 ... 391
7(2a) ... 391
9(2) ... 391
Regulation 1419/2006 ... 375, 379, 381
Regulation 864/2007 (on law applicable to non-contractual obligations (Rome II)) ... 33

**International Conventions and Rules**

Arrest Convention 1952 (International Convention relating to the Arrest of Seagoing Ships) ... 21, 273, 320, 349, 350
Art 1(1) ... 22
(2) ... 349
7 ... 22
23 ... 22
24 ... 22
Athens Convention 1974 (relating to the Carriage of Passengers and their Luggage by Sea) ... 147 *et seq*, 208, 319, 321
Art 1 ... 148
(5) ... 208
Athens Convention 1974 (relating to the Carriage of Passengers and their Luggage by Sea)—*continued*
Art 3 ... 148
7 ... 148
13 ... 148
16 ... 148
17(2) ... 148
2002 Protocol to the Athens Convention ... 148–149, 342
Basel Convention 1989 (Convention on the Control of the Transboundary Movements of Hazardous Wastes and Their Disposal) ... 291
Art 1.1(a) ... 291
1.3 ... 291
1.4 ... 291
2.1 ... 291
2.8 ... 294
2.10 ... 291
2.11 ... 292
2.14, 2.15 ... 291
2.16 ... 292
2.17 ... 292
2.18 ... 291
2.19 ... 292
2.3 ... 291
4 ... 292
4.2 ... 291, 294
4.3 ... 292, 294
4.4 ... 294
4.5, 4.7 ... 292
6, 6.1, 6.9, 6.11 ... 292
9.1, 9.2, 9.3 ... 292
Annex 1 ... 291
3 ... 291
V Pt A ... 292
Pt B ... 292
Basel Liability Protocol 1999 ... 293
Art 4 ... 293
4.5(a), (b), (c), (d) ... 293
5 ... 293
6.2 ... 293
11 ... 293
Brussels Convention 1924 (Int'l Convention for the Unification of Certain Rules of Law Relating to Bills of Lading) ... 1
Protocol 1968 ... 1
1979 ... 1
Brussels Convention 1963 ... 290
Brussels Salvage Convention 1910 ... 162
CLC Convention (International Convention on Civil Liability for Oil Pollution Damage 1992) ... 191, 210, 254, 255 *et seq*, 318, 358
Art I(1) ... 257, 269
(2) ... 257
(5) ... 256
(6) ... 258, 265
(a) ... 270

CLC Convention (International Convention on Civil Liability for Oil Pollution Damage 1992)—*continued*
Art I(7) .......... 258
(8) .......... 257, 258, 269
II .......... 256, 270
(b) .......... 256
III(1), (4), (5) .......... 257
(2) .......... 259, 264, 265
(3) .......... 259, 260
(4) .......... 260, 271
(5) .......... 259
IV .......... 257
(3) .......... 271
V .......... 262
(8) .......... 265
(11) .......... 261, 262
VI(1)(b) .......... 263
(2) .......... 263
VII(1) .......... 261
(8) .......... 259, 260, 261
(12) .......... 260
VIII .......... 259
IX(1) .......... 263
(3) .......... 264
X .......... 264, 267
XI .......... 257
CMR Convention (Convention on the Contract for International Carriage of Goods by Road) Geneva, 1956 .......... 122
Collisions Convention 1910 .......... 158–159
Collision Jurisdiction Convention 1952 (International Convention on Certain Rules Concerning Civil Jurisdiction in Matters of Collision) .......... 21, 158, 350
COLREGS (Convention on the International Regulations for Preventing Collisions at Sea 1972) .......... 159, 319, 321
r 10 .......... 215
Convention for the Suppression of Unlawful Acts against the Safety of Navigation (Rome 1988) .......... 311, 319
Convention on Facilitation of International Maritime Traffic 1965 .......... 318
Convention on the High Seas 1958 .......... 299
Art 2(2) .......... 302
3 .......... 305
5 .......... 309, 310
6 .......... 308
22 .......... 310
23 .......... 311
24 .......... 304
Convention on the International Maritime Satellite Organisation 1976 .......... 319
Convention on the Prevention of Marine Pollution by Dumping of Wastes and Other Matter (London Convention 1972) .. 291,295, 320
Convention on the Territorial Sea and Contiguous Zone (Geneva 1958) ...... 303 *et seq*
Art 16(3) .......... 303
COTIF (Convention concerning International Carriage by Rail), Berne 1980 .......... 122
FUND Convention 1992 (International Convention on the Establishment of an International Fund for Compensation for Oil Pollution Damage .......... 210, 319
Art 4(1)(b) .......... 265
(4)(c) .......... 266
(6) .......... 266
(10)(c) .......... 265
6(1) .......... 265
7(3) .......... 267
(5) .......... 267
(6) .......... 265
Hague Convention 2005 (Convention on Choice of Court Agreements) .......... 11
Art 2 (f), (g) .......... 11
17 .......... 11
Hague Rules .......... 23, 40, 41, 45, 47 *et seq*, 52, 230
Art III r1 .......... 48, 52, 335
2 .......... 48
6 .......... 41, 48, 54
8 .......... 48, 335
IV r2 .......... 48, 53
4 .......... 60
5 .......... 48
IV *bis* rr1–4 .......... 48
V .......... 49
Hague-Visby Rules .......... 23, 27, 28, 39–41, 45 47–51, 52, 93–94, 107, 230
Art III .......... 2
r1 .......... 52, 119, 120, 335
2 .......... 119, 120
3 .......... 109, 111 *et seq*
4 .......... 110, 111
5 .......... 110
6 .......... 54, 96, 109
8 .......... 107, 114, 118, 119, 120, 335
IV r2 .......... 53, 110, 121
4 .......... 60, 123
5 .......... 96, 121, 122
V .......... 49
X .......... 39
Hamburg Rules .......... 21, 41, 45, 47 *et seq*
Art 2.3 .......... 49
5 .......... 48
6 .......... 48
7.1, 7.2 .......... 48
8 .......... 48
20 .......... 2, 48, 54
21 .......... 23, 26
HNS Convention 1996 (Civil Liability and Compensation for Damage in Connection with the Carriage of Hazardous and Noxious Substances by Sea) .......... 275 *et seq*, 320
Art 1(1) .......... 278, 280
(2) .......... 280
(3) .......... 280

HNS Convention 1996 (Civil Liability and Compensation for Damage in Connection with the Carriage of Hazardous and Noxious Substances by Sea)—*continued*
Art 1(5) .... 278
(6) .... 278, 279
(8) .... 279, 281
(9) .... 280
4 .... 279
(1) .... 279, 288
(3) .... 279
(4), (5) .... 278
5(3), 5(4) .... 278
7(1) .... 280
(2), (3), (4), (5) .... 281
(3) .... 285
(6) .... 280
8(1) .... 280, 282
(2), (8) .... 282
9 .... 281, 282
(2) .... 282, 283
(3) .... 283
10(1), (2) .... 283
11 .... 283
12(1), (2), (4) .... 281
(8) .... 280, 281
(10) .... 281
13 .... 285
14(1) .... 285
(2) .... 286
(3), (4) .... 285
(5), (6) .... 286
16(1), (2) .... 287
19 .... 287
21(2) .... 290
37(1) .... 283
(2) .... 286
(3) .... 284
(4) .... 284, 286
38(1), (2), (5) .... 284
(4) .... 287
39(1) .... 286, 287
(2) .... 286
(5) .... 287
(7) .... 284
40 .... 284
(1) .... 284, 285
(2) .... 284, 286
41 .... 286
43 .... 288
Hovercraft (Convention on Limitation of Liability for Maritime Claims (Amendment) Order 1998 .... 206
IMO Convention 1948 .... 309
Arts 12, 13 .... 314
15, 16, 17, 18, 19 .... 314
21, 22, 23, 24, 26, 27, 28, 30, 32, 37, 38, 39, 40 .... 315
Art 34 .... 316
Arts 42–46 .... 316
Art 52 .... 316
IMO Convention 1948—*continued*
Art 63 .... 316
International Convention on Civil Liability for Bunker Oil Pollution Damage, 2001 .... 255, 268 *et seq*, 320
Art 1(1) .... 270
(3) .... 268, 270
(5) .... 269
(7) .... 271
(8) .... 269
(9) .... 272
(a) .... 270
2 .... 270
3(1), (2) .... 270
(3)(a) .... 270
(b) .... 270
(4) .... 270
(5) .... 271
4(1) .... 269
(2), (3), (4) .... 271
6 .... 272
7 .... 268
(1) .... 273
(10) .... 268, 272
8 .... 271
9 .... 273
(2), (3) .... 273
10(1) .... 273
(2) .... 273
International Convention for the Control and Management of Ships' Ballast Water and Sediments (London 2004) .... 316, 320
International Convention on the Control of Harmful Anti-fouling Systems on Ships, 2001 ... 320
International Convention Relating to Intervention on the High Seas in Cases of Oil Pollution Casualties (Brussels 1969) .... 176, 191, 252, 318
Art 1 .... 252
V .... 191
International Convention on Load Lines, 1966 ... 318
International Convention on Maritime Liens and Mortgages, 1993 .... 319, 362
International Convention on Maritime Search and Rescue, 1979 .... 319
International Convention on Oil Pollution Preparedness, Response and Cooperation, 1990 .... 319
International Convention on Tonnage Measurement of Ships, 1969 .... 216, 318
International Convention for Safe Containers, 1972 .... 319
International Convention on Salvage, 1989 .... 162, 163–176, 319, 336, 363
Art 1a .... 163
1(1) .... 185
2, 3, 4 .... 163
5(2) .... 169
6 .... 173

International Convention on Salvage, 1989—*continued*
Art 6(2) .................................. 171, 173, 179
7 .................................................... 171
8 .................................................... 164
(1)(d) ............................................ 172
(2) ................................................. 187
10 .................................................. 165
11 .................................................. 176
12 .......................................... 165, 185
(3) ................................................. 169
13 .................. 165, 166, 167, 173, 174, 185, 187, 363
14 .................. 166, 167, 168, 173, 174, 175, 187, 210, 363
(1) ................................................. 167
(3) ................................................. 167
(5) ................................................. 168
16 .................................................. 165
17 .......................................... 168, 185
18 ............................ 164, 165, 174, 185
20 .................................................. 169
21(3) ............................................. 165
30 .................................................. 163
31(1) ............................................. 163
32 .................................................. 163
International Convention on Standards of Training, Certification and Watch-keeping, 1995 (STCW95) ............... 230, 236 *et seq*, 319, 339
IOPC Fund Convention (International Fund for Compensation for Oil Pollution Damage) ..... 254 *et seq*, 264 *et seq*, 277
Art 1(3) ............................................ 266
10(1) ............................................. 266
Limitation Convention 1924 ..................... 202
Limitation Convention (International Con-ven-tion on the Limitation of Liability of Owners of Sea-Going Ships, Brussels 1957) .......................... 9, 28, 29, 202, 230
LLMC (Convention on Limitation of Liability for Maritime Claims) 1976 ...... 10, 29–30, 149–150, 202, 204, 319, 339
Art 1(2) ...................................... 218, 271
(5) ................................................. 207
2 ............................................. 205, 269
(2) .......................................... 207, 210
3 .................................................... 221
(c) ................................................. 290
4 ......................................... 13, 211, 230
6(1) ............................................... 272
(2) ................................................. 272
8 .................................................... 220
9 .................................................... 218
10(1), (2) ........................................ 224
11 .......................................... 219, 222
12(2) ............................................. 221
13 .................................................. 223
14 .................................................. 222
15(2) ............................... 205, 206, 218
(4) ................................................. 206
LLMC (Convention on Limitation of Liability for Maritime Claims) 1976—*continued*
Art 15(5) .......................................... 206
LLMC (Convention on Limitation of Liability for Maritime Claims) 1996 ...... 9, 28, 150, 165, 170, 191, 202 *et seq*, 262, 269, 358, 359
Art 1 ................................................ 202
(2) ................................................. 202
(5) ................................................. 202
(6) ................................................. 204
2 ..................................... 204, 207, 276
(1) ................................ 207, 208 *et seq*
3 ............................................. 210, 220
(2) ................................................. 272
(d) ................................................. 290
4 ..................................... 200, 211, 215
5 .................................................... 219
6 ............................... 204, 211, 220, 221
(1) ................................................. 217
(2) ................................................. 217
7 ............... 150, 204, 208, 217, 220, 283
8 .................................................... 220
(1) ................................................. 221
(2), (3) ........................................... 221
10(1), (2) ........................................ 224
11 ................................... 204, 219, 222
(1) ................................................. 220
(2) ................................................. 221
12 .................................................. 204
(2) ................................................. 221
(4) ................................................. 221
13 .......................................... 220, 223
(1), (2), (3) .................................... 222
14 .................................................. 222
15(1) ............................................. 204
(3) *bis*) ................................ 208, 217
Lugano Convention ............................. 5, 17
Arts 21–23 ........................................... 8
Art 57 ................................................ 21
Maritime Labour Convention 2006.... 240 *et seq*
Arts III, IV, VIII .................................. 241
MARPOL 1978 (International Convention for the Prevention of Pollution from Ships) .... 253, 319
Annex I ............................................. 322
Annexes I–VI...................................... 253
MCNM Convention 1971 (Civil Liability in the Field of Maritime Carriage of Nuclear Material) .................................... 275, 319
Montreal Convention 1999 (Convention relating to International Carriage by Air) ...... 122
Nairobi Wreck Removal Convention 2007 .. 190 *et seq*, 259, 295, 320
Arts 2, 3, 9, 10 .................................... 191
Art 3(2) ............................................. 192
10(2) ............................................. 209
New York Convention on the Recognition and Enforcement of Foreign Arbitral Awards 1958 .................................................. 3

NUCLEAR 1971 (International Convention Relating to Civil Liability in the field of Maritime Carriage of Nuclear Material) ... 290
Paris Convention 1960 (Convention on Third Party Liability in the field of Nuclear Energy) ........ 210, 290
Rome Convention 1980 (Convention on the Law Applicable to Contractual Obligations) ..... 15, 32, 33–43, 107
Art 1(2) ........ 34–35
(3) ........ 35
3 ........ 37, 41, 43
(1) ........ 35–36
(2) ........ 39
(3) ........ 39
(4) ........ 37
4 ........ 39, 41
(1), (2), (3), (4), (5) ........ 41–43
7(1) ........ 39
(2) ........ 39, 40
8, 9, 11 ........ 37
8(1) ........ 38
(2) ........ 38
18 ........ 33
21 ........ 41
SOLAS Convention (Safety of Life at Sea Convention) ........ 52, 227 *et seq*, 243, 319, 339
Chap V ........ 235
V, reg 13 ........ 235
V, reg 19.2.4 ........ 232
XI ........ 234
XI-2 ........ 253
XI-3 ........ 232
XI-6 ........ 232
Special Trade Passenger Ships Agreement 1971 .. 318
Statute on the International Regime of Maritime Ports (Geneva 1923) ........ 306
Art 2 ........ 306
Transfrontier Shipment of Waste Regulations 1994 ........ 294
UN Convention on the Carriage of Goods by Sea 1978 ........ 1
UNCLOS (United Nations Convention on the Law of the Sea) ........ 176, 298, 300 *et seq*
Art 3 ........ 303, 355
Arts 7–10 ........ 303
Art 11 ........ 305
18 ........ 306
19 ........ 307
(2) ........ 307
21 ........ 251
(2) ........ 251, 207, 322
24(1) ........ 307, 308
UNCLOS (United Nations Convention on the Law of the Sea)—*continued*
Art 24(2) ........ 307
25(1) ........ 307
(3) ........ 303, 307
26(1) ........ 307
28 ........ 357
33 ........ 304
38(1), (2) ........ 303
41(3) ........ 322
46 ........ 304
53 ........ 304
(8) ........ 322
56 ........ 190
(1), (2) ........ 304
58 ........ 302
(1), (2) ........ 304
73 ........ 325
76, 78 ........ 305
86 ........ 304
87(2) ........ 302
89 ........ 302
91 ........ 308, 310
92 ........ 308
110 ........ 310
(1) ........ 311
111 ........ 311
149 ........ 193
292 ........ 323 *et seq*
303 ........ 193
Part IV ........ 303
V ........ 251, 304
VI ........ 302
XI ........ 305
XII ........ 251
XV ........ 298
XIII ........ 302
Annex VI ........ 298
UNESCO Convention on the Protection of the Underwater Cultural Heritage 2001 .. 193
United Nations Convention on the Carriage of Goods by Sea 1978 ........ 320
United Nations Convention on Conditions for the Registration of Ships (Geneva 1986) ..... 310, 320
Vienna Convention on the Law of Treaties ...... 300, 317–318, 3231
Art 1 ........ 203
9(2) ........ 317
10(b) ........ 317
14 ........ 318
18 ........ 318
York-Antwerp Rules ........ 333 *et seq*
r A.1 ........ 333
E.3 ........ 336
G.3 ........ 334

CHAPTER 1

# The Conflict of Laws

*PROFESSOR YVONNE BAATZ*

## 1. INTRODUCTION

When an international dispute arises out of a maritime contract or incident such as a collision, it is necessary to consider at the outset which law applies to the dispute; which tribunal has jurisdiction to determine the dispute on its merits; whether there is any time bar and whether the claimant can obtain security for its claim. Many maritime contracts contain express governing law and jurisdiction clauses. This chapter will consider the extent to which the English courts will give effect to party choice, the limits on that choice as a result of the maritime conventions and what the position is where no choice has been made. First the reason why these issues matter will be explored.

In order to advise a party on their rights and obligations in any situation it is necessary to establish which law governs those rights and obligations. Whether a contract is governed by one law rather than another may mean the difference between total success by the claimant or total defeat if, for example, one law does not recognise a cause of action or provides the defendant with a complete defence, whereas the other does recognise a cause of action and there is no defence.[1]

The issue of jurisdiction may be of great tactical significance as there may be more than one court which has jurisdiction to determine the dispute and then the claimant must make sure that it commences proceedings in the jurisdiction which is most advantageous to it. In maritime disputes there are a number of reasons why one jurisdiction may be more favourable to one party than the other. One of the aims of this chapter when dealing with jurisdiction is to highlight the differences that can occur in one jurisdiction rather than another, due to the different maritime conventions which States are parties to. This creates an incentive to forum shop. For example, different limits of liability for a cargo claim may apply in different jurisdictions depending on whether the Hague,[2] Hague-Visby[3] or Hamburg Rules[4] apply.[5] A second example is that different tonnage

1. See, e.g., *Mauritius Oil Refineries Ltd v Stolt-Nielsen Nederlands BV (The Stolt Sydness)* [1997] 1 Lloyd's Rep 273 discussed at p. 41 of this chapter.
2. The International Convention for the Unification of Certain Rules of Law Relating to Bills of Lading, Brussels, 25 August 1924.
3. The International Convention for the Unification of Certain Rules of Law Relating to Bills of Lading signed at Brussels on 25 August 1924 as amended by the Protocol signed at Brussels on 23 February 1968 and by the Protocol signed at Brussels on 21 December 1979.
4. The UN Convention on the Carriage of Goods by Sea 1978. See *The Ratification of Maritime Conventions* (LLP, 2007). See also Chapter 2, p. 48, for the differences between these Conventions.
5. See pp. 23, 28 and 40 of this chapter.

limits may apply depending on which convention on tonnage limitation, if any, applies.[6] In any case, whether maritime or not, one court may award more interest; award more legal costs; have more favourable procedural rules, for example, in relation to disclosure of documents; proceed to judgment faster, and so on. If one jurisdiction is more advantageous to one party, the other party would probably prefer to litigate in the other available jurisdiction and this may create a race between the parties to commence proceedings first in the jurisdiction of choice. Such races have resulted in a diver being hired to dive down and pin court proceedings on a ship which had sunk in the territorial waters of Singapore to ensure the jurisdiction of the Singapore court as the tonnage limits were lower there.[7] If the arbitration award or judgment that a party would obtain in one jurisdiction is significantly different from that which the other party would be liable for elsewhere, it may be very difficult to settle the case until the issue of jurisdiction has been resolved.

It is of critical importance to commence proceedings in the correct jurisdiction against the correct party within any time limit. Many maritime disputes are subject to relatively short time limits. For example, the Hague, Hague-Visby or Hamburg Rules may apply to a bill of lading or may be incorporated voluntarily into a charterparty and they have a one- and two-year time bar respectively.[8] If the bill of lading provides for London arbitration and the Hague-Visby Rules apply mandatorily, the cargo receiver must identify the carrier[9] and commence arbitration proceedings in London within the one-year time bar, otherwise the carrier is discharged from all liability.[10]

A party must also consider how to secure its claim as soon as any such claim arises. There is no purpose in expending time, effort and expense in obtaining a favourable court judgment or arbitration award if there are no assets against which to enforce that judgment or award. Thus the claimant should try to obtain security for its claim right at the outset of the dispute. In a maritime dispute there may be a right to arrest a ship[11] or an arrest may be threatened in order to obtain alternative security in the form of a P&I Club letter of undertaking[12] or bank guarantee. Alternatively, if no security is forthcoming there may be a judicial sale of the ship and the proceeds of sale distributed amongst the creditors.[13] If there can be no arrest, perhaps because the ship has sunk and is an actual total loss, the claimant may be able to find assets such as the proceeds of the hull and machinery insurance or funds in the shipowner's bank account which can be frozen by means of a freezing injunction.[14]

This chapter will consider first which tribunal, either arbitration tribunal or court, has jurisdiction to determine the dispute on its merits and then how the English court determines which law is applicable to the dispute. The parties may

6. See pp. 9 and 10, 12 and 13 and 28–30 of this chapter.
7. See *Owners of the Herceg Novi v Owners of the Ming Galaxy (The Herceg Novi and the Ming Galaxy)* [1998] 2 Lloyd's Rep. 454 (CA), discussed at p. 29 of this chapter.
8. Article III rule 6 of the Hague and Hague-Visby Rules and Article 20 of the Hamburg Rules.
9. See Chapter 3, pp. 104–107.
10. See fn. 1 of this chapter.
11. See Chapter 11, pp. 349–364.
12. See Chapter 10, p. 344.
13. See Chapter 11, pp. 358–361.
14. See Chapter 11, pp. 364–370.

have chosen which tribunal has jurisdiction to determine their disputes. Many maritime contracts provide for arbitration. If there is no agreement to arbitrate, the parties may have agreed on a court to determine their disputes but, if they have not, it will be necessary to consider which court will have jurisdiction to determine the dispute on its merits.

## 2. ARBITRATION

Arbitration in London is a popular choice of dispute resolution in maritime contracts. Thus, for example, many standard form charterparties,[15] international sale contracts, salvage contracts,[16] reinsurance contracts and P&I Club Rules provide for London arbitration. Many bills of lading incorporate the arbitration clause in the charterparty under which the bill is issued.[17]

Arbitration is perceived to have advantages over court litigation including speed, limited right of appeal,[18] lower cost, the parties may choose their own arbitrators and procedure[19] and confidentiality. This last criterion may be very important, for example, to large companies who do not wish to have their trade secrets aired in the public proceedings of the court. Furthermore, arbitration awards are confidential and cannot be published except with both parties' consent. If such consent is given they may be published in *Lloyd's Maritime Law Newsletter*. Although they are not binding precedent they may provide very useful guidance.

The United Kingdom is a party to the New York Convention on the Recognition and Enforcement of Foreign Arbitral Awards 1958 and it gives effect to its international obligations under that convention in the Arbitration Act 1996. Sections 5 and 6 of the Arbitration Act 1996 set out the formalities that have to be complied with for there to be a valid arbitration agreement. Where a charterparty containing an arbitration clause has been drawn up and signed by both parties it will satisfy those formalities. Where arbitration proceedings are commenced by one party and the other party does not consider it is bound by an arbitration agreement in the contract, the respondent should object to the jurisdiction of the arbitration tribunal before it contests the merits of the matter.[20] The arbitration tribunal may rule on its own substantive jurisdiction.[21]

It will be necessary to determine whether a contract which incorporates the terms of another contract, such as a bill of lading incorporating the terms of the charterparty pursuant to which it is issued or a reinsurance contract which incorporates the terms of the primary insurance contract,[22] validly incorporates the arbitration clause in that contract. General words of incorporation will not successfully incorporate an arbitration clause.[23] If, however, specific words of

15. See, e.g., cl. 17 of NYPE 1946, cl. 45 of NYPE 1993, cl. 19 of Gencon 1994.
16. Clause I of Lloyd's Open Form 2000.
17. See, e.g., the Congenbill.
18. Sections 69(2) and (3) and 70(2) and (3) of the Arbitration Act 1996.
19. The London Maritime Arbitrators Association has very experienced maritime arbitrators. They offer varying types of procedure depending on the amount at stake.
20. Section 31 of the Arbitration Act 1996.
21. Section 30 of the Arbitration Act 1996.
22. *Trygg Hansa Insurance Co. Ltd v Equitas Ltd* [1998] CLC 979.
23. *Skips A/S Nordheim v Syrian Petroleum Company (The Varenna)* [1983] 2 Lloyd's Rep 592. See also fn. 48 of this chapter.

incorporation are used (i.e. the arbitration clause is specifically referred to in the words of incorporation in the bill of lading), that will successfully incorporate that clause into the bill of lading. This will be so even if it is necessary to manipulate the wording of the charterparty clause, because, for example, that clause refers "all disputes arising out of this charterparty" to arbitration.[24] As the parties have made clear their intention by the specific words that the arbitration clause is to be incorporated into the bill, the court will add the words "and under any bill of lading issued hereunder".

Where a party to an arbitration clause,[25] which provides for arbitration in England or abroad, commences proceedings in the English court, the court is obliged to stay the court proceedings if the other party applies for a stay, unless satisfied that the arbitration agreement is null and void, inoperative, or incapable of being performed.[26] Where, however, a ship has been arrested, the court granting the stay has a discretion to order that the property arrested be retained or that alternative security be provided for the satisfaction of any arbitration award.[27] The court may also grant a freezing injunction in support of the arbitration proceedings.[28]

Where a party to a London arbitration agreement commences or threatens to commence proceedings elsewhere in breach of the arbitration agreement, the other party to the agreement may apply to the English court for an anti-suit injunction to restrain the first party from commencing or pursuing the proceedings elsewhere.[29]

## 3. COURT JURISDICTION

If there is no arbitration agreement it will be necessary to determine whether the English court has jurisdiction either because it has been chosen by the parties or on some other ground. Maritime contracts, such as bills of lading, marine insurance policies[30] and international sales contracts often provide for the exclusive jurisdiction of the High Court in London. We shall consider how effective such a clause is, both where at least one of the parties to it is domiciled in an EC Member State and where neither of the parties is. We shall also consider the position where there is no jurisdiction clause and either the defendant is domiciled in an EC Member State or it is not.

24. *Daval Aciers d'Usinor et de Sacilor v Armare S.R.L. (The Nerano)* [1996] 1 Lloyd's Rep 1; *The Delos* [2001] 1 Lloyd's Rep 703 and *The Epsilon Rosa* [2003] EWCA Civ 938; [2003] 2 Lloyd's Rep 509.
25. Sections 9–11 apply even if the seat of the arbitration is outside England and Wales or Northern Ireland or no seat has been designated or determined (s. 2(2)(a)).
26. Section 9(4) of the Arbitration Act 1996. *Halki Shipping Corp v Sopex Oils Ltd* [1998] 1 Lloyd's Rep 465.
27. Section 11 of the Arbitration Act 1996.
28. Section 44 of the Arbitration Act 1996, which applies regardless of the location of the seat of the arbitration (s. 2).
29. See pp. 30 and 31 of this chapter.
30. Marine insurance contracts on the MAR forms contain an exclusive English court jurisdiction clause, as do some P&I Club Rules.

### (a) The EC Jurisdiction Regulation

The first issue is whether Council Regulation (EC) No 44/2001 of 22 December 2000 on Jurisdiction and the Recognition and Enforcement of Judgments in Civil and Commercial Matters ("the EC Jurisdiction Regulation") or the EFTA Convention on Jurisdiction and the Enforcement of Judgments in Civil and Commercial Matters, 1988 (the "Lugano Convention") applies. The EC Jurisdiction Regulation replaced the latest Accession Convention to the Convention on Jurisdiction and the Enforcement of Judgments in Civil and Commercial Matters 1968 ("the EC Jurisdiction Convention"). The EC Jurisdiction Convention and the EC Jurisdiction Regulation are often referred to as the Brussels Convention or Brussels Regulation, but that description is not used here to avoid confusion as many maritime conventions were concluded in Brussels. The rules under the EC Jurisdiction Regulation, the Lugano Convention and the EC Jurisdiction Convention shall be treated as if they are identical unless specifically stated otherwise.

The EC Jurisdiction Regulation seeks to determine the international jurisdiction of the courts of the EC Member States so that all Member States are bound by the same rules and will therefore recognize and enforce each other's judgments speedily. It provides for certain and predictable rules with very little discretion. In its recent decision in *Color Drack GmbH v Lexx International Vertriebs GmbH*[31] the European Court of Justice stated that the aim of the EC Jurisdiction Regulation is that the claimant should be able "to identify easily the court in which he may sue and the defendant reasonably to foresee before which court he may be sued". It applies to "civil and commercial matters"[32] with some exceptions and those exceptions which are particularly relevant to maritime disputes are where there are proceedings relating to the winding up of insolvent companies[33] or arbitration.[34]

The basic rule is that a defendant domiciled in a Member State must be sued in that State.[35] It does not matter where the claimant is domiciled.[36] Thus if a Japanese claimant sues a defendant domiciled in France, the EC Jurisdiction Regulation applies and the defendant must be sued in France, unless an exception applies. If the Japanese claimant were to sue the French domiciled defendant in England, the defendant could ask for a stay of the English proceedings. Furthermore, in *Owusu v Jackson*[37] the European Court of Justice held that Article 2 will apply if the defendant is domiciled in a Member State, in that case England, even if the only other court involved is that of Jamaica, a non-Member State. The importance of predictability and certainty was stressed. Thus the

31. Case C-386/05 [2007] I L Pr 35 at paras. 19, 20, 32 and 33.
32. Article 1.
33. Article 1(2)(b).
34. Article 1(2)(d). See fns 170 and 171 of this chapter.
35. Article 2.
36. Case C-421/98 *Société Group Josi Reinsurance Company SA v Compagnie d'Assurances Universal General Insurance Company* [2000] 2 All ER (Comm) 467.
37. Case C-281/02 [2005] ECR I-1383; [2005] 1 Lloyd's Rep 452. Noted by E. Peel, "Forum Non Conveniens and European Ideals" [2005] LMCLQ 363 and A. Briggs, "Forum Non Conveniens and Ideal Europeans" [2005] LMCLQ 378; A. Briggs, "The Death of Harrods: Forum Non Conveniens and the European Court" (2005) 121 LQR 535; D. Jackson, "Jurisdiction in Europe – and forum non conveniens", *Shipping and Transport Lawyer International*, Vol. 5, No. 2, p. 33, and C. Hare, "Forum Non Conveniens in Europe: Game Over or Time for Reflexion?" [2006] JBL 157.

English court could not decline the jurisdiction conferred on it by Article 2 on the ground that the Jamaican court would be a more appropriate forum for the trial of the action.

Article 60 of the EC Jurisdiction Regulation provides that a company is domiciled at the place where it has its "statutory seat" or "central administration" or "principal place of business".[38] The date on which the domicile of a defendant has to be established is the date on which the proceedings are issued.[39]

There are a number of exceptions to the basic rule,[40] most notably for present purposes where the parties have chosen the court of an EC Member State to have exclusive jurisdiction. Party autonomy is recognised as an important principle, although it is limited in relation to insurance (but not marine insurance),[41] consumer and employment contracts, as the insured, the consumer and the employee are given consumer protection.[42]

Autonomy in this context relates to a jurisdiction agreement. It is irrelevant that the parties have chosen the law applicable to the agreement as this does not found jurisdiction under the EC Jurisdiction Regulation.[43] Therefore if the parties have provided that their contract shall be governed by English law this will not give the English court jurisdiction under the EC Jurisdiction Regulation.

*(i) A jurisdiction clause – Article 23 of the EC Jurisdiction Regulation*

The important exception of party autonomy is addressed by Article 23 of the EC Jurisdiction Regulation. That Article deals with two different situations. The first is where at least one of the parties to a jurisdiction agreement is domiciled in an EC Member State and the parties have chosen the court of an EC Member State. That court shall have exclusive jurisdiction.[44] It does not matter whether it is the defendant who is domiciled in the EC Member State as both the claimant and the defendant are bound by the agreement. Thus if a Japanese seller is sued by a German buyer and their sale contract contains an exclusive English jurisdiction agreement, the English court could not refuse jurisdiction in favour of the courts of another Member State, nor would the courts of another Member State have jurisdiction. The second situation is where neither party is domiciled in an EC Member State, and they have chosen the court of an EC Member State. In that event Article 23(3) does not provide that the court chosen shall have jurisdiction, but does provide that the courts of other Member States shall have no jurisdiction, unless the court chosen has declined jurisdiction. In this situation the court chosen may apply its own national law to determine whether it has jurisdiction and may decline jurisdiction.[45] We shall consider the English common law below

38. *The Rewia* [1991] 2 Lloyd's Rep 325 (CA).
39. *Ministry of Defence and Support of the Armed Forces for Iran v Faz Aviation Ltd* [2007] EWHC 1042 (Comm); [2007] I L Pr 42.
40. See also Article 22 which provides for exclusive jurisdiction, Article 24 and Article 71 (international conventions – as to which see pp. 21–23 of this chapter).
41. Article 13(5).
42. See Recital 14.
43. *Cf.* the position at common law under Part 6, rule 20(5)(c) of the Civil Procedure Rules. See p. 23 of this chapter.
44. Article 23(1).
45. See Article 4 and p. 23 of this chapter.

and we shall see that the difference is that instead of the certain rule in the first situation, the English court would have a discretion in the second situation. Although the English court will usually exercise its jurisdiction when it is chosen, it may in rare cases decline to do so, where there are multiple proceedings already commenced in another jurisdiction between multiple parties, some of whom are not bound by the English jurisdiction clause.[46]

The parties will only have made a choice within Article 23 if the jurisdiction agreement satisfies certain formalities. It must be either:

> "(a) in writing or evidenced in writing, or
> (b) in a form which accords with practices which the parties have established between themselves, or
> (c) in international trade or commerce, in a form which accords with a usage of which the parties are or ought to have been aware and which in such trade or commerce is widely known to, and regularly observed by, parties to contracts of the type involved in the particular trade or commerce concerned."

The claimant must show that it has a good arguable case that the jurisdiction clause satisfies these formalities.[47]

Whether there is a jurisdiction clause that satisfies these requirements may be a complex question. Consider the example of a transferable bill of lading. A bill of lading will often be on a standard form usually only signed by one party, very often the Master on behalf of the carrier. There may be no signature by or on behalf of the shipper, let alone by the third party holder of the bill of lading to whom it has been delivered and indorsed. The Master's signature is usually on the face of the bill of lading but the jurisdiction clause may be one of many printed conditions on the reverse of the bill. Alternatively, in a charterparty bill of lading the jurisdiction clause is frequently incorporated into the contract by reference to the terms of the charterparty.[48]

To address these difficulties paragraph (c) of Article 23(1) was added when the United Kingdom acceded to the EC Jurisdiction Convention. The reason that the United Kingdom wanted an amendment to the EC Jurisdiction Convention was to safeguard the jurisdiction of the High Court in London, which is chosen in many international standard form contracts, including bills of lading. The requirement to satisfy the formalities is to ensure that there is real consent on the part of the parties. However, consensus is presumed where there is a commercial usage in the relevant branch of international trade or commerce of which the parties are or ought to have been aware.[49]

The European Court of Justice has held[50] that the validity of a jurisdiction clause in a bill of lading must be assessed by reference to the relationship between

46. See pp. 25–28 of this chapter.
47. *Bols Distilleries v Superior Yacht Services Limited* [2006] UKPC 45; [2007] 1 WLR 12.
48. This will only be successful if the words of incorporation in the bill of lading specifically refer to the court jurisdiction clause in the charterparty: *Siboti K/S v BP France SA* [2003] EWHC 1278; [2003] 2 Lloyd's Rep 364. For incorporation of arbitration clauses, see pp. 3 and 4 of this chapter.
49. Case C–106/95 *Mainschiffahrts-Genossenschaft eG v Les Gravières Rhénanes (MSG)* [1997] All ER (EC) 385 and Case C–159/97 *Trasporti Castelletti Spedizioni Internazionali SpA v Hugo Trumpy SpA* [1999] I L Pr 492.
50. Case 71/83 *Tilly Russ v Nova* [1983] ECR 2417, para. 24; Case C-159/97 *Castelletti v Trumpy* [1999] ECR I-1597, paras. 41 and 42, and Case 387/98 *Coreck Maritime GmbH v Handelsveem BV* [2000] ECR 1-09337, para. 27.

the original parties to the contract, the shipper and the carrier. Furthermore, if the clause is effective as between those parties,[51] it is also effective between the carrier and a third party bill of lading holder who was not an original party to the bill of lading, provided that the third party holder of the bill of lading succeeded to the shipper's rights and obligations under the applicable national law when it acquired the bill of lading. The question as to which national law is applicable is not one of interpretation of the Convention. It falls within the jurisdiction of the national court which must apply its rules of private international law.[52] Under English law the "lawful holder" of a transferable bill of lading does have transferred to it the rights and obligations under the bill of lading pursuant to sections 2(1) and 3 of the Carriage of Goods by Sea Act 1992.[53]

If the third party bill of lading holder does not succeed to the rights and obligations of the shipper under the applicable national law when it acquired the bill of lading, it must be established whether it agreed to the jurisdiction clause in accordance with the requirements in the first paragraph of Article 23. In *Dresser UK v Falcongate Ltd* [54] the Court of Appeal held that, even where the doctrine of bailment on terms applied, it could not satisfy the requirements of Article 17 of the EC Jurisdiction Convention (now Article 23 of the EC Jurisdiction Regulation).

### (ii) *Multiple proceedings*

Section 9 of the EC Jurisdiction Regulation (Articles 27 to 30)[55] contains provisions which seek to prevent multiple proceedings and thus avoid differing judgments being given in more than one jurisdiction. This last situation might lead to non-recognition of a judgment on the ground that it is irreconcilable with a judgment given in proceedings between the same parties in the Member State in which recognition is sought.[56]

The classic case of multiple proceedings would be where a seller sues the buyer in England for non-payment of the purchase price and the buyer sues the seller in another Member State for a declaration that it is not liable under the contract. In those circumstances Article 27 of the EC Jurisdiction Regulation provides for a simple, cut and dried rule that has been described as "first come first served". Where the proceedings involve the same cause of action, are between the same parties and are brought in the courts of different Member States, any court other than the court first seised shall of its own motion stay its proceedings until such time as the jurisdiction of the court first seised is established. Once the jurisdiction of the court first seised has been established, any court other than the court first seised shall decline jurisdiction in favour of the court first seised. Even if the requirements of Article 27 are not satisfied, Article 28 provides that any

51. The court chosen does not have to be determined on the wording of the jurisdiction clause alone. If the clause states the objective factors on the basis of which the parties have agreed to choose the court (e.g. the country of the carrier's principal place of business) sufficiently precisely, the court seised can determine jurisdiction by the particular circumstances of the case: Case 387/98 *Coreck Maritime GmbH v Handelsveem BV* [2000] ECR 1-09337, para. 15.
52. Case 387/98 *Coreck Maritime GmbH v Handelsveem BV* [2000] ECR 1-09337, para. 30.
53. See Chapter 3, pp. 95–104.
54. [1992] 1 QB 502.
55. Section 8 of the EC Jurisdiction and Lugano Conventions (Articles 21–23).
56. Article 34(3) of the EC Jurisdiction Regulation or Article 27(3) of the EC Jurisdiction Convention.

court other than the court first seised may stay its proceedings where related actions are brought in the courts of different Member States. Actions are "related" where they are so closely connected that it is expedient to hear and determine them together to avoid the risk of irreconcilable judgments resulting from separate proceedings.[57] Article 29 further provides that where actions come within the exclusive jurisdiction of several courts, any court other than the court first seised shall decline jurisdiction in favour of the court first seised. Under Articles 27 and 29 a stay is mandatory, whereas under Article 28 it is discretionary. Article 30 provides that a court is seised when proceedings are commenced.[58]

To determine whether the proceedings involve the same cause of action under Article 27 the courts must look to the substance of the matter and not simply to the form.[59] The French version of the same cause of action is "*le même objet et la même cause*". The "*objet*" is "the end the action has in view" and the "cause" comprises the facts and the rule of law relied on as the basis of the action. Thus if in one set of proceedings in the Netherlands the carrier seeks a declaration that it has no liability under a bill of lading and in England the cargo interests seek damages from the carrier for breach of the bill of lading contract, the proceedings will involve the same cause of action. This was the decision of the European Court of Justice in *The Maciej Rataj*.[60] The reason that the cargo interests preferred to sue in England rather than the Netherlands, was that, at that time,[61] the Netherlands applied the 1957 International Convention relating to the Limitation of the Liability of Owners of Sea-Going Ships ("the 1957 Limitation Convention"). Under that Convention the owners would be entitled to limit their liability to

57. Article 28(3) of the EC Jurisdiction Regulation. See, e.g., Case C-406/92 *The Tatry* (*sub nom. The Maciej Rataj*) [1994] ECR I-5439; [1995] 1 Lloyd's Rep 302; *Maersk Olie & Gas A/S v firma M de Haan en W de Boer* [2004] ECR I-9657; [2005] 1 Lloyd's Rep 210; *Bank of Tokyo-Mitsubishi Ltd v Baskan Gida Sanayi Ve Pazarlama* [2004] EWHC 945 (Ch), [2004] 2 Lloyd's Rep 395 and *JP Morgan Europe Ltd v Primacom AG* [2005] EWHC 508; [2005] 2 Lloyd's Rep 665.
58. See, e.g., *Tavoulareas v Tsaviliris* [2005] EWHC 2140, [2006] 1 All ER (Comm) 109 and *Royal & Sun Alliance v MK Digital FZE* [2005] EWHC 1408 (Comm); [2005] 2 Lloyd's Rep 679. Article 30 was an amendment to the EC Jurisdiction and Lugano Conventions. Under those Conventions when a court is seised is a matter for the national law of each State: *Zelger v Salinitri (No. 2)* [1984] ECR 2397. That led to different solutions in each Contracting State. In England the English court was seised when the claim form was served and not when it was issued: *The Freccia del Nord* [1989] 1 Lloyd's Rep 388; *Dresser UK Ltd v Falcongate Freight Management Ltd (The Duke of Yare)* [1992] 2 All ER 450; *Neste Chemicals SA v D K Line SA (The Sargasso)* [1994] 2 Lloyd's Rep 6; *Internationale Nederlanden Aviation Lease BV v The Civil Aviation Authority* [1997] CLC 43; *Phillips v Symes* [2001] CLC 1,673 and *Tavoulareas v Tsaviliris* [2004] EWCA Civ 48, [2004] 1 Lloyd's Rep 445.
59. E.g. Case 144/86 *Gubisch Maschinenfabrik KG v Giulio Palumbo* [1987] ECR 4861; *Sarrio SA v Kuwait Investment Authority* [1997] 4 All ER 929 (HL); [1997] 1 Lloyd's Rep 113 (CA); [1996] 1 Lloyd's Rep 650; Case C-111/01 *Gantner Electronic GmbH v Basch Exploitatie Maatschappij BV* [2003] ECR I-4207 and Case C-39/02 *Maersk Olie & Gas A/S v firma M de Haan en W de Boer* [2005] 1 Lloyd's Rep 210.
60. Case C-406/92 *The Tatry* (*sub nom. The Maciej Rataj*) [1994] ECR I-5439; [1995] 1 Lloyd's Rep 302. Although the English courts were previously hostile to negative declarations of liability, they appear to have overcome their antipathy to this remedy: see, e.g., *Boss Group Ltd v Boss France SA* [1996] 4 All ER 970; *Maas Logistics (UK) Ltd v CDR Trucking BV* [1999] 2 Lloyd's Rep 179; *Messier-Dowty Ltd v Sabena SA* [2000] 1 Lloyd's Rep 428; *Phillips v Symes* [2001] CLC 1,673, para. 38; *Bristow Helicopters Ltd v Sikorsky Aircraft Corporation* [2004] EWHC 401 (Comm); [2004] 2 Lloyd's Rep 150 and *Bhatia Shipping v Alcobex* [2004] EWHC 2323 (Comm); [2005] 2 Lloyd's Rep 336, paras 24–26. L. Collins, "Negative Declarations and the Brussels Convention" (1992) 108 LQR 545; A. Bell, "The Negative Declaration in Transnational Litigation" (1995) 111 LQR 674.
61. The Netherlands ratified the 1976 LLMC in 1990 but has not ratified the 1996 Protocol referred to in fn. 62 of this chapter.

approximately US$1.25m, whereas under the 1976 Convention on Limitation of Liability for Maritime Claims ("1976 LLMC") which applied in England,[62] the limit of owners' liability would be more than three times as much, at approximately US$4.225m. This would be of enormous significance in this claim because the total of the cargo owners' claim could amount to approximately US$3.5m, i.e. almost three times the Dutch limitation figure.

In contrast in *Maersk Olie & Gas A/S v firma M de Haan en W de Boer*[63] the European Court of Justice held that an application by shipowners for limitation of their liability under the 1957 Limitation Convention in the courts of the Netherlands did not involve the same subject matter and cause of action as an action for damages for damage to their oil and gas pipelines in the North Sea brought by Maersk against the shipowner before the Danish courts. The subject matter was clearly not the same, as an action for damages seeks to have the defendant declared liable, whereas an application to limit liability is designed to ensure that, in the event the defendant is found liable, such liability will be limited.[64] The cause of action comprises the facts and the legal rule invoked as the basis for the application. Even if it were assumed that the facts underlying the two sets of proceedings were identical, the legal rule which formed the basis of the application was different. The action for damages was based on the law governing non-contractual liability, whereas the application for the establishment of a limitation fund was based on the 1957 Limitation Convention and the legislation of the Netherlands giving effect to it.[65]

Where one party commences proceedings in the court of a Member State and the defendant in those proceedings brings proceedings in the court of another Member State on the ground that there is an exclusive jurisdiction agreement in favour of the court second seised, that court must stay its proceedings until the court first seised has determined whether it has jurisdiction or not. This is as a result of the judgment of the European Court of Justice in *Erich Gasser GmbH v MISAT SRL*.[66] This decision was met with dismay in England,[67] as the London High Court is often the court chosen in commercial contracts including maritime contracts, and it has been argued that the court chosen should be the court which determines whether there is a valid jurisdiction clause rather than the court first seised. The disadvantage of the decision is that an unscrupulous debtor who wishes to delay payment may deliberately[68] commence proceedings in breach of a clear

62. The Protocol of 1996 amending the Convention on Limitation of Liability for Maritime Claims of 19 November 1976 (London, 2 May 1996) (1996 LLMC) is now in force in the UK – see Merchant Shipping Act 1995, ss. 185–186. The amended 1976 LLMC will be referred to as the 1996 LLMC. See pp. 28–30 of this chapter and pp. 170 and 201–226 of Chapter 6.
63. Case C-39/02 *Maersk Olie & Gas A/S v firma M deHaan en W de Boer* [2004] ECR I-9657; [2005] 1 Lloyd's Rep 210. See also the decision of Longmore J in *The Happy Fellow* [1997] 1 Lloyd's Rep 130, discussed at pp. 12 and 13 of this chapter (although the case went to the Court of Appeal, the issue on "same cause of action" was left open – [1998] 1 Lloyd's Rep 13). See also *Dresser UK Ltd v Falcongate Ltd* [1991] 2 Lloyd's Rep 557 and *The Volvox Hollandia* [1988] 2 Lloyd's Rep 361.
64. *Ibid.*, para. 35.
65. *Ibid.*, para. 38.
66. Case C-116/02 [2003] ECR I-14693; [2005] QB 1.
67. See, e.g., A. Briggs, "The Impact of Recent Judgments of the European Court on English Procedural Law and Practice," *Zeitschrift fur Schweizerisches Recht* 124 (2005) II 231.
68. This appeared to be the case in *JP Morgan Europe Ltd v Primacom AG* [2005] EWHC 508 (Comm); [2005] 2 Lloyd's Rep 665. Noted in R. Swallow and R. Hornshaw, "Jurisdiction Clauses in Loan Agreements: Practical Considerations for Lenders", *Bankers Law*, Vol. 1, No. 2, 18. See also *Bank*

jurisdiction agreement in a jurisdiction which is known to be slow and benefit from the sluggish procedure of the court first seised. This tactic has been dubbed the "Italian torpedo".[69]

The complexity of a dispute as to whether there is a valid jurisdiction agreement in a bill of lading and the length of time it takes to resolve is illustrated by *Trasporti Castelletti Spedizioni Internazionali SpA v Hugo Trumpy SpA*.[70] That case took some 10 years to proceed through the Italian courts and obtain a judgment from the European Court of Justice. That was still not the end of the matter as the European Court of Justice can only determine issues of interpretation. It cannot resolve issues of fact, which would have to go back to the national court. In *Gasser* the European Court of Justice rejected any exception to their decision that the court second seised, even if chosen, must stay its proceedings in favour of the court first seised, even if there were excessive delay by the court first seised.

Article 27 provides for a simple and inflexible rule based on the chronological order in which proceedings are brought and the rule does not bend for jurisdiction clauses or delays. Thus, even if there is a clear jurisdiction clause, the party wishing to rely on the clause is in a stronger position if it can seise the court chosen first.

The EC Jurisdiction Regulation is currently being reviewed[71] and the Commission will report on its application and if necessary submit proposals for amendments. The 2005 Hague Convention on Choice of Court Agreements has recently been concluded.[72] However, even if the Convention comes into force,[73] it does not apply to the carriage of goods.[74]

The current defects and delays in the courts of some Member States in determining the preliminary issue of jurisdiction are unacceptable. It is simply not good enough for a claimant with a clear jurisdiction agreement to have to wait many years for the court first seised to decide on its jurisdiction. This gives the unscrupulous debtor a wholly unfair advantage. It is clearly incumbent on the Member States to improve their procedures for determining the preliminary issue of jurisdiction, so that they deserve the trust that the European Court of Justice demands that all Member States accord each other. With the great expansion of the European Union and further States waiting to join, it is important that this issue is addressed.[75] The system is only as good as its weakest link. The problem

---

*of Tokyo-Mitsubishi Ltd v Baskan Gida Sanayi Ve Pazarlama* [2004] EWHC 945 (Ch); [2004] 2 Lloyd's Rep 395, para. 49, a case of multiparty litigation where two parties sought a declaration of non-liability in Italy and alleged an Italian jurisdiction clause. Lawrence Collins J stayed the English proceedings for contractual claims (but not for tortious claims) under Articles 27 and 28 until the Italian court had determined whether it had jurisdiction.

69. See A. Briggs, "The Impact of Recent Judgments of the European Court on English Procedural Law and Practice", *Zeitschrift fur Schweizerisches Recht* 124 (2005) II 231–262, n. 24.
70. Case C–159/97, [1999] I L Pr 492.
71. Recital 28 of the EC Regulation and Article 73.
72. On 30 June 2005 the final Act of the Twentieth Session of the Hague Conference on Private International Law was signed including the Convention on Choice of Court Agreements. See *www.hcch.net/index_en.php?act=conventions.text&cid=98.*
73. Article 31.
74. Article 2(f) excludes the carriage of passengers and goods and Article 2(g) excludes marine pollution, limitation of liability for maritime claims, general average and emergency towage and salvage. The Convention does, however, apply to contracts of insurance and reinsurance that relate to such matters (Article 17).
75. See A. Dickinson, "A Charter for Tactical Litigation in Europe?" [2004] LMCLQ 273.

is not limited to jurisdiction clauses. In any case where the court second seised must stay its proceedings, whether there is a jurisdiction clause or not, the court first seised must determine the preliminary issue of jurisdiction swiftly. Indeed the issue of delays in some Member States only serves to highlight why litigants wish to include a jurisdiction clause.[76]

Article 27 also requires the parties in the different sets of proceedings to be identical. In *The Maciej Rataj* the carrier had commenced proceedings in Rotterdam against some, but not all, the cargo interests. Some of the cargo interests had commenced proceedings in England by arresting a sister ship of the carrying ship. Article 27 applied to those proceedings where the cargo interests were involved in both the Dutch and the English proceedings but not to those where the cargo interests were only involved in either the Dutch or the English proceedings, but not both.

The European Court of Justice looks at the substance of the issue rather than the detail of procedure and also held in *The Maciej Rataj* that *in rem* proceedings in England against the ship were against the shipowner and therefore involved identical parties as proceedings commenced in Rotterdam by the shipowner.[77] Similarly, an insured shipowner and its hull underwriter will be treated as the same party where the insurer is exercising its subrogated rights and stands in the shoes of the insured, provided the interests of the insured and the insurer do not conflict.[78]

### *(iii) Related actions*

As we have already seen if Article 27 does not apply because, for example, the cause of action is not the same or the parties are not identical in both sets of proceedings in different Member States, the court second seised may stay its proceedings if the proceedings are related.[79] Article 28 applied to the proceedings in *The Maciej Rataj* brought by the cargo interests who had not been sued in Rotterdam but had sued in England. All the proceedings were related as they involved alleged contamination of the soya bean oil cargo on the same voyage on bills of lading in the same form.

We have already seen that the European Court of Justice has held that liability and tonnage limitation proceedings in different jurisdictions are not the same cause of action within Article 27, but they may well be related actions. This issue arose in *The Happy Fellow*.[80] The ships *Happy Fellow* and *Darfur* were in collision on the river Seine. The *Darfur* was arrested at Le Havre. Seven claimants, including the owners of the *Happy Fellow*, commenced proceedings in Le Havre against the owners of the *Darfur*, which they were entitled to do both because the collision occurred in France and because the ship had been arrested there. After the collision the time charterers of the *Darfur*, Baco-Liner, agreed an exclusive

76. See, for example, *Phillips v Symes* [2001] CLC 1,673 where a final hearing in Greece might not take place for some seven years, whereas Hart J thought that a trial in England could be achieved within two years (para. 53).
77. See Chapter 11, p. 351.
78. Case–351/96 *Drouot Assurances SA v Consolidated Metallurgical Industries* [1998] All ER (EC) 483. See also *Kolden Holdings Ltd v Rochette Commerce Ltd* [2008] EWCA Civ 10; [2008] I L Pr 20 (assignor and assignee).
79. See pp. 8 and 9 of this chapter.
80. [1998] 1 Lloyd's Rep 13 (CA); [1997] 1 Lloyd's Rep 130.

English law and jurisdiction clause. They commenced proceedings in London claiming damages for breach of the charterparty. The owners of the *Darfur* accepted service of the writ and instituted limitation proceedings in the same court. They purported to constitute a limitation fund. The Court of Appeal held that a limitation action in England and liability proceedings in France were related actions and that Longmore J at first instance had clearly exercised his discretion correctly to stay the English proceedings in favour of the French courts. Longmore J did not, however, consider that liability and limitation proceedings will always be related actions. He said:

"... it does not seem to me necessarily to follow that any action in which it is alleged that a shipowner is liable must inevitably be related to any action in which a shipowner is seeking to limit his liability. If, for example, it is clear that the Court trying the liability action does not consider itself seised of the issue of limitation and the main issue in the liability action is, for example, whether a duty of care is owed by the defendant to the plaintiff, it might well be that the actions would not be related actions..."[81]

However, on the facts of the case he held that the French proceedings and the English limitation proceedings were related for two main reasons. First, at the time of the first instance hearing the owners of the other ship involved, the *Darfur*, had not admitted liability.[82] Thus the issues of the failure of the *Darfur*'s steering gear, the reasons for the failure and the owners' fault and the degree of such fault would be raised in the French proceedings. Very similar issues would arise in the limitation action, which would consider whether the claimant's loss resulted from the personal act or omission of the shipowners "committed recklessly and with knowledge that such loss would result" within Article 4 of the 1976 LLMC. Secondly, the French court would regard itself as seised of limitation as well as liability.

It is worth noting that the reason that one party wanted the limitation proceedings to be determined in France, rather than in England, was that, although the courts of both countries would apply the 1976 LLMC, it was thought that it would be easier to break the limits in France than in England, as it was believed that the French courts apply a more objective approach to the test for breaking the limits under Article 4, than the subjective approach followed in the English courts. If this perception was correct, this does illustrate how even if two States are parties to the same Convention, there may still be reason to forum shop if those two States interpret that Convention differently.

### *(iv) No jurisdiction clause*

Where none of the exceptions to the rule that the defendant must be sued where it is domiciled apply, such as a jurisdiction clause, the claimant may have a choice to sue the defendant where it is domiciled or, if there is sufficient link with another Member State, in that State. Section 2 of the EC Jurisdiction Regulation entitled Special Jurisdiction gives the claimant additional choices where there is a particularly close connection between the subject matter of the dispute and the courts

81. [1998] 1 Lloyd's Rep 130, 135–136.
82. Such an admission had been made by the time the appeal was heard. The Court of Appeal held that this should not be taken into account.

of a particular place. Some of these provisions are particularly relevant to maritime disputes. Thus Article 5 gives the claimant the option to sue the defendant "in matters relating to a contract, in the courts for the place of performance of the obligation in question" (Article 5(1)); "in matters relating to tort, delict or quasi-delict in the courts for the place where the harmful event occurred or may occur" (Article 5(3)); "as regards a dispute arising out of the operations of a branch, agency or other establishment, in the courts for the place in which the branch, agency or other establishment is situated" (Article 5(5)) or "as regards a dispute concerning the payment or remuneration claimed in respect of the salvage of a cargo or freight, in the court under the authority of which the cargo or freight" has been arrested or could have been so arrested but security has already been provided (Article 5(7)). Article 6 provides for multiple defendants, third party proceedings and counterclaims and Article 7 deals with tonnage limitation.

As the special jurisdiction is a derogation from the basic rule that the defendant must be sued where it is domiciled, Articles 5 to 7 must be interpreted restrictively.[83] The provisions must be given a European interpretation rather than in accordance with national law as the aim is to seek a uniform interpretation throughout the EC Member States so that each State has equal jurisdiction.[84]

### *(v) Contract claims – Article 5(1)*

Article 5(1) may be very useful where the place of performance of the obligation in question is in a different Member State from the place where the defendant is domiciled and the claimant would prefer to sue there. For example, if an English seller sells goods to a French buyer it has a choice to sue in France where the buyer is domiciled or the place where the goods were delivered. If the goods were delivered in England, the seller has a choice of England or France.

For Article 5(1) to apply, there must be a contractual relationship between the parties. In *Réunion Européenne SA v Spliethoff's Bevrachtingskantoor BV*,[85] the lead insurer brought proceedings exercising its subrogated rights for damage to pears. The pears were carried from Melbourne to Rotterdam on the *Alblasgracht VOO2* under a bill of lading issued by Refrigerated Container Carriers Pty Ltd (RCC) and on their headed note paper. RCC had its registered office in Sydney. The pears were actually carried by Spliethoff's Bevrachtingskantoor BV, the actual carrier, who were not mentioned on the bill of lading and whose registered office was in Amsterdam. The pears were discharged in Rotterdam and then carried by road under an international consignment note to Rungis in France, where the insured consignee had its registered office. The insurers sued RCC, the actual carrier, and the Master of the carrying ship, who resided in the Netherlands, in the French courts. The first issue before the European Court of Justice was whether the claim against the actual carrier was based on the contract of

83. *Kalfelis v Bankhaus Schroder, Munchmeyer, Hengst & Co* [1988] ECR 5565.
84. See, e.g., Case C-51/97 *Reunion Europeenne SA v Spliethoff's Bevrachtingskantoor BV* [1999] CLC 282.
85. Case C-51/97, [1999] CLC 282. See A. Briggs, "Claims against Sea Carriers and the Brussels Convention" [1999] LMCLQ 333.

transport and whether the claim for that or any other reason fell within the scope of "matters relating to a contract" within the meaning of Article 5(1). The European Court of Justice held that it did not. The bill of lading disclosed no contractual relationship freely entered into between the consignee and the actual carrier or the Master of the ship.

As the words must be given a European interpretation, this may result in there being a contractual relationship even if under the stricter English law requirements, e.g. on consideration, there would not be.[86]

The English courts have distinguished between the situation where a contract is void, for example, for illegality or *ultra vires* and where the contract is voidable, for example, for misrepresentation or non-disclosure.[87] Thus in *Kleinwort Benson Ltd v Glasgow City Council*[88] a majority of the House of Lords[89] held that the bank's claim for restitution where a contract was void for *ultra vires*, was not a matter relating to a contract within Article 5(1). In *Agnew v Lansforsakringsbolagens AB*[90] a majority of the House of Lords held that claims for alleged pre-contractual non-disclosure and misrepresentation in a reinsurance contract which make the contract voidable, fell within Article 5(1). It is not clear, however, whether *Agnew* can be distinguished from the decision of the European Court of Justice in *Fonderie Officine Meccaniche Tacconi SpA v Heinrich Wagner Sinto Maschinenfabrik GmbH*.[91] There it was held that Article 5(1) did not apply where the claim was that the defendant had broken off negotiations for a contract in breach of good faith with the result that no contract was ever concluded.

The parties are free to agree the place of performance but that place must bear some relation to the actual performance of the contract. The parties cannot provide for a place of performance which does not reflect the performance which is actually required by the contract. *Mainschiffahrts-Genossenschaft eG v Les Gravières Rhénanes*[92] concerned an oral agreement for the charter of an inland waterway vessel. The European Court of Justice held that where there is no valid jurisdiction clause, an oral agreement that Germany is the place of performance, which was designed not to determine the place where the person liable is actually to perform its obligations (which was France), but solely to establish that the courts for a particular place have jurisdiction, was not valid under Article 5(1). The place of performance designated had no real connection with the reality of the contract. Otherwise it would be open to a party to circumvent the formalities required by Article 23. Thus an oral agreement on the place of performance which is designed solely to establish that the courts for a particular place have jurisdiction is not governed by Article 5(1), but by Article 23, and is valid only if it complies with the formalities of the latter Article.

86. Similar issues could arise under, e.g., the Rome Convention which only applies to contractual disputes and the EC Regulations on Unfair Terms in Consumer Contracts 1999.
87. See ss. 17–20 of the Marine Insurance Act 1906 discussed at Chapter 10, p. 329.
88. [1997] 4 All ER 641 (HL); [1996] 2 All ER 257 (CA); *Barclays Bank v Glasgow City Council* [1994] 4 All ER 865 (Hirst J). See E. Peel, "Jurisdiction over Restitutionary Claims" [1998] LMCLQ 145 and A. Briggs, "Jurisdiction over Restitutionary Claims" [1992] LMCLQ 283.
89. Lord Goff, Lord Clyde and Lord Hutton with Lord Mustill and Lord Nicholls dissenting.
90. [2000] 1 Lloyd's Rep 317 (HL); [1997] 4 All ER 937 (Court of Appeal); [1996] 4 All ER 978 (Mance J). See H. N. Bennett, "Mapping the doctrine of utmost good faith in insurance contract law" [1999] LMCLQ 165, 193–196.
91. Case C-334/00 [2002] ECR I-7357. *Cf.* Article 1(i) of the Rome I Regulation (see fn. 179 of this chapter) and Article 12 of Regulation (EC) No. 864/2007 (see p. 33 of this chapter).
92. Case C-106/95 [1997] All ER (EC) 385.

Article 5(1)(b) provides that, unless otherwise agreed, in the case of sale of goods and provision of services, the place of performance of the obligation in question shall be where, under the contract, the goods were delivered or should have been delivered or the services were provided or should have been provided. This provision was new in the EC Jurisdiction Regulation and was intended to provide as the place of performance the place where the obligation which characterises the contract is to be performed.[93] It may be difficult to determine where the place of delivery under a sale contract is.[94] The goods may be delivered or the services provided in different Member States; or the contract may be for both delivery of goods and provision of services in different Member States.

Article 5(1)(b) does not apply where the contract is neither for goods nor services or, if it is, the place of performance is in a non-EC Member State. In that event, the "obligation in question" is the obligation arising under the same contract and forming the basis of the proceedings commenced by the claimant and not the obligation which characterises the contract.[95] Where there are a number of obligations in issue the principal obligation will determine the court's jurisdiction.[96] If several obligations are in dispute but there is no principal obligation, there will only be jurisdiction in State A for the claim in respect of the obligation to be performed in State A and jurisdiction in State B for the obligation to be performed in State B.[97] Although this would lead to the fragmentation of the litigation, the claimant always has the option to sue for all its claims where the defendant is domiciled under Article 2.

The place of performance of the obligation in question is determined as a matter of national law.[98]

### *(vi) Tort claims – Article 5(3)*

Article 5(3) provides that "in matters relating to tort, delict or quasi-delict" the courts for the place where the harmful event occurred shall also have jurisdiction. The European Court of Justice has held that the concept of "matters relating to tort, delict or quasi-delict" is an autonomous one. *Kalfelis v Bankhaus Schroder, Munchmeyer, Hengst & Co*[99] involved claims against three defendants, based on contractual liability for breach of the defendants' duty to provide information, on tort and for unjust enrichment. The court held that in order to ensure uniformity

93. Case C-386/05 *Color Drack GmbH v Lexx International Vertriebs GmbH* [2007] I L Pr 35.
94. *Scottish & Newcastle International Limited v Othon Ghalanos Limited* [2008] UKHL 11; [2008] 1 CLC 186.
95. Case 14/76 *Ets A de Bloos SPRL v Société en Commandite par actions Bouyer* [1976] ECR 1497; Case 266/85 *Shenevai v Kreischer* [1987] ECR 239; *Atlas Shipping Agency (UK) Ltd v Suisse Atlantique Société D'Armement Maritime SA (The Gulf Grain and El Amaan)* [1995] 2 Lloyd's Rep 188; Case C-106/95 *Mainschiffahrts-Genossenschaft eG (MSG) v Les Gravières Rhénanes Sarl* [1997] All ER (EC) 385; *Domicrest Ltd v Swiss Bank Corp* [1998] 3 All ER 578; *Viskase Ltd v Paul Kiefel GmbH* [1999] Comm 641 (CA); *RPS Prodotti Siderurgici SRL v The Owners of the Sea Maas (The Sea Maas)* [1999] 2 Lloyd's Rep 281.
96. *Union Transport Group plc v Continental Lines SA* [1992] 1 All ER 161; *Source Ltd v TUV Rheinland Holding AG* [1997] 3 WLR 365; and *AIG Group (UK) Ltd v The Ethniki* [2000] 1 Lloyd's Rep 343.
97. Case C-420/97 *Leathertex Divisione Sintetici SpA* [1999] CLC 1983.
98. Case 12/76 *Tessili v Dunlop* [1976] ECR 1473; Case C-256/00 *Besix* [2002] ECR I-1699. Case C-440/97 *GIE Groupe Concorde v The Master of the vessel Suhadiwarno Panjan* [1999] CLC 1976.
99. Case 189/97.

in all the Member States the concept covers all actions which seek to establish the liability of a defendant and which are not related to "contract" within the meaning of Article 5(1). The English courts have, however, interpreted this as meaning that the liability referred to must be interpreted as connoting liability in tort, delict or quasi-delict and not as a catch-all provision for any liability other than in contract. In *Barclays Bank plc v Glasgow City Council*[100] the House of Lords held that the bank's claim for restitution did not fall within Article 5(3). A claim based on unjust enrichment did not, exceptional circumstances apart, presuppose either a harmful event or a threatened wrong.

In *Kalfelis* the European Court of Justice went on to hold that where a court has jurisdiction under Article 5(3) over an action in so far as it is based on tort or delict, it does not have jurisdiction over that action in so far as it is not so based. Simply because the court has jurisdiction over a claim in tort it will not also have jurisdiction over a claim between the same parties based on contract. This can lead to fragmentation of claims so that a party can rely on Article 5(3) to bring its claim in tort, for example, in England but as regards any claim in contract it would have to rely on Article 5(1), and if the place of performance of the obligation in question was France, it would have to bring its contract claim there and could not bring it in England. This is clear from *Domicrest Ltd v Swiss Bank Corp*,[101] a case on the Lugano Convention. There Rix J held that Domicrest could sue in England under Article 5(1) on its contractual claim against the bank for failure to honour a payment order. However, Domicrest also had claims in tort alleging negligent misrepresentation by the bank as to the effect of the payment order and the client's credit. Rix J held that the place where the harmful event occurred was Switzerland and Italy. Therefore Domicrest could not pursue both its contract and tort claims in England. The solution for Domicrest, if it did not wish to pursue different aspects of the same dispute in different courts, would have been to pursue all its claims in Switzerland, where the bank was domiciled.

In *Bier v Mines de Potasse d'Alsace*[102] the European Court of Justice held that the "place where the harmful event occurs" has an autonomous meaning and covers both the place where the damage occurs and the place of the event giving rise to that damage. If those places are different the claimant can choose to bring proceedings in either of them.

In *Réunion Européenne SA v Spliethoff's Bevrachtingskantoor BV*[103] the European Court of Justice held that the cargo insurers' claims against the actual carrier and the master of a ship did not fall within Article 5(1) as there was no contractual relationship between the parties. Therefore, following *Kalfelis v Schröder*,[104] the court held that such an action must be a matter relating to tort, delict or quasi-delict within Article 5(3). On the question of "the place where the harmful event occurred", the consignee could bring proceedings against the actual carrier either before the courts of the place where the damage occurred or the courts of the place of the event giving rise to it. The problem for the consignee was that in an international transport operation of this kind, where the goods

100. [1997] 4 All ER 641 (CA); see Leggatt LJ [1994] 4 All ER 865 (Hirst J).
101. [1998] 3 All ER 578.
102. Case 21/76 [1976] ECR 1735.
103. Case C–51/97, [1999] CLC 282.
104. See fn. 99. See also p. 20 of this chapter.

had been carried by sea to Rotterdam but then on-carried by road to Rungis in France, the consignee might not be able to determine where the event giving rise to the damage occurred. The place where the damage occurred cannot be either the place of final delivery, which can be changed in mid-voyage, or the place where the damage was ascertained. To allow the consignee to bring the actual carrier before the courts for the place of final delivery would in most cases mean attributing jurisdiction to the plaintiff's domicile and would depend on uncertain factors. Therefore the place where the damage arose in this type of international transport operation could only be the place where the actual maritime carrier was to deliver the goods, as that place meets the requirements of foreseeability and certainty imposed by the Convention.

The courts have given a narrow interpretation to the place where the damage occurs and the European Court of Justice held in *Kronhofer v Maier*[105] that it does not refer to the place where the claimant is domiciled or where "his assets are concentrated" by reason only of the fact that he has suffered financial damage there resulting from the loss of part of his assets which arose and was incurred in another State. For example, in a claim for misrepresentation it is not the place where the misrepresentee had a bank account and made a payment in reliance on the misrepresentation. Thus in *Domicrest Ltd v Swiss Bank Corp*[106] Rix J considered whether Domicrest could sue in England for claims in tort alleging negligent misrepresentation by the bank as to the effect of the payment order and the client's credit. Domicrest argued that the relevant event which gave rise to the damage was the receipt by Domicrest in England of the statements and assurances which the bank intended Domicrest to rely upon and which Domicrest did rely upon. As for the damage itself, England was the place where the economic loss was suffered, for it was where Domicrest maintained its bank account, where it received and acted upon the assurances, and where its commercial operations were based. Rix J considered that the place giving rise to the damage in a case of negligent misstatement occurs where the misstatement originates and not the place of receipt and reliance, i.e. in this case Switzerland. The place where the damage itself occurs may be somewhere other than the place of the event giving rise to the damage and is quite likely to be where the misstatement is heard and relied upon. However, on the facts of the case he did not consider that that place was in England but was in Switzerland and in Italy where the goods had been released to the bank's customer in reliance on the bank's assurances that the bank would pay the purchase price.

*Domicrest* was approved in *Sunderland Marine Mutual Insurance Co Ltd v Wiseman (The Seaward Quest)*[107] which involved a choice of jurisdiction between England and Scotland and therefore Schedule 4 to the Civil Jurisdiction and Judgments Act applied.[108] Rule 3(c) of that Schedule is equivalent to Article 5(3). A mutual insurance company pleaded that the three defendants had conspired to

105. Case C-168/02 *Rudolf Kronhofer v Marianne Maier and Others* [2004] ECR I 06009.
106. [1998] 3 All ER 578. See also *ABCI v Banque Franco Tunisienne* [2003] 2 Lloyd's Rep 146 at para. 41; *London Helicopters Ltd v Heliportugal LDA-INAC* [2006] EWHC 108 and *Newsat Holdings Ltd v Zani* [2006] 1 Lloyd's Rep 707.
107. [2007] EWHC 1460 (Comm), [2007] 2 Lloyd's Rep 308.
108. Which applies *intra* United Kingdom.

sink the *Seaward Quest* deliberately and had fraudulently misrepresented the circumstances of the loss to the insurers who had paid out under the insurance policy. Langley J held that the "harmful event" alleged occurred in Scotland. The conspiracy to scuttle the ship and alleged misrepresentations were made there. The only connection with England was that that was the place where the insurers made the decision to pay the claim and it was assumed that payment was made from there.

In *Anton Durbeck GmbH v Den Norske Bank ASA (The Tropical Reefer)*[109] the claimant cargo interests alleged that a Norwegian bank, the mortgagee of the ship *Tropical Reefer*, had wrongfully interfered with the claimants' contracts for the carriage of a cargo of bananas by arresting the ship in Panama. Nigel Teare QC held that the English court did not have jurisdiction to determine the claimants' claim for damages for wrongful interference with the cargo under Article 5(3) as Panama, rather than London, was the place where the event which gave rise to the damage occurred.

### *(vii) Agency – Article 5(5)*

A person domiciled in a Contracting State may also be sued in another Contracting State "as regards a dispute arising out of the operations of a branch, agency or other establishment, in the courts for the place in which the branch, agency or other establishment is situated".

In *Anton Durbeck GmbH v Den Norske Bank ASA (The Tropical Reefer)*[110] the Court of Appeal held that the decision by the London branch of a Norwegian bank to arrest the *Tropical Reefer* in Panama meant that the dispute arose out of the activities of the London branch within Article 5(5). The activities which had given rise to the dispute had arisen out of the London banking business conducted by the defendant's London branch. The loan in respect of which the security over the ship had been taken had been negotiated in London; the decision to enforce the security had been taken in London; and the London branch had given instructions to enforce the security and the power of attorney to enable it to be done. Therefore the English court had jurisdiction under Article 5(5) but the Court of Appeal stayed the proceedings on the grounds of *forum non conveniens*, in favour of Panama.

### *(viii) Remuneration for salvage of cargo or freight – Article 5(7)*

The claimant may sue for remuneration for salvage of cargo or freight in the court where the cargo or freight has been arrested or could have been arrested and bail or security has been provided (Article 5(7)).

### *(ix) Multiple defendants – Article 6(1)*

Where there is more than one defendant, the courts for the place where any one of the defendants is domiciled are recognised as having jurisdiction "provided the claims are so closely connected that it is expedient to hear and determine them

109. [2002] EWHC 1173; [2002] All ER (D) 67. The case subsequently went to the Court of Appeal but not on this point – [2003] EWCA Civ 147; [2003] 2 All ER (Comm) 411.
110. [2003] EWCA Civ 147; [2003] 2 All ER (Comm) 411.

together to avoid the risk of irreconcilable judgments resulting from separate proceedings". The words in quotes did not appear in Article 6(1) of the EC Jurisdiction and Lugano Conventions but they reflect the decision of the European Court of Justice in *Kalfelis v Schröder*.[111] Thus if, for example, a carrier brings proceedings against different cargo interests, A, B, and C, seeking a declaration that it is not liable for cargo damage to cargo shipped on the same voyage under bills of lading in the same terms, and A is domiciled in England, B is domiciled in France and C is domiciled in Spain, the carrier can sue all three cargo interests in either England, France or Spain. The claimant must establish a good arguable case that the defendant is domiciled in England.[112]

Until *Freeport plc v Olle Arnoldsson*[113] it had been debated whether it was possible to apply Article 6(1) in a situation where claims were brought against two or more defendants and one action was based in contract, whereas the other was based in tort. In *Freeport* Mr Arnoldsson sued Freeport because of an agreement that he would be paid a fee by a company which was to become the owner of a factory shop in Sweden. This company was subsequently incorporated under Swedish law as Freeport AB. Mr Arnoldsson brought proceedings in Sweden against both companies. Freeport argued that the action against it had a contractual basis, whereas the action against Freeport AB was based in tort, delict or quasi-delict since there was no contractual relationship between Mr Arnoldsson and that company. As the legal bases of the actions against Freeport and Freeport AB were different, Article 6(1) could not apply as it could not be shown that the two actions were connected. The European Court of Justice held that Article 6(1) can apply if the *Kalfelis* test is satisfied, "without there being any need for the actions brought to have identical legal bases".[114]

A valid jurisdiction clause within Article 23 of the EC Jurisdiction Regulation prevails over the special jurisdiction of Article 6(1) of the EC Jurisdiction Regulation.[115] Therefore if three defendants, A, B and C, are domiciled in England, France and Spain respectively but C has agreed to jurisdiction in Germany, the claimant could sue both A and B in either England or France but must sue C in Germany in accordance with Article 23. The claimant could not sue A, B and C in Germany as only C has agreed to jurisdiction there and none of the defendants is domiciled there, so Article 6(1) does not apply.

### *(x) Third party proceedings – Article 6(2)*

Article 6(2) provides that an action against a third party may be brought in the court seised of the original proceedings. There must be a close connection between the proceedings commenced by the original claimant and the third party proceedings

111. See fn. 99. See also, e.g., *Roche Nedeland and others* [2006] ECR I-6535; *FKI Engineering Ltd v Dewind Holdings Limited* [2008] EWCA Civ 316 and Case C-103/05 *Reisch Montage AG v Kiesel Baumachinen Handels GmbH* [2007] I L Pr 10.
112. *Canada Trust Co v Stolzenberg & Co. KG (No 2)* [2002] 1 AC 1; *Bols Distilleries v Superior Yacht Services Limited* [2006] UKPC 45; [2007] 1 WLR 12; *Benatti v WPP Holdings Italy SRL* [2007] EWCA Civ 263; [2007] I L Pr 33 at paras [37]–[44].
113. Case C-98/06 [2007] WLR (D) 252.
114. *Ibid.*, para. 46.
115. *Deforche (Société) v Tomacrau (Société)* [2007] I L Pr 25 (French Court De Cassation).

commenced by the original defendant.[116] There was not such a close connection in *Barton v Golden Sun Holidays Ltd*.[117] There the claimants were a group of holidaymakers and the defendant was a tour operator. The tour operator admitted liability when the holidaymakers became ill and settled the case with the amount of costs to be agreed at a later date. The tour operator applied to serve third party proceedings on the hotelier in Cyprus. It was held that the claim brought by the holidaymakers was for causes of action and remedies based solely in English law for the protection of English consumers, whereas the claim against the hotelier had consequences under Cypriot law. Furthermore, as the claim between the claimant and defendant had been settled and was no longer active, there was no realistic prospect that the claim between the claimant and the defendant and the third party would be tried together. Therefore there was no risk of irreconcilable judgments.

Again, where the third party and the defendant have a jurisdiction agreement that satisfies Article 23, that will prevail over Article 6(2).[118]

### *(xi) Limitation – Article 7*

As the EC Jurisdiction Regulation seeks to minimise the risk of irreconcilable judgments and ensure that liability and limitation proceedings are determined by the same court, Article 7 provides that a court of a Member State which has jurisdiction in "actions relating to liability from the use or operation of a ship" shall also have jurisdiction over claims for limitation of such liability. So, for example, if the shipowner is domiciled in Greece, the court of that State would have jurisdiction where the shipowner is sued for liability for a collision. Without Article 7 the shipowner would not be able to commence a limitation action in Greece but would have to sue where the other party or parties were domiciled. Article 7 allows the shipowner to bring proceedings to limit where it could be sued.[119]

### *(xii) Other international conventions*

Article 71[120] provides that the EC Jurisdiction Regulation shall not affect any Conventions to which the Member States are parties and which in relation to particular matters, govern jurisdiction. A number of conventions may be of great significance in maritime matters such as the International Convention for the Unification of Certain Rules Relating to the Arrest of Seagoing Ships of 1952 (the "Arrest Convention"), the International Convention for the Unification of Certain Rules Concerning Civil Jurisdiction in Matters of Collision 1952 ("the Collision Convention"), and the Hamburg Rules.[121]

116. C-365/88 *Kongress Agentur Hagen GmbH v Zeehaghe BV* [1990] ECR 1-1845.
117. [2007] I L Pr 57.
118. Case C-77/04 *Groupement D'Intérêt Economique (GIE) Réunion Européenne v Zurich España* [2005] I L Pr 456.
119. See gen. ed. D. R. Thomas, *Liability Regimes in Contemporary Maritime Law* (Informa, 2007), chapter 16 by N. Meeson on "Jurisdictional Aspects of Limitation of Liability for Maritime Claims", pp. 306–308.
120. Article 57 of the EC Jurisdiction and Lugano Conventions.
121. See fn. 4 of this chapter.

The Arrest Convention is of particular significance as Article 7 gives the English courts jurisdiction on the merits of the dispute if a ship is arrested in England. Therefore, if it is possible to arrest the ship in respect of which the claim arose or a sister ship when it comes into territorial waters, the English court will have jurisdiction on the merits of the dispute, even though the shipowner is domiciled in another EC Member State. The ship must be arrested for the Arrest Convention to apply.[122] It is not sufficient that an arrest has been threatened and security, for example, by means of a P&I Club letter of undertaking or bank guarantee, has been provided in order to avoid arrest. If the claimant agrees not to arrest it should ask the shipowner to agree to English jurisdiction within Article 23 or submit to the jurisdiction within Article 24.[123]

The Arrest Convention may be contrasted with the Collision Convention, Article 1(1) of which provides that a collision action can only be brought before the courts there set out including the court where the ship or a sister ship has been arrested or could have been arrested but bail or other security has been provided.[124]

The EC Jurisdiction Regulation and the other international convention must be read together where that is possible. Where, however, there is a conflict between the EC Jurisdiction Regulation and the other convention, the latter will prevail. The European Court of Justice considered whether there was a conflict between the Arrest Convention and the EC Jurisdiction Convention in *The Maciej Rataj*.[125] There a sister ship had been arrested in England so that England had jurisdiction on the merits under the Arrest Convention. However, proceedings had already been brought in relation to the same claim in Rotterdam and the shipowner argued that the English court, as the court second seised, must stay its proceedings because of the multiple proceedings provisions in the EC Jurisdiction Convention. The European Court of Justice held that as the Arrest Convention does not contain any multiple proceedings provisions there was no conflict and the multiple proceedings provisions of the EC Jurisdiction Convention applied. Therefore the English court, as the court second seised, had to stay its proceedings in favour of the court first seised, Rotterdam, in so far as they were between the same parties.

The English court has held that there is a conflict between Article 17 of the EC Jurisdiction Convention, now Article 23 of the EC Jurisdiction Regulation (which provides that the court chosen shall have jurisdiction), and the Arrest Convention (which provides that the courts of the country in which the arrest was made shall have jurisdiction),[126] but the English court exercised its discretion at common law to stay its proceedings in favour of the court chosen.[127] Therefore the Arrest

122. *The Deichland* [1989] 2 All ER 1066. The claimant can arrest to found jurisdiction even if the shipowner has acknowledged issue of the writ *in rem* and filed a bail bond (*The Prinsengracht* [1993] 1 Lloyd's Rep 41) or entered a caveat against the arrest of the ship (*The Anna H* [1995] 1 Lloyd's Rep 11).
123. E.g., by acknowledging service of a writ *in rem* and by providing a bail bond – *The Prinsengracht* [1993] 1 Lloyd's Rep 41.
124. Article 1(1)(b). See *The Po* [1991] 2 Lloyd's Rep 206. *Cf.* Article 7 of the International Convention on the Arrest of Ships 1999 which is not yet in force and Article 5(7) of the EC Jurisdiction Regulation.
125. Case C-406/92 [1995] 1 Lloyd's Rep 302. See pp. 9, 10 and 12.
126. *The Bergen* [1997] 1 Lloyd's Rep 380. *Cf. The Bergen (No. 2)* [1997] 2 Lloyd's Rep 710 on *forum non conveniens*.
127. *The Bergen (No. 2)* [1997] 2 Lloyd's Rep 710. See pp. 24–28 of this chapter on *forum non conveniens*.

Convention prevailed. Another example of an international convention prevailing would be where the Hamburg Rules apply to a bill of lading which provides for the exclusive jurisdiction of the courts of a Member State. Article 21 of the Hamburg Rules provides that the cargo claimant can choose from a number of different fora including the court chosen and this would prevail over Article 23 which provides that the court chosen shall have exclusive jurisdiction.

It is doubtful whether the Hague-Visby Rules would fall within Article 71 as it may be argued that they do not govern jurisdiction.[128] In *The Morviken*[129] the House of Lords struck out a jurisdiction clause where the court chosen would have applied the Hague Rules which would have imposed a lower package limit than that under the Hague-Visby Rules which applied mandatorily under English law.

### (b) Common law

If the defendant is not domiciled in a Member State, pursuant to Article 4 of the EC Jurisdiction Regulation, the English courts determine their jurisdiction in accordance with the common law, i.e. the Civil Procedure Rules[130] and case law.

At common law jurisdiction is founded as of right for *in personam* proceedings where a defendant is served with proceedings within the jurisdiction in accordance with Part 6 of the Civil Procedure Rules.

Where the defendant is not within the jurisdiction the claimant requires the permission of the court in order to serve proceedings on the defendant outside the jurisdiction. The application for permission is made by the claimant without notice to the defendant. Part 6 rule 20 of the Civil Procedure Rules sets out the grounds on which such permission may be granted. The claimant must state in its application which ground or grounds it relies on. Those most likely to apply to maritime contractual claims are under paragraph 5 where the claim is made in respect of a contract which (a) was made within the jurisdiction; or (b) was made by or through an agent trading or residing within the jurisdiction; or (c) is governed by English law; or (d) contains a term to the effect that the court shall have jurisdiction to determine any claim in respect of the contract. Alternatively, the claim may be made under paragraph 6 in respect of a breach of contract committed within the jurisdiction or paragraph 7 for a claim for a declaration that no contract exists where if it was found to exist it would comply with the conditions set out in Part 6 rule 20(5).

128. *Cf.* J. Cooke, T. Young and A. Taylor, *Voyage Charters* (3rd ed, Informa, 2007) – ("*Cooke*"), para. 85.27 expresses the view that the Hague-Visby Rules would probably override Article 23 of the EC Jurisdiction Regulation; R. Aikens, R. Lord, and M. Bools, *Bills of Lading* (Informa, 2006) ("*Aikens*") expresses the view that the Hague-Visby Rules are not within the terms of Article 71 – see para. 10.50, n. 73 and para. 14.43; and G. Treitel and F. Reynolds, *Carver* (2nd ed, Sweet & Maxwell, 2005) ("*Carver*"), paras. 9-077, n. 92, which suggests that "such a jurisdiction clause would however now normally require to be accepted by virtue of Art. 17 [*sic* – presumably 23] of Council Regulation 44/2001 on Civil Jurisdiction and Judgments".
129. [1983] 1 AC 565. See pp. 28 and 40 of this chapter. The decision can only apply if the Hague-Visby Rules apply compulsorily – see *The Komninos S* [1991] 1 Lloyd's Rep 370 and *Trafigura Beheer BV v Mediterranean Shipping Co SA (The MSC Amsterdam)* [2007] EWCA Civ 794 discussed at pp. 40 and 41 of this chapter, and see Chapter 3, p. 108.
130. The Civil Procedure Rules replaced the Rules of the Supreme Court in April 1999. The Civil Procedure Rules will be referred to except where case law is discussed which was decided on the Rules of the Supreme Court.

Although there is some overlap these grounds differ considerably from the grounds of jurisdiction under Articles 23, 5(1) and 5(5) of the EC Jurisdiction Regulation. Both Article 23 of the EC Jurisdiction Regulation and Part 6 rule 20(d) recognise party autonomy. However, there is nothing in the EC Jurisdiction Regulation which confers jurisdiction on the basis of where the contract is concluded, or the governing law of the contract or where the breach of contract is committed. At common law where, for example, a bill of lading provides for English law, the court may grant permission to serve a claim form outside the jurisdiction in Canada, as in *The Spiliada*.[131]

The claimant must show that it is, or has become, a party to the bill of lading contract, for example, if it is the transferee of a bill of lading that it is the holder of the bill and that rights have been transferred to it by virtue of section 2 of the Carriage of Goods by Sea Act 1992[132] or where there is an implied contract on the terms of the bill of lading.[133]

### (i) *Forum non conveniens*

In a case where the defendant has been served within the jurisdiction a stay will only be granted on the ground of *forum non conveniens* where the defendant can show that England is not the natural or appropriate forum for the trial and that there is another available forum which is clearly or distinctly more appropriate than England, i.e. the case may be tried more suitably for the interests of all the parties and the ends of justice.[134] Thus in *Caltex Singapore Pte Ltd v BP Shipping Ltd,*[135] BP were served as of right in England as they were resident in England, but they sought a stay of the English proceedings on the ground that Singapore was the natural or appropriate forum. The burden was on BP to show that England was not the appropriate forum. BP admitted liability for the damage caused when their ship, the *British Skill*, collided with Caltex's jetty in Singapore, so that only the issues of quantum and limitation remained. Considering such factors as whether there was any connection with England; the place of the tort (Singapore); where the parties were based (Singapore and England); the applicable law (Singapore); where it would be more convenient to have the trial (Singapore as all the witnesses of fact as to the damage to the Caltex jetty were in Singapore); and existing proceedings elsewhere, Clarke J held as a first stage that Singapore was the natural forum for the determination of the issues in the action. At the second stage he asked whether the plaintiff had established that there was some special circumstance as a result of which justice required that the action be allowed to proceed in England.[136]

Where, however, the defendant is outside the jurisdiction the court will not grant permission unless satisfied that England and Wales is the proper place in which to bring the claim. The burden of proof is on the claimant.[137] In *The*

131. *Spiliada Maritime Corp v Cansulex Ltd (The Spiliada)* [1987] AC 460 – see pp. 24 and 25 of this chapter.
132. See Chapter 3, p. 98.
133. *Brandt v Liverpool* [1924] 1 KB 175. See Chapter 3, pp. 102 and 103.
134. *The Spiliada* [1987] AC 460.
135. [1996] 1 Lloyd's Rep 286.
136. This is the correct question but his conclusion was subsequently overruled in *The Herceg Novi,* discussed at p. 29 of this chapter.
137. Part 6 rule 21(2A) CPR.

*Spiliada*[138] shipowners claimed against Canadian shippers, Cansulex, for alleged corrosion and pitting of the holds and tank tops of their ship due to a cargo of wet sulphur. The bills of lading provided that the bills were to be construed and governed by English law. Leave was obtained by the shipowners to issue and serve a writ upon Cansulex in Canada on the ground that the contract was governed by English law under Order 11 rule 1 of the Rules of the Supreme Court, which has now been replaced by Part 6 rule 20 of the Civil Procedure Rules. Cansulex applied for an order to set aside such leave. A very similar action was at that time proceeding in the Admiralty Court in London in which Cansulex were also defendants. That action concerned a ship called the *Cambridgeshire*. After reviewing the authorities, Lord Goff, in a judgment with which all the other Law Lords agreed, stated that where the defendant is outside the jurisdiction the claimant is seeking to persuade the court to exercise its discretionary power to permit service on the defendant outside the jurisdiction. That jurisdiction may be exorbitant. His Lordship also considered that the court should not be deterred from granting a stay of proceedings, or from exercising its discretion against granting leave under Order 11 simply because the plaintiff would be deprived of a legitimate personal or juridical advantage, provided that substantial justice would be done in the available appropriate forum. The plaintiffs were time barred in Canada. The House of Lords upheld the judge's exercise of discretion that England was the appropriate forum. The factors which he had taken into account included the availability of witnesses, the multiplicity of proceedings and the *Cambridgeshire* factor, i.e. the fact that experienced teams of lawyers and experts were already aware of the issues involved and this would contribute to efficiency, expedition and economy and, in Lord Goff's view, to promoting the possibility of settlement. Lord Goff indicated that, even if the judge had erred in exercising his discretion, he would only have set aside the proceedings on the condition that Cansulex waive their right to rely on the time bar in British Columbia.

#### *(ii) Jurisdiction agreement*

As seen above, the common law rules will apply where neither party to the English jurisdiction clause is domiciled in a Member State. This is as a result of the application of Articles 4 and 23(3) of the EC Jurisdiction Regulation. Thus if, for example, a receiver domiciled in Singapore wishes to rely on an English jurisdiction clause in a bill of lading with a carrier domiciled in a non-Member State, and the carrier has commenced proceedings in the court of its domicile, the English court will apply their common law rules under which it has a discretion.

The decision in *Gasser* may be contrasted sharply with the position at English common law, where the English court has adopted a robust defence of English jurisdiction clauses in most circumstances. Thus the English court will uphold a jurisdiction clause unless there are strong reasons for staying the proceedings in the forum in which the parties have agreed that they will be litigated.[139] This is the case even though proceedings have already been commenced elsewhere, as

138. [1987] AC 460. See also *Connelly v RTZ Corporation plc* [1997] CLC 1357. See also *Lubbe v Cape plc* [2000] 1 Lloyd's Rep 139 and *Carlson v Rio Tinto plc* [1999] CLC 551.

139. *The Eleftheria* [1970] P 94; *The El Amria* [1981] 2 Lloyd's Rep 119; *The Bergen (No. 2)* [1997] 2 Lloyd's Rep 710 and *Donohue v Armco Inc* [2001] UKHL 64; [2002] 1 Lloyd's Rep 425.

the court chosen would be the appropriate forum, unless there are multiple proceedings between multiple parties in the other forum, some of whom have not agreed to English jurisdiction.[140]

Two recent decisions on bills of lading illustrate this, even in the face of legislation in the other jurisdiction which would make the English jurisdiction clause invalid. In *OT Africa Line Ltd v Magic Sportswear Corp,*[141] O. T. Africa Line Ltd (OTAL), an English company which also had offices in Toronto, carried goods from New York on their ship *Mathilde Maersk* to Monrovia. OTAL issued a bill of lading in Toronto where the ocean freight was payable. The bill of lading named Magic Sportswear Corporation (Magic), a Delaware corporation with business interests in New York, as the shippers and the intended receivers were Blue Banana, a Liberian corporation. It was alleged that the goods were short delivered and Magic and Blue Banana commenced proceedings in Toronto in August 2003. The instigators of those proceedings were the Canadian cargo insurers exercising their subrogated rights to bring the claims in the name of the insured, as Magic and Blue Banana were dormant.

The bill of lading contained an English law and exclusive English court jurisdiction clause. The basis on which the jurisdiction of the Canadian courts was invoked was section 46(1)(b) and (c) of the Canadian Marine Liability Act 2001. Although Canada does not give the force of law to the Hamburg Rules, this section is a similar jurisdiction provision to Article 21 of the Hamburg Rules, which provides that the cargo claimant has an option to bring proceedings in a number of places including the place designated by the contract of carriage. The Canadian legislation is more favourable to the cargo claimant in that it permits an action to be brought if the defendant has *a* place of business, branch or agency in Canada, rather than *the* principal place of business or the habitual residence of the carrier provided for by the Hamburg Rules. The rationale for section 46 included giving Canadian importers and exporters the right to pursue cargo claims in Canada and an attack on what was perceived to be a monopoly of the British courts over such claims. The Canadian court retained a discretion to refuse jurisdiction on grounds of *forum non conveniens* and the choice of law provision remained effective. The Hamburg Rules are not in force in England and Wales and there are no current plans to change this. The case therefore challenged the principle of the supremacy of party autonomy, long recognised by the English courts.

The Court of Appeal held that the conflict between the provisions of the Canadian legislation and the agreed jurisdiction of England was to be resolved by the rules of private international law of the court in which the question has to be resolved, i.e. the English court. One of those rules is that questions of interpretation and enforcement of contracts are resolved by reference to the proper law of the contract, which was English law.[142] The Court of Appeal concluded that there

140. *Bouygues Offshore SA v Caspian Shipping Co* [1998] 2 Lloyd's Rep 461 and *Donohue v Armco Inc* [2001] UKHL 64; [2002] 1 Lloyd's Rep 425. For the converse situation where the English court refuses to enforce a foreign jurisdiction agreement because of multiple proceedings see *Citi-March Ltd v Neptune Orient Lines Ltd* [1996] 2 All ER 545; [1997] 1 Lloyd's Rep 72; *The MC Pearl* [1997] 1 Lloyd's Rep 566; and *obiter Konkola Copper Mines plc v Coromin* [2006] EWCA Civ 5; [2006] 1 Lloyd's Rep 410 and R. Asariotis, Y. Baatz and N. Gaskell, *Bills of Lading: Law and Contracts* (LLP, 2000) ("*Gaskell*"), paras 20.213–20.219.

141. [2005] EWCA 710; [2005] 2 Lloyd's Rep 170.

142. The court relied on the decision of Thomas J in *Akai Pty Ltd v People's Insurance Co Ltd* [1998] 1 Lloyd's Rep 90.

was no strong reason not to hold the parties to the English jurisdiction clause. Furthermore, the Court of Appeal upheld the anti-suit injunctions to restrain the defendants from pursuing the Canadian proceedings.[143] The Canadian court ultimately stayed the shippers' action in Canada.[144]

*Magic Sportswear* has been followed in *Horn Linie GmbH & Co v Panamericana Formas E Impresos SA, Ace Seguros SA (The Hornbay).*[145] The claimants, a German ship owning company that operated a liner service to South America, loaded a cargo of printing machinery on board the *Hornbay*. The cargo was shipped on board at Hamburg for delivery in Cartagena, Colombia. Due to bad weather it was necessary to land the goods at Le Havre where they were found to be a constructive total loss. The bill of lading provided for English law and the exclusive jurisdiction of the High Court in London. The bill of lading also expressly incorporated the Hague-Visby Rules and a Himalaya Clause.

The second defendants were the cargo insurers, ACE, who had procured proceedings to be issued in Colombia against Maritrans, the claimants' agents in Colombia, seeking judgment for the full value of the cargo. The claim was founded upon the contract of carriage and provisions of the Colombian Code of Commerce which the defendants argued imposed liability on Maritrans as agent of the shipowners. The defendants challenged the jurisdiction of the English court in the proceedings for a negative declaration brought by the claimants contemporaneously with the commencement of the Colombian proceedings. The claimants sought an anti-suit injunction against the defendants in respect of the Colombian proceedings. The commercial significance of the dispute on jurisdiction was that, if it remained in England, the cargo interests would be likely to recover nothing because of the one-year time bar. Morison J held that there was no exceptional reason why the English court would not exercise the jurisdiction conferred on it and granted an anti-suit injunction. He joined ACE as a necessary and proper party to the proceedings pursuant to CPR 6.20(3)(c) and (d), as an injunction against them would be more effective than against the first defendants alone. The claimants were also permitted to join Maritrans as a party and to amend their claim for a negative injunction to plead the time bar point.

Thus where the English courts apply their common law rules, a litigant will usually be able to rely on an exclusive English jurisdiction clause, even if proceedings have already been commenced in a non-Member State. This would also be the situation where there is a London arbitration clause where the London arbitrators would have jurisdiction to determine their own jurisdiction.[146] If the EC Jurisdiction Regulation applies, however, the litigant can only rely on the exclusive English jurisdiction clause or indeed an exclusive jurisdiction clause choosing the courts of any Member State, if the court chosen is also first seised, or once the court first seised, but not chosen, declines jurisdiction.

The English court will also uphold a foreign jurisdiction clause unless there is strong cause not to, for example, because there are multiple proceedings already in existence in England.[147] This assumes the jurisdiction agreement is valid. It

143. See p. 30 of this chapter.
144. *OT Africa Line Ltd v Magic Sportswear Corp* [2007] 1 Lloyd's Rep 85.
145. [2006] EWHC 373 (Comm); [2006] 2 Lloyd's Rep 44.
146. Section 30 of the Arbitration Act 1996.
147. See, e.g., *Citi-March Ltd v Neptune Orient Lines Ltd* [1996] 2 All ER 545; [1997] 1 Lloyd's Rep 72 and *The MC Pearl* [1997] 1 Lloyd's Rep 566 and *Gaskell*, paras 20.213–20.219.

will not be if the English court would apply the Hague-Visby Rules[148] and the effect of the jurisdiction clause would be to lessen the carrier's liability. Thus in *The Morviken*[149] the House of Lords held that an Amsterdam court jurisdiction clause was null and void and of no effect in accordance with Article III rule 8 of the Hague-Visby Rules, which applied mandatorily in that case. The Amsterdam court would have applied lower limits than the English court. A forum clause would not always be invalid but would depend on the type of claim brought. For example, a claim by the carrier for freight would not be affected by the Hague-Visby Rules. In *The Benarty*[150] the Court of Appeal gave a stay on the basis of an exclusive jurisdiction clause in favour of the court of Djakarta unless the carrier elected otherwise, on the ground that the carrier sought the benefit of lower tonnage limitation in Indonesia and not lower package limitation, a situation expressly permitted by Article VIII of the Hague-Visby Rules. In that case the defendants had given an undertaking not to rely on the lower package limits applicable in Indonesia. Lord Ackner gave the practice of giving such an undertaking his approval.[151] In *Baghlaf Al Zafer Factory Co v Pakistan National Shipping Co*[152] the shipowners gave an undertaking that they would not rely on the lower limits applicable in Pakistan where the Hague Rules apply and the limit is £100 sterling per package rather than £100 gold value. Had they not done so, Phillips LJ, with whom the other members of the Court of Appeal agreed, said that any application to stay English proceedings where there was an exclusive Pakistan jurisdiction agreement would have been doomed to failure, as the jurisdiction agreement would have had no effect.[153] Subsequently it transpired that it might not be possible to waive the time bar under Pakistani legislation and therefore the English Court of Appeal lifted the stay.[154]

### *(iii) Tonnage limitation*

As we have already seen, a major cause of forum shopping is where a claimant in a maritime incident prefers one jurisdiction rather than another due to the differences in the tonnage limits applicable.[155] There is not a level playing field internationally in relation to tonnage limits. Some States give effect to the 1996 Protocol to the 1976 LLMC with high limits but which may be difficult to break, whereas other States give effect to the 1957 Limitation Convention with lower limits but which may be easier to break.[156]

148. As to when the Hague-Visby Rules apply, see pp. 40 and 41 of this chapter and Chapter 3, pp. 107 and 108.
149. [1983] 1 AC 565. See pp. 23 and 40 of this chapter.
150. [1984] 2 Lloyd's Rep 244.
151. *Ibid.*, p. 249.
152. [1998] 2 Lloyd's Rep 229, and see J. Edwards, "Exclusive Jurisdiction Clauses and Forum Non Conveniens" [1998] IJOSL 193. See also *Pirelli Cables Ltd v United Thai Shipping Corporation Ltd* (unreported, 5 April 2000 (Langley J)).
153. *Ibid.*, p. 238.
154. *Baghlaf Al Zafer Factory Co v Pakistan National Shipping Co. (No 2)* [2000] 1 Lloyd's Rep 1.
155. On tonnage limitation see pp. 9, 10, 12 and 13 of this chapter.
156. See *Jurisdiction and Forum Selection in International Maritime Law Essays in Honor of Robert Force,* gen. ed. M. Davies, Chapter 5 by J. Hare, "Shopping for the Best Admiralty Bargain"; P. Griggs, R. Williams and J. Farr, *Limitation of Liability for Maritime Claims* (4th ed, LLP, 2005); gen. ed. D. R. Thomas, *Liability Regimes in Contemporary Maritime Law* (Informa, 2007), Chapter 16 by N. Meeson on "Jurisdictional Aspects of Limitation of Liability for Maritime Claims".

The English courts have held that where proceedings have been commenced elsewhere first and then in England and the other forum is the natural or appropriate forum, the English court should stay its proceedings in favour of the natural forum, even though that forum will apply the 1957 Limitation Convention, rather than the 1976 LLMC which would have been applied in England. In *The Herceg Novi and Ming Galaxy*[157] the *Herceg Novi* and the *Ming Galaxy* were involved in a collision in the Straits of Singapore. Two days after the collision the Taiwanese owners of the *Ming Galaxy* commenced proceedings in Singapore. They subsequently sought to limit their liability. The writ *in rem* was served by fixing it to the mast of the *Herceg Novi* where she had sunk inside Singapore waters. Ten days after the collision the Maltese owners of the *Herceg Novi* issued a writ *in rem* against the *Ming Galaxy* which was served on a sister ship, the *Ming South*, two days later at Felixstowe. The *Herceg Novi* owners' claims amounted to US$10,353,000, but they could not recover that in either Singapore, where the 1957 Limitation Convention applied,[158] or England, where the 1976 LLMC applied, as there was no suggestion that the limit could be broken under either Convention. The *Ming Galaxy*'s limit in England was US$5,800,000, whereas it was US$2,900,000 in Singapore. In addition, the *Herceg Novi* cargo owners had claims of US$4,000,000. Thus the owners of the *Herceg Novi* had every reason to want the English court to determine limitation. The *Ming Galaxy*'s claim did not exceed the limit of the *Herceg Novi* under either Convention, but they obviously preferred the issue of limitation to be resolved in Singapore to minimise their liability. They applied for a stay of the English proceedings.

The Court of Appeal gave an unconditional stay of the English action. Sir Christopher Staughton, giving the judgment of the court, said that it was accepted that England was not the natural or appropriate forum. Singapore was clearly and distinctly a more appropriate forum than England. Therefore there ought to be a stay of the English action unless that course would deprive the owners of the *Herceg Novi* of some juridical advantage so as to justify the refusal of a stay. The Court of Appeal did not accept that there was a juridical advantage for three reasons. First, the 1976 LLMC has not received universal acceptance and thus is not "an internationally sanctioned and objective view of where substantial justice is now viewed as lying". Secondly, the IMO is not a legislature and cannot be found to have enacted an international consensus. Lastly it is quite impossible to say that substantial justice is not available in Singapore. The preference for the 1976 LLMC has no greater justification than for the 1957 regime.

*Bouygues Offshore SA v Caspian Shipping Co*[159] concerned multiple parties, two of whom had agreed English jurisdiction and governing law. The Court of Appeal stayed the English proceedings on liability in favour of South Africa where the court had jurisdiction over all the parties, but refused a stay of the limitation actions in England and in this way gave effect to the English jurisdiction agreement. The difference between the two jurisdictions was acute as the whole of the claim for £50 million might be recovered in South Africa which applied the 1957 Limitation Convention with lower limits but which are easier to break, whereas the limit in England was one hundredth of the amount of the claim.

157. [1998] 2 Lloyd's Rep 454.
158. Singapore now gives effect to the 1976 LLMC but not the 1996 Protocol.
159. [1998] 2 Lloyd's Rep 461.

In *Seismic Shipping Inc v Total E&P UK plc (The Western Regent)*[160] the Court of Appeal has held that the 1976 LLMC does not require liability proceedings to have been commenced in England before the shipowner can invoke limitation.

### (c) Anti-suit injunctions

The English court has a discretion to grant an anti-suit injunction to restrain a party from commencing or continuing proceedings in a foreign court if such proceedings would be an abuse of process under section 37 of the Supreme Court Act 1981.[161] It is important to stress that the injunction restrains the defendant to the English court proceedings and not the foreign court. Nevertheless the foreign court may take the view that such an order is an interference with its sovereignty,[162] and the European Court of Justice has held in *Turner v Grovit*[163] that an anti-suit injunction should not be granted to restrain a defendant from pursuing proceedings in another Member State as there should be mutual trust between all the Member States. Furthermore, as a result of the decision in *Erich Gasser*[164] an English court which is second seised would have to stay its proceedings until the court first seised has declined jurisdiction and therefore could not grant an anti-suit injunction to enforce an English jurisdiction agreement if the court first seised is within a Member State.

However, the use of anti-suit injunctions to restrain a defendant from pursuing proceedings in a court of a non-Member State is permissible.[165] Different considerations apply where there is no mutual agreement as to jurisdiction between two States.[166] The House of Lords stated in *Donohue v Armco*[167] that the English courts will usually exercise their discretion and grant an anti-suit injunction to enforce a jurisdiction agreement unless the party suing in the non contractual forum can show that there is strong reason for suing in that forum.[168] However, in that case an anti-suit injunction was not granted to enforce an exclusive English jurisdiction clause as there were already proceedings between multiple parties in New York, some of whom were not bound by the English jurisdiction agreement.[169]

What is not clear is whether the English court can grant an anti-suit injunction to restrain a defendant from pursuing court proceedings in a Member State or

160. [2005] 2 Lloyd's Rep 359. See Chapter 6, p. 225.
161. *Turner v Grovit and Others*, 2004 WL 5400365, House of Lords.
162. The Dusseldorf Court of Appeal held that an English anti-suit injunction could not be served on the ground that it was unconstitutional and interfered with its sovereignty: *Re the Enforcement of an English Anti-Suit Injunction* [1997] I L Pr 320.
163. Case C-159/02 *Turner v Grovit* [2004] ECR I-3565; [2005] 1 AC 101.
164. Case C-116/02 *Erich Gasser GmbH v MISAT Srl* [2003] ECR I-14693; [2005] QB 1.
165. See, e.g., *OT Africa Line Ltd v Magic Sportswear Corp* [2005] EWCA 710; [2005] 2 Lloyd's Rep 170 and *Horn Linie GmbH & Co v Panamericana Formas E Impresos SA, Ace Seguros SA (The Hornbay)* [2006] EWHC 373 (Comm); [2006] 2 Lloyd's Rep 44, both bill of lading cases discussed on pp. 26 and 27 of this chapter; and in the context of an insurance contract an anti-suit injunction was granted in *Goshawk Dedicated Ltd v Roo Inc* [2006] EWHC 1730; [2006] Lloyd's Rep IR 711.
166. See, e.g., A. Briggs in Chapter 12, "Anti-Suit Injunctions in a Complex World" in *Lex Mercatoria, Essays on International Commercial Law in Honour of Francis Reynolds*, ed. F. Rose (LLP, 2000).
167. [2001] UKHL 64; [2002] 1 Lloyd's Rep 425.
168. See, e.g., Lord Bingham at para. 24.
169. See also *Bouygues Offshore SA v Caspian Shipping Co* [1998] 2 Lloyd's Rep 461.

Lugano Contracting State if they are in breach of a London arbitration agreement. This issue is currently pending before the European Court of Justice.[170] The English court has until now frequently granted such injunctions on the basis that arbitration proceedings fall outside the scope of the EC Jurisdiction Regulation as they are excluded by Article 1(2)(d).[171] However, the court does have a discretion and has not granted such an injunction where the cargo insurers exercising their subrogated rights seek recovery for cargo loss from the ship's P&I Club by way of direct action granted by statute.[172] The English court clearly does have a discretion to grant such an injunction to restrain a defendant from pursuing court proceedings in a State which is not a Member State or Lugano Contracting State.[173]

### (d) Damages for breach of a jurisdiction agreement

Where the common law rules apply, a party to an exclusive jurisdiction agreement which has been breached may be able to recover damages for breach of contract[174] or for the tort of procuring a breach of contract.[175] Where the EC Jurisdiction Regulation rules apply, the claimant in the English proceedings will seek to recover its costs of successfully contesting the jurisdiction of the court first seised from the court first seised. However, recovery of costs in full or in part may not be possible and the claimant may seek damages in the English proceedings. If the claimant in the English proceedings is not successful in contesting the jurisdiction of the court first seised, it may seek to recover damages from the English court representing the difference between what it recovers in the court first seised and what it would have recovered in England. However, there are great difficulties in seeing how the English court could award damages for breach of contract if a court first seised in a Member State has determined that there was no English jurisdiction clause.[176]

170. *West Tankers Inc v RAS Riunione Adriatica di Sicurta (The Front Comor)* [2007] UKHL 4, [2007] 1 Lloyd's Rep 391.
171. Case C-190/89, *Marc Rich & Co AG v Societa Italiana PA (The Atlantic Emperor)* [1992] 1 Lloyd's Rep 342; *The Heidberg* [1994] 2 Lloyd's Rep 287 at pp. 298–303; *Toepfer International GmbH v Societe Cargill France* [1998] 1 Lloyd's Rep 379; Case C-391/95 *Van Uden Maritime BV v Kommanditgesellschaft in Firma Deco-Line* [1999] All ER (EC) 258 ECJ; *Navigation Maritime Bulgare v Rustal Trading Ltd (The Ivan Zagubanski)* [2002] 1 Lloyd's Rep 106 and *Through Transport Mutual Insurance Association (Eurasia) Ltd v New India Assurance Co Ltd (The Hari Bhum)* [2004] EWCA (Civ) 1598; [2005] 1 Lloyd's Rep 67; *A v B* [2006] EWHC 2006 (Comm), [2007] 1 Lloyd's Rep 237 but not in *Verity Shipping SA v NV Norexa (The Skier Star)* [2008] 1 CLC 45.
172. See fn. 171. See also *Markel International Co Ltd v Craft (The Norseman)* [2006] EWHC 3150 (Comm), [2007] Lloyd's Rep IR 403.
173. *Kallang Shipping SA v Axa Assurances Senegal (The Kallang)* [2006] EWHC 2825; [2007] 1 Lloyd's Rep 160; *Noble Assurance Co v Gerling-Konzern General Insurance Co* [2007] EWHC 253 (Comm); [2007] 1 CLC 85; *C v D* [2007] EWHC 1541 (Comm); [2007] 2 All ER (Comm) 557.
174. *Union Discount Co v Zoller* [2002] 1 WLR 1517; *Donohue v Armco Inc* [2001] UKHL 64; [2002] 1 Lloyd's Rep 425 at paras [36], [48] and [75].
175. See Morison J in *Horn Linie GmbH & Co v Panamericana Formas E Impresos SA, Ace Seguros SA (The Hornbay)* [2006] EWHC 373 (Comm); [2006] 2 Lloyd's Rep 44 at para. [26].
176. See A. Briggs, "The Impact of Recent Judgments of the European Court on English Procedural Law and Practice", *Zeitschrift fur Schweizerisches Recht* 124 (2005) II 231 and R. Swallow and R. Hornshaw, "Jurisdiction Clauses in Loan Agreements: Practical Considerations for Lenders" *Bankers Law*, Vol. 1, No. 2, 18 at p. 21.

A party may recover indemnity costs where the other party has acted in breach of a jurisdiction clause, an arbitration clause or an anti-suit injunction.[177]

## 4. GOVERNING LAW

Our purpose in this section is to consider how the governing law of maritime contracts such as charterparties, bills of lading and marine insurance contracts should be determined in the light of the Convention on the Law Applicable to Contractual Obligations of 1980 ("the Rome Convention"). Although it is usual for such contracts to contain an express jurisdiction and governing law clause or for a bill of lading to incorporate the jurisdiction and governing law clause contained in any charterparty pursuant to which the bill of lading has been issued, this is not always the case. Furthermore, even where there is an express clause, as we shall see, the parties' choice may be subject to restrictions. Where there is no choice we need to consider what guidelines are available to determine the governing law.

The governing law chosen is usually, but not always,[178] the law of the place which the parties have chosen to have jurisdiction. Thus where, for example, a bill of lading provides for jurisdiction in the country of the carrier's principal place of business, it will also usually provide for the law of this country to apply. This is simply for the common sense reason that a tribunal is best placed to adjudicate on its own law with which it is familiar, rather than on a foreign law. It is much quicker and cheaper for the High Court in London to apply English law than to hear evidence from foreign lawyers on the law of another country and then determine that law. Proper law and jurisdiction may therefore be inextricably linked. An express choice of jurisdiction may indicate the parties' choice of governing law. However, if the parties have chosen English Court jurisdiction and the English courts determine that Italian law applies, they will apply Italian law.

Following the harmonisation of the rules as to when a court of an EC Member State had jurisdiction by the EC Jurisdiction Convention, the rules as to how such a court should determine what law governs a contract were also harmonised in the Rome Convention. Section 2 of the Contracts (Applicable Law) Act 1990 gives the force of law to the Rome Convention, as amended by subsequent accession Conventions, with the exception of Articles 7(1) and 10(1)(e). It came into force on 1 April 1991. A Regulation to replace the Rome Convention will be adopted in 2008, except by the United Kingdom, Ireland and Denmark.[179]

177. *Kyrgyz Mobil v Fellowes International* [2005] EWHC 1314 (Comm.) (London arbitration agreement); *Travelers Casualty and Surety Company of Canada v Sun Life Assurance Company of Canada (UK) Ltd* [2006] EWHC 2885 (Comm); *A v B (No 2)* [2007] EWHC 54 (Comm); [2007] 1 Lloyd's Rep 358 (Swiss arbitration subject to the jurisdiction of the Swiss courts); *National Westminster Bank v Rabobank Nederland RV* [2007] EWHC 1742 (Comm) (breach of jurisdiction clause and anti-suit clause), but not in *C v D* [2007] EWCA Civ 1282.

178. See, e.g., the Bermuda Form for liability insurance which provides for London arbitration and New York law which was considered in *C v D* [2007] EWCA Civ 1282.

179. Regulation of the European Parliament and the Council on the Law Applicable to Contractual Obligations (Rome 1), Brussels, 15.12.05, COM (2005) 650 final, 2005/0261 and PE-CONS 3691/07 dated 31 March 2008. The United Kingdom Government has recommended that the UK should opt in to the Rome I Regulation. See Consultation Paper CP05/08 dated 2 April 2008 – *www.dfpri.gov.uk*.

Section 3(1) of the Contracts (Applicable Law) Act 1990 provides that any question as to the meaning or effect of any provision of the Conventions set out in the schedules to the Act shall be referred to the European Court in accordance with the Brussels Protocol or determined in accordance with the principles laid down by, and any relevant decision of, the European Court. In addition the report on the Rome Convention by Professor Mario Giuliano and Professor Paul Lagarde which is reproduced in the Official Journal of the Communities of 31 October 1980 may be considered in ascertaining the meaning or effect of any provision of the Convention.

Article 18 of the Convention further provides that in the interpretation of the rules of the Convention regard shall be had to their international character and to the desirability of achieving uniformity in their interpretation and application.

### (a) The scope of the Rome Convention

The Rome Convention only applies to contractual obligations.[180] Whether a contractual obligation is involved raises similar issues in other contexts such as a whether a claim relates to a contract in Article 5(1) of the EC Regulation or the Regulations on Unfair Terms in Consumer Contracts and case law in those contexts may assist here.

If the dispute between the parties involves, for example, a collision and the claim is in tort the governing law will be determined, not by the Rome Convention, but by sections 9 to 15 of the Private International Law (Miscellaneous Provisions) Act 1995. However, from 11 January 2009 the EC Regulation No 864/2007 on the law applicable to non-contractual obligations (Rome II) will come into effect.[181]

Any contract concluded after 1 April 1991 which involves "a choice between the laws of different countries"[182] will be subject to the Contracts (Applicable Law) Act 1990, unless it is specifically excluded. Most bills of lading involve such a choice in a peculiarly acute form. This is because the number of different countries involved may be considerable: the nationality of the carrier, shipper, consignee or indorsee; the flag of the ship; the place of loading and discharge; the governing law of any charterparty under which the bill of lading has been issued and any governing law chosen by the parties may all be in different countries. Reinsurance contracts similarly may also involve many different countries, for example, because of the different nationalities of the reinsurer, reinsured and primary insured, the risks may be situated in many different countries, the governing law of the primary insurance and the choice of law of the reinsurance policy may all be different.

The application of the Rome Convention is not limited to contracts which have some connection with a Contracting State. In this respect the Rome Convention may be contrasted with the EC Jurisdiction Regulation, the application of

180. *Base Metal Trading Ltd v Shamurin* [2002] CLC 322.

181. Except for Article 29 (which requires Member States to notify the Commission of international conventions to which one or more Member States are parties at the time when the Regulation is adopted and which lay down conflict of law rules relating to non-contractual matters), which shall apply from 11 July 2008.

182. Article 1(1).

which is generally triggered by the domicile of the defendant in a Member State. The Rome Convention will apply to a contractual obligation within its scope which comes before the court of a Contracting State provided it involves a choice between the laws of different countries, i.e. any countries and not simply those countries which are Contracting States. Thus, for example, if the English court has to determine whether Japanese or New York law applies to a charterparty it will apply the Rome Convention.

Article 1(2) of the Rome Convention excludes certain obligations from its scope. The first exclusion which may be relevant to bills of lading is that in Article 1(2)(c): "obligations arising under bills of exchange, cheques and promissory notes and other negotiable instruments to the extent that the obligations under such other negotiable instruments arise out of their negotiable character". The main reason for this exclusion is that many Member States, although not the UK, are parties to the Geneva Conventions which deal with these matters. The issue of interest to us is that it has been suggested that this exclusion may cover some bills of lading. Clearly those bills of lading which are not negotiable, e.g. because they are stated to be "non-negotiable" or where delivery is to a named consignee, are not caught within the exclusion. Where the bill is negotiable because, for example, it is an order bill, it is still not a negotiable instrument. If this is so, it would appear that the Rome Convention applies to all bills of lading.

By Article 1(2)(d) the rules of the Convention do not apply to arbitration agreements and agreements on the choice of court. The reason for this exclusion is that such agreements are subject to other international conventions such as the New York Convention on the Recognition and Enforcement of Arbitral Awards and Article 23 of the EC Jurisdiction Regulation. It is necessary to distinguish the governing law of the underlying contract and the arbitration agreement which is a separable and separate agreement.[183] Although the law of the underlying contract, the arbitration agreement and the law of the place where the arbitration is to be conducted will often be the same, they may not be. A contract may be governed by one law but the arbitration governed by a different law. It would be rare for the law of the arbitration agreement and of the seat of the arbitration to be different. For example, in *C v D*[184] an insurance policy provided for London arbitration and was governed by New York law. The parties had further agreed that the seat of the arbitration was London and the law of the arbitration was English law. The US insurer applied to the arbitration tribunal to correct its award alleging that the award was manifestly in disregard of New York law and it threatened to commence proceedings in a US Federal Court. The Court of Appeal upheld the anti-suit injunction granted by Cooke J. By choosing London as the seat of the arbitration, the parties must be taken to have agreed that proceedings on the award should be only those permitted by English law. Proceedings in a US Federal Court would negate the whole framework in which the arbitration took place and was vexatious and oppressive, unconscionable and an abuse of process.[185] As the arbitration provision expressly referred to English

183. *Premium Nafta Products Ltd v Fili Shipping Co Ltd* [2007] UKHL 40. *Fiona Trust & Holding Corporation v Privalov* [2008] 1 Lloyd's Rep 254.
184. [2007] EWCA Civ 1282; [2008] 1 Lloyd's Rep 239.
185. Applying *Noble Assurance Co v Gerling-Konzern General Insurance Co* [2007] EWHC 253 (Comm), [2007] 1 CLC 85.

law and the Arbitration Act 1996 the parties had not only agreed to arbitration itself but also that any challenge to an award would only be made to the courts of the place agreed as the seat of the arbitration.[186] The choice of New York law as the governing law of the insurance policy did not mean that the parties had replaced the framework of the Arbitration Act 1996.[187]

"The question whether an agent is able to bind a principal, or an organ to bind a company or body corporate, or unincorporate, to a third party" is excluded by Article 1(2)(f). Such an issue may arise in relation to bills of lading, e.g. whether a forwarding agent had actual or ostensible authority to sign a bill of lading on behalf of the carrier.

The Rome Convention does not apply to "contracts of insurance which cover risks situated in the territories of the Member States of the European Economic Community" (Article 1(3)). The English court must apply its own law in order to determine whether a risk is situated in these territories. The reason for this exclusion is that such risks are covered by the EC Second Directive on Non Life Insurance which has its own special rules on governing law which are similar to those in the Rome Convention.

Contracts of reinsurance are not covered by Article 1(3) (Article 1(4)). So, for example, if a risk is situated in Denmark, the contract of insurance covering such risk is not governed by the Rome Convention, whereas the reinsurance of such risk or the insurance of a risk situated in India, would be governed by the Convention.

Where the Convention does not apply, for example, because the charterparty was concluded before 1 April 1991, or the issue is one excluded under Article 1(2), the common law rules in relation to conflicts of law apply. The proper law of the contract means the system of law which the parties intended to apply to the contract. The parties may express their intention or where there is no express written choice their intention may be inferred from the terms and nature of the contract. So, for example, where the contract contains a choice of forum clause, but no express choice of law clause, the court will infer that the parties intended the contract to be governed by the law of the forum where disputes are to be tried unless there are strong indications that they did not intend or may not have intended this result.[188]

Where the intention of the parties as to the law governing it is not expressed and cannot be inferred from the circumstances, the contract is governed by the system of law with which the transaction has its closest and most real connection.[189]

### (b) Freedom of choice

The basic principle enshrined in Article 3(1) of the Rome Convention is that the contract is to be governed by the law chosen by the parties. The choice must be

186. Applying *A v B* [2006] EWHC 2006 (Comm), [2007] 1 Lloyd's Rep 237 and *A v B (No 2)* [2007] EWHC 54 (Comm); [2007] 1 Lloyd's Rep 358.
187. Applying *XL Insurance Ltd v Owens Corning* [2000] 2 Lloyd's Rep 500.
188. *Compagnie D'Armement Maritime SA v Compagnie Tunisienne de Navigation SA* [1971] AC 572; *The Al Wahab* [1983] 2 Lloyd's Rep 365 and *Hellenic Steel Co v Svolamar Shipping Co Ltd (The Komninos S)* [1991] 1 Lloyd's Rep 370.
189. See, e.g., *Compagnie D'Armement Maritime SA v Compagnie Tunisienne de Navigation SA* [1971] AC 572 and *Trade Indemnity plc v Forsakringsaktiebolaget Njord* [1995] 1 All ER 796.

express or demonstrated with reasonable certainty by the terms of the contract or the circumstances of the case. Thus if a charterparty expressly provides that English law is to govern the contract, that choice clearly falls within Article 3(1) and will be the applicable law, unless one of the restrictions dealt with below applies.

Standard form bills of lading are intended to be used by parties of any different nationality. They may therefore seek to retain a degree of flexibility rather than providing for any one law to govern. Many, but not all, standard bills of lading forms are more advantageous to the carrier than to the consignee as they often provide for the jurisdiction and governing law to be that of the principal place of business of the carrier.[190] Thus the carrier will have the comfort of knowing that any disputes will be determined by the courts in its own country in accordance with the law of that country. Such a clause does demonstrate with reasonable certainty what the choice of law is, provided that the identity of the carrier and its principal place of business can be ascertained.[191]

If the contract contains no express choice of law provision the parties may still have demonstrated their choice with reasonable certainty. Where, for example, the parties have chosen a particular forum this may demonstrate with reasonable certainty that they wanted the law of that forum to govern the contract. In *Egon Oldendorff v Libera Corporation*[192] Clarke J had to consider whether the London arbitration clause in the charterparty on the NYPE form demonstrated with reasonable certainty that the parties had chosen English law within Article 3 of the Rome Convention. He also had to consider a Memorandum of Agreement ("MOA") in the Norwegian Sale Form to be attached to the charterparty which provided for arbitration in a city to be specified by the parties and the contract to be subject to the law of the country agreed as the place of arbitration. A footnote in the standard wording provided that if the line was not filled in, it was understood that arbitration would take place in London in accordance with English law. The clause further provided for three arbitrators. Another footnote provided that if the parties did not complete who was to appoint the third arbitrator, the third would be appointed by the London Maritime Arbitrators' Association (LMAA) in London. It was held that there was no reason to disregard the footnotes and that therefore the parties had agreed London arbitration and that the MOA was to be subject to English law as the country agreed as the place of arbitration.

Clarke J concluded that the parties had demonstrated their choice in the charterparty with reasonable certainty. On all the facts of the case, when set in the context of the terms of the contract as a whole and of the circumstances of the case, the arbitration clause was a strong indication of the parties' intention to choose English law as the applicable law as well as the curial law. Having agreed English arbitration for the determination in London of disputes arising out of a well known English language form of charterparty which contains standard clauses with well known meanings in English law, it was to be inferred that the parties intended that law to apply. Having agreed a neutral forum the reasonable

190. See, e.g., clause 3 of the Conlinebill.
191. The facts of *The Rewia* [1991] 2 Lloyd's Rep 325 illustrate how difficulties may arise on both these issues.
192. [1996] 1 Lloyd's Rep 380.

inference is that the parties intended the forum to apply a "neutral" law, namely English Law and not either German or Japanese law. The parties made a tacit choice of English law as the applicable law of both the charterparty and the MOA, which was not surprising as they undoubtedly chose English law in the case of the MOA and it was an express term of their Agreement that the MOA would be attached to the charterparty.

Clarke J accepted that the plaintiff's case would have been even stronger if the charterparty had contained wording similar to the MOA providing for arbitration in London by LMAA arbitrators or London brokers or by a local association or exchange. The charterparty clause here simply provided that all arbitrators were to be conversant with shipping matters.

In *Gan Insurance Co Ltd v Tai Ping Insurance Co. Ltd*[193] the Court of Appeal upheld the decision of Cresswell J that there was an implied choice of English law demonstrated with reasonable certainty by the terms of the contract which contained the clauses commonly used in the London market within Article 3 of the Rome Convention. Although the reinsurance slip stated "as original" it did not incorporate all the terms of the Taiwanese insurance policy including the Taiwanese choice of law clause, but only the provisions which defined the extent of the risk insured.

Some bills of lading specifically incorporate the choice of law clause in the charterparty pursuant to which the bill of lading is issued.[194] It is probable that, as a result of the Court of Appeal decision in *The Nerano*, where the bill of lading makes specific reference to the charterparty choice of law clause this will be an effective incorporation of that clause, even if the clause states, e.g. that the charterparty shall be governed by English law. The English courts will probably be prepared to manipulate the wording in the charterparty to apply to the bill of lading. That case concerned the incorporation of an arbitration clause, not a choice of law clause, but there does not appear to be any distinction in principle.

If there is a dispute as to the validity of a contract or as to the validity of the choice of law clause, e.g. on the grounds that the incorporation is ineffective, what law applies to determine this issue? Article 3(4) provides that the existence and validity of the consent of the parties as to the choice of the applicable law shall be determined in accordance with the provisions of Articles 8, 9 and 11. Article 8 provides that the existence and validity of a contract, or of any term of a contract, shall be determined by the law which would govern it under the Rome Convention if the contract or term were valid (rule 1). Nevertheless, a party may rely upon the law of the country in which it has its habitual residence to establish that it did not consent if it appears from the circumstances that it would not be reasonable to determine the effect of its conduct in accordance with the law specified in rule 1 (rule 2). Mance J considered both rules of Article 8 in *Egon Oldendorff v Libera Corporation.*[195] There German charterers alleged that they had concluded a charterparty with Japanese owners. The latter argued that the agreement was subject to two conditions which had not been satisfied. One of those conditions was subject details of a previously concluded fixture which provided for London arbitration. Mance J held that if the arbitration clause was

193. [1999] CLC 1270.
194. E.g. Congenbill 1994, Heavyconbill, HIBL and Orevoybill.
195. [1995] 2 Lloyd's Rep 64.

validly incorporated, any contract which was validly made was subject to English law and not Japanese law. Therefore, English law applied to determine whether the subject details had been lifted. Even on the assumption in the Japanese owners' favour that Japanese law would have reached a different conclusion, Mance J held that they could not rely on Article 8(2). He thought that the onus must be on the party who sought to invoke Article 8(2) to negative consent, to bring himself within the provisions of that Article. Whether or not that was right, there were very strong grounds for regarding it as unreasonable to determine the effect of the owners' conduct on either the formation of a valid contract or the agreement on a valid arbitration clause in accordance with Japanese law. The natural implication of the London arbitration clause in the charterparty on which the negotiations were based was that English law governed. It would be contrary to ordinary commercial expectations to ignore that clause when everything suggested that the owners must have considered and accepted the clause and, even if they had not done so, should have done. Furthermore, the arbitration clause was precisely the sort of clause which they might have expected in such an international charterparty (indeed the charterparty form which the owners had originally proposed was amended to provide for London arbitration).

Similarly in *Welex AG v Rosa Maritime Ltd (The Epsilon Rosa)*[196] the Court of Appeal upheld the decision of Steel J that, assuming that English law was applicable under Article 8(1) and applying that law, the arbitration clause referred to in an executed charterparty was incorporated into the bill of lading. In *Welex AG v Rosa Maritime Ltd (The Epsilon Rosa) (No 2)*[197] the claimant sought to rely on Ukraine or Swiss law to establish it did not consent to incorporation by virtue of Article 8(2) of the Rome Convention. Steel J held that the burden was on Welex to displace the effect of Article 8(1). The shippers presented the Congenbill to the Master for signature; it was not suggested that there was anything unreasonable in holding Welex to the contract of carriage as a whole; an arbitration clause was commonplace in contracts of this kind; in due course Welex succeeded to the shippers' rights and obligations; and there was nothing "eccentric" let alone unjust in the English law to hold that both shipper and consignee were bound by the terms of the dispute resolution clause. The transaction was an entirely conventional one, nothing in the circumstances rendered it unreasonable to determine the effect of Welex's conduct by reference to English law.

The parties can choose the law applicable to the whole or a part only of the contract.[198]

The parties must choose the law of a country. A reference to Sharia law does not refer to any particular country's laws; as such it falls outside the Contracts (Applicable Law) Act 1990. Although it is possible to incorporate provisions of foreign law as terms of the contract, it is important to identify specific aspects of Sharia intended to be incorporated into the agreement. The reference to Sharia

196. [2003] EWCA Civ 938; [2003] 2 Lloyd's Rep 509; [2002] EWHC 762 (Comm). See also *Raffeisen Zentralbank Osterreich Aktiengesellschaft v National Bank of Greece SA* [1999] 1 Lloyd's Rep 408 at pp. 412 and 413 and *Horn Linie GmbH & Co v Panamericana Formas E Impresos SA, Ace Seguros SA (The Hornbay)* [2006] EWHC 373 (Comm); [2006] 2 Lloyd's Rep 44. On a letter of credit *Marconi v PT Pan Indonesia Bank Ltd TBK* [2004] 1 Lloyd's Rep 594.

197. [2002] 2 Lloyd's Rep 701.

198. *Centrax Ltd v Citibank NA* [1999] 1 All ER (Comm) 557 (CA).

law in *Shamil Bank of Bahrain EC v Beximco Pharmaceuticals Ltd*[199] was therefore repugnant to the choice of English law and could not be given effect to.

Article 3(2) provides that the parties may at any time agree to vary the law which previously governed the contract. Thus, for example, where the parties had already agreed that Italian law should govern the contract, they could at any time thereafter agree that the contract should be governed by English law. Similarly, if the contract did not contain any choice of law either express or demonstrated by reasonable certainty, the contract would have an applicable law which would fall to be determined in accordance with Article 4 of the Rome Convention but the parties would be free to agree a new applicable law. There may be a floating proper law which is objectively ascertainable.[200]

### (c) Limits on party choice

Where the Act applies, there are a number of limitations on the parties' freedom to choose the proper law. Article 3(3) provides that the fact that the parties have chosen a foreign law, whether or not with a foreign jurisdiction clause, shall not, where all the other elements relevant to the situation at the time of the choice are connected with one country only[201] prejudice the application of mandatory rules of that country. Mandatory rules are rules of law which cannot be derogated from by contract, e.g. the Hague-Visby Rules. This article will only apply to a bill of lading which is for inter-State coastal trade where the ship is registered in that State and all the parties to the bill of lading are nationals of that State. In such a situation if the parties have chosen the law of a different State to apply, e.g. because the foreign State does not give effect to the Hague, Hague-Visby or Hamburg Rules, the mandatory rules of the port of shipment will still apply if the dispute comes before the courts of a Contracting State to the Rome Convention.

Article 7(1) concerns the mandatory rules of another country with which the situation has a close connection but is not in force in the United Kingdom.

However, Article 7(2) of the Rome Convention goes further as it provides that nothing in the Convention shall restrict the application of the rules of the law of the forum in a situation where they are mandatory irrespective of the law otherwise applicable to the contract. An issue which is particularly relevant to bills of lading is whether, applying the law of the forum, the Hague-Visby Rules apply mandatorily even if they would not apply under the law chosen by the parties. The Hague-Visby Rules are given the force of law by the Carriage of Goods by Sea Act 1971 and apply mandatorily where the provisions of section 1 of the Carriage of Goods by Sea Act 1971 or Article X of the Rules are satisfied. Prior to the coming into force of the Contracts (Applicable Law) Act 1990, the parties' express or inferred choice of law could be rendered null and void where the Hague-Visby Rules applied mandatorily and the effect of the choice of law would have been to render the carrier's liability less than that which would have been imposed by the

199. [2004] EWCA Civ 19; [2004] 2 Lloyd's Rep 1.
200. *Bhatia Shipping v Alcobex* [2004] EWHC 2323 (Comm); [2005] 2 Lloyd's Rep 336.
201. See the dicta of Longmore J in *Bankers Trust International plc v RCS Editori SpA* [1996] CLC 899 at pp. 904–905, and, in particular, *obiter* at p. 905H where the judge doubted whether all the elements relevant to the situation were connected with Italy. *Ingmar GB Ltd v Eaton Leonard Technologies Inc* [1999] ECC 49 (CA).

Hague-Visby Rules. In *The Morviken*[202] a bill of lading expressly applied "the law of the Netherlands in which the Hague Rules ... are incorporated". It further provided for the exclusive jurisdiction of the Amsterdam court unless the carrier elected otherwise. The shippers commenced an action *in rem* in England as a sister ship belonging to the carrier was within the jurisdiction of the Admiralty Court. The carriers sought a stay on the grounds of the foreign jurisdiction clause. The carrier preferred to have the case tried in the Netherlands where its liability would be about £250 under the Hague Rules, whereas if the English court applied the Hague-Visby Rules, the limit would be approximately £11,000. The Hague-Visby Rules have the force of law in the United Kingdom and thus are to be treated as if they are part of directly enacted statute law. The rules applied as the bill of lading was both issued in a Contracting State and it covered a contract for carriage from a port in a Contracting State within Article X(a) and (b). The House of Lords held that the choice of law provision purported to lessen the carrier's liability and was therefore null and void and of no effect in accordance with Article III rule 8 of the Rules.

The effect of Article 7(2) of the Rome Convention would be the same as that of the decision in *The Morviken*. The law otherwise applicable to the contract as determined under Articles 3 or 4, could not restrict the application of the Hague-Visby Rules where they apply mandatorily. It is important to stress that Article 7(2) of the Rome Convention would not apply where the Hague-Visby Rules only apply contractually to a contract, as opposed to mandatorily. For example, the Hague-Visby Rules never apply mandatorily to a charterparty, although they are often incorporated voluntarily into standard form charterparties.[203] Although they frequently apply mandatorily to bills of lading, this is not always the case. It should be noted that the fact that English law governs the contract, does not necessarily trigger the application of the Hague-Visby Rules. Thus in *Trafigura Beheer BV v Mediterranean Shipping Co SA (The MSC Amsterdam),*[204] 360 tonnes of copper cathodes were shipped from South Africa to China. The bill of lading was expressly governed by English law and the clause paramount provided:

> "(a) For all trades,..., this B/L shall be subject to the 1924 Hague Rules with the express exclusion of Article IX, or, if compulsorily applicable, subject to the 1968 Protocol (Hague-Visby) or any compulsory legislation based on the Hague Rules and/or said Protocols...."

South Africa was not a Contracting State to the Hague-Visby Rules although its legislation, the South African Carriage of Goods by Sea Act 1986, does apply the Hague-Visby Rules to any shipment from a South African port. The Court of Appeal held that the Hague Rules and not the Hague-Visby Rules were applicable. In order to determine whether the Rules are compulsorily applicable one had to look to the proper law of the contract and not the law of the country of shipment or of destination. The law of the forum might also have to be considered. The Court of Appeal held that Aikens J had correctly held that English statute law

202. [1983] 1 AC 565.
203. See Chapter 2, p. 49.
204. [2007] EWCA Civ 794; [2007] EWHC 944 (Comm). See also *The Komninos S* [1991] 1 Lloyd's Rep 370. See also the *obiter dicta* of Tuckey LJ with whom Aldous LJ agreed, Rix LJ dissenting, in *Parsons Corporation v CV Scheepvaartonderneming "Happy Ranger" (The Happy Ranger)* [2002] 2 Lloyd's Rep 357, para. 19.

did not make the Hague-Visby Rules applicable and therefore neither the proper law nor the law of the forum made the Hague-Visby Rules compulsorily applicable and they did not therefore apply to the bill of lading.

Furthermore, Article 21 of the Rome Convention provides that the Convention shall not prejudice the application of international conventions to which a Contracting State is, or becomes, a party. This would include the Hague-Visby Rules but again only if they apply mandatorily to a bill of lading.

Where a charterparty incorporates foreign legislation, for example, the US Carriage of Goods by Sea Act 1936, which gives effect to the Hague Rules, the question of construction of the legislation must be determined by the proper law of the contract. Thus in *The Stolt Sydness*[205] it made a difference whether the time bar in the US Carriage of Goods by Sea Act 1936, which was incorporated into the voyage charterparty, was interpreted under English law or United States law. Under the latter "suit" in Article III rule 6, which is reproduced in section 3(6) of the US Act, was confined to litigation and did not extend to arbitration. By contrast under English law suit includes arbitration and thus arbitration must be commenced within the one year time limit.[206] As the charterparty expressly provided for London arbitration and English law, Rix J held that the English law interpretation applied and the claim was time barred as arbitration had not been commenced within the one year time limit.

Where the Hamburg Rules are incorporated into a bill of lading, or where the proper law is that of a Contracting State to the Hamburg Rules where that law would mandatorily apply the Hamburg Rules, the English courts would apply those Rules provided they impose a greater liability on the carrier than that under the Hague-Visby Rules. The parties are free to increase their liabilities but not to seek to lessen them. The effect of the Hamburg Rules is that they would usually impose a greater liability on the carrier than the Hague-Visby Rules.

### (d) No choice

Where the parties have not chosen the law applicable to the contract in accordance with Article 3, Article 4 rule 1 provides that the contract shall be governed by the law of the country with which it is most closely connected. That Article further provides that a severable part of the contract which has a closer connection with another country may be governed by the law of that other country.

In order to determine which country the contract is most closely connected with, there are a number of presumptions in Article 4(2), (3) and (4), all of which may be disregarded in accordance with Article 4(5) if it appears from the circumstances as a whole that the contract is more closely connected with another country. Article 4(3) relates to immovable property and is not therefore relevant for present purposes. There is a special presumption in Article 4(4) for contracts for the carriage of goods and that provision states that single voyage charterparties and other contracts, the main purpose of which is the carriage of goods, shall be treated as contracts for the carriage of goods. In such a contract if the country in which

205. *Mauritius Oil Refineries Ltd v Stolt Nielsen Nederland BV (The Stolt Sydness)* [1997] 1 Lloyd's Rep 273.
206. *The Merak* [1964] 2 Lloyd's Rep 527.

the carrier has its principal place of business, is also the country in which the place of loading or the place of discharge or the principal place of business of the consignor is situated, it shall be presumed that the contract is most closely connected with that country. The time for applying this test is when the contract is concluded as we look to the formation of the contract. Thus if an Italian charterer who is also the carrier issues bills of lading for carriage of goods from Rotterdam to Genoa, the presumption is that Italian law applies, unless it appears from the circumstances as a whole that the contract is more closely connected with another country. However, there will frequently be no presumption as often the principal place of business of the carrier is not the same as the loadport, discharge port or principal place of business of the consignor. It is common for bills of lading to contain express clauses providing for jurisdiction in the courts of and the governing law of the principal place of business of the carrier. If, however, the parties have not made an express choice nor demonstrated it with reasonable certainty by choosing the jurisdiction, one of three other factors must point to the principal place of business of the carrier for the presumption to apply.

If the contract is not for the carriage of goods but is, for example, an international sale contract, time[207] or demise charterparty, insurance contract to which the Rome Convention applies, reinsurance contract or letter of credit, the presumption in Article 4(2) applies. This involves first working out what the characteristic performance of the contract is. This will be the performance in return for which payment is promised.[208] Thus, for example, the performance characteristic of a contract of insurance is the provision of insurance cover,[209] not payment of the premium, and of a sale contract the delivery of the goods, not payment of the purchase price

Where the contract is entered into in the course of the trade or profession[210] of the party who is to effect the performance characteristic of the contract, the presumption is that the governing law of the contract is that of the country where that party has its principal place of business or, where under the terms of the contract the performance is to be effected through a place of business other than the principal place of business, the country in which that other place of business is situated.

The presumptions will apply unless it appears from the circumstances as a whole that the contract is more closely connected with another country.[211] Circumstances such as where the performance of all the contractual obligations is

207. *Quaere* trip time charterparty, if the main purpose is the carriage of goods.

208. See also *Print Concept GmbH v GEW (EC) Ltd* [2001] EWCA Civ 352; [2002] CLC 352; [2001] ECC 36 (distributorship agreement). See also *Iran Continental Shelf Oil Co v IRI International Corp* [2002] EWCA Civ 1024; [2004] 2 CLC 696. On letters of credit see *Bank of Baroda v Vysya Bank Limited* [1994] 2 Lloyd's Rep 87 (letter of credit between the confirming and the issuing bank); *PT Pan Indonesia Bank Ltd TBK v Marconi Communications International Limited* [2005] EWCA Civ 422; [2004] 1 Lloyd's Rep 594 (letter of credit between the beneficiary and the confirming bank). *Tavoulareas v Tsaviliris* [2005] EWHC 2140, paras. 49–52.

209. *Credit Lyonnais v New Hampshire Insurance Co* [1997] 2 Lloyd's Rep 1 applied in *American Motorists Insurance Co v Cellstar Corporation Welex* [2003] EWCA Civ 206; [2003] Lloyd's Rep IR 295 (CA); EWHC 421 (Comm); [2002] 2 Lloyd's Rep 216. *Dornoch Limited v The Mauritius Union Assurance Company Ltd* [2006] EWCA Civ 389; [2006] 2 Lloyd's Rep 475, paras. 41–43, the characteristic performance of a reinsurance contract was payment in the event of a claim.

210. If not, the habitual residence or, in the case of a body corporate or unincorporate, its central administration.

211. Article 4(5).

to be given and the governing law of an independent but interconnected contract may be relevant.[212] In *Definitely Maybe (Touring) Ltd v Marek Lieberberg Konzertagentur GmbH*[213] the characteristic performance of the contract was for Oasis to perform in two concerts in Germany and thus the presumption under Article 4(2) was that as the party to effect the characteristic performance was located in England, English law would be the governing law of the contract. However, the defendant established factors which showed the contract had a closer connection with Germany than with England as the contract required performance of contractual obligations by both parties in Germany. Therefore the presumption did not apply and German law applied.

In *Gan Insurance Co Ltd v Tai Ping Insurance Co Ltd*[214] the Court of Appeal agreed with Cresswell J at first instance that if there were no choice within Article 3 of the Rome Convention,[215] the reinsurance had its closest connection with English law under Article 4(2) and it did not appear from the circumstances as a whole that the reinsurance contracts were more closely connected with Taiwan under Article 4(5).

212. *Bank of Baroda v Vysya Bank Limited* [1994] 2 Lloyd's Rep 87 (letter of credit between the confirming and the issuing bank). See also *HIB Ltd v Guardian Insurance Co Inc* [1997] 1 Lloyd's Rep 412. The decision of the Court of Appeal in *Crédit Lyonnais v New Hampshire Insurance Co* [1997] CLC 909 is relevant to Article 4. Although the court was there considering the Second EC Directive on Non Life Insurance, it recognised that there are many similarities between the Rome Convention and the second directive (p. 913).

213. [2001] 2 All ER (Comm) 1. See also *Iran Continental Shelf Oil Co v IRI International Corp* [2002] EWCA Civ 1024; [2004] 2 CLC 696; 2002 WL 1310773 (CA (Civ Div)); [2002] CLC 372; *Samcrete Egypt Engineers and Contractors SAE v Land Rover Exports Ltd* [2001] EWCA Civ 2019; [2002] CLC 533; *Ennstone Building Products Ltd v Stanger Ltd* [2002] EWCA Civ 916; [2002] 2 All ER (Comm) 479; Applied by *Waldwiese Stiftung v Lewis* [2004] EWHC 2589 (Ch); 2004 WL 2652645 (Ch D); *Kenburn Waste Management Ltd v Bergmann* [2002] EWCA Civ 98; [2002] CLC 644; *Caledonia Subsea Ltd v Micoperi SRL* [2003] SC 70 (Inner House Court of Session) and *Ophthalmic Innovations International (UK) Ltd v Ophthalmic Innovations International Incorporated* [2004] EWHC 2948 Ch, [2005] I L Pr 10.

214. [1999] CLC 1270, *per* Beldam LJ at p. 1,279 and *per* Cresswell J [1998] CLC 1,072 at p. 1,082. See also *Raffeisen Zentralbank Osterreich Aktiengesellschaft v National Bank of Greece SA* [1999] 1 Lloyd's Rep 408 at pp. 412 and 413 and *Ferguson Shipbuilders v Voith Hydro GmbH and Co KG* [2000] SLT 229, a decision of the Scottish Outer House. *ISS Machinery Services Ltd v Aeolian Shipping SA (The Aeolian)* [2001] 2 Lloyd's Rep 641.

215. See p. 37.

CHAPTER 2

# Charterparties

*PROFESSOR YVONNE BAATZ*

## 1. INTRODUCTION

A shipowner will wish to ensure that it makes as much profit from its ship as it possibly can. One means of achieving this aim is to charter the ship either on a time charter or on a voyage charter. A demise charterparty is a time charterparty usually for a long term such as 10 years and the ship is in the possession of the demise charterer who crews, maintains and insures the ship. Demise charters are often entered into for tax reasons. They are in a small minority of charters and this chapter will focus on the more usual time and voyage charterparties. In both these cases the ship remains in the possession of the owner who crews, maintains and insures the ship. However, there are very significant differences between time and voyage charterparties, most notably the manner in which the owner is paid. Under a time charterparty the ship is placed at the disposal of the time charterer for a period of time and the time charterer pays hire for every minute that it is so placed, unless the ship is off hire. Under a voyage charterparty the contract is for a voyage and the charterer pays freight and, if the time allowed at either the load or discharge port for the process of loading and discharging the cargo is exceeded, usually demurrage.

This chapter will consider the role of shipbrokers. It will focus on charterparties between commercial parties. Such parties enjoy freedom of contract and can contract on such terms as they have the commercial muscle to obtain. The Hague, Hague-Visby or Hamburg Rules, which impose minimum obligations on carriers under bills of lading that cannot be contracted out of, do not apply mandatorily to charterparties. However, the parties may voluntarily provide for such conventions to apply to their charterparty. Whether they have done so will be considered so that the terms of the charterparty can be identified before the parties' obligations are discussed.

Standard form charterparties, both time and voyage, almost invariably contain express terms imposing obligations on the owner to make the ship seaworthy; to perform its contractual obligation with reasonable despatch; and not to deviate from the contractual voyage. If there were to be no such express terms each of these obligations would be implied. These obligations will be considered together with the impact of any Rules which apply to the charterparty. The remedies that are available to the charterer for breach will be considered. The charterer's obligations in relation to safe ports will be discussed, before considering the circumstances in which a charterparty can be frustrated. Issues specific to time charterparties will then be explored before turning to such issues in relation to voyage charterparties. Time charterparties are considered first as if there are both time and voyage charters in relation to the same ship, the time charter will usually have come into existence first. Finally the issue of liens both over cargo and sub freights to enforce payment under the charterparty will be considered.

## 2. SHIPBROKERS

Both the owner and the charterer may each instruct a chartering shipbroker, who will have the best knowledge of the current chartering market. Shipbrokers will often specialise in different types of ships such as oil tankers or general cargo ships. This is both because the owners and charterers of these ships are different and because the standard form contracts which usually form the basis of the negotiations and tailor made clauses vary according to which type of ship is involved. There are numerous standard form charterparties, both time and voyage, and in each case, for different types of cargo. Thus for a time charterparty for the carriage of general cargo the New York Produce Exchange ("NYPE") form 1946 or 1993 is commonly used, whereas for the carriage of oil a specialist form such as the Shelltime 3 or 4 may be used. For voyage charterparties the Gencon charterparty 1994 is widely used for general cargo and the Asbatankvoy form is used for oil. These particular standard forms will be referred to throughout this chapter to give examples of typical provisions and the problems they may give rise to. Both the NYPE form 1946 and the Asbatankvoy charterparties are now old forms. Although they are both still widely used, they are often extensively amended and numerous additional typed clauses will probably be appended to the standard form. The broker will advise its principal on how to tailor the standard form to the individual transaction.

It is important to determine whether the broker has contracted as agent for its principal or in its personal capacity as principal.[1] If the broker acts as an agent for its principal, there will be an agency contract between the broker and the party on whose behalf it is acting. That contract will impose obligations on the broker to act, for example, with reasonable skill and care. If the broker fails to comply with those obligations it may be liable to its principal in either contract for breach of the agency contract or in tort for breach of its tortious duty of care. The principal can choose whether to sue in contract or in tort depending on which cause of action is most favourable[2] because, for example, the damages may be assessed differently; the time limit is different in contract and tort[3]; jurisdiction may be different.[4] Where the claim in contract and in tort is concurrent and both the contractual and tortious duty are coextensive, as they are both to exercise reasonable skill and care, the broker could rely on the defence of contributory negligence.[5]

Provided that the broker has actual or ostensible authority to act on behalf of its principal, when the charterparty is concluded, its principal is bound to the other party to the charterparty. The broker has no obligations under the charter-

1. *Polish Steamship C v A J Williams (Overseas Sales) Ltd (The Suwalki)* [1989] 1 Lloyd's Rep 511.
2. *Henderson v Merrett* [1994] 3 All ER 506.
3. *Ibid.*
4. See pp. 13–19 of Chapter 1.
5. *Vesta v Butcher* [1988] 2 All ER 43.

party as it has acted merely as agent. Were the broker not to have authority to contract on behalf of its principal, it could not bind its principal to the charterparty and would be liable to the other party in tort for breach of warranty of authority. The broker can also incur liability to the other party to the transaction if it makes a misrepresentation in its personal capacity rather than on behalf of its principal, for example, as to the creditworthiness of its principal. This was the situation in *The Arta*[6] where the charterer's broker indicated to the owner's broker at the commencement of negotiations for a voyage charterparty that the charterer was "okay", meaning that it could meet its financial commitments under the charter. The charterer subsequently failed to pay the freight and the brokers were held liable in tort for breach of their duty of care as they had failed to carry out checks on their new client's creditworthiness. In establishing whether the broker was in breach of its duty of care the court would consider the rules by which the broker was bound, for example, those of the Institute of Chartered Shipbrokers, and the extent to which a broker could rely on information supplied to it by another broker.

The broker is paid commission and the charterparty will usually contain a clause providing who will pay what commission to which broker.[7] The broker is not a party to the charterparty contract. If the party obliged to pay the commission fails to do so, then if that party is the broker's own principal, the broker can sue its own principal in contract under its agency agreement. However, if the other party to the charterparty owes the commission, the broker may be able to overcome the problem of lack of privity if the Contracts (Rights of Third Parties) Act 1999 applies, either because the charterparty expressly provides that the broker may enforce the charterparty[8] or, which is more likely, the term in the charterparty purports to confer a benefit on the broker.[9] In *Nisshin Shipping Co Ltd v Cleaves & Co Ltd*[10] Colman J held that chartering brokers had the right to enforce commission clauses in charterparties between their principals and the shipowners pursuant to section 1 of the Contracts (Rights of Third Parties Act) 1999 and had the right and the obligation to refer the disputes to arbitration as provided for in the charterparties. Alternatively, the broker can sue both parties to the charterparty as co-defendants to enforce a constructive trust of the commission of which it is beneficiary.[11]

## 3. THE HAGUE, HAGUE-VISBY AND HAMBURG RULES

Some time and voyage charterparties provide that the Hague, Hague-Visby or Hamburg Rules apply to the charterparty. The charterparty may contain a clause paramount or set out sections of the rules in the charterparty or provide that any set of Rules that applies to any bill of lading issued under the charterparty shall also apply to any cargo claim under the charterparty.

6. *Markappa Inc v N W Spratt & Son Ltd (The Arta)* [1985] 1 Lloyd's Rep 534.
7. See, e.g., cl. 24 of the Baltime form, cls 27 and 28 of NYPE 1946 and cls 43 and 44 of NYPE 1993.
8. Section 1(1)(a).
9. Section 1(1)(b). The broker must be identified in accordance with s. 1(3).
10. [2004] 1 Lloyd's Rep 38.
11. *Les Affreteurs Reunis v Walford* [1919] AC 801.

The development of the Hague, Hague-Visby and Hamburg Rules will be outlined. In the nineteenth century shipowners included wide exclusions of liability in their contracts. This was perceived as unacceptable for bills of lading where the third party consignee or indorsee of the bill of lading, who was not an original party to the bill of lading and had not had an opportunity to negotiate its terms, might find that it had paid for a cargo but had no rights against the shipowner for damage to or loss of that cargo because of those exclusions. Following the lead of the US Harter Act 1893,[12] the international community agreed to the Hague Rules in 1924. Those Rules impose certain minimum obligations on carriers which they cannot contract out of,[13] such as the duty to exercise due diligence to make the ship seaworthy before and at the beginning of the voyage[14] and to care for the cargo.[15] In return the shipowner has certain exemptions or immunities, such as the right to rely on the list of exceptions in Article IV rule 2, provided that it has complied with its seaworthiness obligation; to limit its liability for cargo loss or damage[16] and to be discharged from liability one year after discharge of the goods.[17] Once the Hague Rules had been in force for about four decades it became apparent that there were some criticisms of the rules, not least that the package limits had become very low. Therefore in 1968 the Visby Protocol was agreed. It is given the force of law in the United Kingdom by the Carriage of Goods by Sea Act 1971. It follows the format of the Hague Rules but made amendments principally to the limits of liability which were increased; the method of calculation of the limit[18] and the right to break the limit;[19] an extended time limit for indemnity claims;[20] extending the defences and limits of liability to tort claims[21] and to servants and agents of the carrier.[22]

In 1978 the Hamburg Rules were agreed, which seek to give greater protection to cargo interests. Major differences from the Hague-Visby Rules include a different regime of liability;[23] higher limits[24] (but they can be broken[25] and the defences and limits of liability of the carrier are extended to claims in tort[26] and to the servant or agent of the carrier[27]); a two-year time bar[28] and jurisdiction provisions.[29]

There is no international harmony on which rules apply compulsorily to bills of lading. Some States still give effect to the Hague Rules (most notably the United States of America by its US Carriage of Goods by Sea Act 1936 ("US COGSA 1936"), but this Act applies the Rules to both inward and outward shipments).

12. See cl. 24 of NYPE 1946.
13. Article III rule 8.
14. Article III rule 1.
15. Article III rule 2.
16. Article IV rule 5.
17. Article III rule 6.
18. Article IV rule 5.
19. Article IV rule 5(e) and Article IV*bis* rule 4.
20. Article III rule 6*bis*.
21. Article IV*bis* rule 1.
22. Article IV*bis* rules 2 to 4.
23. Article 5 of the Hamburg Rules.
24. Article 6 of the Hamburg Rules.
25. Article 8 of the Hamburg Rules.
26. Article 7.1 of the Hamburg Rules.
27. Article 7.2 of the Hamburg Rules.
28. Article 20. Article 20 rule 5 of the Hamburg Rules also provides for indemnity claims.
29. Article 21 and 22. See p. 23 of Chapter 1.

Other States give effect to the Hague-Visby Rules (including most EC Member States) and yet other States give effect to the Hamburg Rules. National legislation which gives effect to a set of Rules may provide for some local variation or a combination of more than one set of Rules. In a final bid for international unity the United Nations Commission on International Trade Law is currently reviewing a further draft convention on the carriage of goods.

Although the consignee of a non-transferable bill of lading[30] or the third party transferee of a transferable bill of lading deserves protection, there is no reason to restrict the parties' freedom of contract for charterparties. Therefore, neither the Hague, Hague-Visby nor Hamburg Rules apply mandatorily to charterparties.[31] However, the parties to the charterparty may wish to ensure that the obligations under both the charterparty and the bill of lading are the same. Some standard form charterparties seek to achieve this by incorporating a clause paramount into the charterparty and providing that it must be incorporated into any bill of lading issued under the charterparty.[32]

Provided a charterparty, either voyage or time, makes clear the parties' intention to incorporate a clause paramount into the charterparty, the English courts will give effect to that intention, even though this may involve some manipulation of the wording of the clause paramount and even though it may mean some of the Rules referred to in the clause paramount have to be ignored. In *The Saxon Star*[33] the charterparty in its original form was a voyage charterparty which had been amended to cover as many consecutive voyages as the ship could perform within 18 months. It provided that the clause paramount was "to be incorporated in this charterparty". The clause paramount itself provided as follows:

> "This bill of lading shall have effect subject to the provisions of the Carriage of Goods by Sea Act of the United States, approved Apr. 16, 1936, which shall be deemed to be incorporated herein, and nothing herein contained shall be deemed a surrender by the carrier of any of its rights or immunities or an increase of any of its responsibilities or liabilities under said Act. If any term of this bill of lading be repugnant to said Act to any extent, such term shall be void to that extent, but no further."

The House of Lords held that the charterparty did incorporate US COGSA[34] and that the wording in the clause paramount could be manipulated to read "This charterparty" rather than "This bill of lading" in view of the parties' clear intention to apply the statute to the charterparty as well as the bill of lading,[35] despite the fact that US COGSA itself provides that it does not apply to charterparties.

30. *J I MacWilliam Co Inc v Mediterranean Shipping Co SA (The Rafaela S)* [2005] UKHL 11; [2005] 1 Lloyd's Rep 347.
31. Article V of the Hague and Hague-Visby Rules and Article 2 rule 3 of the Hamburg Rules.
32. E.g. cl. 24 of NYPE 1946 and cl. 31 of NYPE 1993.
33. *Adamastos Shipping Co v Anglo-Saxon Petroleum Co (The Saxon Star)* [1959] AC 133.
34. This statute gives effect to the Hague Rules with some amendments. See G. Treitel and F. Reynolds, *Carver* (2nd ed, Sweet & Maxwell, 2005) ("*Carver*"), para. 9-089 on the "peculiarities" of this statute and R. Aikens, R. Lord, and M. Bools, *Bills of Lading* (Informa, 2006) ("*Aikens*"), para. 10.19.
35. This may be contrasted with the incorporation of charterparty clauses into bills of lading where it is not permissible to manipulate the wording of the charterparty clause to make it applicable to the bill of lading – *Miramar Maritime Corporation v Holborn Oil Trading Ltd (The Miramar)* [1984] 2 Lloyd's Rep 129, unless specific words of incorporation are used, e.g. *Daval Aciers D'Usinor et De Sacilor v Armare SSL (The Nerano)* [1996] 1 Lloyd's Rep 1, discussed at p. 4 of Chapter 1.

Applying the decision in *The Saxon Star,* Staughton J held that US COGSA was effectively incorporated into a time charter by the printed clause paramount in clause 24 of the NYPE form in *The Satya Kailash.*[36] Staughton J dismissed the argument that the parties could not have intended to incorporate the duty to exercise due diligence to make the ship seaworthy in US COGSA as they had already provided for an absolute obligation of seaworthiness.

Whereas initially the clause paramount only referred to the Hague Rules or national legislation giving effect to those Rules, clause paramounts in more recently drafted standard form charterparties have become more complicated because the Hague-Visby Rules or the Hamburg Rules or some national legislation giving effect to them may apply mandatorily to the bill of lading.[37] A clause paramount may provide, for example, that the bill of lading is to be subject to the Hague Rules or the Hague-Visby Rules where they are compulsorily applicable.[38]

It will then be necessary to determine which set of Rules applies to the charterparty or to which voyage or voyages under the charterparty. Sometimes it may not matter whether the Hague or the Hague-Visby Rules apply because, for example, in both cases there is a duty to exercise due diligence to make the ship seaworthy before and at the beginning of the voyage[39] and a list of exceptions in Article IV rule 2.[40] However, in other cases, as we have already seen, there may be significant differences depending on which set of rules applies. It will be a question of construction of both the words of incorporation and the clause paramount itself as to whether the same Rules that apply to each bill of lading issued under the charterparty are to apply to the voyages covered by such bill of lading under the charterparty[41] with the result that, for example, different voyages under a time charterparty are governed by different Rules. An alternative construction would be that the default position under the clause paramount is to apply to all the voyages under the charterparty, with the result that the charterparty and the bill of lading may not be back to back. More sophisticated recent standard form charterparties do not seek to incorporate the clause paramount into the charterparty, but only into any bill of lading issued under that charterparty. There is an express clause stating that the Rules that apply to the bill of lading are also to apply to cargo carrying voyages under the charterparty.[42]

Where the charterparty incorporates foreign legislation giving effect to the Hague Rules, such as US COGSA, the construction of the legislation must be

36. *Seven Seas Transportation Ltd v Pacifico Union Marina Corporation (The Satya Kailash and Oceanic Amity)* [1982] 2 Lloyd's Rep 465. Although the case went to the Court of Appeal – [1984] 1 Lloyd's Rep 588 (as discussed at p. 54 of this chapter) – this point was not appealed. See also *Grimaldi Compagnia Di Navigazione SPA v Sekihyo Lines Ltd (The Seki Rolette)* [1998] 2 Lloyd's Rep 638.
37. See, e.g., cl. 31 of NYPE 1993.
38. See, e.g., *Trafigura Beheer BV v Mediterranean Shipping Co SA (The MSC Amsterdam)* [2007] EWCA Civ 794; [2007] 2 Lloyd's Rep 622, discussed at pp. 40 and 41 of Chapter 1.
39. However, if the owner is in breach of this obligation, the owner can limit its liability – *Parsons Corporation and Others v CV Scheepvaartonderneming "Happy Ranger" and Others (The Happy Ranger)* [2002] 2 Lloyd's Rep 357. The limits differ under the Hague and Hague-Visby Rules and can be broken under the latter.
40. Thus in *Whistler International v Kawasaki Kisen Kaisha Ltd (The Hill Harmony)* [2001] 1 Lloyd's Rep 147 the charterparty incorporated three clauses paramount but no point arose on their application or on which one was relevant as their effect was to incorporate the exception in Article IV rule 2(a) – *per* Lord Hobhouse at p. 154.
41. London Arbitration 2/97 LMLN 450.
42. See, e.g., clause 27(c)(ii) of the Shelltime 4 charterparty as amended in December 2003.

determined as a question of the proper law of the contract. In *The Stolt Sydness*[43] that was English law rather than US law.

Sometimes the parties use shorthand and simply provide for "Paramount Clause to be incorporated herein" or "US Clause Paramount" or "Canadian Clause Paramount". In *The Agios Lazaros*[44] the Court of Appeal held that "paramount clause" meant that all the Hague Rules applied. Although this decision was before the Hague-Visby Rules came into force, the words will still mean the Hague Rules unless a party can adduce evidence that shipping men would now understand these words to mean the Hague-Visby Rules,[45] which seems unlikely, as if the Hague-Visby Rules are required, the wording "general clause paramount" is used.[46]

Where the Rules are incorporated into the charterparty, there may be difficulties of construction as to whether the clause paramount prevails over other clauses in the charterparty.[47] The clause paramount may state that in case of inconsistency the rules are to prevail.[48] Alternatively there may be a provision to the opposite effect.[49]

## 4. SEAWORTHINESS

If there were no express provision in the charterparty as to seaworthiness, there is an implied obligation of seaworthiness at common law. It is an absolute obligation that the ship will be fit for the purpose intended. However, nowadays one would expect a standard form charterparty to contain express provisions as to seaworthiness, although the word "seaworthiness" may well not be present.[50] For example, the New York Produce Exchange form 1946 expressly provides that on her delivery the ship shall be "ready to receive cargo with clean swept holds and tight, staunch, strong and in every way fitted for the service ... with full complement of officers, seamen, engineers and firemen for a vessel of her tonnage".[51]

43. See *Mauritius Oil Refineries Ltd v Stolt Nielsen Nederlands BV (The Stolt Sydness)* [1997] 1 Lloyd's Rep 273, discussed at p. 41 of Chapter 1.
44. *Nea Agrex SA v Baltic Shipping Co Ltd ( The Agios Lazaros)* [1976] 2 Lloyd's Rep 47.
45. *Seabridge Shipping AB v AC Orssleff's Eftf's A/S (The Fjellvang)* [1999] 2 Lloyd's Rep 685.
46. See *Lauritzen Reefers v Ocean Reef Transport Ltd SA (The Bukhta Russkaya)* [1997] 2 Lloyd's Rep 744 for the meaning of this wording which is similar in effect to the clause paramount in the Congenbill 1994. On the facts of this case, the Hague Rules applied rather than the Hague-Visby Rules and the charterer's claim for an indemnity for its liability for cargo damage on the voyage in question was therefore time-barred.
47. See *Marifortuna Naviera v Government of Ceylon (The Mariasmi)* [1970] 1 Lloyd's Rep 247 at p. 255; *Nea Agrex SA v Baltic Shipping Co Ltd (The Agios Lazaros)* [1976] 2 Lloyd's Rep 47, *per* Lord Goff at p. 53; and *Seven Seas Transportation Ltd v Pacifico Union Marina Corporation (The Satya Kailash and Oceanic Amity)* [1984] 1 Lloyd's Rep 588; *Finagra (UK) Ltd v OT Africa Line Ltd* [1998] 2 Lloyd's Rep 622 and *Dairy Containers Limited v Tasman Orient Line CV (The Tasman Discoverer)* [2004] UKPC 22; [2004] 2 Lloyd's Rep 647. *Carver*, para. 9-091; J. Cooke, T. Young, A. Taylor, *Voyage Charters* (3rd ed, Informa, 2007) ("*Cooke*"), paras. 85.14–85.18 and *Aikens*, para. 10.33 and n. 38.
48. See, e.g., cl. 24 of NYPE 1946 (Appendix 2).
49. See, e.g., *Parsons Corporation and Others v CV Scheepvaartonderneming "Happy Ranger" and Others (The Happy Ranger)* [2002] 2 Lloyd's Rep 357.
50. *Hong Kong Fir Shipping Co Ltd v Kawasaki Kisen Kaisha Ltd* [1962] 2 QB 26; [1961] 2 Lloyd's Rep 478.
51. Lines 21–24. See also cl. 2 of NYPE 1993.

Although this provision is clearly confined to the time of delivery in addition there will probably be a description of the ship at the time the charterparty is concluded in the preamble of the charterparty which covers matters such as the ship's class, her capacity, and her speed and consumption.[52] Further details may be given in additional typed clauses. There is also a continuing obligation to maintain the ship[53] and a clause paramount which incorporates US COGSA.[54]

Assuming that the Hague or Hague-Visby Rules are incorporated into a charterparty they may have a significant effect on the seaworthiness obligation. If the charterparty provides for an absolute obligation of seaworthiness, the effect will be to reduce the obligation to one to exercise due diligence. This was the effect of the clause paramount in *The Saxon Star*. Although that case concerned a consecutive voyage charterparty the better view is that it applies by analogy to a time charterparty.[55] Article III rule 1 has three parts. First, Article III rule 1(a) requires the ship to be seaworthy. For example, the ship must not leak and her machinery, such as her engines and steering gear, must be in good working order. Second, Article III rule 1(b) requires the ship to be properly manned, equipped and supplied. Her crew must be sufficient, qualified and trained. The requirements in relation to the number of the crew to be employed on board a particular ship are determined by the ship's flag State. Furthermore the crew must be properly qualified to perform the duties which they are actually employed to perform on the relevant ship. Finally the crew must be properly trained to carry out those duties. The Standards of Training, Certification and Watchkeeping of Seafarers 1995, which is part of the Safety of Life at Sea Convention,[56] require that the crew must be continuously trained to keep abreast of new developments and technology. In *The Star Sea*[57] the ship *Star Sea* was found to be unseaworthy as the Master, despite being qualified and very experienced, had not been trained to use the fire-fighting equipment on the ship. When a fire broke out he did not use the carbon dioxide fire fighting system quickly enough, and, when he did give instructions that it should be deployed, he did not order that all the $CO_2$ be used to flood the hold on fire, as he should have done, but only part of the $CO_2$, with the result that the fire was not extinguished and the ship became a constructive total loss. The Master was held to be incompetent and therefore the ship was unseaworthy.

Third, Article III rule 1(c) requires the ship to be fit and safe to carry her cargo. The test of unseaworthiness is subjective and not objective, i.e. this ship must be fit to encounter the perils of the sea for the contractual voyage and not any other voyage. The perils of a voyage carrying timber on deck across the Atlantic in February are very different from those of a reefer vessel carrying frozen prawns in its refrigerated holds in the Mediterranean in June.

52. Lines 3–11.
53. Clause 1. See also cl. 6 of NYPE 1993.
54. Clause 24. See also cl. 31 of NYPE 1993.
55. See Wilford, *Time Charters* (5th ed, Informa, 2003) ("*Wilford*"), para. 34.5, discussing the effect of the incorporation of US COGSA into the NYPE 1946 by cl. 24.
56. See pp. 236–240 of Chapter 7.
57. *Manifest Shipping Co Ltd v Uni-Polaris Insurance Co Ltd (The Star Sea)* [1995] 1 Lloyd's Rep 651. Although the case went to the House of Lords the decision of Tuckey J at first instance that the ship was unseaworthy was not appealed. The case concerned s. 39(5) of the Marine Insurance Act 1906.

The burden of proving unseaworthiness is on the claimant who must also show that the ship was unseaworthy before and at the beginning of the voyage. If the claimant can establish that, the burden of proof then shifts to the owner to establish that it exercised due diligence to make the ship seaworthy before and at the beginning of the voyage.[58] This is a fairly heavy burden as the duty cannot be delegated.[59] It is not enough for the owner to say that it exercised due diligence in selecting, for example, reputable ship repairers or surveyors. The owner must also establish that those ship repairers or surveyors themselves exercised due diligence. In *The Fjord Wind* the ship was on voyage charter and after leaving her loadport the ship grounded as a result of engine problems. The engines required lengthy repairs and the cargo had to be transshipped. The issue was whether the charterparty had been frustrated or whether the owner was in breach of its seaworthiness obligation. The Court of Appeal had to reconcile an initial seaworthiness clause and the scheme of the Hague Rules. It was held that the owner's obligation as to seaworthiness at each stage was the same, i.e. to exercise due diligence. The owner had failed to exercise due diligence to make the ship seaworthy. Although maintenance work had been carried out on the main engines by two representatives of the engine manufacturers at Durban, the problem for the owner was that it was unable to prove that the representatives had exercised due diligence when making the repairs to the engines and the burden of proof was on the owner to do so.

It is still not clear, however, under a time charter when the obligation to exercise due diligence under the Hague or Hague-Visby Rules bites. The better view is that it applies at the beginning of each voyage under the charterparty.[60] This is supported by the continuing obligation to maintain the ship which, although it may appear to be an absolute obligation, is read together with the Rules to become a duty to exercise due diligence.[61] Therefore more modern standard form charterparties expressly provide that the owner shall exercise due diligence to maintain the ship throughout the charter service.[62]

Provided the owner has exercised due diligence to make the ship seaworthy it may rely on the exceptions in Article IV rule 2 of the Hague and Hague-Visby Rules. The exception for "act neglect or default of the Master, mariner, pilot or the servants of the owners in the navigation or the management of the vessel" in Article IV rule 2(a), may be of great significance to the owner, not least because the general exception clause in the charterparty may not cover negligent errors of navigation, whereas the Article IV rule 2 exception does. Thus, provided the owner has exercised due diligence in employing a Chief Officer who is properly qualified and trained, if the Chief Officer makes a negligent error of navigation while he is on watch, the owner will not be liable.

58. Article IV rule 1. *The Hellenic Dolphin* [1978] 2 Lloyd's Rep 336.
59. *Riverstone Meat Co v Lancashire Shipping Co (The Muncaster Castle)* [1961] 1 Lloyd's Rep 57; *Eridania SpA v Rudolf A Oetker (The Fjord Wind)* [2000] 2 Lloyd's Rep 191; [1999] 1 Lloyd's Rep 307.
60. *Scrutton on Charterparties* (20th ed, Sweet & Maxwell, 1996) ("*Scrutton*"), p. 364, and *Wilford*, paras 34.5 and 34.15 and 38.129 on cl. 27(c)(ii) of Shelltime 4.
61. See *Wilford*, para. 34.5, discussing the effect of the incorporation of US COGSA into the New York Produce Exchange form 1946 by cl. 24 but see the words of caution of Mustill J in *Nitrate Corporation of Chile Ltd v Pansuiza Compania de Navegacion SA (The Hermosa)* [1980] 1 Lloyd's Rep 638 at p. 648.
62. See, e.g., cl. 3 of Shelltime 4. See *Golden Fleece Maritime Inc v ST Shipping & Transport Inc (The Ellie and the Frixos)* [2007] EWHC 1890 (Comm); [2008] 1 Lloyd's Rep 262.

The exceptions have been interpreted as applying to the wider range of services which are to be provided under a time charterparty than those which would be provided in relation to the loading, handling, stowage, carriage, custody, care or discharge of the goods under a bill of lading. Thus in *The Satya Kailash*[63] the owner of the *Satya Kailash* chartered the *Oceanic Amity* to lighten the *Satya Kailash*. During the lightening operation damage was caused to the *Satya Kailash* as a result of the negligent navigation of the Master of the *Oceanic Amity*. The Court of Appeal held that the owner of the *Oceanic Amity* could rely on the exception of negligent navigation.[64]

The time bar is also extremely important. The time limit within which claims must be brought under a charterparty is generally six years from the breach of contract, unless the parties have expressly agreed a shorter time limit.[65] However, where the Hague or Hague-Visby Rules apply to the charterparty they contain a one-year time bar in Article III rule 6 and the Hamburg Rules provide for a two-year time bar in Article 20. Many charterparties contain a provision referring all disputes to arbitration[66] and therefore the arbitration must be commenced within the time limit. The time bar is of even greater import now that section 12 of the Arbitration Act 1996 has narrowed the grounds on which an extension of time can be obtained.[67]

Not all claims under a charterparty will be caught by the time bar in the Rules as there must be a real connection between the loss or damage claimed and the goods being carried, and not just a very tenuous link.[68] Thus, for example, in *The Standard Ardour*[69] Saville J, as he then was, held that the charterer's claim for an indemnity for claims due to delays in the release of bills of lading which the charterer alleged were caused by the failure of the owner to provide a ship properly equipped to measure the quantities loaded, was not time barred. The loss was connected with the shipping documents and not the goods.

Some standard form charterparties limit the application of the Rules to cargo claims.[70] In *The Stena Pacifica*[71] Evans J concluded that the limited terms of

63. *Seven Seas Transportion Ltd v Pacifico Union Marina Corporation (The Satya Kailash and Oceanic Amity)* [1984] 1 Lloyd's Rep 588 upholding the decision of Staughton J in that case at first instance and *Industrie Chimiche Italia Centrale SpA v Nea Ninemia Shipping Co SA (The Emmanuel C)* [1983] 1 Lloyd's Rep 310 that the mutual exceptions clause, cl. 16, of the NYPE form, does not cover negligent errors.
64. See also *Aliakmon Maritime Corporation v Transocean Continental Shipping Ltd and Frank Truman Export Ltd (The Aliakmon Progress)* [1978] 2 Lloyd's Rep 499; *Actis Co Ltd v The Sanko Steamship Co Ltd (The Aquacharm)* [1982] 1 Lloyd's Rep 7; *Bayoil SA v Seawind Tankers Corporation (The Leonidas)* [2001] 1 Lloyd's Rep 533 and *Whistler International v Kawasaki Kisen Kaisha Ltd (The Hill Harmony)* [2001] 1 Lloyd's Rep 147 (HL); [1999] 2 Lloyd's Rep 209.
65. See, e.g., *Babanaft International Co SA v Avant Petroleum Inc (The Oltenia)* [1982] 2 Lloyd's Rep 99 (CA); [1982] 1 Lloyd's Rep 448.
66. E.g. cl. 17 of NYPE 1946 and cl. 23 of the Baltime form.
67. *Grimaldi Compagnia Di Navigazione SpA v Sekihyo Lines Ltd (The Seki Rolette)* [1998] 2 Lloyd's Rep 638 where Mance J did not grant an extension under s. 12 of the Arbitration Act 1996.
68. *Goulandris Brothers Ltd v B Goldman and Sons Ltd* [1957] 2 Lloyd's Rep 207; *Interbulk Ltd v Ponte dei Sospiri Shipping Co (The Standard Ardour)* [1988] 2 Lloyd's Rep 159; *Cargill International SA v CPN Tankers (Bermuda) Ltd (The Ot Sonja)* [1993] 2 Lloyd's Rep 435 (voyage charter – charterers suffering financial loss and expense due to loading delayed due to necessity of cleaning dirty tanks and due to analysis of suspected contamination of cargo); *Noranda Inc v Barton (Time Charter) Ltd (The Marinor)* [1996] 1 Lloyd's Rep 301; *Grimaldi Compagnia Di Navigazione SpA v Sekihyo Lines Ltd (The Seki Rolette)* [1998] 2 Lloyd's Rep 638; *Linea Naviera Paramaconi SA v Abnormal Load Engineering Ltd* [2001] 1 Lloyd's Rep 763.
69. *Interbulk Ltd v Ponte dei Sospiri Shipping Co (The Standard Ardour)* [1988] 2 Lloyd's Rep 159.
70. E.g. cl. 27(c)(ii) of the Shelltime 4 form.
71. [1990] 2 Lloyd's Rep 234. See also *Borgship Tankers Inc v Product Transport Corporation Ltd (The Casco)* [2005] EWHC 273 (Comm); [2005] 1 Lloyd's Rep 565.

incorporation meant that Article III rule 6 did not apply to claims outside the Hague Rules obligations.

## 5. REMEDIES FOR OWNER'S BREACH

We shall now consider the remedies that the charterer will have if the ship does not comply with its description or is not seaworthy.

Where the owner has made a representation of fact to the charterer during the negotiations for the charterparty, probably through its broker, which induced the charterer to enter into the charterparty, and the representation is false, the charterer has a right to elect to avoid the charterparty. It must make an election to avoid or affirm the contract once it is aware that it has such a right, or it will be taken to have waived its right and the contract will be affirmed. If the charterer does elect to avoid, it is as if the charterparty had never existed. The charterer is entitled to be put back in the position it was in before the representation was made and it was induced to enter into the contract, as it never would have entered into this contract had it not been misled.

The charterer may also be entitled to damages for misrepresentation. Where the misrepresentation made by the misrepresentor induces the misrepresentee to enter into a contract with the misrepresentor, the Misrepresentation Act 1967 applies. If the owner cannot show that it had reasonable grounds to believe and did believe in the truth of the representation, it will be liable for damages as if the representation were fraudulent under section 2(1). Thus in *Howard Marine & Dredging Co Ltd v Ogden & Sons (Excavations) Ltd*[72] the owner misrepresented the carrying capacity of its two barges. It had relied on incorrect figures given in Lloyd's Register. The Court of Appeal held that it was not reasonable to rely on those figures as the ships' documents giving the true figures were in the owner's possession.

The great advantages of section 2(1) of the Misrepresentation Act 1967 are twofold: the reverse burden of proof on the misrepresentor and the fiction of fraud, which means that the misrepresentee can recover damages as if the misrepresentor were fraudulent, although this is controversial.[73] If the owner could prove that it did have reasonable grounds to believe and did believe in the truth of the representation, the charterer could seek damages in lieu of rescission under section 2(2) of the Misrepresentation Act 1967 but this is at the discretion of the court.

Where the misrepresentee is induced to enter into a contract with a third party rather than the misrepresentor, the Misrepresentation Act 1967 does not apply. This was the case, for example, in *The Arta*[74] referred to above where the charterer's broker made a representation in its personal capacity, rather than as agent on behalf of the owner, and induced the owner to enter into a contract with the charterer, rather than itself. If the charterer can prove that the misrepresentation

72. [1978] QB 574.
73. *Royscot Trust Ltd v Rogerson* [1991] 3 All ER 294, but see the doubts of the House of Lords in *Smith New Court Securities Ltd v Scrimgeour Vickers Asset Management Limited* [1997] AC 254.
74. *Markappa Inc v N W Spratt & Son Ltd (The Arta)* [1985] 1 Lloyd's Rep 534, discussed at p. 47 of this chapter.

was made fraudulently, it will be entitled to damages for the tort of deceit for all direct losses, whether foreseeable or not. There is no defence of contributory negligence[75] and the liability cannot be excluded.[76] However, the burden of proof is a heavy one and if it cannot be satisfied the misrepresentor may sue for the tort of negligence.[77] In that case the misrepresentee must establish that the misrepresentor owes it a duty of care. The burden of proving negligence in breaching that duty of care would be on the misrepresentee and it must show that the loss was foreseeable. The owner could rely on the defence of contributory negligence[78] and the liability could be excluded by a contractual term.[79]

Where the failure complained of is a breach of a term of the charterparty the charterer has a number of contractual remedies. The first to consider is whether the charterer can cancel the charterparty. Almost all standard form charterparties give the charterers an express right to cancel if the ship is not delivered ready or in every way fitted for the service by a specific time.[80] This provision is of great importance to the charterer as it may cancel the contract,[81] regardless of fault by the owner and the right is therefore not affected by whether the owner's obligation is absolute or one of due diligence. The only question the charterer has to ask is whether the ship is in the condition contracted for by the time prescribed. If it is not, the charterer may cancel. The charterer does not have to ask why not, unless it also wishes to claim damages, in which case it must show a breach of charterparty.

Where one party has failed to comply with an obligation under the contract, either express or implied, it is in breach of contract. The remedy that the innocent party will have for that breach will depend on the importance of the obligation breached. Provided that the innocent party can show that it has suffered a loss caused by the breach which is not too remote, it will always be able to claim damages for breach. However, if the breach is fundamental, the innocent party not only has the right to damages, but also has the right to elect to terminate the contract, thereby discharging the parties from their future obligations under the contract.

Therefore if the charterer accepts delivery of the ship it may never have another chance to terminate the charterparty at common law, even if the ship is defective, unless it can prove a fundamental breach that is either a breach of condition or an innominate term where the consequences of the breach go to the root of the contract; or there is another express right to terminate or cancel. It is therefore necessary to be able to determine whether the term breached is a condition or an innominate term.

The parties may expressly provide that a clause in the charterparty is a condition. However, this is neither sufficient nor necessary. Even if the parties have neither expressly stated that an obligation is a condition nor spelled out the consequences

75. *Standard Chartered Bank v Pakistan National Shipping Corporation (No 2)* [2003] 1 Lloyd's Rep 227.
76. *HIH Casualty and General Insurance Ltd v Chase Manhattan Bank* [2003] 2 Lloyd's Rep 61.
77. *Hedley Byrne v Heller* [1964] AC 465.
78. See, e.g., *Vesta v Butcher* [1988] 2 All ER 43.
79. See, e.g., *Howard Marine & Dredging Co Ltd v Ogden & Sons (Excavations) Ltd* [1978] QB 574.
80. E.g. cl. 21 of the Baltime 1939 (as revised 2001); cl. 14 of NYPE 1946; cl. 16 of NYPE 1993 and cl. 5 of Shelltime 4.
81. See further below at pp. 67 and 68 of this chapter.

of breach, the court may find that the term was of such importance in the contract that it is a condition. In *The Seaflower*[82] a time charterparty for a period of 11 months, maximum 12 months at the charterers' option, contained the following clause 46:

"Vessel is presently MOBIL (expiring 27/1/98) CONOCO (expiring 3/2/98) and SHELL (expiring 14/1/98) acceptable. Owners guarantee to obtain within 60 days (sixty) days EXXON approval in addition to present approvals. On delivery date hire rate will be discounted USD 250...for each approval missing...If for any reason, Owners would lose even one of such acceptances they must advise charterers at once and they must reinstate same within 30 (thirty) days from such occurrence failing which Charterers will be at liberty to cancel charterparty... Hire rates will be reinstated once Owner will show written evidence of approvals from Major Oil Companies."

The Court of Appeal unanimously held that the requirement to obtain approval from Exxon within 60 days was a condition, breach of which entitled the charterer to elect to terminate the charterparty. The clause could have been better drafted. One of the charterer's problems was that the clause did not spell out whether the charterer had the right to cancel the charterparty if the Exxon approval was not obtained within 60 days. It only expressly provided for such a right if an acceptance were lost and not reinstated within 30 days. That right clearly applied to the loss of Exxon approval once such approval was obtained. Thus the charterer treated the majors' approval as important and the clause treated a failure to reinstate a lost approval as a breach of condition. The parties should be assumed to have intended to be consistent about the importance of obtaining and maintaining majors' approvals. Thus there should be no inconsistencey between the loss of some majors' approvals and that of Exxon or between having the approval at the outset of the charterparty and losing the approval after the commencement of the charter period. It did not matter that the charterparty did not expressly state that the requirement was a condition. As held by the House of Lords in *Bunge Corporation v Tradax Export SA*[83] a provision for performance of an obligation within a certain time limit in a mercantile contract (but not the time for payment of time charter hire),[84] particularly if the other party's performance of the contract is dependent on performance of that obligation by a certain time, is presumed to be a condition. The word "guarantee" used in this provision served to emphasise the importance of the provision although it would not on its own justify the conclusion that the provision was a condition.[85]

A term may be an innominate term where the consequences of breach could vary from being very significant to inconsequential. In *The Hong Kong Fir*[86] the Court of Appeal held that the obligation as to seaworthiness is an innominate term and therefore breach of that term would only give rise to a right to elect to terminate if the consequences of the breach are so serious that they deprive the innocent party of substantially the whole of the benefit that it was intended to obtain under the contract – in other words if the breach is fundamental or goes to the root of the contract. This is because of the range of consequences that can result from breach of such a term. At one end of the spectrum the consequences

82. *BS & N Ltd (BVI) v Micado Shipping Ltd (Malta) (The Seaflower)* [2001] 1 Lloyd's Rep 341.
83. [1981] 1 WLR 711; [1981] 2 Lloyd's Rep 1.
84. See p. ??? of this chapter.
85. *Per* Jonathan Parker LJ at para. 102.
86. *Hong Kong Fir Shipping Co. Ltd v Kawasaki Kisen Kaisha Ltd (The Hong Kong Fir)* [1962] 2 QB 26; [1961] 2 Lloyd's Rep 478.

of breach may be very trivial. For example, the radar of the ship may break down. Nevertheless the ship is navigated safely into port without any difficulty. On arrival in port an electrical engineer is requested to fix the radar which is repaired within a matter of hours and no delay is caused to the ship's operations as cargo operations are performed throughout the repairs. At the other end of the spectrum, the ship's steering gear fails in heavy seas and the ship becomes a total loss on the rocks.

The disadvantage of the classification of the term as an innominate one rather than a condition is that, instead of being able to elect to terminate the charterparty immediately on breach, the charterer has to wait to see what the consequences of the breach are. This may be commercially very inconvenient as is illustrated by *The Hong Kong Fir*. There the charterparty was for a term of 24 months. The ship suffered a number of engine breakdowns and it was necessary for repairs to be carried out over a period of five months. The Court of Appeal held that the breach by the owner of the seaworthiness provision did not entitle the charterer to elect to terminate the charterparty as it had not been deprived of substantially the whole benefit it had contracted for: the charterer had lost the use of the ship for five months out of 24.

Commercially the charterer may be in a very difficult position if it does not have the use of the ship for a period of time. This will be exacerbated by the fact that when the ship gets into difficulties it may not initially be clear how long it will take to sort the problem out. For example, if the engines break down and it is necessary to obtain spare parts from the manufacturer and perhaps have the manufacturer's personnel attend the ship to advise on the necessary repairs, it may take some time to estimate how long the repairs will take. This may play havoc with the charterer's planning. The charterer may well have to make decisions such as whether to charter in a substitute ship to perform its contractual commitments to sellers and purchasers and may not know how long to charter such substitute for, so that it will have to enter into voyage charters. Until it becomes clear how long the difficulties will last, or it becomes clear that the difficulties will cause a significant delay, the charterer cannot elect to terminate the charterparty. This is even more frustrating if the market is falling and the charterer would much prefer to charter in a reliable and cheaper substitute ship.

It is for this reason that many of the more sophisticated time charterparties, and particularly those with the oil majors, contain express cancellation clauses entitling the charterer to cancel the charterparty if the owner does not rectify a problem within a specified time[87] and provide for an indemnity.

If a party has a right to elect to terminate the charterparty it must make that election by clearly communicating it, unless its non-performance of the contract clearly demonstrates its election to terminate.[88] It does not matter why the innocent party elects to terminate. It may wish to escape the contract for purely commercial reasons; for example, it could now go out into the market and charter in another ship at a better rate. If the innocent party does make an election to terminate both parties are discharged from future performance of their primary obligations under the contract. The party in fundamental breach has a secondary obligation

87. E.g. cl. 3(iii) of the Shelltime 4 form and additional typed clauses as in *The Seaflower,* discussed above at p. 57 of this chapter.
88. *Vitol v Norelf (The Santa Clara)* [1996] AC 800.

to pay damages for that breach. The contract itself is not to be disregarded. Indeed, the contract will establish what the liability of the party in fundamental breach is. It will be a question of construction whether clauses of the contract such as exemption clauses, limitation clauses and liquidated damages clauses, are drafted widely enough to apply even to the fundamental breach of contract.[89] If the parties litigate their dispute they will still be bound by any jurisdiction or arbitration clause in the contract.

The election to terminate is irrevocable and once made the innocent party cannot subsequently change its mind. Both parties will be liable for other breaches which occurred prior to the fundamental breach.

The innocent party may prefer to elect to affirm the contract, especially if the market has fluctuated so that it would now be more expensive, for example, for the charterer to charter a substitute ship. In that event both parties must continue to perform the charterparty. The party in fundamental breach will be liable for damages for that breach and both parties will be liable for any previous breaches. Once the innocent party has communicated its affirmation it is irrevocable unless the party in breach persists with its non-performance or commits a new fundamental breach, in which case the innocent party can elect to terminate.[90] In extreme cases where the party in breach can show that the innocent party has "no legitimate interest, financial or otherwise, in performing the contract rather than claiming damages" there will be no right to affirm.[91]

If the term breached is neither a condition nor an innominate term, it will be a warranty and the only remedy for breach of warranty is damages.

Off hire is another important remedy for a time charterer.[92] The charterer of the *Hong Kong Fir* did not have to pay hire for the ship during the period that time was lost while repairs to the engines were carried out. Furthermore, some charterparties expressly provide that the charterer is entitled to add off hire periods to the period of the charterparty, as in *The Hong Kong Fir*,[93] so that the charterer does actually have the use of the ship for the time originally contracted for.

## 6. REASONABLE DESPATCH

There is usually an express term in a charterparty providing that the owner must exercise reasonable despatch, all convenient despatch,[94] utmost despatch[95] or due despatch.[96] Where a contract does not provide for the time within which an obligation must be performed at common law it will be implied that the obligation must be performed within a reasonable time.

89. *Photo Production v Securicor* [1980] 1 All ER 856.
90. *Johnson v Agnew* [1980] AC 369.
91. *Clea Shipping Corp v Bulk Oil International Ltd (The Alaskan Trader)* [1983] 1 Lloyd's Rep 315 and *Ocean Marine Navigation Ltd v Koch Carbon Inc (The Dynamic)* [2003] 2 Lloyd's Rep 693.
92. See pp. 76 and 77 of this chapter.
93. See also *Petroleo Brasileiro SA v Kriti Akti Shipping Co SA (The Kriti Akti)* [2004] EWCA Civ 116, [2004] 1 Lloyd's Rep 712, discussed at p. 70 of this chapter.
94. See, e.g., cl. 1 of Asbatankvoy.
95. See, e.g., cl. 8 of NYPE 1946.
96. See, e.g., cl. 8 of NYPE 1993.

## 7. DEVIATION

A charterparty may provide for a particular route to be followed or under a time charterparty the time charterer may give express instructions as to the route.[97] If there is a contractually agreed route, the shipowner must follow that route unless an exception applies. If there is no contractually agreed route it is presumed that the contractual route is the direct geographical route, unless the owner can prove that there is a customary route.[98]

Many charterparties contain an express liberty to deviate.[99] Such a clause will be interpreted restrictively against the owner.[100] If the charterparty incorporates the Hague or Hague-Visby Rules Article IV rule 4 of both sets of Rules provides that the carrier shall not be liable for any loss or damage resulting from any deviation in saving or attempting to save life or property or any reasonable deviation.[101] The Rules do not permit the owner to contract out of the minimum obligations imposed by the Rules,[102] and where there is both a wide express liberty clause and the Rules apply, the question arises whether the liberty clause is an attempt to lessen the owner's obligations and is thus void, or defines the scope of the owner's obligations in which case it is valid. The latter interpretation seems likely.[103]

If there is no express liberty clause and the Rules do not apply to the charterparty, the owner can rely on the justifications for deviation at common law. These are narrower than those under the Rules and cover deviation to save human life or to communicate with a ship in distress where there is a risk of loss of life (but not for the sole purpose of saving property);[104] to avoid danger to the ship or her cargo, even if the danger was caused by the ship being unseaworthy when she went to sea;[105] or where deviation is necessary due to the fault of the charterer.

Unjustified deviation is a fundamental breach of contract and the charterer has the right to elect to terminate or affirm the contract.[106] The breach was treated at common law as of such a serious character as to go to the root of the contract and, if the charterer elected to terminate the contract, the owner could no longer rely on any of its terms, including any exception clauses. This is the doctrine of fundamental breach. That doctrine no longer survives in general contract law as a result of the decision of the House of Lords in *Photo Production v Securicor*.[107] However, in that case Lord Wilberforce left open the question whether maritime contracts are of a special type and therefore whether the doctrine should survive in relation to them.[108] The better view is that it does not.[109] Historically the reason

97. See, e.g., *Whistler International v Kawasaki Kisen Kaisha Ltd (The Hill Harmony)* [2001] 1 Lloyd's Rep 147.
98. *Reardon Smith Line v Black Sea and Baltic General Insurance* [1939] AC 562.
99. See, e.g., cl. 3 of Gencon 1994.
100. *Glynn v Margetson* [1893] AC 351 and *Stag Line v Foscolo, Mango & Co* [1932] AC 328.
101. See *Stag Line v Foscolo, Mango & Co* [1932] AC 328 and *Lyric Shipping Inc v Intermetals Ltd (The Al Taha)* [1990] 2 Lloyd's Rep 117.
102. Article III rule 8 of the Hague and Hague-Visby Rules.
103. *Renton v Palmyra Trading Corp* [1956] 1 QB 462 at p. 510, approved in *Jindal Iron & Steel Limited v Islamic Solidarity Shipping Co (The Jordan II)* [2005] 1 Lloyd's Rep 57.
104. *Scaramanga v Stamp* (1880) 5 CPD 295, *per* Cockburn CJ at p. 304.
105. *Kish v Taylor* [1912] AC 604.
106. *Hain Steamship Company Ltd v Tate & Lyle Ltd* [1936] 2 All ER 597.
107. [1980] AC 827.
108. *Ibid.*, at p. 845.
109. See, e.g., the view of Lloyd LJ in *The Antares* [1987] 1 Lloyd's Rep 424 at p. 430. C. Debattista, "Fundamental Breach and Deviation in the Carriage of Goods by Sea" [1989] JBL 22.

for the draconian response to deviation was that the insurer was discharged from liability if there was a deviation.[110] Nowadays the standard form insurance contracts hold the insured covered if there is a deviation.[111] If the doctrine of fundamental breach no longer survives, it would be a question of construction whether an exemption clause is drafted widely enough to cover the fundamental breach which has occurred.

Where the Hague or Hague-Visby Rules apply to the charterparty, the time bar will probably still apply[112] even if the owner has deviated and the owner can rely on the limits of liability,[113] although it may be possible to break those limits where the Hague-Visby Rules apply.

## 8. SAFE PORTS

A charterparty either time or voyage will usually provide that the ship may only be ordered to safe ports or places.[114] In some more sophisticated charterparties, the charterer's obligation is limited to one of due diligence to ensure that the ship is only employed between and at safe places.[115] At common law there is an implied obligation on a time or voyage charterer only to nominate a safe port.

The classic statement of what constitutes a safe port is that of Sellers LJ in *The Eastern City*:[116]

> "... a port will not be safe unless, in the relevant period of time, the particular ship can reach it, use it and return from it without, in the absence of some abnormal occurrence, being exposed to danger which cannot be avoided by good navigation and seamanship ..."

Thus a port may be unsafe because the ship cannot safely get to it, for example, because her draft is too great; there is ice; the anchorage is unreliable;[117] or there is no adequate system of monitoring the channel.[118]

Simply because there are hazards at a port does not necessarily make that port unsafe as it may be possible to avoid them with good navigation and seamanship. There must be a safe system in the port to warn of hazards and to avoid them. Thus a port is still safe if it is prone to bad weather and it is necessary for the ship to leave the port during such weather, if there is an adequate system for forecasting bad weather, sufficient tugs and pilots, adequate sea room to manoeuvre and an adequate system of making sure that adequate sea room is always available

110. Sections 45 and 46 of the Marine Insurance Act 1906. H. Bennett, *The Law of Marine Insurance* (2nd ed, Oxford University Press, 2006) ("*Bennett*"), paras. 18.34–18.37.
111. *Bennett*, paras. 18.111–18.114.
112. *Cf. The Antares* [1987] 1 Lloyd's Rep 424, 429.
113. *Cf. Daewoo Heavy Industries Ltd v Klipriver Shipping Ltd (The Kapitan Petko Voivoda)* [2003] EWCA Civ 451; [2003] 2 Lloyd's Rep 1; *Scrutton*, pp. 435, 447–449 and 452; A. Diamond, "Hague-Visby Rules" [1978] 2 LMCLQ 225, 246–247.
114. See, e.g., cl. 6 of NYPE 1946; cl. 5 of NYPE 1993; cl. 1 of Gencon 1994 and cls. 1 and 9 of Asbatankvoy.
115. See, e.g., cl. 3 of Shelltime 3 and cl. 4 of Shelltime 4.
116. *Leeds Shipping Co v Société Francaise Bunge (The Eastern City)* [1958] 2 Lloyd's Rep 127 at p. 131.
117. *Ibid.*
118. *Independent Petroleum Group v Seacarriers (The Count)* [2006] EWHC 3173.

to manoeuvre.[119] A port may also be unsafe for political reasons, for example, as a result of the outbreak of hostilities so that the ship is trapped at her discharge port.[120]

When a time charterer gives voyage instructions its obligation is to nominate a port which is prospectively safe, i.e. the port will be safe at the time that the ship arrives there, uses it and leaves. The port does not need to be safe at the time the order is given, provided it will have become safe for this ship by the time she arrives, for example, because the ice currently at the port will have melted. The charterer is liable for the normal characteristics of the port whether they were known to it or not. However, it does not guarantee the safety of the port, as it will not be liable for abnormal and unexpected events. Thus the charterer was not liable in *The Evia (No 2)*[121] when the ship was trapped in the Shatt al Arab waterway as a result of the outbreak of war between Iran and Iraq. In *The Saga Cob*[122] the ship was attacked by Eritrean guerrillas in Massawa. The Court of Appeal held that it was impossible to say that such an attack or even the risk of an attack was a normal characteristic of the port. The attack was an abnormal and unexpected event. The charterer's duty in that case was one of due diligence and the Court of Appeal thought that there was a strong argument that the test should be if a reasonably careful charterer would on the facts known have concluded that the port was prospectively unsafe.[123] What happened after the attack would also be relevant on the question of due diligence.

The House of Lords also held in *The Evia (No 2)* that if the port which was prospectively safe subsequently becomes unsafe, the charterer has a secondary obligation to order the ship to a new safe port. Where the ship is already at the port no such secondary obligation can arise where it is not possible for the ship to leave, as was the case in *The Evia (No 2)*. In *The Lucille*, however, the ship could not enter the port due to congestion and the port became prospectively unsafe. The charterer should have ordered the ship to leave and was therefore in breach of its secondary obligation. It is not clear whether the secondary obligation is an absolute one or is based on due diligence or reasonable care or on the actual knowledge of the charterer.

The House of Lords also left open the question as to whether the secondary obligation applies to a voyage charterer. A voyage charterparty may expressly provide that the ship is to proceed to a named port or ports, so that the parties have agreed in advance the contractual ports. In *The Archimidis*[124] the Court of Appeal held that the express typed provision for "1 safe port Ventspils" constituted a warranty by the charterer of the safety of the port, as opposed to an agreement by both parties that the port was safe. *The Livanita*[125] concerned a "time charter trip via St Petersburg". The hull of the ship was damaged by ice blocks created by ice breakers which assisted her as she left St Petersburg. The charterer contended that there was no relevant express warranty because the risk of the ship

119. *The Khian Sea* [1979] 1 Lloyd's Rep 545.
120. *Kodros Shipping Corp v Empresa Cubana de Fletes (The Evia (No 2)* [1982] 2 Lloyd's Rep 307.
121. *Ibid.*
122. *K/S Penta Shipping A/S v Ethiopian Shipping Lines Corporation (The Saga Cob)* [1992] 2 Lloyd's Rep 545.
123. *Ibid.*, p. 551.
124. *AIC Limited v Marine Pilot Limited (The Archimidis)* [2008] EWCA Civ 175.
125. *STX Pan Ocean Co Ltd v Ugland Bulk Transport A.S. (The Livanita)* [2007] EWHC 1317 (Comm).

encountering ice at St Petersburg was a risk the owner had agreed to bear by agreeing to a charterparty with St Petersburg as a named port in winter. Langley J held that where a charterparty expressly names a loading port and also contains a safe port warranty that warranty applies to the named port. No case was made by the charterer of variation, estoppel or waiver. There was no evidence that either party knew or ought reasonably to have anticipated that the port was unsafe at the time the charter was entered into, nor that it was unsafe in a reasonably predictable and expected way.

When a charterer gives voyage instructions under a time charterparty to proceed to an unsafe port the owner is entitled to reject the order as invalid and ask for valid voyage instructions. An analogy may be drawn with the situation where the charterer gives an order to go on an illegitimate last voyage.[126] Thus if the charterer were to insist on invalid voyage instructions, the charterer would be in repudiatory breach of charterparty and the owner would have the right to elect to terminate the charterparty. Where the owner is not aware that the port is unsafe, but it subsequently becomes clear that that is the position, the owner may refuse to enter the port.

Where, however, the owner is aware that the port is unsafe but accepts the order to proceed there, the owner cannot then change its mind although it may still have a right to damages for breach of contract.[127] Where the Master ignores obvious danger and proceeds to enter the agreed port, this may constitute a break in the chain of causation so that the owner cannot recover damages from the charterer as the loss resulted from the choice of the owner's servant rather than the charterer's breach.

When the charterer is in breach of its safe port obligation it will be liable in damages for the consequences of its breach such as physical damage to the ship, additional costs incurred at the port, for example, if the ship is unable to enter due to her draught being excessive and it is necessary to lighten her. Where the consequence is delay the time charterer would continue to be liable for time charter hire and other expenses incurred such as additional insurance premiums while the delay continued, whereas a voyage charterer would be liable for damages for detention.

## 9. FRUSTRATION

In *National Carriers Ltd v Panalpina (Northern) Ltd*[128] Lord Simon stated:

> "Frustration of a contract takes place when there supervenes an event (without fault of either party and for which the contract makes no sufficient provision) which so significantly changes the nature (not merely the expense or onerousness) of the outstanding rights and/or obligations from what the parties could reasonably have contemplated at the time of its execution that it would be unjust to hold them to the literal sense of its stipulations in the new circumstances; in such case the law declares both parties to be discharged from further performance."[129]

126. See p. 72 of this chapter and see *The Peonia*, *per* Lord Bingham at p.107 and *The Gregos*.
127. *Motor Oil Hellas Refineries SA v Shipping Corp of India (The Kanchenjunga)* [1990] 1 Lloyd's Rep 391.
128. [1981] AC 675 (HL).
129. *Ibid*., at p. 700.

In the maritime context frustration may occur if the ship is destroyed, requisitioned,[130] seized[131] or trapped due to outbreak of war.[132] Simply because it is more expensive and time consuming[133] to perform the contract will not frustrate it. Thus in *Tsakiroglou & Co Ltd v Noblee Thorl GmbH*[134] a sale contract was not frustrated by the closure of the Suez Canal, even though the freight rate was much higher and it took twice as long to perform the voyage as the ship had to take the route round the Cape of Good Hope. The contract could still be performed. This would not be the case if the ship could not arrive within the contractual delivery date or the cargo would perish on the longer voyage.

Where an event causes delay in performance of contractual obligations it may be possible to say immediately that the prospective delay is so great that the contract is frustrated. In other situations, however, it may be necessary to wait to see whether the delay that has already occurred, and is likely to occur in the future, is so great as to frustrate the contract. The party alleging frustration will seek the earliest frustration date possible and will no doubt argue that it was predictable at an early stage that the delay would be frustrating. It is for the tribunal of fact, properly informed as to the law, to decide the effect of the delay.[135]

It will be necessary to consider the impact of the event on each individual contract. The same event may have a different impact on different contracts depending on what obligations remain to be performed under each contract and whether the contract has provided for the event which has occurred. For example, the outbreak of war between Iran and Iraq on 22 September 1980 frustrated the time charterparty in *The Evia*[136] on 8 October 1980 as, soon after the outbreak of war, it became clear that it would be a long, slow war of attrition and as the ship had completed discharge of her cargo on the day war broke out, the only obligation remaining to be performed by charterers was to redeliver the ship, which was not possible. In *The Agathon*,[137] however, the charterparty could still be performed after the outbreak of war, as the ship could still continue to discharge her cargo, albeit slowly, thus her charterparty was not frustrated until December that year, when discharge was completed.

In *The Sea Angel*[138] Tsavliris, salvors, chartererd the *Sea Angel*, a small ship, to transfer the cargo of crude oil from the *Tasman Spirit* which had grounded in the approaches to the port of Karachi, as part of the salvage operation of the *Tasman Spirit*. The time charter of the *Sea Angel* was for 20 days. The *Sea Angel* completed the transfer of the cargo and was due to leave Karachi on 9 September for redelivery at Fujairah three days later. However, the Karachi Port Trust (KPT) refused to grant a No Demand Certificate so she could not leave. KPT demanded that Tsavliris pay about $11million. The ship was detained for 108

130. *Anglo Northern Trading Company Limited v Emlyn Jones & Williams* [1917] 2 KB 78; *Bank Line Limited v Arthur Capel & Co* [1919] AC 435.
131. *Tatem v Gamboa* [1939] 1 KB 132.
132. *Kodros Shipping Corp v Empresa Cubana de Fletes (The Evia) (No 2)* [1982] 2 Lloyd's Rep 307.
133. *Davies Contractors Ltd v Fareham Urban District Council* [1956] AC 696.
134. [1962] AC 93.
135. *Pioneer Shipping Ltd v. BTP Tioxide Ltd (The Nema)* [1982] AC 724 (strike).
136. *Kodros Shipping Corp v Empresa Cubana de Fletes (The Evia (No 2)* [1982] 2 Lloyd's Rep 307.
137. *Kissavos Shipping Co SA v Empresa Cubana de Fletes (The Agathon)* [1982] 2 Lloyd's Rep 211 (CA).
138. *Edwinton Commercial Corporation v Tsavliris Russ (Worldwide Salvage & Towage) Ltd (The Sea Angel)* [2007] EWCA Civ 547; [2007] 2 Lloyd's Rep 517.

days until 26 December. The Court of Appeal upheld the decision of Gross J at first instance that the contract was not frustrated. Tsavliris argued on appeal that the delay which had already taken place by 13 October of about five weeks added to the prospective delay amounted to a total, ongoing, indefinite delay of such unreasonable and inordinate length, especially when compared with the length of the charter and the very short time unexpired, as to frustrate the contract. It was argued that this comparison was the main test to apply. Rix LJ rejected that argument as although it is an important consideration it was on the facts "only the starting point".[139] Rix LJ distinguished the cases on requisition, seizure or trapping as there is no possibility in such cases of negotiating or litigating one's way out of such consequences of war. A special factor included the foreseeability of the general risk of the unreasonable detention of a ship participating in salvage services, which was recognised within the salvage industry. The requirement of justice was not an additional test for frustration but was "a relevant factor" and "provides the ultimate rationale of the doctrine". It could be used as "a reality check".[140]

The event may not only have been foreseen by the parties but there may be some express provision in the charterparty.[141] It will be a question of construction whether any provision is sufficient to cover the very serious circumstances which have occurred or whether the supervening event goes beyond the risk assumed under the contract and renders performance radically different[142] from that contracted for.

The supervening event must not be due to the fault of either party. Thus if the event is caused by the fault or breach of either party the contract cannot be frustrated and this is referred to as self-induced frustration. For example, in *The Fjord Wind*[143] the ship ran aground and it was necessary to transship her cargo. The owner argued that the voyage charterparty was frustrated. However, as the grounding was due to the owner's failure to exercise due diligence to make the ship seaworthy there could not be frustration. Furthermore, where it is impossible to perform the contract due to a choice or election made by one of the parties this is self-induced frustration. Thus in *The Super Servant Two*[144] a contract could be performed by one of two ships. The owner allocated one ship to perform another contract and the second ship was lost. The charterparty was not frustrated as it could not be performed due to the owner's choice to use the first ship to perform a contract with a third party rather than using it to perform this contract. The solution would have been for the owner to provide in the contract that it had an option as to which of the ships was to perform the contract. Once such an option was exercised, if the ship chosen is lost the contract could be frustrated, but the owner cannot keep its option open and claim frustration if only one ship is lost.

139. *Ibid.*, para. 118.
140. *Ibid.*, para. 132.
141. *Ocean Tramp Tankers Corporation v V/O Sovfracht (The Eugenia)* [1963] 2 Lloyd's Rep 381 (CA); *W J Tatem, Ltd v Gamboa* (1938) 61 Ll L Rep 149; *BTP Tioxide Ltd v Pioneer Shipping Ltd and Armada Marine SpA (The Nema) (No 2)* [1981] 2 Lloyd's Rep 239 (HL).
142. *Per* Lord Radcliffe in *Davies Contractors Ltd v Fareham Urban District Council* [1956] AC 696 at p. 729.
143. *Eridania SpA v Rudolf A Oetker (The Fjord Wind)* [2000] 2 Lloyd's Rep 191.
144. [1990] 1 Lloyd's Rep 1.

The consequence of frustration is that the contract is terminated automatically as from the date of frustration, i.e. both parties are discharged from their contractual obligations without either party making any election. At common law any sums that were due by the date of frustration were still due and any sums which had been paid before the date of frustration could not be recovered. Any sums which would have become due after the date of frustration no longer had to be paid. In *Fibrosa v Fairbairn*[145] the House of Lords held that a payment which had been made prior to frustration could be refunded if there was a total failure of consideration.

The Law Reform (Frustrated Contracts) Act 1943, which seeks to apportion losses between the parties, applies to time charters and charterparties by demise, but not to voyage charters and bills of lading. Where a time charterparty is frustrated the hire which has been paid in advance may be repayable under section 1(2) of the Act, although the court has a discretion to allow hire to be retained by the owner where it has expended money in or for the performance of the contract. Section 1(3) provides that where a valuable benefit has been conferred on a party by partial performance of the contract, the court has a discretion to award compensation to the party conferring the benefit. Such compensation cannot exceed the value of the benefit conferred and should take into account the expenses which the party obtaining the benefit has incurred in performing the contract and any circumstances which may have affected the value of the benefit.[146]

## 10. TIMING AT THE BEGINNING OF THE CHARTERPARTY

Although the ship may already be at the loadport when the charterparty is concluded, this will not usually be the case. The owner will wish to conclude the next fixture in good time before the completion of the current charterparty, so that there is no possibility of the ship being unemployed. The charterer will need to know when the ship will be delivered and ready to load so that it can make arrangements to have the cargo ready at the loadport at that time. The charterer may well have other contractual commitments, such as sale or purchase contracts or a sub charterparty, to perform and the timing of those contracts and the charterparty must be carefully linked. Thus, for example, the charterer may be the f.o.b. buyer of goods under a contract which provides for shipment within a five-day window. It may also have sold the goods on c.i.f. terms with shipment within the same five-day window. The charterer will wish to have the ship arrive at the appropriate time to enable the ship to load within that window. The charterer will not wish the ship to arrive too early when there is no cargo available if the risk of delay is for the charterer. If this were the case a time charterer would be liable for time charter hire or laytime would commence under a voyage charterparty but the charterer cannot yet use the ship. Furthermore, the charterer will not wish the ship to arrive so late that the charterer cannot load within the window.

145. [1943] AC 32.
146. *BP Exploration v Hunt* [1982] 1 All ER 925.

The charterer will therefore be protected by a number of clauses in the charterparty. First the charterparty may well record where the ship is at the time that the charterparty is concluded.[147] The charterparty may state "now trading" or "present position". Such a provision will be a condition of the charterparty so that if the ship is elsewhere the charterer would be entitled to elect to terminate the charterparty.[148] In addition the charterparty may state when the ship is "expected ready to load".[149] In *The Mihalis Angelos*[150] the Court of Appeal held that such a provision is also a condition so that if the owner gives a date without any honest belief that the ship will arrive by that date or without any reasonable grounds for it, again the charterer is entitled to elect to terminate the contract. The charterer in that case was entitled to elect to terminate, even though the reason that it gave for terminating the contract was an entirely different one – it sought to rely on a *force majeure* clause in the contract as it could not provide a cargo.

The "expected ready to load" date is not, however, a guarantee that the ship will definitely arrive by the date given. Provided the date given is both honest and reasonable at the time it was given, the owner will not be in breach of that provision if the ship is then delayed, for example, by an unforeseen tug strike or there is bad weather. Therefore, it is usual for both time and voyage charterparties to provide for a cut off date so that if the ship has not arrived by that date, the charterer has an express right to cancel.[151] The period of time starting from the earliest date at which hire will commence under a time charter or the earliest time from which laytime can start counting under a voyage charter and the latest time by which the ship can tender a notice of readiness without the risk of being cancelled is often called the laycan.

In *The Niizuru*[152] Mance J held that a clause requiring the owner to narrow the laycan to a 15-day spread 25 days prior to the narrowed laycan was a condition precedent to delivery of the ship under a time charterparty. However, the Court of Appeal held in *Universal Bulk Carriers Ltd v Andre Et Cie*[153] that an obligation on the charterer to narrow the laycan in a voyage charterparty was not always a condition precedent to an obligation to nominate a vessel and was not in that case.

So that the charterer is kept informed of progress it is common for the charterparty to provide that the owner must give notices, for example, 72, 48 and 24 hours before the ship's arrival at the delivery point.

The cancellation clause may only give a right to cancel on the cancelling date and not before. In *The Mihalis Angelos*[154] a majority of the Court of Appeal, Lord Denning dissenting, held that the charterer could not exercise its express right to cancel until the cancelling date specified in the clause, even though it was clear some days earlier that the ship would not arrive by the cancelling date. If the charterer purports to cancel before the right to cancel accrues, the charterer will

147. *SK Shipping Co Ltd v BB Energy (Asia) Pte Ltd* [2000] 1 All ER (Comm) 810.
148. *Behn v Burness* (1863) 3 B & S 751.
149. See Box 9 of Gencon.
150. *Maredelanto Compania Naviera SA v Bergbau-Handel GmbH (The Mihalis Angelos)* [1970] 2 Lloyd's Rep 43.
151. E.g. cl. 14 of NYPE 1946, cl. 16 of NYPE 1993 and cl. 5 of Asbatankvoy.
152. *Hyundai Merchant Marine Co Ltd v Karander Maritime Inc (The Niizuru)* [1996] 2 Lloyd's Rep 66.
153. [2001] EWCA Civ 588; [2001] 2 Lloyd's Rep 65 (CA). London Arbitration 5/01 LMLN 557.
154. [1970] 2 Lloyd's Rep 43.

be in repudiatory breach of charterparty, unless it has a right at common law to elect to terminate the charterparty for a breach by the owner. As we have already seen the owner was in breach of the expected ready to load provision in *The Mihalis Angelos* and the charterer was entitled to rely on its right to elect to terminate for that breach. Even if the charterer were in repudiatory breach of charterparty, the owner's damages for that breach would be nominal if the charterer would beyond doubt have exercised its right to cancel when the ship did not arrive by the cancelling date.[155]

A simple cancelling clause may be problematic for the owner as, even if it is clear that the ship will not arrive by the cancelling date, the owner is still obliged to proceed to the loadport with reasonable, due or convenient dispatch, knowing that the charterer may choose to cancel when the ship does not arrive on time. The charterer is not obliged to tell the owner in advance whether it will cancel or not. Therefore the more sophisticated cancellation clauses oblige the charterer to advise whether it wishes to cancel if the owner asks prior to the cancellation date, failing which the cancellation date is extended.[156]

The express right to cancel is a very valuable remedy for the charterer. Not only does the ship have to be at the right place by a specified deadline, but she must also be ready. Thus in *The Madeleine*[157] the charterer was entitled to cancel the charterparty in the Baltime form which required the ship to be "in every way fitted for ordinary cargo service" because she did not have a deratisation certificate. However, in *The North Sea*[158] the ship was "in every way fitted for container service" by the cancelling date but did not have the amount of bunkers on board stipulated in the charterparty until two hours after the cancelling time. The Court of Appeal agreed with Mance J that breach of the bunker clause could easily be remedied by a claim for damages and did not attract the more draconian remedy of cancellation, although it could if the ship lacked bunkers to the extent which meant that she was not in every way fitted for her service.

Like an off hire clause,[159] the cancellation clause is a no fault provision. The charterer does not have to ask why the ship is not there or is there, but not ready. All the charterer has to ask is whether the ship is there and ready and if she is not, the charterer can cancel. However, that is the only remedy the clause gives. If the charterer also wishes to claim damages, then the charterer would have to show that the owner was in breach of charterparty, for example, if the ship had failed to proceed to the loadport with reasonable despatch[160] and cannot rely on the exceptions clause or had broken down enroute due to unseaworthiness.

155. *The Mihalis Angelos. Fercometal Sarl v MSC Mediterranean Shipping Co SA (The Simona)* [1988] 2 All ER 742; [1988] 2 Lloyd's Rep 199 (HL).
156. See, e.g., cl.9 of Gencon 1994.
157. *Cheikh Boutros Selim El-Khoury and Others v Ceylon Shipping Lines, Ltd (The Madeleine)* [1967] 2 Lloyd's Rep 224.
158. *Georgian Maritime Corporation plc v Sealand Industries (Bermuda) Ltd (The North Sea)* [1999] 1 Lloyd's Rep 21.
159. See p. 76 of this chapter.
160. *The Baleares* [1993] 1 Lloyd's Rep 215. London Arbitration 13/02 LMLN 594; London Arbitration 12/96 LMLN 445; *The West Islands*, LMLN 461; *The North Sea* [1999] 1 Lloyd's Rep 21; Inspection London Arbitration 8/97 LMLN 459.

## 11. TIME CHARTERPARTIES

Under a time charterparty, other than a demise or bareboat charter, the ship remains in the possession of the owner and is not actually delivered to the charterer. Nevertheless the terminology commonly used is that the ship is delivered to the time charterer and redelivered by it at the end of the charter period. What is meant by this is that the ship is placed at the disposal of the charterer, in the sense that the time charterer can give voyage instructions to the owner as to where the ship is to go and what cargoes she is to carry, provided that the instructions are within the limits provided in the contract. In return the time charterer pays hire for the whole time that the ship is placed at its disposal and for the bunkers.

### (a) For how long does the time charterer have the use of the ship?

It will be of immense significance to both parties to know how long the charterer has the ship at its disposal. As we have already seen the charterparty will no doubt provide the earliest date on which the charterer will become liable for time charter hire and contain an express cancellation clause entitling the charterer to cancel the charterparty without asking why the ship is late if it is not delivered ready by a specified time.[161]

The charterer must redeliver the ship within the contractual period, failing which it will be in breach of charterparty and liable for damages. There is often some leeway as to when the ship must be redelivered as it is difficult for the charterer to predict exactly how long any particular voyage will take. Any number of factors may disrupt the best laid plans, for example, the weather or a strike. Therefore when fixing the length of the charter period the parties will often allow a degree of flexibility. For example, they may provide for a period of about 6 months; 12 months 15 days more or less in charterer's option; minimum 4 months maximum 6 months; "about 50 to maximum 70 days"[162] or for a trip time charter where the period of the charterparty is the length of time it takes to perform a particular trip.

If the express terms of the charterparty do not provide any flexibility the courts will imply a margin or tolerance, unless the charterparty imposes an absolute obligation to redeliver the ship by a certain date.[163] Where the charterparty already provides for an express margin the courts will not extend the period further by adding an implied margin.[164] Thus in London Arbitration 12/02 LMLN 594 the charterparty in the NYPE form provided for a period of 11 to 14 months. The vessel was redelivered five days before the 11 months had expired. The arbitrators held that there was no implied margin allowing the charterer to redeliver before the eleven months had expired.

The parties may provide that the period is "without guarantee". In *The Lendoudis Evangelos II*[165] Longmore J held that where a time charter trip provided

161. See p. 67 of this chapter.
162. *Torvald Klaveness A/S v Arni Maritime Corporation (The Gregos)* [1995] 1 Lloyd's Rep 1, where the arbitrator held that "maximum 70 days" did not allow for a margin.
163. *Alma Shipping Corp. of Monrovia v Mantovani (The Dione)* [1975] 1 Lloyd's Rep 115 (CA).
164. *Ibid. Mareva Navigation Co v Canaria Armadora SA (The Mareva AS)* [1977] 1 Lloyd's Rep 368 and *Arta Shipping Co. Ltd v Thai Europe Tapioca Shipping Service Ltd (The Johnny)* [1977] 2 Lloyd's Rep 1 (CA).
165. *Continental Pacific Shipping Ltd v Deemand Shipping Co Ltd (The Lendoudis Evangelos II)* [1997] 1 Lloyd's Rep 404. London Arbitration 5/97 LMLN 458.

"duration about[166] 70/80 days without guarantee"–the charterer was only under an obligation to make the estimate of the duration of the trip in good faith and not on a reasonable basis. The trip took over 103 days. The arbitrator found that, as the owner had alleged, the charterer made the estimate negligently, but it was never alleged that the charterer did not have a genuine belief in the estimate and therefore it was not liable.

Sometimes the charterparty gives an express right to the charterer to add any periods of off hire to the charter period. In *The Kriti Akti*[167] the Court of Appeal had to consider how to calculate the final terminal date where the charter was "for a period of 11 (eleven) months, 15 days more or less in Charterers' option ..." and the charterer had an option to extend the charter period by any period of off hire. It held that a final voyage was legitimate which would finish within eleven months plus any off hire period plus 15 days.

When the charterer will wish to redeliver the ship is often dictated by what the market is doing. Obviously if the market has risen sharply the charterer would be wise to keep the ship until the latest possible date permitted under the charterparty ("the final terminal date"), as the charterparty rate of hire is lower than the rate the charterer would have to pay for another ship. On the other hand, if the market has fallen, the charterer will wish to redeliver the ship as early as it is contractually entitled to ("the earliest terminal date"), so that it can charter in another ship at the lower market rate.

#### *(i) Early redelivery*

If the ship is redelivered prior to the earliest terminal date, the charterer is in breach and is liable for damages. If there is an available market, the measure of damages is the difference between the charterparty rate of hire and the market rate of hire from the date of redelivery until the earliest date on which the charterer was entitled to redeliver. If there is no available market, the measure of damages is the normal and direct loss to the owners caused by the breach.

Damages for early redelivery were considered by the House of Lords in *The Golden Victory*.[168] The owner chartered its ship for seven years with one month more or less in charterer's option. In repudiatory breach the charterer redelivered the ship almost four years too early. The charterparty gave the charterer a right to cancel the charterparty if war broke out between any two or more of a number of countries including the United States, the United Kingdom and Iraq. The second Gulf War began some 14 months after the charterer's repudiation and some 32 months before the charterparty would have expired. There was at the time of the repudiation an available market for the charter of ships such as the *Golden Victory*. The arbitrator found that at the time of the acceptance of the repudiation a reasonably well informed person would have considered war between the United States, the United Kingdom and Iraq "merely a possibility" but not "inevitable or even probable"; and that the charterer would have exercised

166. The arbitrator gave a tolerance of 10% for the word "about", *viz.* eight days.
167. *Petroleo Brasileiro SA v Kriti Akti Shipping Co SA (The Kriti Akti)* [2004] EWCA Civ 116, [2004] 1 Lloyd's Rep 712.
168. *Golden Strait Corporation v Nippon Yusen Kubishka Kaisha (The Golden Victory)* [2007] UKHL 12; [2007] 2 Lloyd's Rep 164.

the right to cancel had the ship remained on charter to it at the outbreak of the second Gulf War. A majority of the House of Lords[169] held that the owner could only recover damages until the outbreak of the war. The principle applicable to time charters was that the innocent party should be placed, so far as damages could achieve it, in the position it would have been in had the contract been performed. If the contract would have terminated early on the occurrence of a particular event, the chance of that event happening had to be taken into account. If it was certain that the event would happen, the damages had to be assessed on that footing. They did not therefore apply the general rule that damages for breach of contract were to be assessed as at the date of breach, as that rule could be subject to another date where that more accurately reflected the overriding compensatory rule.

In *Miranos International Trading Inc v Voc Steel Services BV*[170] Cooke J held that where a time charter trip provided that "The charterers guarantee a minimum 35 days' duration", and the charterer redelivered earlier than 35 days, the arbitrator's decision that the owner was entitled to hire for 35 days without giving credit for any benefit it received from the use of the ship between the actual and charter redelivery dates was wrong. The guarantee of minimum duration cannot amount to a guarantee of remuneration. The breach of the guarantee is the same as a breach of warranty that the charter voyage would be of a certain length and the relief to be granted in respect of such a breach is damages. Where the owner was able to earn the freight under its next fixture one and a half days earlier than it would have done had the ship been delivered on time, the arbitrator must find as to the owner's loss by reference to market rate or to normal and direct loss, if there is no such rate.

### *(ii) Late redelivery*

If the charterer gives instructions to the shipowner for a final voyage which may reasonably be expected to result in redelivery by the final terminal date, this is a legitimate final voyage order and the owner must comply with it. In *The Gregos*[171] the House of Lords held that the legitimacy of the order must be judged not at the time the order is given but at the time for performance. In that case the charterer ordered the ship to proceed from Matanzas to Palua and load a cargo of iron ore for carriage to Italy. At the time the order was given before the completion of her penultimate voyage, compliance with the order could reasonably have been anticipated to allow redelivery by the final terminal date. However, by the time the *Gregos* completed discharge at Matanzas another ship had grounded in the River Orinoco and was obstructing the navigable channel between Palua and the river mouth. Redelivery would have been two to four days late. The charterer was not entitled to insist on the voyage. This decision can make life difficult for the time charterer. It will wish to fix a cargo in good time before the ship completes her current voyage and not wait until the time for performance of the last

169. Lord Scott, Lord Carswell and Lord Brown; Lord Bingham and Lord Walker dissenting.
170. [2005] EWHC 1812 (Comm).
171. *The Gregos* [1995] 1 Lloyd's Rep 1. See also B. Davenport and M. White, "Last Voyage Orders – Again (The Gregos)" [1994] LMCLQ 154.

voyage with the risk of the ship being unemployed. However, the time charterer takes all the risk of events delaying the anticipated final voyage between the time the last voyage order is given and the time for performance of that order.

If the charterer gives instructions for a voyage which cannot reasonably be expected to be completed by the final terminal date, the owner is entitled to refuse such instructions. The owner cannot at this point elect to terminate the charterparty but must ask for valid voyage instructions. Only if the charterer fails to give valid voyage instructions will it be in repudiatory breach of charterparty and the owner could then elect to terminate or affirm the charterparty. Lord Mustill (with whom three other Law Lords agreed) held in *The Gregos* that the issuing of an invalid order, for example, for an illegitimate last voyage is not an automatic ground of discharge. Lord Mustill saw it as depending "not on the invalid order which was given, but on the valid order which was not". The original order given by the charterer had become ineffectual as at the time for performance it was no longer possible to perform the voyage and redeliver by the final terminal date. The charterer was therefore obliged to replace the original order with one which it was entitled to give. The persistence by the charterer in the order after it had become invalid showed that it did not intend to perform the obligations under the contract. This was an anticipatory breach of contract and the owner was entitled to elect to terminate the contract.

In *The Gregos* it was not necessary to express a firm conclusion as to the nature of the charterer's obligation to redeliver on time. However, Lord Mustill (with whom three other Law Lords agreed)[172] inclined to the view that it was an innominate term and that a short delay in redelivery would not justify the termination of the contract. In practice if there is a cargo on board at the final terminal date the owner would probably not wish to elect to terminate the charterparty as the owner will still have obligations to deliver the cargo under the bill of lading or in tort or in bailment.[173]

Whether or not the order was legitimate, if the owner performs it and the ship is redelivered after the final terminal date, the charterer is in breach of charterparty, even though the delay was not due to any fault on its part. The owner is entitled to damages for the period between the final terminal date and redelivery ("the period of overlap") at the charterparty rate or the market rate, whichever is the higher[174] and losses it has suffered under its next fixture. In *The Achilleas*[175] the owner had fixed its next charterparty for about four to six months at a rate of US$39,500 per day. When it realised that the *Achilleas* was going to be redelivered late, it obtained an extension of the cancelling date under its next fixture but at a reduced charter rate of US$31,500 per day, as the market had in the meantime fallen. The owner claimed damages of US$1,364,584.37 representing $8,000 per day for the period of its next fixture less the additional sums earned by reason of the late redelivery. The Court of Appeal held that the owner was entitled to that sum and not simply to the difference between the market rate and the charter rate during the period of overlap.

172. Contrast the view of Lord Templeman, at p. 3, who held that the time for redelivery is of the essence.
173. See p. 95 of Chapter 3.
174. *Hyundai Merchant Marine Co. Ltd v Gesuri Chartering Co Ltd (The Peonia)* [1991] 1 Lloyd's Rep 100 (legitimate final voyage).
175. *Transfield Shipping Inc v Mercator Shipping Inc (The Achilleas)* [2007] EWCA Civ 901; [2007] 2 Lloyd's Rep 555. Leave has been granted to appeal to the House of Lords.

The parties may include an express clause entitling the charterer to complete any last voyage even if it runs beyond the final terminal date without being liable for damages and only paying hire at the charterparty rate until the actual date of redelivery, unless the delay in completion was due to the charterer's breach of some other term.[176] Thus in *The Peonia* a provision that "Charterers have further option to complete last voyage ..." was held to give the charterers the right to complete a legitimate last voyage without any liability for damages for the period of overlap. The clause would not have entitled the charterer to order the ship to perform an illegitimate last voyage. By contrast in *The World Symphony*[177] the Court of Appeal held that the crucial addition of the wording at the beginning of clause 18 of the Shelltime 3 form that it was "notwithstanding" the charter period meant that it overrode the charter period and the charterer could give an order for a voyage which would not enable the ship to be redelivered by the final terminal date and pay at the charter rate until she was redelivered. Such a clause would be of great advantage to a charterer in a rising market. Such clauses will be even more important now in the light of the decision in *The Achilleas*.[178]

### (b) The charterer's obligation to pay hire

The time charterer agrees to pay hire for every minute that the ship is at the charterer's disposal from her delivery until redelivery. The hire is usually stipulated at a daily rate and payable in advance.[179] It is of great importance to the owner in financing the operation of its ship to receive the hire on time and for the right amount. The shipowner will need to meet outgoings such as any principal and interest due under any loan which it took out to finance the purchase of the ship;[180] insurance premiums and P&I Club calls;[181] maintenance and crew wages. There may be grave consequences for the owner if it cannot meet those outgoings on time. For example, if the owner fails to pay the principal and interest due to its bank on any loan it has taken out to buy the ship, the bank might have the right to sell. In order to encourage the charterer to comply with the obligation to pay hire promptly, the standard form time charterparties give the owner an express right to withdraw the ship, i.e. to terminate the charterparty if the hire is not paid. This section will consider the owner's right of withdrawal; the special typed clauses which are frequently inserted to give the charterer some measure of protection known as anti-technicality clauses; off hire clauses and the charterer's limited right to make deductions from hire.

A time charterparty will typically provide that the charterer must pay the hire "in cash"[182] by the due date. "Cash" includes inter-bank transfers with the correct

176. *Hyundai Merchant Marine Co v Gesuri Chartering Co (The Peonia)* [1991] 1 Lloyd's Rep 100 (CA) and *Marimpex Mineraloel-Handelsgesellschaft GmbH & Co KB v Compagnie de Gestion et d'exploitation Ltd (The Ambor and the Once)* [2001] 1 All ER (Comm) 182.
177. *The World Symphony and the World Renown* [1992] 2 Lloyd's Rep 115 (CA), applied in *Petroleo Brasileiro SA v Kriti Akti Shipping Co SA (The Kriti Akti)* [2004] EWCA Civ 116; [2004] 1 Lloyd's Rep 712.
178. See fn. 175.
179. Clauses 4 and 5 of NYPE 1946 and cl. 6 of Baltime 1939.
180. The bank will usually have taken an assignment of the hire as security for the loan.
181. The bank will require the owner to have insurance under the loan agreement and will usually take an assignment of the insurance proceeds as security for the loan.
182. Clause 5 of NYPE 1946 form and cl. 6 of Baltime 1939.

value date and bankers drafts.[183] Time charter hire will usually be paid by an inter-bank transfer and the money must be in the account of the owner designated in the charterparty value the due date. If the due date falls on a weekend or a bank holiday the charterer must make sure that the hire is paid on the last banking day before the due date.[184]

### (c) Withdrawal

If the hire is not paid by the due date, or too little hire is paid by that date, most standard form charterparties provide that the owner has the right to withdraw the ship. This means that the charterparty is terminated, i.e. that both parties are released from future performance of their obligations under the charterparty. The reason for including such a clause is that at common law the time for payment of hire is not a condition of (or not of the essence of) the contract, unless expressly stated to be so. Thus late payment of hire would not entitle the owner to terminate the charterparty, unless the late payment constituted a repudiatory breach by the charterer because, for example, the charterer had evinced an intention not to perform and had said that it would not pay or could not pay. Late payment by the charterer does not deprive the owner of its right to withdraw,[185] but the owner must then return the hire payment.

There is no right to withdraw temporarily unless the contract so provides.[186] If the contract does not so provide, this may place the owner in difficulties. If the hire falls due but is not paid and the ship is about to load a cargo, the owner would prefer not to load until it has been paid, as once the cargo has been loaded the owner will probably be obliged to issue a bill of lading which will impose on it obligations to carry the cargo to the discharge port, whether or not the time charter hire has been paid. Even though the hire has not been paid the owner cannot refuse to load the cargo. It is all or nothing: the owner is entitled to withdraw or it must perform. There is no halfway house. Therefore, more modern charterparties may expressly allow the owner to withhold performance while awaiting payment of hire.[187]

The right to withdraw must be exercised promptly. Otherwise the owner will waive its right to withdraw for that payment of hire.[188] However, should there be a later failure to pay the hire on time or for the correct amount, a new right to withdraw will arise.

The right to withdraw may in certain circumstances be a draconian remedy. In *The Scaptrade*[189] the charterer argued that there should be equitable relief from forfeiture, as is the case in a lease. The House of Lords distinguished a lease as the charterer, unlike the lessee of land, does not have possession of the ship and held that there is no equitable relief from forfeiture. The position is different under a

183. *The Chikuma* [1981] 1 Lloyd's Rep 371.
184. *The Laconia* [1977] 1 Lloyd's Rep 315.
185. *Ibid.*
186. *The Mihalios Xilas* [1978] 2 Lloyd's Rep 186. London Arbitration 10/97 LMLN 460.
187. See, e.g., lines 153–158 of cl. 11 of NYPE 1993.
188. *More OG Romsdal Fylkesbatar AS v The demise charterers of the Ship Jotunheim* [2005] 1 Lloyd's Rep 181.
189. [1983] 2 Lloyd's Rep 253.

demise charter where the charterer does have possession of the ship. In *More OG Romsdal Fylkesbatar AS v The demise charterers of the Ship Jotunheim*[190] Cooke J held that the court was in principle entitled to grant relief from forfeiture in the case of a demise charter, but that that was not an appropriate case for doing so.

As the withdrawal clause may operate very harshly against the charterer, especially where the failure to pay hire is not due to any fault on its part, but is due, for example, to a bank error in transmission of the hire as in *The Afovos*,[191] it is usual to include an anti-technicality clause to protect the charterer.[192] Such a clause requires the owner to give notice to the charterer when default has occurred so that the charterer has an opportunity to rectify any error. Unless the charterer expressly provides when such a notice may be given the charterer has the whole of the due date to pay the hire and therefore the owner can only give the anti-technicality notice the following day. If the owner gives the notice as soon as banking hours close on the due date, it will not have given a valid notice and were it then to withdraw the ship, the owner would be in repudiatory breach of the charterparty.[193]

An anti-technicality notice must be in the form of a clear and unambiguous ultimatum that unless the hire overdue is paid within the specified period the owner will withdraw the ship. In *The Li Hai*[194] the anti-technicality notice did not contain such an ultimatum and it was confusing as to what hire was outstanding. Therefore, the owner was not entitled to withdraw the ship and was liable to the charterer for the difference between the market rate and the charter rate for the balance of the charter period.

The right to withdraw is an extremely important one for the owner. If the market is rising steeply the owner will be waiting to pounce the moment the charterer makes any small non-payment of hire so that it can withdraw the ship and go out into the market to obtain a new charter at a much higher rate of hire. The sum in dispute in *The Li Hai* was only US$500, but as the market for such a ship had risen about two and a half times the charter rate in 10 months it was extremely tempting for the owner to get out of the charter if it could. This was "commerce, red in tooth and claw".[195] However, the owner will not always wish to exercise its right to withdraw. It may take into account factors such as whether the market is rising or falling; the creditworthiness of the charterer; its obligations to third parties under, for example, a bill of lading;[196] whether it has a right to lien the cargo or sub-freights in respect of any sums which have not been paid[197] or whether it can obtain security for sums unpaid, for example by arrest or freezing injunction.[198]

190. [2005] 1 Lloyd's Rep 181.
191. *The Afovos* [1983] 1 Lloyd's Rep 335.
192. See, e.g., cl. 11(b) of NYPE 1993 and cl. 9(a) of Shelltime 4.
193. *The Afovos* [1983] 1 Lloyd's Rep 335, but see also *Schelde Delta Shipping BV v Astarte Shipping Ltd (The Pamela)* [1995] 2 Lloyd's Rep 249 and London Arbitration 3/01 LMLN 555.
194. *Western Bulk Carriers K/S v Li Hai Maritime Inc (The Li Hai)* [2005] EWHC 735; [2005] 2 Lloyd's Rep 389 and *Schelde Delta Shipping BV v Astarte Shipping Ltd (The Pamela)* [1995] 2 Lloyd's Rep 249.
195. *Ibid., per* Jonathan Hirst QC sitting as Deputy Judge of the High Court, at para. 1.
196. *Vantage Navigation Corp v Suhail and Saud Bahvan Building Materials (The Alev)* [1989] 1 Lloyd's Rep 138.
197. See pp. 88–91 of this chapter.
198. See Chapter 11.

### (d) Off hire

Standard forms of time charter provide that hire will cease to be payable on the occurrence of certain events which prevent the full working of the ship such as a breakdown of her engines, or the ship running aground, or detention by average accidents (an accident which causes damage),[199] either for the time lost[200] to the charterer as a result of such event or during the period that the event continues.[201] The off hire clause will not depend on the fault of the shipowner. If the shipowner is actually at fault it may also be in breach of charterparty and the charterer may have remedies such as the right to terminate the charterparty or claim damages in addition to, or in substitution for, the ship being off hire. If the off hire event is caused by a breach of charterparty by the charterer, the ship may still be off hire but the owner will be able to recover damages for the breach including any off hire.

The charterer is obliged to pay hire continuously unless it can show that the wording of the off hire clause applies to the event which has occurred. Where the clause is a net loss of time clause the burden of proof is on the charterer to show not only that the off hire event occurred but also that time has been lost as a result. Once the ship is again in full working order, the ship is no longer off hire even if time is lost thereafter.[202]

Some charterparties provide for a list of specified events which will trigger the off hire clause and culminate in the wording "or any other cause preventing the full working of the vessel".[203] The words "preventing the full working of the vessel" apply to all the causes and it should first be determined whether the cause does prevent the full working of the vessel. This will be the case, for example, if the ship is arrested[204] or free pratique (medical clearance) is delayed due to suspected typhus on the ship at her previous port,[205] but not where the ship is trapped by a boom across the Yangtze river[206] or her draft is too great for the Panama canal.[207] "Any other cause" will be construed *ejusdem generis*, that is, it will be limited to the same type as those events which have been specifically identified in the list which has gone before or at least as Rix J, as he then was, said in *The Laconian Confidence*[208] "in some limited way reflecting the general context of the charter and clause". In that case the type of causes were "internal" to the ship as opposed to "external" or "extraneous" and did not therefore include delay caused

199. *The Laconian Confidence* [1997] 1 Lloyd's Rep 139; *Nippon Yusen Kaisha Ltd v Scindia Steam Navigation Co Ltd (The Jalagouri)* [2000] 1 Lloyd's Rep 515.
200. Clause 11 of the Baltime form, cl. 15 of NYPE 1946 and cl. 17 of NYPE 1993. See *The Marika M* [1981] 2 Lloyd's Rep 622; *The Pythia* [1982] 2 Lloyd's Rep 160; *The Ira* [1995] 1 Lloyd's Rep 103; London Arbitration 6/99 LMLN 504; *The Houda* [1994] 2 Lloyd's Rep 541; London Arbitration 11/96 LMLN 442; *Action Navigation Inc v Bottigliere di Navigatione SpA (The Kitsa)* [2005] EWHC 177; [2005] 1 Lloyd's Rep 432; LMLN 660; *Bottiglieri di Navigazione Spa v Cosco Qingado Ocean Shipping Co (The Bunga Saga Lima)* [2005] EWHC 244; [2005] 2 Lloyd's Rep 1, LMLN 661.
201. See, e.g., cl. 21 of Shelltime 4 form and *The Bridgestone Maru No 3* [1985] 2 Lloyd's Rep 62.
202. *Vogemann v Zanzibar* (1902) 7 Com Cas 254 (CA); (1901) 6 Com Cas 253 and *The Marika M* [1981] 2 Lloyd's Rep 622.
203. See, e.g., cl. 15 of NYPE 1946.
204. *The Mastro Georgis* [1983] 2 Lloyd's Rep 66.
205. *The Apollo* [1987] 1 Lloyd's Rep 200.
206. *Court Line v Dant & Russell* (1939) 44 Com Cas 345.
207. *The Aquacharm* [1982] 1 Lloyd's Rep 7.
208. See fn. 199.

by an unforeseeable interference by the port authorities regarding disposal of residual sweepings. Where the word "whatsoever" is added after the words "any other cause" there is no limit on the causes, although it must still satisfy any express requirement that it prevents the full working of the vessel.

The charterparty may expressly provide for the situation where the ship has to deviate and state that she will be off hire until she is again in an efficient state to resume her service and in a position not less favourable to the charterer than that at which such loss of time commenced.[209] The ship will come on hire again when she is again in an efficient state and in a position not less favourable even though there is some external cause which will still delay her such as a sunken barge restricting shipping movements in the Mississippi.[210]

Tailormade off hire clauses may be included in the charterparty. Thus in *The Doric Pride*[211] a charterparty in the NYPE form contained a special off hire clause as follows:

> "Should the vessel be captured or seized or detained or arrested by any authority or by any legal process during the currency of this Charter Party, the payment of hire shall be suspended until the time of her release, and any extra expenses incurred by and/or during the above capture or seizure or detention or arrest shall be for Owners account, unless such capture or seizure or detention or arrest is occasioned by any personal act or omission or default of the charterers or their agents or by reason of cargo carried or calling port of trading under this charter."

The ship was detained on her way to call at New Orleans, her loading port, on the orders of the captain of the port, pursuant to the Marine Transportation Safety Act 2002, US legislation designed for security purposes. Under that legislation the ship had been designated as a "High Interest Vessel". She was a first time caller to the United States and there was a US Coast Guard policy to inspect first time callers to any US port. Unfortunately, while the ship was at anchor awaiting the coastguard boarding team, there was a serious collision between two other ships which led to the closure of the south-west pass. The available resources of the US Coastguard were engaged in search and rescue operations with the result that the inspection of the ship was delayed. The owner argued that this was a simple case of detention by reason of "calling port of trading under this charter" and fell within the proviso to the clause. The Court of Appeal held that the real problem lay in the ship's status and not in the charterer's trading and the ship was therefore off hire within the main part of the clause.

The charterparty may expressly provide that the charterer has an option to add any period of off hire on to the end of the charter period.[212]

### (e) Deductions from hire

It will be of vital importance to the cash flow of the charterer to be able to deduct claims from the hire rather than to have to pay the hire in full and subsequently seek to recover its claims from the owner. The charterer must be careful not to

209. E.g. cl. 21(c) of Shelltime 4.
210. *Poseidon Schiffahrt GmbH v Nomadic Navigation Co Ltd (The Trade Nomad)* [1998] 1 Lloyd's Rep 57 at p. 65; [1999] 1 Lloyd's Rep 723 (CA).
211. *Hyundai Merchant Marine Co Ltd v Furness Withy (Australia) Pty (The Doric Pride)* [2006] EWCA Civ 599; [2006] 2 Lloyd's Rep 175.
212. See, e.g., *The Hong Kong Fir* and *Petroleo Brasileiro SA v Kriti Akti Shipping Co SA (The Kriti Akti)* [2004] EWCA Civ 116; [2004] 1 Lloyd's Rep 712. See pp. 59 and 70 of this chapter.

make wrongful deductions as this would entitle the owner to withdraw the ship. The charterer can make deductions from the hire in two situations: where there is an express right to do so or where there is an equitable right of set off. If there is no such right, the charterer must pursue its claim against the owner and, if it is not paid, bring court or arbitration proceedings. This may take considerable time and meanwhile the charterer should seek security for its claim.

It is usual for the charterer to have an express right to deduct a number of different claims from the hire including advances for the ship's disbursements made by the charterer on behalf of the owner;[213] off hire periods (but not anticipated off hire periods);[214] fuel used while the ship is off hire;[215] the cost of diesel oil consumed for domestic consumption;[216] speed and performance claims;[217] and the cost of bunkers on board on redelivery from the last hire payment.

If there is no express provision in the charterparty permitting the charterer to make a deduction from hire for a particular sum, English law recognises limited circumstances in which the time charterer is entitled to deduct from hire by way of equitable set off. This contrasts sharply with the position of the voyage charterer who has no such right to deduct from freight.[218] Where the owner of the ship is in breach of time charter and the effect of such breach is wrongly to deprive the charterer of the use of the ship or to prejudice the charterer in the use of it, the time charterer is entitled to deduct the claim for such breach from hire.[219] Thus the time charterer may deduct a claim for speed and performance from the hire,[220] failure to load a full cargo in breach of charterer's instructions,[221] but not a cargo claim,[222] or claim for misappropriation of the charterer's bunkers,[223] or fee incurred by the charterers because a delivery of bunkers was cancelled.[224]

Whether the deduction is made pursuant to an express clause or by way of equitable set-off it must be a reasonable assessment made in good faith.[225] The amount does not have to be agreed by the owner.[226]

## 12. VOYAGE CHARTERPARTIES

Under a voyage charterparty the owner pays for the maintenance of the ship, insurance, crew wages and the bunkers. The charterer pays freight to have its

213. Line 66 of NYPE 1946.
214. *The Lutetian* [1982] 2 Lloyd's Rep 140; *Western Bulk Carriers K/S v Li Hai Maritime Inc (The Li Hai)* [2005] EWHC 735 (Comm); [2005] 2 Lloyd's Rep 389.
215. Clause 20 of NYPE 1946.
216. *Ibid. The Sounion* [1987] 1 Lloyd's Rep 230.
217. *The Al Bida* [1987] 1 Lloyd's Rep 124.
218. *Aries v Total Transport* [1977] 1 All ER 398 and *Bank of Boston Connecticut (formerly Colonial Bank) v European Grain & Shipping Ltd (The Dominique)* [1989] 1 Lloyd's Rep 431 (HL).
219. *Federal Commerce and Navigation Ltd v Molena Alpha Inc (The Nanfri, Benfri and Lorfri)* [1978] 2 Lloyd's Rep 132.
220. *Ibid.* See also London Arbitration 5/08 LMLN 739.
221. *Compania Sud Americana De Vapores v Shipmair BV (The Teno)* [1977] 2 Lloyd's Rep 289.
222. *Federal Commerce & Navigation Co Ltd v Molena Alpha Inc (The Nanfri)* [1978] QB 927 (CA), *per* Lord Denning at p. 976.
223. *Leon Corporation v Atlantic Lines and Navigation Co Inc (The Leon)* [1985] 2 Lloyd's Rep 470.
224. *Western Bulk Carriers K/S v Li Hai Maritime Inc (The Li Hai)* [2005] EWHC 735 (Comm); [2005] 2 Lloyd's Rep 389.
225. *The Nanfri* [1978] 2 Lloyd's Rep 132.
226. *Ibid. SL Sethia Liners Ltd v Naviagro Maritime Corp (The Kostas Melas)* [1981] 1 Lloyd's Rep 18.

goods carried from the loadport to the discharge port. The freight due under a voyage charterparty usually covers the preliminary voyage to the loadport. Sometimes, however, the charterparty will provide for the charterer to pay a ballast bonus for the preliminary voyage. The freight will also cover the voyage from the load port to the discharge port and a limited period to load and to discharge at the loading and discharge ports respectively. That limited period of allowed time is called laytime or laydays. If the charterer exceeds the laytime it is in breach of the charterparty and will be liable to pay damages to compensate the shipowner for that breach. It is usual for the shipowner and the charterer to agree in advance the amount of damages due for such breach. Such liquidated damages are called demurrage. The amount of demurrage agreed will depend on the market rate payable for the ship at the time of fixing the charterparty. The shipowner will not be entitled to terminate the charterparty as a result of the charterer's failure to load or discharge within the laytime, unless the breach is repudiatory (for example, the charterer says that it will not load); or the delay amounts to a frustrating delay; or it is clear that a frustrating delay will occur or there is an express contractual right to terminate.[227]

Some of the most complex problems under voyage charterparties arise as a result of the complicated clauses which the parties may include in an attempt to allocate the risk of delay during the loading and discharging operations between themselves. When it is known at the time the fixture is concluded where the load and discharge ports are it is possible to draft the clauses specifically to deal with any known or anticipated delays which may occur at those ports. Where the ports are not known, for example, because the charterer has the right to nominate a port from a wide range of ports, the shipowner must try to cover itself for all the eventualities that could occur in such ports.

As the freight includes the laytime the charterer pays for the stipulated amount of time allowed for the loading and discharging operations. If that time is not used, it is common for general cargo charters to provide that the owner will pay the charterer despatch. Despatch is often half the rate of demurrage.[228]

### (a) Freight

The charterparty will provide what the freight is: it may be a lump sum; or in a tanker charter ascertained by reference to Worldscale; or be calculated by reference to the amount of cargo. In the latter case it is important to know whether the freight rate is to be calculated by reference to the intake quantity,[229] bill of lading quantity or delivered quantity. If the charterer fails to load the amount of cargo agreed it may be liable for deadfreight to compensate the shipowner for the freight that it would have earned had the charterer loaded the agreed amount of cargo.[230]

At common law the freight is due on delivery of the cargo. By that time the owner has performed the whole of its obligations under the contract. Therefore it

227. See, e.g., cl. 7 of Gencon 1994.
228. See, e.g., *Glencore Grain Ltd v Flacker Shipping Ltd (The Happy Day)* [2002] 2 Lloyd's Rep 487.
229. See cl. 2 of Asbatankvoy.
230. *China Offshore Oil (Singapore) International Pte Ltd v Giant Shipping Ltd (The Posidon)* [2001] 1 Lloyd's Rep 697; *Pentonville Shipping Ltd v Transfield Shipping Inc (The Johnny K)* [2006] EWHC 134 (Comm); [2006] 1 Lloyd's Rep 666 and *AIC Limited v Marine Pilot Limited (The Archimidis)* [2008] EWCA Civ 175.

is usual for the charterparty to provide expressly that at least part of the freight is to be paid in advance, so as to have a better balance between the parties. A distinction must be drawn between the date on which the freight becomes due and that on which it becomes payable. Once the freight is due the owner will not lose its right to be paid the freight even if the ship is lost with all her cargo on board.

Unlike the time charterer who can make deductions from hire by way of equitable set off, there is no such right of deduction from freight.[231] There will only be a right to make deductions if the charterparty expressly permits deductions, for example, for the value of cargo remaining on board where the ship carries a crude oil cargo.[232] In *The Dominique* the charterer had to pay the freight which had become due without deduction even though subsequently the ship was arrested by creditors at Colombo and it was unlikely that she would leave Colombo under the same ownership, as the shipowner would not be able to put up security to release the ship from arrest.

### (b) When does laytime start?

Subject to the express terms of the charterparty laytime will begin to run when three requirements have been satisfied: first the ship is an "arrived ship" at the load port; secondly notice of readiness has been given in accordance with the charterparty terms; and thirdly the ship is in fact ready. The shipowner will be anxious to get the laytime clock ticking as early as possible for as soon as the laytime expires the shipowner will start earning demurrage. The charterer, however, will seek to ensure that the laytime starts counting as late as possible so that the ship never comes on demurrage. The classic illustration of this is the case of *The Happy Day*, which will be considered below, where not only did the charterer argue that laytime never started, but it also claimed despatch for the laytime never used.

#### *(i) Arrived ship*

To determine when the ship is arrived it will be necessary to see where the charterparty stipulates the ship has to proceed to. It may provide for the ship to proceed, for example, to one safe port or one safe berth or sea mooring buoy. If the charterparty provides that the ship is to proceed to a port, the area of that port may be very large and on arrival the ship may be required to anchor while she waits for her berth to become available. The anchorage may be some distance from her berth. However, she will be an arrived ship when she is within the limits of the port and is at the immediate and effective disposal of the charterer so that when a berth becomes available, the ship can proceed straight to it. There is a presumption that the ship is at the disposal of the charterer when she is at the usual waiting place in the port, although that presumption is rebuttable. Thus even if the ship is about 17 miles away from her berth she is an arrived ship if she is at

231. *The Aries* [1977] 1 Lloyd's Rep 334; *The Dominique* – see fn. 218.
232. See London Arbitration 3/08 LMLN 734.

the usual waiting place,[233] provided that she is within the limits of the port.[234] This is tough on the owner if the usual waiting place is outside the port limits or the ship cannot get into the port due, for example, to congestion. Thus the owner may insist on an express clause entitling it to give notice of readiness "whether in port or not".

Tanker charterparties may provide that notice of readiness can be given "upon arrival at customary anchorage at each port of loading or discharge ... berth or no berth".[235] London arbitrators have accepted that this provision entitles notice of readiness to be tendered at a customary anchorage which is outside the port.[236] Although it has been argued that the ship has not arrived until she has anchored at the designated anchorage as her sea voyage has not yet come to an end,[237] an alternative view is that there is nothing in the express wording of Asbatankvoy which requires the ship to have anchored.[238] All she has to have done is arrive at the customary anchorage. Indeed, she may never anchor. It may not be necessary to anchor as the terminal is expecting her and she can proceed straight into berth. It has also been asked whether in such circumstances the ship should proceed via the customary anchorage in order to tender notice of readiness. It is likely that in such circumstances the ship will arrive in the berth and laytime will start counting before the expiry of six hours from giving notice at the customary anchorage.[239]

Where the charterparty provides that the ship is to proceed to a berth, the ship is not arrived until she is in berth. This is dangerous from the owner's point of view as the owner usually has no control over the allocation of the berth but takes the risk that there is a delay in getting into berth for whatever reason.[240] The charterer may have some contractual link with the shipper or receiver of the goods and the sale and purchase contract for the goods will usually contain laytime and demurrage clauses so that the seller or buyer can recover demurrage if the shipper or receiver is slow in providing a berth. Therefore even if the charterparty provides that the ship must proceed to a berth, a number of clauses may be used to reallocate the risk of delay in getting into berth back to the charterer.

The first is the berth "reachable on arrival" provision found in clause 9 of the Asbatankvoy charterparty. This was considered by the House of Lords in *The Laura Prima*[241] and it was held that the charterer was in breach of the obligation to designate and procure a berth reachable on arrival where the berth was congested. It has subsequently been held that matters such as lack of tugs and bad weather[242] or lack of pilots and prohibition of night navigation,[243] which were traditionally considered to be the owner's risks, would also mean that the berth was not reachable on arrival so that the charterer was in breach of this obligation.

233. *The Johanna Oldendorff* [1973] 2 Lloyd's Rep 285.
234. *The Maratha Envoy* [1977] 2 Lloyd's Rep 301.
235. E.g. cl. 6 of Asbatankvoy.
236. See (2007) 725 LMLN 2, and see *Cooke*, para. 57.4.
237. See J. Schofield, *Laytime and Demurrage* (5th ed, LLP, 2005), paras. 3.289–3.297.
238. See (2007) 725 LMLN 2.
239. London Arbitration (2006) 698 LMLN 1.
240. *The Isabelle* [1984] 1 Lloyd's Rep 366 (CA); [1982] 2 Lloyd's Rep 81 (Mr Justice Robert Goff).
241. *Nereide SpA di Navigazione v Bulk Oil International (The Laura Prima)* [1982] 1 Lloyd's Rep 1.
242. *Palm Shipping Inc v Kuwait Petroleum Corp (The Sea Queen)* [1988] 1 Lloyd's Rep 500.
243. *K/S Arnt J Moerland v Kuwait Petroleum Corporation (The Fjordaas)* [1988] 1 Lloyd's Rep 336.

An alternative is to provide that time is to count "whether in berth or not". This provision was considered by the House of Lords in *The Kyzikos*.[244] It does not provide the owner with as great protection as the berth "reachable on arrival" provision as time will only count if a berth is not available. If a berth is available, but cannot be reached, for example due to fog, time will not count. Another possibility is to have the provision "time lost waiting for a berth to count as loading ... time"[245] or a clause tailormade for delays which are anticipated at a specific port.[246] The parties may agree to split certain delays of getting into berth between themselves.[247]

### *(ii) Notice of readiness*

The charterer requires notice of the arrival of the ship so that it can arrange to load the ship promptly. Indeed the charterparty may provide that the shipowner is also to give notice of the ship's expected time of arrival, e.g. 72, 48 and 24 hours prior to her estimated time of arrival so that the charterer has additional time to ensure that the cargo is ready and a berth is available as soon as the ship arrives. Many standard forms of charterparty provide that laytime will not commence until six hours after notice of readiness has been tendered or received or until the ship has berthed, whichever is the earlier.[248]

An initial question is whether the notice of readiness can be given outside the laycan, i.e. prior to the commencement date or after the cancelling date given in the charterparty. As we have already seen[249] the charterer will not want laytime to start before a specified time, which will usually be the start of the window allocated within the shipper's loading schedule, as it will have no use for the ship. If the ship arrives before that window the owner may invite the charterer to take the ship early and agree that laytime will commence early. The charterer may approach the shipper and if there is some flexibility in the loading schedule, for example, because another ship is late, the shipper may be able to bring forward the loading and the charterer can then agree with the owner to accept notice of readiness early.

The charterparty usually provides that laytime shall not commence before the commencement date, except with the charterer's sanction.[250] If the charterer requests the ship to tender notice of readiness and berth before the earliest lay-day, then the charterer has sanctioned the earlier commencement of laytime.[251] The charterparty may not provide what is to happen if notice of readiness is given before the commencement date. If the charterer does not want the ship to load early notice of readiness and the six hours after notice of readiness may run

244. *Seacrystal Shipping Ltd v Bulk Transport Group Shipping Co (The Kyzikos)* [1989] 1 Lloyd's Rep 1. *Glencore Grain Ltd v Flacker Shipping Ltd (The Happy Day)* [2002] 2 Lloyd's Rep 487. See also London Arbitration (2006) 690 LMLN (2).
245. Clause 6 of Gencon. See *Aldebaran Compania Maritima SA v Aussenhandel AG (The Darrah)* [1977] AC 157.
246. See, e.g., *Ellis Shipping Corp v Voest Alpine Intertrading (The Lefthero)* [1992] 2 Lloyd's Rep 109.
247. E.g. the Conoco Weather Clause.
248. See, e.g., cl. 6 of Asbatankvoy.
249. See pp. 66–68 of this chapter.
250. E.g. cl. 5 of Asbatankvoy.
251. *Tidebrook Maritime Corporation v Vitol SA (The Front Commander)* [2006] 2 Lloyd's Rep 251 (CA) at para. 45, *per* Rix LJ.

before the commencement date,[252] so that laytime would commence at 0001 hours on the first day of the laycan. Other charterparties expressly provide that laytime shall not commence before 0600 hours on the commencement date.[253]

The owner is obliged to proceed "with all convenient despatch" to the loadport even if it is clear that the ship will not arrive by the cancellation date and may be cancelled. The charterer has no right to cancel before the cancelling date even though it may be clear to the charterer for some days beforehand that the ship will not arrive by the cancelling date. If the charterer does not cancel the ship even though the ship is late, the charterer may find that it has to pay for all the time spent waiting for a berth. In *The Nikmary*[254] the Court of Appeal held that the delay resulted from the charterer's failure to have cargo ready for loading.

The charterparty will usually provide for the form in which notice of readiness must be given (for example, in writing, by fax); to whom (for example, to the charterer's load port agents or the loading terminal); and when.[255] Thus it is common in a charterparty for general cargo to find that notice of readiness can only be tendered during working hours and not on a weekend or holiday. By contrast most oil terminals operate 24 hours 7 days a week and notice of readiness can usually be tendered at any time of the day or night. However, in *The Petr Schmidt*[256] the charterparty provided that notice of readiness must be tendered between 0600 and 1700 hours. If a notice of readiness was given outside those hours, the notice could not start time counting at the time it was given but, provided it was a truthful notice at the time it was given it was not a nullity. Therefore, when working hours started again time would start counting as long as the notice remained truthful and the ship was still ready. It was not necessary to tender a further notice.

### *(iii) Readiness*

Thirdly, the notice of readiness must contain accurate statements that the ship has arrived and is ready at the time the notice is given. If the statements are inaccurate the notice is a nullity,[257] unless it is accepted by the charterer[258] or its agents[259] or there is a waiver of the requirement for a notice of readiness. The fact that the ship becomes ready or becomes an arrived ship[260] after the notice is given does not give the notice of readiness any subsequent effect. In *The Mexico I*[261] notice of readiness was given when the charterer's cargo was overstowed with the owner's cargo and the ship was therefore not ready to discharge the charterer's cargo until the owner's cargo had first been discharged. No further notice of

252. *Ibid.*
253. Clause 13(a) of ExxonMobil VOY2000 and cl. 13(1)(a) of Shellvoy 6.
254. *Triton Navigation Ltd v Vitol SA (The Nikmary)* [2003] EWCA Civ 1715; [2004] 1 Lloyd's Rep 55.
255. See, e.g., cl. 6 of Asbatankvoy and cl. 6(c) of Gencon.
256. *Galaxy Energy International Ltd v Novorossiysk Shipping Co (The Petr Schmidt)* [1998] 2 Lloyd's Rep 1 (CA).
257. *Compania de Naviera Nedelka v Tradex International (The Tres Flores)* [1973] 2 Lloyd's Rep 247.
258. *Sofial SA v Ove Skou Rederi (The Helle Skou)* [1976] 2 Lloyd's Rep 205.
259. *Ocean Pride Maritime Ltd Partnership v Qingdao Ocean Shipping Co* [2007] EWHC 2796 (Comm).
260. *TA Shipping Ltd v Comet Shipping Ltd (The Agamemnon)* [1998] 1 Lloyd's Rep 675.
261. *Transgrain Shipping BV v Global Transporte Oceanico SA (The Mexico 1)* [1990] 1 Lloyd's Rep 507 (CA).

readiness was given when discharge of the owner's cargo was completed. The Court of Appeal rejected the owner's arguments that the notice of readiness was inchoate and became effective when the ship became ready or when the charterer knew, or ought to have known, that the ship was ready. In that case the charterer conceded that laytime would commence when discharge actually commenced. Mustill LJ indicated that he thought the concession was correctly made.

However, in *The Happy Day*[262] no such concession was made. The ship arrived off Cochin and was unable to enter the port because she missed the tide. Nevertheless the Master purported to give a notice of readiness. As the charterparty was a berth charterparty and a berth was available, this was an invalid notice of readiness. The ship entered the port and commenced discharging the following day but discharge was not completed until almost three months later. The shipowner claimed demurrage for the extensive delay. The charterer argued that as no valid notice of readiness had ever been given, laytime never commenced. This despite the fact that the charterer had used the ship for some three months. To add insult to injury, the charterer claimed despatch. This would have been such an unappealing result that the Court of Appeal held that where notice of readiness valid in form had been served on the charterer or receiver prior to the arrival of the ship; the ship thereafter arrived and was or was accepted to be ready to discharge to the knowledge of the charterer; and discharge thereafter commenced to the order of the charterer or receiver without either having given any intimation of rejection or reservation in respect of the notice of readiness previously served, or any indication that further notice of readiness was required before laytime commenced, the charterer could be deemed to have waived reliance on the invalidity of the original notice as from the time of commencement of discharge and laytime would commence as if a valid notice of readiness had been served at that time.

Where the shipowner is in doubt as to whether a notice of readiness is valid, it should tender another notice of readiness when it is clear that the ship is arrived and is ready. There could still be significant delays after giving a valid notice of readiness until the commencement of cargo operations and the shipowner needs to protect its position in respect of such time. If a valid notice of readiness is never given, the owner should clearly plead waiver and request the tribunal at first instance or the arbitrator for clear findings of fact upon which waiver can be based.

The ship must actually be ready[263] when the notice of readiness is given, subject to *de minimis*. Thus she must have clean holds,[264] and be ready to receive cargo, clear customs[265] and receive free pratique (medical clearance). The consequence that the notice of readiness will be void if the ship is not ready, even though the Master thought she was ready, can be hard on the owner if the ship is not inspected on arrival at the loadport and is kept waiting for a berth. Only when a berth is finally allocated and the ship is inspected is the owner told that

262. *Glencore Grain Ltd v Flacker Shipping Ltd (The Happy Day)* [2002] 2 Lloyd's Rep 487. See also *The Mass Glory* [2002] 2 Lloyd's Rep 244; *Alphapoint Shipping Ltd v Rotem Amfert Negev Ltd (The Agios Dimitrios)* [2005] 1 Lloyd's Rep 23; and *Ocean Pride Maritime Ltd Partnership v Qingdao Ocean Shipping Co (The Northgate)* [2007] EWHC 2796 (Comm).

263. *The Tres Flores* [1973] 2 Lloyd's Rep 247; *The Virginia M* [1989] 1 Lloyd's Rep 603.

264. *Cobelfret NV v Cyclades Shipping Co Ltd (The Linardos)* [1994] 1 Lloyd's Rep 28.

265. *The Antclizo (No 2)* [1992] 1 Lloyd's Rep 558.

the ship is not ready and no time will count at all until she is actually ready, even though it may not take long to make her ready. Therefore, the charterparty may expressly provide that laytime will count even if it is subsequently found that the ship is not ready, except the time making her ready.[266] In *The Linardos*[267] Colman J held that it was necessary to imply a term into such a provision that the notice of readiness must be given in good faith.

### (c) The calculation of laytime

The period of laytime may be provided for in the charterparty in a number of different ways, for example, a specified period of time or a formula such as a fixed amount of cargo per day. Thus a tanker voyage charter usually provides for 72 hours laytime to cover both the loading and discharging operations or alternatively, for 36 hours laytime at the loadport and 36 hours laytime at the discharge port. The former would be preferable from the charterer's point of view as if only 30 hours were used at the loadport there would still be 42 hours available at the discharge port, whereas the provision for 36 hours at each port is non-reversible.

Unless provided otherwise, laytime will run continuously from the time the notice of readiness expires. Exceptions must be clear and a general exceptions clause will not usually create an exception from laytime, although it is a question of construction.[268] In a general cargo charterparty it is usual to exclude days which are not worked at the port from the computation of laytime, such as Saturdays and Sundays, or Thursday afternoons and Fridays in Muslim countries, and holidays. Only "working days" or "weather working days" may count as laytime. In a tanker charterparty there are not likely to be such exceptions to laytime as an oil terminal is likely to operate 24 hours a day 7 days a week. However, there will be other express exceptions to laytime such as the time it takes to shift the ship from her anchorage to her berth (in a berth charterparty this will be considered as part of the voyage even though the charterparty has allowed the notice of readiness to be given earlier than on the arrival in berth) or deballasting (as this is a ship operation to make the ship ready to load).

Where the charterparty provides that the charterer must designate a berth reachable on arrival the charterer cannot rely on any exceptions from laytime until it has designated such a berth.[269]

The charterer has paid for the laytime in the freight. Therefore, the charterer is entitled to keep the ship for the whole of the laytime even though it could have loaded in less time.[270] The charterer is entitled to order the Master not to berth immediately on arrival at the loadport, so that if the Master acts in breach of those orders the owner will be liable for the charterer's loss.[271] However, once loading or discharging has been completed, laytime comes to an end, even if the cargo operations have been concluded within the laytime allowed and there is

266. See fn. 264 and *United Nations Food and Agriculture Organisation World Food Programme v Caspian Navigation Inc (The Jay Ganesh)* [1994] 2 Lloyd's Rep 358. See also cl. 6 of Gencon 1994.
267. [1994] 1 Lloyd's Rep 28.
268. *Cero Navigation Corporation v Jean Lion & Cie (The Solon)* [2000] 1 Lloyd's Rep 292.
269. *Nereide SpA di Navigazione v Bulk Oil International (The Laura Prima)* [1982] 1 Lloyd's Rep 1.
270. *Margaronis Navigation Agency Ltd v Henry W Peabody & Co of London Ltd* [1965] 2 QB 430.
271. *Novorossisk Shipping Co v Neopetro Ltd (The Ulyanovsk)* [1990] 1 Lloyd's Rep 425.

unexpired laytime. Thus if loading is completed within the laytime allowed but the ship is delayed, for example, due to the charterer's failure to give the Master instructions or because cargo documents are delayed, the charterer will be liable for damages for detention.[272]

Some charterparties contain express provisions as to when laytime ends. For example, most tanker charterparties provide that laytime shall run until hoses are disconnected[273] or until cargo documents have been received on board.[274]

### (d) The calculation of demurrage

Once the laytime has expired the charterer is in breach and would be liable for damages for detention. However, most standard form voyage charterparties provide for damages at an agreed rate called demurrage. The maxim "once on demurrage always on demurrage" means that time counts for demurrage unless the parties have unambiguously provided otherwise.[275] Thus in the Asbatankvoy charterparty the allowance of six hours after giving of notice of readiness does not apply if the ship is already on demurrage when notice of readiness is given.[276] Exceptions to laytime do not constitute exceptions to demurrage unless they are expressly stated to be exceptions to demurrage as well.[277] A general exceptions clause is unlikely to be specific enough.[278] Furthermore, if the wording of the exception is ambiguous it will be construed against the charterer, as the party seeking to rely on it. The burden of proof is on the charterer to show that the terms of the exception apply.

Clear exceptions may include fire; storm; strikes or lockouts; "causes beyond the control of the Merchant" which will cover the breakdown of loading equipment as a result of bad maintenance on the part of the operator, who was an independent contractor of the charterer;[279] or "breakdown of machinery or equipment in or about the plant of the Charterer, supplier, shipper or consignee of the cargo".[280]

Time does not run during the periods where cargo operations have been delayed by the shipowner's fault. This derives from the principle that nobody can benefit from their own wrong. It has been argued that time will run if the shipowner can prove that during that period, no cargo operations would have taken place but *The Stolt Spur*[281] has decided the issue against the owner. Demurrage will, however, continue to accrue where the delay is not due to the fault of either shipowner or charterer, unless an express exception applies.

272. *Owners of the Steamship Nolisement v Bunge and Born* [1916] CC 135.
273. E.g. cl. 11 of Asbatankvoy.
274. Clause 9 of Intertankvoy. *Cf.* cl. 13(c) of ExxonMobil VOY2000. See 1993 LMLN 358.
275. See, e.g., cl. 8 of Asbatankvoy.
276. *Nippon Yusen Kaisha v Marocaine de L'Industrie du Raffinage (The Tsukuba Maru)* [1979] 1 Lloyd's Rep 459. Contrast, e.g., clause 7.3.2 of BPVOY 4.
277. *Dias Compania Naviera SA v Louis Dreyfus* [1978] 1 All ER 724. *Nippon Yusen Kaisha v Marocaine de L'Industrie du Raffinage (The Tsukuba Maru)* [1979] 1 Lloyd's Rep 459.
278. *The Lefthero*, fn. 246.
279. *The Mozart* [1985] I Lloyd's Rep 239 and *A Meredith Jones & Co Ltd v Vangemar Shipping Co Ltd (The Apostolis) (No 2)* [1999] 2 Lloyd's Rep 292 at pp. 300–301.
280. *Portolana Cia Nav v Vitol SA (The Afrapearl)* [2004] 2 Lloyd's Rep 305.
281. *Stolt Tankers Inc v Landmark Chemicals SA (The Stolt Spur)* [2002] 1 Lloyd's Rep 786.

### (e) The distinction between demurrage and damages for detention

It may be important to determine whether a claim is one for demurrage or for damages for detention for a number of reasons. First the rate of damages is at an agreed rate for demurrage but not for damages for detention, unless the charterparty expressly provides otherwise. Therefore the owner would have to prove its loss. Secondly, charterparties sometimes require presentation of all documentation relating to a demurrage claim within quite a short time limit, failing which the claim is time barred.[282] If the time bar applies to demurrage claims, but not claims for damages for detention, the latter claim will be subject to the general contractual time bar of six years from the breach of contract. Section 12 of the Arbitration Act 1996 has narrowed the grounds on which an extension of time can be obtained.[283] Thirdly, most charterparties provide for a lien for certain claims. Unless the charterparty expressly provides for a lien for demurrage and damages for detention there will be no lien for either of the claims not expressly referred to.[284]

Demurrage is the agreed amount of damages due to the shipowner if the charterer is in breach of charterparty because the laytime, i.e. the agreed time for loading or discharging the ship, is exceeded. If the charterer is in breach of the charterparty in other respects and delay is caused the charterer will not be liable for demurrage but for damages for detention. Thus, for example, if the charterer delays the ship at the loadport once loading has been completed either because it has not paid its agents and therefore the ship is prevented from leaving, or the charterer fails to nominate the discharge port, the charterer is not entitled to use the ship as floating storage space and will be liable for damages for detention. The charter may provide that the demurrage rate applies[285] but if it does not, the owner must prove its loss and adduce evidence (for example, from a chartering broker) as to the market rate for the ship. If the market has risen this will be to the owner's advantage as the owner may well be able to recover more than the demurrage rate. However, if the market has fallen, the owner may recover less than the demurrage rate.

### (f) Termination for non-payment

A relatively recent development in voyage charterparties is the provision for an express right to terminate the charterparty for non-payment of demurrage, such as clause 7 of Gencon 1994. This provision is similar to the right to withdraw under a time charterparty for non-payment of hire. However, the right to terminate under clause 7 of Gencon is restricted to the situation where the ship is at or off the loadport. This no doubt reflects the practical reality that once the ship has loaded and left the loadport the owner may well have an obligation to a third

282. *Babanaft International Co SA v Avanti Petroleum Inc (The Oltenia)* [1982] 2 Lloyd's Rep 99 (CA) and [1982] 1 Lloyd's Rep 448 (Bingham J); *Evergos Naftiki Eteria v Cargill plc (The Voltaz)* [1997] 1 Lloyd's Rep 35 for the construction of a time bar for "any claim", and *Waterfront Shipping Co Ltd v Trafigura AG (The Sabrewing)* [2008] 1 Lloyd's Rep 286.

283. *Cathiship SA v Allanasons Ltd (The Catherine Helen)* [1998] 2 Lloyd's Rep 511; London Arbitration 21/98 LMLN 493; and *Bocimar NV v Mira Oil Resources of Tortola (The Obo Venture)* [1999] CLC 819, [1999] 2 Lloyd's Rep 101. See also fn. 67 of this chapter.

284. See p. 88 of this chapter.

285. See, e.g., cl. 4(c) of Asbatankvoy.

party to carry the cargo to the discharge port under a bill of lading and it will not therefore wish to terminate the charterparty.

## 13. LIENS

At common law there is a lien for freight payable on delivery, general average contribution and expenses of preserving goods. Most standard form charterparties, both time and voyage, contain an express contractual right to lien the cargo which is much wider than that at common law. For example, time charters may well provide for a lien on the cargo "for any amounts due under this Charter"[286] and voyage charterparties "for freight, deadfreight, demurrage, claims for damages and for all other amounts due under this Charter Party including costs of recovering same".[287] If, however, the charterparty does not expressly provide for a lien for a claim such as damages for detention, there is no lien for such claim.[288]

### (a) On cargo

Most charterparties provide for a lien on "the cargo".[289] The lien on cargo is a possessory lien. The owner has possession of the cargo and the lien, whether at common law or contractual, gives the owner a right to retain possession until it has been paid the sums which the lien covers. If the owner parts with possession it will lose its lien.[290] Usually the owner will wish to discharge the cargo as soon as possible under a voyage charterparty so that the ship can be delivered under its next fixture, rather than just sitting as floating storage at the discharge port. Laytime and demurrage will continue to run during the time that the cargo is retained while the lien is exercised, provided such exercise is valid. However, if there is already a problem with payment of, for example, demurrage, the owner will not wish further demurrage to accrue while its ship is idle. The owner may therefore decide that the best course of action is to discharge the cargo to its own agents at the discharge port. This is only possible if there are suitable facilities to receive the cargo, such as segregated shore tanks or barges for an oil cargo, or dry, secure warehouse facilities for a general cargo, which is not always the case. The owner can then seek to recover such costs of exercising the lien either if the express terms of the lien clause cover them or as damages from the charterer for failure to pay the sums due.

Where the cargo is owned by the charterer, the owner has the right to lien the cargo under the express terms of the charterparty. Where, however, the cargo is owned by a third party the owner must check that it has the right to lien the

286. Clause 18 of NYPE 1946 and cl. 23 of NYPE 1993.
287. Clause 8 of Gencon 1994.
288. E.g. cl. 21 of Asbatankvoy.
289. E.g. cl. 8 of Gencon 1994.
290. *Cf.* the wording of cl. 21 of Asbatankvoy which states that the "lien shall continue after delivery of the cargo into the possession of the Charterer, or of the holders of any Bills of Lading covering the same or of any storagemen". It is not clear what the effect of this wording is – see *Cooke*, para. 79.3.

cargo *vis-à-vis* the cargo owner, who cannot be bound by the terms of the charterparty as it is not a party to that contract. The bill of lading may contain a lien clause or, if the bill of lading incorporates the charterparty terms,[291] even general words of incorporation will incorporate the lien clause from the charterparty,[292] as that clause relates to the shipment, carriage and discharge of the goods. Then the owner can lien the cargo, even though the bill of lading holder does not have a personal liability for the sums due. Thus in *The Miramar*[293] owners sought to argue that they could lien against the bill of lading holder for demurrage due under a charterparty as the bill of lading incorporated the charterparty terms, including the lien clause. The demurrage clause in the charterparty provided that the demurrage was payable by the charterers. At first instance Mustill J, as he then was, held that there was no obligation to pay demurrage on the bill of lading holders, but that the owners could recover under a letter of guarantee that had been provided by the bill of lading holders to lift the lien as they were entitled to exercise the lien which was incorporated into the bill of lading. Mustill J's decision that owners could exercise the lien was not appealed but the Court of Appeal and the House of Lords upheld the decision that the wording of the charterparty demurrage provision could not be manipulated to impose the obligation to pay demurrage on the bill of lading holders.[294]

Where the bill of lading does not contain a lien or incorporate the charterparty lien clause there are conflicting decisions. Mocatta J held in *The Agios Giorgis*[295] that although the charterparty provided for a contractual lien on "all cargoes", this could not give the owner the right to lien cargo which did not belong to the charterer and the owner was in breach of the charterparty when it instructed the Master to refuse discharge. Donaldson J took a different view in *The Aegnoussiotis*.[296] He held that if the cargo is owned by a third party and not the charterer, the latter is obliged to make sure that there is a contractual lien in favour of the owner. If the charterer does not do this, the owner can still exercise the lien as against the charterer who cannot rely on its own breach of contract. The charterer would remain liable for hire during the period that the lien had been exercised. The bill of lading holder, however, would have a claim against the owner.

The owner is not entitled to protect its lien by refusing to issue bills of lading unless they incorporate the charterparty lien clause and are stamped "freight prepaid". In *The Nanfri*[297] the House of Lords held that the owner would be in repudiatory breach of charterparty if it failed to issue bills of lading in the form chosen by the charterer.

In order to exercise the lien the owner must give a notice stating that it is exercising a lien and stating the sum that must be paid or setting out how that sum

291. E.g. the Congenbill.
292. *Miramar Maritime Corporation v Holborn Oil Trading Ltd (The Miramar)* and *Santiren Shipping Ltd v Unimarine SA (The Chrysovalandou Dyo)* [1981] 1 Lloyd's Rep 159.
293. *Ibid.*
294. [1984] 2 Lloyd's Rep 129. See also *Tradigrain SA v King Diamond Shipping SA (The Spiros C)* [2000] 2 Lloyd's Rep 319.
295. *Steelwood Carriers Inc of Monrovia v Evimeria Compania Naviera SA of Panama (The Agios Giorgis)* [1976] 2 Lloyd's Rep 192.
296. *Aegnoussiotis Shipping Corporation v A/S Kristian Jebsens Rederi (The Aegnoussiotis)* [1977] 1 Lloyd's Rep 268.
297. [1979]1 Lloyd's Rep 201 at p. 211.

can be calculated. A lien can only be exercised for sums which are already due.[298] The owner cannot exercise a lien on the way to the discharge port[299] but can exercise it off the discharge port.[300] The owner must also consult a local lawyer to ascertain whether the local law permits the exercise of the lien; whether, the cargo may be sold if the sums due are not paid and, if so, in accordance with what procedure.[301]

### (b) On sub-freight

Some charterparties also provide for a lien on "all sub-freights".[302] The nature of this right is very different from the lien on cargo which is founded on the owner's right to retain possession. The owner's right over the sub-freight is to intercept freight due to the charterer under a sub-charterparty or under a bill of lading issued by the charterer, but not hire under a sub-time charterparty.[303] The owner must give a notice to the sub-charterer or bill of lading holder demanding payment of the freight due before the payment is made. If the sub-charterer has already paid the freight before it receives the notice from the owner, the lien is lost. In *The Spiros C*[304] the time charterer failed to pay time charter hire and the owner therefore gave notice of the exercise of a lien on subfreights to Tradigrain, the subcharterers of the ship and the shippers under the bills of lading. Owners' bills of lading provided that freight was payable as per charterparty and incorporated "all terms and conditions liberties and exceptions" of the sub-charterparty. Tradigrain had already paid the freight in accordance with the sub-charterparty to the account designated in the subcharterparty. Tradigrain had made deductions from the freight. The deductions for commission and extra insurance were expressly permitted by a clause in the subcharter which was in turn incorporated into the bill of lading. However, deductions had also been made in respect of a cash advance to the Master and ship's disbursements at the loadport which had been paid by Tradigrain on account of the time charterer for which there was no express right to deduct although the time charterers and the sub-charterers had agreed that such sums could be set off. The Court of Appeal reversed Colman J's decision that it was not open to Tradigrain unilaterally to alter the payment terms of the bill of lading to accommodate collateral arrangements it may have made with the disponent owner for deductions from the sub-charter freight.

If the party receiving the owner's notice is not sure whether the freight should be paid to the owner or to the charterer with whom it has a contract, it can interplead and pay the money into court.[305]

298. *The Fort Kipp* [1985] 2 Lloyd's Rep 168.
299. *International Bulk Carriers (Beirut) SARL v Evlogia Shipping Co SA, and Marathon Shipping Co Ltd (The Mihalios Xilas)* [1978] 2 Lloyd's Rep 186.
300. *Santiren Shipping Ltd v Unimarine SA (The Chrysovalandou Dyo)* [1981] 1 Lloyd's Rep 159.
301. Under English law see CPR 25, r25.1(m) and the Torts (Interference with Goods) Act 1977, s. 12.
302. E.g. cl. 18 of NYPE 1946 and cl. 23 of NYPE 1993 and cl. 8 of Gencon 1994, but not cl. 21 of Asbatankvoy.
303. *Itex Itagrani Export SA v Care Shipping Corp (The Cebu) (No 2)* [1990] 2 Lloyd's Rep 316.
304. See fn. 294.
305. Part 35 CPR. For priority of claims see *Samsun Logix Corporation v Oceantrade Corporation, Deval Denizeilik VE Ticaret AS v Oceantrade Corporation, Samsum Logix Corporation* [2007] EWHC 2372 (Comm).

Voyage charterparties often also contain cesser clauses either as part of the lien clause or separately. The purpose of the cesser clause is to provide that the charterer's liability to pay demurrage ceases but only to the extent that the owner has been able to obtain payment of it by exercising the lien on the cargo.[306] The Court of Appeal has held that the right of lien must be enforceable and effective at the time of discharge for the charterer's liability to cease.[307] The local law may not permit a lien to be enforced or it would be "practically ineffective" if no lien could be exercised ashore and any attempt to exercise it on board would have resulted in the ship being sent to the end of the queue of waiting ships.[308] There are conflicting *obiter dicta* as to whether the charterer or the owner has the burden of proving that the lien was ineffective but the better view is that it lies on the charterer as the cesser clause seeks to exempt or limit the charterer's liability.[309]

306. E.g. cl. 8 of Gencon 1994.
307. *Overseas Transportation Co v Mineralimportexport (The Sinoe)* [1972] 1 Lloyd's Rep 201.
308. *The Tropwave* [1981] 2 Lloyd's Rep 159.
309. See *Cooke*, paras 17.12 and 17.13.

CHAPTER 3

# Cargo Claims and Bills of Lading

*PROFESSOR CHARLES DEBATTISTA*

## 1. CARGO CLAIMS – THE GENERAL PICTURE

Cargo claims are brought by cargo-interests against carriers when the cargo in which they have an interest is not delivered, is delivered short or is delivered damaged. Those cargo-interests may be the shippers of the goods; they may be the receivers (or, in the case of non-delivery, the intended receivers) of the goods; they may be charterers or sub-charterers of the vessel on which the cargo was shipped; they may even be banks who have extended a line of credit against the security of the cargo. The carriers sued may be shipowners or charterers. Lurking behind those interests and those carriers, there will typically be insurance entities, cargo-insurers or Protection and Indemnity Clubs. The terms on which the cargo-interest will claim against the carrier may also vary: in some circumstances, the claim will be brought on the terms of a bill of lading – a document which comes in many shapes and forms; in other circumstances, the claim will properly be brought on the terms of a charterparty. Finally, the law governing the claim will differ according to what the relevant contract of carriage says about the choice of law and other circumstances of the particular case.

The complexities are, it will readily be appreciated, many. The objectives of the parties to the claim, however, are simple: the cargo-claimant has suffered a loss which it seeks to cover through an award of damages against the carrier; the carrier, for its part, seeks to deny, exclude or limit liability for that loss. Moreover, whether the vessel on which the goods were carried is or is not under charter, and where it is, whether the claim is brought by a charterer or a non-charterer, the bill of lading will play a central role in the cargo-claim.

In this chapter, we shall follow the progress of a cargo claim governed by English law. Despite the complexities referred to above, there are a number of questions which any adviser working on a cargo claim needs to answer. These are:

(1) Does the claimant have *title to sue* the defendant?
This question conceals two quite different but related issues:
  (a) The claimant's title to sue.
  (b) The identity of the responsible carrier.
(2) Do the *Hague-Visby Rules* apply to the cargo-claim?

Having established that the right claimant has the right defendant in its sights, the next issue is whether the Hague-Visby Rules (the main international regime governing cargo claims) apply to the claim. The reason this needs to be tackled at this early stage is that the answers to the questions which follow will, at any rate in part, depend on whether the claim is subject to the Hague-Visby Rules.

(3) If the right parties are in play, then can the claimant *prove its loss*?

With the stage now set for the cargo-claim – with the right parties in the right court and with the proper law identified – the claimant needs to prove its loss, the basic reason for the claim. This question focuses on the function of the bill of lading as a receipt: in essence, the claimant is saying that the carrier has failed to discharge what the latter had stated it had shipped in the bill of lading. The evidential force of the bill of lading is consequently of great significance at this stage of the claim.

(4) If the claimant has proved its loss, then can it prove that the loss has been caused by a *breach* by the carrier of a duty owed by the carrier to the claimant?

Proof of loss is not enough: to drive home its claim, the claimant needs to prove that that loss has been caused by the carrier's breach of a duty owed to the claimant in law, whether in contract or in bailment or in tort. Behind this question, there lurk two important questions:

(a) Where are the terms of the contract of carriage between the claimant and the carrier: are they in the bill of lading or in a charterparty?
(b) If the terms of the claimant's contract of carriage are in the bill of lading, what are the carrier's duties regarding
   (i) the vessel; and
   (ii) the care of the goods?

(5) If the claimant has been able to prove that its loss was caused by the carrier's breach of contract, can the carrier *exclude or limit* its liability?

These questions explain the main headings to this chapter:

- The claimant's title to sue
- The identity of the carrier
- Do the Hague-Visby rules apply?
- Proving the claimant's loss
- Proving the carrier's breach
- Excluding or limiting the carrier's liability

There is a last heading which will be dealt with, at any rate briefly, in this chapter. While not technically part of a cargo claim, a claimant does need to be aware of how its role as claimant in a cargo claim may expose it to liabilities towards the carrier.

- The claimant's potential liability towards the carrier.

## 2. THE CLAIMANT'S TITLE TO SUE

### (a) Who cares about title to sue?

The heading here may give the impression that it is always the claimant who is more interested in establishing its title to sue: without title to sue, the claimant lacks legitimacy – commonly called *locus standi* – against the carrier and the claim is thrown out. It is necessary to point out immediately, however, that the carrier too is concerned about the claimant's title to sue – and not always or only for the obvious reason that demolishing the claimant's *locus standi* is the quickest escape route from the claim for the carrier.

The claimant may have more than one route through which to claim against the carrier. The most obvious is through a contract of carriage, either made or acquired by the claimant. The claimant may, however, have other arrows in its quiver. In certain circumstances, the claimant may bring an action against the carrier in one of two relevant torts recognised by English law, i.e. conversion or negligence. If the carrier fails to deliver goods to which the claimant can prove that it has certain rights, then the carrier is liable to the claimant in conversion. Again, if the carrier short-delivers or damages goods to which the claimant can prove it has certain rights, then the carrier is liable to the claimant in the tort of negligence. Moreover, if the circumstances are such that the carrier is the cargo-interest's bailee, holding physical possession of goods to which the cargo-interest has a right to possession (commonly called constructive possession) then another possible route – bailment – opens itself up to the cargo interest, outside any contract of carriage that may exist between the parties to the claim.

These different routes, tort and bailment, have two things in common. First, they are not special to the law of carriage of goods by sea. They are simply carriage equivalents of more general grounds of liability which arise, for example, when a theatre-goer entrusts his overcoat and umbrella to the theatre cloakroom attendant: the latter must, as a matter of common law, return the same number of items to the same theatre-goer in the same condition in which they were entrusted to the theatre: and failure to do so exposes the theatre to liability in tort or bailment. Secondly, both routes are alternative to contract in two senses, i.e. (a) that either route may be available even if there *is* no contract of carriage; and (b) that either route may be available *in addition* to the claimant's contractual route of recovery where there *is* a contract of carriage between the claimant and the carrier.

It is in this latter instance that the carrier may, far and away from *denying* the claimant's title to sue in contract, become – somewhat perversely – the party interested in *establishing* it. Where a carrier is threatened by a claim outside the contract of carriage – either because there appears to be *no* contract of carriage or because there *is* one, but the requirements for recovery in tort or bailment *also* are satisfied – then the carrier is actually assisted if it can establish the cargo-interest's *locus standi* in contract. This is not because the carrier can dictate which weapon the cargo-interest uses: in English law, choice of weapon is very much up to the claimant. The point is that, while the claimant can choose whether to go in contract, tort or bailment (and claimants typically go in all three, on a belt-and-braces basis), the carrier too can, for its part, choose its shield: whichever sword the claimant chooses to wield, a carrier proving a contract with the claimant can use that contract – in its defence. And here lies the rub: liability, even if grounded in tort or bailment, is limited not only by the *general* rules of causation, remoteness and time-limitation applicable by law, but *also* by the *special* terms of any contract existing between the parties. And, in the nature of things, the terms of that contract, particularly in the liner trade where there are many cargo-interests shipping their goods onto one vessel, is a contract the terms of which will have been dictated by (and therefore more likely favour) the carrier. Thus, for example, a cargo claimant may wish to bring its claim against the carrier in tort or bailment two years after discharge of the goods: the general law would allow such a claim in tort or bailment. However, if the parties are bound by a contract of carriage governed by the Hague-Visby Rules, then the carrier can have the claim thrown out on the basis that the claim is barred by the lapse of one year from delivery under Article III rule 6 of those Rules. Alternatively, a cargo claimant may wish to recover its entire loss, "at large" and without any limitations of *quantum*, other than the general rules of causation and remoteness: a carrier, however, who can establish a contract between it and the claimant, a contract again covered by the Hague-Visby Rules, can limit its exposure through the so-called "package and unit limitation" provided for in Article IV rule 5 of the same Rules.

For these reasons, both parties to a cargo claim care about the cargo-interest's title to sue: the claimant, because it provides the claimant's legitimacy in the claim; the carrier, either because it destroys that legitimacy and throws out the claim, or because it allows the carrier to use a friendly contract shield against a hostile *non*-contractual sword.

### (b) Where there is no doubt about title to sue

Given the serious interests at stake in establishing or denying the claimant's title to sue in contract, it is not surprising that this first topic is frequently hotly disputed between parties to a claim. It is important, however, to state that there are two instances where there is no mileage at all in disputing the claimant's *locus standi*.

*Charterers.* The first is where the cargo claimant is a charterer or a sub-charterer of a chartered vessel. There is no doubt here that the claimant has title to sue the party from whom it has chartered the vessel, which may be the shipowner or another charterer, under the terms of the charterparty concluded between the claimant and the respondent carrier. The charterer may be the shipper of the goods (in which case it will, if the goods are the subject of a sale contract, be, for example, a c.i.f. seller) or it may be the receiver of the goods (in which case, again if the goods are the subject of a sale contract, the receiver-charterer will likely be an f.o.b. buyer). In either event, the point is that if the claimant is a charterer, its *locus standi* is unassailable: once a charterer, as it were, always a charterer.

*Shippers.* The second case where there is no problem with the claimant's *locus standi*, at any rate until the moment when the bill of lading issued by the carrier is transferred by the shipper to the receiver, is where the claim is brought by the shipper who has concluded the contract of carriage. This is true whether the goods are carried on a chartered vessel (the situation we have just examined) or not. Thus where, for example, S books space with C for the carriage of 10 containers on C's vessel, then it is that contract between S and C which provides S with *locus standi* to bring a cargo claim against C: for S to establish its title to sue, it needs satisfy no further condition, for example the issue or presentation of a bill of lading. If such a bill of lading *is* issued and transferred, then the shipper will, as we shall see later in this chapter, lose its title to sue. It is not quite here once a shipper *always* a shipper: it is true to say, however, that a shipper of goods derives its title to sue the carrier from its role as a shipper, not from the issue or presentation of a bill of lading; it is equally true to say, however, as we shall see, that letting go of any bill of lading issued will extinguish that shipper's *locus standi*.

Charterers, then, are always safe, as far as concerns title to sue; and shippers are too, at any rate until they transfer the bill of lading. In which circumstances, therefore, might there be a question mark over the cargo interest's title to sue the carrier in contract – and over the carrier's ability to defend itself through the terms of the same contract?

### (c) Where problems with title to sue arise

*The privity problem*

The problem of the cargo claimant's title to sue the carrier has been closely associated with English law and other systems in the common law tradition because of the common law's strictures regarding privity of contract. If only those who are parties to a contract can sue on it, then a cargo interest who had not actually itself concluded the contract of carriage cannot sue the carrier on it despite the fact that the loss caused by the carrier's breach of contract was actually incurred by the third party rather than by the cargo interest who concluded the contract with the carrier.

Thus, if S makes a contract of carriage with C for the carriage of goods which S sells to B, and if B pays S the purchase price of the goods against tender of a bill of lading by S to B, whether under a c.i.f. sale or under an f.o.b. sale providing that S is to make the carriage arrangements, and if C damages the goods in transit, then the doctrine of privity of contract causes B serious difficulties. B is technically a third party to S's contract with C; the doctrine of privity thus bars him from suing C; S, however, has no interest in suing C, despite having been the initial cargo interest privy to the contract of carriage, because of the simple reason that B has paid S in full and S will have suffered no loss. B, however, the receiver of damaged goods for which B has paid the full price of sound goods under the sale contract when the bill of lading was tendered, is a third party to the contract – and is therefore left out in the cold. The consequence is that the person with title to sue, S in this example, suffers no loss; but the person who *has* suffered a loss, here B, has no title to sue.

English law sought to resolve this problem in the context of cargo claims very early on, in the shape of the Bills of Lading Act 1855, now repealed. Indeed, in 1999, English law sought to resolve the *general* problem of privity of contract across the area of contract law through the Contracts (Rights of Third Parties) Act 1999, an Act which, however, was explicitly denied impact in the context of the carriage of goods by sea.[1] The particular Act now seeking to resolve the difficulties caused by the doctrine of privity of contract in the *special* context of cargo claims is the Carriage of Goods by Sea Act 1992.

### *The Carriage of Goods by Sea Act 1992*

The effect of section 2 of the 1992 Act is to provide the following three types of cargo interest with rights of suit against the carrier: (a) lawful holders of transferable bills of lading; (b) parties for the time being named as consignees on sea waybills and straight bills; and (c) parties to whom the carrier undertakes to deliver the goods under a ship's delivery order.

Each of the terms used in that brief summary of the effect of the Carriage of Goods by Sea Act 1992 – in particular each of the three shipping documents captured by the Act – is carefully defined in the Act. These definitions are important because, where a particular document falls outside them, it becomes necessary to examine whether there is any other basis for title to sue under the common law.

*Lawful holders of bills of lading.* The first type of cargo interest with title to sue the carrier is the lawful holder of a "bill of lading", a phrase which, for the purposes of this Act, is assumed in section 1(2) to include only transferable bills of lading, that is to say, bills of lading which are either made out to bearer, or simply to order, or to the shipper's or to a named consignee's order. Moreover, for the claimant to have rights of suit under the Act, it must be a "lawful holder" of the bill of lading, a term defined in section 5(2) of the Act as a person with possession of the bill *and*, unless the bill is made out to bearer, either (a) named as consignee on the bill, or (b) to whom the bill is endorsed either in full or in blank.

It is clear that the way the bill of lading is "made out" or endorsed is crucial to the transfer of rights of suit under the Act, at any rate where the bill is not a "bearer" bill.

*Bearer bills.* Where the bill simply names the "bearer" as the consignee, it is the mere holding of the bill – without any need of endorsement by any cargo-interest – which endows the holder with rights of suit against the carrier. That holder may be any one of a number of persons, e.g. a buyer of the goods, a bank extending a line of credit to the buyer, or indeed a person who simply comes across the bill. This flexibility provides at once the greatest strength and the greatest weakness of bearer bills. On the one hand, bearer bills facilitate the transfer of rights of suit down a string of buyers or through a chain of banks through simple physical transfer of the bills with no requirement of endorsement in one form or another. On the other hand, bearer bills carry with them the risk that they may end up in the wrong pair of hands, those of a holder who simply comes across the bill and presents it under the Act: although the Act does, at section 2(1), somewhat piously, require the holder to be a "lawful" holder, it is difficult to see how a carrier can in practice be expected to assess such a holder's good faith when the bill is presented for delivery of the goods. It is presumably for this reason that bearer bills are far less commonly used in practice than bills of lading made out to the order of a named person, normally the buyer.

1. See s. 6(5)(a) of the Contracts (Rights of Third Parties) Act 1999.

*Shipper's Order Bills.* Before we come to bills made out to the order of the buyer, however, we need to look at bills of lading made out to the order of the shipper itself. The consignee box in such bills may be completed in one of the following ways: "To Order", "To Shipper's Order" or "(To the Shipper's name) or Order". In these cases, the carrier has agreed to carry the goods and to deliver them to any person to whom the shipper orders the carrier to deliver the goods. The question is: how does the carrier ascertain the shipper's order regarding any particular cargo? Bills made out "to order" are issued in order to dispense with repeated undertakings by the carrier to deliver: their issue constitutes what is called an *a priori* attornment, i.e. acknowledgment by the carrier, and it can hardly be concluded that where a bill of lading is made out simply "to Order", the intention of S and C is that C needs to "attorn to" (i.e. acknowledge) every transfer of the bill. The more likely conclusion to draw from the completion of a bill of lading to Shipper's Order in any of the three ways described here is that the shipper's instructions to deliver the goods to a particular person can safely be inferred by the carrier from the fact that that person holds the bill and physically presents it for delivery of the goods at the agreed discharge port. Looked at from this perspective, there seems to be little difference between bills of lading made out to the order of the shipper and bearer bills. With both types of bill, the holder of the bill of lading has rights of suit under the 1992 Act, with no endorsements required for those rights of suit to travel down a string to the eventual receiver. The strengths – and the weaknesses – of bearer bills are consequently shared with bills of lading made out to the order of the shipper.

*Bills of lading made out to a named consignee who is not the shipper.* This brings us to somewhat safer – but rather less flexible – transferable bills made out to the order of a named person, normally (but not always) the buyer of the goods. The paradigm example would be where S ships goods on C's ship and has the bill of lading made out to the order of B, the buyer of the goods. Here, if B physically presents the bill of lading at the discharge port, he is the lawful holder of the bill of lading and has rights of suit against the carrier under section 2(1) of the 1992 Act. If, however, B sells the goods on to B1 while the goods are still in transit to the discharge port agreed between S and C, then *B1* is the lawful holder of the bill of lading for the purposes of the Act and consequently has rights of suit against the carrier if two conditions are satisfied: (a) if B endorses the bill to B1, typically on the reverse side of the bill, either in full (by signing it and explicitly naming B1) or in blank (by simply signing the bill), and (b) physically transfers the bill of lading to B1 so that B1 can present the bill of lading at the discharge port.

Although the person named as consignee will typically be the buyer of the goods, this is by no means always the case. Where banks extend a line of credit to the applicant under a letter of credit, typically the buyer of the goods, it may well be a condition of the letter of credit that bills of lading be made out to the order of the bank: the bank would here be securing itself against the buyer's default with the letter of credit by ensuring that it, the bank, has direct rights over the goods as against the carrier. This situation has a direct impact on how the bill of lading needs to be endorsed and on who becomes the holder of the bill of lading for the purposes of the 1992 Act – and when.

Before we leave transferable bills of lading, we should say that once S, the shipper, transfers the bill of lading to B, its buyer, S loses its rights of suit against

C, the carrier. Where there are several sellers and buyers down a string, each seller transferring a bearer bill or endorsing a bill of lading made out to a named consignee's order down a string also loses its own rights of suit against the carrier. In most situations, this tallies precisely with all the parties' commercial expectations: once a seller transfers a bill of lading to a buyer, it no longer expects to be interested in the performance of the contract of carriage by the carrier – and consequently loses interest in, and the rights under, the contract of carriage. It should be remembered, however, that, as we saw earlier, a charterer never loses its title to sue its contractual carrier. Consequently, if S, the original shipper, or any of the sellers down a string, happens to be a charterer, then they retain title to sue under the charterparty even after transferring the bill of lading to their buyer.

*Sea waybills and straight bills of lading.* Bearer bills, bills made out to the order of the shipper and bills of lading made out to the order of a named consignee all share one feature: by issuing the bill of lading in any of these three forms, the carrier has agreed to deliver the goods to a person who is not necessarily identified on the bill at the time the bill is issued. Even in the third case, where the bill is made out to the name of an identified consignee, typically the buyer, the carrier has agreed to deliver the goods to the named buyer *or* to an endorsee from that buyer – and such endorsees are not identified in the bill at that time.

There may be circumstances, however, where the identity of the *only* party to whom the shipper wants the goods delivered is known when the bill of lading is issued. Thus, for example, where one company in a group ships mechanical equipment to another company overseas in the same group, then it is not typically envisaged that the equipment will be sold in transit. In this case, C, the carrier, happily agrees with S, the shipper, that it will deliver the equipment to B – and only to B. That agreement can be recorded on a shipping document called – and calling itself – a sea waybill. B here has rights of suit against C, in terms of the 1992 Act, solely through it being named as consignee. The way in which the named consignee here acquires rights of suit against the carrier is different from the way in which a lawful holder of a bearer or order bill acquires such rights in two important ways. First, there is no need for any endorsement of the sea waybill by S to B: S and C have agreed that the equipment be delivered to B – and that, as it were, is the end of the line and there is no need for C to have any further evidence (through endorsement) of S's desire that the equipment be delivered to B. For much the same reason, B does not need to be a lawful *holder* of the sea waybill for B to acquire rights of suit: B's identity was known to S and to C at the time the sea waybill was issued. Consequently, the only credentials C needs to see before handing the goods over to B, and exposing itself to rights of suit under the contract of carriage contained in the sea waybill, is proof that B is who it says it is, i.e. B. While with a bearer or order bill – a bill intended to be and capable of being transferred down a string – the best credentials the carrier can look for in order to ensure that the goods are delivered and rights of suit are transferred to the right person is the physical holding of the bill of lading, the same cannot be said of a sea waybill which clearly on its face envisages delivery of the goods to one person and to one person only, the singularly named consignee.

We have assumed so far in this part of the chapter that the carrier has issued a document calling itself a sea waybill. What has been said in respect of sea waybills is also, however, true of documents calling themselves bills of lading but not made out to bearer or to anyone's order. Such bills of lading are commonly called straight or non-transferable bills of lading. These are used – or at least they are best used – where it is not envisaged that the goods shipped will be sold in transit. Just as with sea waybills, B's exclusive identity is known to C at the time C issues the bill to S and rights of suit in B exist because of its named role as B and because B can prove its identity as B at the discharge port, not because of any endorsement and physical transfer of the bill of lading by S.

It is clear that the main advantage of sea waybills and straight bills is that rights of suit against C can travel from S to B without physical transfer of the bill of lading: the relationship between B and C is not consequently held up by any delay in the physical transfer of the sea waybill or the straight bill of lading by S to B. There are, however, three possible consequences of the use of such documents which need to be weighed up against this advantage. First, because B's rights of suit against C depend exclusively on its being named as consignee on the document, those rights of suit vanish as soon as B stops being named as consignee – and S can, so far as concerns its contract of carriage with C, name another person as consignee at any time until the goods are discharged: B's rights of suit against C are consequently precarious in that S can deprive B of such rights through the simple expedient of giving alternative delivery instructions to C. B may, of course, have rights of action against S under the sale contract in such circumstances, but such rights may provide recourse which is both too little, too late, and possibly in a foreign jurisdiction. Secondly – and this may be of concern to C – whereas C is free of liability towards S where S transfers a bearer or order bill to B, the same is not true where C issues a sea waybill or a straight bill. Section 2(1) of the 1992 Act makes it clear that S's rights of suit against C co-exist with the rights of suit which B has against C arising out of B's role as named consignee. Thirdly, while it is clear that an order bill of lading is, in stipulated circumstances which we shall examine later on in this chapter, governed by the Hague-Visby Rules, the circumstances in which those Rules apply to a sea waybill and a straight bill of lading are somewhat more complex: we shall return to this later in this chapter.

*Ship's Delivery Orders.* Apart from lawful holders of bills of lading and consignees named on sea waybills and straight bills of lading, the third type of cargo interest to whom the Carriage of Goods by Sea Act 1992 transfers rights of suit against the carrier is any person to whom the carrier acknowledges (or "attorns") a right to delivery under a ship's delivery order. Such documents are used where a cargo shipped in bulk needs to be split. So, for example, where S ships 10,000 metric tonnes of rice covered by one bill of lading and then sells 5,000 metric tonnes to each of B and B1, S now needs two shipping documents to tender under its sale contracts to B and B1. Rather than asking C, the carrier, to re-issue two bills of lading each for 5,000 metric tonnes, S asks C to issue two ship's delivery orders, in which C undertakes to each of B and B1, both explicitly named on their respective documents, that C will deliver 5,000 metric tonnes of rice. Here, by virtue of section 2(1)(c) of the 1992 Act, B and B1 each have rights of suit against C.

As with sea waybills and straight bills of lading, B and B1 have rights of suit because they are named, normally as "consignees", on the ship's delivery orders. The delivery orders consequently do not need to be endorsed to B or B1 for either party to acquire rights of suit; neither do they need physically to be held or presented by B or B1, who simply need to satisfy C, the carrier, that they are the party identified on the ship's delivery order as consignee. Again as with sea way-bills and straight bills of lading, S, the shipper does not lose its own initial rights of suit against the carrier if he transfers the ship's delivery order to either or both of B and B1.

### (d) Where problems with title to sue are not solved by the 1992 Act

*The* Brandt v Liverpool *contract*

The 1992 Act was passed in order to resolve title to sue issues in as many different situations as were considered to be common at the time of the passing of the Act. This did not mean, however, that other situations might not arise, falling outside the Act, where either a cargo interest or a carrier might seek to establish or deny title to sue. Thus, for example, a cargo interest may be named as consignee not on a *ship's* delivery order, but on what is sometimes called a trader's or mere delivery order, a warrant issued not by C (the carrier) but by S (the shipper) undertaking to B (the buyer) that C (the carrier) will deliver, say, 5,000 metric tonnes of rice. Here, there is no direct undertaking by C towards B; the document is not, therefore, covered by section 1(4) of the 1992 Act and section 2(1) of the same Act does not give B rights of suit. Again, if "B's bank or order" rather than B itself is named as consignee on a bill of lading, and B's bank hands the bill of lading to B but fails to endorse it, B, though in possession of the bill, is not its lawful holder within the terms of section 5(2) of the Act, being neither a consignee nor an endorsee of the bill. In these and other circumstances, B is left out in the cold by the Act, bereft of title to sue C, the carrier, at any rate in contract. Moreover, if B could seek recovery on a cause of action outside contract, then C could not plead the terms of a contract of carriage in its defence. Thus if B could prove that he owned the particular goods damaged at the time the damage was caused, B's cause of action in the tort of negligence would not be subject to any of the contractual defences which would have been available to the carrier had B had contractual title to sue.

The problem in either of the above two cases is technical and legal: privity rears its head again and a factual situation lying ever so slightly outside the precise terms of the 1992 Act leaves cargo and vessel unconnected by contract. However, carriers and cargo interests at discharge ports frequently raise their sights above such technicalities and proceed as if there was no problem. Despite the fact that a particular document falls outside the precise strictures of the 1992 Act, the carrier may deliver the goods to a cargo interest which will, for its part, tender the document in its possession to the carrier and pay the carrier any outstanding shipping charges. The courts have for many years recognised in this factual exchange of goods for documents and charges an implied contract of carriage, a contract of carriage sometimes called a *Brandt v Liverpool* contract, after the case which most famously recognised such a contract.[2] The 1992 Act was designed to make recourse to such implications by the common law unnecessary: the Act did not, however, exclude such an implication where a situation arises which falls

2. *Brandt v Liverpool Brazil & River Plate Steam Navigation Co Ltd* [1923] All ER Rep 656 (CA).

outside the Act and consequently where the Act fails to work, legal advisers will seek facts which support the implication of a contract at common law.

### *The party with title to sue claiming for the benefit of another*

The *Brandt v Liverpool* solution to a privity problem had its limitations: the cases where the device worked all involved the surrender of some form of shipping document and the payment of some form of shipping charge by the receiver to the carrier, and the handing over of some goods by the carrier to the receiver. Where one of these factors was absent, the exchange of consideration between the parties to a contract was missing and no amount of judicial ingenuity could solve the privity problem. Section 2(4) of the 1992 Act hands the cargo interest a life-line: where a bill of lading, a sea waybill or straight bill of lading or a ship's delivery order has been issued but B, a buyer, does not acquire rights against C (a carrier) through section 2(1) of the Act, but such rights of suit reside in another person, say S (the shipper), then S can bring an action against C for the benefit of B. The idea here is to allow the party *with* title to sue a right to bring an action against C with any damages recovered from C to be held by S for the benefit of B. It is important to note two limitations to the effect of this subsection. First, for the section to apply, one of the three documents to which the Act applies – a bill of lading, a sea waybill or a ship's delivery order – must still be issued: the section does not apply where no such document is issued. Secondly, B's position against C here clearly depends on S's co-operation: if that co-operation is not forthcoming, as it may not be, say, where the damage to the goods has provoked not only a dispute between the receiver and the carrier under the alleged contract of carriage but also one between the buyer and the seller under the sale contract, then B is not assisted by the subsection, which simply states that S is entitled to sue for the benefit of B, not that S is obliged so to do.

### *The f.o.b. seller and title to sue*

So far we have focused on the buyer's title to sue the carrier, a question which arises every time a seller who has made the contract of carriage with the carrier then seeks to transfer its rights against the carrier to a buyer, typically where the sale contract is concluded on c.i.f. terms or on f.o.b. terms where the parties to the sale contract agree that the seller is to make the initial contract arrangements. As we shall see when we look at the role of shipping documents in international trade contracts in Chapter 4, however, there are other types of f.o.b. contracts of sale. The parties to the sale contract may agree that the seller, S, will make the carriage arrangements with C (the carrier), not as principal but as agent for B (the buyer). In this situation, either cargo interest's title to sue the carrier is clear, B having *locus standi* under the carriage contract as principal and S as agent.

More difficult is the situation where the seller and the buyer agree that the buyer will make the carriage arrangements. Here, there is clearly no problem with establishing the buyer's *locus standi*: the buyer has made the carriage contract and is and will remain (at any rate until it transfers those rights on to an on-buyer through transfer of the bill of lading) an initial cargo party to the contract of carriage. The difficulty lies with the seller. Circumstances may arise where the seller, S, suffers a loss through the carrier's breach of the contract of carriage which C (the carrier) makes with B (the buyer). Thus, for example, where C simply fails to ship goods in space booked by B, S suffers a loss in that, as we shall see in Chapter 4, it will have failed to ship goods free on board the vessel by a date stipulated in the sale contract. Were S to be found liable to B in damages, could S recover such a loss from C under a contract of carriage? The doctrine of privity again threatens S's *locus standi*: if the contract of carriage was concluded by B, then S has no right to sue C on that contract, to which it, S, was not a party. In *Pyrene v Scindia*[3] however, Devlin J came remarkably close to recognising a contract for the benefit of a third party: S had title to sue either because, in a situation broadly analogous to that here described, B was a third party clearly envisaged by C and B when making their contract of carriage as being a party intended to be benefited by that contract; or because it was possible to imply, at any rate where goods were damaged during shipment, a contract of the type recognised in *Brandt v Liverpool.*

## 3. THE IDENTITY OF THE CARRIER

It may appear strange, outside a shipping law context, that the identity of the carrier should be a problem at all: surely if a claimant's claim is in contract, then the appropriate defendant is simply the claimant's contractual counterparty. The difficulty here, however, is that it is sometimes difficult to identify precisely who that contractual counterparty is. Part of the problem lies in the way ships are used, the way they are chartered and sub-chartered down several layers of charterparties. Another part of the problem – and a part of the solution – lies in the way bills of lading are signed and by whom.

The problem typically arises in the following manner. S ships its goods on a ship chartered by O, the shipowner, to C; the same ship is sub-chartered by C to C1, which itself sub-sub-charters it to C2; S then transfers the bill of lading to B. If the goods are damaged in transit, B needs to know against which defendant to bring its claim: O, the shipowner or one of the three charterers, C, C1 or C2. Life may become more complex where, for example, S is itself a charterer of the vessel and where S itself may therefore join the identity parade facing B as a potential defendant. The problem of the identity of the carrier may also arise in a totally different set of circumstances where there is no charterparty at all: imagine S ships its goods onto O's vessel from which the goods are then transhipped onto O1's vessel: again here, B faces two possible defendants, O and O1: which is B to sue? Which *can* it sue?

### (a) Is this a problem?

In a sense, of course, it may seem strange to present this as a problem: surely having more than one possible defendant is a bonus, not a problem. Moreover, the decision is and should be a commercial, tactical one, rather than a purely legal

3. *Pyrene Co Ltd v Scindia Steam Navigation Co Ltd* [1954] 1 Lloyd's Rep 321.

one. The claimant would be well-advised to claim against the defendant with the deepest pocket, with assets in the friendliest, most accessible and most litigation-efficient jurisdiction. While all of these factors no doubt play a part in every claimant's choice of defendant, it is still important to get the choice right in terms of law. Getting it wrong – pursuing a defendant who then successfully points elsewhere – not only involves unnecessary cost, but also runs the risk of allowing a time-bar to lapse *vis-à-vis* the proper defendant. The claimant's objective is to establish that the defendant against whom it *wishes* to claim (for all the tactical reasons indicated earlier on) is the defendant against whom it *can*, as a matter of law, bring a claim.

Who then *is* the proper defendant? Who is the contractual carrier? The answer depends in large part on the bill of lading covering the goods. There is one situation, however, where the bill of lading will not indicate the identity of the carrier and we need to deal with that situation first.

### (b) Where the claimant is a charterer

Where the claimant in a cargo claim is a charterer, then its carrier is the party from whom it chartered the vessel. Thus, where S, the shipper, ships goods on a vessel sub-chartered to C by O, the shipowner, S's defendant is C not O. C and S have contracted for the carriage of goods on the chartered vessel; the charter-party is the only contract to which they are both party; and C is consequently S's defendant in a cargo claim. The bill of lading will, as we shall see when we come to proving the claimant's loss, play a part in that claim, but it will not establish who S's defendant is: it will simply help establish S's loss.

### (c) Where the claimant is not a charterer

Where the claimant is not a charterer, then the identity of its carrier will depend on the logo or banner heading of the bill of lading covering the goods and on the manner in which the bill of lading is signed. The latter factor has been particularly significant in providing relatively quick answers to most "identity of the carrier" questions since 1994, when the UCP 500, the Uniform Customs and Practice for Documentary Credits, came into force. Those Rules have now, as we shall see in Chapter 4, been superseded by the UCP 600, but for present purposes, there is no relevant difference between the two versions of the Rules. For a bill of lading to be accepted by a bank under a letter of credit, Article 20 of the UCP 600 requires it to "indicate the name of the carrier" and to be signed in one of a number of ways detailing the name of the signatory and the capacity in which it signs the bill.

It is not surprising that a set of banking rules requires such detail: the bill of lading frequently acts as security for the bank against non-payment by the buyer as applicant under a letter of credit and, in such circumstances, the bank has an interest in identifying clearly who physically has the goods represented by the bill of lading. A presumably unintended, but nonetheless welcome, consequence of these banking rules is that it is now relatively easy to identify the carrier for the purpose of identifying the carrier in a cargo claim. The link between the UCP 500 and the significance in particular of the signature at the foot of a bill of lading was explicitly recognised by the House of Lords in *The Starsin*,[4] where the evidence of identity provided by the signature on a bill of lading was held to prevail over an express "identity of the carrier" clause appearing on the reverse of a bill of lading: in effect, what was good enough for a document checker in a bank should be good enough for a cargo claimant when it comes to identifying the contractual carrier responsible for the safe carriage of goods.

The main identifier, then, in discovering whom the claimant can pursue in a cargo claim is the signature at the foot of the bill of lading, assisted by the banner logo at the top of the bill of lading. Consequently, in our example above, where B faced four possible defendants, O (the owner), C (the head-charterer), C1 and C2 (two sub-charterers), B's legal advisers would need to look at the bill of lading, focusing first on the signature at the toe and then at the logo (if there is one) at the top. Given the rigours required by the banking rules, it is now extremely likely that this fairly mechanical scrutiny will answer the carriage question as to the identity of the carrier.

To this, three caveats need to be added. First, if the head-charter between O and C is a demise or bareboat charterparty (as to which see Chapter 2), then O falls out of B's range: one of the effects of such a charterparty is that C acts as disponent owner of the vessel and O is out of everyone's sight other than C's. Secondly, it must be recalled that this entire question is a matter of contract and that it is therefore subject to any clear contra-indication: thus, for example, it is conceivable that a clear and obvious clause on the front of the bill may upset the presumptions raised at the top and toe of the bill of lading. Thirdly, and by the same token, in the rare situation where the logo and the signature fail clearly to identify the carrier, the courts have developed a number of presumptions on which to fall back, the most important of which is that a master is deemed to have signed on behalf of the shipowner rather than a charterer.

### (d) Claiming against the "actual" carrier

So far, we have looked at the problem of the identity of the carrier in the context of chartered vessels. The problem may, however, also arise where S, a shipper, contracts with O, a shipowner, for the carriage of goods which are then transhipped onto O1's vessel: who can B sue, O, the contractual carrier, or O1, the so-called "actual" carrier?

It is clear that B can sue O, with whom B has a contract. What, however, if O is not worth suing: can B claim against O1, with whom it has no contract? The answer to this question is quite obvious and unremarkable: B can claim against O1 if B can establish a tort committed by O1 or a breach by O1 of O1's duties as B's bailee. Broadly speaking, if B can prove that O1 failed in its duty of care towards B at a time when B owned or was entitled to the possession of the goods, then B has title to sue O1 in tort or bailment.

The real problem is not with B's sword, but with O1's shield. If B could sue O1 in tort or bailment, would O1 be able to use in its defence the terms of the bill of lading issued by O to B or of any bill of lading issued by O1 to O? If the answer to

4. *Homburg Houtimport BV v Agrosin Private Ltd (The Starsin)* [2003] 1 Lloyd's Rep 571.

this question was "No", the result would be that, even where they *could* sue O, claimants would choose to sue O1 at large and in a claim uncluttered by the contractual defences which would affect an action against O. This consequence is avoided by the decision in *The K H Enterprise*[5] which held that where O's contract with S allowed O to tranship the goods on any terms, O1 could, if sued by S or B, plead in its defence the terms of a bill of lading issued by O1 to O, i.e. the terms of the bill of lading under which the goods were transhipped by the actual carrier.

## 4. DO THE HAGUE-VISBY RULES APPLY?

As we proceed through the cargo claim, we shall see that a number of matters depend on whether or not the Hague-Visby Rules[6] apply: we have already alluded to some such matters, like the one-year time-bar and the package/unit limitations under the Rules. These Rules, brought into force in the UK by the Carriage of Goods by Sea Act 1971, represent a patchwork quilt of compromises between the interests of cargo claimants and those of carriers. Thus, for example, while time-bars and the cap on recoverable damages obviously favour the carrier, the bar on bill of lading clauses which seek to exclude or limit the carrier's liability other than as provided in the Rules (contained in Article III rule 8) is obviously important to cargo interests. It follows that it is difficult to predict before a dispute arises and the claim starts playing itself out which of the two parties to a cargo claim will be arguing for the application of the Rules: this will really depend on which party needs which article in the Rules to drive home the claim or to extinguish or limit it.

We saw in Chapter 1 that the general rules whereby English courts decide which law applies to a particular dispute are now to be found in the Contracts (Applicable Law) Act of 1990 which brought into effect the Rome Convention on the law applicable to contractual obligations. We saw there that an express choice of law determines the law applicable to a contractual dispute and one might have thought that, given that most bills of lading contain choice of law clauses, the matter would be relatively uncontroversial: the Hague-Visby Rules would apply only where the parties had expressly incorporated them or, failing that, where the contract of carriage had a close connection with the UK, a Hague-Visby State.

Ever since the decision of the House of Lords decision in the *The Morviken*,[7] however, a decision made before the 1990 Act but which has, perhaps rather surprisingly, stood since then, the English position regarding the law applicable in particular to cargo claims has been rather special. In summary, rather than following the usual conflicts path of first finding out which national law applies (through the conflicts rules contained in the Contracts (Applicable Law) Act 1990) and then, if English law applies, finding out which *part* of English law applies to the particular dispute (e.g. the Carriage of Goods by Sea Act 1971), the courts will

5. *Owners of cargo lately laden on board the KH Enterprise v Owners of the Pioneer Container (The KH Enterprise)* [1994] 1 Lloyd's Rep 593.
6. For a brief history of the Hague-Visby Rules, see Chapter 2, pp. ???
7. *Owners of cargo on board the Morviken v Owners of the Hollandia (The Morviken)* [1983] 1 Lloyd's Rep 1.

use the 1971 Act itself to decide whether the English Carriage regime applies to the cargo claim. In other words, the conflict rules used for cargo claims are contained in the Carriage of Goods by Sea Act 1971 rather than in the Contracts (Applicable Law) Act 1990. The effect is that if any one of a number of triggers in the 1971 Act is triggered, then the Hague-Visby Rules will apply, even without an express choice of law clause saying so, and indeed (as was the case in *The Morviken* itself), in the teeth of an express choice of law clause choosing some other regime.

The 1971 Act contains four such triggers. The Rules will apply to any bill of lading if (a) the bill of lading is issued in a Hague-Visby contracting State;[8] or if (b) the carriage starts from such a State; or if (c) the bill of lading incorporates the legislation of a State giving effect to the Rules; or if (d) the bill of lading expressly incorporates the Rules through what is commonly called a clause paramount. Triggers (a), (b) and (c) only apply to bills of lading covering the carriage of goods between ports in different States and do not apply to the carriage of live animals or to goods carried on deck and stated on the bill so to be carried. Trigger (d), however, applies, by virtue of sections 1(6)(a) and 1(7) of the 1971 Act whether or not the carriage is international and even to live animals and goods carried on deck and stated so to be carried. The effect of using these triggers as conflict rules for cargo claims is that cargo claims in England will almost certainly attract the application of the Hague-Visby Rules as enacted in the Carriage of Goods by Sea Act 1971 even where there is precious little connection between the contract and this country and even if (as was the case in *The Morviken*) the parties choose another law in the bill of lading.[9]

It will be noted that for the Rules to apply, the starting point is that a bill of lading is required. However, three caveats need to be added to this default position. First, it was held in *Pyrene v Scindia*[10] that, where an f.o.b. seller claimed against a carrier in respect of goods damaged by the carrier during shipment, the carrier could plead the terms of the Rules despite the fact that no bill of lading had actually been issued. Secondly, by virtue of section 1(6)(b) of the 1971 Act, the Rules can, in large part, be made to apply to a non-negotiable receipt through a clause incorporating the Rules into such a document: this would cover a sea waybill containing a so-called "clause paramount". Thirdly, it is now clear since *The Rafaela S*[11] that the Rules apply to straight bills of lading, i.e. bills of lading made out to a named consignee but not to its order.

In the rest of this Chapter, we will follow the progress of a cargo claim on the assumption that it is governed by the Hague-Visby Rules.

8. It is not enough for the bill of lading to be issued in, or for the goods to be shipped from, a State which has enacted into its domestic law, but has not signed, the Hague-Visby Rules. See *Trafigura Beheer BV and Another v Mediterranean Shipping Company SA (The MSC Amsterdam)* [2007] 2 Lloyd's Rep 622 (CA).
9. In effect, the Hague-Visby Rules are treated as mandatory rules for the purposes of Article 7(2) of the Rome Convention: See Sched. 1 of the Contracts (Applicable Law) Act 1990.
10. *Pyrene Co Ltd v Scindia Steam Navigation Co Ltd*, see fn. 3.
11. *J I Macwilliam Co Inc v Mediterranean Shipping Co SA (The Rafaela S)* [2005] 1 Lloyd's Rep 347 (HL).

## 5. PROVING THE CLAIMANT'S LOSS

Having established its own *locus standi* as claimant and having identified the carrier as a proper defendant, the claimant, whether it be S, the shipper, or B, the buyer of the goods, now needs to prove its loss. In effect, this means that it is up to the claimant to establish that the carrier has failed to deliver what the carrier shipped. This involves a comparison between two photographs or snapshots of the goods: the goods as they were shipped and the goods as they were discharged.

### (a) Notice of loss at discharge

To start with the second of the snapshots, the snapshot at discharge, it is of course important for the cargo interest to preserve, as it were, the evidence. Article III rule 6 of the Hague-Visby Rules provides an incentive: notice of loss or damage must, failing joint inspection when the cargo interest receives the goods, be given in writing to the carrier at the discharge port before or when the cargo interest takes the goods into its custody or, where such loss or damage is not apparent, within three days. If the cargo interest fails to give such notice, in effect presenting a snapshot of damaged goods on discharge, the carrier is *prima facie* assumed to have delivered the cargo as described in the bill of lading. Such an assumption would not necessarily destroy the cargo claim, but it does seriously wrong-foot the claimant who would now have to upset the presumption by proving one of two negatives, i.e. either that the goods were *not* delivered in the condition or quantity described in the bill of lading or that the goods were not damaged ashore after discharge. Clearly an Article III rule 6 notice, the receiver's "discharge snapshot", is of considerable evidential importance in getting a cargo claim off the ground.

### (b) Where the shipper claims: a *prima facie* presumption

It is, however, the difference between that photograph, taken at discharge, and the photograph taken on loading in the bill of lading which provides real substance to the cargo claim because it is that difference, that discrepancy, which constitutes the claimant's evidence of loss. It is clear that the carrier must, on the shipper's demand, provide the shipper with a snapshot after receiving the goods into its charge, showing among other things, the quantity of the goods as furnished in writing by the shipper (whether by way of the number of packages or pieces or by weight, as appropriate); the apparent order and condition of the goods; and the leading marks necessary for the identification of the goods as furnished in writing by the shipper.[12] It will be noticed that the shipper plays an important role in the taking of this photograph. Thus, the quantity of the goods and the leading marks originate with the shipper: this is hardly surprising, as the shipper is at least as likely as the carrier to have this information.

Once the bill of lading is issued and signed by the carrier, however, the photograph becomes the carrier's: by signing the bill, by autographing the snapshot, the carrier states that the goods identified by the indicated loading marks have

12. Article III rule 3 of the Hague-Visby Rules.

been loaded (hence "bill of 'loading'") in the quantity and apparent condition stated in the bill. That statement raises a *prima facie* presumption against the carrier that the goods *were* so loaded, a presumption which the carrier can, if the cargo claim is brought by the shipper, rebut through evidence contradicting the statements on the bill as to loading marks, quantity and apparent condition. Given that the information as to loading marks and quantity originates with the shipper and given that both the shipper and the carrier are both physically present at the loading port, it makes sense for the presumption raised against the carrier in a claim by the shipper to be relatively weak, i.e. rebuttable by contrary evidence intended to show that the carrier loaded goods in the quantity and apparent condition in which they were discharged, not the quantity and apparent condition stated on the bill of lading. The evidential playing field as between the carrier and the shipper is sensibly level, or at any rate only slightly tilted in the carrier's favour.

### (c) Where a third party claims: conclusive evidence

A third party to whom the bill of lading has been transferred, however, needs stronger protection. B, the buyer of goods to whom the bill of lading has been endorsed and transferred, was not the party with whom information about the goods originated; neither was B at the shipment port, nor does B have easy access to evidence as to what was shipped at that port. To allow C, the carrier, to upset the *prima facie* presumption raised against C by the bill of lading in a claim brought by B would be unfairly to skew the balance in C's favour. This is why Article III rule 4 of the Hague-Visby Rules bars proof contradicting the statements as to quantity, apparent condition and leading marks contained in the bill of lading when the bill has been transferred to a third party acting in good faith, here B, the buyer of the goods: the bar raises an estoppel against the carrier, making the bill of lading conclusive evidence of what it says about the goods. The result is that if B can show that the goods were discharged in a smaller quantity or in a worse apparent condition than that in which they were stated in the bill of lading to have been shipped, it will have proved its loss and the cargo claim is well on its way to success. Given the fact, however, that some of the information to which the carrier is bound – leading marks and quantity – originates with S, the shipper, the Rules provide C with an indemnity against S for all loss, damages and expenses resulting from any inaccuracies in any such particulars.[13]

Before we leave the apparently strong presumption which the Hague-Visby Rules raise in Article III rule 4 in favour of third party transferees of bills of lading against the carrier, it is important to point out that the Article does not apply where the goods are covered not by a transferable bill of lading (a bearer bill or a bill of lading made out to order) but by a sea waybill. Section 1(6)(b) of the Carriage of Goods by Sea Act 1971 makes it clear that where goods carried by sea are covered by a non-negotiable receipt marked as such (in modern practice, a sea waybill), statements on the document regarding leading marks, quantity and apparent condition are not conclusive. Three points need to be made. The

13. Article III rule 5 of the Hague-Visby Rules

first is that where a sea waybill is issued, it will not necessarily be – and it does not need to be – transferred to the person named as consignee. We have already seen that the consignee acquires its rights of suit against the carrier through being named as consignee not through transfer of the document. Secondly, although the document does not need to be transferred to the consignee, it may be – and where this happens, it may come as a surprise to the consignee that the carrier is not bound by the statements on the sea waybill regarding the goods, particularly given that the sea waybill envisaged in section 1(6)(b) is one which expressly provides that the Rules are to govern the contract as if the sea waybill were a bill of lading. Thirdly, it is not clear whether the transferee of a straight bill of lading – as opposed to a sea waybill – is similarly deprived of the advantages of Article III rule 3 of the Hague Rules. In *The Rafaela S*,[14] the House of Lords held that the Rules applied to such bills of lading on the basis either that a straight bill of lading was nonetheless a bill of lading or that it was a "similar document of title" within the definition of "contract of carriage" in Article II(b) of the Rules. The specific issue in the dispute was whether the carrier could limit its liability rather than whether the bill of lading provided conclusive evidence in the hands of the consignee. It would seem to follow from the decision that the Rules apply to straight bills, however; that a straight bill *does* provide the consignee with conclusive evidence of what it says about the goods, although, as we have seen, a sea waybill, curiously, does not.

### (d) Why the estoppel is weaker than it seems

The stage seems set for an evidential victory for B, with C having a residual indemnity against S: this would, however, be too simplistic a summary of the position. The effect of Article III rule 4 of the Hague-Visby Rules is to bind C to what is stated about quantity, apparent condition and leading marks in the bill of lading and if the bill of lading states nothing much in this regard, then there is little to which to bind C. Now no carrier is likely to issue a bill of lading saying nothing about the quantity and apparent condition of the goods shipped, for much the same reason that it is unwise to issue a blank cheque in general commercial life: blanks can be filled in later with information which would not assist C. Carriers do, however, so qualify their statements as to make them of little use to B: like all estoppels, the estoppel raised by Article III rule 4 of the Hague-Visby Rules is only as strong as the statements on which it is based and if those statements are weak, then so is the estoppel. Statements as to apparent condition are weakened by so-called "clausing"; those as to quantity, by "weight and quantity unknown" clauses.

### (e) Clausing bills

Bills of lading typically state in pre-printed wording that the goods have been shipped in apparent good order and condition. The statement says nothing, of course, about the commercial value or specifications of the goods – it is limited to the *apparent* condition of the goods. This is all that a carrier can reasonably be

14. See fn. 11.

held to, the carrier not being a trader in the particular goods or commodities being shipped.

The shipment of goods in apparently good condition is, of course, what both C, the carrier, and S, the shipper – and most definitely B, the buyer – hope *will* happen. C, however, is also wary of being bound to such a statement if it is not true, of being held hostage to a photograph showing goods to have been shipped in good condition when they were not: such a "clean" photograph would give B, the buyer, an unfair advantage in a cargo claim, unfair because the goods were simply not, on this hypothesis, ever shipped in apparently good condition. If the goods are shipped in less than good order and condition, the carrier will therefore want to "clause" the bill qualifying the statement that the goods were shipped in apparent good order and condition, adding words such as "torn bags noted" or "evidence of rust on shipment".

This type of clausing has an unwelcome impact on a c.i.f. seller, who is under an implied duty to tender a clean bill of lading:[15] the clausing of a bill by C in effect puts S in breach of its duties under the sale contract and will also prejudice its chances of payment under any letter of credit. In order to avoid this, S will attempt to persuade C to issue a clean bill where a claused one is warranted, normally by offering to hold C harmless against any consequences of issuing a clean bill. Two issues arise: first, is S actually *entitled* to a clean bill of lading; and second, can C safely issue a clean bill in these circumstances against a letter holding it harmless against the consequences of so doing?

As for the first issue, it is clear that a shipper is *not* entitled to a clean bill where the goods are shipped in less than *good* order and condition. All that Article III rule 3 of the Hague-Visby Rules gives the shipper is the right to demand on shipment of the goods a bill of lading stating the apparent order and condition of the goods, not one stating the apparent good order and condition of the goods. It is for the shipper to ask for, but for the carrier to issue, a clean bill of lading – and if the carrier does so issue, then, of course, as we have seen, the carrier is held to that photograph in a cargo claim brought by any transferees of the bill of lading. This is why carriers who *do* issue clean bills in such circumstances will normally do so only against a letter of indemnity ("LOI") in which the shipper holds them harmless against the consequences of so doing – and this brings us to the second issue: how secure are these LOIs?

There are two problems here. First, the LOI is only, of course, as good as its issuer and a carrier would need to feel sure, before issuing a clean bill in these circumstances, that the issuer is both solvent and easily accessible: this is why carriers frequently ask for an LOI backed by a bank guarantee. Secondly, however, there is some doubt as to whether such an LOI is actually enforceable under English law: in a majority decision, the Court of Appeal held in *Brown Jenkinson & Co Ltd v Percy Dalton (London) Ltd*,[16] that such an indemnity is unenforceable where its purpose is to make a fraudulent representation as to the apparent condition of the goods – which, it would appear, would be the case by definition in the circumstances here envisaged. It is for these reasons that disputes quite regularly arise between shippers and carriers as to whether goods shipped are or

15. *M Golodetz & Co Inc v Czarnikow-Rionda Co Inc (The Galatia)* [1980] 1 Lloyd's Rep 453 (CA).
16. *Brown Jenkinson & Co Ltd v Percy Dalton (London) Ltd* [1957] 2 Lloyd's Rep 1.

are not in apparent good order and condition – and as to whether carriers are or are not entitled to clause bills of lading see, for example, the disputes which arose in *The David Agmashenebeli*[17] and *The Sea Success*.[18]

### (f) "Weight and quantity unknown" clauses

If there are problems with bills clausing the statement as to the apparent order and condition of goods shipped, there are many more problems with statements on bills regarding the quantity of goods shipped. Bills are not always claused: they are only claused when carriers observe obvious problems with the goods on shipment. The shipper's figures as to quantities are, however, always qualified as a matter of course by carriers, in pre-printed wording varying in ingenuity: "weight and quantity unknown", "shipper's figures, for information only", "said to contain", "said to be", "STC", "STB", etc. Two issues arise: first, what is the effect of such qualifications; second, is the carrier entitled so to qualify the figures given to it by the shipper?

As for the first issue, it is clear that the effect of such qualifications is to deprive the bill of lading of any evidential force regarding the quantity of goods shipped in a cargo claim brought either by a shipper or by a third party transferee of the bill of lading. A statement can only raise a presumption of its truth, whether *prima facie* or conclusive, if a statement is made; a statement as to quantity involves stating that goods have been shipped in such-and-such a quantity; a statement stating that goods *may* have been shipped in such a quantity, but then again may *not* have, is no statement at all and consequently no presumption arises.

As for the second issue, four things are clear. First, the carrier is entitled so to qualify the statements as to quantity where, in the words of Article III rule 3, "he has reasonable ground for suspecting not accurately to represent the goods actually received, or which he has no reasonable means of checking". Secondly, however, this is the extent of the leeway allowed to the carrier. It is equally clear from the article that "on demand of the shipper", the carrier "shall" issue a bill of lading giving the quantity of the goods shipped. Consequently, the shipper does have the right, when faced with a bill of lading qualifying out of existence the statement on it as the quantity of goods shipped, to demand that the offending part of the qualification be deleted. Thus, for example, where the bill of lading states that 20,000 mts of a commodity have been shipped, "weight and quantity unknown", the shipper is entitled to ask for the deletion of the qualification, leaving the statement ready to acquire conclusive evidence in the hands of the transferee. Thirdly, and again however, the shipper is highly unlikely to exercise its rights of demand under Article III rule 3: the reality is that a shipper in receipt of a bill of lading is far likelier to tender it for payment to the buyer than to complain to the carrier about the precise effect of the qualifications as to the quantity of goods shipped: the shipper's objective is to get paid as quickly as possible rather than to return the bill of lading to the carrier for deletion of the qualification. Fourthly, where the qualification is not deleted (as is, for the reason just stated, most likely)

17. *Owners of cargo lately laden on board the David Agmashenebeli v Owners of the David Agmashenebeli (The David Agmashenebeli)* [2003] 1 Lloyd's Rep 92.
18. *Sea Success Maritime Inc v African Maritime Carriers Ltd (The Sea Success)* [2005] 2 Lloyd's Rep 692; [2005] 2 All ER (Comm) 445.

the qualification cannot, it is suggested, be struck down by Article III rule 8, the Article which bars clauses, covenants or agreements which relieves or lessens the carrier's liability under the Rules: a qualification of a statement of fact is not a clause, covenant or agreement and therefore falls outside the effect of Article III rule 8.

The net result is that where a cargo claim for short delivery is brought by a transferee of a bill of lading, the transferee has no clear photograph of the quantity of goods shipped and will consequently need to prove not only the quantity in which the goods were discharged (which the transferee can easily do so long as notice of loss is given on discharge) but also the quantity in which the goods were shipped. The estoppel raised by the Rules is consequently of little use to the transferee – and the buyer of commodities where quantity discrepancies are common may need to protect itself against such losses through means other than the contract of carriage, as we shall see in Chapter 4.

## 6. PROVING THE CARRIER'S BREACH

Proving that the goods discharged were not the goods stated to have been shipped, comparing the difference between the discharge and the loading snapshots, is necessary but not sufficient for the success of the cargo claim. For the claimant to succeed, it needs to prove that its loss was the direct result of a breach by the carrier of any one of three possible sources of obligation, i.e. contract, tort or bailment. We have already seen the requirements for success in tort or bailment, namely a link between the claimant and the particular goods damaged at the time of damage. It is with proof of breach of contract that this part of the chapter is concerned – and this issue revolves around two central questions:

(a) Where are the terms of the contract of carriage between the claimant and the carrier: are they in the bill of lading or in a charterparty?
(b) If the terms of the claimant's contract of carriage are in the bill of lading, what are the carrier's duties breach of which might give success to the cargo claimant?

### (a) Where are the terms of the contract of carriage?

If the cargo claimant needs to prove that its loss has been caused by a breach by the carrier of a particular term of a particular contract, it becomes crucial for the claimant to identify the contract on which the claim is being brought. It is easy to draw the conclusion from the fact that the claimant holds a bill of lading, whether as shipper or as transferee, that the terms of its contract with the carrier are contained in the bill of lading and that the claimant's task is to declare the carrier in breach of a term contained in the bill of lading. This conclusion is, however, too simplistic. In identifying the claimant's contract of carriage, there are four possible sources:

#### *(i) The contract itself*

It may seem tautological to say that the contract of carriage on which the claim is based is in the contract of carriage: there is, however, a fundamental truth hidden in this circularity. Where a cargo claim is brought by a non-charterer shipper of goods who has actually concluded the contract of carriage with the carrier, then the terms of the contract of carriage are contained in the agreement which they have concluded. The contract pre-exists – and is not exclusively contained in – any bill of lading which may later be issued. The bill of lading is issued after the goods are shipped, performing its role as a snapshot of shipment. Shipment occurs, however, in performance of a contract which already exists – and some of whose terms will already therefore have been agreed, e.g. freight and time of shipment. Those terms will be contained in a variety of exchanges and possibly documents, e.g. telephone or email exchanges and published schedules or booking notes. Other terms will be left to the bill of lading, which will, when it is issued, provide good evidence of the parties' agreement. It is not, however, the only or even the prevailing source of evidence, in the sense that if parties have agreed terms which do not tally with a particular term of the bill of lading, then it is the specially agreed term which prevails over the bill of lading term, not because one is special and the other general, but because the contract exists before the issue of the bill of lading. Thus if, for example, the parties agree that shipment will be direct without calls at intermediate ports, that agreement will prevail over a term in the bill of lading giving the carrier a liberty to call at intermediate ports. The basic point is that the shipper's contract is in the contract evidenced by, but not contained in, the bill of lading.

Who is the shipper here? Two situations are quite simple. first, we are envisaging here a shipper who is not also a charterer: we shall see presently that a shipper who is a charterer contracts with the carrier on charterparty terms, despite the fact that the charterer also holds a bill of lading. Secondly, the shipper will typically be either a shipper shipping goods for its own account, without selling the goods on, or a c.i.f. seller making the contract of carriage and actually shipping the goods it is selling to a buyer. In either case, the terms of the shipper's contract of carriage are in its contract of carriage with the carrier.

The third situation is a little more complex. We have already looked at the case *Pyrene v Scindia*,[19] where an f.o.b. seller claimed against a carrier in respect of goods damaged by the carrier during shipment: the carrier successfully pleaded the terms of the Rules despite the fact that no bill of lading had actually been issued. We shall see in Chapter 4 that in f.o.b. sales, the party who will typically (but not always) make the contract of carriage is the buyer – this type of f.o.b. contract is normally called a straight f.o.b. contract and the sale contract in *Pyrene v Scindia* was on such terms. Now, on the assumption that the buyer is not a charterer, the straight f.o.b. buyer's contract of carriage is contained in its agreement with the carrier: the buyer is here the contractual shipper making its contract of carriage with the carrier, with the bill of lading providing evidence of, but not containing, the terms of that contract. What if, however, a claim is brought against the carrier not by the buyer, the carrier's contractual shipper, but by the seller, who will most likely be the *actual* shipper of the goods? We have already seen that Devlin J recognised the actual shipper's title to sue the carrier; we also saw that the carrier could, in defence to such a claim, plead the terms of a bill of lading which was never issued. This must mean that, as between a

19. See fn. 3.

straight f.o.b. seller and a carrier, the terms of the contract of carriage are contained in, not just evidenced by, the bill of lading which would have been issued had goods been shipped.

### *(ii) The bill of lading*

This brings us to more typical situations where the contract terms are contained in the bill of lading. Again leaving to one side situations where the goods are carried on a chartered vessel, the buyer of goods from a c.i.f. seller, or from an f.o.b. seller where the seller has agreed to conclude and to transfer a contract of carriage to the buyer, obtain, as we saw at the start of this chapter, rights of suit against the carrier through the Carriage of Goods by Sea Act 1992 – and those rights of suit are in a real sense *contained in*, rather than simply evidenced by, the bill of lading. Consequently, any terms of the contract of carriage specially agreed between the seller/shipper and the carrier do not travel to the buyer. To return to the example used earlier, if a shipper agrees with the carrier that there will be no intermediate calls, that term prevails over a bill of lading term permitting such calls; once the bill of lading is transferred, however, and a claim is brought against the carrier by the transferee, then the bill of lading permitting intermediate calls prevails.

### *(iii) A charterparty*

So far, we have not considered situations where the goods are carried on a chartered vessel. The issue here is whether either party to a cargo claim, the claimant or the carrier, can plead terms contained in the charterparty or in the bill of lading issued when the goods were shipped. It is impossible to predict which party to a claim will want which document to dictate the terms of the contract on which the claim is brought. The reality is that the parties are not after a *document*: they are after a particular term in a particular document which happens to suit the way the claim has progressed. Thus, for example, a carrier will want a particularly short time-bar in a charterparty to prevail over the longer one-year time bar affecting the bill of lading through the Hague-Visby Rules. For its part, the claimant may be after a London arbitration clause in the bill of lading in preference to a possibly less attractive jurisdiction clause contained in the charterparty.

The problem – which document, which contract – arises because the same transaction frequently spawns both a charterparty (clearly a contract of carriage) and a bill of lading (the reverse page of which looks uncannily like a contract). If the resulting but only apparent confusion is to be cleared up, it is helpful to make two crucial points. First, a charterparty is – and can only be – a contract of carriage: it can never perform any other functions: it does not provide a snapshot of the goods on shipment, and neither can it be passed down a string of buyers, transferring rights of suit as it goes. Secondly, although a bill of lading can, in certain circumstances, contain the terms of a contract of carriage, this is not the only function it performs – and it is not a function it *always* performs. We have already seen that in the contractual shipper's hands, the bill of lading evidences but does not contain the contract of carriage. And whether or not it does contain the terms of the contract, the bill of lading will always perform its original snapshot or receipt function and may, where the requirements of the Carriage of Goods by Sea Act 1992 are satisfied, transfer rights of suit to a succession of buyers of the goods it covers. In sum, a charterparty does one thing; a bill of lading can do different things at different times.

Given this fundamental difference between the two documents, it ceases to surprise that a charterer may hold at one and the same time two documents, a charterparty and a bill of lading, both of which look as though they contain a contract of carriage. The truth is that, in a charterer's hands, only one of those documents contains the terms of its contract of carriage with the carrier: the charterparty. The reason the charterer also holds a bill of lading is that the charterer needs a receipt for the goods shipped, whether for its own reassurance or because it needs to tender such a snapshot under a sale contract with its buyer; a second reason the charterer needs the bill is because it may need the means whereby to transfer to its buyer rights of suit against the carrier. Were such transfer not to happen, however, and were the claim to be brought by the charterer against the carrier, the contract terms covering that claim would be contained in the charterparty not in the bill of lading, and this despite the fact that the bill of lading would still, in that same cargo claim brought by the charterer against the carrier, perform its useful function as a receipt. In essence, the practical consequence is that a c.i.f. seller/charterer and an f.o.b. buyer/charterer bring their cargo claim against the carrier on the terms of the charterparty; a c.i.f. buyer/receiver, however, and (as we have seen) a straight f.o.b. seller, bring their cargo claim against the carrier on the terms of the bill of lading.

### *(iv) A bill of lading incorporating charterparty terms*

There is one additional complication to the issue of whether a cargo claim is brought on bill of lading or charterparty terms: what if the appropriate document is, on the basis of the principles summarised above, the bill of lading, but that bill of lading contains a clause incorporating one, some or all terms from a charterparty? In this situation, is the cargo claim subject to bill of lading or to charterparty terms?

It is common for bills of lading to incorporate terms from a charterparty, largely but not exclusively, in the commodity trades. Where commodities are shipped requiring the full capacity of a single ship, the c.i.f. seller or f.o.b. buyer will typically charter the vessel and the bill of lading issued will typically be a so-called short-form bill of lading, marked "for use with charterparties" and incorporating all terms from a charterparty. These bills of lading are commonly called "charterparty bills of lading". Incorporation of charterparty terms into bills of lading is not unknown, however, in the liner trade, where a full form bill of lading is issued, not intended exclusively for use with a charterparty, but incorporating but one term, e.g. freight or arbitration "as per charterparty".

In either case, where the claim is brought by the charterer, the incorporation of charterparty terms causes no problem: as we have seen, a claim brought against the carrier by the charterer will be on charterparty terms in any event. It is when the bill of lading is transferred to a non-charterer that a problem of known unknowns arises: the bill of lading tells the transferee that charterparty terms are incorporated, but those terms are unknown to the transferee, who was not a party to – and played no part in negotiating – the charterparty. It may seem harsh on the transferee to bind it into charterparty terms in the conclusion of which it played no part and to sight of which at any rate in the absence of express stipulations, it has no right under the sale contract.

It is with these considerations of fairness – in essence considerations of privity of contract and notice – that the courts in England have developed a number of tests intended to protect third party transferees from the untoward effect of unseen contractual terms. First, where the words of incorporation in the charterparty are general in ambit, only those terms which are germane to the carriage of goods are susceptible of incorporation into the bill of lading: thus, for example, while time-bars and limitation clauses would travel into the bill of lading from the charterparty, a bunkering clause or a safe port warranty would not. Secondly, where more specific terms of incorporation are used in the bill of lading, only those charterparty terms which come strictly within the ambit of the terms of incorporation and which can, with a limited degree of verbal manipulation, be intelligibly applied within the bill of lading, are susceptible of incorporation. Thus, for example, if the bill of lading incorporates "freight" or "destination" as per charterparty, then it is only freight and destination clauses which can travel from the charterparty into the bill of lading, sensibly substituting, for example, the word "shipper" for "charterer". Thirdly, and perhaps most importantly, even if a charterparty term travels successfully from a charterparty into a bill of lading, incorporation does *not* work if an inconsistency results from such incorporation within the bill of lading. Thus, for example, if a bill of lading incorporates a charterparty London arbitration clause, but contains, say, its own Paris arbitration clause, then the charterparty arbitration clause is not incorporated into the bill of lading. This is a particularly obvious form of inconsistency. A less obvious, but possibly more important, form of inconsistency may arise through the Carriage of Goods by Sea Act 1971. We have already seen that Article III rule 8 of the Hague-Visby Rules strikes down bill of lading clauses which relieve or lessen the carrier's liability under the Rules. Where a charterparty term successfully negotiates its way through the tests just described, it becomes, for the purposes of the cargo claim to which it now becomes relevant, a bill of lading clause. If the bill of lading is subject to the Hague-Visby Rules, the result is that if the incorporated charterparty clause falls foul of Article III rule 8 (as it would do, for example if it provided for a nine month time-bar) then the charterparty time-bar is in effect not incorporated into the bill of lading.

### (b) Breach of which term in the contract of carriage?

Given the complexity involved in identifying the terms of the contract of carriage on which the cargo claim is based, it is obvious that it is impossible to generalise on which particular term the claimant will use to ground its claim: it is in the nature of a cargo claim that a claimant will collect the facts which can plausibly be argued to have caused the loss, and then attempt to characterise those facts as the reverse of a particular term in the claimant's contract of carriage with the carrier.

Having said that, however, where a claim is brought on the terms of a contract of carriage contained in or evidenced by a bill of lading governed by the Hague-Visby Rules, it is clear that the claimant will need to establish facts which put the carrier in breach of one of two types of obligation, those going to the vessel, set out in Article III rule 1, and those going to the custody of the goods, set out in Article III rule 2. Moreover, there are tactical advantages for the claimant in pursuing the first route rather than the second.

*Seaworthiness and care of goods*

Article III rule 1 requires the carrier, before and at the beginning of the voyage, to exercise due diligence to make the ship seaworthy, in a broader sense than simply the sea-going viability of the ship: the carrier needs also to ensure that the vessel is properly manned and equipped and that its holds are fit to receive the cargo. Not only is the carrier barred by Article III rule 8 from inserting terms in its bill of lading lessening its duties in this regard, but the decision of the House of Lords in *The Muncaster Castle*[20] prevents the carrier from escaping from this liability on the simple ground that that due diligence was exercised in selecting a competent independent contractor to make the ship seaworthy. Finally, once the fact of unseaworthiness is established by the claimant, the burden of proof shifts very sharply onto the carrier to prove that it exercised due diligence to make the ship seaworthy.

Article III rule 2 requires the carrier properly and carefully to load, handle, stow, carry keep, care for, and discharge the goods carried, "[s]ubject to the provisions of Article IV". The reference in Article III rule 2 to Article IV provides the claimant with the tactical advantage of Article III rule 1 over Article III rule 2. Article IV rule 2 contains a long litany of exceptions to the carrier's liability, e.g. acts of God, perils of the sea, strikes, etc. Where the claimant can only prove facts which would put the carrier in breach of Article III rule 2, the carrier could seek to exclude its liability by proving facts which come within one or more of the exceptions to liability described in Article IV rule 2. Where, on the other hand, the claimant can prove facts which put the carrier in breach of its broad seaworthiness duties under Article III rule 1, those exclusions are not available to the carrier, given that Article III rule 1 does not start (as Article III rule 2 does) with the words "[s]ubject to the provisions of Article IV".

Thus, for example, if containers go overboard during a storm, a peril of the sea for which liability is excluded by Article IV rule 2(c), and the lashing equipment on board is found to have been defective, the carrier's position will depend on what the claimant can prove. If the claimant can establish that the lashing equipment was defective at the beginning of the voyage, this would put the claimant in breach of Article III rule 1: the vessel would be unseaworthy under that article, which is not subject to Article IV and the carrier cannot, consequently, exclude its liability because of the peril of the sea. Alternatively, if the claimant can prove only that the lashings had become defective during the voyage, although this too would be a breach of contract, it is one from which the carrier can escape through

20. *Riverstone Meat Co Pty Ltd v Lancashire Shipping Co Ltd (The Muncaster Castle)* [1961] 1 Lloyd's Rep 57; [1961] AC 807.

the peril of the sea exception in Article IV rule 2. The net result is that it generally pays the claimant to base its claim on unseaworthiness under Article III rule 1 rather than a simple breach of care of the goods under Article III rule 2.

There is, since the House of Lords decision in the *The Jordan II*,[21] an additional tactical advantage for the claimant in Article III rule 1 over Article III rule 2. While it is clear that Article III rule 8 bars the carrier from excluding or lessening its duties or liabilities to provide a seaworthy vessel under Article III rule 1, it is now clear that it is open to the carrier to craft a term in the bill of lading which allocates the duty of stowage to the cargo interest rather than to the carrier. Such a clause was considered by the House of Lords to be one defining the parties' obligations rather than one relieving or lessening an obligation imposed by the Rules.

## 7. EXCLUDING OR LIMITING THE CARRIER'S LIABILITY

We have reached the end of the cargo claim. With the right claimant establishing, in a claim against the right defendant, that its proven loss was caused by a breach by the carrier of a term in their contract of carriage or of an obligation owed by the carrier to the claimant in tort or bailment, the claimant will succeed. The carrier will, of course, have fought the claimant all the way: contesting the claimant's title to sue; claiming that it is not the claimant's contractual carrier; disputing evidence of loss; denying a breach of any duty owed towards the claimant. If none of these counter-attacks works, however, there are a few remaining routes out of liability or, at any rate, out of as much recovery as the claimant would like. The carrier could extinguish the claim, either by arguing that the claim has been time-barred or by pleading one of the exceptions to liability allowed by the Hague-Visby Rules. If neither of those escape routes are available, the carrier could limit its liability through the so-called package and unit limitation imposed by the Rules, a privilege of which the claimant could deprive the carrier through one of two means, i.e. either deviation or by proving that the damage was caused intentionally by the carrier.

Before we deal with these escape routes from and limitations to liability, it would be useful to make one methodological point. Viewed from one perspective, it makes sense to deal with these matters at the end of this chapter on Cargo Claims: escape routes and limitations should logically come after having established liability. From a more practical perspective, however, it frequently makes sense to examine the facts going to the time-bar, exceptions and limitation as soon as the dispute hits the desk. The matters previously discussed in this chapter going to title to sue, proof of loss and liability are obviously crucial: whether the bottom line looks attractive, however, whether anything much at all can be recovered if liability is established, makes it easier to decide whether it is worth pursuing the claim vigorously – or settling it.

### (a) The one-year time-bar

The normal limitation period for civil liability in English law is six years: cargo claims under the Hague-Visby Rules, however, must be brought within one year

21. *Jindal Iron & Steel Co Ltd and Others v Islamic Solidarity Shipping Co Jordan Inc (The Jordan II)* [2005] 1 Lloyd's Rep 57.

of the delivery of the goods or of the date on which the goods should have been delivered. For the reason stated in the immediately preceding paragraph, it is crucial to ensure, at a very early stage of the claim, whether the time-bar has lapsed and, if it has, to see whether agreement can be reached with the carrier to extend or waive the time-bar.

### (b) Exceptions to liability

We have already referred to Article IV rule 2 of the Hague-Visby Rules as the Article containing a long litany of exceptions to the carrier's liability. Some of these exceptions are quite typical of any contracts of carriage, whether covered by a bill of lading or by a charterparty and whether or not governed by the Hague-Visby Rules: acts of God, acts of war, strikes or lockouts etc. Others, however, are quite particular to the Rules and are part of the patchwork compromise between the interests of cargo and carrier arrived at in the Hague-Visby Rules. Thus, for example, it may come as a surprise to a cargo claimant that an act, neglect or default in the navigation or management of the ship has pride of place as the very first exception to the carrier's liability. Moroever, while in most contracts, a list of exclusions of liability is normally closed, the list in Article IV rule 2 ends with an open-ended exclusion: any other cause arising without the actual fault or privity of the carrier, the burden of proving the absence of fault or privity falling on the carrier.

### (c) Quantification and limitation of loss

Assuming that neither the time-bar nor Article IV rule 2 provides the carrier with an escape route from liability, the claimant's next task is to quantify its loss. If the parties have agreed that loss, in what is commonly called an *ad valorem* box in the bill of lading, then the issue of *quantum* is resolved, at any rate *prima facie*. In effect, the claimant's loss has been liquidated in advance and the cargo claimant is tied to that declared value as the sum of its loss. In order to guard against inflated valuations, however, the presumption raised by the *ad valorem* declaration is not conclusive against the carrier, who can, therefore, prove that the goods shipped were worth less than the valuation. Moreover, if the carrier can prove that the shipper *knowingly* mis-stated the value of the goods, then the carrier is simply not liable at all, according to Article IV rule 5(h).

On the other hand, if the value of the claimant's loss has not been agreed beforehand, or if the valuation has been set aside by the carrier, then there are two stages to be gone through under the Hague-Visby Rules, the first being the usual process of quantification of damages for breach of contract and the second being the limitation of those damages.

First, the basic objective here, as with any award in damages, is to place the claimant, through damages, in the position in which it would have been had the contract been performed, i.e. had the goods arrived in a sound condition. In the context of a contract of carriage, this translates into the following formula: the claimant is entitled to the difference between the market value of the goods had they arrived in sound condition and their value in the condition in which they actually arrived. The formula is used in Article IV rule 5(b) of the Hague-Visby Rules.

Secondly, once that sum is arrived at, the damages need to be limited by the so-called "package/unit limitation" contained in Article IV rule 5(a)(c) and (d). The basic principle is that liability is limited to the higher of the following two quantities, either 666.67 special drawing rights of the International Monetary Fund per package or unit or 2 special drawing rights per kilogramme of gross weight of the goods lost or damaged. It is important to point out that Article IV rule 5(a) does not provide two formulae, one for goods in units or packages and the other for commodities shipped in bulk. The single formula has two alternatives, both of which need to be worked out whatever the cargo – and the applicable limit is the higher of the two.

Moreover, where goods are consolidated in a container, pallet or such like and the bill of lading quantifies the goods as, say, "one container said to contain 10,000 pairs of shoes", then the multiplier for the purpose of the package/unit limitation in Article IV rule 5(a) is 10,000 rather than one. The effect of "said to contain" clauses has already been covered: the evidential force of the bill of lading is emasculated in the sense that no binding photograph exists as to what was shipped. If a cargo claim has reached the stage of quantification, however, this must mean that the claimant has overcome the resulting evidential difficulties by actually proving what was shipped, through tally sheets, alternative exchanges between the parties, oral evidence etc: the carrier will, as it were, have failed in its attempt to qualify the statement as to quantity on the bill of lading. Having failed in that attempt, the carrier does not get a second bite at the cherry: the claimant having proved that 10,000 pairs of shoes were in fact shipped, the carrier cannot now use 1 as the enumerator for limitation purposes.[22] To allow the carrier to do so would be to allow the carrier in effect to nullify the evidential gain already made by the claimant.

Finally on limitation, it is important to emphasise that the limitation amounts here described relate to claims brought on bills of lading for the carriage of goods by sea. Other conventions provide different levels of limitation for the carriage of goods by other means[23] and, where carriage is multimodal, bills of lading will frequently contain clauses limiting damages according as to whether the location of the loss is or is not known.

### (d) Breaking limitation

Limitation of liability is, of course, not something the claimant gladly accepts: it does mean that he may well be left with an uncovered exposure to loss which may or may not be covered by a cargo insurance policy on the goods. The claimant's instinct, at this late stage of the cargo claim is to break or "bust" limitation and there are two recognised means of doing so. The first is the less controversial but also, in English law, the less frequently used. Article IV rule 5(e) states that liability cannot be limited where the damage to the goods results from an act or

22. See Article IV rule 5(c) of the Hague-Visby Rules and, under the Hague Rules, *The River Gurara* [1998] 1 Lloyd's Rep 225 (CA).
23. *Cf.* Arts. 22 to 25 of the Convention for the Unification of Certain Rules for International Carriage by Air, Montreal, 28 May 1999; Art. 23 of Convention on the Contract for International Carriage of Goods by Road (CMR Convention), Geneva, 19 May 1956; Arts. 30(2) and 31 of the Convention concerning International Carriage by Rail (COTIF), Berne, 9 May 1980.

omission of the carrier done with intent to cause damage or recklessly and with knowledge that damage would probably result. The critical point here is proof of *intent*, a difficult and, in the context of civil liability, an unusual thing for English lawyers to concern themselves with in quantifying damages: and this may be why the article has been somewhat under-utilised in our litigation.

A far more traditional method of breaking limitation is to prove that the carrier has deviated from the contract voyage. The meaning of deviation has already been covered in the context of Charterparties in Chapter 2. All Article IV rule 4 of the Hague-Visby Rules adds to the sum of knowledge on deviation is that deviation is permissible not only for the saving of life or property but also for any reasonable cause. The relevance of deviation to the breaking of limitation lies, however, outside the Rules. The position traditionally held in English law is that a carrier who deviates steps outside the contract of carriage and that it consequently cannot plead any of the contractual defences to which it would normally be entitled. This is commonly known as the "deviation rule". Its effect is draconian, leaving the carrier open to liability at large, unrestricted by the package/unit limitation or indeed any of the other defences under the Hague-Visby Rules, like the time-bar, whether or not the claim was based on or the loss caused by the deviation. It has been argued, but so far not successfully in litigation, that the deviation rule is a carriage equivalent of the so-called "doctrine of fundamental breach" in general contract law, a doctrine given burial by the House of Lords in *Photo Production Ltd v Securicor Transport Ltd*.[24] Despite these discussions, largely restricted to the legal journals, it is still wise for a cargo claimant faced by unwelcome limitation, to argue that limitation is unavailable where the carrier has deviated from the contract voyage.

## 8. THE CLAIMANT'S POTENTIAL LIABILITY TOWARDS THE CARRIER

It may seem strange to end a chapter on cargo claims against the carrier with a brief consideration of claims by the carrier against cargo-interests. The carrier may be owed freight; the carrier may wish to recover for, say, warehousing charges where the receiver fails to collect; or for damage to the vessel caused by the cargo, whether prohibited, dangerous or neither. Now there are two types of cargo interest who are never beyond the reach of a carrier for these types of losses. First, a charterer from the carrier will always be open to attack by the carrier: that charterparty survives any transfer of a bill of lading by or to the charterer. Secondly, even where there is no charterparty, a carrier never loses its rights of suit against the original shipper with whom the carrier first contracted, again despite the fact that the shipper may have transferred the bill of lading to a third party. The problem arises when a carrier wishes to pursue a claim not against either of these two parties, a charterer or a shipper, but against a lawful holder

24. *Photo Production Ltd v Securicor Transport Ltd* [1980] 1 Lloyd's Rep 545. See also C. Mills, "The Future of Deviation" [1983] 4 LMCLQ 587; C. Debattista, "Fundamental Breach and Deviation" [1989] JBL 22; F. Reynolds, "The Butterworth Lectures 1990–91" (London: Butterworths, 1991), reviewed by Johan Steyn in [1993] LMCLQ at pp. 272–273; M. Dockray, "Deviation: A Doctrine All at Sea" [2000] LMCLQ 76.

of a bill of lading, a person named as consignee on a sea waybill or a person to whom a carrier acknowledges a right of delivery under a ship's delivery order. Does the fact that these cargo interests have rights of suit against the carrier mean that the carrier can pursue them under the relevant document? If the answer to this question was yes, difficulties would be caused to banks: a bank named in any of these capacities on any one of the three documents mentioned above would be a likely and attractive defendant for carriers and the result would be that bills of lading and associated shipping documents would become unattractive security documents for banks extending a line of credit to buyers through letters of credit. Section 3 of the Carriage of Goods by Sea Act 1992 consequently makes it clear that for a carrier to have rights of action against a lawful holder of a bill of lading, a consignee named as such on a sea waybill and a party to whom the carrier acknowledges a right of delivery on a ship's delivery order, that person must do one of the following: it must either take or demand delivery of any of the goods to which the document relates or make a claim under the contract of carriage to which the document relates. This means that for the cargo interest to expose itself to liability towards the cargo interest needs first to activate liability by exercising its own rights under the 1992 Act. An unintended consequence follows from this: a cargo interest can simply avoid any liabilities towards the carrier under the carriage contract through the simple expedient of failing to receive goods in which it has, for some reason or other, lost interest under the sale contract. This leads us to Chapter 4, where we shall deal with the use of shipping documents in international sales and letters of credit.

CHAPTER 4

# International Trade and Shipping Documents

*FILIPPO LORENZON*

## 1. INTRODUCTION: SHIPPING AND INTERNATIONAL TRADE

Thousands of commercial vessels sail daily across the oceans, operated by companies incorporated in different jurisdictions, under charterparties and bills of lading imposing duties and liabilities on all parties concerned. These vessels are built by hundreds of shipbuilding facilities and have to comply with a multitude of international, regional and national regulations in order to call safely at a world-wide network of commercial ports. The shipping industry as a whole employs millions of people worldwide and feeds a great number of service providers and public servants. However, the purpose of the world's commercial fleet, the main reason why vessels are built, registered, chartered and insured, is not *maritime* at all: vessels sail to carry goods bought on one market to be sold on another. The real purpose of the entire commercial shipping industry and its regulatory and contractual framework is to make *international trade* possible, safe and efficient.

This chapter will give a brief overview of the basic concepts of international commercial sales on shipment terms in order to provide the reader with the commercial background to better understand shipping law as a whole.

## 2. INTERNATIONAL COMMERCIAL SALES ON SHIPMENT TERMS

International trade law is a quite specialist area of commercial law dealing with the sale of goods for commercial purposes. Contracts for the international sale of goods may be further divided into three main groups depending on the mode and place of delivery of the consignment sold: *E terms*[1] (or ex works contracts), *D terms*[2] (destination/arrival or delivered contracts); and *Shipment terms*.[3] Broadly speaking, the delivery of the goods is made at the seller's premises in *X terms*, at the buyer's premises in *D terms* and on board a vessel at the loading port in *shipment terms*. The following pages are dedicated to the identification of the main features of this latter type of commercial sales, where the link between the sale contract and the shipping documents becomes more complex.

1. EXW in Incoterms 2000 language. Common in practice are also "ex store" and "ex warehouse".
2. The current Incoterms D terms are as follows: DAF (Delivered At Frontier), DES (Delivered Ex Ship), DEQ (Delivered Ex Quay), DDU (Delivered Duty Unpaid) and DDP (Delivered Duty Paid).
3. C.i.f., c&f and f.o.b. contracts; in Incoterms 2000 language the shipment sales for maritime transport are CIF, CFR, and FOB; for other means of transport FCA, CPT and CIP should be used.

### (a) The contract and its terms

In current commercial practice, sale contracts are concluded by exchanges of short emails, faxes or telexes, *confirmation notes* focusing mainly on the description of the goods to be sold and the main delivery and payment terms. Very often, though, these notes provide for express incorporation of one of the Incoterms[4] and/or longer and considerably more detailed standard forms such as the ones provided by trade associations as GAFTA[5] and FOSFA.[6] These forms – when correctly incorporated by reference – constitute a second layer of contractual clauses with an equally binding effect between seller and buyer. It is not uncommon for these forms to incorporate further terms from other standard forms or in-house models, rules and/or procedures which will come to form a third layer of contractual clauses.[7] In this *millefoglie* of contractual clauses, identifying the exact terms agreed upon by the parties may not be an easy task to achieve.

The importance of the correct ascertainment of the parties' intention is, however, paramount since it is essential at the very early stages of any claim to establish, for example, the correct law applicable to the contract and the correct forum where the claim should be brought.[8] Because of the number of contractual layers forming the agreement of the parties, it is not unusual to have clauses in the confirmation note interacting with clauses in one or more of the standard forms or rules incorporated by reference. In these circumstances it becomes crucial to identify correctly the relationship between the various layers of the contract. The basic principle here is that the arbitrator or judge will try to identify the intention of the parties as it appears from the contract.[9] Hence, if the contract contains a clear hierarchy clause making one layer prevail over the others, the clause will be given full effect.[10] Where no hierarchy clause is drawn up, however, the principle is that where there is an established conflict between two clauses,[11] specially negotiated terms would prevail over standard terms and conditions of sale.[12] Occasionally the courts have refused to uphold the validity of the incorporation of unusual[13] or unreasonable[14] clauses but – it is submitted – this string of authorities should be read cautiously and with reference to the special circumstances of the cases concerned.

It may be worth at this stage discussing the incorporation of the International Chamber of Commerce's (ICC) *Official Rules for the Interpretation of Trade Terms* (more commonly known as the *Incoterms*[15]) and the effect of their incorporation

4. See below.
5. The Grain and Feed Trade Association.
6. The Federation of Oils, Seeds and Fat Associations Ltd.
7. E.g. FOSFA 54, lines 31–33.
8. See Chapter 1.
9. *Charles Robert Leader and Henrietta Ada Leader v George F. Duffey and Amyatt Edmond Ray* (1888) LR 13 App Cas 294 (HL).
10. *Pagnan SpA v Tradax Ocean Transportation SA* [1987] 2 Lloyd's Rep 342 (CA).
11. English courts, however, will seek to construe every contract as a whole and if a reasonable commercial construction of the whole could reconcile two provisions (whether typed or printed) then such a construction could and should be adopted; *Bayoil SA v Seawind Tankers Corp (The Leonidas)* [2001] 1 Lloyd's Rep 533.
12. *Indian Oil Corporation v Vanol Inc* [1991] 2 Lloyd's Rep 634.
13. *OK Petroleum AB v Vitol Energy SA* [1995] 2 Lloyd's Rep 160.
14. *Ceval Alimentos SA v Agrimpex Trading Co Ltd (The Northern Progress) (No 2)* [1996] 2 Lloyd's Rep 319.
15. International Chamber of Commerce, *Incoterms 2000 – ICC official rules for the interpretation of trade terms* (Paris, 1999), ICC publication no. 560.

into the contract. The Incoterms (2000, in their latest edition) are a set of standard trade terms compiled by the ICC. They are not, nor they are meant to be, an international convention and are regarded – at any rate under English law – as just another set of standard forms. From this it follows that under English law the mere agreement that a contract is fixed "on c.i.f. terms" is not enough to trigger the application of Incoterms and that, once correctly incorporated, they become just another layer of the contract to which the ordinary rules of construction discussed above apply.[16] It is therefore crucial for the parties who intend to make use of Incoterms not only to incorporate expressly the right Incoterm[17] of the right vintage[18] but also to draft a detailed confirmation note to record the special terms agreed between them for the particular transaction at stake.

### (b) C.i.f. and f.o.b. contracts and carriage arrangements

Once the terms and conditions of the agreement between the parties are identified, it is now necessary to illustrate the main features of commercial sales on shipment terms. First of all it must be made clear that both c.i.f. and f.o.b. sales are *shipment* contracts where the duty of the seller as to the delivery of the cargo is fulfilled by shipping goods on board a vessel or procuring goods shipped on board a vessel rather than by handing them over to the buyer at the port of discharge. But whereas the duty to procure the cargo rests always with the seller, the duty to fix a vessel suitable to carry the cargo from the port of loading to the port of discharge does not always follow. Generally speaking in c.i.f. (or c.& f.) agreements it is the seller who is under the obligation to fix the vessel whereas in bare (or straight) f.o.b. sales such duty falls on the buyer. Particular care, however, should be taken with regard to f.o.b. contracts where – in practice – such default position is often amended by way of contractual variations the most common of which is often referred to as "f.o.b. of the classic type". In its "classic" form the f.o.b. contract provides for the seller to conclude a contract of carriage as an agent for the buyer, at all material stages the original party to the contract of carriage with the carrier; the commodity will be still invoiced by the seller at f.o.b. rate but a commission for the fixture is usually added as a separate item. Another common alternative may be referred to as "f.o.b. with additional carriage services" where the seller fixes the contract of carriage with the carrier in his own name and then transfers his contractual position endorsing the bill of lading. In this case again the commodity is invoiced at f.o.b. rate and freight and commission are charged separately or specifically itemised. Distinguishing between c.i.f. sales and the various subtypes of f.o.b. terms is crucial both for (i) understanding the apportionment of the risk of market fluctuations between seller and buyer, and (ii) for the identification of the terms of the contract of carriage governing the cargo claim in case of loss of or damage to the cargo.[19]

16. For a recent case of construction where CIP Incoterms 2000 were incorporated together with a set of rules for the specific trade concerned see *Stora Enso Oij v Port of Dundee* [2006] CSOH 40, [2006] 1 CLC 453.
17. In case of carriage by air on c.i.f. terms, for example, it would be advisable to incorporate the CIP Incoterms 2000 rather than the CIF term, specifically designed for maritime transport.
18. Incorporation of CIF Incoterm may in fact not be enough to prefer Incoterms 2000 over Incoterms 1990 whereas – it is suggested – reference to the "CIF Incoterm in force at the date of the conclusion of the contract" would indeed suffice.
19. See Chapter 3.

*(i) The risk of market fluctuations*

Because of the timing of international commercial transactions – where sale contracts (and price) may be agreed upon long before or indeed long after the actual date of shipment – and the high volatility of the freight and insurance markets, selling on c.i.f. terms means retaining the risk of fluctuations of effectively three separate markets (the one for the commodity itself, the freight and the insurance) where opting for an f.o.b. solution leaves fluctuations in the freight and insurance markets for the buyer to bear. This is particularly significant when comparing a sale on "f.o.b. terms with additional carriage services" with a c. & f. contract: both arrangements see the seller providing the fixture and paying for it as agreed with the carrier; however, where the c. & f. contract involves an all-in quote by the seller who carries the risk of any increase (and the benefit of any reduction) in the cost of carriage, the f.o.b. seller would go immune from any such fluctuations: he may well have negotiated and paid for the contract of carriage but the risk and the benefits of variations in the freight market would clearly be for the buyer's account.[20]

*(ii) The parties to the contract of carriage*

Identifying correctly which of the parties to the sale contract is also a party to the carriage contract allows for the correct identification of the terms on which this contract is concluded, i.e. the terms on which the carrier may be eventually sued to recover losses arisen in transit.[21] From what we have seen above it follows that in c.i.f. and c.f.r. contracts the seller is the original party to the carriage contract – e.g. a voyage charterparty, a contract of affreightment or liner booking – and the terms of his agreement with the carrier will always be found in that original contract.[22] However, as soon as a negotiable bill of lading is transferred by the seller to the buyer in exchange for payment, the buyer acquires rights of suit under the contract evidenced in the bill.[23] In this situation both seller and buyer will have an enforceable contract with the carrier but the terms of such contract will be contained in different documents, the seller's agreement being recorded in the charterparty (or other agreement arrived at between them) and the buyer's in the bill of lading. The situation changes considerably when the sale contract is concluded on f.o.b. terms. In the case of bare f.o.b. contracts, where the charterparty is negotiated and fixed by the buyer as charterer, the buyer is and will always be the carrier's original contractor and the terms of the agreement between buyer and carrier will be – at all material times – contained in the charterparty, whether or not a bill of lading is issued and tendered.[24] The situation remains factually unaltered in f.o.b. classic arrangements when the charterparty is concluded

20. *Scottish & Newcastle International Ltd v Othon Ghalanos Ltd* [2008] UKHL 11, at [35] (HL).
21. See again Chapter 3.
22. *Rodocanachi, Sons & Co v Milburn Brothers* (1887) LR 18 QBD 67 (CA).
23. *Tate & Lyle, Ltd v Hain Steamship Company Ltd* [1936] 2 All ER 597, (1936) 55 Ll L Rep 159 (HL). Where a "straight consigned bill of lading" or a seawaybill is issued the buyer acquires rights of suit under that contract at the time of issue by virtue of being identified as the consignee by the document itself and transfer of the document will not be necessary; see COGSA 1992, s. 2(1)(b).
24. *President of India v Metcalfe Shipping Ltd (The Dunelmia)* [1970] 1 QB 289, [1969] 2 Lloyd's Rep 476 (CA).

by the seller as agent for the buyer. However, if additional carriage services are added to the f.o.b. seller's duty the situation is reversed and the buyer – non-charterer – will only become a party to a contract of carriage through transfer of the bill of lading and on the terms of such bill.

## 3. THE PASSING OF RISK AND PROPERTY IN THE GOODS

The parties to every sale contract are concerned about the quality and condition of the goods they trade but – when the sale involved is an international one – there is a further cause for concern: to reach their buyers the goods sold have to be carried across international political and geographical boundaries. It may well happen that such goods are shipped in lorries at the producers' plant, transhipped onto barges or lighters, transhipped again on a seagoing vessel to be discharged at destination only several weeks after they left the seller. While carried, the goods are in the control of a network of carriers, independent contractors working neither as agents of the seller nor for the buyer. But what happens if the goods are damaged or lost in transit? Although both the carrier (or his liability insurer) and the cargo insurer will provide compensation for transit losses, within the framework discussed elsewhere in this work,[25] the identity of the party which will be actually damaged by the loss depends on the answer to a rather different question: who bears the risk of loss of or damage to the goods while in transit?

According to the maxim *res perit domino* only the owner of the cargo can suffer an actual loss out of his cargo being lost or damaged. And in fact section 20 of the Sale of Goods Act 1979[26] clearly states that: "Unless otherwise agreed, the goods remain at the seller's risk until the property in them is transferred to the buyer [...]." However, when goods are sold on shipment terms the situation is more elaborate and risk and property are very seldom transferred at the same time.

### (a) Risk passes on or as from shipment

Given the key importance of risk in international trade transactions it may happen that the parties expressly clarify the allocation of transit risks in their contracts with *ad hoc* clauses saying, for example, that "risk ... shall pass to Buyers at the loading port or terminal as the oil passes the loading vessel's permanent hose connection". In such cases it is clear that risk of transit loss will pass to the buyer at that very precise moment in time. On the other hand, if the parties have not given special consideration to the issue of risk, risk will pass according to the kind of contract stipulated by the parties.

In *ex works* contracts the seller's duty is to place the goods at the disposal of the buyer for collection at the seller's or another named place (warehouse/factory, etc) not loaded on any collecting vehicle,[27] whereas the buyer has the duty to take delivery of them and to make his own transit arrangements from that point to their final destination.[28] The main consequence of this is that the risk of transit loss rests with the buyer from the point of collection at seller's premises

25. See Chapters 3 and 10.
26. (c. 54). The Act covering the sale of goods in the UK.
27. Incoterms 2000 EXW, A4.
28. *Ibid.*, B4.

onwards.[29] At the opposite end of the spectrum, in contracts concluded on *D terms* the seller undertakes to arrange the carriage of the goods to the named destination in the country of import, whereas the buyer has to take delivery only if the goods he receives at destination are as agreed in the contract. From this it follows that the risk for transit damage to or loss of the goods whilst being carried rests squarely with the seller.[30] If the sale is concluded on *shipment terms* either the seller (in c.i.f. and c. & f./CFR sales) or the buyer (in f.o.b. sales) may undertake to make transport arrangements but delivery of the goods takes always place on board the nominated vessel at the port of shipment.[31] If the obligation of the seller is one to deliver the goods on board a vessel – in other words to *ship* the goods – it must follow that the risk of transit loss of such goods passes from the seller to the buyer from that moment on, i.e. *on (or as from) shipment* irrespective of where the property in the goods lies.[32] The fact that the buyer does bear such a significant risk is, however, balanced by some degree of control over the goods through the documents which the seller has delivered to it: by holding a bill of lading which gives constructive possession of the goods, the buyer can ask the carrier for the goods and sell them on; by becoming a party to the contract of carriage with the carrier, it acquires title to sue the carrier in case the goods are damaged in transit[33] and finally by being the beneficiary under the contract of insurance, the buyer has recourse against the insurer for transit loss.[34]

The rule that risk in goods passes on or *as from shipment* also responds to the commercial reality that a seller might have shipped goods before it has reached a binding agreement with a buyer or situations where a trader might have sold goods it has yet to buy. In these cases, if the goods are lost or damaged in transit prior to the conclusion of the contract of sale, it is still the buyer who bears retroactively the risk for such loss and its duty to pay the seller against conforming documents remains unaffected. But what if a buyer of goods in transit with knowledge that the goods have perished sells on to another buyer? Does this on-buyer inherit retroactively a risk which has already materialised in a loss? It is here suggested that whether the seller's duty is one to ***ship*** *goods of the contract description* or one to *procure the same goods* ***shipped*** *as promised*, the obligation of the seller under a sale contract on shipment terms is one to *ship* the goods, never one to deliver them at destination. Hence, in order to understand whether the risk has passed to the buyer, the right questions to be asked should be: (a) did the seller procure goods that – *at the time of shipment* – conformed to the requirements set in the sale contract? (b) Do the documents tendered evidence that goods of the contract description were in fact shipped? Were both questions answered in the affirmative the seller has performed his duty and risk lies with the buyer.[35]

29. *Ibid.*, A5 and B5.
30. E.g. "Ex Ship deliveries: The risk and property in the crude oil delivered under the agreement shall pass to the Buyer as the crude oil passes the Vessel's permanent hose connection at the Discharge Port". See also Incoterms 2000 DES, A5 and B5.
31. Incoterms 2000 CIF, A4; CFR, A4 and FOB, A4.
32. *The Julia* (1948–49) 82 Ll L Rep 270, at p. 271; the presumption made by s. 20(2) of the Sale of Goods Act 1979 (hereinafter "SOGA 1979") is that the risk passes together with property is defeated by the express choice of the parties of contracting on shipment terms.
33. See COGSA 1992 and Chapter 3.
34. See Chapter 10.
35. *Manbre Saccharine Co Ltd v Corn Products Co Ltd* [1919] 1 KB 198; *C Groom Ltd v Barber* [1915] 1 KB 316. To the same conclusion Debattista, *The Sale of Goods Carried by Sea* (2nd ed) (London,

### (b) The exceptions to the rule

The rule that risk passes on or as from shipment is not without exceptions which – if triggered – would relieve the buyer from bearing all or part of the risk of transit loss or damages. Such exceptions may be divided into two main categories: (i) the *contractual exceptions* arising out of express agreement between the parties, and (ii) the *legal exceptions*, when they find their source in statutory provisions or in the Common Law. They will be dealt with in turn.

#### *(i) Contractual exceptions*

In the exercise of their freedom of contract the parties may well decide to allocate the risks associated with the carriage of the goods sold as they see fit. In practice this is usually done with specifically drafted *out turn* clauses commonly related to the quantity,[36] quality or condition[37] of the cargo at the port of discharge. Such clauses usually provide for an adjustment in price in case the commodity reaches destination falling short – in quantity, quality or condition as the case may be – of the contract specifications with the effect of reversing the risk of such losses back onto the seller's shoulders.[38] *Out turn* clauses are interpreted strictly *contra proferentem* by the courts and hence do not cover the total loss of the consignment.[39]

#### *(ii) Legal exceptions*

Whether or not the contract contains specific clauses on the reallocation of risks, both the Sale of Goods Act 1979 and the Common Law provide for a limited number of exceptions to the rule that risk passes on or as from shipment. The legal exceptions are five: (i) where delivery has been delayed through the fault of the seller any loss which might not have occurred but for such fault is for the seller's account;[40] (ii) where the seller acts as bailee or custodier of the goods, losses caused by breach of the duty to take reasonable care of such goods is for the seller's account;[41] (iii) where the seller has failed to make a reasonable contract of carriage for the benefit of the buyer, the loss of or damage to the goods is also

---

1998), (hereinafter "*Debattista*"), chap. 4; and Sassoon, *c.i.f. and f.o.b. contracts* (4th ed) (London, 1995), (hereinafter "*Sassoon*"), para 253. *Contra*, for cases of total loss in c.i.f. contracts only see *Couturier v Hastie* (1856) 5 HLC 673. See also Goode, *Commercial Law* (3rd ed) (London, 2004), (hereinafter "*Goode*"), at pp. 942–943; and Guest (ed), *Benjamin's Sale of Goods* (7th ed) (London, 2006), (hereinafter "*Benjamin*"), para. 19-113.

36. E.g. providing for the out turn quantity "to be settled at the market price of the last day of discharge of the last ship to arrive", FOSFA 54, cl. 16, l. 171.
37. Typically providing for a discount proportional to the deterioration in the quality or condition of one or more items of the description; e.g. GAFTA 119, cl. 5.
38. The seller at this stage has probably lost its title to sue the carrier under s. 2(5) of the Carriage of Goods by Sea Act 1992 and care shall be taken to ensure the out turn clause provides expressly for an assignment back of the buyer's action against the carrier.
39. *Soon Hua Seng Co Ltd v Glencore Grain Ltd* [1996] 1 Lloyd's Rep 398 (QBD), *per* Mance J at p. 405: "If the goods covered by the shipping documents and invoice are lost in transit and do not arrive at all, the risk of loss remains on the buyers and no question of any adjustment to the payment due against the commercial invoice can arise."
40. SOGA 1979, s. 20(2) and *Gatoil International Inc v Tradox Petroleum Ltd (The Rio Sun)* [1985] 1 Lloyd's Rep 350.
41. SOGA 1979, s. 20(3).

for the seller to bear;[42] (iv) if the seller has failed to pass on information to enable the buyer to insure goods during their sea transit, again the goods will be at the seller's risk during such sea transit;[43] and finally (v) if the consignment gets damaged or lost in transit because its condition at the time of shipment was such as to make it unlikely to withstand normal sea transit, they will be at seller's rather than at buyer's risk.[44]

### (c) Property passes when intended to pass

Although the transfer of risk is certainly a more significant issue to traders, there are circumstances in which it may be important to establish where property in the goods lies, the most obvious being where it is necessary to start a tortious action against the carrier[45] or where either of the parties becomes insolvent. The default position under the Sale of Goods Act is that property will pass at such time as the parties to the contract intend it to be transferred,[46] such intention to be ascertained having regard to the terms of the contract, the conduct of the parties and the circumstances of the case.[47]

So, where the contract makes it clear that the property in the goods shall only pass on payment of the price or on delivery of the relevant shipping document then the situation is clear. In case the contract is silent about the transfer of property, it will be necessary to refer to section 18 of the Act which provides a series of rebuttable presumptions, the most relevant for international commercial sales being that where there is a contract for the sale of unascertained or future goods by description, and the goods are unconditionally appropriated to the contract through delivery to a carrier, the property in the goods passes to the buyer at the time of delivery to such carrier.[48]

## 4. PERFORMANCE OF THE CONTRACT

The Sale of Goods Act states very clearly that a sale contract is an agreement by which the seller undertakes to deliver the goods in accordance with the terms of the contract of sale.[49] However, in international commercial sales on shipment terms *physical* delivery of the goods is not enough to discharge the seller's duty as to delivery: he has also a *documentary* duty to tender the documents agreed upon in the contract.[50] The duties to deliver goods and documents are separate and independent from each other[51] and will be dealt with in turn.

42. SOGA 1979, s. 32(2); see also F Lorenzon, "When is a CIF seller's carriage contract unreasonable? – section 32(2) of the Sale of Goods Act 1979" (2007) 13 JIML 241 (hereinafter "*Lorenzon*").
43. SOGA 1979, s. 32(3).
44. *Mash & Murrell Ltd v Joseph I Emanuel Ltd* [1961] 2 Lloyd's Rep 326 (CA).
45. *Leigh & Sillivan Ltd v Aliakmon Shipping Co Ltd (The Aliakmon)* [1986] AC 785; [1986] 2 Lloyd's Rep 1 (HL).
46. SOGA 1979, s. 17(1).
47. *Ibid.*, s. 17(2).
48. *Ibid.*, s. 18, Rule 5(1). For goods shipped commingled see Rule 5(3) and (4).
49. *Ibid.*, s. 27.
50. *Arnhold Karberg & Co v Blythe, Green, Jourdain & Co* [1916] 1 KB 495 (CA).
51. *Kwei Tek Chao & Others v British Traders and Shippers Ltd* [1954] 2 QB 459; [1954] 1 Lloyd's Rep 16.

### (a) The seller's physical duties

On the physical side the seller must (a) ship *contractual goods*, (b) *as agreed* in the sale contract. What the expression "contractual goods" actually means under English law and how accurately it needs to follow the shipping instructions agreed in the contract will be the subject of the following paragraphs.

#### *(i) Shipping contractual goods ...*

The most obvious obligation imposed on the seller by any sale contract is the duty to ship *exactly* the goods it has promised. However, the extent of precision with which the seller has to perform this basic obligation and the remedies of the buyer for breach of such duty vary according to the *nature* of the contractual term at stake. Under English law, contractual terms relating to the goods are in fact considered either by express choice of the parties, by the relevant market and/or by the law as being so crucial to the trade concerned that their breach gives the buyer the option of rejecting the goods and terminate the contract.

Traditionally contractual clauses have been classified in three different categories: (a) *warranties*, the breach of which entitles the innocent party to a claim in damages; (b) *conditions*, the breach of which gives the innocent party the further option to bring the contract to an abrupt end; and (c) *intermediate* (or *innominate*) terms, whose breach may afford the innocent party the right to terminate provided it may prove that the breach in question went to the root of the contract concerned. Since this classification has very powerful effects on the life itself of the transaction it is crucial for both buyer and seller to be able to identify which terms of their contract are conditions and which are not. The test to be applied here has been authoritatively summarised in *Chitty on Contracts*[52] and recently approved by the Court of Appeal in *The Seaflower*[53] as follows:

"... a term of a contract will be held to be a condition:
(i) If it is expressly so provided *by statute*;
(ii) If it has been so categorised as the result of *previous judicial decision* [...];
(iii) If it is so designated *in the contract* or if the consequences of its breach, that is, the right of the innocent party to treat itself as discharged, are provided for expressly in the contract; or
(iv) If the nature of the contract of the subject-matter or the circumstances of the case lead to the conclusion that *the parties must, by necessary implication, have intended that the innocent party would be discharged* from further performance of his obligations in the event that the term was not fully and precisely complied with."[54]

If a term in a contract falls within any of the four limbs of this definition, then the parties' rights and liabilities are sharp and clear.

*Conditions by contract*: Limbs (iii) and (iv) above may be collectively defined as *conditions by contract* on the ground that they find their source in the freedom of the parties to determine the terms of their agreement although it must be said that judges are increasingly reluctant to imply conditions under limb (iv). The

52. H G Beale (ed), *Chitty on Contracts* (29th ed) (London, 2004), (hereinafter "*Chitty*"), para [12-040].
53. *B S & N Ltd (BVI) v Micado Shipping Ltd (Malta) (The Seaflower) (No 1)* [2001] 1 Lloyd's Rep 341.
54. *Ibid.*, at p. 348.

bottom line here is that if a particular feature of the goods to be shipped is of crucial importance to the buyer it should be proactive and draft a clause in his contract whereby delivery of goods without such feature would give it the right to reject the consignment.

*Conditions by law*: On the other hand, clauses falling within limbs (i) and (ii) of the test may be collectively classified as *conditions by law* as they find their source either in statutory provisions or in the Common law. Under English law the Sale of Goods Act 1979 implies three types of conditions into all sale contracts.

(1) *Terms describing the goods*: Section 13 of the Sale of Goods Act 1979 states that where there is a contract for the sale of goods by description, there is an implied condition that the goods will correspond with the description.[55] The key here is that the contract prevails and that if the parties have agreed to allowances and/or price adjustments in their agreements the courts will infer that that particular item of the description was not regarded by the parties as a condition at all. However, where the contract is silent, the court will make its decision on the basis of evidence from the market as to whether the description of the goods in the contract went to the identity of the commodity sold.[56]

(2) *The goods must be of satisfactory quality*: Section 14 of the Sale of Goods Act 1979 further provides that where the seller sells goods in the course of a business, there is an implied term that the goods supplied under the contract are of satisfactory quality;[57] this implied term is a condition.[58] In the attempt to clarify what it is intended by satisfactory quality, the Act regards as satisfactory the quality of goods meeting "the standard that a reasonable person would regard as satisfactory, taking account of any description of the goods, the price (if relevant) and all the other relevant circumstances".[59] Moreover, the quality of the goods is said to include their state, condition, fitness for all the purposes for which goods of the kind in question are commonly supplied, appearance and finish, freedom from minor defects, safety, and durability.[60]

(3) *The case of goods sold as per sample*: The third implied condition established by the Sale of Goods Act 1979 relates to the special case of goods sold per sample. A contract of sale is a contract for sale by sample where there is an express or implied term in the contract to that effect.[61] In this case there is an implied condition that the bulk will correspond with the sample in quality[62] and that the goods will be free from any qualitative defect which would not be apparent on reasonable examination of the sample.[63]

Having examined the three conditions implied by the Act, the next question to be addressed is whether any breach – however slight – of these terms entitles the

55. SOGA 1979, s. 13.
56. *Tradax Internacional SA v Goldschmidt SA* [1977] 2 Lloyd's Rep 604.
57. SOGA 1979, s. 14(2).
58. *Ibid.*, s. 14(6).
59. *Ibid.*, s. 14(2A).
60. *Ibid.*, s. 14(2B); on durability in the context of shipment sale as to capability to withstand normal sea transit see again *Mash & Murrell v Emanuel*, fn. 44.
61. SOGA 1979, s. 15(1).
62. *Ibid.*, s. 15(2)(a).
63. *Ibid.*, s. 15(2)(c).

buyer to terminate the contract or whether, together with the term, the law implies also a leeway: the current position is not entirely clear. Section 15A of the Act,[64] provides that where the buyer has the right to reject goods by reason of a breach on the part of the seller of a term implied by sections 13, 14, or 15 of the Act but the breach is so slight that it would be unreasonable for it to reject them[65] (burden on the seller[66]), the breach may be treated as a breach of warranty.[67] If the discrepancy falls within the known *de minimis* allowance implied by common law the buyer would not be allowed to reject the goods.[68] It is, however, clear that section 15A is an attempt to broaden considerably the scope of the *de minimis* allowance to avoid so-called technical rejections. On the other hand, this section only applies unless a contrary intention appears in, or is to be implied from, the contract[69] and this is almost invariably the case in commodity sales where allowances and adjustments are commonly catered for or incorporated by reference.

Apart from the Sale of Goods Act itself, the Common law has also made substantial contributions to the categorisation of terms in sale contracts. So terms about the time[70] and place[71] of shipment and the quantity[72] of the goods to be shipped have traditionally been considered as part of the description of the goods and as such held to be conditions. As far as the quantity of the goods is concerned the Sale of Goods Act (in its amended version) softened the harshness of the buyer's remedy by adding that it may not reject the whole consignment for short nor excess delivery if such shortfall or, as the case may be, excess is so slight that it would be unreasonable for it to do so.[73] This subsection being subject to any usage of trade, special agreement or course of dealing between the parties[74] – it is submitted – should not ordinarily apply to c.i.f. and f.o.b. sales.

### *(ii) ... as agreed in the sale contract.*

Selecting the goods for shipment represents of course only part of the physical duties owed by the seller to his buyer: such goods now need be *delivered as agreed* in the sale contract. This obviously *physical* duty in shipment sales – both on c.i.f. and f.o.b. terms – is performed by loading the goods on board the vessel fixed by seller or buyer respectively. Section 32(1) of the Sale of Goods Act in fact provides that where the seller is required to send the goods to the buyer, delivery of the goods to a carrier for the purpose of transmission to the buyer is *prima facie* deemed to be a delivery of the goods to the buyer.[75] Two issues are crucial here: (i) this is

64. Inserted by the Sale and Supply of Goods Act 1994, s. 4(1).
65. SOGA 1979, s. 15A(1)(a).
66. *Ibid.*, s. 15A(3).
67. *Ibid.*, s. 15A(1)(b).
68. *Arcos Ltd v. E A Ronaasen & Son* (1933) 45 Ll L Rep 33, [1933] AC 470, at p. 479, *per* Lord Atkin: "No doubt there may be microscopic deviations which businessmen and therefore lawyers will ignore", (HL).
69. SOGA 1979, s. 15A(2).
70. *Bowes v Shand* (1876–77) LR 2 App Cas 455 (HL).
71. *Petrograde Inc v Stinnes Handel GmbH* [1995] 1 Lloyd's Rep 142.
72. *In Re an Arbitration between Keighley Maxted & Co and Bryan Durant & Co* [1893] 1 QB 405, (1894) 7 Asp MLC 418.
73. SOGA 1979, s. 30(2A).
74. *Ibid.*, s. 30(5).
75. *Ibid.*, s. 32(1). In the context of f.o.b. sales, see *Scottish & Newcastle International Ltd v Othon Ghalanos Ltd* [2008] UKHL 11 (HL).

and remains at all material times a *physical* duty to load and stow the cargo in the manner and on the vessel agreed in the sale contract; and (ii) the remedy available to the buyer for breach of such duty will depend entirely on the terms of the sale contract.

As already discussed the duty to make transport arrangement may fall on either the seller or the buyer depending on the terms on which the shipment sale has been concluded. In f.o.b. sales where the contract of carriage is concluded directly by the buyer, the physical duties related to the choice of the vessel her route and – often – the details of the loading operations will be agreed upon by the buyer itself at the outset and are unlikely to cause any disputes, at any rate between the parties to the sale contract. On the other hand, where the shipping and carriage arrangements are made by the seller, he ought to comply with the prescriptions contained in the purchase agreement. The seller's duties with regards to the terms of the contract of carriage, at any rate when English law applies to such contract, are to be found in the contract of sale itself (or in the letter of credit) and in section 32(2) of the Sale of Goods Act 1979.

*The sale contract*: Naturally the buyer is entitled to carriage arrangements it has stipulated for in the contract of sale. So if the sale contract provides for a vessel of a given class or tonnage, imposes restrictions on previous cargos or flag, reefer temperatures or any other specific requirements, the seller shall make the transport arrangement it promised. The fact that the promise is contained in the confirmation note or any of the incorporated standard forms or rules is clearly irrelevant as they are all part of the same agreement.

*The letter of credit*: A letter of credit is a promise by a bank to pay to the beneficiary – *qua* seller – up to the amount of the credit against presentation of the documents stipulated therein.[76] As the agreed method of payment of the contract price, the credit will invariably contain – expressly or through incorporation of the UCP 600[77] – details relating to the carriage documents to be presented by the seller in order to collect payment. This has two consequences: (i) the bank will honour payment only to a seller who tenders the documents as required by the letter of credit[78] and consequently (ii) shipment will have to be made so as to allow the issue of such documents or certificates. An example may clarify this matter: if shipment on a vessel of a specific class was not required by the sale contract but the letter of credit requires tender of a given class certificate issued by an, for example, IACS[79] member, the bank will honour the credit only if the seller tenders such a certificate and hence duty to ship as agreed in the contract can only be performed by shipping on board a vessel classed by a member of the Association.

Section 32(2) of the Sale of Goods Act 1979 provides that any other features of the contract of carriage tendered by the seller must be "reasonable having regard to the nature of the goods and the other circumstances of the case" and, if they are not, risk does not pass to the buyer leaving the seller responsible for transit

76. *United City Merchants (Investments) Ltd v Royal Bank of Canada (The American Accord)* [1982] 2 Lloyd's Rep 1, [1983] 1 AC 168 (HL); see below.
77. ICC Uniform Customs and Practice for Documentary Credits, 2007 Revision, ICC Publication No. 600 (hereinafter "*UCP 600*").
78. UCP 600, Article 2 and 14(a).
79. The International Association of Classification Societies.

loss.[80] The authorities available appear to suggest that the word "reasonable" in this section has a three-fold meaning: the seller must provide a contract of carriage (a) on usual terms,[81] (b) giving the buyer "protective rights"[82] against the carrier, and (c) which is appropriate[83] to grant sufficient protection to the goods while in transit.[84] At this stage, it may also be interesting to notice the different choice of wording made in the Incoterms 2000. The corresponding provisions there – e.g. Article CIF A3(a) – describes the seller's duty as one to tender a contract of carriage on "usual terms". However, the Article further prescribes that the carriage of the goods must be made "to the named port of destination by the usual route in a seagoing vessel of the type normally used for the transport of goods of the contract description"[85] which clearly indicates that – under the Incoterms – the choice has been made to allow the seller to arrange for whatever transport arrangement the market regards as "usual" in the trade concerned, provided it meets the above requirements.

If it is certainly true to say that the seller must make a contract of carriage which conforms to the contract of sale (or the letter of credit) and which is reasonable or usual as the case may be, it is also true to say that this does not imply that the seller guarantees to the buyer any degree of success in an action against the carrier[86] who is certainly entitled to all the protection and exclusion offered to it by the applicable national and international legislation.[87]

### (b) The seller's documentary duties

Shipping goods as agreed in the sale contract only fulfils part of the seller's duties under the sale contract; in order to get paid for his goods the seller will also have to tender to the buyer the documents it has promised. The duty to tender documents together with (and at times instead of) goods is deeply embedded in the concept of shipment sale which are also referred to as *documentary* sales on shipment terms. The matter is hardly one of definition, both the physical and documentary tenders being essential parts of the performance of the sale contract.

Which documents will have to be tendered by the seller will clearly depend on the wording of the relevant agreement. Confirmation notes and standard form contracts will invariably list a number of documents to be tendered and will often spell out some of the characteristics these documents will have to have. In general terms, however, it can be said that two documents are essential to every shipment sale: the *commercial invoice* with which the seller quantifies his credit and a clean shipped on board *bill of lading*. If the goods are sold on c.i.f. terms the seller will also need to tender an *insurance policy* covering marine risks and any

80. SOGA 1979, s. 32(2).
81. *The Northern Progress (No 2)*, fn. 14; and the other authorities cited in *Lorenzon*, at pp. 242 *et seq.*
82. *Elof Hansson v Hamel and Horley* [1922] 2 AC 36, (1922) 10 Lloyd's Rep 507 (HL).
83. *Texas Instruments Ltd and Others v Nason (Europe) Ltd and Others* [1991] 1 Lloyd's Rep 146; *Gatoil International Inc v Tradax Petroleum Ltd (The Rio Sun)*, see fn. 40.
84. *Thomas Young and Sons Ltd v Hobson and Partner* (1949) 65 TLR 365.
85. CIF Incoterms 2000, Art. A3(a).
86. *M Golodetz & Co Inc v Czarnikow-Rionda Co Inc (The Galatia)* [1979] 2 Lloyd's Rep 450, approved by the Court of Appeal at [1980] 1 Lloyd's Rep 453.
87. See Chapter 3 and *Jindal Iron and Steel Co Ltd and Others v Islamic Solidarity Shipping Co Jordan Inc (The Jordan II)* [2004] UKHL 49; [2005]1 Lloyd's Rep 57 (HL).

additional risks agreed for in the sale contract.[88] The importance of the documents is crucial to both seller and buyer for different reasons: as far as the seller is concerned, it will only be paid if it can tender the documents promised under the sale contract, physical performance being insufficient to trigger the buyer's duty to pay the price. For the buyer – on the other hand – the documents provide it with evidence of physical performance, possessory rights over the goods and contractual rights against the carrier and the insurer. Where a letter of credit has been agreed as the method of payment for the goods in question, the credit itself will ask for a list of documents to be tendered, each with specific requirements.

Among the many documents which may be asked for in exchange for payment, the most complex and important is the bill of lading for it performs three crucial functions: (1) it provides evidence of a contract of carriage with the carrier and title to sue such carrier on its terms; (2) it gives constructive possession of the goods and hence the right to control and dispose of them; (3) it functions as a receipt for the goods shipped. Most aspects of the law relating to bills of lading have already been discussed in the preceding chapter on cargo claims.[89] It will be recalled that the focus there was on the rights and liabilities of the carrier *vis-à-vis* cargo interests and on how such action can be brought under English law. The following paragraphs will focus on an entirely different, although connected, issue: what kind of bill of lading is the seller to tender to his buyer in order to be entitled to payment? The answer to this question will depend entirely on the method of payment agreed between the parties: "net cash against documents" or via a letter of credit governed by the UCP 600.

*(i) To the buyer under the sale contract in cash against documents transactions*

If there is no letter of credit, the seller is bound to tender to the buyer the documents listed in the sale contract.[90] It must be emphasised that very often the confirmation note contains some specific requirements regarding the most obvious or crucial documents to be tendered. However, often several documentary requirements are contained in standard forms incorporated by reference; in such cases the buyer will be entitled to all documents provided for in the note plus every additional document listed in the standard form's documents clause. It is worth noting that when the parties incorporate Incoterms 2000, the requirement becomes one to tender the "usual proof of delivery" if the contract is on FOB terms or the "usual transport document" in case of CFR or CIF sales. In the latter scenario the transport document tendered must:

- cover the contract goods;
- be dated within the period agreed for shipment;
- enable the buyer to claim the goods from the carrier at the port of destination; and
- unless otherwise agreed, enable the buyer to sell the goods in transit by the transfer of the document to a subsequent buyer or by notification to the carrier.[91]

88. See Chapter 10.
89. See Chapter 3.
90. *Bergerco USA v Vegoil Ltd* [1984] 1 Lloyd's Rep 440.
91. Incoterms 2000, CFR and CIF terms, A8.

In case the sale contract refers only to the "usual shipping documents" it will be necessary for the party (and the arbitrator or judge) to ascertain what is usual between the parties to that contract, the custom of the particular trade concerned and – where English law applies to the contract – the English common law. The most relevant requirements the bill must have to be acceptable to the buyer are that the bill must cover the goods which are the subject matter of the contract,[92] be made out in transferable form,[93] give the buyer a right of action against the carrier[94] and be clean.[95]

*Time of presentation.* If the sale contract provides for tender by a given time, the documents must be tendered within such time, the provision being regarded as a condition of the contract.[96] If the contract is silent, the seller must tender as soon as possible after shipment.[97]

When the contract stipulates for payment to be made via a letter of credit, all the above will have only very limited relevance to ascertain the seller's documentary duties under the sale contract.

*(ii) To the bank under the letter of credit*

In commercial sales of commodities the parties commonly agree for the buyer to pay via letter of credit; in such cases the only way for the seller to get to the contract money is through tender of the documents to the bank instructed by its buyer.

LETTERS OF CREDIT AND THE WAY THEY WORK

A letter of credit is – in essence – a series of contracts involving the buyer, one or more banks and the seller,[98] allowing documents and money to change hands in opposite directions, giving the buyer rigorous documentary screening before payment is made on its behalf and giving the seller an additional solvent debtor within its own jurisdiction. The system works as follows: the buyer instructs its bank to open a credit in favour of the seller for the amount of the purchase price. Naturally the buyer must open a credit which conforms to the specifications spelled out in the sale contract. This *issuing* bank will then correspond with a bank within the seller's jurisdiction, which will either *advise* the seller of the opening of the credit in its favour, or *confirm* the credit opened by the issuing bank adding its own direct undertaking to pay the purchase price. At this stage the advising or confirming bank will send the letter of credit to the seller – the beneficiary under the credit – containing a list of documents to be presented in order to obtain release of the money.

Once the letter of credit is received by the seller, the banks' promise becomes irrevocable[99] and the payment mechanism becomes active. This is not to say that

92. *In Re an Arbitration between Keighley, Maxted & Co and Bryan, Durant & Co*, see fn. 72.
93. *Soproma SpA v Marine and Animal By-Products Corp* [1966] 1 Lloyd's Rep 367. For a full list see Halsbury's Laws of England, Vol. 41, *Sale of goods and supply of services* (4th ed) (London, 2005), para. 332.
94. *Buckman v Levi* (1813) 3 Camp 414; *Lorenzon*, at p. 246.
95. *The Galatia*, fn. 86; see Chapter 3.
96. *Toepfer (Hamburg) v Lenersan-Poortman NV (Rotterdam)* [1980] 1 Lloyd's Rep 143 (CA).
97. *C Sharpe & Co Ltd v Nosawa & Co* [1917] 2 KB 814.
98. *The Bank of Baroda v The Vysya Bank Ltd* [1994] 2 Lloyd's Rep 87, at p. 90.
99. UCP 600, Art. 2.

the beneficiary itself is bound by it as yet: the letter of credit is a unilateral contract which – as payment – may well be rejected *vis-à-vis* the buyer if it does not meet the requirements set for it in the sale contract. So, where the credit was agreed to be confirmed and it is not, or where it requires tender of different documents from the ones agreed in the sale contract, the seller would be certainly entitled to reject it and withhold shipment of the goods.[100] In other words, the buyer is not entitled to amend the seller's documentary duties after the contract of sale has been concluded. On the other hand acceptance of a non-conforming credit – both express or through conduct – has been held to amount to a new agreement capable to modify the contract of sale itself.[101]

Once accepted, the letter of credit becomes the only method of payment available to the seller. Hence, tender of the document provided for in the letter of credit has a dual effect: on the one hand (i) it constitutes documentary performance under the sale contract, and on the other (ii) it triggers the bank's duties under the credit. At this stage the bank will carefully examine the bundle to make sure to part with money only where the documents presented comply with the applicant's instructions as they appear in the credit. If they do, the confirming bank will release the funds and pass on the documents to the issuing bank for reimbursement and then eventually to the buyer; if they do not the bank will refuse payment and return the documents. But what criteria will the bank follow to make such a crucial decision?

## THE UCP 600

The Uniform Customs and Practice for Documentary Credits are – in essence – standard terms setting out duties and liabilities of the parties to the letters of credit in which they are incorporated.[102] They are drafted and regularly amended by the International Chamber of Commerce in Paris and they have no international nor – as far as England is concerned – national standing at all. This notwithstanding, their incorporation in letters of credit is almost universal and their acceptance by bankers and traders alike makes them an essential tool to understand international commercial sales and supply agreements. In its current edition in force from 1 July 2007 (the UCP 600) they apply to any documentary credit "where the text of the credit expressly indicates that it is subject to these rules. They are binding on all parties thereto, unless expressly modified or excluded by the credit";[103] in practice they are the universal rule of the game, the instructions the seller has to follow to convert documents into hard cash.

The duties and liabilities of the bank as to the examination and scrutiny of the documents – collectively referred to as *presentation* – are scrupulously defined and limited by the UCP 600 and the decision on whether to accept them or not must be made strictly "on the basis of the documents alone".[104] At common law

100. *Soproma SpA v Marine and Animal By-Products Corp*, fn. 93.
101. *Panoutsos v Raymond Hadley Corp of New York* [1917] 2 KB 473 (CA); *Enrico Furst & Co v W E Fischer Ltd* [1960] 2 Lloyd's Rep 340; *W J Alan & Co Ltd v El Nasr Export & Import Co* [1972] 2 QB 189 (CA); *Ficom SA v Societad Cadex Ltda* [1980] 2 Lloyd's Rep 118; *Glencore Grain Rotterdam v Lebanese Organisation for International Commerce (The Lorico)* [1997] 4 All ER 514; [1997] 2 Lloyd's Rep 386 (CA).
102. UCP 600, Art. 1.
103. *Ibid.*
104. UCP 600, Arts. 5 and 14(a).

the position is clear: the presentation is acceptable only if made in *strict compliance* with the terms set in the letter of credit; as Lord Sumner once put it: "There is no room for documents which are almost the same, or which will do just as well…."[105] This case was, however, decided by the House of Lords in 1926, in a pre-UCP banking era.

Under the UCP 600 the strict duty imposed by the Common law is heavily corrected by a series of carefully drafted clauses according to which banks must examine the presentation to determine whether or not the documents appear *on their face*[106] to be in accordance with the terms and conditions of the credit, the UCP 600 themselves and international standard banking practice.[107] Moreover, in documents other than the commercial invoice the description of the goods, services or performance, may not be stated at all or be in general terms not conflicting with their description in the credit.[108] Furthermore, banks assume "no liability or responsibility for the form, sufficiency, accuracy, genuineness, falsification or legal effect of any documents …".[109] These "disclaimers" have two main functions: (i) on the one hand they have the clear intent to protect the banks from liabilities which the duty of strict compliance would undoubtedly impose on them; (ii) on the other they allow banks a certain amount of flexibility hence permitting to the credit to be a reliable and prompt payment mechanism.

BILLS OF LADING UNDER THE UCP 600

A full account of all detailed requirements the UCP set for the acceptability of bills of lading goes beyond the scope of this work.[110] What must be clarified is that the bank, by opening the letter of credit and parting with money against documents, exposes itself to the risks of being unable to be reimbursed by its customer, either because the applicant declines a non conforming presentation or becomes insolvent. In this case the bank will have an actual – as opposed to vested – interest in getting as much security as it can from the documents and that is where the terms on which shipping documents are issued become extremely important.[111] For these reasons, the UCP 600 list several requirements bills of lading have to comply with in order to be acceptable under the credit. Such requisites may be usefully grouped according to the kind of security the bank (and its customer) may be interested in obtaining from the document in: (a) requirements related to the bill as a contract of carriage giving enforceable rights against a contracting carrier; (b) requirements connected to the bill as a document of title to goods; and (c) particulars concerning its function as a receipt.

Broadly speaking, (a) as a *contract of carriage* the bill of lading to be acceptable has to:

105. *Equitable Trust Co of New York v Dawson Partners Ltd* (1926) 25 Ll L Rep 90.
106. UCP 600, Art. 14(a).
107. *Ibid.*, Art. 2.
108. *Ibid.*, Art. 14(e).
109. *Ibid.*, Art. 34.
110. For a full account see C Debattista, "The New UCP 600 – Changes to Tender of the Seller's Shipping Documents under Letters of Credit" (2007) 4 JBL 329.
111. For a full discussion on shipping documents as a form of security for banks involved in letters of credit see C Debattista, "Banks and the Carriage of Goods by Sea: Secure Transport Documents and the UCP 500" [1994] BJIBFL 329.

(i) appear to indicate the name of the carrier;[112]
(ii) indicate that the goods have been actually shipped on board;[113]
(iii) be made out from the port of loading to the port of discharge indicated in the credit;[114]
(iv) contain the terms of the contract of carriage.[115]

It must be noted, however, that the UCP 600 do not require the bill to be made out in such a way to give title to sue the carrier under COGSA 1992: detailed indication on how and to whom the bill will have to be made out is left to the applicant and the bank to decide and hence are invariably contained in the letter of credit itself rather than the UCP.[116] Once the credit makes such stipulation, the bank will only pay against a bill complying with it.

Secondly, in case something goes wrong with the reimbursement arrangement, the bank has a clear interest in being able to sell the bill of lading on and recover its losses. This may only be achieved if the bill of lading is (b) a negotiable *document of title* giving the bank constructive possession of the goods. Again here the UCP 600 does not contain express requirements on the issue other than for the fact that the bill has to be the sole original or, if issued in set, it must be tendered as a full set.[117]

Finally, (c) as a receipt the bill must:

(i) describe the goods in a way which is not inconsistent with the description of the goods in the credit;[118]
(ii) contain data which is not conflicting with data in other parts of the document, any other stipulated document or the credit;[119] and
(iii) bear no clause or notation expressly declaring a defective condition of the goods or their packaging.[120]

THE DECISION TO PAY OR NOT TO PAY

It is now been seen that the bank is called to decide on the basis of the documents alone whether the presentation has been made in accordance to the requirements expressly set in the letter of credit, the UCP 600 when incorporated and international standard banking practice. To reach its decision, the UCP 600 Article 14(b) gives the bank "a maximum of five banking days following the day of presentation". Delay in deciding whether or not to pay may well lead to the bank being estopped from denying that the documents conform to the credit.[121] If the bank decides that one or more of the documents tendered are not in compliance with the terms and conditions of the credit, in order to avoid liability for breach of contract *vis-à-vis* the applicant it will have to reject the documents.

112. UCP 600, Art. 20(a)(i).
113. *Ibid.*, Art. 20(a)(ii).
114. *Ibid.*, Art. 20(a)(iii).
115. *Ibid.*, Art. 20(a)(v) and (vi).
116. See Chapter 3.
117. UCP 600, Art. 20(a)(iv).
118. *Ibid.*, Art. 14(e).
119. *Ibid.*, Art. 14(d).
120. *Ibid.*, Art. 27.
121. *Ibid.*, Art. 14(f).

*Time for presentation.* It is clear that where the letter of credit stipulates a period for tender from the shipment date, the seller must tender the transport document by that date. Article 6(e) of UCP 600 provides that documents must be presented on or before such expiry date. If any of the above dates fall on a non-business day, then the documents must be tendered on the subsequent banking day.[122]

## 5. REJECTION: THE BUYER'S REMEDY AND THE SELLER'S RIGHT TO CURE

In c.i.f. and f.o.b. contracts, cancellation by rejection may be much more complex than in ordinary sales on delivery terms as the seller actually performs *two* types of delivery, the *documentary* tender and the *physical delivery* of goods. Moreover, whereas the law considers physical delivery the one which takes place at the place and time of shipment, the buyer will have the right to inspect its cargo only several days or weeks later at the port of discharge, at a time when – possibly – it has already taken delivery of the documents, directly or through its bank. Finally, the costs of rejecting the consignment at the port of discharge are significant and would involve further negotiations (and expenses) aimed at rerouting the vessel to a new buyer or storing the unwanted cargo at the original discharge port awaiting resale.

Moreover, it will be remembered that the physical duty to ship the consignment on board the vessel and the documentary duty to tender the agreed documentation run neatly separate and independent from each other and have been independently dealt with above. From this follows that serious breaches of each one of them will give the buyer separate and independent rights of termination: a physical breach of condition will entitle to rejection of the goods and termination of the sale contract where a breach of the documentary duty to tender contractual documents will entitle the buyer (and the bank) to reject the presentation, withhold payment and terminate the contract in its own right.[123] The further practical difficulty is that documents and goods will rarely reach the buyer at the same time making it even more difficult for it to decide whether or not it actually wishes to terminate: if documents reach the buyer before arrival of the goods, in spotting a documentary defect the buyer may actually wish to withhold its right to reject them awaiting physical inspection of the actual cargo, particularly against a rising market. At the opposite side of the spectrum the buyer may have no option to reject the documentary tender as the documents may well be in order, whereas the goods – on discharge – may tell a completely different story. Moreover, where banks are involved with the scrutiny of documents, the decision as to whether the presentation is complying or not with the terms of the credit will be based exclusively on the examination of the documents and no regard will be paid to the condition of the goods on shipment.[124] For this reason the position of buyers and banks with regard to rejection will be dealt with separately.

122. UCP 600, Art. 29(a).
123. *James Finlay & Co Ltd v Kwik Hoo Tong Handel Maatschappij* [1929] 1 KB 400, (1928) 32 Ll L Rep 245; *Kwei Tek Chao & Others v British Traders and Shippers Ltd*, fn. 51.
124. UCP 600, Art. 5.

### (a) Rejection of goods and documents by the buyer

The right to reject documents is completely separate and independent from the right to reject goods. The position under English law is quite clear: accepting the documentary tender does not have any implications on the separate and independent right to reject the physical tender on inspection.[125] This principle, however, is not absolute but has two important exceptions: (i) when the contract of sale provides for physical performance to be exclusively evidenced by documents, and (ii) when the buyer accepts a documentary tender providing clear evidence of a fatal defect in the *physical* tender. The two exceptions will be dealt with in turn.

#### *(i) Documentary final evidence of physical performance*

The duties to ship the consignment within a certain date or in a given quantity or again to load goods of a specific description are clearly all physical duties the seller has to perform. These duties have been all classified as conditions of the sale contract, breach of which entitles the buyer to reject the goods and declare termination. However, while the seller performs these duties at the time and place of shipment, the buyer will be able to verify physical compliance only much later, at the time and place of discharge. Moreover, in order to rightfully reject the cargo the buyer will have to provide evidence that the goods were non-conforming to the contractual specs at the time and place of shipment, when – at best – it was not there to check. It is hence very common for sale contracts – in particular in commodity trades – to provide for *documentary evidence of physical performance* and to make such evidence *"final" between the parties*: non-rebuttable. So the date of shipment may well be said to be "final as per bill of lading" and the quantity and quality of the goods "final as per certificate issued by independent surveyor", so to provide both parties with conclusive evidence of what has been shipped.

When the parties have agreed upon such terms, breach of the physical duty in question may only be evidenced through the stipulated documents and where the documents indicate correct physical performance the buyer will not be entitled to refuse delivery of a non conforming cargo: it is *estopped (by convention)* from doing so unless it can prove fraud[126] on the part of the seller or a procedural breach in the collection or examination of the samples.[127]

#### *(ii) Acceptance of documents evidencing a physical repudiatory breach*

The other exception to the doctrine of independence of the physical and documentary duties arising under a sale contract is based on the Court of Appeal decision in *Panchaud Frères*.[128] In this case the buyers accepted and paid for documents among which there was a bill of lading indicating shipment within the shipment period and a certificate of inspection indicating that samples were collected at the port of loading ashore, *after* the last day allowed for shipment. The bill of lading was clearly antedated and the presentation could have been rejected as a whole, as evidencing shipment outside the permitted time window. On arrival the buyer

125. *Kwei Tek Chao & Others v British Traders and Shippers Ltd*, fn. 51.
126. *Gill & Duffus SA v Berger & Co Inc* [1984] AC 382; [1984] 1 Lloyd's Rep 227 (HL).
127. *Soon Hua Seng Co Ltd v Glencore Grain Ltd*, fn 39.
128. *Panchaud Frères SA v Etablissements General Grain Co* [1970] 1 Lloyd's Rep 53.

rejected the goods for breach of the *physical* duty to ship the consignment within the time stipulated in the contract. The buyers then sued the seller to recover the price paid against tender of documents but the claim was unsuccessful: Lord Denning MR held that by accepting documents indicating a defective condition of the goods the buyers are now *estopped (by conduct)* from rejecting the goods on the same grounds.

A last point needs to be made at this stage: what if the goods delivered are only in part compliant with the terms of the contract and the rest is not? Would it be possible for the buyer to take delivery of the good consignment and reject the bad one? The situation is considered by section 35A of the Sale of Goods Act which – in such cases – allows the buyer an option: reject the non-conforming goods while accepting the rest. The section provides as follows:

"If the buyer has the right to reject the goods [...] but accepts some of the goods, including, where there are any goods unaffected by the breach, all such goods, he does not by accepting them lose his right to reject the rest."

### (b) Rejection of documents by the bank

The bank's obligation with regard to honouring the credit is determined by the UCP 600 as one to honour[129] a complying presentation or refuse to honour a non-complying one.[130] The bank can hence commit either of two breaches: (a) paying against a non-complying presentation; or (b) refusing to pay against a complying presentation. Should the bank pay against defective documents, it will clearly have no action against the issuing bank or the applicant for reimbursement.[131] Should the bank refuse to pay under conforming documents the beneficiary will have a direct action for breach of the promise contained in the letter of credit.

In order to try and avoid such liabilities banks have two devices: if presented with non-complying documents the confirming bank may in its sole discretion approach the issuing bank and – in turn – the applicant for an advanced waiver of the discrepancy.[132] Once permission to pay is granted upstream the bank can safely pay the beneficiary without responsibility. Another way of avoiding liabilities for wrongful payment has been created through the practice of paying "under reserve" against documents known to be defective. However, where the bank is inclined to pay under reserve it has to take great care to clarify its rights and liabilities *vis-à-vis* the beneficiary in the under reserve arrangement itself so to avoid difficulties when the time to enforce such arrangement comes.[133]

Where the bank intends to reject, however, it is crucial it follows strictly the prescriptions contained in Article 16(c) of the UCP 600 according to which the bank *must* give a single notice of rejection containing three fundamental elements: (i) a statement that the bank is refusing to honour the credit; (ii) a list of each discrepancy in respect of which the rejection is grounded, and (iii) a declaration

129. UCP 600, Art. 15(a).
130. *Ibid.*, Art. 16(a).
131. *Credit Agricole Indosuez v Generale Bank and Seco Steel Trading Inc and Considar Inc (No 2)* [2000] 1 Lloyd's Rep 123.
132. UCP 600, Art. 16(b).
133. *Banque de l'Indochine et de Suez SA v JH Rayner (Mincing Lane) Ltd* [1983] 1 All ER 1137; [1983] 1 Lloyd's Rep 228; *Cooperative Centrale Raiffeisen-Boerenleenbank BA v Sumitomo Bank (The Royan, The Abukirk, The Bretagne, The Auvergne)* [1988] 2 Lloyd's Rep 250 (CA).

indicating what the bank is currently doing with the unsuccessful presentation. The importance of the formalities of such notice are signified by the draconian consequences the bank will have to face in case of failure to act in accordance with the provisions of the article: the bank shall in fact be precluded from claiming that the documents do not constitute a complying presentation and hence will be forced to pay or defend an action for non-payment by the beneficiary.[134]

### (c) The seller's right to cure a defective tender

The last question to be addressed is whether – on rejection – the seller has the right to cure physical and/or documentary defects. This issue is particularly relevant since were the buyer allowed to cure his defective performances the seller would still be bound to accept the new conforming performance and pay the contract price.

*Curing physical performance*: It is quite clear on the authorities and indeed on the wording of the Sale of Goods Act that if the physical tender was made in breach of condition the remedy available to the buyer is an absolute one: termination of contract.[135] Once the contract is terminated, the seller would be allowed to retender only if it can reach a new agreement with the buyer: in substance a new contract.

*Curing documentary tender in cash against documents transactions*: It is clear that when the sale contract allows or – more commonly – prohibits the seller to cure a defective tender, the court will give effect to such term. If the contract is silent, however it is here submitted that – at any rate where the parties did not provide for a time window for the tender of documents – it would not be possible for the seller to tender a complying presentation after a first non-conforming tender has been rejected. This is argued on the ground that documentary tender *is* performance of the contract and once the document tendered evidences (or is itself) a repudiatory breach, documentary performance is non-contractual and the buyer's remedy remains termination. On the other hand, where the contract provides for a time window for presentation of documents then the seller appears to be entitled to re-tender,[136] the documentary duty becoming a rather different one: to tender conforming documents *within the last available day*. On these terms there can be no breach until the time has elapsed.

*Curing documentary tender in letters of credit transactions*: It is clear that where the bank decides to reject the presentation, the seller has the right to re-tender provided it does so within the timeframe allowed by the credit. This is where the notice of rejection the bank must give[137] becomes most relevant as it notifies the beneficiary of the grounds on which payment has been refused and hence allows the seller to cure the documents and re-tender what should then be a complying presentation. The promise of the bank under the credit in fact still stands and a new complying presentation will still entitle the beneficiary to full payment provided such new tender is effected within both the expiry date of the credit[138] and the last day for presentation of documents.[139]

134. UCP 600, Art. 16(f).
135. SOGA 1979, ss. 13, 14 and 15; and discussion above.
136. *SIAT di Dal Ferro v Tradax Overseas SA* [1980] 1 Lloyd's Rep 53.
137. UCP 600, Art. 16(c).
138. *Ibid.*, Art. 6(e).
139. *Ibid.*, Art. 16(c).

CHAPTER 5

# Carriage of Passengers

*RICHARD SHAW*

## 1. INTRODUCTION

Claims arising as a result of accidents to passengers on ships have provided a fertile field for maritime lawyers since the loss of the *Titanic* in 1912.[1] An important distinction must, however, be drawn between *international* and *domestic* carriage of passengers. States with extensive ferry services as part of their transport network such as Norway and Greece tend to have elaborate domestic laws governing the liabilities of their passenger carriers. These are not the principal subject of this chapter.

Carriage of passengers between different States has, however, been governed for many years by the Athens Convention 1974 relating to the Carriage of Passengers and their Luggage by Sea, which entered into force in 1987.[2] Although this Convention is regarded by many governments as seriously out of date, attempts to introduce a new regime based on the Protocols of 1990 and 2002 have met with very limited success. A careful study of the Athens Convention 1974 is therefore a necessary starting point. The United Kingdom has incorporated the terms of the Athens Convention 1974 into the Merchant Shipping Act 1995[3] and applied its provisions, subject to increased limits, to the domestic carriage of passengers.[4]

## 2. THE ATHENS CONVENTION 1974 RELATING TO THE CARRIAGE OF PASSENGERS AND THEIR LUGGAGE BY SEA

This Convention has governed international carriage of passengers by the majority of major ship owning nations for the last 20 years and is generally considered to work satisfactorily, apart from the fact that the limits of liability are now seriously out of date. A major revision has been carried out by the 2002 Athens Protocol (see below) but there are serious doubts whether this protocol will ever enter into force.

1. White Star Line sought to limit their liability in the United States to the value of the life boats which were recovered and brought to New York with the survivors on board the "Carpathia" [1912] 209 Fed Rep 501, *New York Times*, 26 May 1912.
2. It has now (2008) been ratified or acceded to by 32 States.
3. Schedule 6.
4. MSA 1995, Schedule 6. See The Carriage of Passengers and their Luggage by Sea (Domestic Carriage) Order 1987, SI 1987 No 670 and also SI 1998 No 2917 by which the limit is now 300,000 SDRs per passenger.

### (a) Basis of liability

Article 3 of the Athens Convention 1974 relating to the Carriage of Passengers and their Luggage by Sea ("the Athens Convention") starts by reciting the common law position that the carrier is liable for damages caused by the death or injury of a passenger caused by the fault or neglect of its servants or agents acting within the scope of their employment. However, paragraph 3(3) provides that such fault or neglect is *presumed* if the death or injury arose from or in connection with shipwreck, collision, stranding, explosion, fire or defect in the ship, i.e. the burden of proof is reversed. However the burden of proving that the incident causing the loss or damage occurred in the course of the carriage still lies with the claimant.[5]

Article 1 provides that the Convention applies to the period while the passengers and their luggage are on the ship and not while they are, for example, in a terminal ashore, but it does extend to passage by launch to and from the ship if that service is provided by the carrier. Note also that it only applies to injuries suffered as a result of "marine" risks but not to "hotel" risks such as cabins and food.

### (b) Limit of liability

Article 7 provides for a limit of the carrier's liability of 46,666 Special Drawing Rights (SDR) per carriage.[6] The 1990 Protocol attempted to increase this to 175,000 SDR ($285,200) but this has not achieved any ratifications.[7] The UK has, however, unilaterally increased the limit per passenger to 300,000 SDR ($488,928 or £245,940), following the *Herald of Free Enterprise* casualty.

Article 13 provides for *loss of the right to limit liability* in the event of intentional harm or recklessness in terms similar to Article 4 of the 1976 Limitation Convention.[8]

Article 16 provides for a *two-year time-bar* for the bringing of legal proceedings, unless an extension of time has been agreed in writing, and Article 17 contains elaborate provisions as to the jurisdiction in which the claimant may sue; but note that Article 17(2) permits the parties to agree *after* the incident causing the damage, to any jurisdiction or to arbitration.

## 3. THE 2002 PROTOCOL TO THE ATHENS CONVENTION

The need for revision of the limits in the Athens Convention was recognised by the International Maritime Organization ("IMO"),[9] and a diplomatic conference in 2002 adopted the Protocol to the Athens Convention, which attempts to make a number of important changes to the regime. Liability to passengers for injury resulting from shipping accidents[10] (i.e. not "hotel risks") is strict (the claimant does not have to prove negligence on the part of the carrier or his servants) up to

5. Article 3, para. 2.
6. Equivalent in April 2008 to £38,257 or US$76,055. For latest equivalent rates see *www.imf.org/external/np/fin/data/rms_five.aspx*
7. This figure has been adopted by the Scandinavian countries.
8. See Chapter 6, p. 211.
9. See Chapter 9, p. 312.
10. Defined in Article 3, para. 5, a remarkably cumbersome piece of drafting.

250,000 SDRs, with the possibility of further liability up to a maximum figure of 400,000 SDR but with the burden of proof on the claimant. The Protocol[11] does, however, allow States to provide in their national law for liability to be higher, or unlimited.

The Protocol also contains provisions, similar to those in the Oil Pollution Liability Conventions, for compulsory liability insurance of passenger carriers and with direct action against the insurer.[12] A Certificate of Financial Responsibility will be required for each passenger ship carrying more than 12 passengers.

These provisions, combined with the higher limits, caused considerable concern in the world of marine liability insurance, particularly in the International Group of P&I Clubs.[13] The steadily increasing size of passenger ships has raised the spectre of a major accident on a ship carrying more than 3,500 passengers and 1,500 crew. At the Diplomatic Conference in 2002 a leading underwriter stated that insurance to meet the Protocol's requirements, particularly with unlimited reinstatements after a casualty, was simply not available on the market. Subsequent events have proved this to be correct, and States which have signed the Protocol have been unable to bring it into force because they are unable to issue the Certificates of Financial Responsibility required.

At the October 2006 meeting of the IMO Legal Committee a set of guidelines were adopted to enable States to implement the Athens Convention as amended by the 2002 Protocol.[14] These permit States to ratify the Protocol subject to a reservation limiting the Certificate to the level of insurance available, but the outcome is still uncertain.

## 4. INTERACTION BETWEEN THE ATHENS CONVENTION AND THE 1976 AND 1996 CONVENTIONS ON LIMITATION OF LIABILITY FOR MARITIME CLAIMS

The topic of limitation of a shipowner's liability will be covered in detail in Chapter 6 (*Liabilities of the Vessel*), but it is important to understand how the limitation provisions in the Athens Convention will interact with those applicable under the general regime of shipowner's limited liability. As has been explained, the underlying principle of the Athens Convention is a presumption of fault on the part of the carrier if the death or injury of a passenger is caused by a maritime accident,[15] but that liability is limited to 46,666 SDR per passenger. However, the 1976 Convention on Limitation of Liability for Maritime Claims ("1976 LLMC") contains a different structure. The liability of the carrier must be established before that convention can apply at all, and only then will the carrier be entitled to the benefit of its provisions. In brief there are two limitation funds under 1976 LLMC, one for death and injury claims and a smaller fund for "ordinary" damage claims. Each fund is calculated by reference to the tonnage of the ship[16] multiplied

11. Article 6.
12. See Chapter 8, p. 254.
13. See Chapter 10, p. 340.
14. IMO Circular letter no 2758 dated 20 November 2006 and annexed documents at *www.imodocs.imo.org*
15. Shipwreck, collision, stranding explosion or fire (Art. 3(3)).
16. Calculated in accordance with the 1969 Tonnage Convention.

by a sliding scale of SDR,[17] but in addition there is a ceiling of 46,666 SDR multiplied by the number of passengers which the ship is *authorised to carry*, irrespective of the number of passengers actually on board at the time of the accident, or 25 million SDR whichever is the less.

In a case in which a small number of passengers suffer serious injury, the total amount of their claims will be limited by reference to the total number of passengers which the ship is licensed to carry or the 25 million SDR maximum, so in reality their claims are unlikely to be reduced by these provisions. However, in addition, unless they are on a British or Scandinavian ship, they are likely to have their claims reduced to the limit of 46,666 *per capita* if the Athens Convention applies.

The 1996 Protocol to 1976 LLMC ("1996 LLMC") contains an important modification to this regime in Article 7 by allowing States Parties to adopt legislation on claims for loss of life or personal injury which are more favourable than those provided in Article 7 of the Protocol. Some States, notably Japan, have removed this ceiling altogether.

In the UK on the other hand, until the Merchant Shipping Act 1995 applied the limitation provisions of the 1976 LLMC to vessels which are not sea-going, the provisions of the Athens Convention and 1976 LLMC did not apply to them. Thus the claims of the passengers on the Thames Cruise Boat *Marchioness*, which sank following collision with the dredger *Bowbelle* in 1989,[18] were not subject to any limitation regime.

## 5. THE REAL WORLD

The resultant effects of these provisions are not as harsh in reality as they may seem. Students will note that there are in fact very few reported cases of death and injury claims being pursued through the courts. This is because such claims are invariably covered by the carrier's Protection and Indemnity ("P&I") insurance, and it is the policy of the P&I Clubs which insure virtually all the world's fleet of passenger ships to seek amicable settlement of such claims out of court. The principal value of the limitation provisions in the Athens and LLMC Conventions is therefore to curb the excess zeal of claimants' legal advisors, and to foster realistic settlements.

## 6. QUANTUM OF DAMAGES FOR DEATH AND INJURY

The English courts have always been somewhat ungenerous to death and injury claimants, particularly when compared with the awards in other jurisdictions such as the United States.

The following are the principal heads of claim available to personal injury plaintiffs in the English courts:

(a) medical expenses;
(b) pain and suffering (past, present and future);

17. Article 6.
18. With the loss of 51 lives.

(c) loss of amenity;
(d) lost earnings (past, present and future).

In the case of *death*, the claim will be made by the personal representatives of the deceased, and will include:

(a) medical, funeral and testamentary expenses, including expenses in connection with a coroner's inquest;
(b) the deceased's pain and suffering prior to death;
(c) damages under the Fatal Accidents Acts (currently £11,800) to specified dependents;
(d) dependency claims by those (e.g. spouse, children or aged parents) whom the deceased was supporting prior to death. Such claims will reflect the likely duration of such payments if the deceased had survived, taking into account their circumstances and state of health.

## 7. FORUM SHOPPING

The level of death and injury awards in the United States courts (most of which are assessed by a jury) means that in any marine casualty with an international dimension the lawyers acting for death and injury claimants will always explore the possibility of pursuing their claims in the USA. The key question will be whether the accident involves a "US element" sufficient to justify the establishment of US jurisdiction.

The advantages of bringing a claim in the US from the plaintiffs' point of view include:

(a) higher levels of damages;
(b) lawyers will accept instructions on a contingency fee basis (now available in the UK in some circumstances);
(c) penetrating discovery procedures;
(d) no liability to pay the defendant's costs;
(e) class actions.

The possibility of obtaining an award of "punitive damages" in a shipping case in the USA is a myth. There is no recorded maritime case in the US where such damages have been awarded, but it is fair to say that no defendant (or their insurance company) wants to be the first.

The threat of such proceedings in a case involving a maritime casualty in Europe has in many cases led to a "Mid-Atlantic Settlement" at a figure substantially higher than that obtainable in the English courts.

## 8. THE EU PACKAGE TRAVEL DIRECTIVE

This Directive[19] was introduced in 1990, and is a part of the law of all Member States of the European Union. It applies to all travel which is part of a prearranged set of services sold or offered for sale at an inclusive price covering a

19. Directive 90/314/EEC incorporated into English Law by the Package Travel, Package Holidays and Package Tours Regulations 1992, SI 1992 No 3288.

period of more than 24 hours or including an overnight stay and which combines at least two of:

- transport;
- accommodation;
- any other tourist services not related to transport or accommodation which account for a significant proportion of the package price.

Thus, for example, the purchase of a ticket for the transport sector of a holiday alone will not be covered by this Directive.

Articles 4 and 5 of the Directive provide protection to consumers in relation to descriptive matters and the contents of brochures; Article 6 sets out circumstances in which particulars in a brochure are to be binding on an operator. Articles 7 and 8 impose on the operator the obligation in a timely way to provide certain appropriate information. Article 9 sets out certain minimum requirements as to the contents and form of the relevant contract, including the provision that "all the terms of the contract are set out in writing or such other form as is comprehensible and accessible to the consumer". Articles 10 to 14 provide the consumer with protection in relation to the transfer of bookings, price revision, significant alteration of essential terms and significant proportion of services not provided.

Article 15 provides:

"Liability of other party to the contract for proper performance of obligations under contract

(1) The other party to the contract is liable to the consumer for the proper performance of the obligations under the contract, irrespective of whether such obligations are to be performed by that other party or by suppliers of services ...

(2) The other party to the contract is liable to the consumer for any damage caused to him by the failure to perform the contract or the improper performance of the contract ...

(3) In the case of damage arising from the non-performance or improper performance of the services involved in the package, the contract may provide for compensation to be limited in accordance with the international conventions which govern such services.

(4) In the case of damage other than personal injury resulting from the non-performance or improper performance of the services involved in the package, the contract may include a term limiting the amount of compensation which will be paid to the consumer, provided that the limitation is not unreasonable."

The interaction between this Directive and the Athens Convention has been the subject of two legal decisions in UK County Court which are difficult to reconcile with each other and with the Convention. In the first case, *Lee and Another v Airtours Holidays Ltd and Another*,[20] decided in April 2002, Judge Hallgarten QC held that the provisions of the Directive were part of UK domestic law and should be applied unless the provisions of the Convention were specifically referred to in the contract, which they were not on the facts of that case (where a booking was made by internet).

However, in *Norfolk v My Travel Group plc*,[21] Judge Overend in the Plymouth County Court held in August 2003 that the Athens Convention was given the force of law in the UK by section 183 of the Merchant Shipping Act 1995, and that the Athens Convention therefore applied even where there was no express

20. [2004] 1 Lloyd's Rep 683.
21. [2004] 1 Lloyd's Rep 106.

reference to it in the contract. He also held that the two-year time-bar in the Convention did not conflict with the terms of the Directive.

Judge Overend did not refer to the decision in *Lee v Airtours* in the course of his judgment nor indeed to the cases cited by Judge Hallgarten, although that case had been decided one year earlier. He did, however, rely heavily on the comments of Lord Hope in the House of Lords case of *Sidhu and Others v British Airways plc, Abnett (known as Sykes) v British Airways plc*,[22] which concerned the interaction of the Warsaw Convention and common law claims by passengers in an aircraft, and which was not cited in *Lee v Airtours*.

On a broader basis, there is an apparent conflict between the terms of the Directive and the express terms of Articles 11 and 14 of the Athens Convention, which demonstrate that it is intended that the code contained in the Convention applicable to claims against a carrier should also apply to claims against the servants or agents of the carrier, and, more important, that no claims by passengers should be brought otherwise than in accordance with the Convention. Judge Overend relied on these provisions in *Norfolk v My Travel*. It is strongly arguable that the provisions of the EU Directive, to the extent that they conflict with it, amount to a breach by the member States of their treaty obligations to the other States parties to the Athens Convention.

It is noteworthy that at the time of writing (April 2008) the decisions in *Lee v Airtours* and *Norfolk v My Travel* have not been cited judicially in any other reported case.

22. [1997] 2 Lloyd's Rep 76; [1997] AC 430 (HL).
23. In an article ([2004] JIML 10(3) 243) the author commented that the need for a distinction between the protection of a passenger by sea and a passenger by sea as part of a package holiday was "curious and probably unconvincing".

CHAPTER 6

# The Liabilities of the Vessel

*RICHARD SHAW AND DR MICHAEL TSIMPLIS*

## 1. INTRODUCTION[1]

This chapter deals with liabilities arising from the vessel's operation. These are usually called "wet" topics, to contrast with what are called the "dry" aspects of maritime law which usually refer to cargo and charterparty claims. In this book contracts for the carriage of passengers and cargo as well as charterparty claims are dealt with in separate chapters.[2] Marine pollution which includes an expanding body of rules and international conventions is also described separately.[3]

The aspects of liability we consider in this chapter are those arising from collisions, salvage and towage as well as liability for wreck removal, damage to harbours and damage occurring when the vessel is under the command of a pilot. The final section of this chapter discusses the privilege granted to shipowners and others to limit their liability in respect of some types of claim.

## 2. COLLISIONS

### (a) Introduction

Collisions between ships inevitably lead to claims, and frequently to litigation.[4] The cases reported in the law reports are principally concerned with the establishment of what exactly occurred – what the lawyers call "the facts" – and the application to those facts of well-established principles of law. The cause of action pleaded in every collision case is that of negligence. In English law that is defined as the breach of a recognised duty of care owed to a person who may reasonably be foreseen to suffer loss as a direct result of that breach.[5]

The principal procedural issue in every case is the choice of jurisdiction for the collision litigation. In most cases this issue is resolved by agreement between the parties, or, more frequently, between their insurers, since the financial consequences of collision are invariably covered in large measure by the insurances on the ships involved.[6]

1. Sections 1, 4 and 5 have been written by Richard Shaw and sections 2, 3, 6 and 7 by Michael Tsimplis.
2. In Chapters 5, 2 and 3 respectively.
3. See Chapter 8.
4. The leading legal textbook on collision litigation is *Marsden on Collisions at Sea* (13th ed) (Sweet & Maxwell, 2003). This is an extremely detailed treatment of this topic, and is not suited to student study.
5. *Donoghue v Stevenson* [1932] AC 562.
6. See Institute Time Clauses (Hulls) 1.10.83, clauses 6.2.3 and 8.

### (b) Insurance interests concerned

In arriving at an understanding of the practical working of collision litigation it is important to understand the involvement of the insurance interests concerned. These may be summarised as follows:

(i) Hull Underwriters
- repairs to damage suffered by the insured ship;
- voyage and port expenses at port where repairs can be effected;
- salvage and General Average – insured ship's proportion;
- RDC – 3/4ths of third party liability for damage to the other colliding ship and cargo.[7]

(ii) P&I Club[8]
- 1/4th RDC, if not covered by the hull insurer;
- death and/or personal injury claims;
- pollution;
- liability (if any) to cargo on entered vessel;
- other entered risks.

(iii) Defence (FD & D) Club[9]
Proportion of legal fees attributable to recovery of owner's loss of earnings claim and other uninsured items of claim.

(iv) Shipowner
Loss of earnings due to detention for collision damage repairs.

As the collision litigation evolves it will be important for the lawyer to keep each of these interests advised of significant developments, and to seek their approval to any major step, such as a choice of venue for the litigation or the terms of any proposed settlement.

In the immediate aftermath of a collision there are many important arrangements to be made, and the lawyer will probably be the coordinator of most of those arrangements including surveys, security, the collection of all relevant ship's documents and the taking of statements from the ship's witnesses.

### (c) Surveys

(i) damage suffered by the client ship as a result of the collision;
(ii) damage suffered by the opponent's ship as a result of the collision (without prejudice to liability);
(iii) speed and angle of blow – based on the damage to both ships.

### (d) Security

A letter of guarantee is usually issued by the P&I Club of the ship concerned to guarantee payment of whatever damages are due and payable at the conclusion of the litigation. The form of such a guarantee is negotiable, but in English practice

7. Some hull insurers, notably those in France, Germany and Scandinavia, usually cover 4/4ths RDC.
8. See Chapter 10, p. 337.
9. Usually called "Freight Demurrage and Defence Association".

all collision security is now given on the terms of the standard forms published by the City of London Admiralty Solicitors Group.[10]

### (e) Investigation of a collision

Following a major accident such as a collision at sea it is imperative that the facts should be established with reasonable certainty as quickly as possible. The lawyer conducting such an investigation, usually a solicitor or experienced legal executive, must assemble all the ship's documents including log books, charts and any automatic data logging devices installed on the ship. They will then interview the officers and crew members on watch on the bridge and in the engine room, and any other member of the crew who saw anything relevant, and prepare a written statement of each witness's evidence. Such statements are, according to the English Civil Procedure Rules, *privileged.* That is to say that the statements cannot be forcibly disclosed to the other parties to the litigation without the agreement of the party on whose behalf they were made.[11] In practice most such statements are disclosed in English collision proceedings and treated as evidence of the facts described, except where the witness is called to give oral evidence. This results in a significant saving of time and costs.

### (f) Independent evidence

Such evidence is always of considerable value in a collision case, but it is not always easy to obtain. The Speed and Angle of Blow Survey Report is in a sense independent, since it is based on the crumpled metal of both ships, but it is always also an expression of professional opinion, albeit that of an experienced engineer surveyor. Better evidentiary value will be given by, for example, a video-tape recording of the radar showing movements of the ships concerned made by an official body such as Dover Coastguard[12] or other Vessel Traffic Surveillance (VTS) service.[13] The lawyer should act quickly to ensure that the recordings are preserved. Most such bodies will take a scrupulously neutral stance, making the information and tapes available to all parties involved.

Occasionally independent evidence may be obtained from the officer on watch on another ship in the vicinity of the collision, who may have observed the movements of the two ships on radar. Although discovering the existence of such evidence may be difficult, the wise practitioner is well advised to spend time, and if necessary money, to follow up such enquiries, since the value of such independent evidence can be very significant.

### (g) Choice of jurisdiction

This is usually established by agreement, but in the absence of such agreement there may be an unseemly amount of manoeuvring by the parties to establish a

10. Available free of charge from *www.admiraltysolicitorsgroup.com*
11. In the United States such statements are disclosable, unless they can be categorised as "attorney's work product".
12. Which monitors and records all traffic passing though the Dover Strait from Langton Battery on the cliffs above Dover.
13. Such services are to be found in many major ports such as London and Southampton.

jurisdiction which favours their case.[14] This will require the appraisal of a range of factors, the most important of which is whether the ship for whom the lawyer is acting is likely to be the *recovering* or the *paying* party in the litigation. If the former, then the most desirable jurisdiction will be one in which a fair and objective judgment can be obtained as quickly as reasonably possible which will be such as can be enforced without undue procedural delays. The latter case would require a jurisdiction where the courts are not likely to be swayed by the large sums involved and where the principles of Limitation of Liability[15] will be applied effectively.

Such an appraisal will require an informed estimate both as to the probable division of blame between the two ships[16] and also of the likely amount of the damages ultimately recoverable. Neither of these will be available in the immediate aftermath of the collision, and the practitioner is therefore obliged to carry out continuous reappraisal of both as further information comes in from surveyors, shipowners and other parties involved in the litigation.

The English courts now recognise the principle, originally developed in civil law jurisdictions, of *forum non conveniens*. Where a court has to choose between one jurisdiction and another it will weigh many factors including the availability of witnesses, particularly pilots if they were on the bridge of one or both ships, or other sources of important evidence.[17]

The Collision (Civil Jurisdiction) Convention 1952[18] contains a number of rules for the establishment of jurisdiction in collision cases, but since these are expressly subject to contrary agreement between the parties, this convention is hardly ever applied in actual cases.

## (h) Principles of liability for collision

### *(i) The 1910 Collision Convention*

This Convention, incorporated into English law by the Maritime Conventions Act 1911,[19] introduced into England for the first time the principle of liability in proportion to blame, and thus the concept of contributory negligence. The owner of a ship involved in a collision is liable to make good the damage suffered as a result of the collision in proportion to that ship's *fault*.[20] The Convention does not define fault but it is recognised by the courts throughout the world that this effectively means a breach of the principles set out in the International Regulations for Preventing Collisions at Sea, which will be discussed below.

The two other important legal principles were established by this convention. firstly that where two or more ships involved in collision are in fault liability for death and personal injury shall be joint and several, subject to a right of recourse

14. See Chapter 1.
15. See below, p. 201.
16. As to which see below, Principles of liability.
17. *Owners of the Atlantic Star v Owners of the Bona Spes (The Atlantic Star and The Bona Spes)* [1973] 2 Lloyd's Rep 197 (HL) and *Owners of the Las Mercedes v Owners of the Abdin Daver (The Abidin Daver)* [1984] 1 Lloyd's Rep 339 (HL).
18. 439 UNTS 217, entered into force in 1955.
19. Now s. 187 of the Merchant Shipping Act 1995 (MSA1995).
20. Art. 4.

between the ships themselves,[21] and secondly that the time limit for bringing legal proceedings arising out of a collision shall be two years.[22]

It is significant that of all the maritime conventions adopted by the international shipping community in the twentieth century, the 1910 Collision Convention is the only one for which no amending convention or protocol has been sought internationally.

### *(ii) The International Regulations for Preventing Collisions at Sea*

These are a series of rules, agreed internationally under the 1972 IMO COLREGs Convention,[23] which form the basis for conduct to avoid collision between ships, and, where they fail in that regard (i.e. a collision takes place) for the assessment of blame for the collision.[24]

These rules have existed for centuries, but the latest version was produced in 1972, and is revised regularly, most recently in 2001.[25]

The cardinal principle is that ships "drive on the right" – when two ships are approaching each other in a narrow channel, or on opposite courses, they must pass port to port, keeping to the starboard side of mid-channel (Rule 9) and must alter course to starboard when approaching end-on (Rule 14). In a crossing situation the ship which has the other on her starboard side must give way (Rule 15).[26]

The 1972 Rules introduced for the first time (in Rule 10) the concept of "Traffic Separation Schemes" in congested waters such as the English Channel. In such schemes the traffic is channelled into one-way lanes separated by a zone through which normal traffic does not pass. Special lanes for coastal traffic are maintained on either side of the English Channel. There is no doubt that this scheme has significantly reduced the number of collisions in this busy seaway.

Special rules (set out in Rule 19) apply in restricted visibility, which is when most collisions take place. The steering and sailing Rules 11 to 18 apply *only* to vessels *in sight* of one another, and not to vessels navigating by reference to one another by radar in fog.

The Collision Regulations also contain detailed rules concerning lights and shapes to be displayed by vessels (Rules 20–30), and sound signals to be given by them (Rules 34–35).

### *(iii) Claims by the owners of cargo damaged or delayed by collision*

Cargo damaged as a result of a collision leads to the possibility of claims against the two colliding vessels:

21. Section 188 of the MSA 1995.
22. Art. 7 incorporated into English Law by s. 190 of the MSA 1995; this provision has given rise to a series of decisions, not easily reconciled, over whether the craft concerned was a "ship", including *Steedman v Scofield and Another* [1992] 2 Lloyd's Rep 163 and the decision of Lord Phillips CJ in *R v Goodwin (Mark)* [2005] EWCA Crim 3184 and [2006] 1 Lloyd's Rep 432, both of which involved collisions between personal watercraft sometimes called "jet-skis". For a detailed review of the subject see *http://webjcli.ncl.ac.uk/2006/issue2/grant2.html*
23. Convention on the International Regulations for Preventing Collisions at Sea, 1972.
24. To be found at *www.imo.org/Conventions/contents.asp?doc_id=649&topic_id=257*
25. Under the IMO "tacit acceptance procedure" – see Chapter 9. Entered into force in November 2003.
26. Note that the principles of "Common Sense" are preserved by Rule 2.

- a claim in tort against the *non-carrying* vessel, which should lead to recovery of that proportion of the claim which is equivalent to the proportion of blame falling on that ship;
- a claim in contract against the *carrying* vessel. Such a claim may well be met with the defence of negligence in the navigation of the vessel under Article 4 Rule 2(a) of the Hague and Hague-Visby Rules, unless the collision resulted from the incompetence of a watch-keeping officer amounting to unseaworthiness, or from a failure of the ship's equipment which itself rendered the ship unseaworthy.

### (i) The "Innocent Cargo" Rule in the USA

In the USA until 1975 blame in collision litigation was either 100% on one or other of the two colliding vessels, or divided equally. In 1975 the proportional fault principle was adopted by the US Supreme Court in the "*Reliable Transfer*" decision.[27] However, US law has always treated cargo as "innocent", and thus entitled to recover 100% of its claim from the non-carrying vessel if that vessel is in any way to blame, leaving the owners of that vessel to claim contribution from the other.

Such a recourse action would defeat the exoneration of the carrying vessel from the consequences of negligent navigation which is to be found in the US COGSA and the Hague and Hague-Visby Rules. Thus the "both to blame collision clause" was drafted whereby the carrying ship may claim recourse against the owners of cargo carried on board her for the proportion of the claim of any such cargo which is attributable to the blame of the carrying ship and which is included in the claim of the non-carrying ship against the carrying ship.[28]

Such a clause, whose tortuous wording has puzzled many a lawyer, finds its way into many charterparties, e.g. GENCON 1994, Cl. 11; ASBATANKVOY, Cl. 20(b)(iv).[29]

### (j) Remoteness and causation

If negligence is found by the court on the part of the crew of a colliding vessel, it will *only* be taken into consideration in the assessment of the division of blame if it is *causative* of the collision. Any negligence which is found by the court to be non-causative will be left out of the reckoning.[30]

In the assessment of blame the court will also take into account the "agony of the moment". If a wrongdoing ship causes another ship to take urgent manoeuvres to avoid collision, those manoeuvres will not be judged too harshly.[31]

### (k) Collision litigation in the Admiralty Court

In England collision cases are allocated to the Admiralty Court, which is part of the Queen's Bench Division of the High Court of Justice.[32] The applicable procedural

27. 421 US 397 (1975).
28. For the full text of this clause see *www.jseinc.org/document/bl/n&b.pdf*
29. Clause 3 of the Institute Cargo Clauses (A, B and C) covers cargo interests for this liability.
30. *Owners of the Global Mariner v Owners of the Atlantic Crusader (The Global Mariner and Atlantic Crusader)* [2005] 1 Lloyd's Rep 699.
31. *The Eglantine, Credo and Inez* [1990] 2 Lloyd's Rep 390.
32. Supreme Court Act 1982, s. 20.

rules are set out in Part 61 of the Civil Procedure Rules (CPR) and in the Admiralty Practice Direction.[33]

A detailed study of this procedure is beyond the scope of this work, but no study of collision litigation would be complete without a reference to two significant features of these rules. The document known as the "Collision Statement of Case", formerly known as the Preliminary Act, plays a unique role. It contains a series of questions relating to the circumstances of the collision, which each party is required to complete and file at the court without knowing the answers given by their opponents. Answers to the questions are considered to be admissions of fact by the party filing it, and that party cannot advance a case which is inconsistent with their Collision Statement of Case without the leave (permission) of the judge.

The second is the use of Elder Brethren of Trinity House, who are retired ships' masters who sit with the Admiralty Judge as Nautical Assessors, and advise him on matters of ship handling and seamanship. It is therefore not normally necessary for the parties to call expert evidence on these aspects.[34]

It is the usual practice in collision cases in England for the question of liability (the division of blame) for the collision to be decided separately from the quantum of damages. The sums recoverable in most collision cases are negotiated and settled directly between the solicitors for the parties, but in the event of failure to agree, the disputed item(s) will be decided by the Admiralty Registrar.[35]

## 3. SALVAGE

### (a) Introduction

The sea can be a dangerous place. A ship in difficulties cannot rely, unless very close to the coast, on assistance coming from land. The responsibility of the coastal States may be non-existent in areas beyond their jurisdiction or it may be only to assist by saving lives without any interest in preserving the ship or its cargo. In addition there is no general duty to save property at sea. Thus, historically, assistance was most likely to come from other passing ships, or from ships prepared to leave the safety of the port and willing to risk severe weather conditions in order to assist stricken vessels.[36]

In order to facilitate and encourage this practice public policy has been developed encouraging assistance to endangered vessels. This public policy consisted of three elements. First, by recognising that such assistance entitles the salvors of the property to a salvage reward; second, that the right to a salvage reward arises at the time of rendering assistance irrespective of any contract; and third, that this right is protected by a maritime claim of the highest priority, the salvage lien, and a right to arrest the salved property by an action *in rem*.

33. Note also the special rules applicable to collision cases in CPR 61.4 including those in paras 10–12 regarding recoverable legal costs following an offer to settle the division of liability.
34. For the way in which the advice of Nautical Assessors is used by the judge see *Owners of the Bow Spring v Owners of the Manzanillo II (The Bow Spring and the Manzanillo II)* [2005] 1 Lloyd's Rep 1.
35. See para. 13 of the Admiralty Practice Direction.
36. The public policy to encourage and reward assistance to endangered property is ancient. For more information see Hassan S Khalilieh, Admiralty amd Maritime Laws in the Mediterranean Sea (ca. 800–1050): the Kitab Akriyat al-Sufun *vis-à-vis* the Nomos Rhodion Nautikos, Brill, Ledien, 2006, n. 2 at p. 205.

The liability to pay the reward is incurred by the owners of the salved property in proportion to the relative values of their property. Thus the liability will not only attach to the shipowner but also to the cargo owners whose cargo has been saved from danger.

Problems also arise between the salvor and the shipowner. Clearly the recognition of a right to a salvage reward does not by itself resolve the manner in which the operation should be performed; the respective obligations of the salvor and the salved property; the place and the time when the property or ship is to be redelivered to its owner; or the provision of financial security to the salvor who is also worried that cargo owners may resist the payment of salvage. Moreover, negotiating the salvage reward cannot be made, in a situation of danger, at arm's length. For these reasons specialised salvage contracts providing solutions to the practical difficulties and setting out clearly the obligations of the parties, while leaving aside the determination of the salvage reward, have developed. The most influential of them, the Lloyd's Open Form (LOF), leaves open the reward to an arbitrator appointed by Lloyd's, thus avoiding negotiations and delays in helping the casualty. The LOF contract is associated with the No Cure–No Pay principle which reflects the general position in salvage that only where property is salved is there an entitlement to a salvage reward.

During the last 40 years marine pollution from shipping incidents has made salvage operations crucial not only for the preservation of property but also for the protection of the marine environment. However, it soon became clear that under the traditional salvage arrangements where no property was salved the salvor would not be able to get any reward, even where the salvor had made significant efforts to prevent marine pollution thus benefiting the owners and users of coastal resources and reducing the liability exposure of the shipowner.

As a response to pressure from salvage operators the 1980 LOF contract was modified to permit the recovery of the salvor's expenses where the salvage operation concerned oil tankers if the salvage reward under the No Cure–No Pay principle was insufficient. In addition the CMI with the encouragement of the IMO, salvors, and the International Groups of P&I Clubs started the process of reviewing pre-existing salvage law[37] and eventually developed the Montreal Draft Convention which provided for the foundations of the International Salvage Convention 1989 (hereinafter "The Salvage Convention").[38] The Salvage Convention significantly modified the reward scheme for salvage.

The Salvage Convention is presently consolidated in Schedule 11 to the Merchant Shipping Act 1995 after originally being enacted through the Merchant Shipping (Salvage and Pollution) Act 1994. The Salvage Convention is the salvage law for England overriding all pre-existing law of salvage. Only where the Salvage Convention is unclear or is silent there may be some freedom to get guidance from the pre-existing law of salvage. However, because international

37. The Convention for the Unification of Certain Rules of Law respecting Assistance and Salvage at Sea 1910 – the Brussels Salvage Convention 1910. Some Articles of this Convention were enacted into English Law by the Maritime Conventions Act 1911, ss. 6–8, but the Convention was never formally incorporated into English Law. See R Shaw, "The 1989 Salvage Convention and English Law" [1996] 2 LMCLQ 202.

38. Originally developed by the CMI. See: R Shaw, "The 1989 Salvage Convention and English Law" [1996] 2 LMCLQ 202.

conventions are exactly that, i.e. international, it is suggested that only where the pre-existing English law can be said to reflect international law such argument can be persuasive.[39] It is at least comforting to observe that the Salvage Convention is to an extent consistent with pre-existing English salvage law thus facilitating its interpretation.[40]

### (b) The Salvage Convention

The Salvage Convention applies in all cases where salvage matters are brought before an English court or an arbitration panel seated in England.[41] Thus it applies irrespective of the flag of the ships[42] involved or the area of the sea the salvage operation is undertaken. The UK has reduced the scope of the application of the Salvage Convention by excluding salvage operations that take place in inland waters[43] where all vessels involved are vessels of inland navigation, and excluding salvage in inland waters where no ships are involved.[44] The definition of inland waters provided within the same section excludes waters "within the ebb and flow" of the spring tide and any docks connected with such waters. When a vessel is one of inland navigation is unclear. The wording may have various meanings for example it may mean a vessel designed solely for inland navigation or one that is only employed in inland navigation, or one which was employed in inland navigation at the time of the incident necessitating salvage assistance.

Ships, craft and other structures capable of navigation as well as other property not permanently and intentionally attached to the shore can be the objects of salvage. Freight at risk is also subject to salvage. Pipelines and jetties are excluded from salvage because they are permanently and intentionally attached to the shore. By contrast cargo adrift or sunken would be subject to the salvage.[45] Drilling platforms whether floating, fixed or mobile are expressly excluded[46] from the application of the Salvage Convention when they are on location and engaged in their specific operation of drilling. However, when under way these structures are subject to salvage.[47]

For an operation to fall under the definition of salvage the relevant property must be in danger.[48] The Salvage Convention does not define the term danger.

39. Art. 31(1) The Vienna Convention on the Law of Treaties, 1969 requires that: "A treaty shall be interpreted in good faith in accordance with the ordinary meaning to be given to the terms of the treaty in their context and in the light of its object and purpose." While supplementary means of interpretation, such as the working documents of the treaty, are allowed under Art. 32 in special circumstances, reference to any national law or pre-existing Convention is arguably not permitted.
40. N Gaskell puts it as strongly as that the 1989 Salvage Convention effectively codifies pre-existing English law of salvage. The Merchant Shipping Act 1995, *Current Law Statutes Annotated.*
41. Art. 2.
42. Warships and State-owned vessels are generally excluded from the Salvage Convention unless a government has provided otherwise: Art. 4.
43. For the position before the Salvage Convention 1989, see *The Goring* [1988] 1 AC 631.
44. The UK entered a reservation under Art. 30 of the Convention which was then enacted in English law by Schedule 11, Part II, s. 2.
45. For the earlier narrower position under English law see *Wells and Another (Paupers) Appellant v The Owners of the Gas Float Whitton No 2 Respondents (The Gas Float Whitton No 2)* [1896] P 42 (CA), [1897] AC 337 (HL).
46. Art. 3.
47. *Owners of the Maridive VII, Maridive XIII, Maridive 85 and Maridive 94 v Owners and Demise Charterers of the Key Singapore* [2004] EWHC 2227; [2005] 1 All ER (Comm) 99; [2005] 1 Lloyd's Rep 91; 2004 WL 2458650.
48. Art. 1(a).

Under pre-existing English law the requirement was one of real danger, reasonably apprehended, and this appears to be accepted as the correct interpretation under the Salvage Convention too[49] in spite of the argument that the meaning should be given an international interpretation. The danger does not need to be present at the time of the sustained damage provided that it is reasonably expected that it will arise before self-help can remedy the situation. Thus, a ship immobilised by engine failure is generally in danger, even if the weather is calm or it is anchored, if there is no possibility for effective repairs to be performed.[50] A vessel breaking one mooring line and swinging around its mooring point may also be in danger if there is a risk of collision with a buoy,[51] or if it is unable to turn around in a strong current.[52] Whether the vessel is in danger or not is to be decided objectively by the judge or arbitrator. The Master's opinion is not conclusive in this respect[53] even if he is the person who will request or accept an offer for salvage assistance.

The salvor is under a duty to perform the salvage operation with due care and in doing so to minimise environmental damage and to seek assistance from other salvors if needed. If the salvor fails to fulfil these duties it may receive a reduced reward or no reward at all.[54] The owners of the property in danger are under an obligation to co-operate fully with the salvor; to prevent or minimise environmental damage and to accept redelivery at a place of safety. It is unclear what are the consequences if the owner of the property or the Master does not fulfil these obligations. If, for example, the owner fails to provide information of the cargo's nature to the salvor, and as a result the vessel and cargo are lost, would then the salvor be entitled to a salvage reward or some compensation? Similar questions can be posed in respect of the environmental duties of the salvor and the owner or Master. If there is no property salved then it is clear that no salvage award could be due. Thus the only available remedies to the salvor would arguably be either breach of the salvage contract, if there is one, or breach of the duties under Article 8 of the Salvage Convention 1989. However, the Salvage Convention 1989 does not specify such remedies.[55] In a similar example what would the sanctions be if the salvage is successfully performed but no party pays any attention to environmental protection, for example, by unnecessarily discharging oil at sea in order to refloat a grounded vessel? Within the Salvage Convention there does not appear to be any penalty for the owners of the property. For the salvor, one could argue that a smaller reward may be the penalty in view of the criteria for reward which will be discussed below.

49. *Owners of the Hamtun v Owners of the St John (The Hamtun and the St John)* [1999] 1 Lloyd's Rep 883.
50. *Owners of Cargo Lately Laden on Board the Troilus v Owners, Masters and Crew of the Glenogle (The Troilus and the Glenogle)* [1951] AC 820; [1951] 2 All ER 40; [1951] 1 Lloyd's Rep 467; [1951] 2 TLR 22; (1951) 95 SJ 465; 1951 WL 11359; *Tsavliris Salvage (International) Ltd v Guangdong Shantou Overseas Chinese Materials Marketing Co (The Pa Mar)* [1999] 1 Lloyd's Rep 338, 1997 WL 1102429.
51. *The Hamtun and the St John*, see fn. 49.
52. *Owners and/or Demise Charterers of the Tug Sea Tractor v Owners of the Tramp (The Tramp)* [2007] EWHC 31 (Admlty) [2007] 2 Lloyd's Rep 363; 2007 WL 261207; 2007 WL 261207.
53. *The Hamtun and the St John*, see fn. 49. See Mr Peter Gross QC, judgment on p. 889, col. 1.
54. Art. 18. *Owners of the Maridive VII, Maridive XIII, Maridive 85 and Maridive 94 v Owners and Demise Charterers of the Key Singapore*, see fn. 47.
55. See R Shaw (fn. 38) at pp. 225–226 for a discussion on the subject.

The obligation of the owners of property to accept redelivery, when the property is at a place of safety, is also problematic. The Salvage Convention does not define what a place of safety is. One could suggest alternative definitions. For example, a place of physical safety can be a place where the property can stay without being under immediate threat of the elements of nature even if it cannot be repaired and returned into service. Under pre-existing English law an interpretation, requiring that the place of safety does not only need to be physically safe but also to have appropriate facilities to put the vessel back into service, appears to be the correct one.[56] However, it is strongly arguable that the natural meaning of the term, on which its interpretation should be based, is the former.[57] One may also argue that once the vessel has been brought into physical safety, cheaper methods for its transportation to a place of repair, for example towage, could and should, if available, be employed.[58]

When a salvage operation has a useful result then a right to a reward arises (Article 12). The Salvage Convention does not define what a useful result is. The term *useful* may imply an improvement of the condition/value or quantity of the property salved and not simply that some property has been salved. If, for example, the salvors save some property but as a matter of fact the same property would have been saved without their assistance then arguably no useful result has been achieved and no salvage reward should be given.[59] An alternative interpretation may be that the salvage of any property in itself is a useful result, subject to the reservation that where the salvor has not exercised due care or has not been efficient the salvor may face a reduced reward under the relevant criteria of Article 13, or a reduction in or full deprivation of the reward under Article 18. It is submitted that because it would have been easy to state that "where property is salved a right to a reward arises", the more complicated wording of Article 12 suggests that the word "useful" implies more than the mere salvage of property.[60]

Saving of people at sea alone does not by itself create a right to a salvage award. This is partly a result of Article 16 of the Salvage Convention which provides that salved people are not under an obligation to pay salvage. This arrangement does not affect any national law provisions. English law does not recognise a right to a reward for saving life.[61] Thus where life is saved but no property is saved there is no right to a salvage award.

However, where life is saved together with property the Salvage Convention provides for a fair share of the amount paid for salvage. In addition, if this amount is not sufficient, the Secretary of State can award an appropriate amount

56. *The Troilus and the Glenogle*, see fn. 50
57. See also Art. 21(3), where the requirements for security are linked to a right of detention at the "port or place where the property first arrives".
58. This is clearly a matter of interest for all property owners and in particular for cargo interests.
59. Under English Law salvors are liable for damages caused by their negligence and shipowners can recover against salvors for such damage. See *The Tojo Maru* [1972] AC 242 concerning a salvage contract. However, the salvor's liability is limited under the general limitation provisions of Sch. 7 to the Merchant Shipping Act 1995 enacting the 1976 Limitation Convention as amended by the 1996 Protocol.
60. See R Shaw (fn. 38) for the view that useful result is the same as the requirement of success under English Law before the Salvage Convention 1989.
61. *The Renpor* (1883) LR 8 PD 115 (CA). The 1989 Salvage Convention does impose (Art. 10) an obligation on Masters (only) of ships, to render assistance when life is endangered, and on the contracting States to legislate for this (see s. 3 of Part II of Sch. 11 to the 1995 MSA). Ss. 92 and 93 of the 1995 MSA.

in respect of salvage operations within UK waters or anywhere in the world if the salvor of life is acting from a UK ship.[62]

### (c) The salvage reward

Two ways of calculating the salvor's remuneration are provided under the Salvage Convention. Where there is a useful result the "no cure–no pay" principle is applied on the basis of various performance-related criteria (Article 13) and a salvage reward is due. The criteria used include the value of the salved property; the skills of the salvors in minimising environmental damage; the nature and extent of danger, the measure of success and the general skills of the salvors as expressed in the response time; the risks undertaken; the availability of vessels; the promptness and length of the salvage service and the time spent. The various criteria listed under Article 13 are not in an hierarchical order and can only be considered as indicators for the adjudicators of the salvage reward. Thus it cannot be said *a priori* which of these criteria is the one that determines the amount of the reward. As a result judges and arbitrators have significant discretion in determining the amount awarded. What is certain is that if there is no valuable property salved there will be no reward.[63] It is arguable that the point in time at which the reward is earned is on redelivery of the property to the owners, or if the owners are avoiding redelivery, the time at which redelivery should have been accepted.[64]

The salvage reward is payable by the owners of the property salved and in proportion to the value of the salved property.[65] Thus, for example, if the ship's salved value is $8,000,000, the salved cargo's value is $90,000,000, the bunkers cost $1,000,000 and the freight at risk another $1,000,000, then, a salvage reward of $100,000 under Article 13, will be payable as follows: the owner of the ship will pay $8,000, the cargo owner $90,000, the owner of the bunkers $1,000 and the party benefiting from the unpaid freight for the salved cargo another $1,000.

The second way by which the salvage reward is to be calculated under the Salvage Convention applies only in certain circumstances is called "special compensation" and is described under Article 14. The special compensation is the most significant modification introduced by the 1989 Salvage Convention in the Law of Salvage and aims at providing incentives for the salvors to get involved in incidents where pollution is threatened, even if there is a risk that very little or no property will eventually be salved.

Before describing the method of calculation of the special compensation it is worth explaining when this special compensation becomes payable. The Salvage Convention defines "Damage to the environment" as "substantial physical damage to human health or to marine life or resources in coastal or inland waters or areas adjacent thereto, caused by pollution, contamination, fire, explosion or similar

62. Section 5, Part II, Sch. 11 to the 1995 MSA imposes the obligation on ship Masters.
63. Art. 13(3).
64. Arguably it is at that time that the "useful" result can be assessed, although difficulties may arise if the property is brought in a place of safety but it becomes lost between that time and redelivery to the owners.
65. Art. 13(2).

major incidents".[66] This definition is restrictive in many ways. First, damage to the environment is only covered in coastal or inland waters and adjacent areas. Thus, it is arguable that any damage occurring away from the coastal areas, presumably within the EEZ but certainly when it is on the high seas is not subject to this definition.[67] The second restrictive characteristic of the definition is that it requires "substantial" physical damage, a term which is not clear. Presumably the "substantial" nature of the damage will depend not only on the extent of the damage but also on the importance and rarity of the marine life and resources affected. The third way in which the definition is restrictive is the required link with major incidents indicating that where the physical damage to the environment is substantial but the incident is not a major one, the environmental damage will probably not be covered by the definition.

Where the salvor has participated in a salvage operation in which there was a threat of environmental damage then there is an entitlement to special compensation. Two situations are provided for. The first occurs where the salvor has been unsuccessful in his attempts to prevent or minimise damage to the environment. In such a case the special compensation will be equivalent to the salvor's expenses.[68] The second situation is where the salvor has been successful in preventing or minimising damage to the environment. In such a case the salvor can recover his expenses plus an increase by anything up to 100%.[69] The extent of the increase is to be decided on the basis of the same reward criteria that apply for the salvage reward under Article 13.

The special compensation is only payable to the extent that it exceeds the ordinary Article 13 reward. Only the shipowner is liable for the payment of special compensation. This is arguably a fair arrangement as it is usually the shipowner who restricts his pollution liability exposure by the actions of the salvor.

While the whole idea of a special compensation appears at first reading as sound and workable, its practical application has led, under English law, to two significant problems. The first problem is the way in which the salvor's expenses are to be calculated. The Salvage Convention itself under Article 14(3) specifies a way of calculating these expenses. Thus, actual payments made reasonably by the salvor, for example for hiring equipment, fall under the "out of pocket" expenses and are to be included in the expenses on the basis of which the special compensation is to be calculated.[70] However, Article 14(3) also requires the inclusion in the salvor's expenses of "... a fair rate for equipment and personnel actually and reasonably used in the salvage operation". While it is clear that the intention of the Salvage Convention was to provide reasonable compensation for

66. Art. 1(d).
67. An alternative reading would be to restrict the definition of coastal areas and areas adjacent thereto only in respect of resources thus permitting all damage to human health and marine life to be covered by the definition.
68. Art. 14(1).
69. Note that the text of the Convention under Art. 14(2) is badly drafted and does not make sense. The wording of Art. 14(2) can probably be taken to mean that the special compensation should in general be up to 130% of the salvor's expenses and only in exceptional cases should it be increased to 200%.
70. Art. 14(3). See also *Semco Salvage & Marine Pte Ltd v Lancer Navigation Co Ltd (The Nagasaki Spirit)* [1997] AC 455; [1997] 2 WLR 298; [1997] 1 All ER 502; [1997] 1 Lloyd's Rep 323; [1997] CLC 507; [1997] 6 Re LR 305; 1997 AMC 1989; (1997) 141 SJLB 43; *The Times* (10 February 1997); WL 1106227.

the use of the salvor's equipment whether "fair rate" should be reflecting market prices or be decided on some other commercial basis has caused practical problems. The issue was resolved by the House of Lords in *The Nagasaki Spirit* where it was decided that the term "fair rate" referred to expenditure and did not include an element of profit. The assessment of the fair rate in such a way may need the involvement of accountants, an unnecessary and impractical exercise in a market where decision making on whether to get involved in pollution threatening incidents must be encouraged by providing certainty of an appropriate reward.

The second unclear point regarding Article 14 is whether special compensation is payable only during the period in which a threat of environmental damage is present and is not payable as soon as the environmental damage is averted or whether, once it becomes payable, it is to be calculated until the redelivery of the property to its owners. The House of Lords confirmed in *The Nagasaki Spirit* that, if Article 14 applies, the calculation of the special compensation continues until the redelivery of the property to its owners.[71]

The special compensation can be reduced if the salvors act negligently or in breach of their environmental duties under the Salvage Convention.[72]

### (d) Who can claim a salvage reward?

Public policy supports salvage and as a result when assistance is rendered at sea a salvage reward is likely. However, certain categories of claimant are not entitled to claim salvage, largely for public policy reasons. For example, it is reasonable to exclude from the right to claim salvage persons who deliberately create danger in order to gain a salvage reward. Thus, in general, the Master and the crew of the salved vessel, as well as pilots and tugs under contracts of towage will not be able to claim while performing the services contracted for. The Salvage Convention requires that "the services rendered exceed what can be reasonably considered as due performance of a contract entered into before the danger arose".[73] However, when the services provided do exceed the contractual arrangement, for example when the vessel is abandoned by order of the Master, then one would expect that the crew members may act as salvors.[74] Similarly, during the performance of a towage contract if the situation becomes dangerous then towage may turn into salvage. For example, where the tow line parts and the weather conditions put the tow in danger, the service may turn into a salvage operation which in practice means that the towage contract is displaced and the salvage obligations and reward come into play.[75]

Two other categories of person who may find difficulty in claiming salvage are salvors employed by governmental or public services and the governmental or

71. *Ibid.*
72. Art. 14(5).
73. Art. 17.
74. See *The San Demetrio* (1941) 69 Ll L Rep 5, and *The Warrior* (1862) Lush 476. See also *The Albionic* (1942) 72 Ll L Rep 91.
75. *The Texaco Southampton* [1983] 1 Lloyd's Rep 94; 1983 WL 216285 (CA New South Wales), *Owners of the Maridive VII, Maridive XIII, Maridive 85 and Maridive 94 v Owners and Demise Charterers of the Key Singapore*, see fn. 47; *The Hamtun and the St John*, see fn. 49. Note, though, that while this is tempting for the tugs, it may be difficult to prove.

public services themselves, for example the Navy or the Coastguard. In respect of salvors employed by governmental authorities or performing salvage under the control of such authorities Article 5.2 of the Salvage Convention 1989 expressly entitles them to salvage. while in respect of the governmental and public services themselves the issue is subject to the national law of the State in which the public service is situated.[76]

The general encouragement of salvage requires that a shipowner can provide salvage assistance to another of its ships.[77] This is consistent with the pre-existing law of Salvage[78] under which in the appropriate circumstances a salvage reward may be due to the shipowner or the cargo owner.[79]

### (e) Financial security

The right to the salvage reward is supported by a maritime lien of the highest priority[80] and by a possessory lien. However, especially in respect of the special compensation, salvors need to know as early as possible that payment for their services will be forthcoming and that the shipowner will be capable of paying. Thus the provision of financial security at an early stage is important for the salvors.

The Salvage Convention leaves unaffected maritime liens existing under national law as well as liens under other international conventions. The only restriction imposed is that where security is provided the maritime lien cannot be exercised.[81] However, the amount of the required security is not specified but needs to be "satisfactory" by reference not only to the reward itself but to interest and costs. The duty for the provision of financial security is put upon the owners of the property. However, the shipowner, apart from the obligation to provide financial security for the part of the reward for which he is responsible, is also under a duty to exercise best endeavours in ensuring that the cargo interests will also provide security in respect of their part of the reward.

To enhance the probabilities of recovery for the salvor the Salvage Convention provides that the ship or other property salved should not be moved from the port prior to the provision of security. However, these words do not create robust obligations because there are no sanctions provided under the Salvage Convention to cover the situation where, for example, the cargo is removed from the ship and the port. Moreover, it is unclear how the person permitting the unauthorised release of the property can become liable to the salvors. Similarly, the general requirement about the provision of satisfactory security does not spell out what the salvor's options are where such security is not provided.

76. MSA 1995 s. 230(2), entitles the Crown to claim salvage.
77. Art. 12(3).
78. See, e.g., *The Troilus and the Glenogle*, fn. 50.
79. *The Sava Star* [1995] 2 Lloyd's Rep 13.
80. *The Bold Buccleugh* (1851) 7 Moo PC 267; *Owners of the Carbonnade v Owners of the Ruta (The Ruta)* [2000] 1 WLR 2068; [2001] 1 All ER 450; [2000] 1 All ER (Comm) 847; [2000] 1 Lloyd's Rep 359; [2000] CLC 784; [2000] ICR 1024; (2000) 97(12) LSG 39; (2000) 144 SJLB 135; *The Times* (21 March 2000); WL 191231; 2000 WL 191231. It is doubtful whether the salvage maritime lien covers Special Compensation. The maritime lien exists independently of the 1989 Salvage Convention. Thus its scope depends on its characteristics under pre-existing English law.
81. Art. 20.

The arrangement under Article 14 is supported by a non-binding Code of Practice between the International Group of P&I Clubs and the International Salvage Union (ISU) regarding the provision of security.[82]

### (f) Apportionment of the salvage reward

Where more than one salvor is involved in the salvage operation, the question on how the salvage reward should be distributed becomes important. Article 15 of the Salvage Convention requires that any salvage reward or special compensation is to be divided between the salvors in accordance with the criteria of Article 13. In addition the distribution of the salvage reward between crew members is subject to the law of the flag of the salvor's ship. Where salvage is not performed from a ship, the law of the contract between the salvor and its employees will decide how the reward should be split. Of course if there are sub-contracts between the head salvor and other contributors, it is usual that both the law and jurisdiction, and probably the substantive part of the payment, has been agreed.[83]

A different problem arises where the ship performing the salvage is under a demise or time charter. The question whether and to what extent the salvage reward will be split between owners, demise-charterers and other charterers will depend on the relevant charterparty.[84]

### (g) Time bar and limitation of liability

The time bar for any action relating to payment under the Salvage Convention is two years from the time the salvage operation has been terminated.[85] The period can be extended by the defendant in a salvage claim. Indemnity claims are subject to the time bars for actions under the national law of the State party. In England this is six years.[86]

Limitation of liability issues are not dealt with under the 1989 Salvage Convention but under the 1996 Limitation of Liability for Maritime Claims Convention (1996 LLMC).[87] It is sufficient to clarify here two points. First, that the salvage reward and the Special Compensation are, under English law, not subject to limitation of liability.[88] Second, that under the 1996 LLMC, the salvors' liability is limited to that of a shipowner of a vessel of 1,500 tons.[89]

82. The Funding Agreement 1989. See R Shaw, fn. 38, at p. 228 for a discussion on the issues of obtaining security under the Convention.
83. The International Salvage Union provides standard forms of sub-contracts which can be found at *www.marine-salvage.com/documents/*
84. See, for example, Barecon 1989, cl. 17, where the benefit and repairs are for the demise charterer and Baltime where under cl. 19 the net profits are to be equally split between owner and charterer.
85. Art. 23.
86. Limitation Act 1980, s. 5.
87. Convention on Limitation of Liability for Maritime Claims (London, 19 November 1976) (1976 LLMC) and the Protocol of 1996 amending the Convention on Limitation of Liability for Maritime Claims of 19 November 1976 (London, 2 May 1996) (1996 LLMC); see ss. 185–186 of the 1995 MSA. See the section on *Limitation of liability*.
88. 1996 LLMC, Art. 3.
89. Which is 2 million SDR for loss of life and personal injury and 1 million SDRs for property damage. See section on *Limitation of liability* at p. 201.

### (h) Salvage contracts under the Salvage Convention 1989

The right to a salvage reward arises independently of whether there is a contract or not. However, salvage contracts when appropriately drafted can significantly clarify the duties of the parties during the salvage operation. Provisions for the place of redelivery, the conditions under which salvage can be terminated including agreement on the forum and the law of the contract can avoid further disputes and expenses. The Salvage Convention permits exclusion of many of its provisions by contract. The default position under the Salvage Convention is that it only applies to the extent that salvage contracts do not provide otherwise. Thus salvage contracts can substantially alter most of the conditions under the Convention including the payment options, the time bar etc. However, the rights granted to courts to review salvage contracts (Article 7) and the environmental obligations put on the salvor and the salved property cannot be contracted out.

Liability for a salvage reward can be a significant financial burden for the shipowner and the cargo owner. Thus it is not surprising that where the Master has signed a salvage contract the cargo interests have sought to avoid liability for salvage by claiming that the salvage contracts is not binding to the cargo owners because it has not been agreed with them. Of course, where a situation of danger exists, and assistance is successfully provided, the right to claim part of the salvage reward from the cargo owners arises independently of the salvage contract.

Under the Salvage Convention binding authority to sign salvage contracts is granted to the master of the vessel. This authority is binding both for the shipowner and the cargo owner.[90] The wording of Article 6(2) provides binding authority only for the conclusion of contracts concerning salvage operations which must involve a ship or property in danger (Article 1(a)). As a result where danger is not present, salvage operations, as defined under the Salvage Convention, cannot take place and the Master arguably has no authority to bind the cargo if he chooses to sign a salvage contract.

The extent of the Master's authority under Article 6(2) has not yet been interpreted by the courts. However, it appears that after a reasonable contract of salvage is concluded, further modifications agreed between the shipowner and the salvor will not necessarily be binding on the cargo owners.[91] Similarly, it can be argued that where the Master breaches the contract of salvage, for example, by unreasonably replacing the salvor, then the cargo owners would probably not be considered in breach of the original salvage contract[92] nor bound by the new contract leaving the shipowner to pay for the contractual breaches.

90. This is an important modification of the pre-existing English law under which the Master of the ship did not in general have authority to bind the cargo interests to a salvage contract, except where a situation creating an "agency of necessity" was created. The creation of the agency of necessity occurs when there is a situation of danger making salvage necessary, coupled with difficulties in communicating with the owners of the cargo such that obtaining their instructions is reasonably impractical. In addition the actions of the Master must be *bona fide* for the interests of cargo and also reasonable in entering the contract. *Industrie Chimiche Italia Centrale v Alexander G Tsavliris & Sons Maritime Co (The Choko Star)* [1996] 1 WLR 774; [1996] 1 All ER 114; [1995] 2 Lloyd's Rep 608; [1995] CLC 1461; *The Times* (8 August 1995); *The Independent* (4 September 1995) (CS); 1995 WL 1081833.

91. *Tsavliris Salvage (International) Ltd v Guangdong Shantou Overseas Chinese Materials Marketing Co (The Pa Mar)* [1999] 1 Lloyd's Rep 338.

92. Unless, probably, where they have consented to the breach committed by the Master.

### (i) Dismissal of salvors

Situations may arise where a more competent or cheaper salvor can be found and then the Master or the shipowner may wish to replace the original salvor. The Salvage Convention does not give such a right to either the Master or shipowner. However, it imposes an obligation on the salvors to accept the assistance and collaboration of other salvors when reasonably requested by the Master. If it is later shown that such intervention was unnecessary then the reward of the original salvor "would not be prejudiced",[93] probably meaning that the shipowner would have to remunerate fully the first salvor and also pay salvage to the second salvor. However, if the salvor is dismissed it is not clear what the consequences are under the Salvage Convention. Under pre-existing salvage law it was arguable that there was compensation for loss of opportunity and a reward for the period during which the salvor contributed to salvage.[94] However, this depended on the final success of the salvage operation.

By contrast where a salvage contract has been signed, a dismissal of the salvor is a breach of contract for which the salvor is entitled to claim damages, sounding in the amount of salvage that would have been received had he completed the salvage operation minus any expenses and costs that would have been incurred by the salvor.[95] This decision is a consequence of the law of contract and it should remain unaffected by the Salvage Convention.[96]

### (j) The Lloyd's Open Form – "No Cure–No Pay"

One of the most extensively used salvage contract forms is the Lloyd's Open Form. This has developed over more than a century, and its development and flexibility has been a contributor to the dominant role English salvage law has. The LOF form has repeatedly adjusted to accommodate the needs of contemporary salvage in anticipation of developments of national or international law which always took much longer. Thus the LOF 1980 included the first departure from the "No Cure–No Pay" salvage principle by entitling the salvor of a stricken tanker who had failed to recover an ordinary salvage reward to recover its costs plus 25% uplift of those costs. The 1990 version of the LOF incorporated the Salvage Convention six years before it came into force. The LOF 2000 introduced the first attempt to overcome the difficulties of the Salvage Convention by providing the option to incorporate the Special Compensation P&I Club's (SCOPIC) Clause.

In brief, the most recent LOF 2000 contract consists of a short form which incorporates a number of standard sets of clauses, namely, the Lloyd's Standard and Arbitration Clauses (LSSA) the Lloyd's procedural rules and, when the option is exercised, the SCOPIC Clause. Signing the LOF implies determination of the award and any conflicts through arbitration.[97]

93. Art. 8(1)(d).
94. *The Unique Mariner (No 2)* [1979] 1 Lloyd's Rep 37.
95. *Ibid.*
96. Such a claim was held in *The Tesabu* [1982] 1 Lloyd's Rep 397 not to be "in the nature of salvage"; but see Merchant Shipping (Salvage and Pollution) Act 1994, Sched. 2, para. 6, amending s. 20 of the Supreme Court Act 1981 and extending the Admiralty Jurisdiction of the High Court to such claims.
97. The website *www.lloydsagency.com* has information on such arbitrations and on a new form of fixed Cost Arbitration.

The main provisions of the LOF 2000 contract are set out in the short form which provides for identification of the parties to the contract and the property to be salved, place and date of the agreement, the agreed place of safety and an agreed currency for an arbitration award. Most importantly, the LOF 2000 provides the option to the parties to have the SCOPIC clause incorporated or not. This option radically changes the effects of the contract.

Whether the SCOPIC Clause is incorporated or not a contract subject to English law and Lloyd's Arbitration comes into existence when the LOF 2000 is signed. The basic obligation of the LOF 2000 is the salvage of the named property and the redelivery to the agreed place of safety (Clause A). If the salvors bring the ship and/or the property to the agreed place of safety then, if the property does not need salvage assistance and the port or government regulations do not require the presence of salvors any further, the salvors have fulfilled their part of the deal (Clause H).

While performing the contract the salvors should use best endeavours to prevent or minimise damage to the environment (Clause B). Note that the term "best endeavours" has been argued to be more burdensome than the obligation under Article 8 of the Convention to "exercise due care".[98] Other views are also arguable and best endeavours can be taken to mean a subjective measure of care that depends on the particular salvor while due care reflecting the standard of professional care and skill required of professional salvors.[99]

Interestingly, where a LOF 2000 is agreed it applies retrospectively to all previous services rendered.[100] Express obligations are imposed on the owners of the property in danger to provide reasonable use of the machinery onboard the ship and also to provide all necessary information to the salvors and help in obtaining permission for entry into the designated place of safety.

The LOF 2000 provides that the Master has authority to act as agent of the property interests (Clause K). Clearly, this is a contractual undertaking from the shipowner, it is actionable against the shipowner alone and cannot replace the Salvage Convention's authority of the Master under Article 6.2.[101]

The LOF 2000 also provides for an obligation on the shipowner to inform the cargo owners of the salvage agreement and for the latter to provide security when salvage is successful.[102]

Where the SCOPIC clause is not incorporated, the two types of remuneration under the Salvage Convention, namely the reward under Article 13 and the Special Compensation under Article 14, are available to the salvor.[103]

98. N Gaskell, The 1995 Merchant Shipping Act, *Current Law Statutes Annotated*, p. 390.
99. Consistent with the judgments in *The Tojo Maru* [1972] AC 242.
100. This naturally raises the query whether or not the consequences of a breach of the LOF before it is agreed are also retrospectively actionable.
101. There is, of course, the question whether the Master's authority can be removed by contract because the Salvage Convention does not exclude the possibility that Art. 6 of the Salvage Convention may itself be excluded by contract. Even if this were the case, it is suggested that only a salvage contract can have this effect and exclusions of such authority in other contracts, for example time charterparties, cannot exclude such authority to bind the cargo against a salvor, although they may constitute grounds for damages to be paid under the time charterparty. In such a case, as well as in the case that the above interpretation is wrong, and the authority of the Master to sign salvage contracts can be removed by other than salvage contracts, the existence of agency of necessity discussed above at fn. 90 above will become relevant again.
102. Important Note 1 giving notice of Clause 4 of the LSSA Clauses.
103. See Clause D.

However, where the SCOPIC 2007[104] clause is incorporated, the Article 14 special compensation is in general excluded as a potential remuneration.[105] Thus, the salvor can only rely on the Article 13 reward until the salvor decides to invoke, in writing, the SCOPIC clause. From the time the SCOPIC clause is invoked, it replaces the calculation of the Special Compensation under Article 14 of the Convention. However, any services provided before the SCOPIC Clause was invoked remain subject to the salvage reward under Article 13 of the Convention. It is important to note that the SCOPIC reward does not depend on the existence of any threat of damage to the environment nor is it restricted to a particular jurisdictional or physical area of the seas.[106] Thus it is a more general and readily available compensation for the salvors in all cases in which they may become worried about the possibility of a satisfactory Article 13 reward. The remuneration under SCOPIC is based on set tariffs[107] contained in a separate Appendix (A) to the clause. There is a standard bonus of 25% on top of the tariffs.[108] Thus, the calculation of the SCOPIC reward is simple and easy to make. The standard of conduct under the SCOPIC clause is, as under the LOF, to use best endeavours (Clause 10) for salving the property and in doing so to prevent or minimise damage to the environment.[109]

The SCOPIC reward is only payable by shipowners and only to the extent it exceeds the Article 13 reward under the Salvage Convention. However, there is a discount to the Article 13 reward if the salvor has unnecessarily invoked the SCOPIC clause in a situation where the Article 13 reward would have been larger. In such a case the Article 13 reward is reduced by 25% of the difference between the salvage reward and the SCOPIC remuneration (Clause 7). For this reduction the SCOPIC remuneration is calculated from the beginning of salvage irrespective of the day on which it was actually invoked. This retrospective extension maximises the SCOPIC remuneration and minimises the difference to a calculated Article 13 award thus making the penalty's application more unlikely.[110]

Apart from the difference in the salvor's remuneration, the invocation of SCOPIC has several other consequences. First, the owners are obliged to put up a bank guarantee or P&I security for US $3,000,000 within two working days.[111] This initial security can be adjusted later as needed or by the arbitrator if there is a

104. Apart from increasing the tariff rates, SCOPIC 2007 also incorporates Art. 18 of the Salvage Convention into the contract.
105. SCOPIC, s. I.
106. This is beneficial to salvors both in terms of avoiding the difficulties of Art. 14 but also by ensuring that the SCOPIC remuneration is equally high whether the salvage is undertaken in the expensive developed world or the relatively cheap developing world.
107. The rates are agreed by the International Salvage Union and the International Group of P&I Clubs and endorsed by property underwriters and owners. The latest update applies to LOF contracts entered into after 1 July 2007 and will continue until 31 December 2010. The increase was 25% of the previous applicable SCOPIC rates for tugs and other craft. Rates for Salvor's own portable salvage equipment have increased by 15%, and rates for personnel have increased by 5% as there was an earlier increase of 10% in 2006.
108. SCOPIC, Cl. 5. Where the salvor has higher salvage tugs and equipment at rates higher than those set out in the SCOPIC tariffs he will receive either the actual costs plus 10% bonus or the tariff rate plus the 25% bonus, whichever is higher.
109. SCOPIC, Cl. 10.
110. Arguably it would have been easier in such a case just to replace the Art. 13 reward with that chosen by the salvor that is the SCOPIC remuneration.
111. SCOPIC, Cl. 3.

dispute. If security is not provided the salvor can withdraw from SCOPIC and revert to the LOF including Article 14.[112]

Second, a Special Casualty Representative (SCR) is appointed. The SCR is a salvage specialist acting as an independent advisor to the shipowner, who pays for him, and assesses for the owner the efficiency and the reasonableness of the salvage operations undertaken under the SCOPIC agreement and provides the shipowner with daily estimates of the SCOPIC remuneration. The SCR is to be selected from a list of specialists.[113] Appendix B of SCOPIC sets out the rules of conduct for the SCR. Two other Special Representatives, one for Hull and one for Cargo interests can be appointed under the SCOPIC clause. They are required to be technical men and not practising lawyers. Their role is set out in Appendix C. The role of the SCR and the Special Representatives is to provide transparency of the salvage operations thus removing fears that salvors would unnecessarily prolong salvage in order to achieve higher SCOPIC remuneration. However, the control of the salvage operation remains with the salvage master.

Third, the SCOPIC clause provides for rights of termination of the SCOPIC clause and the LOF contract for the salvor where the SCOPIC remuneration plus the value of the property that can be salved are lower than the costs of the services provided.[114] The shipowner can also terminate at any time by giving five days notice and paying for five days (or as long as needed for demobilisation) salvage remuneration. But the rights to termination only exist if the salvor is not restricted from ceasing the salvage services by the government or the port authorities.[115]

The SCOPIC clause is supported by two non-binding Codes of Practice, one applying to the International Group of P&I Clubs and the ISU regarding the provision of SCOPIC security, and the other applying to the International Group of P&I Clubs and the London Property Underwriters and the ISU regarding the contribution to the payment of fees of the SCR by the P&I Clubs and the property insurers.

The SCOPIC Clause has so far been considered successful, resolving most of the problems present in the Salvage Convention. It is a further example of a successful and well-designed intervention by the salvage industry to avoid the difficulties developed by the Salvage Convention and responding to the needs of the market.

### (k) Public law issues of salvage

There are several public law issues related to salvage of which three will be discussed here briefly. The three issues are the control of salvage operations by the coastal State; the (non-existent) obligation of the coastal State to provide a place of refuge; and finally the liability of salvors for pollution during salvage operations.

### (l) The control of the salvage operation by the coastal State

The Salvage Convention preserves any rights available under international law to the coastal State to take measures for coastal protection and pollution prevention and to intervene and give direction in relation to salvage operations.[116] Such

112. SCOPIC, Cl. 4.
113. *www.lloyds.com/Lloyds_Worldwide/Lloyds_Agents/Salvage_Arbitration_Branch/Salvage_contacts/Special_Casualty_Representatives/Special_Casualty_Representatives.htm*
114. SCOPIC, Cl. 9.
115. *Ibid.*, Cl. 9.
116. Art. 9.

rights may arise under UNCLOS[117] or from the Intervention Convention 1969[118] or under regional or international conventions or customary international law.

Thus the coastal State is under no obligation to permit the salvors to enter to a place where salvage can be more efficient, but on the contrary can order them to move the stricken vessel away from the coast.[119] The freedom of the coastal State is not restricted by the obligation imposed under Article 11 of the Salvage Convention to take into account, when deciding on the provision of a place of refuge, the need for cooperation between salvors, other interests and the coastal State.

In UK the Secretary of State appoints the Secretary of State's Representative "SOSREP" with powers to oversee, control and intervene in salvage operations within UK waters involving vessels or fixed platforms where there is significant risk of pollution. The powers of the SOSREP are set out in the MSA 1995, Schedule 3A, as amended by the Marine Safety Act 2003.

The European Directive 2002/59/EC[120] establishes a system of national authorities in each Member State which collects information regarding ship movements and incidents and to which application for entries into ports of refuge should be submitted. Each Member State must, under Article 20, designate appropriate places of refuge.

The UK position is more flexible and the SOSREP considers that every coastal place may, in appropriate circumstances, be considered a place of refuge. To facilitate decision-making, a list of ports and anchorages and their facilities is available to the SOSREP.[121]

### (m) Responder immunity

Salvors have been campaigning for a right to what is called "responder immunity", that is, a protection from criminal liability or strict civil liability for pollution caused through their intervention. The International Salvage Union is particularly concerned with the criminal aspect of this liability in particular in light of the EU Directive on Ship Source Pollution (2005/35/EC). A case is pending in the European Court of Justice which will decide whether it is legitimate for the EC to legislate in excess of what international standards set through the IMO provide for. However, a first challenge to the legitimacy of the use of criminal liability to assist environmental protection has failed as the use of criminal sanctions in support of environmental protections was considered as within the EU competence even if criminal liability in general is not within the EU ambit.[122]

117. See Chapter 9, p. ???.
118. International Convention Relating to Intervention on the High Seas in Cases of Oil Pollution Casualties (Brussels, 29 November 1969). See Chapter 8.
119. *The Castor* and *The Prestige* are recent examples. In *The Prestige* case it appears that the decision of the Spanish Government to order the vessel away from the coast was disastrous in enhancing the spatial extent of the pollution caused. See *www.Tsavliris.com/htmls/services/salvagedetail.asp?sid=111* for the facts on *The Castor* and *www.ibiblio.org/maritime/Scheepvaartnieuws/Pdf/scheepvaartnieuws/2002/juni/10-06-2002A.PDF*. See also the IOPC Fund 2006 Annual Report at *www.iopcfund.org/npdf/AR06_E.pdf* on *The Prestige*.
120. Directive 2002/59/EC of the European Parliament and of the Council of 27 June 2002 establishing a Community vessel traffic monitoring and information system and repealing Council Directive 93/75/EEC. See also the relevant IMO Resolution A 949 (23).
121. See *www.mcga.gov.uk/c4mca/mcga-environmental/mcga-dops_cp_environmental-counter-pollution/mcga-dops_cp_sosrep_role/internet-_dops-_counterpollution-places_of_refuge__/dops_-_sosrep_-_ports_and_anchorages_hq-newpage-1003083.htm*
122. See Chapter 9.

## 4. TOWAGE

### (a) Introduction

Towage has been defined as "the employment of one vessel to expedite the voyage of another when nothing more is required than the accelerating of her progress".[123] However, tugs are employed for many more tasks than this definition would imply. Primarily tugs still accompany or speed up the voyage of larger vessels especially at their entry, manoeuvring and departure from ports where restrictions in the movement and heavy traffic can pose risks to the bigger ships. However, tugs are also used for towing dead ships or unmanned barges between places and they also supply services and assistance to the offshore industry. Thus, modern towage entails many more varieties of service and as a result the original definition appears now as restrictive and can only be considered as a starting point for the discussion of towage.

Tugs can also be employed for salvage assistance, pollution prevention or clean up operations. However, such services are not usually in the nature of towage but are remunerated under the legal regime of Salvage or under clean-up arrangements with the coastal State.

Towage law involves two different aspects which must not be confused. The first concerns the contractual relationship between the tug and tow. This is a matter for the towage contract and any implied terms or statutory interventions relevant to this contract.

The second aspect concerns tug and tow liability to third parties in collision or pollution cases. The legal basis of this and the liability *vis-à-vis* the third party are governed by the law of torts and any statutory regimes concerning pollution. The fact that the tug and the tow are physically connected or commanded by the same person can create problems when one tries to identify to whom liability attaches. The third party is not, in general, affected by the towage contract between the tug and the tow; thus even where the contract puts liability solely on one party this is not effective *vis-à-vis* the third party which can recover under tort from whichever party has been negligent. However, because the limits of liability for the tug are many times smaller than those for the tow it is to the advantage of the third party to attempt to attach negligence and consequential liability on the tow thus improving the amount of recovery available to them.

### (b) The contract of towage

Various standard forms of towage contracts are available. However the arrangements under these forms are not restrictive and the parties can agree on any terms they wish subject to restrictions imposed by statute, for example by the Unfair Contract Terms Act, 1977.[124] Having said that, the commercial reality is quite different. Port services in many cases are monopolised by tugowners working as a group offering exactly the same contractual terms. In addition standard forms are convenient because they are supposedly better thought out and tested in practice than new arrangements.

123. *The Princess Alice* (1849) 3 W Rob 138 at p. 139.

124. However, this Act is more relevant where towage is provided as a service to small boat or yacht owners who can be considered as consumers.

In the absence of a written contract the courts would imply certain terms and conditions.[125] As the contract of towage is one for the provision of services the Supply of Goods and Services Act 1982 (SGSA 1982) would apply to such contracts. The SGSA 1982 implies an obligation to perform the service with reasonable care and skill (section 13) and within reasonable time (section 14). However, these implied terms can be excluded under section 16(1) by express contractual agreement, or by a course of dealing or a usage binding between the tug and the tow. These implied terms are very similar if not identical to the requirements under earlier case law implying the use of "best endeavours"[126] or showing the "proper skill and diligence".[127] These obligations have been detailed to involve a tug appropriately fitted and manned, acting with reasonable and proper skill, and an obligation to stay with the tow if the towing line breaks and use at least the appropriate skill or possibly best endeavours to reconnect with it.[128]

Several examples of application of these obligations exist in case law. In a case where the tug, fearing a collision, let the towing line go and as a result the tow collided with another ship the tug was held to be under an obligation to reconnect and continue the towage.[129] In another case where the towline broke, the tug was in breach of contract because it did not stand by the tow but sailed away in order to get a new tow line.[130] The obligation to stand by the tow is of course concerned with the safety of the tow. Thus, it is probably not surprising that where a vessel was towed from the anchorage to a berth but could not berth, towage was not finished until the vessel was taken back to the anchorage.[131] In short, towage can only be abandoned if it becomes impossible to perform.[132]

Obligations are not only imposed on the tug but on the tow as well. Thus, the tow is also under an obligation to be fit for towage and appropriately manned. In addition the persons on board the tow must demonstrate proper skill and diligence in respect of the tow's actions during towage.[133] Thus, where the tow collides and sinks the tug because of negligence in its navigation, the tow is liable for breach of the towage contract.

The law is unclear on whether the standard of the duty imposed in respect of the fitness of the tug is an absolute one, akin to the obligation of a common carrier to provide a seaworthy vessel or one of due care to provide a tug fitted to the service.[134] It appears that the stronger view under the English system is the second, while other legal systems favour the first one.[135] There is an exception if the contract of towage is for a specified tug in which case there is no implied warranty as to the fitness of the tug.[136]

The implied duties, or indeed the contractual obligations, come into play when towage starts. Where there is a contract it is the contract itself which would

125. *The Minnehaha* [1861] Lush 335; (1861) 15 Moo PC 133, and *The Julia* [1861] Lush 224.
126. *The Minnehaha, ibid.*
127. *The Julia, ibid.*
128. *The Julia, ibid.*; *The Minnehaha, ibid.*, and *The Maréchal Suchet* [1911] P 1, but see also the discussion in Simon Rainey, *The Law of Tug and Tow* (2nd ed) (Informa, 2002) (hereinafter "*Rainey*").
129. *The Golden Light* [1861] Lush 355.
130. *The Refrigerant* [1925] P 130.
131. *The Aboukir* [1905] 21 TLR 200.
132. *The Minnehaha*, fn. 125.
133. *The Julia*, fn. 125.
134. See the cases above and *The West Cock* [1911] P 208, and the discussion in *Rainey*, n. 128.
135. Discussion in *Rainey*, n. 128.
136. *Fraser & White Ltd v Vernon* [1951] 2 Lloyd's Rep 175.

probably stipulate the time the various obligations must be performed. In the absence of express contractual stipulation towing starts at the time the towing line is passed and ends when the towing line is slipped.[137]

All contractual and pre-contractual remedies available under English law are applicable to a contract of towage. Thus the contract can be frustrated,[138] or remedies for misrepresentation under the Misrepresentation Act 1967 can be available.[139] Issues related to the parties to the contract and the authority of the tug's and tow's Masters to bind their principals are also dealt with on the basis of general contract law. Thus the Master usually has express or implied actual authority in binding his principal to a reasonable contract of towage. It is also arguable that where the vessel is in danger (and therefore the Master has authority under Article 6.2 of the Salvage Convention to bind the owners of property onboard the ship as well as the shipowner) this authority would arguably cover the situation where the agreement is made on towage terms rather than on a standard contract of salvage. The identity of the contractual parties to the towage contract is important not only in respect of the exercise of contractual rights but also in respect of security proceedings, in particular actions *in rem*.[140] To that extent it is important to ascertain whether the contract of towage is binding on the shipowner, the demise-charterer or the time or voyage charterer.

### (c) Standard forms of towage

Special forms of contract have been developed reflecting the needs of, mainly, the towage industry. This is particularly true of harbour towage where monopoly conditions operate in many cases. Exclusions of liability and indemnities are routinely introduced in towage contracts. Under English law such exclusion and indemnity terms are valid, if clearly drafted.[141] Moreover, the Unfair Contract Terms Act 1977, which regulates the use of exemption clauses, excludes from its application towage and salvage contracts,[142] except where such contracts relate to owners of small yachts who are seen as consumers.

The inclusion of wide exclusion and indemnity clauses has led to attempts by shipowners to avoid their consequences by disputing that they are operative in respect of a particular incident because towage has either not started or has already finished. This depends on the construction of the contract and will be discussed in detail when the most common contracts are outlined. In other situations the shipowners try to identify a lack of agency or authority of the party signing

137. *The Clan Colquhoun* [1936] 54 Ll L Rep 221.
138. For example, if the tow is lost without fault of the tug or the tow, or the tow and the tug belong to flag States which come into conflict.
139. For example, where the power of the tug does not correspond to that stated in the negotiations, for an example see the litigation of *Ultisol Transport Contractors Ltd v Bouygues Offshore SA and Comité d'Etudes et des Services des Assureurs Maritimes et Tansports de France (Tigr, Ultisol v Bouyges)* [1996] 2 Lloyd's Rep 140 and *Bouygues Offshore SA v Caspian Shipping Co (No 3)* [1997] 2 Lloyd's Rep 493; [1997] CLC 1443; 1997 WL 1102415, involving several issues. See also *Ease Faith Limited v Leonis Marine Management Limited, Cloudfree Ship Management Limited* [2006] 1 Lloyd's Rep 673 (under TOWCON) where a claim of tow in "light ballast" failed.
140. See Chapter 11.
141. *The President Van Buren* [1924] 19 Ll L Rep 185; [1924] 16 Asp MLC 444. This position is not universally adopted and, in the US such clauses are nullified as against public policy, *Bisso v Inland Waterways* [1955] AMC 899.
142. Sch. 1, para. 2(a).

for the tugowners or themselves. An example would be where a port authority, or terminal operator, or time charterer, makes the towage contract on behalf of independent tug companies.[143]

The parties to these forms are usually termed the "Tugowner" and the "Hirer". The second term is an indication that it is not necessarily the owner of the tow who is party to the contract but probably a charterer, demise-charter or some other entity. The question then would be whether the person signing the contract has the authority of the owner of the tow to sign the towage contract. If it does not have the authority then the owner of the tow is not bound by the contract and, in addition, security measures against the tow may not be available to it.

In order to remedy this situation most standard forms includes a "warranty of authority" clause[144] under which the "Hirer" warranties that it has authority to sign on behalf of the owner of the tow and their binding by the contract is joint and several. While such a term can be the basis for a recourse action against the *Hirer*, where such authority to bind the tow owner does not exist, it cannot on its own bind the owner of the tow to the towage contract.[145]

Below we will use the terms "tug" and "tow" to refer to the parties to the contract. However, this should not be misunderstood as assuming that the Hirer is always the tow owner nor that there is always an implication of liability *in rem* against the tow.

*(i) UK Standard Towing Conditions 1986*

The UK Standard Conditions for Towage and Other Services (UKSCT) goes back to 1933 with several subsequent modifications. In addition to towage the UKSTC 1986 also cover "other services". Thus they can be incorporated where ancillary services to oil rigs and the offshore industry are provided. The reference to the UK does not preclude their application to other parts of the world as these are in essence contractual terms.[146] From the variety of forms available worldwide the UK STC are probably the most favourable to tugowners. The UKSTC include English law and exclusive English jurisdiction except in Scotland where local courts have jurisdiction.[147]

The incorporation of the UKSTC 1986 to the towage contract depends on whether there is express incorporation, for example on fixture communication, or where the conduct of past dealing between the parties indicates an intention to be bound by the standard conditions[148] or because they habitually apply to such contracts and this fact is known and expected.[149]

143. See *Owners of the Borvigilant v Owners of the Romina G (The Borvigilant and Romina G)* [2003] 2 Lloyd's Rep 520, where such an attempt failed. The Contracts (Rights of Third Parties) Act 1999 may now be relevant to assist tug companies.
144. Cl. 2 in the UKSTC and Cl. 22 in the BIMCO TOWHIRE and TOWCON contracts.
145. *Lukoil-Kaliningradmorneft Plc v Tata Ltd and Global Marine Inc* [1999] 1 Lloyd's Rep 365; [1999] 2 Lloyd's Rep 129 (CA).
146. Subject to the law applicable at that State. See, for example, *PNSL Berhard v Dalrymple Marine Services Pty Ltd; PNSL Berhard v The Owners of the Ship Koumala (The Koumala)* [2007] QSC 101 where the exclusions in the 1974 of the UK Standard Conditions of Towage were found to violate the Australian Trade Practices Act 1974 which imposed an implied warranty to provide services with due care and skill (s. 74) and which could not be excluded by contract (s. 68).
147. UKSCT 1986, Cl. 9.
148. *The Tasmania* [1888] LR 13 PD 110.
149. For support of this argument see *British Crane Hire Corp Ltd v Ipswich Plant Hire Ltd* [1975] 1 QB 303. See also *Owners of the Wallumba v Australian Coastal Shipping Commission (The*

The terms provide for two different types of services: towing and other services. Towing is defined as "any operation in connection with the holding, pushing, pulling, moving, escorting or guiding of or standing by the Hirer's vessel",[150] and the contract applies "whilst towing" which covers the period from when the tug is in position to receive orders or to pick up ropes or when the towing line has passed whichever occurred first until the final orders have been performed or the lines have slipped (whichever is later) *and* the tug or any other assisting vessel is safely clear of the tow.[151]

This definition includes in the towage service any period of interruption but it is not free from difficulty. Consider the situation where the tug arrives early on site and the vessel has not yet finished loading or discharging the cargo. If the tug runs into the prospective tow and damages itself and the tow, could it then be protected by the UKSCT?[152] In *The Apollon*[153] Brandon J reviewing the authorities considered that three conditions must be fulfilled for the tug to be "in a position to receive orders direct from the Hirer's vessel ... to pick up lines ... etc". First, that the situation is such that those on board can reasonably expect the tow to give the tug orders or to pick up ropes or lines, second, that the tug is ready to respond to such orders and that the tug can receive these orders directly, that is, the tug is within hailing distance.[154] One may query whether the requirement that the tug should be at a hailing distance is necessary as in practice orders can and are given in many cases through VHF. However, the orders must be "direct", arguably indicating very close proximity rather than being concerned with the way of communication.[155]

Where more than one tug is involved in the towage it is reasonable to suggest that the UKSCT will start applying separately at the time each tug satisfies the *Apollon* conditions.[156] However, the wording of the contractual arrangement will be significant in this sense and may provide otherwise.

---

*Wallumba)* [1964] 2 Lloyd's Rep 387; [1965] 1 Lloyd's Rep 121, an Australian case in which a tug was requested by the central tug control officer of the Port of Melbourne where a pooling arrangement exists between tugowners. The court found that the nomination of the tug gave rise to a contract between the vessel which was to be assisted and the tug providing assistance which was subject to the UKSTC applicable there.

150. UKSCT 1986, Cl. 1(b)(i).

151. Paragraph 1(b)(iv). But it does not include an accidental parting of the towing line (*The Wallumba* [1964] 2 Lloyd's Rep 387; [1965] 1 Lloyd's Rep 121).

152. *The Uranienborg* (1935) 53 Ll L Rep 165; [1936] P 21; see also *The Glenaffaric* (1948–49) 81 Ll L Rep; [1949] 1 All ER 245 where *The Uranienborg* was distinguished.

153. *British Transport Docks Board v "Apollon"* [1971] 1 Lloyd's Rep 476. In this case the tug struck a moored dock gate and sustained propeller damage.

154. In *PSNL Berhard v Dalrymple Marine Services Pty Ltd (The Koumala)*, fn. 146, a recent Australian case, the pilot ordered the two tugs to make fast at the starboard side of the vessel. The tugs crossed ahead of the vessel and turned starboard but one of them lost steering power and collided with the tow. Helman J considered that the tug was not yet in the position to receive orders and thus the UKSCT were not applicable.

155. Without the "hailing distance" requirement the period of the application of the towage contract would expand but arguably not too much. The first and the second conditions of the *Apollon* test require a situation where both tug and tow are ready and a situation in which it is reasonable for the tow to give an order. Thus a situation of proximity would have been implied bound by a criterion of whether it is reasonable or not to give an order rather than whether the tug is at hailing distance.

156. In *Apollon, supra*, fn. 153, two tugs were involved. The first had made fast, the second damaged a dock gate before making fast. The argument that the towage terms applied from the moment the first tug started towing was not made.

The protection of the tug under the UKSCT 1986 is based on the following contractual arrangements. First, under Clause 3, all the employees of the tugowner are deemed to be servants of the tow for the duration of the service. This arrangement provides a defence to any claim by the tow against the tug for negligence of the tugowner's employees. In addition it can provide a cause of action against the tow where the negligence of the tug's crew has caused the damage to the tug. It is important to note again that this contractual arrangement is only binding between the parties to the contract and does not affect third party liability. In other words, *vis-à-vis* a third party, the tugowner's employees remain the source of vicarious liability for the tugowner.

Second, under Clause 4, the liability of the tugowner is expressly exempted. This exemption covers any liability for damages caused either by the tug or the tow and it is effected by use of very wide terms. In addition Clause 4 expressly imposes an obligation on the tow owner to indemnify the tugowner for any damages sustained or paid out to third parties. The indemnity provision in Clause 4(b) is so wide that covers even the loss of the tug caused by negligence of the tugowner or the tug's crew or even cases where the tug is unseaworthy.[157] An additional, comparably more modest exemption, is also introduced under Clause 8 excluding any liability of the tug in respect of losses suffered by the tow and caused by war, war, riots, civil commotions, acts of terrorism or sabotage, strikes, lockouts, disputes, stoppages or labour disturbances, etc.

There are only a few situations under which the liability of the tug is not exempted or is not to be indemnified[158] by the tow. The first situation arises where the tugowner itself or the chief management of the tug or the person in the tug company to which the particular duty has been delegated has failed to exercise reasonable care to provide a seaworthy tug. However, damages arising from the negligence or faults or omissions of any other employees of the tugowner, even if they cause the tug to become unseaworthy and cause the damage suffered, are to be indemnified by the tow.[159] The second situation in which the tow does not have to pay for the tug's faults and the damages arising therefrom concerns situations where the tug has temporarily interrupted the provision of towage or other services and has moved away from the tow, for example to take bunkers or replace a tow line. The third situation arises where loss of life or personal injury is caused by the tug's negligence. The liability of the tug is in such cases not excluded and remains with the tug.

The UKSTC 1986 also provide for the right of the tugowner to substitute tugs or arrange tugs[160] for the tow on behalf of the tow as agent (Clause 5), claim salvage in appropriate circumstances (Clause 6), and limit liability (Clause 6).

### *(ii) TOWHIRE 1985*

Alternatives to the UKSCT 1986 have been produced by BIMCO in order to satisfy the needs arising from long haul towage where the UKSTC conditions are financially

157. *M'Bundis v Waratah Towage*, LMLN [1992] 343. (Note: *The Romina G*, fn. 143, on a slightly different version of the form.)
158. Note that the issue of who are parties to the contract may be relevant when it comes to looking at indemnities: see *Targe Towing Ltd and Another v Marine Blast Ltd* [2004] 1 Lloyd's Rep 721 (CA).
159. UKSCT, Cl. 4(c)(i).
160. Note that the Contracts (Rights of Third Parties) Act 1999 would apply directly to a towage contract as their application is not presumably affected by s. 6(5).

very risky for the tow (the "Hirer"). The developed TOWHIRE[161] and TOWCON[162] forms resemble in many aspects time and voyage charterparties and attempt to provide a more balanced solution to the need of standardised contractual forms.

TOWHIRE is a daily hire towage contract. The first two pages of the form identify the details of the contractual arrangement and the parties to the agreement. TOWHIRE Clause 13 imposes an obligation of due diligence on the tugowner to provide a seaworthy ship at the place of delivery of the tug. A similar obligation of tow-worthiness is placed on the tow owner under Clause 12. In addition the tow owner has to provide a certificate issued by appropriate marine surveyors stating that the vessel is tow-worthy. However, even after such a certificate has been provided the tugowner can still refuse to start the towage if it is not satisfied that the tow is indeed tow-worthy.

Allocation of liabilities under TOWHIRE is on a "knock for knock" basis (see Clause 18). Under this arrangement some damages are allocated to the tug or the tow in relation to which they arose irrespective of whether liability would normally attach to the owner of the tug or the tow respectively. There are three parts of Clause 18, each working in slightly different way. Clause 18(1)(a) provides that the tugowner will indemnify the tow owner for liability arising from loss of life or personal injury of the tug's employees or happening on board the tug. Clause 18(1)(b) similarly provides indemnification to the tugowner for loss of life or personal injury of the tow's employees or people onboard the tow. Clause 18(2) provides that the tugowner will be paying, without having a right of recourse against the tow owner, for loss or damage to the tug or property on board the tug and consequential loss; loss or damage to any other property caused by contact with the tug and consequential loss; wreck removal and pollution liability for the tug. This is coupled with an obligation imposed on the tugowner to indemnify the tow-owner for any such liability imposed on the tow-owner by a court or arbitration decision. The reverse arrangement applies for the tow (Clause 18(2)(b)). Notably the division of damages under Clause 18(2)(b) is stated to be applicable whether or not the damages are "due to breach of contract, negligence or any other fault on the part" of the party to whom liability to pay attaches. Such a statement is not present in the arrangement under Clause 18(1).[163] Note that Clause 18(3) presumably excludes from this division of loss[164] of Clause 18(1) and 18(2) indirect losses of profit, loss of use or production or "… any other indirect or consequential damage for any reason whatsoever".[165]

161. "Towhire" International Ocean Towage Agreement (Daily Hire), can be found at *www. bimco.org/ upload/towhire.pdf*
162. "Towcon" International Ocean Towage Agreement (lump sum), can be found at *www. bimco.org/ upload/towcon.pdf*
163. See *Rainey* for an argument that this difference implies that Cl. 18(1) as well as Cl. 18(3) do not cover situations where the relevant damages are caused by negligence, because exclusion clauses which can be taken to exclude contractual liability will not normally be considered to extend to cover negligence.
164. Note that the exclusion itself contains exclusions in respect of cls 11, 12, 13 and 16.
165. This was the decision in *The Herdentor*, unreported, 19 January 1996, and *Ease Faith Limited v Leonis Marine Management Limited, Cloudfree Ship Management Limited* (under TOWCON), fn. 139. An opposing view is supported by *Rainey*. In the second case the delay in the delivery day of the tug led to increased pilotage expenses as well as docking expense and reduced price for the tow which was sold for scrap. All these damages where recoverable by the tow and were not excluded by Cl. 18(3).

Difficulty arises when the division of financial liability under the knock-for-knock agreement is considered together with the respective obligations of the tug and the tow to provide, respectively, a seaworthy and tow-worthy ship (Clauses 12 and 13). The question which clause prevails would then arise. If the duty of seaworthiness or tow-worthiness is considered as the primary obligation that needs to be fulfilled, this would then mean that when this obligation is breached the knock-for-knock arrangement can be avoided. The alternative interpretation is that the knock-for-knock agreement applies in spite of the breach of the sea-worthiness or tow-worthiness obligation. In *Smit v Mobius*[166] the tow was not entitled to introduce arguments concerning the seaworthiness of the tug in respect of liability arising from a collision between the tow and another vessel because the "knock-for-knock" agreement was a workable allocation of risk and responsibility. Consequently, under a knock-for-knock agreement the significance of the obligation of seaworthiness and tow-worthiness is restricted in respect of the damages included in the knock-for-knock agreement under Clause 18.

However, Clause 18 does not resolve all liability issues. Only where the particular claims referred to are included in the wording of the clause, the clause operates. For example, where the tug is unseaworthy and there are losses not covered by Clause 18, for example by increased bunker consumption, then such operational damages are recoverable provided they are breaches of the contract of towage.

Where the "Hirer" under the TOWHIRE or TOWCON agreement is not the owner of the tow but a charterer then the owner of the tow becomes a third party under Clause 18. Thus, where the tow has been lost and this third party (the owner) sues and recovers from the tugowner in negligence, then the tugowner can obtain an indemnity from the "Hirer", the charterer in this case.[167]

Towhire provides for the creation of a lien on the tow for any unpaid amounts under the contract. However, this will be enforceable only where the tow owner is bound by the towage contract.[168] The exercise of the lien is always dependent on the power to enforce it at the port of destination as it is the law of the place where the assets are located that will determine the issues related to the ownership and possession of property. Thus, even if the contract is under English law, the local court may consider the exercise of the lien as against public policy or unenforce-able, especially where the tow is owned by the port State. In practice this may lead to the tug avoiding going into port or even staying outside territorial waters while exercising its lien.[169] Such delays, if reasonable, do not deprive the tug of the payment of hire, but if unreasonable and there is a date of delivery of the tow, it may result in the payment of damages to the hirer.[170] The contract provides for English law and jurisdiction (Clause 25) and a one-year time-bar (Clause 24).

166. *Smit International (Deutschland) GmbH v Josef Mobius Bau-Gesellschaft (GmbH & Co)* [2001] 2 All ER (Comm) 265.
167. *Targe Towing Ltd. and Another v Marine Blast Ltd*, fn. 158.
168. See *Lukoil-Kalingradnorneft plc v Tata Ltd (No 2)* [1999] 2 Lloyd's Rep 129 (CA) for the proposition, under the TOWCON contract, that under certain circumstances a lien based on bailment can be exercised.
169. In *Ease Faith Ltd v Leonis Marine Management, Cloudfree Ship Management Limited, supra*, fn. 139, this was accepted as consistent with the contract by the parties.
170. *Ibid.*

### *(iii) TOWCON*

This contract is used for towage where payment by lump sum has been agreed. However, the form has flexibility in that it permits part payment to be made at particular times, for example, at the time when the contract is agreed, when lines are passed and when the towage is finished. Thus it determines when the instalment is earned and when and how payment is to be effected. The major differences with TOWHIRE concern the payment provisions under Clause 2, and the place of departure which is more complicated than that of TOWHIRE. As with TOWHIRE, obligations of due diligence to provide a seaworthy tug and a towworthy tow are imposed (Clauses 12 and 13) as well as the knock-for-knock agreement. A duty of reasonable despatch[171] is implied in the contract if no provision about time is contained in it.[172] A tug operating only one of the two engines in order to minimise bunker consumption is in breach of this obligation. The reasoning includes an argument that the towing power of the vessel is included in the consideration of the lumpsum payable, because more powerful tugs cost more, thus in general it is not an option for the tugowner to only use part of the power he has agreed to provide.

English law and jurisdiction (Clause 25), a one-year time-bar[173] (Clause 24) and a warranty of authority exactly the same with that under TOWHIRE are also provided.

Because under TOWCON the risk of delay is on the tug, Clause 17 provides for "Delay Payment" if the delay is due to unsuitability of the tow for towage. The amount is agreed in advance in Box 29 of the form. Under which conditions is the tow unsuitable is a question that is not necessarily answered in exactly the same way as under a time or voyage charterparty.

clause 3

clause 18 & 19.

clause 31.

## (d) Salvage and towage law

Towage services in Admiralty are almost always based on contract.[174] Towing of a vessel in the absence of a contract is only remunerable if it is considered as part of a salvage operation.[175] However, the distinction between salvage and towage services is not always easily defined. The two regimes differ significantly as towage is purely contractual and although it is protected by a statutory action *in rem* entitling the parties to a towage contract to arrest each other's ship, such claim is of lower priority than a claim for salvage which is supported by a maritime lien.[176] In addition the right to a salvage reward arises independently of contract,[177] is payable by the owners of the property in proportion to the relative

171. The contract may provide for "utmost despatch" which is taken to mean the maximum sustainable speed. See *Ease Faith Ltd v Leonis Marine Management Ltd*, supra, fn. 139.
172. *Ease Faith Ltd v Leonis Marine Management Ltd*, supra, fn. 139.
173. *Rowan Companies Inc & Ors v Lambert Eggink Offshore Transport Consultants VOF & Ors* [1998] CLC 1574 (CA).
174. The action of towing another vessel which is in difficulty without remuneration is not uncommon, especially in respect of small yachts or between sister ships. In such cases there is no contract but the courts will impose an obligation to both tug and tow to exercise reasonable care in respect of their contribution to the service. For the principle applied see, for example, the Canadian case *Maurice Federation v Stewart (The West Bay III)* [1969] 1 Lloyd's Rep 158.
175. As defined under Art. 1(1) of the 1989 Salvage Convention. See section on *Salvage* for details.
176. See Chapter 11.
177. Art. 12 of the 1989 Salvage Convention.

value of their property[178] and the final remuneration, when no contract of salvage has been signed, or when the salvage contract is in a form similar to the Lloyd's Open Form depends on several criteria[179] and it is by no means fixed as payment under a towage contract.

For the right to salvage reward to arise the ship must be in danger. This does not exclude the possibility that a ship in danger may enter into a towage contract, provided that a willing tug is found. This is in practice the preferred, and usually cheaper, option for shipowners and cargo owners and is feasible in situations where there is no imminent danger to the vessel, for example where the engines have broken down but the vessel is away from the coast and the weather conditions are fair. The acceptance of a contract of towage arguably excludes the possibility for the tug-owner to claim salvage unless the situation significantly changes.[180]

The restriction arises from Article 17 of the Salvage Convention which states that a salvage reward is only payable where "... the services rendered exceed what can be reasonably considered as due performance of a contract entered into before the danger arose". It must be presumed that a ship under towage, even if disabled, is not in danger and that a situation of danger in respect of the tow should arise. The scope of this provision has not been tested in the English courts. However, there is agreement between commentators[181] that the provision does not appear to change the pre-existing salvage situation. Cases before the Salvage Convention suggest that one must look at the contractual towage arrangement to see whether the rendered services exceed those agreed. For example, operational difficulties, including interruptions of the towage service, which are normal and expected, for instance the parting of the tow line or the deterioration of weather by itself, would not take the tug outside the towage service into salvage.[182] Arguably the test pre-dating the 1989 Salvage Convention is one based on the development of new circumstances which create a dangerous situation for the tow and which cannot reasonably be considered as covered by the existing towage contract.[183]

In a recent case a number of tugs were employed in towing an oil rig between two locations. The hawser of one of the tugs parted under deteriorating weather conditions. The arbitrator held that on the facts a situation of danger arose when the hawser parted and that the services from then on amounted to salvage services even if the situation of danger was brought about partly by negligence of the tugs.[184] The appeal to the High Court did not include the dispute on Article 17 but only in relation to the consequences of the salvor's negligence under Article 18.[185]

178. Art. 13 of the 1989 Salvage Convention.
179. *Ibid.*
180. Cl. 6 of the UK Standard Conditions for Towage and other services expressly preserve the rights of the tugowner and the crew in claiming salvage. Contrast with TOWHIRE AND TOWCON Cl. 15 where the tug should make all reasonable efforts to reconnect with the tow where the towing line parts without claiming salvage. In addition the tugowner and his servants are expressly authorised to seek salvage assistance where needed.
181. See *Kennedy and Rose on the Law of Salvage* (6th ed) (Sweet & Maxwell, 2001); *Brice on Maritime Law of Salvage* (4th ed) (Sweet & Maxwell, 2002) and *Rainey*.
182. *The Minnehaha, supra*, fn. 125.
183. See *Rainey*, n. 128.
184. A reduction of the salvage reward under Art. 18 of the Salvage Convention was the consequence for the negligent salvor.
185. *The Owners, Masters and Crews of the Tugs Maridive VII, Maridive XIII, Maridive 85 and Maridive 94 v Owners and Demise Charterers of the Oil Rig Key Singapore her Equipment, Stores and Bunkers*, fn. 47.

Where a towage service changes into salvage the fate of the towage contract must be considered. The dominant view is that the towage contract is "suspended" until the time when "... the special and unexpected danger is over, and then the salvage service would end, and the towage service would be resumed...".[186] The alternative interpretation is that salvage starts when the towage contract becomes impossible to perform at which point in time the towage contract is abandoned.[187] Arguably, it is more practical for the parties to accept redelivery under salvage at sea, even if redelivery is by the tug, as a salvor, to the same tug under the towage contract and proceed directly to the destination of the contract of towage. The law before the Salvage Convention appears to impose this solution to the parties.[188] One must be aware that complications are bound to arise where the towage contract and the salvage contract are subject to the law of different countries and disputes at the period of suspension arise.

The right to the salvage reward under the Salvage Convention requires a "useful result" and is not subject to redelivery at a place of safety, which is only mentioned under the obligation of the property owners (Article 8.2) to accept redelivery in such a place. To this extent and regarding the criteria for fixing the salvage reward under Article 13 there is no difficulty in accepting that, unless the owners refuse redelivery at sea, the English law solution that the towage contract is suspended during the performance of the salvage services is not in conflict with the 1989 Salvage Convention and is thus still applicable.

However, where Special Compensation under Article 14 is also to be earned there appears to be a problem in respect with the House of Lords decision in *The Nagasaki Spirit*[189] where it was held that the application of Article 14 continues until the salvage operation is completed. To impose on the salvors an obligation to abandon their right of remuneration under Article 14 because of a pre-existing towage contract which has been "suspended" is to our view not justifiable when the purpose of the 1989 Salvage Convention is taken into account[190] and, in any case, cannot be confirmed without consideration of the situation by the courts. In order for the "suspended contract" solution to remain valid one must assume that the "suspended" contract imposes on the tug an obligation to redeliver from the salvage operations and return back to the towage contract as soon as practicable which is far from obvious. Thus the fate of the towage contract when special compensation is payable is to our view unclear and we consider the common law position as problematic and in need of revision. It is submitted that the towage contract ends at the point where a situation of salvage arises and that the towage contract can be reinstated by agreement by both parties but subject to rights and obligations created by the 1989 Salvage Convention.

186. *The Minnehaha, supra*, fn. 125; *The Leon Blum* [1915] P 90; [1915] P 290 (CA).
187. This is a neater, easier to apply and more easy to describe as part of contract law solution. However, it has significant drawbacks in relation to the exact point in time at which a new towage contract is reintroduced.
188. *The Leon Blum, supra*, fn. 185.
189. *Semco Salvage & Marine Pte Ltd v Lancer Navigation Co Ltd (The Nagasaki Spirit)* [1997] 1 Lloyd's Rep 323 (HL).
190. One should also take into account that the Salvage Convention imposes additional obligations on the parties in respect of environmental protection which cannot be excluded by contract. The resurrection of the pre-existing towage contract under the common law position cannot arguably remove such obligations.

By contrast it is clear that where salvage operations have started, whether under a salvage contract or not, the services cannot turn from salvage services to become towage services without an express agreement between the property owners and the salvors.

### (e) Towage and carriage of goods by sea

Where unmanned barges or ships are towed, or where a riding crew is put onboard the tow by the tug, then the tug has physical possession of the tow and can be considered to be in the position of the tow as a bailee.[191] This legal relationship, which is relevant to towage only where the tug has the physical possession of the tow, imposes on the tugowner the strict liability of a bailee. This is a much heavier duty than the reasonable care and skill implied in common law or imposed statutorily by the Supply of Goods and Services Act 1982 to a contract of towage.

The existence of such a relationship of bailment will also be important for the tow-owner who is not a party to the towage contract but can be considered as bound by bailment on terms or sub-bailment.[192]

### (f) Collisions during the towage operation

Liability for collision damage between the tug and tow would almost always be governed by their contractual arrangements.

Collision or pollution liability will be based on tort[193] or on special pollution liability regimes.[194] The contractual or other relationship between the tug and the tow will not affect the relationship of either of them with the third party.

However, there are issues which complicate the relationship between the tug and the tow *vis-à-vis* third parties. First, there is the issue of limited liability. Because the tug is usually a much smaller vessel than the tow, it also has much lower limits of liability. Thus, a third party claimant would be in a better position if it can establish the liability of the tow or if possible the liability of both the tow and the tug.[195]

The second related issue regards the commanding of the towing operation. English case law has in the past used the misleading expression the "tug is the servant of the tow"[196] and this was considered to be the position as a matter of law. It has now been clarified that this position is wrong and the issue of command and liability is a matter of fact not a matter of law.[197] Perhaps the best way to explain the position is by considering three proposals. First, that the tug is an independent entity. Second, that liability of the tug or the tow *vis-à-vis* a third

191. *Lukoil-Kalingradmorneft Plc v Tata Ltd (No 2)* [1999] 1 Lloyd's Rep 365. See also *Targe Towing Ltd and Another v Marine Blast Ltd* (see *supra*, fn. 158), where the issue was partly discussed.
192. *Owners of Cargo lately Laden on Board the KH Enterprise v Owners of the Pioneer Container (The Pioneer Container, The KH Enterprise)* [1994] 1 Lloyd's Rep 593; [1994] 2 AC 324 (PC).
193. See the section on *Collisions*, p. 155.
194. See Chapter 8.
195. See *The Bramley Moore* [1964] P 200; [1964] 2 WLR 259; [1964] 1 All ER 105; [1963] 2 Lloyd's Rep 429; (1963) 107 SJ 980; 1963 WL 21234.
196. *Owners of the SS Devonshire v Owners of the Barge Leslie and Others (The Devonshire)* [1912] AC 634 (HL).
197. *Ibid.*

party will arise when any of them acts or fails to act in accordance with the required "good seamanship" standard.[198] Third, that in addition to the liability of the party that acted negligently, whether this was the tug or the tow, liability may also attach to the other party[199] (tow or tug respectively) if that party was in command of the towage operation and acted negligently in this capacity.[200] Of course causation of damage flowing from the negligent command or actions must be proved in all cases for rights of compensation to arise. Limitation of liability would then depend on the entitlement of each liable party in this respect.[201]

Where the third party's vessel is innocent then the liability of the tug and tow will be joint and several. Where the third party's vessel navigates negligently and contributes to the collision then liability for property damage will be apportioned between the wrongdoers[202] while in respect of loss of life and personal injury liability will be joint and several.[203]

## 5. WRECK REMOVAL

### (a) Introduction

Wrecked ships are a form of pollution of the marine environment, and most developed systems of maritime law contain provisions empowering governments, usually coastguard, port or lighthouse authorities, to remove wrecks which amount to an obstruction or danger to navigation. In England the relevant provisions are sections 252–254 of the Merchant Shipping Act 1995, which not only empower the relevant agency to remove the wreck, but also to recover the cost of doing so from the owner.[204]

The insurance coverage of the costs and expenses of removal, destruction, lighting or marking of a wrecked ship are usually among the risks covered by the Protecting and Indemnity Association ("P&I Club") in which the ship is entered.[205] The wreck of a ship may well include the cargo laden on board, and the shipowner's P&I Club cover will also extend to the removal of such wreckage where the cost of such removal is compulsory by law or the costs are recoverable from the shipowner.[206]

The relevant statutory provisions[207] usually give the governmental agency the power to sell the ship or any material recovered from her to defray the costs of the removal operation, and to recover any unrecovered balance from the shipowner.

198. See the section on *Collisions*, pp. 155 *et seq.*
199. For examples see *Owners of the Steam Barge Trishna v Owners of the Motor Tug Panther (The Panther)* [1957] 1 Lloyd's Rep 57; [1957] 1 All ER 641; *San Jose v Socrates and Champion (The Socrates and the Champion)* (1923) 15 Ll L Rep 196 (CA); [1923] P 162.
200. *The Niobe* [1888] LR 13 PD 55; [1888] 59 LT 257; [1891] AC 401 (HL).
201. *The Bramley Moore* [1964] P 200; [1964] 2 WLR 259; [1964] 1 All ER 105; [1963] 2 Lloyd's Rep 429; (1963) 107 SJ 980; 1963 WL 21234.
202. Section 187, MSA 1995. This applies also where the wrongdoer is not physically in contact with any other vessel. *The Cairnbahn* [1914] P 25 (CA).
203. Section 188, MSA 1995.
204. Similar powers are conferred by s. 56 of the Harbour Docks and Piers Clauses Act 1847.
205. For full details of P&I Clubs and the risks they cover, see Chapter 10, pp. 337–344.
206. See, for example, s. 18 of the Rules of the UK P&I Club.
207. E.g., s. 252(2)(c) and (d) of the MSA 1995.

Although the statutory definitions rarely state so explicitly,[208] a wreck is, by its nature, a thing of no commercial value. Were it to have such a value, the salvage industry would no doubt undertake its removal and sale in return for a suitable salvage reward. However, a valueless wreck will not yield proceeds of sale equal to the costs involved in its removal, and since most ships are owned by a one-ship company, the prospects of a coastal State recovering by legal proceedings expenses which it has incurred in removing a wreck are very poor. This position will change radically when the Nairobi Wreck Removal Convention 2007 enters into force internationally. This will be discussed below.

In the majority of cases the shipowner and its P&I Club will, once the fact that a ship has become a wreck has been established by appropriate surveys, probably take the initiative and arrange for its removal. Standard forms of contract for this purpose, such as the WRECKFIXED, WRECKSTAGE and WRECKHIRE forms, have been developed by the International Salvage Union, the International Group of P&I Clubs and other interested parties. These are published by The Baltic and International Maritime Council ("BIMCO").[209]

What happens when the owner of a wrecked ship (or its insurer) takes no action to remove it? If the wreck is *within* the waters under the jurisdiction of a coastal State (its internal waters or territorial sea), that State is likely to invoke its domestic law to issue a Wreck Removal Order, and eventually to undertake the removal itself[210] in order to maintain the safety of others using the waters in which the wreck lies. It will then, as previously mentioned, seek to recover the costs from the shipowner, but if they have no other assets that may prove very difficult. Recovery direct from the P&I Club in which the ship is entered will generally be defeated by the "pay to be paid" rule in the club cover.[211]

### (b) The Nairobi Wreck Removal Convention 2007

These difficulties led to the drafting and eventual adoption of the 2007 Nairobi Wreck Removal Convention, but another significant impetus for that instrument was the need to confer on coastal States jurisdiction to take appropriate action to remove wrecks which present a danger to navigation or to the marine environment in the Exclusive Economic Zone ("EEZ"). That is the zone beyond the territorial sea over which the Article 56 of the UN Convention on the Law of the Sea ("UNCLOS") confers limited jurisdiction[212] on the coastal State.

The waters in a coastal State's EEZ are, by definition, well offshore, and in most cases deep. Ships sunk in such waters rarely pose problems to other navigators, but leaking fuel oil, or, in the case of a tanker oil cargo, may create a sufficient threat of environmental hazard that action is required. The techniques developed by the offshore oil industry have made it possible to take effective measures to mitigate those hazards,[213] but the legal regime to give the coastal State effective powers to compel such action in the EEZ did not exist.

208. E.g. in s. 255(1) of the MSA 1995.
209. See *www.bimco.org/* and follow links to documents.
210. Or, more probably, to employ a professional salvage contractor to do so.
211. This will be discussed in Chapter 10, p. 342 – see *The Fanti and Padre Island* [1989] 1 Lloyd's Rep 239.
212. See Chapter 9, p. 304.
213. As was demonstrated by the removal of the cargo oil and bunkers from the *Erika* and *Prestige*.

A precedent was found in the 1969 Intervention Convention[214] which conferred limited rights on a coastal State to take action on the *High Seas* if it was threatened by oil pollution from a maritime casualty. Article I gave the right to take such intervention measures only where the danger of pollution of their coastline was "grave and imminent", followed upon a "marine casualty" and was "expected to result in major harmful consequences". Article V required the measures taken to be "proportionate to the damage actual or threatened" and not to "go beyond what is reasonably necessary to achieve the end mentioned in Article I". These phrases have found their way into Article 2 of the Wreck Removal Convention, and reflect the concern internationally not to grant to a coastal State unfettered rights to take action to remove a wreck in its EEZ.

The debates in the Legal Committee of the IMO which eventually led to the drafting of the 2007 Wreck Removal Convention were long and complex, but the text finally adopted contains four principal elements:

(1) the grant of rights to the coastal State to remove a wreck from its EEZ if it represents a hazard to safe navigation or to the marine environment;[215]
(2) the right of a State party to declare that the provisions of the Convention will apply to wrecks within its territory including the territorial sea and to notify the IMO that it has done so – the so-called "opt in" provision;[216]
(3) strict liability on the shipowner for the costs of reporting, marking and removing a wreck if required to do so by the coastal State;[217]
(4) compulsory insurance of liability for wreck removal charges, and a right of direct action against insurers, up to the limit of the shipowner's liability calculated in accordance with the 1996 Protocol to the 1976 International Convention on Limitation of Liability for Maritime Claims. These provisions are modelled on the equivalent provisions of the 1992 CLC Convention.[218]

The Nairobi Wreck Removal Convention requires ratification by 10 States for entry into force, and it seems likely that the major European maritime States will indeed ratify it. The figure of 10 ratifications is relatively small in comparison with other conventions, and this does suggest that there was a broad consensus of States in favour of this convention at the Diplomatic Conference in Nairobi.

States which exercise the option to extend the provisions of the Wreck Removal Convention to wrecks in their internal waters and territorial sea will have to accept the general constraints of reasonableness imposed by Article 2, and the more specific requirements of Article 9, in return for the financial security which the Convention provides. In view of the potential problems of enforcing claims for reimbursement of wreck removal expenses discussed above, it will be apparent that the advantages of accepting those constraints will in most cases outweigh any disadvantages.[219]

214. International Convention Relating to Intervention on the High Seas in Cases of Oil Pollution Casualties, 1969. See Chapter 8.
215. Article 2.
216. Article 3.
217. Article 10.
218. Article 12. The International Convention on Civil Liability for Oil Pollution Damage 1992.
219. A detailed review of the evolution of the Nairobi Wreck Removal Convention and a commentary on its principal articles can be found at [2007] 13 JIML 429.

Moreover, on a broader front, the existence of a certificate of financial responsibility provided for in the Nairobi Wreck Removal Convention may well have an impact on the topical question of Places of Refuge. State and port authorities will be justifiably concerned at the risk of a ship in distress sinking and obstructing navigation of their waterways. If their government has exercised the option in Article 3(2) to extend the application of the Wreck Removal Convention to its internal and territorial waters, this should allay their concerns that they may be left with a valueless wreck and no prospects of recovery from her owners. At the time of writing (February 2008) the topic of Places of Refuge is under discussion in the Comité Maritime International[220] in the European Union,[221] and at the IMO. Delegates would be wise to recognise the linkage with the Nairobi Wreck Removal Convention.

### (c) Historic wrecks[222]

This is a separate subject since such wrecks rarely interfere with navigation nor create a risk of damage to the environment. However, the increasing sophistication of SCUBA diving equipment and remotely operated submersibles has placed virtually all sunken vessels within the reach of researchers and would-be salvors. This has raised some difficult questions of law. English law takes the position that title to a wreck remains in the owner of the ship at the time of her sinking and that she remains under the jurisdiction of her flag State if she lies outside territorial waters. This has led to the enactment of statutes to prevent unrestricted "salvage" of historic wrecks where their preservation is considered necessary, in particular the Protection of Wrecks Act 1973 which enables the Secretary of State to designate such wrecks as protected wrecks if they are of historical, archaeological or artistic value. Military wrecks are protected by the Protection of Military Remains Act 1986 which applies to military wrecks outside the UK, but the protection is limited since the sanctions in that Act can only apply to British persons and those operating from British ships.

While these statutes create a legal regime of regulation, is very difficult in practice to enforce such provisions, due to the isolated location of most of the wrecks concerned.

Another problem is that by designating a wreck under the Protection of Wrecks Act 1973, the exact location of the wreck becomes a matter of public record, thus depriving the wreck of the secrecy which is in many cases its best protection.

The Merchant Shipping and Maritime Security Act 1997 contains in section 24 provisions enabling the Secretary of State to implement international agreements relating to the protection of wrecks. In 2003 an order was made under that section with respect to the RMS Titanic,[223] which gives effect to an agreement between the governments of Britain, Canada, France and the USA.

220. This is on the agenda of the October 2008 Athens Conference of the CMI.
221. In discussion of the Traffic Monitoring Directive.
222. For a detailed treatment of this interesting subject see Chapter 13, "Interests in Wreck", written by Prof N Gaskell and Prof S Dromgoole in N Palmer and E McKendrick (eds) *Interests in Goods* (2nd ed) (LLP, 1998). Also the annotations by Prof N Gaskell to the Merchant Shipping and Maritime Security Act 1997 in *Current Law Statutes*.
223. The Protection of Wrecks (RMS Titanic) Order 2003, SI 2003 No 2496.

### (d) International conventions

Article 303 of UNCLOS 1982 places a duty on States to protect archaeological and historic objects found at sea and to cooperate for that purpose. Article 303(3) expressly reserves the rights of identifiable owners, the law of salvage, or other rules of admiralty, and cultural exchange agreements. Article 149 provides that articles and objects found in the High Seas shall be preserved or disposed of for the benefit of mankind as a whole.

The UNESCO Convention on the Protection of the Underwater Cultural Heritage 2001[224] was intended to provide an internationally agreed basis for preserving underwater cultural objects, and expressly provides that these shall not be subject to the law of salvage. This convention, which requires 20 ratifications for entry into force, has been criticised in many quarters, notably by the CMI,[225] and the extent to which it will achieve acceptance internationally remains in doubt.

## 6. PORTS AND HARBOURS

### (a) Introduction

The legal provisions regarding the establishment of port authorities and their supervision by central government are largely administrative, and thus beyond the scope of this book, but no work on maritime law would be complete without a brief treatment of the legal provisions dealing with ports and harbours.

The safety of navigation in British waters, formerly the entire responsibility of Trinity House (in England and Wales), the Commissioners of Northern Lighthouses (in Scotland) and the Commissioners of Irish Lights (in Northern Ireland), has, since the Ports Act 1991, been divided between them and the relevant Statutory Harbour Authorities.[226] The maintenance of lights, lighthouses and buoys has now been taken over by the latter in the waters subject to their jurisdiction, while the former, now collectively referred to as General Lighthouse Authorities, are responsible for the waters not within the jurisdiction of harbour authorities.

### (b) Port safety management

The principles applicable to matters of safety in port operations are now set out in The Port Safety Code published between November 2005 and March 2006[227] following an extensive review of the laws relating to port authorities and pilotage. This code is not written in mandatory terms, but represents a clear statement of best practice in all aspects of port operations, and is likely to be accepted by courts as the yardstick by which port authorities will be judged if civil claims are brought against them.

224. The full text is at *http://portal.unesco.org/en/ev.php-URL_ID=13520&URL_DO=DO_TOPIC&URL_SECTION=201.html*
225. See the report in the 2002 CMI Year Book at p. 154, also at *www.comitemaritime.org*
226. Ss 193–223 of the MSA 1995.
227. Full details are available from the website of the Dept for Transport at *www.dft.gov.uk/pgr/shippingports/ports/pmsc/*

### (c) Limitation of liability

The subject of limitation of liability of the owners of ships is dealt with elsewhere in this book,[228] but in the context of the liabilities of port authorities it should be noted that English law contains an exceptional provision, now in section 191 of the Merchant Shipping Act 1995. This entitles a port authority to limit its liability to the amount of the limitation fund of the largest UK ship which is in the port at the time of the damage giving rise to the claim, or has been within the preceding five years. The provision, which does not derive from any international convention,[229] but which would apply to a claim by a foreign claimant as much as a British port authority, is rarely invoked. It would have been applicable to civil claims against the Milford Haven Port Authority[230] arising out of the *Sea Empress*[231] case.

### (d) Claims by port authorities

One of the last vestiges of the nineteenth century statute applicable to port authorities is to be found in section 74 of the Harbours Docks and Piers Clauses Act 1847, which creates strict liability on the owner of any vessel causing damage to the harbour dock or pier. That liability is independent of any negligence on the part of the shipowner, but does not prevent him from limiting his liability under the Merchant Shipping Acts.

The word "owner" means the registered owner and does not include bare-boat charterer or any other type of charterer.[232] That the wording establishes strict liability was decided in the *The Mostyn*.[233]

The power to raise the wreck and the shipowner's obligation to pay for the wreck removal is covered under the Harbour Docks Piers Clauses Act 1847, section 56. This has been held to apply to the owner at the time of the wreck raising which can cause problems where the ship has been abandoned to the insurers.[234]

### (e) Port State control

One of the most important results of the Merchant Shipping and Maritime Security Act 1997, following the publication of the Donaldson Report[235] in the light of the *Braer* casualty in 1992, was to define the powers of detention by harbour authorities of unsafe ships under the regime of Port State Control established, in

228. See the section on *Limitation of Liability*, p. 201.
229. It was first enacted in the Merchant Shipping (Liability of Shipowners and Others) Act 1900. A similar provision applies to claims against pilots under s. 22 of the Pilotage Act 1987.
230. The MHPA was a public trust set up as statutory body under the Milford Haven Conservancy Act 1958, and as such typical of the port authorities round the coast of the UK, most of which have their own enabling legislation derived from similar nineteenth century statutes incorporating the terms of the Harbour Docks and Piers Clauses Act 1847.
231. *Environment Agency v Milford Haven Port Authority (The Sea Empress)* [2000] JPL 943.
232. See *BP Exploration Operating Co Ltd v Chevron Shipping* [2002] 1 Lloyd's Rep 77, 97, for the history of the section and in particular s. 81.
233. [1928] AC 57. The earlier decision of the HL in *River Wear Commissioners v Adamson* [1877] 2 App Cas 743 is necessarily wrong in respect of the interpretation of s.74.
234. See *The Crystal* [1894] AC 508.
235. Safer Ships, Cleaner Seas Report of Lord Donaldson's Inquiry into the Prevention of Pollution from Merchant Shipping (HMSO, Cm 2560, 1994).

the case of the UK, by the Paris Memorandum.[236] This was a result of the growing concerns by coastal States at the failure of flag States to enforce their own rules regarding ship safety. The coastal States have now given their port authorities very extensive powers of inspection and detention of ships which do not comply with the internationally recognised standards. The results of the inspections are posted, on an open access basis, on the *www.equasis.org* website.

### (f) Places of refuge[237]

The question of the right of the Master of a ship in distress to seek shelter in a place of refuge has become topical as a consequence of two well publicised incidents involving the ships *Castor* and *Prestige*.[238] Both were tankers and both suffered structural failure in heavy weather off the coast of Spain, the *Castor* in the Mediterranean and the *Prestige* in the Atlantic. In both cases permission to enter a Spanish port was refused. The *Castor* was eventually salved successfully after a long and difficult operation, but the *Prestige* broke in two and sank, causing very extensive pollution off the coasts of Spain, Portugal and France.

International law has long recognised the duty of a coastal State to allow entry of a ship in distress,[239] but this right, which was largely based on humanitarian considerations for the safety of the crew, has been eroded by increasing concerns for the protection of the coastal State's marine environment, and by the availability of helicopters to rescue the crews of ships in distress.

The IMO has adopted Guidelines on Places of Refuge[240] which set out clear criteria for the objective assessment of the condition of a ship in distress. The nub of these guidelines states clearly in paragraph 1.7:

> "... granting access to a place of refuge could involve a political decision which can only be taken on a case by case basis with due consideration given to the balance between the advantage for the affected ship and the environment resulting from bringing the ship into a place of refuge and the risk to the environment resulting from that ship being near to the coast."

Again at paragraph 3.12:

> "When permission to access a place of refuge is requested, there is no obligation for the coastal state to grant it, but the coastal state should weigh all the factors and risks in a balanced manner and give shelter whenever reasonably possible."

These guidelines are not mandatory, but they do, it is submitted, represent a clear statement of best practice in a casualty situation, and in the application of

236. See *www.parismou.org/ParisMOU/Organisation/Memorandum+ of+Understanding/xp/menu.3945/default.aspx* For a full review of this subject see the notes by Prof N Gaskell to the Merchant Shipping and Maritime Security Act 1997 in *Current Law Statutes 1997*.
237. The best collection of papers on this subject is in the 2003 CMI Year Book at *www. comitemaritime.org/year/2003/2003_part02_c.htm* and in the 2004 Year Book at pp. 208–247.
238. The facts of these cases are set out in the paper by R Shaw in the 2003 CMI Year Book at pp. 332–333 accessible at the web address cited above.
239. *Kate A Hoff v The United Mexican States (The Rebecca)* (1929) 4 RAAA P 444; *The American Journal of International Law*, Vol 23, No 4 (October 1929), pp. 860–865. The material section of the award is cited by Brown in *The International Law of the Sea* (Ashgate Publishing Co, 1994) at p. 39.
240. Adopted by IMO Resolution A949(23) and the IMO Guidelines on the control of ships in an emergency, adopted as IMO Circular MSC.1/Circ.1251.

any law or convention in which reasonable conduct is required of a ship in distress, a salvor assisting such a ship, and a coastal State requested to admit such a ship to one of its ports, will represent the best evidence of such best practice.

The IMO Legal Committee has not seen fit to treat Places of Refuge as a matter satisfying the criterion of a "compelling need" which would justify active consideration in the Committee's work programme. However, the topic has not been removed from long-term consideration.

In contrast the European Union has taken an active stance[241] in pressing Member States to adopt clear rules, based on the IMO Guidelines, for the admission of ships to places of refuge, and the designation of such places on the coasts of such States.

The CMI has maintained an active Working Group on Places of Refuge and a draft convention has been prepared, which would give greater legal force to the principles set out in the IMO Guidelines, and which would create a presumption of a right of access to a place of refuge for a ship in distress. That presumption would be rebuttable on proof by the coastal State that the risk of environmental damage caused by the admitting a ship to its harbours outweighed the risks of leaving the ship at the mercy of wind and waves in the open sea. The draft convention and the many issues raised by it are on the programme of the CMI Conference in Athens in October 2008.

## 7. PILOTAGE

### (a) Introduction

A pilot is defined to be "any person not belonging to a ship who has the conduct thereof".[242] Pilots are usually Master Mariners with experience and knowledge of particular sea passages or approaches to harbours. They act as advisors under the ship's Master supervision to enhance the safety of navigation in difficult areas. They also act as a "principal source of skill marine advice to the harbour authority".[243]

Pilotage can be compulsory or voluntary[244] and can also be distinguished to coastal and deep sea. Deep Sea pilots are licenced by the Trinity House[245] and coastal pilots by competent harbour authorities. Deep sea pilotage is not compulsory although it may become so in marine protected areas. Compulsory pilotage is much more common in coastal areas and the approaches to harbours where collisions and accidents are more likely to happen. The most important legal issue in respect of pilotage is arguably who has to pay for damages caused by the pilot's negligence when the pilot is employed under compulsory and non-compulsory

241. See Directive 2002/59/EC of the European Parliament and of the Council of 27 June 2002 Establishing a Community Vessel Traffic Monitoring and Information System and Repealing Council Directive 93/75/EEC, OJL 208, 5.8.2002, pp. 10–27, Articles 20 and 21.
242. Pilotage Act 1987, s. 31(1).
243. Paragraph 16 of the *Review of the Pilotage Act 1987*, Summary, Department for Transport.
244. Government ships are not subject to pilotage directions.
245. The Trinity house is also the Lighthouse Authority for England, Wales, the Channel Islands and Gibraltar. S. 23 of the Pilotage Act 1987 gives power to the Secretary of State to authorise bodies to issue deep sea pilotage certificates.

pilotage respectively. This will be discussed after explaining the statutory liability for the appointment, training and management of pilots.

### (b) Statutory provisions

The law related to pilotage has been radically revised under the Pilotage Act 1987 which transferred responsibility from pilotage authorities to certain harbour authorities.[246] Such authorities have the power and the obligation under the 1987 Pilotage Act, to decide whether and what type of pilotage services are needed in their area for each type of ship and whether pilotage should be compulsory.[247] In addition such Harbour Authorities are authorised to provide the pilotage services,[248] to set the qualifications of pilots,[249] to authorise pilots[250] and to disqualify incompetent pilots.[251] Compulsory pilotage is determined by the issuance of *pilotage directions* by the harbour authorities, empowered under the 1987 Pilotage Act.[252] The competent harbour authority may charge for the pilotage services provided.[253]

If a ship is navigated in an area of compulsory pilotage without a pilot or without a Master or first mate holding an exemption certificate then the ship's Master is guilty of an offence and liable summary conviction.[254]

A review of the 1987 Pilotage Act undertaken by the Department of Transport has led to the development of the Port Maritime Safety Code. While the Review and the Maritime Safety Code identified significant improvements that need to be made in respect of the training and licencing of pilots and advocated the use of port passage plans, it did not suggest any changes in the liability regime applicable under the 1987 Pilotage Act, except perhaps in clarifying that the performance required by the competent harbour authorities in order to discharge their statutory obligations under the Act must be consistent with the Port Maritime Safety Code.

246. Only harbour authorities of ports within pilotage districts as decided under the Pilotage Act 1983 and which already have responsibility for the safety of navigation are authorised as competent harbour authorities. 127 harbour authorities presently have pilotage functions, although over 20 appear not to exercise them. Around 800 pilots are employed, many as part timer,s with about 70% of them involved with the 10 larger port authorities. Department of Trade: *Review of the Pilotage Act 1987*, Summary.
247. See *Oceangas (Gibraltar) Ltd v Port of London Authority (The Cavendish)* [1993] 2 Lloyd's Rep 292 for the rejection of an argument that s. 2 imposes a positive liability on the competent authority on which the claimant shipowner can rely for a claim for damages caused by pilot's negligence.
248. Pilotage Act 1987, Art. 2. In deciding so the harbour authority should take into account the risks of the carriage of hazardous and dangerous goods.
249. Pilotage Act 1987, Art. 3.
250. The power of the harbour authority to appoint new pilots is subject to the approval of existing authorised pilots (s. 4).
251. Pilotage Act 1987, Art. 3. Disqualification occurs when there is incompetence or misconduct in the capacity of a pilot or when qualifications have expired. Licences can also be revoked when the number of pilots exceeds the set limits or where it is appropriate to do so. Art. 3(5).
252. Section 7 of the Pilotage Act 1987. If compulsory pilotage concerns areas outside a harbour, the harbour authority should apply under s. 14 of the Harbours Act 1964 to extent the limits of the harbour (s. 7(3)). Exemption certificates may be issued when appropriate (s. 8) and ships less than 20 metres long and fishing boats less than 47.5 metres long are exempted (s. 21(7(3)).
253. Section 9 of the Pilotage Act 1987. Claims for pilotage fees are supported by an action *in rem* under the SCA 1981, s. 20(2), which can lead to the arrest of the ship.
254. Section 15(2) and (3). The offence is heavier where a pilot has offered services and denied. See also s. 17.

### (c) Liability for the faults of ships under pilotage

Where a ship which is under the command of a pilot causes damage the question can be raised on who would be responsible for the damage. The pilot himself, the owner as well as the authorising harbour authority have to be considered.

#### (i) Liability of the pilot

Pilots are liable for acts of omissions which cause "loss, destruction or serious damage" or "personal injury or death"[255] only where they act deliberately or under the influence of drugs or drink or their act or omission amounts to a breach or neglect of duty.[256] In such circumstances fines and prison sentences may be the consequences for the pilot.

The wording of section 21(1) suggests that liability for damages caused by either ordinary negligence or any type of conduct causing minor damage is excluded. In addition the civil liability of the pilot[257] is limited to £1,000 plus the pilotage fee[258] which can be up to a few thousand pounds for larger vessels and which varies between ports. The limits of liability available to the pilot are absolute, that is, there is no provision under which the pilot may lose the right to limit his liability.

The wording of the above described provisions is not restrictive and would arguably apply irrespective of whether pilotage is compulsory or not and whether it is deep sea pilotage or not.

#### (ii) Liability of the harbour authority

The harbour authority is not liable just because it has authorised a pilot whose acts or omissions have caused damage.[259] Fault by the competent harbour authority itself must be demonstrated. Arguably the fault of the competent harbour authority may be based most probably on a breach of its statutory duties.

Pilots have usually a contractual arrangement, normally a contract of employment with the harbour authority.[260] The question then arises whether the negligence of the pilot imposes vicarious liability on the employing harbour authority, or on the shipowner or on both.[261]

In respect of non-compulsory pilotage vicarious liability cannot arise for the harbour authority simply because it does not exercise any statutory power. The

255. Section 21(1).
256. Section 21(1).
257. The limitation of liability applies even where the ship is outside the area of compulsory pilotage provided that she is navigating to or from the usual place where pilots are picked up (s. 22(2)).
258. Section 21(2).
259. Section 22(8).
260. This is not precluded by the fact that the harbour authority discharges statutory duties by employing pilots. See *Transport and General Workers Union v Associated British Ports Limited* [2001] EWCA Civ 2032 (CA).
261. The possibility of joint liability arose only recently: *Viasystems (Tyneside) Ltd v Thermal Transfer (Northern) Ltd and Others* [2006] QB 510 (CA). No pilotage claim has been decided after this case has been considered. However, it is submitted that the interpretation of s. 16 of the Pilotage Act 1987 is probably conclusive in restricting any liability to the shipowner alone, especially as there is no particular policy reason to impose liability on the harbour authority too.

shipowner can employ any advisor he wishes to assist with the ship's navigation. Only where the shipowner requests an appropriately qualified pilot and later it is revealed that the pilot's licence was granted or remained in force in breach of a duty of the licencing authority, liability could potentially arise but not as vicarious liability in respect of the pilot's actions or omissions.

The situation is different when the ship suffers or causes damage while under the command of a compulsory pilot. There is an argument then to be made that vicariously liability for damages to third parties may not attach to the shipowner but to the authority imposing the pilot on the shipowner. Moreover, in such a case it may also be argued that any damage to the property of the licencing authority caused by the pilot's negligence should not be recoverable and moreover the shipowner may be able to recover against the harbour authority.

All the above arguments have been rejected either by court decisions or statutorily. Up to the coming into force of the 1913 Pilotage Act, case law supported the proposition that in respect of compulsory pilotage the shipowner's liability was excluded.[262] However, the introduction of section 15(1) of the Pilotage Act 1913 reversed the position.[263] The relevant section states:

"Notwithstanding anything in any public or local Act, the owner or master of a vessel navigating under circumstances in which pilotage is compulsory shall be answerable for any loss or damage caused by the vessel or by any fault of the navigation of the vessel in the same manner as he would if pilotage were not compulsory."

Thus in *The Esso Bernicia* the House of Lords held that no vicarious liability attaches to the general employer of a pilot for two reasons. First, because the pilot navigates the ship as a principal not as a servant of his general employer,[264] and second because of the application of section 15(1) of the 1913 Pilotage Act.

The relevant provision presently is section 16 of the 1987 Pilotage Act which states:

"The fact that a ship is being navigated in an area and in circumstances in which pilotage is compulsory for it shall not affect any liability of the owner or master of the ship for any loss or damage caused by the ship or by the manner in which it is navigated."

Taken within the historical context of section 15(1) of the 1913 Pilotage Act, section 16 of the 1987 Pilotage Act has been held to impose a liability for negligence of a compulsory pilot on shipowners in respect of claims of third parties and make the pilot the servant of the shipowner in all respects even where this concerns the damages suffered by the shipowner.[265]

Thus it appears clear that whether the pilotage is compulsory or not there is no vicarious liability[266] attaching to the competent harbour authority for actions of the pilot either in respect of claims by third parties or in respect of claims made

262. *The Maria* (1869) 1 W Rob 95.
263. *Workington Harbour and Dock Board v Towerfield (Owners) (The Towerfield)* [1951] AC 112 (HL).
264. *Esso Petroleum Co Ltd v Hall Russell & Co Ltd (The Esso Bernicia)* [1989] AC 643; [1989] 1 Lloyd's Rep 8.
265. *The Cavendish, supra*, fn. 247.
266. An argument based on a contractual agreement between the shipowner and the harbour authority on implied terms was also rejected in *The Cavendish, supra*, fn. 247, where it was held to be no more than an arrangement to facilitate the shipowner to discharge his statutory obligation for compulsory pilotage, no contract existed.

by the shipowner. It follows that the harbour authority is entitled to claim against the shipowner for damage caused by the pilot.[267]

The liability of the competent harbour authority is limited under the 1987 Pilotage Act in respect of loss or damage to the ship under pilotage and any property on it, loss or damage to any other ship or property onboard such ship as well as to any other property or rights.[268] The applicable limits of liability are calculated by multiplying the number of authorised pilots employed by the harbour authority by £1,000. However, the harbour authority loses the right to limit liability if it is proven that the loss or damage was caused by a personal act or omission of the harbour authority which was intentional or reckless and with knowledge that the damage would have probably resulted.[269] The provisions that apply to a competent harbour authority also apply to any agent authorised to undertake pilotage services.[270]

There is no right to limit liability for loss of life or personal injury under the 1987 Pilotage Act thus for such claims the liability of the harbour authority or any authorised agent is unlimited.

Provisions for the payment into court of the limitation amounts and powers granted to the court to distribute these appropriately and stay pending proceedings are provided under section 22(6).

From the wording of the 1987 Pilotage Act the provisions applicable to competent harbour authorities, the exclusions of liability and the relevant limitation of liability do not extend to any body authorised under section 23 in respect of deep sea pilotage. Thus it appears that the liability of such bodies could be unlimited.

### *(iii) Shipowner's vicarious liability*

As explained, section 16 of the 1987 Pilotage Act[271] provides that the liability of the owner and the Master of the ship is not affected in any way for "any loss or

267. *The Sea Empress* case is the most significant recent decision in this context. A tanker laden with 130,000 tons of crude oil, she ran aground on 15 February 1996 while entering the Port of Milford Haven with a duly licensed pilot on board. It was admitted that the pilot, but not the port authority, was negligent. She was eventually salved successfully but only after some 70,000 tons of crude oil had been released into the sea. The Milford Haven Port Authority ("MHPH") was prosecuted under an obscure provision of the Water Resources Act 1991. They pleaded guilty to the offence, which was one of strict liability, and were fined £4,000,000 at first instance, reduced on appeal to £750,000. Although the case was a criminal prosecution, it did involve detailed consideration of the role of a statutory port authority and its relationship with the pilotage service in its waters. In the course of his judgment Steel J said: "The significance of these matters is all the greater in the context of a scheme of compulsory pilotage. Shipowners and Masters must needs engage a pilot. They have to take the training, experience and expertise of the pilot provided at face value. While the Master remains nominally in command, it has to be recognised that the pilot had the 'con' and a Master can only intervene when a situation of danger has clearly arisen. The port authority imposes a charge for pilotage but in the same breath has the added advantage of the pilot being treated for purposes of civil liability as an employee of the shipowner. All this calls for the highest possible standards on the part of the port authority." See the dicta of Steel J in *Environment Agency v Milford Haven Port Authority (The Sea Empress)* [1999] 1 Lloyd's Rep 673. The appeal is reported at [2000] JPL 943.
268. Section 22(3).
269. Section 22(3) where the test to be satisfied is that under Art. 4 of the 1996 LLMC. See section 7 for the meaning of the test.
270. Section 22(4).
271. Under common law the liability of the shipowner was excluded when the ship was under compulsory pilotage (*The Maria, supra*, fn. 262).

damage caused by the ship or by the manner in which it is navigated".[272] As discussed earlier this provision has been deemed to impose liability on the shipowner in respect of the acts or omissions of the pilot during compulsory pilotage and to assimilate it to the long standing position in respect of non-compulsory pilotage that the pilot's actions make the shipowner vicariously liable.[273]

The establishment of limitation rights for the pilots and the competent harbour authority does not affect the right of the shipowner or others to limit liability.[274]

## 8. LIMITATION OF LIABILITY

### (a) Introduction

Shipowners and certain others connected with the operation of a ship enjoy the unusual privilege of limiting their liability.[275] Because liability is limited and known the shipowner can deposit to an appropriate court the full amount he may be liable for and thus can be free of further liability or legal actions and security measures against his property, like ship arrest in respect of these claims. The shipowner can thus avoid multiple litigation and security demands in various jurisdictions and continue trading leaving the claimants and the court managing the limitation fund to arrange for the distribution of the claims.

Limitation of liability was originally developed to reduce the personal exposure of the shipowner and all its property in cases where the ship's Master and crew where negligent or acted intentionally.[276] Such cases risked financial ruin for the shipowners and were catered for by express rights to avoid liability where the ship and freight were abandoned to creditors. This practice was developed in several continental and Scandinavian countries, but was not introduced in England until 1733.[277] Limitation of liability has expanded in time to cover more persons and also to protect these persons more by making it almost an undisputable right.

Presently shipowners (and certain others) are entitled to limit their liability in two different contexts. The original right to limit liability has led to the development

272. Section 16.
273. *The Cavendish*, *supra*, fn. 247.
274. Section 21(7).
275. Arguments for and against limitation of liability can be found in articles by Lord Mustill: "Ships are different – or are they?"[1993] LMCLQ, 4 (November), pp. 490–501 and the response by David Steel, "Ships are different: the case for limitation of liability" [1995] LMCLQ 1 (February), pp. 77–87.
276. This explanation links vicarious liability with the right to limit and naturally leads to the conclusion that where liability of the shipowner is personal then limitation of liability should not be available. See, for example, D C Greenman, "Limitation of liability unlimited" (2001) *Journal of Maritime Law and Commerce*, 3292, pp. 279–315. This arrangement is reflected in the 1851 US Limitation Act and was reflected in the wording of the older International Limitation Conventions, including the 1957 Limitation Convention, and was changed only in the 1976 LLMC.
277. The triggering event was, according to Marsden, *The Law of Collisions at Sea* (11th ed, 1961) the case of *Boucher v Lawson* (1734) Cas Temp Hardw. 85 (cited in *Marsden*, para. 175) in which personal liability of the shipowner was established for the value of a cargo of bullion stolen by the ship's Master. This led to legislation establishing limited rights of liability for such incidents which where gradually in time expanded.

of global limitation regimes for which the only purpose is the establishment of the right to limit without altering the applicable substantive liability rules. By contrast, special liability regimes for, for example, oil pollution, carriage of goods or passengers, also provide for an entitlement to limited liability but this is coupled with liability rules which modify the ordinary legal position. In that context limitation of liability is arguably more justifiable as it forms part of the package deal rather than a separate entitlement. In this section we will deal with global limitation regimes.

Three international Conventions provide shipowners (and certain others) with an almost global ability to limit. These conventions are: the 1924 Limitation Convention; the International Convention relating to the Limitation of Liability of Owners of Sea-Going Ships (Brussels 1957) (1957 Limitation Convention); Convention on Limitation of Liability for Maritime Claims (London 1976) (1976 LLMC) and its Protocol of 1996 amending the Convention on Limitation of Liability for Maritime Claims of 19 November 1976 (London, 2 May 1996) (1996 LLMC). The 1976 LLMC and its 1996 Protocol are in force in the UK.[278] We will refer to the amended 1976 LLMC as the 1996 LLMC.

These Conventions apply whether the claims are classified as occurring in tort or delict, contract, or on some other basis.[279] However, not every claim against a shipowner is subject to limitation of liability under these Conventions.

Shipowners also in practice limit their liability by forming "one ship" companies, however this method is part of the general corporate law and is not in any way unique to shipowners.

### (b) Who is entitled to limit liability

The 1996 LLMC in Article1 prescribes that "shipowners", salvors, persons for whose acts the shipowner or the salvor are responsible and the insurers of particular liabilities have the right to limit their liability. In turn, the registered owner, the charterer, the manager and the operator of a sea-going ship are deemed to be within the convention's definition of shipowner[280] and thus entitled to limit their liability under the 1996 LLMC. The liability of these persons for actions against the ship (*in rem*) is also subject to limitation.[281]

The House of Lords in *The Hopper No 66*[282] held, reversing the decisions of the lower courts, that under the Merchant Shipping Act 1894, sections 503 and 504, the right of the owner of a vessel to limit liability for collision damage was also available to the demise-charterers who were considered as being included in the definition of owner in those particular sections. The inclusion of the term charterer in the definition of owner under Article1(2) of the 1976/1996 LLMC removed

278. Merchant Shipping Act 1995, ss. 185–186.
279. That is how the somehow misleading term "global limitation" has come into existence. Limitation under these regimes is "global" in the sense that the liability of the shipowner does not have to arise from a specific liability head. However, the term "global" also gives the impression that this right is always available against all shipowners' liability which, as we will see later, is not true.
280. Art. 1(2) of the 1996 LLMC.
281. Art. 1(5) of the 1996 LLMC.
282. *Sir John Jackson Ltd v Owners of the Steamship Blanche, her Master and Crew and Others (The Hopper No 66)* [1908] AC 126 (HL).

the need for reliance on the *The Hopper No 66*[283] or statutory provisions as demise-charterers clearly fall within this category.

In the context of arrest of ships, the term "charterer" has been decided, to include a time-charterer[284] and voyage as well as slot-charterers.[285] The same position appears to have been adopted in respect of the 1996 LLMC,[286] regarding the word "charterer", that is, it includes demise-charterers as well as, at least, voyage and time-charterers. The position of the slot charterers is not yet clarified. We submit that slot-charters are also entitled to limit liability for two reasons. First we note that the part of the vessel chartered by a slot charterer may be small or may be a substantial part of the vessel's cargo space and we cannot see how one can differentiate between these two especially if the contractual rights are very similar to those of an ordinary voyage or time-charterparty. Secondly the "ordinary meaning to the words of the treaty"[287] does not permit such a distinction between a voyage and a time-charterer on one hand and a slot charterer on the other.

The ship's managers and operators are also entitled to limit their liability. The ordinary meaning of the words would certainly include the managing owners but it is uncertain whether managers and operators of part the shipping activity for example, recruitment would be covered. The management contract should be valid and not frustrated or repudiated in order for the right of limitation to be available. Where the management of the ship is taken over by a bank or other creditor under a mortgage agreement there could also be difficulties as the mortgagee in possession is not the owner of the ship[288] but may be considered as the operator of the ship.[289] An alternative route is to suggest that the mortgage agreement provides the consent of the owner for the mortgagee to act as managers in particular circumstances and thus mortgagees are entitled to limit liability.

Persons for whose act, neglect or default the shipowner or salvor is responsible are also entitled to limited liability. The purpose of this provision is to avoid circumvention of the right to limit by claimants suing the individual wrongdoer rather than the shipowner.[290] The extension of the right to limit to persons for which the shipowner is responsible clearly covers the Master and crew members when they act within the scope of their employment. However, anyone who can show that he/she is linked with the shipowner in a way that makes the shipowner

283. *Ibid.* In any case, legislatory intervention clarifying the position by extending the right to limit to demise-charterers was enacted immediately after the unfavourable decision of the High Court under the Merchant Shipping Act 1906, s. 71.
284. *The Span-Terza* [1982] 1 Lloyd's Rep 225 (CA).
285. *MSC Mediterranean Shipping Co SA v Polish Ocean Lines (The Tychy)* [1999] 2 Lloyd's Rep 11 (CA).
286. This much can be deducted from *The Aegean Sea*, a voyage charterparty case, and the *CMA CGM SA v Classica Shipping Co Ltd (The CMA Djakarta)* [2003] 2 Lloyd's Rep 50, where the right of the voyage and time-charterers to limited liability was challenged by the shipowners only to the extent that it applied to indemnity claims by the shipowners and not in general. Lord Justice Longmore in the CA stated that the concession, that a charterer when sued by a cargo-owner is entitled to limit, is "obviously correct" – *CMA CGM SA v Classica Shipping Co Ltd (The CMA Djakarta)* [2004] 1 Lloyd's Rep 460.
287. 1969 Vienna Convention on the Law of Treaties, Art. 1.
288. *Collins v Lamport* (1864) 4 De G J & Sim 500; 46 ER 1012.
289. A statement to this effect is included in G Bowtle and K McGuiness, *The Law of Ship Mortgages* (LLP, 2001), at p. 189.
290. This was successful in *Adler v Dickinson and Another (The Himalaya)* [1954] 2 Lloyd's Rep 267 (CA).

responsible would also be entitled to limit liability. Pilots may be subject to this provision because under English law their negligence makes the owner liable.[291] However, in England pilots may also limit their liability under section 22 of the Pilotage Act 1987 to a much lower limit.[292] Independent contractors as well as others involved in the shipping business are arguably not included in the definition. Thus, ship's agents, stevedores and classification societies[293] are probably not entitled to limit their liability.

Salvors are also expressly entitled to limit their liability.[294] When salvors operate from a ship they are shipowners and therefore are entitled to limit their liability. However, when they do not operate from a ship they will not fall under the definition of shipowner.[295] Thus the express statement ensures that salvors are always entitled to limit their liability. The definition of salvors is wide and probably includes persons involved in wreck removal.[296]

Liability insurers of shipowners in respect of claims subject to limitation are also given the right to limit liability under the 1976 LLMC[297] "to the same extent" as the insured.[298]

Persons that do not fall within the Article 1 definitions would not be able to limit liability under the 1996 LLMC.[299] Other entities, in particular port authorities as well as owners of docks and canals can limit liability on the basis of section 191 of the 1995 MSA. The right to limit arises on the basis of the relevant section of the 1995 MSA and is therefore independent from the 1996 LLMC.[300]

### (c) Can owners limit liability against each other?

Persons entitled to limit liability under the 1976 LLMC may of course bring claims against each other. Their contractual relationship will determine the legal

291. See *Esso Petroleum Co Ltd v Hall Russell & Co Ltd (The Esso Bernicia)* [1989] AC 643; [1989] 1 Lloyd's Rep 8 (HL) and s. 16 of the Pilotage Act 1987.
292. £1,000.
293. Classification Societies do not owe a duty of care and do not become liable to third parties for financial losses (*Marc Rich & Co AG and Others v Bishop Rock Marine Co Ltd and Nippon Kaiji Kyokai (The Nicholas H)* [1996] AC 211; [1995] 2 Lloyd's Rep 299 (HL)). However, where loss of life occurs there could be liability put on them (*Perrett v Collins and Others* [1998] 2 Lloyd's Rep 255; [1999] PNLR 77; *The Times*, 23 June 1998 (CA (Civ Div)).
294. Art. 1(1).
295. *NV Bureau Wijsmuller v NV Owners of the Tojo Maru (The Tojo Maru)* [1971] 1 Lloyd's Rep 341 (HL).
296. 1996 LLMC, Article 2, paras 1(d), (e) and (f).
297. This was another innovation of the 1976 LLMC.
298. Art. 1(6). This has been seen as problematic in respect of the interpretation of s. 1 of the Third Parties (Right Against Insurers) Act 1930 in *firma C-Trade SA Respondents v Newcastle Protection and Indemnity Association (The Fanti)* [1990] 3 WLR 78; [1990] 2 Lloyd's Rep 191 (HL). Setion 1 in essence permits direct recovery by claimants from the insurers in cases where the assured has been wound up. However, the House of Lords, in *The Fanti*, considered this right to be subject to the express terms of the contract of insurance which in that case was the requirement that the claimant was paid by the insured for the insured to obtain a right of collecting the insurance from his P&I Club. See Chapter 10, p. 342.
299. Persons who are not residents or do not have a principal place of business in a Party State and would otherwise have been entitled to limit liability can be excluded by a Party State under Art. 15(1). The UK has not provided for any such exclusion.
300. However, the determination of the limits of liability for these entities is based on the tonnage of the largest UK ship that has visited these facilities and are calculated by reference to Arts 6 and 7 of the 1996 LLMC. Similarly, the constitution of a limitation fund is also prescribed on the basis of Arts 11 and 12 of the 1996 LLMC.

basis of such claims. If, for example,[301] there is a cargo claim against the charterer, the charterer would be entitled to limit his liability against the cargo owner. However, if the charterer pays the claim in full and then tries to recover from the shipowner, the shipowner would be entitled to limit his liability against the charterer in exactly the same way as if the claim was directly from the cargo owner against the shipowner. This is consistent with the historical development of the limitation of liability as a protectionist measure for the benefit of the owner and the extension of the shipowners' privilege to other persons. However, when the cargo claim is brought against the shipowner who pays up and then tries to recover from the charterer, in such a case is the charterer also entitled to invoke limitation of liability against the shipowner? Such a result would be a significant expansion of the scope of limitation beyond the protection of the shipowner, who may consequently face limited recovery for damages incurred in the shipping business.

The historical development of limitation of liability suggests that a charterer would only be entitled to limit his liability where it acts "in the shoes" of the shipowner. To this effect were the first instance decisions in *The Aegean Sea*[302] and in *The CMA Djakarta*.[303]

However, the first instance decision in *The CMA Djakarta* was unanimously reversed by the Court of Appeal. The Court of Appeal noted that the construction of any international convention should be made without any English law preconceptions and that it must not be controlled by domestic principles of construction.[304] They also noted that the ordinary meaning of the word charterer includes a charterer whether it acts as a charterer or under any other capacity. Thus charterers as well as managers and operators enjoy the same rights as the shipowners making the effect of the 1996 LLMC to be much wider than shipowners would have expected.

### (d) Which ships are subject to limitation of liability?

The 1996 LLMC applies to the owner of a sea-going ship.[305] However, the UK government extended the application of the right to limit to owners of non-seagoing ships[306] thus removing the need for determining the distinction between sea-going and non-seagoing ships and granting the same right of limited liability to shipowners of non-seagoing ships.

The reference to a ship "includes references to any structure (whether completed or in course of completion) launched and intended for use in navigation as a ship or part of a ship".[307] Under English case law this is usually decided as a matter of

301. The same applies for all claims subject to limitation of liability.
302. *Aegean Sea Traders Corp v Repsol Petroleo and Another (The Aegean Sea)* [1998] 2 Lloyd's Rep 39.
303. *CMA CGM SA v Classica Shipping Co Ltd (The CMA Djakarta)* [2003] 2 Lloyd's Rep 50, fn. 286.
304. *Ibid.* One, can of course counter-argue that the development of limitation of liability and the creation of the 1976 LLMC (and its predecessors) can and should be considered in the light of the preconceptions of English law that are common with the other parties to the 1976 LLMC as they must have been part of the basis of the agreement in forming the Convention.
305. 1976 LLMC, Art. 2.
306. 1995 MSA, Sch. 11, Part II, s. 2. This was based on an express right under the 1976 LLMC Art. 15(2) to legislate for vessels of inland navigation. The extension of the right of a shipowner to limit liability irrespective of whether his vessel is sea-going or not goes back to 1894 (s. 503).
307. 1995 MSA, Sch. 11, Part II, s. 12. Notably, the inclusion of the term "under construction" would extend the right to limit to shipowners of vessels not yet completed but launched. However, it is unclear when, at the end of the life of the vessel, such right is lost. For example, would under any

fact on a case-by-case basis taking into account the use of the particular structure in question in navigation and also the policy reasons or the practicalities that may suggest that a structure should or should not be described as a ship. The term "used in navigation" is arguably not satisfied by "controlled travel over water" but "ordered progression over the water from one place to another".[308] Thus jet skis do not satisfy the "use in navigation" criterion,[309] while a jack-up oil rig was considered under a different statute[310] to fulfil the navigation criteria[311] even if its primary purpose was not navigation.

Special rights are granted under the 1996 LLMC to each Party State in respect of the limitation arrangements for vessels smaller than 300 tons.[312] In the UK the 1995 MSA, Schedule 7, Part II, section 5, sets out the limits of liability for ships smaller than 300 tons. Government ships are also subject to the 1996 LLMC.[313]

The 1976 LLMC expressly excludes, aircushion vehicles, and floating platforms for the exploration and exploitation of natural resources.[314] However, as the 1995 MSA does not include the particular article, it follows that the exclusion is not operative in England. The question whether such structures can be considered as ships remains and may restrict the application of the convention to such structures. In respect to hovercraft, specific legislation making part of the 1996 LLMC applicable to them has been enacted.[315]

Ships engaged in drilling, whether specifically constructed for this purpose or adapted, while engaged in drilling may be excluded from the 1996 LLMC if national legislation provides for higher limits of liability or when the particular State is party to a specialised convention applicable to such ships.[316] These provisions are not enacted in the 1995 MSA and therefore such craft, provided that they fulfil the definition of ship, are also subject to the application of the 1996 LLMC.

### (e) Claims subject to limitation of liability

Claims under Article 2 and not excluded by Article 3 are subject to limitation. Qualifying claims are subject to limitation, whether the liability arises in contract,

---

circumstances a claim by injured workers involved in the dismantling of the ship give a right to limitation to the owner, probably the shipyard? Arguably, while the vessel is still in the water the right would exist. It is also arguable that even if she is outside the water and retains the characteristics of a ship (able to float and capable of use in navigation) the right still exists and is only lost when the structure no longer falls within the definition of ship.

308. *R v Goodwin (Mark)* [2006] 1 Lloyd's Rep 432 (CA) citing with approval *Steedman v Scofield and Another* [1992] 2 Lloyd's Rep 163, and considering *The Von Rocks* [1998] 2 Lloyd's Rep 198, *Clark (Inspector of Taxes) v Perks* [2001] EWCA Civ 1228 and *Curtis v Wild* [1991] 4 All ER 172 which contain *dicta* favouring a wider interpretation of the term navigation. Thus, it was held in that case that "the words 'used in navigation' excluded from the definition of 'ship or vessel' craft that were simply used for having fun on the water without the object of going anywhere, into which category jet skis plainly fell".
309. *R v Goodwin (Mark)*, *ibid.*; *Steedman v Scofield and Another*, *ibid.* Arguably this is so for most small recreational vessels not capable of navigating long distances.
310. Merchant Shipping Act 1894.
311. *Clark (Inspector of Taxes) v Perks* [2001] 2 Lloyd's Rep 431.
312. Art. 15(2) of the 1976 LLMC.
313. Section 192 of the MSA 1995.
314. 1976 LLMC, Art. 15(5).
315. Hovercraft (Civil Liability) Order 1986, amended by the Hovercraft (Convention on Limitation of Liability for Maritime Claims (Amendment) Order 1998.
316. 1976 LLMC, Art. 15(4).

tort or by statute[317] and whether they are enforced by personal action against the owner or other person or against the ship.[318] Provided that the claims are within the words of Article 2(1), they will be subject to limitation of liability even if brought by way of recourse or for indemnity under a contract.[319]

Loss of life, personal injury, loss of or damage to property claims as well as consequential losses are all subject to limitation provided that they occur either on board or in direct connection with the operation[320] of the ship or the salvage operations. While damages on board are rather well defined, the extent of the term "direct connection with the operation of the ship" is not as easy to determine. The term expresses the "necessary linkage" between the loss suffered and "the ship in respect of which a claim is made".[321] However, which damages and when are in direct connection with the ship's operation is unclear.

In *The Caspian Basin*, Mr Justice Rix considered whether a claim for loss of a tow arising in part out of misrepresentation as to a tug's bollard pull and b.h.p. was a claim "occurring ... in direct connection with the operation of the ship" within Article 2.1(a) of the 1976 Convention. His decision was based on the fact that the loss claimed was that of the tow which he held to be in direct connection with the operation of the ship.[322]

In *The Breydon Merchant*[323] Sheen J held that a claim by the charterer for salvage contribution is subject to Article 2.1(a) even if not accompanied with physical damage to the cargo. The point was conceded in *The Darfur*.[324]

In *The Aegean Sea*[325] destruction of the bunkers, pollution damage and clean-up costs arising when a vessel grounded on rocks because of the breach of a safe port warranty under an ASBATANKVOY charterparty "were also in direct connection with the operation of the ship".

In *The CMA Djakarta* cargo claims arising from the shipment of undeclared dangerous goods under a charterparty were also considered to be in direct connection with the operation of the ship and thus subject to limitation.[326]

Both in *The Aegean Sea*[327] and *The CMA Djakarta*[328] which involved indemnity claims by the shipowners against the charterers, all five judges considered the wording of Article 2(1)(a) as incapable of including in the limitation right damages suffered by the ship by reference to which the limits of liability are calculated.[329]

317. *The Breydon Merchant* [1992] 1 Lloyd's Rep 373.
318. 1976 LLMC, Art. 1(5).
319. *Ibid.*, Art. 2(2).
320. The term "operation of the ship" was considered in *The Aegean Sea* to include everything that goes to the operation of the ship.
321. See the judgment of Rix L in *Caspian Basin Specialised Emergency Salvage Administration and Another v Bouygues Offshore SA and Others (The Caspian Basin)* [1997] 2 Lloyd's Rep 507 at p. 522, upheld by the Court of Appeal [1998] 2 Lloyd's Rep 461 at p. 472.
322. See section on Towage, p. 177.
323. *The Breydon Merchant*, *supra*, fn. 317.
324. *Blue Nile Shipping Company Ltd and Another v Iguana Shipping and Finance Inc and Others, (The Darfur)* [2004] 2 Lloyd's Rep 469.
325. *Supra*, fn. 301, [1998] 2 Lloyd's Rep 39.
326. *CMA CGM SA v Classica Shipping Co Ltd (The CMA Djakarta)* [2004] 1 Lloyd's Rep 460 reversing the first instance decision.
327. *Supra*, fn. 301, [1998] 2 Lloyd's Rep 39.
328. *CMA CGM SA v Classica Shipping Co Ltd* [2004] 1 Lloyd's Rep 460, in agreement on this point with the first instance decision [2003] 2 Lloyd's Rep 50.
329. Probably a stronger argument is the consequence the opposite decision would have had to other claimants of the limitation fund.

Therefore such claims, usually brought by the owner against the charterer, are not subject to limitation of liability. These decisions also exclude claims related losses consequential to the loss of the ship and in particular salvage expenses and general average incurred by the shipowners[330] and a claim for freight not earned.[331]

In *The Darfur*,[332] following the collision of the *Darfur* with the *Happy Fellow* claims by the charterer of the *Darfur* against the shipowner in respect of the *Darfur* being off-hire, increased insurance costs to cover the deviation after the collision, discharge and transhipment costs for the cargo, loss of use of the relevant containers for the period between the casualty and transhipment, hiring, bunkering and insuring alternative tonnage, loss of business and loss of profit were all considered to be claims consequential to the loss of the vessel and thus not subject to limitation.

The 1996 LLMC under Article 7 covers loss of life and personal injury as well as consequential damage. However, in the UK the application of this is excluded by virtue of the new Article 15(3*bis*) of the 1996 LLMC.[333] As a result in UK law the 1996 LLMC does not cover passengers of sea going vessels.

Under Article 2(1)(b), claims in respect of loss resulting from delay in the carriage by sea of cargo, passengers or their luggage are also subject to limitation of liability. Because, there is no definition of luggage the word arguably encompasses in its ordinary meaning all type of luggage including valuables. The 1974 Athens Convention expressly provides that vehicles are luggage for its purpose.[334] It is doubtful that the ordinary meaning of luggage includes vehicles; however, the 1974 Athens Convention definition may be used as an indication of the internationally acceptable meaning of the term.

Under Article 2(1)(c) claims in respect of other loss resulting from infringement of rights other than contractual rights, occurring in direct connection with the operation of the ship or salvage operations are also subject to limitation of liability. While Article 2(1)(a) is concerned with losses and damages linked with property damage or loss of life this section covers claims from parties that may have suffered losses not linked to property damage. In *The Aegean Sea*[335] loss of use and loss of profit by users of the sea and the coasts in particular owners of fishing boats and yachts, fish and shellfish farm owners, local shop owners, local municipalities, local governments and the coastal State were held to fall in this category. The category is very broad and taking into account that Article 2 is not restricted in general by the legal nature of the claim, the only evident exclusion is that of contractual rights as expressed in the Article itself. Thus, any actionable rights available through national or international law to users of the coastal environment or any relevant infrastructure are probably included in this section and thus subject to limitation. Recovery of freight not earned and lost following damage to the ship has been held not to fall within this category of claims as it is a contractual right.[336]

330. *CMA CGM SA v Classica Shipping Co Ltd (The CMA Djakarta), supra*, fn. 286.
331. If freight is earned it is due in full.
332. *Blue Nile Shipping Company Ltd and Another v Iguana Shipping and Finance Inc and Others (The Darfur), supra*, fn. 324.
333. This was inserted by the Merchant Shipping (Convention on Limitation of Liability for Maritime Claims) (Amendment) Order 1998, which enacts the 1996 Protocol.
334. 1974 Athens Convention, Art. 1(5).
335. *Supra*, fn. 301.
336. *The Aegean Sea, supra*, fn. 301, [1998] 2 Lloyd's Rep 39.

Under Article 2(1)(d) claims in respect of the raising, removal, destruction or the rendering harmless of a ship which is sunk, wrecked, stranded or abandoned, including anything that is or has been on board such ship are also subject to limitation of liability. Wreck raising, removal, etc, differs from other property and consequential claims in the sense that the party claiming could be under a duty to keep the waterways clear of objects[337] and therefore public funding will probably have to meet the costs that exceed limitation. To avoid this consequence[338] the UK has made a reservation in respect of this provision[339] and all claims in respect of wreck raising removal, etc, are not subject to limitation of liability.[340]

Article 2(1)(e) provides that claims in respect of the removal, destruction or the rendering harmless of the cargo of the ship are subject to limitation of liability. This section concerns cargo-related operations in general irrespective of whether the ship is distressed or sunk. It could, for example, cover a claim by cargo owners for the jettison or confiscation of cargo partly infected which makes discharge of the whole cargo, whether infected or not illegal.[341] It would also cover the destruction or raising of a container with toxic substances lost to the sea. Thus, in the UK, because of the reservation made on Article 2(1)(d), the costs for raising or destroying the ship are not subject to limitation of liability; the raising of the cargo would probably be as it also falls under Article 2(1)(e).[342]

Article 2(1)(f) provides for claims of a person other than the person liable in respect of measures taken in order to avert or minimise loss for which the person liable may limit his liability in accordance with this Convention, and further loss caused by such measures to be subject to limitation of liability. These claims are, in essence, assistance services and clean up costs undertaken by persons who cannot be considered as salvors. This section avoids the situation by which a claim would be limited but the claim for prevention of the loss would be unlimited. In *The Breydon Merchant*[343] a claim by cargo owners against the shipowner for salvage liability caused by unseaworthiness was considered to be within this section as it was a claim for measures taken to prevent or minimise the loss to cargo for which (loss to cargo) the shipowner would have been able to limit.

337. In England the MSA 1995, s. 252, describes the powers of the harbour authorities.
338. See *Richard Abel & Sons Ltd v Manchester Ship Canal (The Stonedale No 1)* [1955] 2 Lloyd's Rep 9; [1956] AC 1 for the earlier position.
339. Section 185, MSA 1995, Sched. 7, Part II, para. 3, stating: "Paragraph 1(d) of article 2 shall not apply unless provision has been made by an order of the Secretary of State for the setting up and management of a fund to be used for the making to harbour or conservancy authorities of payments needed to compensate them for the reduction, in consequence of the said paragraph 1(d), of amounts recoverable by them in claims of the kind there mentioned, and to be maintained by contributions from such authorities raised and collected by them in respect of vessels in like manner as other sums so raised by them." No action has been taken by the Secretary of State, thus the reservation is generally applicable.
340. The newly agreed 2007 Nairobi International Convention on the Removal of Wrecks expressly preserves under Art. 10(2) the right of the registered owner to limit liability under any applicable international or national regime such as the 1976 LLMC. However, it is not yet clear whether the UK will subscribe to the Nairobi Convention which is not yet in force and whether as a result of this the domestic law regarding limitation of liability for wreck removal will be changed.
341. See, for example, the facts of *Effort Shipping Co Ltd v Linden Management SA (The Giannis NK)* [1998] AC 605; [1998] 1 Lloyd's Rep 337.
342. One could suggest that Art. 2(1)(d) refers to cargo of stranded vessels while Art. 2(1)(e) refers to cargo of vessels not wrecked or sunk, etc. However, the general wording of Art. 2(1)(e) would arguably be an obstacle to such interpretation.
343. *Supra*, fn. 317.

While in general all claims described above are subject to limitation whether as direct or as indemnity actions, claims under Article 2(1)(d), (e) and (f) are expressly not limited when they relate to remuneration under a contract with the ship-owner.[344] Thus contractors undertaking cargo or ship raising otherwise than in salvage or acting for the minimisation of loss under a contract do not face a defence of limitation when demanding payment. However, it appears that it is only in respect of remuneration that such claims are unlimited. Thus, a claim by a person contracted to raise a lost container who suffers damage will probably be subject to limited liability.

### (f) Claims excluded from limitation

For general policy reasons some claims under Article 2 are expressly exempted from limitation of liability. These exemptions can be found under Article 3. In particular, claims for salvage including Special Compensation under Article 14 of the 1989 Salvage Convention are not subject to limitation. Otherwise salvors may become reluctant to undertake salvage. However the exemption only covers direct[345] claims from salvors and not indemnity claims for salvage expenses under the contract of carriage.[346] Moreover, even claims by salvors must be in the nature of salvage and not otherwise in order to be unlimited.[347]

Claims for oil pollution damage covered by the 1992 CLC[348] are also excluded[349] as the 1992 CLC and the 1992 FUND[350] Conventions contain their independent special liability regime which includes limits of liability. Damages arising from nuclear damage which are subject to national or international legislation are also excluded under Article 3(c). The 1960 Paris Convention[351] and the 1963 Brussels Convention[352] as well as the 1997 Protocol to Amend the Vienna Convention on Civil Liability for Nuclear Damage[353] and the Joint Protocol Relating to the Application of the Vienna Convention and the Paris Convention[354] compose the international liability framework which channels liability exclusively to the operator of a nuclear installation and who is strictly liable and provides for limitation of liability for him. These conventions are applicable to nuclear installations and do not cover liability in respect of nuclear powered ships.[355] Article 3(d) expressly states the liability of the shipowner of a nuclear ship cannot be limited

344. 1976 LLMC, Art. 2(2).
345. Salvage may be contractual or may arise independently as a right under the 1989 Salvage Convention which is presently enacted as Sch. 11 to the 1995 MSA.
346. *The Breydon Merchant*, *supra*, fn. 317.
347. In *The Tesaba* [1982], 1 Lloyd's Rep 397, salvors attempted to arrest a ship because the shipowners permitted the discharge of the cargo before security was provided by cargo interests, in contravention of an agreement with the salvors. However, it was held that for the purpose of an action *in rem* such a claim was not in the nature of salvage.
348. International Convention on Civil Liability for Oil Pollution Damage, London, 2 December 1992. See further Chapter 8, p. 254.
349. In the UK the exclusion can be found in MSA 1995, Art. 4(2) of Sch. 7, Part II.
350. International Convention on the Establishment of an International Fund for Compensation for Oil Pollution Damage. See further Chapter 8, p. 264.
351. Convention on Third Party Liability in the Field of Nuclear Energy of 29 July 1960, Additional Protocol of 28 January 1964 , Protocol of 16 November 1982.
352. Convention of 31 January 1963 Supplementary to the Paris Convention of 29 July 1960, Protocol of 28 January 1964 and Protocol of 16 November 1982.
353. In force but not signed by the UK.
354. In force and ratified by the UK.
355. Art. 1(a)(ii), Convention on Third Party Liability in the Field of Nuclear Energy of 29 July 1960, as amended by the Additional Protocol of 28 January 1964 and by the Protocol of 16 November

under the 1976 LLMC. Notably salvors assisting nuclear ships in distress will be able to limit liability as usual as the exception only covers shipowners.

The final category of claims, Article 2(e) concerns the servants of the owner and salvors. Their claims are not universally excluded from limitation, but it is left to the law governing their contract to decide whether their claims will be in full or limited to any amount which is higher than that under Article 6 of the 1996 LLMC. The provision requires that the servant's duties "are connected with the ship", which would certainly include the Master and crew members. Servants whose duties are only temporarily connected with the ship may also be covered by this provision if they are physically located at the time of the damage on board or in close proximity to the ship. Section 185(4) of the 1995 MSA excludes from limitation of liability personal injury and death as well as property loss claims made by a person employed under a contract of service governed by the law of any part of the UK. However, the application of the particular section of the 1995 MSA depends on whether the established relationship between such parties and the shipowner is a contract of service. In *The Maragetha Maria*[356] the Court of Appeal considered that a claim by the estates of drowned fishermen who were working on the vessel under a share profits arrangement meant that losses as well as profits were to be shared. In addition the deceased paid tax and national insurance on the basis that they were self-employed. These indicated that the deceased were not under a contract of service and their claims were not covered by the exemption under Article 3(3), thus they were subject to the shipowner's right to limited liability.

### (g) When is the privilege to limited liability lost?

Under Article 4, the shipowner loses the right to limited liability if the damages are caused by "his personal act or omission, committed with the intent to cause such loss, or recklessly and with knowledge that such loss would probably result".

This test requires (a) personal act of the shipowner, and (b) culpability which is intentional or almost as bad as intentional.

The personal acts of the shipowner when the shipowner is a company are not always easy to identify and a case-by-case approach is adopted by the courts. The answer depends on the structure of each company[357] and the way responsibilities are distributed within each company.[358] Historically the case law approached the

1982. The 1965 Nuclear Act excludes such ships under Art. 1(1)(a) which restricts the operation of the Act to "any nuclear reactor (other than such reactor comprised in a means of transport, whether by land, water or air)".

356. *Todd and Others v Adams and Chope (t/a Tralewney fishing Co) (The Maragetha Maria)* 2002 WL 498836 (CA (Civ Div)); [2002] CLC 1050; [2002] 2 Lloyd's Rep 293; (2002) 146 SJLB 118; [2002] 2 All ER (Comm) 97; (2002) 99(21) LSG 32; *The Times* (5 March 2002); [2002] EWCA Civ 509.

357. See Lord Mustill's judgment in the Court of Appeal decision in *Société Anonyme des Minerais v Grant Trading Inc (The Ert Stefanie)* [1989] 1 Lloyd's Rep 349.

358. In *Lennard's Carrying Co Ltd Appellants v Asiatic Petroleum Company, Limited Respondents* [1915] AC 705 (HL), Viscount Haldane LC, who delivered the leading judgment, stated: "My Lords, a corporation is an abstraction. It has no mind of its own any more than it has a body of its own; its active and directing will must consequently be sought in the person of somebody who for some purposes may be called an agent, but who is really the directing mind and will of the corporation, the very ego and centre of the personality of the corporation. That person may be under the direction of the shareholders in general meeting; that person may be the board of directors itself, or it may be, and in some companies it is so, that that person has an authority co-ordinate with the board of directors given to him under the articles of association, and is appointed by the general meeting of the company, and can only be removed by the general meeting of the company."

question in a hierarchical way either starting from the top of the company, the owner or the governing board, and coming down or vice versa. More recent case law recognises that certain actions by the company may be delegated to lower ranking officers who do not in general have decision-making authority in respect of the running of the company. This avoids the difficulty that arises if solely the hierarchical approach is used, namely that the delegation of duties to lower ranking officers would exclude the possibility of attributing the faults of these officers to the company itself and consequently ensure an unbreakable right to limit liability. There is significant case law in shipping demonstrating the factual approach adopted by the English courts.

Acts of a member of the board of directors would normally implicate the acts of the company, there could be circumstances under which he may not be representing the company.[359] In the same line, even where there is one person that has ultimate control of a company, this does not necessarily mean that only this person's acts would count as acts of the company.[360]

The Privy Council decision in *Meridian Global Funds Management Asia Ltd v Securities Commission*[361] confirmed the general position that the primary rules of attribution found in the company's constitution and implied by company law together with the secondary rules of attribution, that is the rules of agency, vicarious liability, etc, would determine which were the natural persons whose acts were to be attributed to the company. However, the Privy Council does not end the story there but explains that, in exceptional cases, even where the particular person cannot be properly described as the "directing mind and will" of the company it may be necessary to devise special rules of attribution where the acts of a duly authorised agent or servant of the company will represent the company. Such exceptional cases are distinguishable by reference to the legal substantive provisions imposing obligations on the company. Thus arguments that acts or omissions by a person statutorily required to act for the company in particular respects like, for example, the Designated Person under the ISM code[362] or the "Company Security Officer" under the ISPS code[363] may become the relevant person.

359. Lord Mustill in *The Ert Stefanie*, *supra*, fn. 80, said: "It seems to me at least theoretically possible for a situation to exist where a particular director had been formally excluded from participation in the company's business and where, if nevertheless he did trespass upon that territory, his acts in so doing would not be attributed to the company."
360. *Ibid.*
361. [1995] 2 AC 500.
362. ISM CODE, s. 4. Designated person(s): "To ensure the safe operation of each ship and to provide a link between the Company and those on board, every Company, as appropriate, should designate a person or persons ashore *having direct access to the highest level of management*. The responsibility and authority of the designated person or persons should include monitoring the safety and pollution-prevention aspects of the operation of each ship and ensuring that adequate resources and shore-based support are applied, as required." (Emphasis added.) It is difficult to say whether the conduct of the designated person can cause the shipowner to lose his right to limit liability. This will depend on the role of the designated person within the shipowning company, as explained in *Meridian Global v Securities Commissioner*. A professional ship manager would normally be the employer of the "designated person" under the ship's safety management system. Where the conduct of the designated person satisfies Art. 4, then his employer, the ship manager, could arguably lose his right to limited liability. However, when the registered shipowner remains ignorant of the problem, despite having acted reasonably in appointing a competent ship manager, it would arguably be unfair to deprive the owner (and his P&I Club) of limitation of liability.
363. Where the "Company security officer" is described as "the person designated by the Company for ensuring that a ship security assessment is carried out; that a ship security plan is developed,

However, it is submitted that, only in cases where there is a breach of the ISM or the ISPS Code in respect of the company's obligations to the extent that the right of limitation is challenged and that this obligation was to be discharged by the nominated person himself, then there could be a possibility that *Meridian Global Funds Management Asia Ltd v Securities Commission*[364] could be relied upon to establish that the acts of the relevant person were acts of the company. In such cases it can be argued that the legislation has identified the "alter ego" of the company.

In the absence of these exceptional circumstances there is still a need of search for the "directing will and mind of the company",[365] which involves a hierarchical approach to the company. Thus, acts of the Master or a marine superintendent cannot be considered as personal acts of the company.[366] The acts of the Chief Navigator and his staff in a large State-owned shipping company are not the acts of the company,[367] while the acts of his superior, the director of technical and investment affairs, would, in that particular case, have represented the company.

Fault may also be found in the way the constitution of the company attributes duties. However, such fault would arguably be relevant only where the company directors are in fact aware of the fault and they do not perform the necessary duties.[368]

From a practical point of view, the above would mean that, provided that appropriate procedures are established by the company's management, constitution faults by officers operating or supervising the operation of the vessel would not normally be considered as faults of the company.

The entrusting of the running of the vessel by the registered owner to a management company does not exclude the possibility that there is fault or privity by the registered owners.[369] This position would arguably be also applicable to operating companies.

Where the time or voyage or slot charterer or the salvor tries to limit under a regime that gives them such right[370] the same rules as in respect of the registered owner will also apply.

Having discussed the conditions under which the personal act or omission of the shipowner is established we now need to discuss the type of conduct that needs to be proved in order to deprive the shipowner from his right to limit liability under the 1976 LLMC. If intention can be shown, for example where the vessel is scuttled, the test will be satisfied. However, difficulties arise in the interpretation of the term "recklessly and with knowledge that such damage would probably result".

---

submitted for approval, and thereafter implemented and maintained and for liaison with port facility security officers and the ship security officer."(SOLAS/CONF.5/34, ANNEX 1, Part A, s. 2.7. See Chapter 7.

364. [1995] 2 AC 500.

365. *Lennard's Carrying Co Ltd Appellants v Asiatic Petroleum Co, Limited Respondents*, *supra*, fn. 80.

366. *Arthur Guinness, Son & Co (Dublin) Ltd v Owners of the Motor Vessel Freshfield (The Lady Gwendolen)* [1965] 1 Lloyd's Rep 335; [1965] P 294 (CA) and *The Garden City* [1982] 2 Lloyd's Rep 382.

367. *The Garden City (No 1)* [1982] 2 Lloyd's Rep 382.

368. See, for example, *The Garden City (No 1)*, *ibid.*, at p. 389.

369. *Charlotte v Theory and Others (The Charlotte)* (1921) 9 Ll L Rep 341, *The Lady Gwendolen*, *supra*, fn. 88, *The Marion* [1982] 2 Lloyd's Rep 52, at p. 54 and *The Ert Stephanie*, *supra*, fn. 81, where Lord Mustill said: "While the doctrines of corporate personality call for a ritual nod in the direction of the owners, nobody in practice pays any attention to these one-ship companies registered under flags of convenience; and the law takes the same view when questions of limitation are in issue."

370. The 1976/1996 LLMC does provide for such right.

In interpreting a provision very similar to Article 4 of 1976 LLMC, i.e. Article 25 of the Warsaw Convention, the Court of Appeal in *Goldman v Thai Airways International Ltd*[371] held that the phrase means a person's act which indicates a decision to run the risk or a mental attitude of indifference to the risk's existence.[372] This creates the need to understand the risk involved in order to decide whether a particular act or omission is indeed reckless.[373]

Moreover, it is also needed to show that the wrongdoer had knowledge that damage would probably result. The term "with knowledge" was held to refer to the actual knowledge held by the wrongdoer, in respect of the damage that would probably result and not to knowledge that the wrongdoer ought to have had.[374] The Court of Appeal in *Nugent and Killick v Michael Goss Aviation Ltd and Others*[375] held that anything less than "actual conscious knowledge" cannot satisfy Article 25.[376] Thus "turning a blind eye" knowledge is in essence excluded from the ambit of required knowledge.[377]

The word "probably" has been distinguished from the word "possibly" and was taken to mean "something likely to happen".[378] With "rather less confidence"[379] the Court held in the same case that the word "damage" refers to damage of the same kind as that that had occurred.

The case law on Article 25 of the amended Warsaw Convention can be considered at least as containing persuasive arguments in relation to the interpretation of Article 4 of the 1976 LLMC, although in principle each Convention is independent and has to be interpreted in accordance with its scope.[380] The close similarity of the words and the similar function within each convention of these Articles supports a common interpretation in spite of the modification of the term "loss" to "such loss" in the 1996 LLMC. Arguably the word adds clarification to the need of knowledge of the particular loss that occurred. However, the test may be even narrower than suggested above and may not only refer to the kind of the damage but to the damage actually suffered.

The two possible interpretations have been outlined in respect of the collision between two vessels (A and B). The Court of Appeal stated that in such a situation the required test under Article 4 could have two interpretations: Either that

371. [1983] 1 WLR 1186. Note, however, that the word "such" does not appear before "loss" in the Warsaw Convention.
372. *Goldman v Thai Airways International Ltd* [1983] 1 WLR 1186 (CA) at pp. 1193 and 1194.
373. *Ibid.*
374. An attempt by the claimants in *Gunter and Others v Beaton and Others* [1993] 2 Lloyd's Rep 369, to qualify the knowledge as the knowledge that such damage would occur "if the risk materializes" was expressly rejected by the Court of Appeal.
375. [2000] 2 Lloyd's Rep 222.
376. For two reasons, first that anything less would cause uncertainty and second because the intention of the Convention was taken to be that Art. 25 would be applicable in very rare circumstances.
377. However, the third judge, Pill LJ, considered that the wrongdoer cannot limit his liability just because he made a conscious decision to put the knowledge out of his mind, and he was prepared to infer the general knowledge that an experienced pilot would have. *Nugent and Killick v Michael Goss Aviation Ltd and Others* [2000] 2 Lloyd's Rep 222 (CA).
378. *Goldman v Thai Airways International Ltd*, fn. 372, at p. 1196.
379. *Ibid.*
380. Art. 31 of the 1969 Vienna Convention on the Law of Treaties states that: "A treaty shall be interpreted in good faith in accordance with the ordinary meaning to be given to the terms of the treaty in their context and in the light of its object and purpose." The object and purpose of the liability regime established under the 1929 Warsaw Convention for air carriage is clearly not the same with that of the 1976 LLMC thus, at least in theory, some differences could exist.

the cargo/ship owners of ship A must prove that "... the owner of ship B intended that it should collide with ship A, or acted recklessly with the knowledge that it was likely to do so or that the claimant merely has to prove that the owner of ship B intended that his ship should collide with another ship, or acted recklessly with the knowledge that it was likely to do so".[381] The Court of Appeal did not decide this point which thus remains open. It is unclear whether contributory negligence by the victim is at all relevant in the application of Article 4 and also whether a reckless act that has been taken with knowledge that the particular damage would occur but for the purpose of avoiding a worse evil may also be relevant to the application of Article 4. It is submitted that there is nothing in Article 4 to suggest that counterclaims may affect the right to limit or that the existence of contributory negligence may remove the small possibility from a claimant to satisfy Article 4, although it would certainly affect the damages awarded.[382]

The second situation is more difficult to resolve because, provided there is liability, the literal interpretation would indicate that such liability would not be limited. However, this would, in particular circumstances, discourage efforts to minimise damages because the damages arising from the original negligence could, in a general case, be subject to limitation but the damage from a reckless act to minimise damage would not be.

The burden of proving that Article 4 is fulfilled, is on the claimant,[383] since the shipowner has no interest in proving the fulfilment of conditions under Article 4.

The generally accepted strictness of the test which only slightly lowers the requirement from one of an intentional act has led to the statement that as long as collisions are concerned Article 4 cannot, in general be satisfied and consequently the liability of the shipowner will in all but the most exceptional cases be limited[384] and the court will issue a declaration to this effect, i.e. a limitation decree would be directly available to the shipowner.[385]

In one exceptional case, the limitation decree was not granted. The facts of the case[386] can be summarised as follows: A fishing vessel which routinely[387] navigated the Channel at the wrong side of the traffic separation scheme, under the command of her owner who was also the Master, collided with an oncoming vessel. The owner/Master admitted that the navigation was reckless but claimed that the element of knowledge was missing because the real test was one that required knowledge of the particular loss that occurred, which in this case was collision

381. *Schiffahrtsgesellschaft MS Merkur Sky mbH & Co KG v MS Leerort Nth Schiffahrts GmbH & Co KG (The Leerort)* [2001], 2 Lloyd's Rep 291 (CA).
382. In such a case apportionment of liability may be appropriate, however, the question is whether the loss of the right to limit depends on the conduct of the claimant.
383. See *The Bowbelle* [1990] 1 Lloyd's Rep 532 and *MSC Mediterranean Shipping Co SA v Delumar BVBA (the MSC Rosa M)* [2000] 2 Lloyd's Rep 399; *The Leerort, supra*, fn. 381; *Margolle and Another v. Delta Maritime Co Ltd and Others (The Saint Jacques II and Gudermes)* (Court of Appeal) [2002] EWHC 2452; [2003] 1 All ER (Comm) 102; [2003] 1 Lloyd's Rep 203; 2002 WL 31599631 (QBD (Admlty)). See also the decision of the Court of Appeal in *Goldman v Thai Airways International Ltd, supra*, fn. 372, on the Warsaw Convention which provides for a similar test.
384. *The Leerort, supra*, fn. 381.
385. See Chapter 11.
386. *Margolle and Another v Delta Maritime Co Ltd And Others (The Saint Jacques II and Gudermes), supra*, fn. 383.
387. The judge considered that prior to the accident repetition of the same reckless navigation, i.e. contravening r. 10 of the Collision Regulations, without the occurrence of a collision, did not indicate that such action did not carry with it the probability of damage.

damage caused to the specific vessel[388] and that, as at the time of the collision he was in his cabin sleeping, he did not have such knowledge. The question was whether the limitation decree would be issued without a hearing as suggested for the routine collision cases in *The Leerort*. However, the judge declined to grant the limitation decree as he considered this to be a case where there was a reasonable prospect that Article 4 could be fulfilled. The case was settled before reaching the court. Thus the case provides only an example of what type of conduct may be considered as possibly risking the loss of the right to limit liability and confirms the discretion of the courts to issue a limitation decree, but arguably not much more.

### (h) The limits of liability

The 1996 LLMC which is presently in force in the UK calculates the applicable limits on the basis of the tonnage of the ship[389] as defined under the International Convention on Tonnage Measurement of Ships, 1969.[390] Only in relation to limitation of liability in respect of loss of life and personal injury to passengers a different system based on the number of passengers is used. The limits of liability are shown in Table 1. To determine the limits of liability one has to distinguish between loss of life and personal injury claims on one hand and property damage claims. In case of property damage the limits of liability provide for a smaller fund than where there is also loss of life or personal injury in which case the fund is three times as large. In general the loss of life/personal injury claimants are entitled to 2/3rds of such a fund and any excess of such claims rank equally with property damage in respect of the residual third of the fund.

#### *(i) Limits of liability for property damage*

Where there is only property damage determining the amount of money available to the property claimants is straightforward. Note that in fact the claimants for property damage will have the full amounts described in the Tables only where the loss of life/personal injury claims are fully satisfied by their exclusive part of the limitation fund.

As an example let us consider a ship of 50,000 tons under the 1996 LLMC. The tonnage of the ship spans three ranges, the first of 2,000 tons, the second of 2,001–30,000 tons and also 20,000 in the third range of (30,001–70,000). Thus the first 2,000 tons correspond to 1,000,000 SDR, the next 28,000 tons, up to the 30,000 limit, correspond to 28,000 tons x 400 SDR/ton which equals = 11,200,000 SDR. The 20,000 tons in excess of 30,000 correspond to 20,000 tons x 300 SDR/ton which equals 6,000,000 SDR. Thus the limit of liability for this ship is the sum of 1,000,000 + 11,200,000 + 6,000,000 = 18,200,000 SDR.

388. An arguable option as suggested in *The Leerort*, *supra*, fn. 381
389. Arguably with the exception of liability against passengers where a separate limit per passenger is provided.
390. SI 1997, No 1510 is the latest version adopted under English Law.

### *(ii) Limits of liability for loss of life or personal injury*

FOR NON-PASSENGER CLAIMS

Where there is loss of life or personal injury then the overall limits of liability are almost three times those available for damage to property (see Tables 1 and 2 on page 218). However, the additional two-thirds are earmarked for the exclusive satisfaction of loss of life and personal injury claimants. The other one-third is left to satisfy the property claimants and any unsatisfied balance of claims for loss of life or personal injury not met by the dedicated personal injury fund.

The way this happens is as follows: Article 6(1)(a) provides for the limits of liability for loss of life or personal injury. Article 6(1)(b) provides for the limits of liability for damage to property. Article 6(2) provides for the participation of any unsatisfied loss of life and personal injury claims to the property damage part of the limitation fund.

As an example let's consider again a ship of 50,000 tons under the 1996 LLMC. The limitation fund when only property damage is caused has already been calculated above as being 18,200,000 SDR.

In respect of loss of life or personal injury claims, the limits of liability would be 3,000,000 for the first 2,000 tons, 28,000 x 1,200 = 33,600,000 SDR for the following 28,000 tons and 20,000 x 900 = 18,000,000 SDR for the other 20,000 tons. Thus the limitation fund is then 54,600,000 SDR.

The significance of Article 6(2) can be demonstrated if the property damage is considered to be 18,200,000 SDR and the loss of life/personal injury claims 54,600,000 SDR respectively. In such a case the personal claims will be paid first to cover 36,400,000 SDR. We would then have 18,200,000 SDR of personal claims unpaid as well as an equal amount of property damages. These would rank equally, and will be both paid in proportion from the property related limitation fund. Thus, 9,100,000 SDRs will be paid out to the property claimants and 45,500,000 SDRs to the claims for personal injuries or death.

Thus, the existence of claimants for loss of life/personal injury can significantly reduce the recovery by property damage claimants. The reverse is true only in respect of the 1/3 of the limitation fund.

FOR PASSENGER CLAIMS

A separate limit for loss of life and personal injury of passengers against the carrying ship is established by Article 7 of the 1996 LLMC. The limits imposed are 175,000 SDR per passenger times the number of passengers the ship is authorised to carry. However, Article 15.3*bis* to the LLMC permits the fixing by each State of limits higher than those imposed on the new Article 7 and by implication also permits the removal of limits of liability for loss of life and personal injury of passengers.[391] It is worth noting that the beneficiaries of the inclusion of the passenger fund in the 1976 and 1996 LLMC are not only the passengers themselves but all other claimants who do not have, in cases of passenger loss of life or personal injury, to share the fund under Article 6 with passengers. The UK has restricted the application of Article 7 of the 1996 LLMC thus it is only the 1974 Athens Convention that limits the shipowner's liability for such damages.[392]

391. Each contracting State using Art. 15.3*bis* must inform the Secretary-General in respect of these higher limits or the absence of limits.
392. See Chapter 5.

***Table 1: Limits of liability for property damage and loss of life or personal injury under the 1996 LLMC***

| *Tonnage of Ship* | *SDR* | *SDR/per ton* | *SDR* | *SDR/ton* |
|---|---|---|---|---|
| | *Property damage* | | *Loss of life/personal injury* | |
| <2000 | 1,000,000 | – | 3,000,000 | – |
| 2001–30,000 | 1,000,000 | 400 | 3,000,000 | 1200 |
| 30,001–70,000 | 1,000,000 | 300 | 3,000,000 | 900 |
| >70,000 | 1,000,000 | 200 | 3,000,000 | 600 |

***Table 2: Limits of liability for property damage and loss of life or personal injury under the 1976 LLMC***

| *Tonnage of Ship* | *SDR* | *SDR/per ton* | | *SDR/ton* |
|---|---|---|---|---|
| | *Property damage* | | *Loss of life/personal injury* | |
| <500 | 167,000 | – | 500,000 | – |
| 501–3,000 | 167,000 | 167 | 500,000 | 667 |
| 3,001–30,000 | 167,000 | 167 | 500,000 | 500 |
| 30,001–70,000 | 167,000 | 125 | 500,000 | 375 |
| >70,000 | 167,000 | 83 | 500,000 | 250 |

Article 15(2) of the 1976 LLMC gives the right for a State Party to provide limits of liability for vessels less than 300 tons.[393] For such vessels the limits have been specified to be 1,500,000 SDR for loss of life and personal injury and 500,000 SDR for property damage on its own.[394]

### (i) Multiplicity of defendants and counterclaims

The limits of liability apply to the aggregate of claims occurring during a "distinct occasion".[395] Whether a series of accidents belong to the same or distinct occasions under English law depends on whether the accidents were linked in such a way that the second can be shown to be the natural consequence of the first.[396]

Moreover, the limits of liability established cover the aggregate liability of all persons entitled to limited liability rather than the liability of each defendant. Thus, one limitation fund is available to the claimant(s) irrespective of the number of persons falling under the shipowner definition[397] or the definition of salvor.[398]

393. There is an obligation imposed on each State Party to inform the depositary about the limits of liability for smaller vessels.
394. Merchant Shipping (Convention on Limitation of Liability for Maritime Claims) Amendment Order 1998 (SI 1998 No 1258). Before the coming into force of this amendment (13/5/2004) the previous established limits were 250,000 SDR and 83,333 SDR respectively.
395. 1976 LLMC, Art. 9.
396. See e.g., *Owners of the Lucullite v Owners of the R Mackay (The Lucullite)* (1929) 33 Ll L Rep 186 and *The Harlow* (1922) 10 Ll L Rep 311.
397. 1976 LLMC, Art. 1(2).
398. *Ibid.*, Art. 1(3).

Where counter claims exist, Article 5 provides that the limits of liability apply to the balance of the claim and the counterclaim.[399] For example, where two ships collide and they are both to blame, their claims must be set-off against each other and then the net balance would be subject to limitation of liability of the party that has to pay the net balance.

### (j) Constitution of the limitation fund and priority of claims

Where legal proceedings[400] have been initiated in a State party in respect of claims subject to limitation any person entitled to limit and alleged in these proceedings to be liable is entitled to constitute a limitation fund with one of the courts in front of which proceedings are pending.[401] A fund constituted by one of the persons entitled to limit is considered to be constituted by all persons entitled to limit liability.[402] The provision restricts the establishment of the limitation fund (and therefore the protection available under Article 13) only to courts in States party to the convention. Thus, where a limitation fund is established under a different limitation regimes such limitation fund would not be sufficient for the purpose of the 1976 LLMC. The same applies for a limitation fund established in a 1976 LLMC State party in respect of limitation proceedings and/or arrest of a ship at a 1996 LLMC State party.

Where there are no legal proceedings in any contracting State there are strong arguments supporting the assertion that a shipowner may choose in which contracting State he will constitute the limitation fund and when.[403] This is supported by noting that the purpose of the limitation fund is to provide security up to the limit prescribed and to free the vessel and the shipowner from further inconvenience. Waiting for the initiation of legal proceedings before facilitating this process through the establishment of a limitation fund arguably defeats one of the advantages of limitation of liability. However, such an argument is not sufficient and one should look for support in the text of the 1976/1996 LLMC. Article 11 establishes that where there are legal proceedings the limitation fund may[404] be constituted in one of these courts. This is consistent with the purposive interpretation suggested above because the objective of providing security and releasing the vessel is served better when the limitation fund is established where a claim has been submitted than elsewhere. However, until such an action is established there is no reason to restrict the shipowner's options.

It can also be argued that "legal proceedings" under Article 11 covers not only liability claims against the shipowner but also limitation proceedings and negative

399. 1976 LLMC, Art. 5.

400. Legal proceedings include arbitration proceedings, *ICL Shipping Ltd, Steamship Mutual Underwriting Association (Bermuda) Ltd v Chin Tai Steel Enterprise Co Ltd and Others (The ICL Vikraman)* [2004] 1 Lloyd's Rep 21, following *Afromar Inc v Greek Atlantic Cod Fishing Co (The Penelope II)* [1980] 2 Lloyd's Rep 17.

401. 1976/1996 LLMC, Art. 11(1).

402. 1976/1996 LLMC, Art. 11(3).

403. It is arguable that liability proceedings in a non-contracting State will not be considered as covered by Art. 11 and the options of the shipowner will be the same as when no liability proceedings have been constituted.

404. The wording of Art. 11 is permissive and does not state that the shipowner *must* constitute a limitation fund in one of these courts.

declaratory relief proceedings initiated by the shipowner. Thus, provided that negative declaratory relief is sought by the shipowner at a court of a contracting state that has jurisdiction on the merits, he then becomes automatically entitled to constitute a limitation fund at that State in accordance with Article 11.

It is worth mentioning that Article 11(1) does not question the validity of such proceedings or whether such court has jurisdiction on the merits in respect of claims subject to limitation of liability but only requires the existence of such legal proceedings.

In conclusion, we submit that arguably the most efficient interpretation of the LLMC (1976 and 1996) would recognise a right to establish a limitation fund in any contracting State until proceedings against the shipowner are started. However, if proceedings against the owner have started, then the owner's choice is between the jurisdictions in which proceedings have started, not in every contracting State. This interpretation may mean that the shipowner can wait for suitable actions to begin in a forum convenient for him before establishing a fund. However, such choice may be non-existent if the ship is arrested, in which case a limitation fund would be most efficient at the place of arrest, as will become evident later.

The fund should be for the amounts determined by Article 6 and 7 increased by interest from the day of the incident to the day of the constitution of the fund. The way the interest is calculated is not prescribed in the LLMC but is determined by the national rules.[405] Thus, where there are proceedings in several jurisdictions the shipowner can find some variation of the amounts paid out.

The 1996 LLMC makes it clear that the fund should include interests on the appropriate amount calculated under Articles 6 and 7 for the period between the incident and the establishment of the limitation fund.[406] Thus, payment of the limitation amount without the accrued interest would not be an appropriate fund in accordance with the LLMC and the shipowners would not be entitled to the protection of Article 13.

Depending on the type of the account in which the limitation amount is held the interest gained may be compound or simple.[407] The question is to be answered by national law. English courts can only grant simple interest thus any additional interest is for the shipowner's benefit.[408]

The unit of account for the 1996 and the 1976 LLMC is the Special Drawing Right, a unit defined by the International Monetary Fund.[409] The daily value of this unit is routinely quoted to financial newspapers or can be retrieved through the internet.[410] The value of the fund is determined at the date the limitation fund is established or payment is made or security is deposited.[411] The exchange rates for the currency of countries which are Member States of the IMF is determined

405. In England, the 1995 MSA, Part II, Sch. 8, para. 8(1), states that the Secretary of State may prescribe the rate applied. This is done through appropriate statutory instruments, para. 8(2).
406. The position differs under the 1924 and 1957 Limitation Conventions.
407. This means that the interest itself accumulates interest which is added to the capital invested.
408. *Polish Steamship Co v Atlantic Maritime Co (The Garden City (No 2))* [1984] 2 Lloyd's Rep 37 (CA).
409. 1976 and 1996 LLMC, Art. 8.
410. *www.imf.org/*. See Chapter 5, fn. 6.
411. 1976 and 1996 LLMC, Art. 8.

through the IMF.[412] If a State is not a party to the IMF then that State will have to determine[413] the exchange rate for the SDR and its national currency.[414]

The fund can be constituted either by payment into court of the monies required or "by producing a guarantee acceptable under the legislation of the State Party where the fund is constituted and considered to be adequate by the Court or other competent authority".[415] This wording ensures that where the sum of money corresponding to the limitation fund is paid into court, then the limitation fund is properly constituted but the provision of any other form of financial security or guarantee is possible only where the national court approves it.

### (k) Which claims are paid out of the limitation fund

Claims subject to limitation of liability[416] are paid out of the fund. Where the shipowner or his insurer or any third party settles or pays out a claim which would otherwise have been subject to limitation of liability then the rights of the claimant are subrogated to shipowner or his insurer or to that third party[417] who is entitled to claim against the limitation fund. This means that the shipowner or his insurer cannot always recover the full payment they have made prior to the distribution of the fund but only that part of the claim that would have been paid to the claimant had he retained his claim to the fund.

Provision is also made under the 1996 LLMC for situations where a settlement has not yet been reached at the time the fund is distributed. In situations where the person limiting liability or any other person can show that "he may be compelled to pay, at a later date"[418] such a settlement for which had he paid before the distribution of the limitation fund, he would be entitled to claim against the fund having been subrogated to the claimant's rights the court has discretion to order that a part of the limitation fund should be retained for the payment of the respective proportion of this claim.

Although the 1996 LLMC does not clarify the point it is strongly arguable that litigation costs are not to be paid out of the limitation fund because otherwise the shipowner would be encouraged to embark upon long litigation knowing that he will not have to pay any additional costs.

The fund is distributed proportionally to the "established claims". Apart from the larger amounts available and the priority given in the payment of the loss of life and personal injury claims under Article 6, no other priority is provided for. Thus any priority of claims *in rem* does not affect the distribution of the limitation fund and it does not matter whether the claims are based on maritime liens or other statutory rights *in rem*. This is further clarified in the 1995 MSA where

412. Accessible through the internet at the IMF website, *supra*, fn. 133.
413. Where a State is not a party to the IMF and its national law does not permit the determination of exchange rates the 1976 and 1996 LLMC permit that such a State can declare the limits of liability of Art. 8(2) which use as monetary unit sixty-five and a half milligrams of gold of millesimal fineness nine hundred (Art. 8(3)). The way of converting such units to national currency is left to the law of the State concerned (Art. 8.3).
414. 1976 and 1996 LLMC, Art. 8.1.
415. *Ibid.*, Art. 11(2).
416. That is claims under Art. 2 not excluded under Art. 3 of the 1976/1996 LLMC.
417. 1976/1996 LLMC, Art. 12(2).
418. *Ibid.*, Art. 12(4).

it is stated that "no lien or other right in respect of any ship or property" shall affect the distribution of the fund.[419]

The law applicable to the constitution and the distribution of the fund is the law of the State in which the fund is constituted.[420]

### (l) Consequences of the constitution of the limitation fund

The constitution of a limitation fund which fulfils Article 11 brings immediate protection to the shipowner in respect of any claim made against the fund. Thus all other rights against either the person that has established the fund or on behalf of whom the fund is established, that is all the "shipowners", salvors and their insurers, are barred.[421] The wording is very general and refers to "any rights", thus it is arguable that security proceedings as well as relief by injunction are also barred.

Where the claimant has succeeded in obtaining security through arrest of the ship or attachment of other property or security in any other form before the establishment of the fund, the establishment of the fund may affect the release of the ship or the security depending on the contracting State at which the limitation fund is established. Thus, where the fund is constituted at the first port of call after an incident,[422] or at the place of disembarkation in respect of passengers,[423] or the port of discharge in respect of cargo,[424] or the port where the ship is arrested,[425] then the ship or other property or security should be released. While it is not expressly stated it appears reasonable to assume that the obligation to release any arrested ship or security applies equally to all courts in States which are party to the 1996 LLMC. Both the release of the property and the bar against other actions are subject to the condition that the fund is accessible to the claimant.[426] This means that if, for example, a vessel collides with another vessel at a foreign port and the shipowner establishes a limitation fund at that foreign port, the English courts would have to release any vessel arrested in England in respect of that collision. If the collision takes place outside a port, and the limitation fund is not established at the first port of call either because it is established elsewhere or because the ship is lost because of the collision, the English court has discretion to deal with the release of the ship/security.[427]

This discretion is purely for security ship arrest and attachment of property that has happened before the establishment of the fund. Such rights are barred under Article 13(1) after the establishment of a suitable fund. This provides strong imperatives for the shipowner to establish a limitation fund if he wishes to avoid further arrest or freezing measures for security.

419. 1995 MSA, Sch. 7, Part II, s. 9.
420. 1976/1996 LLMC, Art. 14.
421. *Ibid.*, Art. 13(1).
422. *Ibid*, Art. 13(2)(a), or at the port where the incident happened if it did happen within a port. Presumably the word "port" denotes the administrative characteristics of the port area rather than the physical location within the breakwaters and docks.
423. 1976/1996 LLMC, Art. 13(2)(b).
424. *Ibid.*, Art. 13(2)(c).
425. *Ibid.*, Art. 13(2)(d).
426. *Ibid.*, Art. 13(3): "... only if the claimant may bring a claim against the limitation fund before the Court administering that fund and the fund is actually available and freely transferable in respect of that claim."
427. See *Owners of the Zenatia v Owners of the Putbus (The Putbus)* [1969] 1 Lloyd's Rep 253 (CA) deciding the point in respect of the 1957 Limitation Convention.

Protection of a fund under Art. 13.

The court is authorised to order not only the release of the vessel or the return of bail but also the security provided under contractual terms between the parties,[428] provided that it is subject to that court's jurisdiction.

Where a claim against the limitation fund is made then the claimant is not permitted to enforce his claim against any of the assets of the defendant.[429] This would probably apply whether or not the claim is finally considered to be under the 1996 LLMC. However, if the claim is not under the 1996 LLMC there could be a problem of the action becoming time-barred, in particular where specific claims are subject to exclusive jurisdictions and have to be submitted to courts in countries other than that where the limitation fund is established. Because the wording of Article 13 does not restrict the initiation of proceedings on the merits, but only proceedings against assets arguably providing some sort of pre-trial security, it is wise to start proceedings at the appropriate forum within time irrespective of the position on limitation of liability.

Whether Article13 restricts in any way the right of a claimant to obtain a freezing injunction[430] or any similar restraining order from an English court is questionable. Freezing injunctions are only viewed as orders against the defendant and not as creating rights against the property.[431] Therefore it is unlikely that Article 13 restricts the right to apply for a freezing injunction or prejudices the outcome of the application. However, in order to obtain a freezing injunction, the claimant has to show that there is a risk of removal of assets of the defendant.[432] Where the defendant has already established a limitation fund and the claimant has claimed against the fund it would be virtually impossible to demonstrate that the risk of dissipation of assets exists, so it is unlikely that such an order would be granted.

### (m) Limitation of liability without the constitution of the fund

The constitution of a limitation fund is particularly useful where there are several claimants. In such a case the establishment of a fund acts as the provision of

428. See *The Wladyslaw Lokietek* [1978] 2 Lloyd's Rep. 520, under s. 5 of the Merchant Shipping (Liability of Shipowners and Others) Act 1958. See also *ICL Vickraman* [2004] 1 Lloyd's Rep 21, where the same issue was not challenged.

429. Art. 13 of the LLMC 1976/1996 and see Griggs, Williams and Farr, *Limitation of Liability for Maritime Claims* (4th ed) (LLP, 2005), p. 69.

430. The freezing injunction is a discretionary and interlocutory order aimed in securing funds for the satisfaction of a claim. The purpose is "... to prevent a defendant from taking action designed to frustrate subsequent orders of the court". *Derby & Co and Others v Weldon and Others (Nos 3 and 4)* [1990] Ch 65 (CA). English Procedure is described under CPR r. 25.1. Applications are subject to CPR 23 and CPR 25.3, 25.4. See also Practice Direction 25 CPD-002 in CPR. Any property or other asset that can be used to satisfy the judgment. The property can be situated anywhere in the world (*Babanaft International Co SA v Bassatne and Another* [1990] Ch 13; [1988] 2 Lloyd's Rep 435). A ship can be subject to a freezing injunction as part of an *in personam* action against the shipowner (*The Rena K* [1979] QB 377; [1978] 1 Lloyd's Rep 545) but most probably not in support of an action *in rem* (*The Stolt Filia* [1980] LMLN 15). For more details see S Gee, *Mareva Injunction and Anton Piller Relief* (4th ed) (Sweet and Maxwell, 1998). See Chapter 11.

431. Freezing injunctions are not pretrial attachments and they do not give rise to a lien. *The Cretan Harmony* [1978] 1 Lloyd's Rep 425. See Chapter 11, p. 364.

432. *The Genie* [1979] 2 Lloyd's Rep 184; *Ketchum International plc v Group Public Relations* [1997] 1 WLR 4. The contact and the financial standing of the defendant is relevant as well as the type of assets; see, for examples, *The Genie* [1979] 2 Lloyd's Rep 184; *Ninemia Maritime Corp v Trave Schiffahrtsgesellsschaft mbH The Niedersachsen* [1984] 1 All ER 398. See Chapter 11, p. 366.

security for all claims collectively thus permitting the release of the ship from detention[433] and an assessment of the prospects of recovery for the various claimants. However, where there is only one claimant the constitution of the limitation fund may not be necessary. In such a situation limitation of liability can be used as a defence.[434] Even more, where liability is admitted it is more efficient to order the direct payment of the limitation amount to the sole claimant without the intermediate steps of constituting and administering a fund.

The 1976 and 1996 LLMC provide as the default position, that limitation of liability may be invoked without the constitution of a limitation fund.[435] However, they also provide that the contracting State may in its national law restrict this position by providing that a person is entitled to limit liability only where an appropriate limitation fund has been constituted.[436] Procedure is left to be decided by the contracting State.[437]

The UK has not made use of this option;[438] thus under English law, limitation of liability does not depend on the constitution of a limitation fund.[439] English case law strongly supports the assertion that Article 10 provides a free-standing ground for limitation of liability without the establishment of a limitation fund even where no proceedings have yet started, or are not going to be started, in front of an English court.[440] This interpretation considers the issue of jurisdiction in respect of limitation of liability as completely separate from the issue of jurisdiction on the merits of the dispute, and permits the shipowner entitled to limit liability under English law to pre-empt the limitation issue by applying for a limitation decree in England.[441]

### (n) Jurisdictional issues

Limitation proceedings should be distinguished from any proceedings on the merits of claims which are subject to limitation of liability.[442] The two jurisdictional issues arising from the limitation proceedings will be now discussed. These are: (a) the relevance of limitation of liability proceedings in determining the jurisdiction on the merits of a claim; and (b) the problem of conflicting limitation of liability provisions in parallel proceedings.

433. See Chapter 11.
434. *Ibid.*
435. 1976/1996 LLMC, Art. 10(1).
436. *Ibid.*, Art. 10(1).
437. *Ibid.*, Art. 10(2).
438. Sched. 7, Part 1, of the 1995 MSA only contains the first sentence of the corresponding Article of the Convention and states: "Limitation of liability may be invoked notwithstanding that a limitation fund as mentioned in Article 11 has not been constituted."
439. For a discussion of the procedure and case law, see Chapter 11.
440. See *Seismic Shipping Inc and Another v Total E&P UK plc (The Western Regent)* [2005] 2 Lloyd's Rep 359 (CA) and [2005] 2 Lloyd's Rep 54. See also *The Denise*, unreported, 3 December 2004. There is a contradictory *obiter dictum* in *ICL Vickraman, supra*, fn. 150, which both the High Court and the Court of Appeal in *The Western Regent* have rejected after noting that the working documents of the Convention are in essence neutral on the subject and that the wording of Art. 10 does not permit such restriction to be applied. However, the English courts retain discretion to order the constitution of a limitation fund under CPR 61.11 13(a)(ii).
441. Note that in the case of *The Western Regent* the defendant demise-charterer was registered in England and therefore the English court had personal jurisdiction. Permission to serve out of the jurisdiction is required in other cases which will be discussed in Chapter 11.
442. See Chapter 1, p. 13.

It is beyond the scope of this book to discuss in detail these two very important questions. Thus, only the position under English law will be described.

The English courts consider that a shipowner can start limitation proceedings in respect of any incident as of right even where no claim against him has yet been launched in England.[443] The nature of limitation is not seen as qualifying the substantive right of the claimant.[444] Two consequences follow. First in a case of *forum non conveniens* the fact that the foreign court applies other limitation of liability arrangements is not a contributing factor to grant a stay to the English proceedings.[445]

However, for claims subject to the EC Regulation 44/2001, the English courts will only have jurisdiction in respect of limitation of liability proceedings if Article 7 of the EC Regulation applies, that is only where the jurisdiction on the merits is prescribed for them under the Regulation.[446] Moreover, where another EU court was first seised on the merits of the dispute, the English court may exercise the discretion granted through Article 28 of the EC Regulation 44/2001 and stay its own proceedings.[447] However, such a stay must be surely subject to an assessment of the speed by which the other court is expected to progress. If the foreign court is expected to delay it would arguably be best to determine the limitation of liability issue separately by granting the limitation decree and probably make orders for the establishment of the limitation fund, thus liberating the shipowner from protracted litigation in respect of the limitation of liability. Second, where an English jurisdiction decree is issued its effectiveness would, according to the English courts, be left to the court having jurisdiction on the merits and will not be supported by an anti-suit injunction. However, the last statement is only true where the foreign court is non-EU. For EU courts a limitation decree is directly enforceable under Article 32 of EC Regulation 44/2001.[448]

In respect of limitation decrees issued abroad the position would be as follows: Where a limitation decree has been granted in an EU State this must be recognised and enforced by a UK court.[449] Where a foreign limitation decree from a non-EU country is issued, then its recognition will arguably depend on whether such a decree is from a 1996 LLMC country. Difficulties may arise where a shipowner has lost the right to limit liability in a State applying the 1957 Limitation Convention[450] and then applies for limitation of liability in England.

443. *The Western Regent*, *supra*, fn. 440.
444. "The effect of the Convention ... is not to qualify the substantive right of the claimant against the shipowner, but to limit the extent to which that right can be enforced against the limitation fund." *Caltex Singapore Pte Ltd v BP Shipping Ltd* [1996] 1 Lloyd's Rep 286 at p. 294; approved in *The Western Regent*, *supra*, fn. 440.
445. *The Herceg Novi* [1998] 2 Lloyd's Rep 454. See Chapter 1.
446. This has not been stated in any case law yet; however, there is no obvious alternative formula. Limitation of liability proceedings are in respect of civil and commercial matters. The ECJ has held that there are no jurisdictional Rules in the 1976 LLMC (*Maersk Olie & Gas A/S v Firma M deHaan en W de Boer*, C- 39/02; [2007] I L Pr 5), so Art. 71 does not come into play. Thus, jurisdiction on the merit for limitation of liability proceedings can only be prescribed under Art. 7. In effect the EC Regulation 44/2001 has distributed any jurisdiction in respect of limitation proceedings available under the 1976/1996 LLMC. This, of course reflects in the recognition of the relevant decrees and judgments. See Chapter 1.
447. *Blue Nile Shipping Co Ltd v Iguana Shipping & Finance Inc (The Happy Fellow)* [1998] 1 Lloyd's Rep. 13.
448. *Maersk Olie & Gas A/S v Firma M deHaan en W de Boer*, *supra*, fn. 446.
449. *Ibid.*
450. A shipowner may prefer the 1957 Limitation Convention in view of the lower applicable limits.

Provided that the decision fulfils the common law rules for recognition of judgments the shipowner will probably be estopped from retrying the case because the action will be considered as unconscionable.[451]

451. *Henderson v Henderson* (1843) 3 Hare 100. Section 34 of the Civil Jurisdiction and Judgments Act 1982 states: "No proceedings may be brought by a person in England and Wales or Northern Ireland on a cause of action in respect of which a judgment has been given in his favour in proceedings between the same parties, or their privies, in a court in another part of the United Kingdom or in a court of an overseas country, unless that judgment is not enforceable or entitled to recognition in England and Wales or, as the case may be, in Northern Ireland." This would arguably not apply if a foreign decision removing the right to limit liability from a shipowner has been issued simply because such a judgment cannot be considered as being in his favour. However, if the limitation of liability issue has not been claimed in the foreign or English liability proceedings, there is authority under earlier limitation law that limitation of liability can be raised after the judgment on the merits of *Baltic Shipping Co v Owners of Cargo on the Mekhanik Evgrafov (The Mekhanik Evgrafov and The Ivan Derbenev)* [1988] 1 Lloyd's Rep 330; [1988] 1 FTLR 235; 1988 WL 622963.

CHAPTER 7

# International Regulations for Ship Operators, their Verification and Enforcement

*RICHARD PILLEY AND FILIPPO LORENZON*

## 1. INTRODUCTION[1]

Chapter 7 reviews some of the statutory regulations with which ship operators are required to comply: in particular we look at those which have more recently been introduced. The responsibility for the enforcement of these regulations lies with the flag State administrations but we also examine the role of the port State and of the classification societies. The work of the European safety agency EMSA is also examined.

## 2. THE INTERNATIONAL CONVENTION FOR THE SAFETY OF LIFE AT SEA (SOLAS) 1974

The purpose of the SOLAS Convention is to establish rules which govern the safe construction of ships, the safety equipment with which ships are required to be fitted and the standards to which they should be operated in order to avoid accidents. It is the role of the International Maritime Organisation (IMO) regularly to review the convention and to draft any necessary amendments but the responsibility for enforcement of the provisions of the convention lies with the flag State. The flag State must ensure that the ships which trade under its flag are surveyed when they are first registered, in order to establish that they comply with SOLAS. Thereafter ships are periodically surveyed at stipulated intervals by the flag State, which also issues the certificates prescribed by the convention. The flag States are permitted to delegate these responsibilities to a recognised body such as a classification society.[2] Port States, operating under a memorandum of understanding such as the Paris Memorandum, have authority to inspect those ships which may not be in compliance with SOLAS and if necessary, to detain them.

The first SOLAS Convention was adopted in 1914 following the loss of the *RMS Titanic*. Subsequently several updated versions of SOLAS were adopted at intervals, the fourth version in 1960. In 1974 the current convention was adopted, which incorporated the latest amendments but which also introduced a new amendment procedure intended to ensure that, because the formal procedures

1. Sections 1 to 5 have been written by Richard Pilley and sections 6, 7 and 8 by Filippo Lorenzon.
2. See below, p. 245.

within IMO can be lengthy and time consuming, any necessary amendments could be more quickly brought into force. This procedure is known as the "tacit acceptance procedure" whereby any amendment can enter into force on a certain date, unless objections are received beforehand from an agreed number of Member States. The procedure has, since 1974, been utilised by IMO on a number of occasions, notably with the introduction of the International Safety Management (ISM) Code and the International Ship and Port Security (ISPS) Code.

More detailed and clear information on SOLAS can be obtained from the IMO website[3] or from the "SOLAS Convention", published by IMO.[4]

## 3. THE INTERNATIONAL SAFETY MANAGEMENT (ISM) CODE

The ISM code was adopted by IMO in 1993 and in 1994 it was inserted into the SOLAS Convention as Chapter IX. On 1 July 1998, the code became mandatory for passenger ships, high speed ships, tankers, and bulk carriers of more than 500 gross tonnes. Later, from 1 July 2002, it became mandatory for all other types of ship, excluding only warships, auxiliaries or other government operated ships, used for non-commercial purposes.

The code provided for earlier implementation by Member States where it was deemed appropriate. On 9 December 1995 the Council of the European Union adopted the ISM Code and declared that from 1 July 1996 it would become mandatory for the operators of Ro-Ro passenger ferries operating to or from any port within the European Community. Even before the code became mandatory, it was held by the courts that ISM represented a set of internationally recognised principles embodying best practice in ship management.[5]

The wording of the ISM Code is admirably brief and clear and it sets out principles for ship operators, whether they are owners or managers, requiring them to:

- adopt a Safety Management System (SMS);
- appoint a designated person with responsibility to monitor the implementation of the SMS;
- ensure that adequate resources and support are available;
- establish procedures for all operations and maintenance tasks;
- ensure good safety practices afloat and ashore;
- improve communication between ship and shore;
- establish emergency procedures;
- put in place a system of verification, review and evaluation (internal audits).

It should be noted that while the shipboard aspects of the code are important, equal emphasis is placed upon the role and responsibilities of the operator.

### (a) Certification, verification and control

The flag States are required to institute systems of certification, verification and control, which may be carried out either by the flag State administration or which

3. *www.imo.org*
4. International Convention for the Safety of Life at Sea, 1974 and 1988 Protocol relating thereto, Amendments 2000, International Maritime Organization, London 2001.
5. See *Papera Traders Co Ltd and Others v Hyundai Merchant Marine Co Ltd and Another (The Eurasian Dream) (No 1)* [2002] 1 Lloyd's Rep 719, at paras 143 and 144.

can be delegated to a recognised authority, such as a classification society.[6] Those operators who comply with the Code receive a Document of Compliance (DOC) valid for five years, subject to one intermediate audit. Similarly, each ship, after audit, is issued with a Safety Management Certificate (SMC) valid for five years. Ships are required to carry on board the original SMC and a copy of the DOC as well as a copy of the Safety Management System.

### (b) The designated person

The designated person should be one who is suitably qualified and experienced and who is fully conversant with the company's safety management system and must also have the independence and authority to report all non-conformities to the "highest levels of management". According to the International Chamber of Shipping "Guidelines on the application of the ISM Code", the role of the designated person is a line management responsibility: the designated person will therefore not normally be a member of senior management within the company, but must have access to them and must also have adequate resources, financial, human and material.

When the code was introduced there was concern that the resulting documentation might create a "paper trail" for plaintiffs pursuing litigation, who would seek to find deficiencies in the ship or her management. Obviously many of the certificates and documents required under ISM will be standard items on lists of documents on disclosure, which will also include all records of communications with the designated person, including those between him and his superiors. There will be a presumption that advantage has been taken of this access to the highest levels of management and the burden of proof is likely to rest with higher management to demonstrate, where appropriate, that they were not given relevant information by the designated person.

### (c) Impact on litigation

#### *(i) Disclosure of documents*

The Woolf Report on Access to Justice[7] emphasises that the disclosure of documents must not impose an unfair burden on the court or the parties, but must be confined to the issues as pleaded. The judges are encouraged to take an active role in case management and ensure that the disclosure of documents is controlled.

The ICS "Guidelines on the application of the ISM code" refer to records of maintenance and inspection and to documentation control but the purpose of the code is not that a proliferation of paperwork should be created, adding to the workload of shipboard personnel. The motto of any management control system should be "keep it short and simple" and this applies to the SMS as well as to record-keeping. It might, for example, be perfectly acceptable for an operator when defining his policy on ship-board personnel matters, rather than producing

6. See below p. 245.
7. Access to Justice final Report by The Right honourable the Lord Woolf, Master of the Rolls, July 1996. See *www.dca.gov.uk/civil/final/index.htm*.

a complex document, to state simply that company policy is to comply in every respect with the requirements of the STCW (Standards of Training, Certification and Watch-keeping) Convention 1995.

### *(ii) Cargo claims and unseaworthiness*

The Hague and Hague-Visby Rules require the owner to exercise due diligence to make the ship seaworthy before and at the start of the voyage and are recognised as the standard most widely accepted.[8] The Hamburg Rules impose a higher level of obligation upon the owner[9] but where they apply the ISM Code appears not to make the owner's position any more burdensome. Where the Hague and Hague-Visby rules apply, owners will be unable to benefit from the exceptions from liability for negligence in the navigation or management of the ship or the other exceptions in rule 4, unless they are able positively to demonstrate the exercise of due diligence to make the ship seaworthy. This duty is non-delegable and calls for an effective system of ship and safety management. The ISM Code must now represent the internationally recognised standard of good ship and safety management and failure to comply with the principles of the code (not simply the failure to produce a valid certificate) amounts to a lack of due diligence by the owner. A well-documented safety management system is of considerable help in establishing the exercise of due diligence.

### *(iii) Limitation of liability*

Under the 1957 Limitation Convention, which is no longer in force in England, the right to limit liability is granted to the shipowner "unless the occurrence giving rise to the claim resulted from the actual fault or privity of the owner".[10] The requirement under the ISM code to appoint a designated person with access to the highest levels of management, with express duties to monitor the safety and pollution prevention aspects of the operation of each ship, makes it almost impossible for the owner of a ship claiming limitation of liability under the 1957 Convention to prove the absence of fault or privity if the problems which give rise to the casualty were already known to the designated person.

Under the 1976 Limitation Convention it is more difficult to establish the loss of the right to limit. Article 4 reads: "A person shall not be entitled to limit his liability if it is proved that the loss resulted from his personal act or omission, committed with intent to cause such loss or recklessly and with the knowledge that such loss would probably result." ISM clearly defines the term "company", as including the owner of the ship and any organisation including a professional ship manager or bareboat charterer who has assumed responsibility for the operation of the ship (the "operator.") The question arises whether the "personal fault" of such a manager would be imputed to the owner in the context of the 1976 Convention. The ship manager may well be the employer of the designated person and if that person is found to be at fault, with the true owner ignorant of the problem, it may be considered unfair to deprive him of the right to limit. The

8. See Chapter 3.
9. See Chapter 2.
10. Art. 1.1 of the 1957 Limitation Convention. See Chapter 6, p. 201.

wording of the convention does not assist, although the insertion of the word "personal" may suggest a Rule of Attribution[11] pointing to the owner himself or to the person in a corporate ownership most closely corresponding to the individual shipowner.

The ISM Code requires management arrangements to be more transparent than had formerly been the case and the Code subjects these arrangements to increased scrutiny, meaning that owners' rights to limitation will probably be challenged more frequently.

#### *(iv) Insurance cover*

Section 39(5) of the Marine Insurance Act 1906 excludes liability of the insurer if the ship is sent to sea in an unseaworthy condition with the privity of the assured. The same Rules of Attribution will be applied in deciding the identity of the individual, whose knowledge is to be regarded as that of the assured for the purposes of this section. The designated person nominated under the safety management system is unlikely to be the owner himself. However, since this person is expressly required to have access to the highest levels of management there is surely a presumption that he will use his rights of access to report any problem and to recommend remedial action. Any refusal by the owner to implement such action, which results in a condition of unseaworthiness and leads to a casualty, might well put the ship's insurance cover in jeopardy.

In cases where a total loss is being disputed by hull underwriters, it is certain that their solicitors will demand disclosure of all relevant documentation required by the ISM Code.

### (d) Criminal proceedings

The risk of criminal proceedings against the Master of a ship involved in a casualty is now more real than ever, as evidenced in the cases of both *The Erika* in France and *The Prestige* in Spain. Provided that owners and Masters are able to produce evidence of compliance with ISM by means of certification and documentation, this should help to protect them in such cases.

### (e) Conclusion

It must be stressed that the objectives of the code are "safety at sea and the prevention of marine pollution". The code as has been pointed out earlier is simply drafted and is based upon general principles and objectives. It recognises that no two shipping companies or shipowners are the same and that ships operate under varying conditions. Legal decisions involving the ISM Code have, since it was introduced, been refreshingly few: brief reference to ISM was made in *The Eurasian Dream*,[12] although the code was not in force for that ship at the material time.

The question arises as to whether the ISM code has succeeded in its aim of reducing the number of marine accidents. Some underwriters claim that it has had a positive impact, although it is not clear precisely how this is substantiated.

11. See *Meridian Global Funds Management v Securities Commission* [1995] 2 AC 500 at p. 507.
12. See fn. 5.

Many of those ship operators who willingly embraced the code claim to have benefited in terms of efficiency, economy and safety; others may have regarded the document of compliance as just another trading certificate and may not have adopted the spirit of the code so wholeheartedly. Seafarers not infrequently complain of the extra burden of paperwork involved and it seems likely that, contrary to the spirit of the code, many safety management systems are over-lengthy and over-complicated. Some ship operators have progressed further and have adopted the standards of ISO9000 or ISO14000. Independent tanker owners are encouraged by the oil majors in addition to compliance with ISM, to undergo "Tanker Management Self Assessment" (TMSA) and to establish risk assessment procedures when planning shipboard operations.[13]

## 4. THE IMO INTERNATIONAL SHIP & PORT FACILITY SECURITY (ISPS) CODE

Since 11 September 2001 terrorism has become a threat to the safety of life and property including ships and port facilities. In December 2002, the International Maritime Organization adopted amendments to the SOLAS Convention (Chapters V & XI-2) which require some physical modifications to ships and which relate to ship and port security. The International Ship and Port Facility (ISPS) Code consists of two parts: Part A (mandatory) and Part B (advisory). The ISPS Code covers passenger ships, all types of cargo ships, including high-speed craft, of 500gt and over and mobile offshore drilling units. It applies also to port facilities which handle ships engaged on international voyages but does not apply to warships or other government-operated ships used for non-commercial purposes. There are provisions for contracting governments to reach agreement with others in order to provide alternative security arrangements on ships making short international voyages.

In parallel, the United States of America has enacted the Maritime Transportation Security Act which imposes additional requirements on passenger ships and ships over 500gt calling at United States ports and which makes ISPS (Part B) mandatory for United States flag ships. This Act came into force at the same time as ISPS on 1 July 2004.

### (a) Ship modifications (SOLAS amendments)

- All ships must be fitted with an automatic identification system.[14]
- Display the ship's identification number externally and internally.[15]
- Install a ship security alert system.[16]

### (b) Some ISPS Code provisions

Each ship operator must obtain an International Ship Security Certificate for each ship which must be retained on board the ship at all times. A company security officer must be appointed who is required to carry out a security assessment on

13. Further information on the ISM Code can be obtained from the ICS/ISF booklet *Guidelines on the Application of the ISM Code*, available from Marisec publications.
14. SOLAS, Ch. V, Reg. 19.2.4.
15. *Ibid.*, Ch. XI, Reg. 3.
16. *Ibid.*, Ch. XI, Reg. 6.

each ship and thereafter with the approval of the flag State, formulate a ship security plan. This plan must be available on the ship and will provide for the appointment of a ship security officer who may be the ship's Master and should provide for the appropriate training and exercises. Other duties of the company security officer include assessing likely port security threats and maintaining awareness of terrorist activities. The Master always has the ultimate responsibility for the safety of the ship.

The ship security assessment identifies any existing security measures and any operations where security may be an issue. The plan will vary according to the ship and any potential threats and must be approved by the flag State as must any later amendments. Security plans are not normally subject to inspection by port State Control unless the inspectors have "clear grounds" to believe that ship is not in compliance with the code.

Security levels are controlled by the flag State and are internationally recognised:

- Security Level One: *normal* – the level at which ships and ports will usually operate, with controlled access to the ship, controlled embarkation of all persons and their effects. Restricted areas, including deck areas and areas surrounding the ship must be monitored and the handling of cargo and stores must be supervised.
- Security Level Two: *heightened* – in this case, additional security measures apply as specified in the Security Plan.
- Security Level Three: *exceptional* – the level applying while there is a probable or imminent risk, when further specific measures must be adopted.

If the security level of a port State is higher than that set by the flag State, then the higher level must be adopted before entering port and both parties must be advised.

In addition to the ship security plan and the ISPS certificate, the ship must be provided with a "Continuous Synopsis Record" issued by the flag State. Also on board should be any additional information relating to joining crew, parties to charterparties and those deciding the employment of the ship as well as any security information regarding previous port calls. Records must also be kept of training exercises, any security threats, changes in security level, internal audits, reviews of the ship security plan, amendments to the plan, testing of security equipment and the ship security alert system.

### (c) Continuous synopsis record

This document which must be in English, Spanish or French provides an on-board history of the ship dating from 1 July 2004, including:

- the name of the flag State;
- the date of the ship's registry;
- ship's I.D. number;
- name of ship;
- port of registry;
- name and address of registered owner;

- name and address if applicable, of registered bareboat charterer;
- name and address of the ISM operator;
- classification society;
- the name of the issuing authority of the ISM certificates and the name of the auditor;
- the name of the authority which issued the ISSC and details of the verification process;
- any change of flag.

### (d) Ships entering port

At the earliest opportunity the ship must contact the port facility security officer at the next port of call. Any non-compliance with either the SOLAS regulations or Part A of the ISPS Code or with the requirements of the port State, must be notified before attempting entry into port. The ship is likely to undergo the routine port State inspection but this will not normally include the ship security plan. If officers authorised by the port State have "clear grounds" for believing that the ship does not comply with SOLAS or the ISPS Code, they must inform the ship and the flag State. They may require the ship to undergo further inspection or they may deny entry into port. The ship must be kept fully informed and the Master may decide not to enter that port.

Contracting governments may require further advance information, including the continuous synopsis record, the ship's position, the ETA, details of passenger and crew lists, cargo manifest and any other information required under SOLAS. Further information may be required such as details of the safety security certificate, the security level currently in operation and the security level in the previous ten ports of call, including details of any extra security measures taken in the previous ten ports, records of security measures taken in any port in the territory of a non-contracting government and any "Declarations of Security" entered into with port facilities. Also required may be any records of ship-to-ship activity with ships from a non-contracting government or with ships not required to comply with ISPS. Any information about persons rescued at sea must be reported.

### (e) Declaration of security

The "Declaration of Security" is an agreement between ship and port on the security measures to be adopted during the ship's port call. It might, for example, be required when the ship and port are operating at different levels of security.

### (f) Control measures

Chapter XI of SOLAS describes control measures which will apply to ships from 1 July 2004 including those ships which fly the flag of a State which is not a contracting government and not a party to the 1988 SOLAS protocol. Ships below the convention tonnage must comply with whatever local measures the State may see fit to enforce.

### (g) Obligations of contracting governments

Contracting governments have responsibility for security levels on ships and in port facilities, testing ship security plans, declarations of security, security threats and the provision of the continuous synopsis record. The flag State is also responsible for setting manning levels on all ships within its registry, in accordance with SOLAS Chapter V, Regulation 13, always bearing in mind that any additional workload imposed by the code may require increased manning levels. Contracting governments also have responsibility for approving ship security plans, verifying the compliance of ships, issuing security certificates to ships under its flag and overseeing the obligations of port facilities. All information regarding security must be communicated by contracting governments both to IMO and to registered companies and ships.

### (h) Requirements for ports

SOLAS Chapter XI sets out the requirements for port facilities which are similar requirements to those for ships. Contracting governments must supervise port security assessments and the development of port security plans as well as setting security levels. Each port facility is required to appoint a security officer, similar to that required of companies and ships.

### (i) Commercial and insurance implications of ISPS

When fixing charters, the rights and duties of each party and the apportionment of costs must be taken into account. BIMCO has published ISPS Clauses for both time and voyage charters, which offer a sound framework for the sharing of specific costs and duties. For example, the time charter clause states that owners will, from 1 July 2004 and for the duration of the charter, have to comply with the code. Owners must furnish charterers with evidence of compliance and are accountable for any failure to comply. Some of the owners' obligations can be met only with the cooperation of the charterer: the charterers will be liable for any failure to co-operate. All foreseeable costs are covered by the clause: delays, costs and expenses imposed by a port authority under the code are for the charterers' account. The costs of preparing and complying with the ship security plan are for owners' account.

The trading history of the ship, covering the last 10 voyages, is deliberately not covered in the clause. A wise charterer, before fixing a ship, should ascertain the ship's recent trading history and must, if it emerges that the ship has visited an insecure port, take a commercial decision as to whether to proceed with the charter and to accept the risk of possible delays. United States authorities, for example, are known to maintain records of facilities which are considered to be insecure. Provided that the owners have always complied with the code, then the risk rests with the charterers for the contracted voyage. It is important to include one of the BIMCO clauses, or something similar, in each new charterparty. Other interesting scenarios arise over the question of stowaways. If a ship is found to have stowaways on board, clearly the ship must be in breach of ISPS – does this therefore perhaps mean that the ship is unseaworthy?

P&I Clubs belonging to the International Group of Clubs have made it a condition of cover that ships must have on board and maintain a valid certificate confirming compliance with the code. Failure to do so will result in any claims being paid only at the discretion of the club board of directors.

### (j) Summary and comments

Doubts have been expressed about the practicality of ensuring security on ships and in port facilities, particularly in the face of determined terrorist attacks. Security has not in the past, been a priority for seafarers and many may need extensive encouragement and training to make them more aware of likely security risks. Other concerns include the failure of many ports to comply with the code within the deadline and the possible later consequences for ships calling at such ports. Port operators who are non-compliant may face claims from ship operators who suffer losses as a result of such non-compliance. There has been criticism of some governments who fail to ensure that ports within their jurisdiction are ISPS compliant. Questions have been raised about the consistency of ISPS enforcement and about the practice of appointing the Master as security officer, with some countries stating that they will not approve this. It has also been suggested that while ships may comply with the requirements for automated identification systems, shore-side monitoring stations may not be adequate. Proponents of the code will doubtless contend that, if properly implemented, it should reduce the opportunities for terrorists and others to attack ships or use them in any way to promote terrorist activities and that a strong commitment to the code by all will yield unexpected safety benefits.[17]

## 5. THE INTERNATIONAL CONVENTION ON STANDARDS OF TRAINING, CERTIFICATION AND WATCH-KEEPING AS AMENDED IN 1995 (STCW95)

The aim of this Convention is to ensure that seafarers worldwide are trained to consistent standards and that seafarers' certificates of competency are issued to similar acceptable and consistent standards. The training and certification of seafarers has always been the responsibility of flag administrations and before 1978 when the first STCW convention was drafted, most of the recognised or traditional maritime administrations had in place their own established procedures in order to satisfy these requirements, always to the highest standards. The emergence and growth of non-traditional flag States often not equipped to implement such procedures and sometimes without a robust maritime administration, led to the introduction by the International Maritime Organization (IMO) of an international convention, STCW78, which came into force in 1984.

In the 1990s it became clear that the original convention required further strengthening and clarification if it was to fulfil the perceived needs of the changing

17. More information on the ISPS Code can be obtained from the ICS/ISF booklet *Maritime Security*, available from Marisec publications.

maritime world. Analysis of maritime accidents showed the significance of the human element in most casualties. It became clear that there was a need to raise awareness among shipowners and flag administrations alike of the need to improve training and competency among seafarers and to impose stricter and more precisely defined regulations.

The revised convention, which was published in 1995, and which came fully into force in February 2002, aims to ensure:

- more precisely defined uniform standards of training, certification and competency;
- better procedures to guarantee that STCW is implemented and enforced world-wide; and
- the flexibility to meet the demands of the industry in the twenty-first century.

Both the ISM Code and STCW relate to the human element, both being closely related and complementary to each other. ISM states that: "The company should ensure that each ship is manned with qualified, certificated and medically fit seafarers in accordance with national and international requirements."[18]

It is STCW which defines those international requirements and it may be said that STCW is in some respects an amplification of ISM. Any failure by a shipowner to comply with the requirements of STCW could be construed as a breach of ISM and such a failure, if sufficiently serious in nature, could be interpreted as a major ISM non-conformity.

Unlike the ISM Code, the convention is lengthy. It may be divided broadly into two: that section which applies to flag administrations (the bulk of the convention) and that which applies to shipping companies or operators. Some of the provisions of STCW, applying to shipowners, came into force in February 1997. Other provisions have been in force since August 1998, yet others did not apply until February 2002.

### (a) Responsibilities of shipowners

It may be helpful first to look at the obligations imposed on shipowners, always bearing in mind the significant link between ISM and STWC referred to earlier.

*Documentation*

Companies must not only comply with the new requirements for which they are responsible but also be able to demonstrate compliance. Many of these responsibilities are derived from ISM, the difference being that, STCW requires them to be able to demonstrate implementation in greater detail.

*Certification*

Owners must ensure that officers serving on their ships hold valid certificates of competency for the responsibility which they hold. Ratings also must, when watch-keeping, hold the appropriate certificate. Officers' certificates must be revalidated every five years. All seafarers must, every five years, undergo a

18. ISM Code, para. 6.2.

medical examination recognised by the authority issuing the certificate. Certificates must be endorsed in English to certify that they meet STCW standards. Seafarers must if required, hold recognition endorsements from individual flag States. Officers and ratings employed on certain types of ships, for example tankers, must hold the relevant special endorsements certifying that they are properly trained in that trade. The original certificates must be available for scrutiny on board, not photocopies. All possible precautions must be taken in order to ensure that the certificates are valid.

*Manning*

The seafarers employed on board must hold the certificates stipulated in the Safe Manning Certificate unless they have valid dispensations.

*Record-keeping*

The company must maintain readily accessible records of:

- seafarers' experience (i.e. service record before and during the current employment);
- training received before and during employment;
- medical fitness;
- competence.

*Ship-specific familiarisation*

The company must provide the Master with written instructions on the familiarisation of newly recruited personnel with equipment and operating procedures, ensuring that sufficient time is allocated to the procedure. A responsible crew member must be appointed to ensure that newly joined seafarers receive information in a language that they understand. When this has been completed records must be made and maintained.

*Crew coordination*

Seafarers employed on board must be able to demonstrate that they are able to coordinate their actions in an emergency and communicate in a common language. Drills and exercises simulating various situations must be carried out and recorded.

*Minimum rest periods*

All watch-keeping personnel must be provided with at least the prescribed rest periods. Watch schedules must be posted where they are readily accessible. Part B of the code suggests that records of working hours should be maintained in order to demonstrate compliance.

*Basic safety familiarisation for all seafarers*

All personnel including riding crews and catering staff must undergo elementary training in safety matters, including attending shore-side training courses. Full records of such training must be maintained and be available.

*Basic safety training*

All personnel involved with safety or pollution prevention duties must receive basic training in personal survival techniques, fire prevention and fire-fighting as well as elementary first aid and emergency procedures, pollution prevention and occupational safety. Records must be maintained and personnel must be able to demonstrate that they are competent in these procedures.

*Responsibility*

If a shipowner delegates responsibility for personnel matters to a third party, it must be made clear in the contractual arrangements, who is responsible for compliance with STCW.

### (b) Flag administrations

The new STCW Convention lays down new responsibilities for flag administrations, some of which came into force in 1998 and others which did not come into force until 2002. These responsibilities relate, in the main, to the establishment of suitable training centres, uniform standards of training and competency and measures to ensure uniform, worldwide implementation. Flag States are likely to issue their own certificates of competency to seafarers of their own nationality. Where foreign seafarers are concerned they will either issue their own certificates or issue individual endorsements to any certificates issued by other States. The ultimate responsibilities of the administration cannot be delegated and there is no provision in the convention for flag States to delegate their responsibilities to other parties, such as classification societies.

Flag States are required to have in place an infrastructure, which provides for:

- legislation;
- documentation procedures;
- compliance administration;
- record keeping.

Governments issuing STCW certificates were required, by August 1998, to submit to IMO documentary evidence of compliance with the standards of the convention, in order to facilitate the eventual compilation of the "white list". Information required included:

- details of legal and administrative measures in place to ensure compliance;
- details of all training courses and assessment regimes;
- details of verification procedures.

These reports were to have been submitted in full to IMO by 1 August 1998, after which the "white list" – a list of those administrations that are considered to be in compliance with STCW – was to be published. The list eventually appeared in December 2000.

Since the Convention came fully into force in 2002, governments are required to demonstrate that all training, assessments of competence, certification, endorsement and revalidation activities carried out, whether by themselves or by non-governmental agencies, are monitored through a quality standards system. Even those States, which may have elected to proceed by not issuing their own certificates but by endorsing and recognising the certificates and training provided by other States, still need to establish infrastructures not dissimilar to those of the issuing States. The IMO requires assurances from an endorsing State on the following points:

- What procedures are in place for the recognition of certificates issued by other flags? What standards do they set?
- Do procedures exist for the endorsement of each individual certificate and checking its validity?
- Are there means to maintain records of all certificates endorsed?

Another important feature of STCW is the provision for the involvement of port State control whereby port State control inspectors are authorised to verify the qualifications and competence of seafarers and are encouraged to check that:

- seamen on board hold the appropriate certificates or endorsements;
- the number of seamen on board corresponds with the manning scale.

Following an accident, inspectors will also be empowered to assess the abilities of seafarers, subject to certain provisions.

### (c) Non-compliance and the legal consequences

Earlier, under the section dealing with ISM, reference has been made to the consequences of any failure on the part of a shipowner to comply with ISM. That section referred to unseaworthiness and the likely consequences with respect to cargo claims, prejudice of insurance cover and limitation of liability. Any unseaworthiness arising from a breach of STCW is likely to have similar consequences. A breach of STCW might be construed as non-conformity with ISM.[19]

## 6. THE MARITIME LABOUR CONVENTION 2006

This Convention, adopted in 2006, was the result of a long process of review and research by the International Labour Organization (ILO) over more than five years. The ILO was founded in 1919 soon after the end of the First World War, in order to promote the interests of working people worldwide. It is a United Nations agency which brings together representatives of governments, employers and workers in order to draft and supervise international labour standards.[20] In the maritime field, after the ILO was founded, a series of international conventions were adopted over a period of several years, all of which were concerned with the working conditions of seamen. The current Convention supersedes that previous series of conventions. It seeks, in the words of the preamble, "to create a single, coherent instrument embodying as far as possible all up-to-date standards of

19. Further information about STCW can be obtained from the ICS/ISF booklet *The STCW Convention* (2nd ed), available from Marisec publications.
20. See ILO website *www.ilo.org* for more information.

existing international maritime labour conventions and recommendations, as well as the fundamental principles to be found in other international conventions".[21]

### (a) Entry into force

The Convention will enter into force upon ratification by at least 30 States, which must together represent at least 33% of the world's entire merchant shipping tonnage.[22] As at 11 January 2008, only Liberia and the Marshall Islands have registered their ratifications, respectively on 7 June 2006 and 25 September 2007. In 2005, these two flag administrations accounted for a total of approximately 15% of the world merchant fleet. The EU is actively encouraging its 27 Member States to ratify the Convention.

### (b) Fundamental rights and principles

*Fundamental rights*[23]

- freedom of association and the effective recognition of the right to collective bargaining;
- elimination of all forms of forced or compulsory labour;
- the effective abolition of child labour;
- elimination of discrimination in respect of employment and occupation.

*Employment and social rights*[24]

- every seafarer has the right to a safe and secure workplace that complies with safety standards;
- every seafarer has a right to fair terms of employment;
- every seafarer has a right to decent working and living conditions on board ship;
- every seafarer has a right to health protection, medical care, welfare measures and other forms of social protection;
- each member shall ensure, within the limits of its jurisdiction, that seafarers' employment and social rights as set out above are fully implemented.

"*Explanatory Note to the Regulations and Code of the Maritime Labour Convention*[25]

1. This explanatory note, which does not form part of the Maritime Labour Convention, is intended as a general guide to the convention.
2. The convention comprises three different but related parts: the Articles, the Regulations and the Code.
3. The Articles and Regulations set out the core rights and principles and the basic obligations of members ratifying the convention. The Articles and Regulations can only be changed by the conference in the framework of article 19 of the Constitution of the International Labour Organization (see Article XIV of the convention).

21. The full text of the Maritime Labour Convention is to be found at *www.ilo.org/ilolex/cgi-lex/convde.pl?C186*
22. Art. VIII.
23. Art. III.
24. Art. IV.
25. International Labour Conference, 94th (Maritime) Session, 2006, available at *www.ilo.org/public/english/standards/relm/ilc/ilc94/rep-i-1b.pdf*, p.12

4. The Code contains the details for the implementation of the Regulations. It comprises Part A (mandatory Standards) and Part B (non-mandatory Guidelines). The Code can be amended through the simplified procedure set out in Article XV of the Convention. Since the Code relates to detailed implementation, amendments to it must remain within the general scope of the Articles and Regulations.

5. The Regulations and the Code are organised into general areas under five Titles:

- Minimum requirements for seafarers to work on a ship.
- Conditions of employment.
- Accommodation, recreational facilities, food and catering.
- Health protection, medical care, welfare and social security protection.
- Compliance and enforcement.

6. Each Title contains groups of provisions relating to a particular right or principle (or enforcement measure in Title 5), with connected numbering. The first group in Title 1, for example, consists of Regulation 1.1, Standard A1.1 and Guideline B1.1, relating to minimum age.

7. The Convention has three underlying purposes:

- to lay down, in its articles and regulations, a firm set of rights and principles;
- to allow, through the Code, a considerable degree of flexibility in the way members implement those rights and principles; and
- to ensure through Title 5, that the rights and principles are properly complied with and enforced.

8. There are two main areas for flexibility in implementation: one is the possibility for a member, where necessary (see Article VI, paragraph 3), to give effect to the detailed requirements of Part A of the Code through substantial equivalence (as defined in Article VI, paragraph 4).

9. The second area of flexibility in implementation is provided by formulating the mandatory requirements of many provisions in Part A in a more general way, thus leaving a wider scope for discretion as to the precise action to be provided for at the national level. In such cases, guidance on implementation is given in the non-mandatory Part B of the Code. In this way, members which have ratified this Convention can ascertain the kind of action that might be expected of them under the corresponding general obligation in Part A, as well as action that would not necessarily be required. For example, Standard A4.1 requires all ships to provide prompt access to the necessary medicines for medical care on board ship (paragraph 1(b)) and to carry a medicine chest (paragraph 4(a)). The fulfilment in good faith of this latter obligation clearly means something more than simply having a medicine chest on board each ship. A more precise indication of what is involved is provided in the corresponding Guideline B4.1.1 (paragraph 4) so as to ensure that the contents of the chest are properly stored, used and maintained.

10. Members which have ratified this Convention are not bound by the guidance concerned and, as indicated in the provisions in Title 5 on port State control, inspections would deal only with the relevant requirements of this convention (articles, regulations and the standards in Part A). However, members are required under paragraph 2 of Article VI to give due consideration to implementing their responsibilities under Part A of the Code in the manner provided for in Part B. If, having duly considered the relevant guidelines, a member decides to provide for different arrangements which ensure the proper storage, use and maintenance of the contents of the medicine chest, to take the example given above, as required by the Standard in Part A, then that is acceptable. On the other hand, by following the guidance provided in Part B, the member concerned, as well as the ILO bodies responsible for reviewing implementation of international labour Conventions, can be sure without further consideration that the arrangements the member has provided for are adequate to implement the responsibilities under Part A to which the Guideline relates."

## 7. THE EUROPEAN MARITIME SAFETY AGENCY

It has been seen in this chapter that compliance with international regulatory requirements is evidenced by certificates such as the ISM Document of Compliance (DOC) and the ISM Safety Management certificate (SMC) as well as other certificates confirming compliance with SOLAS.[26] It has also been seen that the responsibility for issuing these certificates, and indeed to control correct implementation of the international conventions concerned, lies squarely with the flag State administrations on one hand and with port State control on the other.[27] The European flag States have a clear interest in coordinating their national processes and in exchanging relevant information about vessels in their fleets and/or calling at their ports and for many years now the EU has been increasingly active in facilitating such exchanges. However, the sinking of the tanker *Erika* in December 1999 with 30,000 tonnes of heavy fuel just off the coast of Brittany further accelerated this process and led in 2002 to the creation of a new European body: the European Maritime Safety Agency (EMSA).

EMSA, now based in Lisbon, was established in the aftermath of the *Erika* disaster as a "specialist branch" of the European Commission[28] for the purpose of ensuring a high, uniform and effective level of maritime safety and prevention of pollution by ships within the Community.[29] Generally speaking, the main function of the Agency is to provide the Member States of the European Union, and the Commission, with the technical and scientific assistance needed in order to help them apply Community legislation in the field of maritime safety and prevention of pollution by ships,[30] to monitor its implementation and to evaluate the effectiveness of the measures in place.[31]

To fulfil its role, Regulation 1406/2002 (as amended) gives EMSA several tasks which may be grouped in four main functions, summarised as follows:

(a) *Assisting the Commission*: EMSA's main function is that of a specialist technical aid to the Commission; as such it shall provide assistance in the preparatory work for updating and developing Community legislation in the fields of maritime safety and maritime security, the prevention of pollution and response to pollution caused by ships, in line with the development of international legislation in that field.[32] Once legislation has been adopted, EMSA shall assist the Commission in its effective implementation by monitoring the overall functioning of the Community port State control regime,[33] performing specific tasks on maritime safety, ship pollution

26. All discussed above.
27. See above.
28. Regulation (EC) 1406/2002 of European Parliament and Council of 27 June 2002, Establishing a European Maritime Safety Agency, OJ L 208, 05.08.2002, p. 1, as amended by Regulation (EC) 1644/2003, OJ L 245, 29.09.2003, p. 10; Regulation (EC) 724/2004, OJ L 129, 29.04.2004; and (EC) 1891/2006 OJ L 394, 30.12.2006; Art. 5.1.
29. Art. 1.1, as amended by Art. 1.1(a) of Regulation (EC) 724/2004.
30. Both accidental and deliberate according to Art. 1.3 of the Regulation, added by Art. 1.1(b) of Regulation (EC) 724/2004.
31. Regulation (EC) 1406/2002, Art. 1.2, as amended by Art. 1.1(a) of Regulation (EC) 724/2004.
32. Art. 2(a), as amended by Art. 1.2 of Regulation (EC) 724/2004.
33. EMSA is expected to provide the Commission with the technical assistance necessary to take part in the work of the technical bodies of the Paris Memorandum of Understanding on Port State Control; Art. 2(b)(ii) as amended by Art. 1.2 of Regulation (EC) 724/2004.

prevention and ship pollution response,[34] and performing the inspection tasks assigned to it pursuant to the Port Facility Security Regulation.[35] EMSA also provides technical and scientific support for participation at meetings in international fora such as the IMO and the IOPC fund.

(b) *Facilitating cooperation between Member States and the Commission*: The Agency's second – but equally important – cluster of functions is that of a facilitator for the cooperation between the Member States and the Commission on several but quite specific matters: namely the development and operation of the EU traffic vessel monitoring and information system[36] and the creation of a common methodology for the investigation of maritime accidents according to agreed international principles.[37]

(c) *Procuring and providing information to the Commission and the Member States*: Thirdly, EMSA is required to provide both the Commission and the Member States with objective, reliable and comparable information and data on maritime safety, maritime security and pollution by ships with the aim of enabling them to take the necessary steps to improve their actions in these fields and to evaluate the effectiveness of existing measures. The Agency will also assist the Commission and the Member States in their activities to improve the identification and pursuit of ships making unlawful discharges.[38]

(d) *Working with Member States*: Lastly, EMSA shall cooperate with the Member States to organise training activities in fields which are the responsibility of the port State and flag State, provide technical assistance related to the implementation of Community legislation and support their pollution response actions in case of accidental or deliberate pollution caused by ships.[39]

As far as its internal organisation is concerned, the Agency's main administrative bodies are its Administrative Board[40] and the Executive Director.[41]

*The Administrative Board* is currently formed by 31 voting members – one representative of each Member State and four representatives of the Commission – and four professionals from the relevant sectors also nominated by the Commission.[42] Professional members have no voting rights.[43] All members of the

34. The focus lies expressly on classification societies, safety of passenger ships, training, certification and watch keeping of ships' crews; Art. 2(b)(iii), as amended by Art. 1.2 of Regulation (EC) 724/2004.
35. Regulation (EC) 725/2004 of the European Parliament and of the Council of 31 March 2004 on Enhancing Ship and Port Facility Security, OJ L 129, 29.04.2004, Art. 9(4).
36. The system has been introduced by Directive 2002/59/EC, OJ L 208, 05.08.2002, p. 10: "with a view to enhancing the safety and efficiency of maritime traffic, improving the response of authorities to incidents, accidents or potentially dangerous situations at sea, including search and rescue operations, and contributing to a better prevention and detection of pollution by ships", Art. 1.
37. Regulation (EC) 1406/2002, fn. 13, above; Art. 2(e), as amended by Art. 1.2 of Regulation (EC) 724/2004. For an example of this kind of activity see the CleanSeaNet satellite service project, on which see *http://cleanseanet.emsa.europa.eu*.
38. Art. 2(f), as amended by Art. 1.2 of Regulation (EC) 724/2004.
39. Art. 2(c)(iii), as amended by Art. 1.2 of Regulation (EC) 724/2004. This may also be done through workshops and/or inspections.
40. Art. 11, as amended by Art. 1.4. of Regulation (EC) 724/2004.
41. Art. 15, as amended by Art. 1.5 of Regulation (EC) 724/2004 and Art. 7(b) of Regulation (EC) 1891/2006, and 16, as amended by Art. 1.6 of Regulation (EC) 724/2004.
42. Art. 11.1, as amended by Art. 1.4 of Regulation (EC) 724/2004.
43. *Ibid.*

Administrative Board will be in office for five years; the term of office may be renewed once.[44] The Board is chaired by a Chairperson elected from among its members for a three-year term.[45] The main functions of the Board are the election of the Executive Director, to report the Agency's activities to the European Parliament, the Council, the Commission, the Court of Auditors and the Member States and to adopt EMSA's work programme and its budget.[46]

*The Executive Director* is – in all relevant respects – the "manager" of the Agency and full independence is expressly guaranteed by Article 15 of the Regulation.[47] The Director is appointed by the Administrative Board:

> "on grounds of merit and documented administrative and managerial skills, as well as competence and experience relevant for maritime safety, maritime security, prevention of pollution and response to pollution caused by ships."[48]

The Director is elected by a four-fifths majority of all voting members, and stays in office for five years, renewable for another five-year term,[49] but can be dismissed by the Administrative Board in accordance with the same procedure.[50] Among the most relevant duties of the Director are the preparation of the Agency's work programme,[51] the estimates of revenue and expenses[52] and – in general – the overall functioning of the Agency.[53]

In conclusion, EMSA evolved from recent major shipping disasters in European waters – such as the sinking of the ferry *Estonia* and the tankers *Erika* and *Prestige* – and is very active and effective in supporting the preparation and implementation of the ever-increasing European intervention in the field of maritime safety and pollution prevention.

## 8. CLASSIFICATION SOCIETIES AND THEIR LIABILITY UNDER DIRECTIVE 94/57/EC

The duties of the flag State to verify, certify and control its fleet for compliance with international safety standards are not always carried out directly by the Maritime Administration – which may or may not have the necessary technical competence – but may be delegated to specialist private bodies known as classification societies.

Classification societies are independent private bodies engaged in the study, development and surveillance of the technical side of ship structural safety and as such, they have achieved a pivotal role within the shipping world. Generally

44. Art. 11.3.
45. Art. 12.
46. The detailed powers of the Board may be found in Article 10 of the Regulation, as amended by Arts. 1.2 of Regulation (EC) 1644/2003; 1.3 of Regulation (EC) 724/2004 and 7(a) of Regulation (EC) 1891/2006.
47. "Without prejudice – in the words of the norm – to the respective competencies of the Commission and the Administrative Board", Art. 15.1.
48. Art. 16.1, as amended by Art. 1.6 of Regulation (EC) 724/2004.
49. Art. 16.2.
50. Art. 16.1, as amended by Art. 1.6 of Regulation (EC) 724/2004.
51. Art. 15.2(a), as amended by Art. 1.5 of Regulation (EC) 724/2004 .
52. Art. 15.2(f).
53. Art. 15.2(c).

speaking, the work of classification societies is based on service contracts with shipowners or shipbuilders alike. However, the importance of class certificates extends well beyond the interests of owners and builders since class documents are relied upon not only by flag States and port State control but also by charterers and traders keen to see their products shipped on board staunch vessels[54] and insurers who need to know the condition of the ships they insure in order to calculate the relevant risks and set their premiums.[55] Buyers of vessels may also need classification certificates to ensure the future employability of the vessel and it does not stop there: other users of the sea, seafarers and coastal interests such as beach resorts and fishing reserves, rely on class certificates almost as a form of guarantee for the safety of the world's fleet.

To better understand the work performed by classification societies and the different liabilities which may arise in respect thereof it is necessary to divide it into two categories: (i) *statutory* work, and (ii) *non-statutory* work.

(i) *Statutory surveys* are performed by classification societies as representatives of the administration under formal authorisation granted by flag States. In performing these surveys classification societies discharge obligations imposed on the flag State by international or national law. These functions comprise the assessment of the flag fleet in order to determine the compliance of registered vessels with the applicable requirements of the international conventions and codes,[56] EU Directives and national legislation and the issue of statutory certificates.

(ii) *Non-statutory surveys* include any other contractual work carried out by classification societies which does not involve the performance of statutory surveys or the issue of statutory certificates.

In order to perform statutory work, classification societies need to go through a special procedure now standardised within the European Union through Directive 94/57/EC.[57] This Directive – in its latest revision[58] – also attempts to unify the liability regime between the authorising States and the classification societies in respect of damages arising from faults of the classification societies in performing statutory surveys.[59] In fact, within the scope of their various tasks and duties, classification societies may make mistakes that can cause damage either to the shipowner or to third parties. The extent of their liability in such cases would vary depending on the applicable legal regime. While performing statutory tasks – where the parties' duties and liabilities are regulated by agreement – the contract itself would probably include clauses to the effect of excluding

54. See Chapter 4.
55. This was, in origin, the *raison d'être* for the development of classification societies.
56. Discussed elsewhere in this chapter.
57. Council Directive 94/57/EC of 22 November 1994, on Common Rules and Standards for Ship Inspection and Survey Organisations and for the Relevant Activities of Maritime Administrations (hereafter "Directive 94/57/EC"), OJ L 319, 12.12.1994, p. 20.
58. Directive 2001/105/EC of the European Parliament and of the Council of 19 December 2001, Amending Council Directive 94/57/EC on Common Rules and Standards for Ship Inspection and Survey Organisations and for the Relevant Activities of Maritime Administrations, OJ L 19, 22.01.2002, p. 9.
59. The attempt, however, can only be partly successful as demonstrated in a recent study by the Institute of Maritime Law of the University of Southampton; see Commission of the European Communities, "Commission working document on the control of recognised organisations by the Commission and on the impact of the civil liability regime in accordance with Directive 94/57/EC", COM (2006) 588 final, 11.10.2006.

or limiting the liability of the surveyor. However, where the classification society is carrying out statutory work, its negligence may lead to claims against the State or the relevant Maritime Authority. In such a case the liability of the State or authority to third parties will depend on national law whereas the recourse action against the class society will depend entirely on the actual wording of the agreement in place between the society and the relevant administration.

When acting on behalf of national administrations the vast majority of recognised organisations in Europe have a contractual arrangement in place, generally called the "Model Agreement". Such agreements do contain a schedule with a full list of all functions which are *delegated* to the organisations by the administration concerned. Generally speaking, the agreements impose a duty of care on the classification societies and a liability towards the Administration for breach of such duty, on the basis either of Directive 94/57/EC as amended or of IMO MSC Circular 710 and MEPC Circular 307. Of course, for a national authority to claim against a classification society under the relevant agreement there must be a breach of the agreement and there must be damage suffered. Damages may be suffered by the authorising State if the classification society has been negligent and the State was sued and found liable to pay damages for such breach of statutory duty. This is where Directive 94/57/EC as amended by Directive 2001/105/EC[60] had a major impact on the European liability regime of classification societies.

In its original text, the Directive imposed on the Member States the obligation to put in place a quality monitoring system[61] for selecting class societies to whom they were allowed to delegate[62] – in full or in part – performance of statutory surveys. Only organisations which met the criteria to obtain recognition as set out in the Annex of the Directive could be authorised to carry out statutory work.[63] The third amendment to this instrument[64] imposed on all Member States to insert in their agreements with such recognised organisations the following clause concerning liability:

"(i) if liability arising out of any incident is finally and definitely imposed on the administration by a court of law or as part of the settlement of a dispute through arbitration procedures, together with a requirement to compensate the injured parties for loss or damage to property or personal injury or death, which is proved in that court of law to have been caused by a wilful act or omission or gross negligence of the recognised organisation, its bodies, employees, agents or others who act on behalf of the recognised organisation, the administration shall be entitled to financial compensation from the recognised organisation to the extent that the said loss, damage, injury or death is, as decided by that court, caused by the recognised organisation;

(ii) if liability arising out of any incident is finally and definitely imposed on the administration by a court of law or as part of the settlement of a dispute through arbitration procedures, together with a requirement to compensate the injured parties for personal injury or death, which is proved in that court of law to have been caused by any negligent or reckless act or omission of the recognised organisation, its employees, agents or others who act on behalf of the recognised organisation, the administration shall be entitled to financial compensation from the recognised organisation to the extent that the said personal injury or death is, as decided by that court, caused by the recognised organisation; the Member States may

60. Directive 94/57/EC, OJ L 319, 12.12.1994, p. 20.
61. Directive 94/57/EC, Art. 11(1) of the original text.
62. Art. 3(2).
63. Art. 4(1) of the original text.
64. Directive 2001/105/EC, OJ L 19, 22.01.2002, p. 9.

limit the maximum amount payable by the recognised organisation, which must, however, be at least equal to EUR 4 million;

(iii) if liability arising out of any incident is finally and definitely imposed on the administration by a court of law or as part of the settlement of a dispute through arbitration procedures, together with a requirement to compensate the injured parties for loss or damage to property, which is proved in that court of law to have been caused by any negligent or reckless act or omission of the recognised organisation, its employees, agents or others who act on behalf of the recognised organisation, the administration shall be entitled to financial compensation from the recognised organisation, to the extent that the said loss or damage is, as decided by that court, caused by the recognised organisation; the Member States may limit the maximum amount payable by the recognised organisation, which must, however, be at least equal to EUR 2 million."[65]

The addition of this clause in the agreements between classification societies and the States may have very serious financial implications indeed exposing classification societies to unlimited financial exposure for negligent acts or omissions. However, it is submitted, the clause cannot be triggered unless two conditions are satisfied: (a) the liability of the Maritime Administration is positively established through (b) the negligence of the class surveyor. If this is true, this situation can only arise in respect of *statutory surveys* where the surveyor is performing inspections by express authorisation of the maritime administration. On the other hand, where a non-statutory survey is performed, the liability of the Administration cannot arise and the classification society will be liable in contract and tort according to the ordinary rules of the law applicable to the relevant claim.

After the recent decision of the Tribunal de Grande Instance de Paris in the *Erika* case[66] it is now clear that – at least under French law – classification societies may be liable to pay huge compensations for pollution damages caused or contributed to by their own negligence. On the other hand they may be able to limit or exclude their liability under specific conventions[67] or national law, as it is clearly the case in England where claims in tort against classification societies have been effectively restricted, mainly on policy considerations.[68] But both the recent *Erika* and *Prestige* decisions appear to be taken on the – with respect, dubious – basis that the class surveyors were negligent in performing *non-statutory* rather than *statutory* surveys. As such, the liability regimes the societies may fall in are far away from being uniform and the distance between the various regimes – even within the European region – are such to encourage shopping for a convenient forum. In particular, following a shipping accident, the defendant classification society may be sued either in the jurisdiction where the shipping accident took place or where the negligent act took place,[69] or again where the organisation has its domicile.[70] The notion of "domicile", in turn, is defined by national law.[71] The domicile of a company is established in the country where it

65. Art. 6.2(b).
66. Tribunal de Grande Instance de Paris, 11ème Chambre – 4ème section, 16.01.2008, unreported.
67. *Reino de España v American Bureau of Shipping et al., sub nom. The Prestige*, US District Court, Southern District of New York, 2 January 2008, Case No. 03 Civ. 3573 (LTS) (RLE), unreported.
68. *Marc Rich & Co AG v Bishop Rock Marine Co Ltd (The Nicholas H)* [1996] AC 211; [1995] Lloyd's Rep 299.
69. Art. 5(3) of Council Regulation (EC ) 44/2001 of 22 December 2000 on Jurisdiction and the Recognition and Enforcement of Judgments in Civil and Commercial Matters, OJ L 12, 16.1.2001, p. 1.
70. Art. 2.
71. Art. 59.

has a statutory seat or central administration or a principal place of business.[72] Thus, it is possible, under some national laws that jurisdiction can be seized on the basis of the registered offices of classification societies in those countries, if those offices may, under that national law, be considered as falling under the scope of Art. 60(1) of Regulation 44/2001/EC.[73] And this without taking into account special conflict provisions contained in specialist conventions.[74]

On the other hand, in the case of statutory surveys – where uniform legislation is put in place by Directive 94/57/EC – uniform results are equally difficult to achieve since the liability provision in Art. 6(2)(b) may only be triggered if the Maritime Administration's liability is established which, in turn, will depend on the court seized and its internal constitutional, administrative and procedural laws.[75]

72. Art. 60(1).
73. *Ibid.*
74. *The Prestige*, see fn. 53.
75. See F Lorenzon, M Tsimplis, "Classification societies and Directive 94/57/EC: Time for rethinking the unlimited liability issue?" (2006) STL 6 (7), 1.

CHAPTER 8

# Marine Pollution from Shipping Activities[1]

*DR MICHAEL TSIMPLIS*

## 1. INTRODUCTION

Despite their extensive use as a safe and quick route for the transportation of goods and their exploitation in respect of their resources, the oceans remain to a large extent unexplored. Marine species while not yet fully documented have become endangered or extinct and several fish populations have collapsed or are on the brink of collapsing. It was the image of big tankers[2] leaking very large quantities of oil, polluting extensive areas and destroying wildlife that raised public awareness about the threats to the environment posed by large scale transportation of oil by sea. The law started from that point onwards to develop into a very distinct and separate field involving both regulatory obligations as well as penal and civil liability.

The exceptional nature of oceanic governance with large areas beyond the jurisdiction of the coastal and other States meant that the only way of providing efficient environment protection, in terms of both prevention and liability, was through the development of international conventions. The development of the 1982 United Nations Convention on the Law of the Sea (UNCLOS) has been the most important legal document in three[3] respects. First, it extended the jurisdiction of the coastal State's rights and obligations to 200 nautical miles from the coast by accepting the Exclusive Economic Zone,[4] second, it imposed general duties on coastal States to protect the marine environment,[5] third it weakened the right of innocent passage by providing that this is to be exercised subject to the protection of the marine environment.[6] However, legislation regarding the construction of ships has to be based on international agreement rather than national standards.[7]

Overall, international policy regarding the protection of the marine environment has been unfocused and in some respects inconsistent. On the one hand framework

1. For a more detailed treatment of the topic see Tsimplis, M N, "Marine Pollution", *Journal of International Maritime Law*, 2008, 2, 1.
2. A detailed review of the history, the well known incidents or the political and financial conflicts involved is beyond the scope of this work. The interested reader is advised to read Colin de la Rue and Charles B Anderson's *Shipping and the Environment* (LLP, 1998), where a good summary of the history is provided.
3. We only refer to the three more important effects here. It should be stressed that UNCLOS has several other provisions affecting the marine environment, but these are dealt with in Chapter 11.
4. Part V of UNCLOS.
5. Part XII of UNCLOS.
6. Art. 21 of UNCLOS.
7. Art. 21(2) of UNCLOS. See Chapter 9.

conventions with subject matters concerning particular qualities of the environment have been developed, for example the Convention on Biological Diversity.[8] On the other hand solutions in particular economic sectors have been sought. More importantly, for the scope of this book, regulation of marine pollution from ships has been based mainly on reactions to particular pollution incidents. Thus, part-solutions to pressing problems have been developed, but the legal framework is, as will become evident, a labyrinth starting with good intentions and ending in many incomplete parts or dead ends.

Apart from the "disaster reaction" syndrome, there are other very serious reasons that make decision-making and enforcement of shipping conventions very difficult. Stating the obvious, ships travel, can change owners and flags and their companies will go wherever the commercial conditions are optimum and maximize their profits and returns while at the same time reducing their liabilities. Thus, in general, ship companies will go to the flag State which offers less regulation, making the running of the ship cheaper and financially more efficient.[9]

However, it is the coastal State rather than the flag State which has an interest to protect its coastal environment and at the same time not restrict trade. Thus the international framework increasingly relies on Port State Control with detentions and fines imposed on vessels which are non-compliant with the environmental norms developed. An important increase of the rights of the coastal State that comes under threat of pollution from a shipping incident has been provided under the Intervention Convention 1969 and its protocols.[10] Under Article 1 of the Intervention Convention 1969 the coastal State is entitled to take measures on the high seas which it thinks necessary in order to avoid grave and imminent pollution threats arising from shipping incidents. In the UK the government's intervention powers can be found in the Merchant Shipping Act 1995.[11]

## 2. SHIP STANDARDS IN CONSTRUCTION, OPERATION AND MANNING

A major component of the legal framework aims at preventing marine pollution. This is achieved in essence by developing five equally important tools. First, improving the construction and maintenance standards for ships so that the carriage of pollutants is more tolerant to the dangers of the sea and to human fault. Second, improving training standards for crew members so that human fault is constrained as much as possible. Third, establishing management systems for the ships, ports and the shipping companies which ensure early identification

8. Signed at the Rio Earth Summit in 1992 by 150 government leaders, and dedicated to promoting sustainable development. The Convention establishes the role of biological diversity for people, food security, medicines, fresh air and water, shelter, and a clean and healthy environment. The CBD covers all biological diversity including the marine environment.
9. For the financial advantages see: D Scorpecci, 2004, *Economic Advantages of Non-Compliance With Pollution Regulations*, OECD, available at *www.amsa.gov.au/Natship_2004/proceedings/danny scorpecci.pdf*
10. International Convention Relating to Intervention on the High Seas in Cases of Oil Pollution Casualties, 1969, came into force 6 May 1975. The original convention covered only some types of oil but its 1973 Protocol extended to other substances. The list of substances has further been revised in 1991, 1996 and 2002 with successive protocols modifying the list of substances to which the convention applies.
11. Schedule 3A was introduced under Schedule 1 to the Marine Safety Act 2003.

and minimisation of risks taken, or, in the alternative, confirmation of knowledge of the risk by those responsible. Fourth, establishing liability regimes which ensure that pollution victims will be compensated and that shipowners and their insurers as well as cargo owners will strive to avoid pollution because of the imposed liability. Fifth, imposing criminal liability and fines for pollution incidents.

Standards for the ship's safety are contained in the International Convention for the Safety of Life at Sea (SOLAS) 1974.[12] SOLAS specifies minimum standards for the construction, equipment and operation of ships, compatible with their safety. Flag and Port State control are utilised as methods of implementation and enforcement. The International Safety Management Code contained in Chapter IX and the International Ship and Port Facilities Security Code (ISPS Code) contained under Chapter XI-2 of SOLAS indicate the breadth of issues covered. SOLAS is the cornerstone of a technical and managerial framework ensuring the safety of ships which in turn also impacts on marine pollution.[13]

Standards for the operations of ships and the reduction of accidental and operational pollution are dealt with under the International Convention for the Prevention of Pollution from Ships, 1973, as modified by the Protocol of 1978 relating thereto (MARPOL 73/78).[14] MARPOL 73/78 has been extended and modified by several successive protocols. It contains regulations for prevention of oil pollution (Annex I), prevention of pollution by hazardous and noxious substances in bulk (Annex II) and harmful substances in packaged form (Annex III), sewage and garbage pollution from ships (Annex IV and V) as well as air pollution from ships (Annex VI).[15] Only the first two Annexes are compulsory for Member States.[16]

Criminal liability and disciplinary procedures are available under these two conventions. Additional criminal sanctions have been imposed by the EU Ship Source Pollution Directive[17] which uses the same definition of illegal, operational or accidental discharges as MARPOL. However, the Directive provides for criminal sanctions when caused intentionally, recklessly or by "serious negligence"[18] by contrast with the similar test under MARPOL which refers to "the owner or the master" acting "either with intent to cause damage or recklessly and with knowledge that damage would probably result".[19] The lower threshold applies to discharges in the territorial sea. In addition, criminal liability under the Directive is not restricted to the owner and the Master of the ship but extends to "any other person involved" which would include many other entities, for example charterers, classification societies and operators presently immune under MARPOL. The Directive applies not just to territorial waters but also exclusive economic zones

12. Which entered into force on 25 May 1980.
13. See Chapter 7.
14. MARPOL 1978, which also includes the 1973 MARPOL, entered into force on 2 October 1983 (along with Annexes I and II).
15. The air pollution regulations relate to sulphur oxide and nitrogen oxide emissions from ship exhausts and prohibit deliberate emissions of ozone depleting substances. Special emission areas are designated. Greenhouse gases from shipping are not regulated under any international or national instrument and are excluded under 1997 Kyoto Protocol, Art. 2.2.
16. The UK is a signatory to all Annexes. General authority to issue orders in this respect is granted under s. 128 of the 1995 MSA. Note also that the International Convention for the Control and Management of Ships Ballast Water & Sediments was adopted by consensus at a Diplomatic Conference at IMO in London on 13 February 2004.
17. Directive 2005/35/EC. See Chapter 9, p. 307.
18. Art. 4, EU Ship Source Pollution Directive 2005/35/EC.
19. Annex I, Regulation 11(b) of MARPOL 73/78.

and the high seas.[20] The Directive was supplemented by European Council Framework Decision 2005/667/JHA which declared that each Member State must take measures necessary to ensure that criminal liability for infringement of Articles 4 and 5 of Directive 2005/35/EC is established.

The Directive 2005/35/EC and the Framework Decision 2005/667/JHA have come under attack by the shipping industry in two respects. The attack on the Framework Decision 2005/667/JHA was based on its constitutional basis and on challenging the availability of criminal sanctions to the EC in respect of environmental protection. The attack was successful so the Framework Decision will have to be reissued under the correct constitutional basis. However, the ECJ held[21] that criminal sanctions in support of environmental measures fall within the ambit of the EC jurisdiction.[22]

An attempt to nullify Directive 2005/35/EC in substance as inconsistent with the 1982 UNCLOS provisions and MARPOL 73/78 is presently pending in front of the ECJ.[23]

## 3. LIABILITY FOR OIL POLLUTION FROM SHIPS

### (a) Civil liability from oil pollution

Civil liability for oil pollution is covered by various international conventions. Oil spills arising from oil carried as cargo or bunkers on board tankers is covered by a two- and for some countries three-tier system of compensation. First the 1969 Civil Liability Convention ("1969 CLC")[24] establishes strict but limited liability for the shipowner, coupled with compulsory insurance and direct action against the insurer. The 1969 CLC convention has been updated by a 1976 Protocol and, in some States including the UK, by the 1992 Protocol which forms the 1992 Civil Liability Convention ("1992 CLC").[25] The 1969/1992 CLC are each supplemented by the International Convention on the Establishment of an International Fund for Compensation for Oil Pollution Damage (IOPCF) 1971/1992 respectively. However, the 1971 Fund Convention ceased to be in force on 24 May 2002. Thus only the 1992 IOPC Fund is presently active. The role of the IOPC Fund is dual. First it provides additional compensation to victims of oil pollution in cases where compensation cannot be received under the CLC because the shipowner's liability is exempted or where the shipowner and his insurer are financially unable to

20. Directive 2005/35/EC, Art. 3.
21. Judgment (Grand Chamber), 23 October 2007, Case C 440/05.
22. By giving as reference: Case C-176/03 *Commission v Council*, para. 48).
23. *The International Association of Independent Tanker Owners and Others*, Case C 308/06 (ECJ). However, the opinion of Advocate General Kokott is that the validity of Directive 2005/35/EC on ship source pollution and the penalties introduced are not in violation of UNCLOS. Albeit not conclusive it is a strong indication of the fate of the case. See Chapter 9, p. 307.
24. International Convention on Civil Liability for Oil Pollution Damage, Brussels, 29 November 1969 which came into force on 19 June 1975. The Protocol to the International Convention on Civil Liability for Oil Pollution Damage, London, 19 November 1976, which came into force on 8 April 1971, has been used as an interim solution to increase the low limits of liability agreed within the 1969 CLC.
25. International Liability Convention on Civil Liability for Oil Pollution Damage, London, 2 December 1992, which is created by the modification of the 1969 CLC in a 1992 Protocol to the 1969 CLC: see Art. 11(2) of the 1992 Protocol and also Art. 12(5). The 1992 Protocol came into force on 30 May 1996.

provide for compensation. In addition it provides compensation to marine pollution victims to limits of liability higher than those available against the shipowner. The CLC/ IOPCF system has been very successful as shown by the wide ratification of the 1992 CLC and the 1992 IOPCF, by 98 States.[26] In addition 40 States are party to the 1992 CLC but not to the IOPCF Convention.

A Protocol to IOPCF 1992 was agreed on 27 May 2003 for the creation of a voluntary third tier of liability for oil pollution. This third tier came into force in 2005. It was produced following recognition that, in spite of successive increases in the limits of liability for oil pollution, the "... maximum compensation afforded by IOPCF 1992 might be insufficient to meet compensation needs in certain circumstances in some Contracting States to that Convention".[27] The Supplementary Fund currently has 15 contracting States. The Supplementary Fund is the third tier of liability which is available only in those States which are party to it. The rationale of the Supplementary Fund is that it provides higher levels of compensation in States which choose to become parties, while enabling States which do not wish to burden their oil importers with the higher levels of contribution involved to remain outside.

Oil spill damage from bunkers and lubrication oils from ships not employed for the carriage of oil are covered by the 2001 Bunker Oil Pollution Convention (2001 BOPC).[28] The 2001 BOPC establishes strict but limited liability for the shipowner and other persons associated with the running of the ship coupled with compulsory insurance and direct action against insurers. However, unlike the CLC/FUND/ Supplementary Fund system, the 2001 BOPC does not provide for a separate "stand-alone" limitation fund but preserves existing rights to limit liability whether under national or international law.[29]

In the UK, the Merchant Shipping Act 1995 rewrites the 1992 CLC (in Chapter III[30]) and the Fund Convention (in Chapter IV) into English law.[31] The 2003 Supplementary Fund has been enacted in the UK through the Merchant Shipping (Oil Pollution Compensation Limits) Order 2003.[32] The 2001 BOPC will come into force on 21 November 2008.

### (b) The 1992 Civil Liability Convention

The 1969 CLC/1971 Fund Conventions apply exclusively to oil pollution damage caused in the territory, including the territorial sea, of a contracting State,[33] and to preventive measures taken to prevent or minimise such damage.[34] There is no restriction regarding the jurisdictional zone in which the preventive measures

26. See the status of International Maritime Organization Conventions at *www.imo.org/*.
27. IMO LEG/CONF.14/20 the Preamble to the Supplementary Fund. The development of the 2003 Supplementary Fund to the IOPCF was initiated as a response to a European Union White Paper on Environmental Liability (Brussels, 9 February 2000, COM (2000) 66).
28. Adopted on 23 March 2001 in London. Closed to signature on 30 September 2002.
29. 2001 BOPC, Art. 6.
30. Sections 152–172, as amended by the Merchant Shipping (Oil Pollution) (Bunkers Convention) Regulations 2006, SI 2006 No 1244. These Regulations will come into force on 21 November 2008.
31. Sections 173–181.
32. By replacing the limits of liability for the Fund under s. 157 of the 1995 MSA.
33. However, there is no requirement that the damage should be only in one contracting State. See also *Landcatch Ltd v International Oil Pollution Compensation Fund* [1999] 2 Lloyd's Rep 316 at p. 328.
34. Art. II.

have to be taken in order to be covered by the 1969 CLC. Following the establishment of the Exclusive Economic Zone as a jurisdictional area under the 1982 UNCLOS, the application of the 1992 CLC/Fund has been extended to cover the new jurisdictional zones. Thus it now also applies to oil pollution damage caused in the exclusive economic zone of a contracting State, established in accordance with international law, or, if the State has not established such a zone, an area beyond and adjacent to the territorial sea of that State extending no more than 200 nautical miles from the baselines from which the breadth of its territorial sea is measured.[35] The 1992 CLC/Fund Conventions expressly provide cover for preventive measures "wherever taken".[36]

The 1992 CLC/Fund defines oil as any persistent hydrocarbon mineral oil such as crude oil, fuel oil, heavy diesel oil and lubricating oil, whether carried on board a ship as cargo or in the bunkers of a ship.[37] However, neither the 1969 CLC nor the 1992 CLC wording defines precisely which types of oil are persistent and thus included within the scope of these Conventions.[38]

The establishment of liability for pollution damage only for persistent oils arises from their evident impact on wildlife, beaches and ecosystems. When the 1969 CLC was developed it was, and still is, assumed that non-persistent oils will dissipate rapidly through evaporation into the atmosphere thus not causing significant damage or cleanup costs.[39] However, it appears wrong to assume that there are no pollution impacts from incidents involving non-persistent oils.[40]

The difficulty of defining the scope of the 1969/1992 CLC is resolved partly by the express reference to some types of oil within the oil definition[41] and partly by the development of a definition of non-persistent oils by the International Oil Pollution Compensation (IOPC) Fund.[42] All oils that do not fall within the non-persistent oil definition are persistent oils and thus subject to the CLC/Fund system. However, the working definition cannot be considered binding on any national court because it does not legally carry the weight of a definition within the meaning of the Convention.

Liquefied natural gas (LNG) and liquefied petroleum gas (LPG) as well as other gas products, gasolines, kerosenes and light distillates are non-persistent oils and are therefore not covered by the CLC/Fund framework.

35. 1969 CLC, Art. II, ss. 152–170, refer to damage and measures in the territory of the UK (s. 153(1)) and to damage and measures in the territory of another CLC State. In turn the UK territory consists of the territorial sea and the British fishery limits set out under the Fishery Limits Act 1976 and the territorial waters and the EEZs (or 200 mile zones) of other CLC States (s. 170(4)).
36. 1992 CLC, Art. II(b).
37. Art. I(5).
38. Section 170(1) of the 1995 MSA specifies "oil" as persistent hydrocarbon mineral oil. The Merchant Shipping (Oil Pollution) (Bunkers Convention) Regulations 2006, which will come into force on 21 November 2008, amend the term to read as "oil" except in the term "bunker oil" means persistent hydrocarbon mineral oil. No practical change is made by this modification.
39. In this context the distinction is not necessary as any claim for damage arising from non-persistent oil would have been difficult to prove.
40. See, for example, Caryn Anderson, "The International Tanker Owners Pollution Federation Limited (ITOPF) Persistent vs Non-Persistent Oils: What you need to know", in *Beacon* (Skuld Newsletter), July 2001, available at *www.itopf.com/_assets/documents/persistent.pdf* where damages to paint coatings in marinas and harbours and to marine organisms are suggested as potential damages arising from non-persistent oils. Atmospheric pollution can also be an issue although it has not at the moment been considered as a consequence that should create civil liability.
41. 1969 CLC, Art. I(5).
42. Caryn Anderson, see fn. 40.

## (c) Imposition of liability

### *(i) What types of vessel are covered?*

The 1992 CLC covers ships defined as "any sea-going vessel and any seaborne craft of any type whatsoever". There is no definition of "seagoing", "vessel", "seaborne" or "craft" in either of the Conventions.[43] The 1992 CLC does not apply to warships and other government ships used for non-commercial activities.[44]

The 1992 CLC applies to oil tankers as well as oil spillage from Oil/Bulk/Ore ships (OBOs) which arguably fulfil the requirement to be constructed for the carriage of oil.[45]

Oil pollution damage arising from barges without steering and propulsion ability, or floating storage units (FSU) as well as floating production, storage and offloading units (FPSO) raises the question of applicability of the 1992 CLC. While for barges with no propulsion or steering it is, under English law, well established that these are to be treated as ships, such an answer is not obvious for the other types of craft and is to be decided on a case-by-case basis.

All structures that fall under the definition of ship under Article I(1) would be subject to the 1969 or 1992 CLC irrespective of their size.

### *(ii) Who is liable?*

The 1992 CLC imposes strict liability on the owner of the ship causing pollution damage.[46] Strict liability in this context means that there is no need for the claimant to prove fault and that only limited exceptions are available to the shipowner.

The owner is defined as the registered owner[47] or, in the absence of registration, the person(s)[48] owning the ship at the time of the incident.[49]

If the oil has escaped or been discharged from two or more ships and pollution damage has resulted, their owners are jointly and severally liable for all damage which is not reasonably separable.[50] Thus, in such a case there is no need for the claimant to prove which ship caused the damage.

### *(iii) When liability may arise*

The 1992 CLC imposes strict liability[51] for pollution damage caused by oil spillage as a result of an incident.[52] "Incident" is defined as any occurrence, or

43. For the UK enactment, see s. 170 of the 1995 MSA.
44. 1969 and 1992 CLC, Art. XI.
45. 1992 CLC, Art. I.I; see also s. 153(3) and (4) of the 1995 MSA.
46. Art. III(1). Section 153 of the 1995 MSA makes reference to the "owner" defined as the "registered owner" under s. 170(1).
47. This will be made express when the Merchant Shipping (Oil Pollution) Bunkers Convention Regulations 2006, SI 2006 No 1244 comes into force. The definition of "registered owner" defined under s. 170(1) corresponds to the present definition of "owner" under the same section.
48. 1969/1992 CLC, Art. I(2). Individuals, partnerships, public and private bodies, corporate or not, including States, are covered by the term "person".
49. See s. 170(2) of the 1995 MSA.
50. Art. IV and s. 153(5) of the 1995 MSA for the UK enactment.
51. In *Landcatch Ltd v International Oil Pollution Compensation Fund*, see fn. 33; at p. 320 the liability was described as "in compensation as distinct from liability in damages at common law".
52. Arts. I(8), III(1), (4). The shipowners can of course pursue third parties for some or all of their resulting losses: Art. III(5).

series of occurrences with the same origin, which cause(s) pollution damage. Under the 1992 CLC, occurrences which create a grave and imminent threat of causing pollution damage are also covered by the term "incident".[53] Thus, preventive measures taken before an incident happens are covered by the 1992 CLC.

"Pollution damage" is defined as loss or damage outside the ship carrying oil caused by contamination resulting from the escape or discharge of oil from the ship, wherever this escape or discharge may occur. It includes the costs of preventive measures and further loss or damage caused by preventive measures.[54] These measures are defined as reasonable measures taken by any person after the incident occurred to prevent or minimise pollution damage.[55]

Under the 1992 CLC, the definition of "pollution damage" also includes the stipulation that compensation for impairment of the environment, other than for loss of profit from such impairment, shall be limited to costs of reasonable measures of reinstatement actually undertaken or to be undertaken.[56]

The wording of the pollution damage definition and in particular the "loss of profit" arising from the impairment of the environment creates rights for recovery of economic losses which are otherwise not recoverable under English law.

The IOPCF practice[57] is that loss of earnings caused by oil pollution suffered by persons whose property has not been polluted (pure economic loss) may be covered. In particular the manual suggests as permissible claims: loss of earnings by fishermen whose nets were not contaminated but who may be prevented from fishing because of the pollution of the area they normally fish; loss of income by hotel owners located close to a contaminated public beach; and even costs of marketing campaigns to prevent or reduce economic losses by counteracting the negative publicity arising from a major pollution incident. The discrepancy between the common law position and the IOPCF practice has led to litigation in order to clarify the extent by which the common law rule of non-recovery has been modified by the introduction of the CLC/Fund legal framework into English law.[58] The English Court of Appeal, in rejecting a claim for secondary/relational economic loss[59] arising from the pollution caused by the grounding of the *Sea Empress*,[60] without deciding the precise scope of the recovery available under the CLC/FUND, accepted that "... damage consisting of economic loss may well be recoverable under the statute by persons such as fishermen accustomed to fish in waters which become contaminated".[61] Thus, the requirement for direct links of the

53. Art. I(8).
54. 1969/1992 CLC, Art. I(6), (7). See s. 153 of the 1995 MSA for the damages for which liability is imposed and s. 170(1) for the statement that "damage" includes "loss".
55. Art. I(7).
56. Art. I(6) and s. 153(3) of the 1995 MSA for the English enactment.
57. IOPCF Manual 2006 Edition at *www.iopcfund.org/npdf/AR06_E.pdf*
58. *Landcatch Ltd v International Oil Pollution Compensation Fund*, see fn. 33; *Smith v Braer Corp*, 1999 GWD 21-1023; *P&O Scottish Ferries Ltd v Braer Corp* [1999] 2 Lloyd's Rep 535; *Skerries Salmon Ltd v Braer Corp*, 1999 SLT 1196; *Alegrete Shipping Co Inc v International Oil Pollution Compensation Fund 1971 (The Sea Empress)* [2003] 1 Lloyd's Rep 327.
59. *The Sea Empress, ibid.* The claim was under the 1995 Merchant Shipping Act. It concerned loss of earnings by a company involved in fish processing and sought to be distinguished from the *Landcatch Ltd* case on the basis that the company relied on provision of fish from the area in which a fishing ban was imposed.
60. The oil tanker *Sea Empress* grounded in the entrance to Milford Haven on 15 February 1996. 72,500 tonnes of oil was spilled and extensive pollution to more than 200 km of the coastline was caused.
61. *The Sea Empress*, see fn. 58, at p. 336, col. 1.

economic loss on one hand and the claimant's activity on the other hand with the polluted area appears to be the primary restriction in the type of claims recoverable.[62]

### *(iv) Exclusion of liability*

No liability for pollution damage will attach to the owner under the 1992 CLC if he proves that the damage resulted from an act or war, hostilities, civil war, insurrection or a natural phenomenon of an exceptional, inevitable and irresistible character; or was wholly caused by a third party's act or omission done with intent to cause damage. Furthermore, no liability attaches where the oil pollution damage was wholly caused by the negligence or other wrongful act of any government or other authority responsible for the maintenance of lights or other navigational aids in the exercise of that function.[63] Contributory negligence is also available as a defence reducing the liability of the registered owner.[64]

Insurers will not be liable if the shipowner's liability is excluded by the abovementioned provisions.[65] The insurer can also avoid liability if he can show that the pollution damage resulted from the wilful misconduct of the owner.[66] However, the insurer is not entitled to take any other defence, apart from the personal wilful misconduct of the shipowner, which he might have been contractually entitled to take in proceedings brought by the owner against him,[67] for example avoidance of the contract for a breach of warranty or for the breach of the duty of utmost good faith under the Marine Insurance Act 1906.[68]

### *(v) Time bar*

Rights of compensation under the Civil Liability Conventions are extinguished unless an action is brought within three years from the date on which the damage occurred.[69] In no case may an action be brought after six years from the date of the incident which caused the damage. The reason for the dual time bar is to cover situations[70] where the pollution does not arise immediately but is for some reason delayed, for example where a fully laden tanker sinks without much oil leaking but subsequently oil is released following the deterioration of the wreck.[71]

62. In *The Sea Empress* (see fn. 59) this was expressed as "the interest and losses of such fishermen could be very closely related to the physical waters and the physical contamination that occurred". But see *Landcatch Ltd v International Oil Pollution Compensation Fund* (fn. 33), where the decisions of the IOPCF were not considered relevant to the interpretation of the CLC.
63. Art. III(2) and s. 155 of the 1995 MSA.
64. Art. III(5) and s. 169 of the 1995 MSA.
65. 1992 CLC, Art. VII(8), and s. 165(2) of the 1995 MSA.
66. Art. III(3) and s. 165(2) of the 1995 MSA.
67. *Ibid.* One of the reasons for the extensive provisions covering insurers in the 1969 and 1992 CLC is that insurance is compulsory for the owners of ships registered in a contracting State carrying more than 2,000 tons of oil in bulk as cargo: Art. VII(1).
68. In addition the UK enactment expressly excludes the compulsory insurance contract from the provisions of the Third Parties (Rights Against Insurers) Act (1930); see s. 165(5) of the 1995 MSA.
69. 1992 CLC, Art. VIII, and s. 162 of the 1995 MSA.
70. See Lord Gill's statement in *Gray and Another v The Braer Corporation and Others and International Oil Pollution Compensation Fund* [1999] 2 Lloyd's Rep 541 at p. 544.
71. The 2007 Nairobi Wreck Removal Convention, when and if it comes into force, will provide the basis for the removal of wrecks which threaten the marine environment. The wreck removal expenses under this Convention are payable by the shipowner or covered by the compulsory insurance the shipowner has to carry. However, the 1992 CLC provisions will continue providing compensation for pollution damage. See Chapter 6, p. 190.

The 1992 CLC provides for a direct right of action by third party claimants against the insurer or other person providing financial security for the owner's liability for pollution damage.[72] This ensures that recovery may be available even if the owner is not financially capable of paying.

The 1992 CLC prohibits in general[73] any claim for pollution damage as defined under the Civil Liability Conventions or otherwise against crew members and other servants or agents of the owner, the pilot (or any other person who, without being a member of the crew,[74] performs services for the ship), any charterer,[75] any manager or operator of the ship, any person performing salvage operations with the consent of the owner or on the instructions of a competent public authority, and any person taking preventive measures to avoid oil pollution damage.[76] Servants or agents of the charterer, manager, operator, salvor or other person taking oil pollution prevention measures are also protected. Thus, for any pollution damage claim the shipowner or his insurer are the only persons a claimant may sue under the 1992 CLC.

Persons not protected under the 1992 CLC, for example shipbuilders and arguably classification societies, can be sued directly, thus potentially becoming exposed to unlimited, fault-based, liability. However, classification societies have been successful in claiming protection under the 1992 CLC before the New York Southern District Court.[77]

By contrast in the first instance decision of *The Erika*[78] the Paris Criminal Court considered the list of the persons protected as restricted. As a consequence it held that the classification society RINA, together with the technical manager of the ship and also Total SA which has vetted the vessel which was then chartered by one of its subsidiaries, were not protected under the 1992 CLC and were liable for damages for the pollution caused on the basis of negligent practices. The case is presently under appeal.

## (d) Limitation of liability

### *(i) Application of the limitation regime*

Under the 1992 CLC scheme limitation of liability is the protection provided to the shipowner for the imposition of strict liability. Thus, limitation of liability under the 1992 CLC may be invoked only in circumstances in which liability is imposed under the 1992 Civil Liability Convention[79] and only for damages covered by the 1992 CLC.

72. Art. VII(8). Government ships used commercially are able to escape this provision and not maintain insurance or other financial security: Art. VII(12) and s. 167(2) of the 1995 MSA.
73. Art. III(4). ".. except insofar as the damage resulted from their personal act or omission, committed with the intent to cause such damage, or recklessly and with knowledge that such damage would probably result". For the meaning of these terms, see p. 211.
74. Art. III(3) and s.156 of the 1995 MSA.
75. "howsoever described" – Art. III.4(c) includes demise, time and voyage as well as slot charterers.
76. 1992 CLC, Art. III(4), but see s. 156 of the 1995 MSA.
77. *Reino de Espana v American Bureau of Shipping*, No 3 Civ. 3573 (LTS)(RLE), 2 January 2008.
78. See the Report on the case submitted by France to the IOPC Fund 92FUND/EXC.40/4/1, 19 February 2008, and a summary provided by the Fund's French lawyer at 92FUND/EXC.40/4.
79. Art. V(1): the liability is stated to be "under this Convention".

### *(ii) Who may limit liability?*

Owners of ships covered by the convention[80] and their insurers are entitled to limit their liability for oil pollution damage.[81] The liability of the insurer is always limited[82] and the insurer can always constitute a limitation fund[83] even if the owner is unable himself to limit liability.[84] The insurer is also entitled to use any defences which the owner would be entitled to use.

### *(iii) What types of vessel may be subject to limitation?*

The types of vessel subject to limitation are the same as those for which liability may arise under the Conventions. Thus there is no size-related restriction in the imposition of strict and limited liability. However, only ships of 2,000 tons or larger are obliged to have oil pollution damage insurance.[85]

### *(iv) The limitation amounts*

When liability is imposed there is a tonnage-based right to limit, as set out in Table 1. The 1976 Protocol to the 1969 CLC increases these limits for States party thereto.[86] The 1992 CLC further increased the applicable limitation of liability limits. The 1992 CLC contains provisions for the amendment of limits without the need of a new Convention.[87]

***Table 1: Limits of liability for the owner of a ship under the CLCs and their protocols***

| | *Minimum liability for ships of 5,000 tons or less* | *Liability per ton in addition to minimum liability* | *Maximum liability* |
|---|---|---|---|
| 1969 CLC | No special provision | 2000 gold francs | 210 million gold francs |
| 1976 CLC Protocol | No special provision | 133 SDR | 14 million SDR |
| 1992 CLC Protocol | 3 million SDR | 450 SDR | 59.7 million SDR |
| 2000 Amendment | 4.51 million SDR | 631 SDR | 89.7 million SDR |

The enacted limits can be found in section 157 of the MSA 1995, as last updated by the Merchant Shipping (Oil Pollution Compensation Limits) Order 2003[88] giving effect to the 2000 Amendment agreed by the IMO.[89]

80. Arts. V(11) and VII(8) provided that the type of damage suffered and the jurisdictional zone in which they have occurred is covered by the relevant Convention.
81. See s. 157(1) of the 1995 MSA for the right of the (registered) shipowner to limit liability and s. 165(3) for the insurer's right to do so.
82. Art. VII(8).
83. Art. V(11) and s. 165(4) for the situation where both the shipowner and the insurer apply to limit their liability.
84. Arts. V(11) and VII(8), and see s. 165(3) of the 1995 MSA.
85. 1969/1992 CLC, Art. VII(1), and s. 163(1) of the MSA 1995.
86. Protocol to the International Convention on Civil Liability for Oil Pollution Damage, London, 19 November 1976. There was also a 1984 Protocol to the 1969 CLC, which was ratified by insufficient countries for it to be in force anywhere. Its provisions have largely been included in the 1992 CLC.
87. 1992 CLC, Art. 15, the so-called "tacit acceptance procedure".
88. SI 2003 No 2559.
89. IMO Legal Committee Resolution Leg. 1/82. The amendment was effected by power given to the Secretary of State under s. 157(2) of the 1995 MSA to give effects to alterations of the limits of liability.

### (e) When does the shipowner lose the right to limit liability?

Only acts or omissions of the owner may remove the owner's right to limit liability under the 1992 CLC. Where, as is the usual case, the shipowner himself is not directly involved in the running of the ship, a search for the "alter ego" of the shipowner in respect of the particular act or omission needs to be undertaken.[90] This must be resolved on a case-by-case basis depending on the structure of each company[91] and the way responsibilities are distributed within each company either by the company's constitution or by statutory responsibility or in fact.[92]

The conduct required for the shipowner's act is intention to cause damage or recklessness coupled with knowledge that such damage would probably result.[93] Thus where the shipowner or his "alter ego" is reckless, but does not have actual knowledge of the particular kind of loss that occurred, the right to limit liability is preserved.[94] The burden of proving the shipowner's conduct is on the claimant.[95]

The condition under which the shipowner may lose his right to limit liability under the 1992 CLC is very similar to the test applied under the 1996 LLMC where a full discussion is provided.[96]

### (f) The shipowner's limitation fund

Under the 1992 CLC the right to limit liability is available to the shipowner and his insurer[97] only after they have constituted a limitation fund which satisfies the following conditions:[98]

- if an action is brought before one or more competent courts or authorities then the limitation fund must be constituted at one of the competent courts or authority;
- if no action is brought in front of a court of a competent jurisdiction the limitation fund can be established at any of the competent jurisdcitions;[99]
- the fund must be for the full limitation sum;

90. However, in the first instance decision in *The Erika* the shareholder of the owning company was held liable for the pollution damage as not covered by the protection of the 1992 CLC. See the Report on the case submitted by France to the IOPC Fund 92FUND/EXC.40/4/1, 19 February 2008. Such a solution is arguably unacceptable under English law where the shareholders are not considered liable for the liability of the company (see, for example, *The Evpo Agnic* [1988] 1 WLR 1090; [1988] 3 All ER 810; [1988] 2 Lloyd's Rep 411.
91. See Lord Mustill's judgment in the Court of Appeal decision *Société Anonyme des Minerais v Grant Trading Inc (The Ert Stefanie)* [1989] 1 Lloyd's Rep 349. Also the judgment of the Privy Council in *Meridian Global Funds Management Asia Ltd v Securities Commission* [1995] 3 All ER 918 at pp. 922–927.
92. See *Lennard's Carrying Company Limited v Asiatic Petroleum Company Limited* [1915] AC 705 (HL).
93. 1992 CLC, Art. V.
94. See Chapter 6, p. 211, for a discussion on whether knowledge of the type of loss caused is enough for the owner to lose the right to limit or whether knowledge of the exact loss that was suffered is required.
95. Art. V(2). It is implicit in the wording.
96. It is very important to note that this has been rewritten under s. 157(3) of the 1995 MSA with a potentially different result. The same modification has also been introduced in the similar test applying to the protection from liability of other persons under s. 156(1)(ii).
97. 1969 CLC, Art. V.11. The insurer has the right to establish a limitation fund even where the shipowner's right to limit liability is challenged or lost. However, the 1992 CLC amendment to this Article clarifies that the establishment of the limitation fund by the insurer does not prejudice a claimant's rights against the owner where the owner has lost the right to limit liability.
98. 1992 CLC, Art. V.
99. For the meaning of a competent jurisdiction, see below, p. 264.

- the fund must be cash or bank guarantee; alternatives are available only where the competent court accepts other type of guarantees.

After the establishment of a limitation fund which satisfies the 1992 CLC conditions and which is accessible to the claimant,[100] and, provided that the right to limit liability has not been lost:

- no other assets of the owner, apart from the limitation fund, can be targeted by claimants;
- the release of any ship or property and relevant security must be ordered.[101]

Where the right to limit has not been lost the limitation fund represents the only asset available for the claimants.[102]

Section 158 introduces two additional provisions. The first permits the court to set a deadline for the submission of claims[103] in addition to the time bar under section 162 of the 1995 MSA. This additional deadline does not replace the time bar and later claims may[104] and arguably must be permitted by the court otherwise the time bar under the convention is in effect reduced. However, if the court has distributed the limitation fund or part of it after the expiration of the deadline but before the three-year time bar a new claimant's action may not be time barred but he may be able to recover less than he is entitled to as the limitation fund may have become exhausted.

The second important aspect of section 158(8) is that it provides that liens or other rights regarding the ship or other property do not affect the amounts recovered by the various claimants.[105] The purpose of this section is to prevent claimants benefiting from (mainly) maritime liens arising after a collision and exhaust the fund thus leaving other claimants for pollution damage unpaid.

The establishment of a limited fund as the only asset of the owner against which rights can be exercised creates conflicts amongst the claimants of an incident. For every new claim introduced against the fund can potentially restrict the amount recoverable by the other claimants. Thus every claimant within the fund can and in practice will, if they have grounds, resist the addition of a new claim.[106]

### (g) Jurisdictional issues

The coastal States which suffer oil pollution damage either in the territorial waters or in the EEZs[107] or where preventive measures have taken place, have

100. 1992 CLC, Art. VI(2).
101. *Ibid.*, Art. VI(1)(b).
102. Unless they can sue other persons not covered or protected by the CLC under other regimes of liability.
103. 1995 MSA, s. 158(4).
104. This argument is based on the decision of the Outer House in *Assuranceforeningen Skuld v International Oil Pollution Compensation Fund (No 1)* [2000] SLT 1333 where the relevant provision under s. 5(3) of the Merchant Shipping (Oil Pollution) Act 1971 was held to be a "procedural provision regulating the making of the claim" and in which the actual time was extended to cover the late claims.
105. 1995 MSA, s. 158(8).
106. See, for example, the Scottish Outer House decision in *Anderson & Ors v International Oil Pollution Compensation Fund* [2001] Scottish Court of Session 34 (14 February 2001) where the right is accepted on the basis of *van Eijck & Zoon v Somerville* (1906) 8 F 22 (HL).
107. 1992 CLC, Art. IX(1). The reference to the Art. II defining zones which are the EEZ or equivalent jurisdictional zones, was made by the 1992 Protocol. Under the 1969 CLC, Art. IX(1), the competent

jurisdiction over claims under the 1992 CLC. These States are termed competent jurisdictions. After the limitation fund is constituted the courts of the State where the fund is constituted have exclusive jurisdiction in respect of the management and distribution of the limitation fund.[108]

Under the 1992 CLC the owner can establish a limitation fund in any of the competent jurisdictions before any claim has been brought. Thus, the jurisdictional initiative, under the 1992 CLC can be with the shipowner who may wish to invoke one of several competent jurisdictions by establishing there a limitation fund.

The UK enactment section 166 restricts the jurisdiction of the UK courts both *in personam* and *in rem* in relation to discharges that do not cause, or threaten to cause, pollution damage and no preventive measures are taken in UK territory. This restriction applies in respect of actions against the shipowner and also in actions against any of the other persons protected under section 156(1)(ii).[109]

Final judgments of a competent court must be recognised by all contracting States.[110]

### (h) The role of the IOPC Fund

The creation of the 1971[111] and the 1992 IOPC Fund Conventions materialise the undertaking of the oil industry and, in particular, oil importers to contribute to the compensation of oil pollution damage. The management and organisation of their contribution is effected by the creation of an intergovernmental organisation: the IOPC Fund. The contribution of the IOPC Fund comes in two forms. First, the Fund contributes where pollution damage exceeds the limited liability imposed on the shipowner by the 1992 CLC, providing compensation to higher limits of liability. Second, the IOPC Fund undertakes to pay compensation for pollution damage where the shipowner is financially incapable of providing compensation or exempt or simply cannot be identified. The financial ability of the Funds to pay compensation arises from obligations imposed on the importers of oil in each contracting State.

#### *(i) Liability for the IOPC Fund*

The 1992 IOPC Fund covers situations in which the owner's liability is excluded under Article III.2 of the 1992 CLC. Thus the Fund will pay out[112] where the pollution damage was caused by a natural phenomenon of an exceptional, inevitable and irresistible character, or was wholly caused by an act or omission done with intent to cause damage by a third party. In addition the IOPC Fund will pay where the damage was wholly caused by the negligence or other wrongful act of any government or other authority responsible for the maintenance of lights or other navigational aids.[113] Thus in the situations mentioned above, although the shipowner

jurisdiction (is) for the actions for compensation for damages or preventive measures in the territorial waters or on land of a contracting State, will be in the courts of such contracting State.

108. 1969 and 1992 CLC, Art. IX(3).
109. Unless the actions of such persons have the consequence that they lose the protection under the test in s. 156(1)(ii).
110. 1969 and 1992 CLC, Art. X, unless obtained by fraud or without reasonable notice to the defendant and a fair opportunity to defend. See also s. 166(4) of the 1995 MSA.
111. The 1971 IOPC Fund ceased to be in force on May 2002.
112. The liability of the Fund in UK is prescribed under s. 175 of the 1995 MSA.
113. Section 175(1)(a)(iii) of the 1995 MSA

will not be liable, an equal amount of compensation will be provided by the IOPC Fund.

The IOPC Fund also covers oil pollution liability in cases where, and to the extent that, the shipowner and its insurer are financially incapable of providing the required compensation under the 1992 CLC Convention[114] or where the damages exceed the owners' liability.[115]

In situations where there is oil pollution damage but the vessel that caused the oil spill has not been identified the claimant can still be compensated by the IOPC Fund if he can prove that the oil that caused the damage came from at least one ship. Thus the Fund is liable for compensation from "mystery" oil spills where the ship that caused the damage is not identified.

However, the IOPC Fund will not be liable where the damage arises from acts of war, hostilities, civil war, insurrection or from a governmental ship used in a governmental mission or where the claimant cannot prove that damage resulted from a ship.[116] In such cases neither the shipowner nor the IOPC Fund have any liability under the 1992 CLC and thus the claimants will have to try and recover against other parties.

The shipowner's expenses for preventive measures falling under the definition of the 1992 CLC Article I.6 rank equally with the pollution damage or clean up claims by other parties. Thus to the extent the shipowner's limit is exceeded these are recoverable from the IOPC Fund[117] in the same way and to the same proportion as other claims.[118]

*(ii) Time bar*

Claims against the IOPC Fund must be brought in front of a court within three years of the incident that caused the pollution.[119] However, situations may arise where it is not evident immediately after the incident that the shipowner is either exempted from liability under Article III.2 of the 1992 CLC or he is unable to pay[120] or simply that damages will exceed the shipowner's limits of liability. To avoid unnecessary claims against the IOPC Fund the Fund Convention enables the claimant to avoid the three year time bar by just providing a notification to the IOPC Fund in a way that will enable the Fund to intervene in the legal proceedings if it decides to do so.[121]

Such notification will be sufficient to avoid the three-year time bar only. However unless the claimant brings a lawsuit within six years from the time the damage occurred the action against the IOPC Fund will be time barred.[122]

114. 1992 Fund Convention, Art. 4.1(b), and s. 175(1)(b) of the 1995 MSA.
115. *Ibid.*, Art. 4.1(c), and s. 175(1)(c) of the 1995 MSA.
116. *Ibid.*, Art. III.2 (a), and s. 175(7) of the 1995 MSA.
117. *Ibid.*, Art. 4.1.
118. 1992 CLC, Art. V.8, and s. 175(6) of the 1995 MSA.
119. 1971/1992 Fund, Art. 6.1. Section 178(1) in the MSA 1995 stated originally that the limit when a note to the Fund is given "not later than three years after the claim against the Fund arose". This has been modified under the Merchant Shipping (Pollution) Act 2006 to "not later than three years after the damage arose". This makes the provision consistent with the wording of the Fund Convention.
120. Under s. 175(5) the owner and the insurer are considered unable to meet their obligations if all the reasonable steps to obtain legal remedies have been taken but were not sufficient to make them pay.
121. 1971/1992 Fund Convention, Art. 7.6.
122. *Ibid.*, Art. 6.1.

*(iii) Limitation of liability for the IOPC Fund.*

Under the 1992 IOPC Fund convention, the claimant will be entitled to recover compensation for pollution damage in addition to the amount received under the 1992 CLC. The limits of liability established by the Fund include the owners' limits of liability under the 1992 CLC. Thus they are the total amounts against which recovery is possible. In cases where the shipowner pays its part the IOPC Fund will "top-up" the amount, while in other cases the whole compensation will be paid by the IOPC Fund. The limits of liability under the various versions of the Fund Convention and Protocols can be seen in Table 2.

***Table 2: Limits of liability for oil pollution damage under the Fund Conventions.***

| *Convention/Protocol* | *Limits of liability (million Sdr)* | *Monetary unit* |
|---|---|---|
| 1971 Fund | 450–900 [a] | Gold francs |
| 1976 Fund Protocol | 60 | SDR |
| 1992 Fund Protocol – not in force | 135 [b] | SDR |
| 2000 Fund Amendment (tacit acceptance) | 203 [c] | SDR |
| 2003 Supplementary Fund | 750 | SDR |

*Notes*:

The 1971 Fund and its 1976 Protocol are no longer in force and are included here for the purposes of comparison. Only the 1992 Fund limits, its Protocol of 2000 and the supplementary Fund are currently applicable.

(a) The original limit was 450 million which was gradually increased to 900 million in accordance with the 1971 Fund, Article 4.6.

(b) The limit is to be raised to 200 million SDR when three States contributing to the Fund receive more than 600 million tonnes of oil per annum.[123]

(c) The limit is to be raised to 300.7 million SDR when three States contributing to the Fund receive more than 600 million tonnes of oil per annum.

The limits of liability for the IOPC Fund can be found in section 176 and appear in Part I of Schedule 5 to the MSA 1995, which has been updated by the Merchant Shipping (Oil Pollution Compensation Limits) Order 2003[124] giving effect to the 2000 Amendment agreed by the IMO.[125]

The 1992 IOPC Fund is supported financially by every oil importer who has imported within a year 150,000 tons or more of contributing oil[126] into a contracting State.[127] Only direct imports by sea or imports by land from a non-contracting State to which they were carried by sea count.[128]

123. 1992 Fund, Art. 4.4(c).
124. SI 2003 No 2559.
125. IMO LEG. 2/82. The amendment was effected by power given to the Secretary of State under s. 176(5) of the 1995 MSA to give effects to alterations of the limits of liability.
126. Contributing oil is defined under Art. 1.3 of the 1992 IOPC Fund Convention to include crude oil and fuel oil. See s. 173(10) of the 1995 MSA for the UK enactment.
127. Section 173 of the 1995 MSA provides for contributions to the Fund and also empowers the Secretary of State to collect the necessary information in order to identify the contributing parties (s. 174). The same section provides for penalties in case of non-compliance or provision of false information in respect of a request for information under this section.
128. 1992 IOPC Fund Convention, Art. 10(1).

*(iv) Jurisdiction for actions under the 1992 IOPC Fund Convention*

Where an action has started before a competent jurisdiction under 1992 CLC, if this State is also a party to the 1992 Fund Convention, then the same court has jurisdiction against the 1992 IOPC Fund. However, where the action has started in a competent jurisdiction, under the 1992 CLC, which is not a party to the 1992 Fund Convention, then the IOPC Fund may be sued either at its place of business (England) or in any of the other competent jurisdictions which are parties to the 1992 IOPC Fund Convention.[129]

There are no provisions in either of the CLCs for multiple proceedings, thus the conflict of laws provisions for each contracting State would apply in such cases.

Final judgments of a competent court must be recognised by all contracting States.[130] However, the IOPC Fund is not bound by judgments in proceedings in which it has not participated.[131]

## (i) The 2003 Supplementary Fund

The 2003 Supplementary Fund was created following major oil incidents off the Spanish and French coasts which made clear that the limits of liability under the two-tier system of the 1992 CLC and Fund were inadequate, especially for coastal areas where the clean-up costs were expensive. Following very strong political pressure from the EU, the IMO has quickly developed a third tier of compensation which is available but not compulsory for all parties to the 1992 CLC and IOPC Fund Conventions. In this way States who may consider that the 1992 IOPC Fund limits are adequate to cover their needs in case of an accident can preserve the expenses imposed on their oil importers without burdening them with the additional costs to support the 2003 Supplementary Fund while other States may opt to include the 2003 Supplementary Fund as a third tier of compensation for oil pollution victims.

The 2003 Supplementary Fund increases the compensation available to victims of oil pollution damage to a total of 750 million SDR.[132] This third tier of compensation is available only to those Contracting States to the 1992 IOPC Fund which are also Contracting States to the 2003 Supplementary Fund. Any importer of 150,000 tons of oil or more, in any given year, to any Contracting State will have to contribute to the Supplementary Fund. In the UK the Merchant Shipping (Oil Pollution) (Supplementary Fund Protocol) Order 2006 incorporates[133] the 2003 Supplementary Fund in the MSA 1995.[134]

129. 1992 Fund Convention, Art. 7.3. The IOPC Fund has also rights to intervene (Art. 7(4)).
130. 1992 CLC, Art. X, unless obtained by fraud or without reasonable notice to the defendant and a fair opportunity to defend. See s. 177 of the 1995 MSA for the UK enactment.
131. 1992 Fund Convention, Art. 7(5).
132. Adopted on 16 May 2003, entered into force on 3 March 2005. Enacted in England by the Merchant Shipping (Supplementary Fund Protocol) Order 2006. The Supplementary Fund Protocol entered into force in the UK on 8 September 2006.
133. According to the final Regulatory Impact Assessment on the Supplementary Fund Protocol (Department of Trade, UK) the worst case scenario will burden the oil importers to the UK by £82.7 million or £1.44 per ton.
134. SI 2006 No 1265 introducing changes in ss 172–178 and adding Schedule 5ZA to the MSA 1995. The Admiralty jurisdiction of the High Court is also modified (s. 20(5a)) to include claims related to the Supplementary Fund.

### (j) STOPIA 2006 and TOPIA 2006

The creation of the 2003 Supplementary Fund has created some tension in the industry because the agreed balance between shipowners and the oil industry was changed as the whole burden of the Supplementary Fund is carried by the oil importers. The issue has been resolved by two private voluntary agreements[135] the Tanker Oil Pollution Indemnification Agreement (TOPIA) 2006 and the Small Tanker Oil Pollution Indemnification Agreement (STOPIA) 2006.[136]

TOPIA 2006 applies in pollution accidents in countries which are members of the 2003 Supplementary Fund. Under this contract the shipowners agree to pay 50% of the money paid out by the Supplementary Fund to which rights are given under Clause XL of this agreement.

STOPIA 2006 covers pollution damage to all States party to 1992 CLC, arising from tankers smaller than 29,548 tons (gross). The owners of such ships are undertaking to voluntarily raise their limit of liability to 20,000,000 SDR. Rights are given to the 1992 Fund under Clause XL. In the case of excessive damage by small tankers in a Supplementary Fund State, both TOPIA 2006 and STOPIA 2006 are relevant.

These arrangements do not affect the rights of claimants for pollution damage and only concern the arrangement between shipowning and cargo interests on who contributes how much in the compensation.

## 4. BUNKER AND LUBRICATING OILS: THE 2001 BUNKER POLLUTION CONVENTION

The 1995 MSA, section 154, provides strict liability to damage caused by persistent oil from non-tankers within UK territory.[137] However, a specialised convention has been agreed and will enter into force on 21 November 2008. The UK has already introduced the 2001 Bunker Oil Pollution Convention into its legislation[138] which will come into force when the 2001 BOPC enters into force.

The 2001 International Convention on Civil Liability for Bunker Oil Pollution Damage (2001 BOPC) establishes strict liability for the registered owner, bareboat charterer, manager and operator of the ship[139] in respect of oil pollution damage from bunker oil. It also establishes compulsory insurance[140] for the registered owner and direct action of third-party claimants against the insurer.[141] The

135. See 92FUND/A.ES.10/131 SUPPFUND/A/ES.2/ February 2006. Both agreements are applicable to ships entered in one of the P&I Clubs which are members of the International Group and reinsured through the pooling arrangements of the International Group. Ships insured by an International Group Club but not covered by the pooling arrangement may agree with the Club concerned to be covered.
136. 92FUND/A.ES.10/131 SUPPFUND/A/ES.2/ February 2006 states that most of the global tonnage is subject to these arrangements.
137. Merchant Shipping Act 1995, s. 154.
138. The Merchant Shipping (Oil Pollution) (Bunkers Convention) Regulations 2006, SI 2006 No 1244, which modify Chapter 3 of Part 6 of the Merchant Shipping Act 1995, implementing Council Decision 2002/762/EC which authorises Member States to sign, ratify or accede to the 2001 BOPC (OJ L 256, 25.9.2002, p. 7).
139. 2001 BOPC, Art. 1(3), and 1995 MSA, s. 153A(7).
140. 2001 BOPC, Art. 7, and 1995 MSA, s. 163A(2).
141. 2001 BOPC, Art. 7(10), and 1995 MSA, s. 165(1A).

Convention does not affect any right of limitation of liability established in national legislation or by international conventions, although it does give a clear suggestion to Parties that the 1996 Protocol to the 1976 Convention on Limitation of Liability for Maritime Claims (LLMC 1996) provides the best background for its application.[142] While the Convention applies to all ships, compulsory insurance applies only to the registered owner of ships larger than 1,000 gt.[143] The amount for which this insurance is required corresponds to the limits of liability available to the shipowner under applicable national law. Thus in States party to the 2001 BOPC where no general limitation of liability is available to the shipowner, the strict liability established by the Convention would be unlimited although the compulsory insurance required by Article 7.1 is limited to the ship's limitation fund under that 1976 LLMC as amended (by the 1996 Protocol).

### (a) The scope and definitions of the Convention

The 2001 BOPC has been developed for the purpose of filling the gap left open by the CLC/IOPCF 1992 scheme regarding pollution from bunkers. There is no overlap between the 1992 CLC and the 2001 BOPC because the latter does not apply to pollution damage as defined by 1992 CLC[144] whether or not compensation can be recovered under 1992 CLC.[145] The avoidance of overlap with the 1992 CLC under English law is achieved by having two sections for liability in the 1995 MSA (section 153, which governs the 1992 CLC, and section 153A, introduced by the Merchant Shipping (Oil Pollution) (Bunkers Convention) Regulations 2006). Section 153A excludes liability for a bunkers from a ship to which section 153 applies. Thus, section 153A creates liability for the owner where the pollution is from a tanker but the 1992 CLC is inapplicable because the bunkers are not within the definition of persistent hydrocarbon mineral oil.

The 2001 BOPC covers only hydrocarbon mineral oils used or intended to be used for the operation or propulsion of the ship as fuel or lubrication as well as the residues from the use of such oil. These are defined as "bunker oil".[146] Thus, the distinction between cargo and bunkers is based on the demonstration of intention of use.

The 2001 BOPC covers liability arising from incidents[147] which either cause pollution damage or create a "grave and imminent threat to cause pollution damage".[148] In turn, "pollution damage" is defined as any loss or damage caused

142. 1995 MSA, s. 168, deems any liability to damages arising from bunker oil pollution damage as defined to be damage to property under paragraph 1(a) of Article 2 of the 1976/1996 LLMC.
143. 2001 BOCP, Art. 7, and 1995 MSA, s. 163A(2). Section 163A(7) creates a right to detention if a ship leaves a port without a valid insurance certificate.
144. CLC 1992, Art. 1.1 This wording is very similar to that of 2001 BOPC but the difference in the two Conventions arises from (a) the definition of ship which under 1992 CLC, Art. 1.1, covers only ships actually constructed for the carriage of oil and actually carrying oil, and (b) from the difference in the terms of "oil" in CLC 1992, Art. 1.5, and "bunker oil" under 2001 BOPC, Art. 1.5.
145. 2001 BOPC, Art. 4.1.
146. 2001 BOPC, Art.1.5.
147. Defined as an event or series of events having the same origin (2001 BOPC, Art. 1.8). This definition is identical to CLC 1969, Art. 1.8. It is unclear whether the definition of incident covers the bunkering process (LEG 74/4/1).
148. 2001 BOPC, Art. 1.8. See s. 153A(1) and (2) of the 1995 MSA, as amended by the Merchant Shipping (Oil Pollution) (Bunkers Convention) Regulations 2006, SI 2006 No 1244, for the UK enactment.

outside the ship[149] by spilled bunker oil[150] and the costs of preventive measures and any further damage caused by the preventive measures. Thus damage by explosion or fire is not covered although the damage arising from the bunker oil spill that followed the explosion or the fire is covered.

Any seagoing vessel and seaborne craft of any type whatsoever is covered by the 2001 BOPC definition of ship.[151]

The 2001 BOPC application is consistent with that of the 1992 CLC.[152] That is, it applies only to pollution damage on the land, the territorial sea or the Exclusive Economic Zone or an equivalent zone[153] of a contracting State.[154] In addition, the 2001 BOPC applies to preventive measures wherever these are taken.[155] It suffices that the pollution damage has been suffered within these jurisdictional zones.

### (b) Liability for bunker oil pollution

The shipowner is strictly liable for pollution damage from bunker oil spilled.[156] The definition of shipowner includes the registered owner, the bareboat charterer, the manager and the operator of a ship.[157] Thus it is much wider than the equivalent definition under 1992 CLC which imposes liability only on the registered owner.

There is no requirement of fault for the liability to arise. The shipowner can only avoid liability if it can prove that the damage was caused by an act of war,[158] an act of God,[159] an act of sabotage,[160] or (wholly) caused by defective navigational aids due to faults of the responsible authority. Contributory negligence or sabotage by the victim of pollution damage may also exonerate the shipowner partly or fully.[161] If only one vessel is involved but more than one persons under the definition of shipowner are liable, the liability is joint and several.[162] This means that State authorities can recover from the financially stronger or more

149. 2001 BOPC, Art. 1.9(a).
150. With the limitation that in relation to the impairment of the environment only loss of profit and reasonable reinstatement measures (undertaken or to be undertaken) are covered (2001 BOPC, Art. 1.9). The definition of pollution damage in 2001 BOPC, Art. 1.9, is identical to CLC 1969, Art. 6.
151. 2001 BOPC, Art. 1.1. See also CLC 1992, Art.1.1. See s. 170(1) of the 1995 MSA for the UK definition.
152. Compare 2001 BOPC, Art. 2, to CLC 1992, Art. 2, and 2001 BOPC, Art. 1.9(a), to CLC 1992, Art. 1.6(a).
153. Art. 2.(a)(ii).
154. Section 153A refers to damage and measures in the territory of the UK (s. 153A(1)) and, if liability arises under the section for liability for damage and measures in the territory of other 2001 BOPC States. In turn the UK territory is defined to consist of the territorial sea and the British fishery limits set out under the Fishery Limits Act 1976 and the territorial waters and the EEZs (or 200-mile zones) of other CLC States (s. 170(4)).
155. Art. 2(b) but for the purpose of prevention of damage from bunker pollution at the territorial waters of a coastal State party to 2001 BOPC.
156. 2001 BOPC, Art. 3.1.
157. 2001 BOPC, Art. 1.3. This definition can be found in the UK enactment in s. 153(7) of the MSA 1995, introduced by the Merchant Shipping (Oil Pollution) (Bunkers Convention) Regulations 2006.
158. 2001 BOPC, Art. 3.3(a): "act of war, hostilities, civil war, insurrection". These words are not defined in the Convention.
159. 2001 BOPC, Art. 3.3(a): "the damage resulted from ... a natural phenomenon of an exceptional, inevitable and irresistible character". Since there is no requirement for the natural phenomenon to be unforeseeable it is presumably correct to argue that the availability of weather forecasts and warnings would not deprive the shipowner of the benefit of this section, unless there is negligence that caused the damage.
160. 2001 BOPC, Art. 3.3(b). See also s. 155, as amended, for the exceptions in the UK enactment.
161. *Ibid.*, Art. 3.4.
162. *Ibid.*, Art. 3.2. As pointed out by the US submission to the IMO (LEG 77/4/3) joint and several liability essentially means that State authorities can ignore litigation between the parties and recover from the financially healthiest shipowner.

accessible shipowner. The 2001 BOPC is the only way to claim against the shipowner.[163] In the UK enactment this is also reflected in section 156(2A) of the 1995 MSA which precludes any recovery other than under the particular section irrespective of whether liability arises or not.

The channelling of claims within the 2001 BOPC is restricted to the shipowner only.[164] However, the UK enactment modifies the 2001 BOPC and excludes from liability any servant or agent of the owner and any person engaged in any capacity on board or performing any service for the ship; salvors, their servants and agents whether acting under the shipowner's or the competent public authority, and any person involved in pollution prevention or mitigation activities and their servants or agents.[165] However, these persons lose their protection under the 2001 BOPC if the damage has resulted by their "... personal act or omission, committed with intent to cause damage, or recklessly and with knowledge that such damage would probably result"[166] but under a slightly varied test under section 156(2A) of the 1995 MSA.

The 2001 BOPC liability does not apply to government vessels used for non-commercial purposes[167] unless the Contracting State so prescribes.[168] All commercial ships whether private or State-owned are subject to liability and jurisdiction as determined by 2001 BOPC.[169]

### (c) Time bar

A six-year absolute time bar from the time of the incident and a three-year bar from the time of the damage are prescribed.[170] The UK enactment contains both time bars in section 162 of the 1995 MSA.[171] The dual time bar reflects the possibility of oil pollution damage arising later than the shipping incidence, for example by leakage of bunker oil from a wreck and the need to provide some leeway for this possibility.

### (d) Limitation of liability

The 2001 BOPC does not set new limits of liability.[172] Nor does it affect the right of the shipowner[173] or the insurer to limit liability "under any applicable national

163. 2001 BOPC, Art. 3.5.
164. By contrast with the equivalent more protective restriction under the 1992 CLC which protects numerous other parties: see Art. III(4) of the 1992 CLC.
165. 1995 MSA, s. 156 (2B), introduced by the Merchant Shipping (Oil Pollution) (Bunkers Convention) Regulations 2006.
166. This is the test included in 1992 CLC, Art. 4.3, and extended to the 2001 BOPC by s. 156(2)(ii) of the 1995 MSA.
167. 2001 BOPC, Art. 4.2. See s. 167 of the 1995 MSA, as amended by the Merchant Shipping (Oil Pollution) (Bunkers Convention) Regulations 2006.
168. 2001 BOPC, Art. 4.3, in which case the Secretary-General of IMO shall be notified of the terms and conditions under which this will happen.
169. 2001 BOPC, Art. 4.4. The Contracting States undertake to waive any rights as sovereign States in respect of these vessels. See s. 167(3) of the 1995 MSA, as amended, for the relevant provision in the UK enactment.
170. 2001 BOPC, Art. 8. As under the 1992 CLC.
171. As amended by the Merchant Shipping (Oil Pollution) (Bunkers Convention) Regulations 2006.
172. This was a much-debated issue. See M Tsimplis, "The Bunker Pollution Convention 2001: Completing and harmonizing the liability regime for oil pollution from ships?" [2005] LMCLQ pp. 83–100, for the various options discussed during the negotiation stages.
173. The definition of the shipowner is identical in LLMC 1976 (Art. 1.2) and Art. 1.3 of the 2001 BOPC, in contrast with CLC 1992 which defines the shipowner more narrowly.

or international regime".[174] The LLMC 1976 is expressly given as such an example.[175] Thus, pollution damage by bunker oil if covered by the 1992 CLC and Fund Conventions is subject to the limits of those Conventions and excluded from the application of 1996 LLMC.[176]

However, if bunker oil pollution damage is not covered by the 1992 CLC it falls under the 2001 BOPC and would be subject to the global limitation of liability regime applicable in each Member State. In the UK case, the applicable regime is the 1996 LLMC. Thus section 168 of the 1995 MSA (as amended) expressly deems liability for damage under section 153A as "property damage" within the meaning of the 1996 LLMC. As the 2001 BOPC does not cover death and personal injury claims[177] the available limits are, at most, one-third of the total limitation fund.[178]

Thus, the imposition of strict liability under the 2001 BOPC results in the inclusion of these claims in the property part of the limitation fund under the 1996 LLMC or any other national limitation regime.

The applicable limits and the procedure for limiting liability would be those which apply in general limitation claims.[179]

The test applicable under the 1996 LLMC for breaking limitation will be relevant in this case.[180]

### (e) Direct action against the insurer

A claimant under the 2001 BOPC can directly sue[181] the insurer[182] whether or not the shipowner is solvent or is in breach of his insurance contract and therefore cannot recover under it.[183] Nevertheless, the insurer is entitled to limit liability even if the shipowner is not.[184] The insurer can invoke all the defences the shipowner would have invoked in an action against the shipowner. In addition the insurer may avoid liability if the pollution was a result of wilful misconduct by the shipowner.[185]

### (f) Jurisdiction and enforcement of judgments

The jurisdictional arrangements mirror those of the 1992 CLC. Thus, courts of contracting States which have suffered damage in their territory, territorial seas

174. 2001 BOPC, Art. 6.
175. *Ibid.* A resolution to include in the 2001 BOPC preamble words encouraging countries to adopt the LLMC 1996 Protocol and denounce all previous Conventions was also agreed (see IMO LEG/CONF.12/14 and LEG/CONF.12/18, also LEG 82/3/2).
176. 1996 LLMC, Art. 3.2.
177. 2001 BOPC, Art. 1.9.
178. LLMC 1976, Art. 6.1, provides limits of liability for (a) personal injury or death (Art. 6.1.1), and (b) other damage (Art. 6.1.2). The limits of liability for personal injury or death are twice the limits of liability for other damage. Nevertheless, these limits are not completely independent. Although the limits of liability for personal injury or death are not available when only other damage takes place, the limits of liability for other damage are available for satisfaction of personal injury or death claims and rank equally with those claims (1996 LLMC, Art. 6.2).
179. See Chapter 11, p. 361. Note that, by contrast with the UK enactment of the 2001 BOPC, the limitation actions under the 1992 CLC are contained in s. 158 of the MSA 1995.
180. 1995 MSA, Schedule 7, Part I, Art. 4.
181. Art. 7.10.
182. Or the person providing financial security (Art. 7.10).
183. See s. 165(1A) of the 1995 MSA, as amended by the Merchant Shipping (Oil Pollution) (Bunkers Convention) Regulations 2006.
184. Art. 7.10 and s. 165(4B) of the 1995 MSA, as amended.
185. Art. 7.10 and s. 165(4A) of the 1995 MSA, as amended.

or their EEZ[186] have jurisdiction[187] to hear any claim against the shipowner and the insurer or provider of security.[188] The Convention does not specify a period of notice of a commenced action to the defendant but only requires that this should be reasonable.[189] Thus the national law periods for service of the claim forms should apply.[190]

The UK enactment implements the above by restricting the jurisdiction of the UK courts to hear actions *in rem* or *in personam* unless bunker pollution damage has occured in UK territory or prevention measures have been undertaken in UK territory.[191]

Final judgments from a State that has jurisdiction under Article 9 should be recognised[192] and enforceable[193] in all contracting States whichever limitation regime applies in the State where enforcement is sought.[194]

Notably there is no mechanism for resolving jurisdictional conflicts under the 2001 BOPC although multiple jurisdictions may be invoked when neighbouring Member States all suffer pollution damage from the same incident. In respect to EU States, Article 27 of the EC Regulation 44/2001 will be applicable[195] and the court first seised will have the right to decide jurisdiction on the merits.

## 5. OTHER LIABILITY FOR OIL POLLUTION

### (a) Liability under section 154 of the 1995 Merchant Shipping Act

The 1992 CLC and its enactment in English law under section 153 of the 1995 MSA and the 2001 BOPC and its enactment under section 153A apply to a "sea-going vessel or sea-borne craft of any type whatsoever".[196] Thus, oil pollution damage from tankers or other vessels which are not sea-going is not covered either by section 153 or section 153A.

Section 154 applies generally to all ships whether sea-going or not[197] and all persistent mineral hydrocarbon oil whether carried as cargo or as bunker oil. However, it excludes from its application all liability arising under sections 153 and 153A. As a result it covers liability for damages for oil pollution from tankers or non-tankers which are non-sea-going vessels. In addition it may cover situations

186. Or the equivalent 200-mile zone under Art. 2(a)(ii).
187. The contracting States are under an obligation to ensure that their courts have such jurisdiction (Art. 9.3).
188. Art. 9.
189. Art. 9.2.
190. Where pollution damage gives the right to arrest the ship, a direct conflict between the 2001 BOPC and the Arrest Convention 1952 exists as the AC 1952 gives jurisdiction at the place of arrest if the national law so provides (Art. 7.1). The ordinary rules for conflict of laws should then apply.
191. Section 166 of the 1995 MSA, as amended.
192. Art. 10.1.
193. When all required formalities are complied with. These formalities should not allow re-opening of the merits of the case (Art. 10.2).
194. Section 166(4) of the 1995 MSA, as amended.
195. *Owners of the cargo lately laden on board the ship Tatry v Owners of the Ship Maciej Rataj (The Maciej Rataj)* ECJ [1994] ECR I-5439, C-406/92.
196. Section 170(1) of the 1995 MSA.
197. Section 154(5) of the 1995 MSA.

where the vessel is a sea-going one, is not a tanker, and the oil pollution damage does not arise from its bunker oil. For example, a car ferry carrying oil tankers and causing pollution from oil spillage from the oil of the tankers. The same section (section 154) also covers liability for bunker oil pollution damage not covered by section 153 until the coming into force of the 2001 BOPC on 21 November 2001 and the implementing Merchant Shipping (Oil Pollution) (Bunkers Convention) Regulations 2006.[198]

The oil[199] pollution damage definition includes damage outside the ship, costs of measures reasonably taken after the discharge and for damage that arises from preventive measures as well as for preventive measures where a grave and imminent threat of oil pollution damage exists.[200] The damage and the threat of imminent damage must have occurred in the UK territory.[201]

Liability under this section attaches only to the registered owner of the ship.[202] The liability of the registered owner arises only under this section and liability under other legal regimes, for example in tort, is excluded.[203] The liability of servants, agents, charterers, manager, operators, salvors and persons performing services on board the ship or taking pollution prevention measures outside the ship as well as the servants or agents of the last three categories of persons are excluded[204] unless the damage has been caused by an action or omission which is either intentional or reckless and in the knowledge that any such damage or cost would probably result.[205] There is no restriction in the size of the ships which are subject to this liability, thus all small ships are covered.

Liability under section 154 is excluded when the damage is caused by an act of war, hostilities, civil war, etc, or wholly caused by actions or omissions of a third party or by omissions or faults by a responsible public authority in respect of navigational lights or aids.[206]

Liability under section 154 is limited under the 1996 LLMC as enacted in the UK by Schedule 7, Part II, of the 1995 MSA.[207] A time bar of three years from the time the damage occurred and an absolute time bar of six years from the occurrence causing the oil discharge apply.[208] Limitation procedures and release of any arrested ship should follow the general limitation proceedings under the Admiralty Jurisdiction of the High Court.[209]

There are no provisions for compulsory insurance in respect of this section. As this is a UK provision, jurisdiction on the merits, recognition and enforcement of judgments should be subject to the normal rules applicable. However, as this section concerns non sea-going vessels in the general case the damages suffered will be

198. SI 2006 No 1244. Note that this came into force on 15 July 2006 in respect of the issuance of insurance certificates under s. 164(1A) of the 1995 MSA, as amended. However, the other regulations will come into force when the 2001 BOPC comes into force in respect of the UK.
199. The term "oil" is defined under s. 170(1).
200. Section 154 of the 1995 MSA.
201. The definition of territory is the same as applied under ss 153 and 153A and can be found in s. 170(1).
202. Section 154(1), as modified by the Merchant Shipping (Oil Pollution) (Bunkers Convention) Regulations 2006, SI 2006 No 1244.
203. Section 156(1), 1995 MSA.
204. Section 156 (2), 1995 MSA.
205. Section 156(1)(ii), 1995 MSA.
206. Section 155, MSA 1995.
207. Section 168 expressly considers pollution damage under s. 154 to be covered by Art. 2(1)(a) of the 1996 LLMC.
208. Section 162, MSA 1995.
209. See Chapter 11 for details.

confined in internal waters and the adjacent coasts. Thus, the involvement of a foreign court would not be likely unless the owner of the ship is a foreign company.[210]

### (b) Oil Pollution damage under EC Directive 2004/35 and other EC provisions

The 2004/35 EC Directive[212] on environmental liability may also affect the liability for oil pollution. The Directive is based on the necessity of sustainable development[212] and aims to establish a liability framework for environmental damage based on the "polluter pays" principle.[213] It imposes strict and unlimited liability for the polluter for environmental damage but does not cover loss of human life or damage to property. The Directive, far from being an independent instrument, interlinks and is based on numerous other Directives and Regulations making it very difficult to assess which parts of the marine environment are subject to it.[214]

The Directive presently excludes from its application[215] damages covered by some of the major conventions concerned with liability for marine pollution arising from carriage of goods by sea, namely the 1992 CLC Convention,[216] the 1992 IOPC Fund Convention,[217] the 2001 BOPC,[218] the 1996 HNS Convention[219] as well as the 1971 MCNM Convention[220] and their future amendments. Thus, the effect of the Directive in respect of the Marine Environment is significantly reduced.

However, the exclusion applies only to the extent that the relevant international convention is in force in the Member State concerned. Thus the Directive directly presents Member State governments with a dilemma: either to ratify the existing international conventions or to abide with the liability framework of the Directive. It is clear that Member States are moving towards ratification of the various Conventions and that the development of the environmental liability directive played a role in pushing towards the coming into force of the 2001 BOPC and the dormant 1996 HNS.

Rights of global limitation of liability under the 1976 LLMC[221] and its future amendments[222] are expressly preserved.[223] This in effect reduces further the

210. Especially one based in an EU country. In such a case the place of domicile of the defendant would be relevant for the determination of jurisdiction (Art. 2 of the EC Regulation 44/2001) although grounds to sue alternatively in the UK (Art. 5.3) will also exist.
211. Directive 2004/35/EC of the European Parliament and of the Council of 21/4/2004 on environmental liability with regard to the prevention and remedying of environmental damage. Official Journal of the European Union L. 143/56.(30/4/2004).
212. Preamble, para. (2).
213. Art. 1.
214. It appears that areas within 1 mile from the coast and in estuaries and river outflows further out would be subject to its application.
215. Art. 4(2) and Annex IV(a–d).
216. Civil Liability for Oil Pollution Convention, 27 November 1992. Annex IV(a).
217. Convention on the Establishment of an International Fund for Compensation for Oil Pollution Damage, 27 November 1992. Annex IV(b).
218. International Convention on Civil Liability for Bunker Pollution Damage, 23 March 2001. Not in force. Annex IV(c).
219. International Convention on Civil Liability and Compensation for Damage in Connection with the Carriage of Hazardous and Noxious Substances by Sea. 3 May 1996. Not in force. Annex IV(c).
220. Civil Liability in the Field of Maritime Carriage of Nuclear Material signed on 17 December 1971. Annex V(e).
221. 1976 Convention on Limitation of Liability for Maritime Claims.
222. This includes the 1996 LLMC, which has come into force on 13 May 2004.
223. Art. 4(3).

significance of the Directive from the point of view of the shipowner as, even if strict liability is imposed under the Directive in respect of a particular incident, the effect would be to share the property damage part of the limitation fund together with any other claimants.

The exclusions of the maritime legal regimes are temporary and will be reviewed together with the whole framework introduced by the Directive in 2013 with a report by the European Council submitted to the European Parliament before 30 April 2014.[224] In the meantime, the Directive will cover environmental liability only for damages that are not covered by the IMO Conventions.

There is a possibility that other EC environmental legislation can be the basis of liability for the shipowner, charterer or other parties involved with the running of the vessel. An example is the Waste Framework Directive[225] which appears to be relevant in some cases.[226] Traders, shipowners and other entities (e.g. salvors) may become liable under such regimes if they can be accused of contributing independently to causing the waste.[227]

### (c) Non-persistent oils

The CLC and Fund Conventions framework covers only persistent oils. Non-persistent oils are not covered by the 1992 CLC so they are not excluded from the 1996 LLMC.[228] Thus the 1996 LLMC limits any damage caused by them. However, the type of damages recoverable and the type of damages to which the 1996 LLMC will apply would depend, the first on the normal rules of recovery in tort and the second on whether the damages fall under Article 2 of the 1996 LLMC. In the future some non-persistent oils may be covered by the Hazardous and Noxious Substances Convention 1996 which is not yet in force. When the 1996 HNS Convention comes into force, strict liability for pollution damage as well as loss of life, personal injury and property damage on board the vessel will be imposed on the shipowner and his insurer with availability of a second tier of compensation in the form of an HNS Fund.

## 6. LIABILITY FOR POLLUTION FROM HAZARDOUS AND NOXIOUS SUBSTANCES

Liability for damages arising from the carriage of hazardous and/or noxious cargo is presently, under English Law, based on tort. Limitation of such liability arising is currently covered by the 1996 LLMC. The 1996 International Convention on Liability and Compensation for Damage in Connection with the Carriage of Hazardous and Noxious Substances by Sea (HNS)[229] has been designed for the

224. Art. 18.
225. Council Directive 75/442/EEC of July 1995, OJ 1975 L 194 amended by Commission Decision 96/350/EC 24 May 1996, OJ 1996 L 135, p. 32, consolidated by Directive 2006/12/EC of 5 April 2006 on waste, OJ 2006 L 114, p. 9.
226. A number of questions arising from *The Erika* have been refered to the European Court of Justice. The case is still pending but the opinion of the Advocate General has been published and highlights the issues. Opinion of Advocate General Kokott, 13 March 2007, Case C-188/07 *Commune de Mesquer v Total France SA and Total International Ltd.*
227. See paras 131 and 132 of the Opinion.
228. See 1995 MSA, Sch. 7, Art. 3(b).
229. Adopted 3 May 1996. Not yet in force. The United Kingdom signed the HNS Convention on 16 October 1996. The Merchant Shipping and Maritime Security Act 1997 contains the necessary enabling legislation.

purpose of establishing strict liability and providing compensation in respect of such damage. The 1996 HNS, although not yet in force, was inserted as Schedule 5A to the 1995 MSA by the 1997 Maritime Security Act which also provided for a power to the Queen to bring Schedule 5 into force by Order in Council which, in turn, has first to be approved by the House of Parliament as a draft Order. A version of the Draft Order[230] can be found within the public consultation documents.[231] The Draft Order amongst other things modifies paragraph 4(1) of Part II of Schedule 7 to the 1995 MSA excluding any claims under the 1996 HNS from the application of the 1996 LLMC.[232] However, the coming into force of the 1996 HNS has been delayed for reasons which will become clear below.

The 1996 HNS was modelled in many aspects on the 1992 CLC/FUND system. Thus, a two-tier system, expressing the joint responsibility of the carrier (first tier) and the traders (second tier), was devised. However, instead of having two independent conventions the 1996 HNS opted for one convention dealing with both tiers.

This choice was made in spite of the fact that there is a very important practical difference between the oil trade and the trade in hazardous and noxious substances. The financial support of the IOPC Fund is based only on fuel oil and crude oil with perhaps 500 traders globally contributing. By contrast around 6,000 types of cargo are covered by the 1996 HNS with perhaps 500,000 traders involved.[233] Thus, significant issues regarding implementation have arisen, in particular in respect of the reporting requirements for imports and the development of methods for collecting the relevant contributions. In addition, from the beginning, conflicts between sectors of HNS traders were developed with the safest cargoes being unwilling to contribute to a general HNS Fund as they feared that they will end up subsidising some accident-prone and relatively unsafe parts of the market. These problems have been identified from the start and continue to impede the wide ratification and the coming into force of the 1996 HNS.

Following extensive discussions within the IOPC Fund which will also manage the HNS Fund it appears that a protocol to the 1996 HNS Convention is probably necessary in order to bring it into force.[234] The protocol is not expected to affect the shipowner's liability regime, which is discussed below.

### (a) Scope of application

The 1996 HNS covers hazardous and noxious substances carried as cargo and in some cases as residuals from previous cargoes. The substances covered by the 1996 HNS are identified by reference to various lists of international codes designed to ensure maritime safety and prevention of pollution.[235] Thus, it covers

230. The Draft Order will also include important provisions regarding the contribution of importers of hazardous and noxious substances.
231. See *www.dft.gov.uk/consultations/archive/2005/pchns* for the output of this consultation.
232. From the time the 1996 HNS comes into force.
233. See the documents in LEG\CONF\1O\6(A).
234. IMO LEG/93/13, 2 November 2007, s. 6.4. The protocol will probably be considered in early 2008 with a view to being adopted as soon as possible after this.
235. It is therefore very different from the 1992 CLC which includes generally persistent oils without specifying exactly which oils are included. Thus the 1996 HNS definition is more precise and, in where a particular substance needs to be included, this can be achieved by amending the relevant list.

cargoes of oils,[236] noxious liquids,[237] dangerous liquid substances,[238] liquefied gases,[239] liquid substances with flashpoint less than 60°C[240] and solid bulk materials possessing chemical hazards[241] as well as residues from previous carriage in bulk.[242] In addition it covers the transport of packaged dangerous hazardous and harmful cargoes covered by the International Maritime Dangerous Goods Code.[243]

It is worth noting that, in general, the cargo covered is referred to as being in bulk. Packaged goods are mentioned only in relation to dangerous hazardous and harmful cargoes covered by the International Maritime Dangerous Goods Code.[244] Thus the 1996 HNS arguably does not apply where hazardous and noxious substances which are not included in the IMDGC are not carried in bulk.

### (b) Which ships are subject to the 1996 HNS?

A "ship" is defined as "any seagoing vessel and seaborne craft, of any type whatsoever".[245] The definition is very wide and not restricted to any particular construction of ship.[246]

State ships, whether belonging to a contracting or non-contracting State, not used in commercial tasks and war ships are excluded from the scope of the 1996 HNS.[247]

Small vessels less than 200 grt employed in coastal trade of a contracting State or employed exclusively in trade between neighbouring States may also be excluded from the application of the 1996 HNS.[248]

### (c) Damages covered

The 1996 HNS covers damage by contamination caused by any of the hazardous and noxious substances carried. Thus, physical damage by contamination to property outside the ship, financial loss arising from damage to the environment,[249] costs for reasonable measures for the reinstatement of the environment[250] and

236. Art. 1.5(a)(i). As defined under Annex I, Appendix I of MARPOL 73/78. This includes persistent and non-persistent oils, for example crude oil, fuel oil, jet oil, gasoline, etc.
237. Art. 1.5(a)(ii). As defined under Annex II, Appendix II of MARPOL 73/78. This includes, amongst others, tetra-ethyl lead, coal tar, styrene monomer, chloroform, sulphuric acid, coconut oil, sodium hydroxide solution, fish oil, etc.
238. 1996 HNS, Art. 1.5(a)(iii). The definition covers substances such as sodium chlorate solution.
239. *Ibid.*, Art. 1(5)(a)(v), covering LPG, LNG ammonia, chlorine, etc.
240. *Ibid.*, Art. 1(5)(a)(vi), for example acetone and ethyl alcohol.
241. *Ibid.*, Art. 1(5)(a)(vii), covered by Appendix B of the Code of Safe Practice for Solid Bulk Cargoes, as amended, to the extent that these substances are also subject to the provisions of the International Maritime Dangerous Goods Code when carried in packaged form, e.g. potassium nitrate, sulphur.
242. 1996 HNS, Art. 1(5)(b).
243. *Ibid.*, Art. 1(5)(a)(iv), for example cyanides, pesticides and ammunition.
244. *Ibid.*
245. 1996 HNS, Art. 1(1).
246. Mobile offshore units although clearly within the definition of ship under the 1996 HNS if they are used for storage rather than transportation would arguably be excluded from the scope of the 1996 HNS.
247. 1996 HNS, Art. 4.4. A contracting State may opt to have the 1996 HNS applicable to their State vessels (Art. 4.5).
248. Arts 5.3 and 5.4.
249. 1996 HNS, Art. 1.6(c).
250. *Ibid.*, Art. 1.6(c).

the costs of and damage caused by preventive measures.[251] These damages are in essence the same as the damages covered by the 1969/1992 CLC.[252]

However, the 1996 HNS also covers two additional heads of damage. First, it covers loss of life and personal injury on board as well as outside the ship[253] only excluding such loss when there is a contract of carriage of passengers.[254] Second, it covers property damage outside the ship. Thus, its scope is much wider than that of the 1992 CLC.[255]

The inclusion of oils both persistent and non-persistent within the scope of the 1996 HNS overlaps with the 1992 CLC/Fund regimes. To avoid the conflict, oil pollution damage covered by the 1992 CLC is excluded from the scope of the 1996 HNS whether compensation is available under the 1992 CLC or not.[256] While the 1992 CLC only covers damage by contamination[257] from persistent oils from tankers there is significant scope for the application of the 1996 HNS in three respects. First, in respect to loss of life and personal injury, second, in respect to property damage outside the ship[258] arising from persistent and non-persistent oils and finally in respect to damage by contamination[259] outside the ship caused by non-persistent oils. This in effect means that separate funds and different limits of liability will be available where loss of life and property damage occurs, in addition to pollution damage.

Where the damage is caused by substances covered by the HNS and by other substances unless the damage is separable it will be wholly covered by the 1996 HNS.[260] Thus if there is an explosion onboard a vessel carrying hazardous and non-hazardous materials then, unless it can be proved that the damage or part of it was caused by the non-hazardous materials, the 1996 HNS will be applicable.

### (d) Where does the 1996 HNS apply?

The application of the 1996 HNS is complicated by a coupling between the type of damage suffered, the jurisdictional zone in which this damage was suffered and the flag of the ship. This is outlined in Table 3 (see page 280). For the EEZ[261] the application of the 1996 HNS is restricted to environmental damage only. In respect of preventive measures these expenses are recoverable wherever they occur subject to the requirement that the preventive measures are taken in respect of pollution damage, actual or threatened,[262] in the territorial waters or the EEZ of a contracting State.

251. 1996 HNS, Art. 1.6(d).
252. 1992 CLC, Art. 1.6.
253. *Ibid.*, Art. 1.6(a).
254. 1996 HNS, Art. 4.1.
255. Warships, naval auxiliaries and other State ships are in general excluded. See Art. 4.
256. 1996 HNS, Art. 4.3.
257. Also including the costs of preventive measures and further loss or damage caused by preventive measures.
258. For example, from an explosion or fire.
259. Including the costs of preventive measures and further loss or damage caused by preventive measures.
260. Art. 1.6. See also Art. 4.3.
261. In the UK case the British fishery limits set out under the Fishery Limits Act 1976.
262. Note that Art. 1(8) defines "incident" as "any occurrence or series of occurrences having the same origin, which causes damage or creates a grave and imminent threat of causing damage". Thus, threatened pollution that does not materialise is covered provided that such threat is "grave and imminent".

***Table 3: Application of the 1996 HNS Convention.***

| | *Contracting State* | | *Non-contracting State* | | *High Seas* |
|---|---|---|---|---|---|
| | Territory and territorial sea | EEZ or equivalent | Territorial sea | EEZ or equivalent | |
| Loss of life on board or outside the ship | All ships | Ships of contracting States | Not applicable | Ships of contracting States | Ships of contracting States |
| Damage to property outside the ship | All ships | Ships of contracting States | Not applicable | Ships of contracting States | Ships of contracting States |
| Pollution damage | All ships | All ships | Not applicable | Not applicable | Not applicable |
| Costs and damages of preventive measures | Everywhere, but has to be related with pollution damage covered by the Convention, that is, pollution damage in the EEZ or the territorial waters of a Contracting State. | | | | |

## (e) Who is liable

The registered[263] owner of a ship[264] carrying hazardous or noxious substances which causes damage is, under the 1996 HNS, strictly liable for such damage.[265] The requirement that the damage must be caused "in connection with the carriage"[266] of hazardous and noxious substances "by sea" imposes restrictions to the claims that fall under the 1996 HNS.

"Carriage by sea" is defined as the period which starts when the hazardous and noxious cargo during loading enters any part of the ship's equipment until the time during discharge they stop being present in any part of the ship's equipment.[267] This definition imposes liability on the shipowner irrespective of who is responsible under the contract of carriage for loading or stowing the hazardous or noxious cargo. However, because the shipowner's rights of recovery against third parties are expressly preserved[268] the shipowner may recover against the party responsible under the contract of carriage.

## (f) Type of liability imposed

Strict liability, that is liability without a requirement on the claimant to prove fault, is imposed on the registered shipowner[269] and his insurer.[270] Joint and several liability is imposed when two or more ships carrying hazardous and noxious substances are involved unless the damage is separable.[271]

263. 1996 HNS, Art.1(3). If there is no registration then persons owning the vessel qualify as owners. For State-owned ships registered by a company the company is the owner. A person includes individuals as well as legal persons at corporate levels as well as States (for the exact wording see Art. 1(2)).
264. 1996 HNS, Art. 1(1). The definition of ship is already treated under section 5(b).
265. *Ibid.*, Art. 7(1).
266. *Ibid.*, Art. 7(1).
267. *Ibid.*, Art. 1(9).
268. *Ibid.*, Art. 7(6).
269. *Ibid.*, Art.7(1).
270. *Ibid.*, Art. 12(8). Compulsory insurance is provided for all ships covered by the HNS (Art. 12(1)).
271. *Ibid.*, Art. 8(1).

Some exceptions are available to the owner, who can escape liability if the damage is caused by "an act of war, hostilities, civil war, insurrection or a natural phenomenon of exceptional, inevitable and irresistible nature".[272] The owner also avoids liability where the damage was wholly caused by an act of a third party with intention to cause damage,[273] or was wholly caused by negligent acts by a government or authority in respect of maintenance of navigational aids.[274] The owner also escapes liability where he was not informed by the shipper of the dangerous and noxious nature of the cargo and that lack of information caused, at least partly, the damage or led to a failure of obtaining the compulsory insurance provided for under Article 9 of the 1996 HNS.[275]

The owner may also avoid liability, partly or fully, where he can prove that intentional acts or omissions by the victim of the incident, with the intent to cause damage, contributed to that person's damage.[276]

The shipowner can be sued under the 1996 HNS Convention only and no claims under any other legal basis are permitted.[277] Protection against claims is provided for the owner's servants or agents, pilots, charters of all types, the manager and operator of the ship, salvors and others involved in preventive measures and the servants and agents of those entities.[278]

### (g) Insurance issues

Compulsory insurance for the owner[279] and direct action against the insurer[280] is provided for by the 1996 HNS. The insurer is entitled to limit its liability[281] and can use the same defences as the owner has available under the 1996 HNS.[282] In addition it is exempted from liability where it can show that it was the owner's wilful misconduct that caused the damage.[283] However, the insurer cannot rely on any other contractual defences which might have enabled him to avoid paying the insured as against a third party initiating a direct action.

### (h) Limitation of liability

#### *(i) The applicable limits*

The liability of the owner and its insurer is limited.[284] The limits, which are applicable per incident,[285] are shown in Table 4 on page 282. The limits are set

272. 1996 HNS, Art. 7.2(a).
273. *Ibid.*, Art. 7.2(b).
274. *Ibid.*, Art. 7.2(c).
275. *Ibid.*, Art. 7.2(d).
276. *Ibid.*, Art. 7.3.
277. *Ibid.*, Art. 7.4.
278. *Ibid.*, Art. 7.5. However, the protection is removed if "... the damage resulted from 'the personal act or omission, of the protected person' ... committed with the intent to cause such damage, or recklessly and with knowledge that such damage would probably result".
279. Art. 12.1. An insurance certificate is required (Art. 12.2) and has to be carried on board (Art. 12.4) otherwise the vessel will not be permitted to trade (Art. 12.10).
280. 1996 HNS, Art. 12.8.
281. *Ibid.*
282. Art. 12.8. The owners' exemptions are set out in Art. 7.2, 7.3 and 7.4 of the 1996 HNS. However, the insurer cannot rely on bankruptcy or winding up of the owner. See above, section 3*(e) Direct action against the insurer*, p. 272, and fns 182–185.
283. 1996 HNS, Art. 12(8).
284. 1996 HNS, Art. 9.
285. "Incident" is defined as "any occurrence or series of occurrences having the same origin which causes damage or creates a grave and imminent threat of causing damage" (Art. 1(8)). Thus, the

on the basis of the tonnage of the vessel rather than the amount of hazardous and noxious substances actually carried. The limits of liability are higher per ton for small ships. Where two or more ships carrying hazardous and noxious substances are involved in an incident the limits of liability are applicable to each vessel independently[286] although the liability may be joint and several.[287]

***Table 4: Limits of liability under the 1996 HNS***

| *Tonnage (T)*[a] *Grt* | *Limitation* *SDR*[288] | *HNS FUND limitation (inclusive of shipowner's limits)*[b] *SDR* |
|---|---|---|
| Less than 2,000 | 10,000,000 | 250,000,000 |
| 2,001–50,000 | 1,500 x (T–2000) +10,000,000 | 250,000,000 |
| 50,001–100,000 | 360 x (T–50,000) +82,000,000 | 250,000,000 |
| 100,001 and over | 100,000,000 | 250,000,000 |

*Notes*:
a Article 9.10 of the 1996 HNS states that the ship's gross tonnage as calculated on the basis of Annex 1 of the International Convention on Tonnage Measurement 1969 is to be used.
b For the HNS Fund, see Section 6 below.

### *(ii) Conduct causing loss of the right to limit liability*

The owner loses its right to limit liability if it is proved by the claimant that the damage resulted from the owner's "personal act or omission (...) committed with the intent to cause such damage, or recklessly and with knowledge that such damage would probably result".[289] Thus the test is very similar to that employed by the 1996 LLMC as well as all the other recent maritime conventions agreed from 1976 onwards.[290] It is worth noting once again that the test is satisfied only when the owner's conduct is intentional in causing damage or where it just falls short of it since it requires recklessness coupled with knowledge of the particular damage that occurred. As a result of its difficulty it will need very special circumstances for the right to limited liability under the 1996 HNS to be challenged.

The liability of the insurer is always limited even where the owner has lost the right to limit liability.[291]

1996 HNS would not apply only where damage has occurred but also where damage is threatened. However, the term "grave and imminent" restricts the application of the Convention to preventive measures in cases of major threats. However, such restrictions do not apply where damage has occurred even where the extent of the damage is small.

286. 1996 HNS, Art. 8(2).
287. *Ibid.*, Art. 8(1).
288. The term unit of account is used in the relevant article (Art. 9) of the 1996 HNS. This is set by default to be the Special Drawing Right (SDR) under Art. 9.9(a) and this is the formula followed in the UK. See Art. 9.9(b) and (c) for the position of states not Party to the IMF.
289. 1996 HNS, Art. 9(2).
290. Information regarding the problems and the application of this test can be found in the section on *Limitation of Liability* in Chapter 6, and section 2(e), above, regarding 1992 CLC.
291. 1996 HNS, Art. 8.8.

### *(iii) Establishment and distribution of the limitation fund*

The provisions of the 1996 HNS related to the establishment of a limitation fund are very similar to those applicable to the 1992 CLC.[292] For the owner to benefit from limited liability a limitation fund should be established[293] in the amount corresponding to the size of his vessel under Article 9.1,[294] in any of the competent courts or authorities[295] in front of which an action has been started.

Where an action has not started the owner can establish the fund in any of the competent courts. Cash or a bank guarantee would be sufficient ways of establishing the fund while other types of guarantee can also be used if they are acceptable under the law of the court at which the limitation fund is established.

When the limitation fund is established by the owner,[296] and provided that the owner is entitled to limit liability and the fund is accessible to any claimant,[297] the ship, if arrested or detained in relation to claims subject to the 1996 HNS, must be released and any security provided by the owner in respect of such arrest should be returned.[298] Moreover, no other assets of the owner should be accessible to claimants.[299] Thus, the practical consequence of establishing the limitation fund is that the owner is able to continue trading as he has in essence discharged his liability in the form of the limitation fund, leaving the claimants and the courts to sort out compensation.

A particularity of the HNS limitation fund is that loss of life and personal injury claims are paid first up to the 2/3rds of the fund.[300] The residual 1/3rd is distributed pro rata between any unpaid loss of life and personal injury claims and all other property, environmental damage and preventive measure claims. This arrangement is similar to that under Article 7 of the 1996 LLMC, however, in that case the 2/3rds of the fund is exclusively reserved for the payment of damages for loss of life or personal injury. Under the 1996 HNS the totality of the fund is available for any type of claims with priority provided for loss of life and personal injury claims in respect of the first 2/3rds of the fund.

## (i) Time bars

A three-year time bar is applicable for claims against the owner or the insurer.[301] In respect of claims against the owner, the starting date for the running of the limitation period is the moment the claimant knows or should reasonably have known of the damage and the identity of the owner.[302]

292. See Section 2(f), p. 262.
293. 1996 HNS, Art. 9.3.
294. See also Table 2.
295. 1996 HNS, Art. 9.2. The competent courts under the convention are those defined in Art. 38. See below, section 5 (j), p. 284.
296. Establishment of a fund by the insurer would not be sufficient.
297. 1996 HNS, Art. 10.2.
298. *Ibid.*, Art. 10.1(b).
299. *Ibid.*, Art. 10.1(a). For a detailed discussion of these provisions which resemble the 1992 CLC, see the previous section.
300. 1996 HNS, Art. 11.
301. *Ibid.*, Art. 37.1.
302. *Ibid.*, Art. 37.1.

An additional time bar of 10 years from the date of the incident[303] is also provided for claims against the HNS Fund to cover cases where the starting date of the time bar period is delayed and is not caught by Articles 37.1 or 37.2 because, for example, the damage is identified late or the identity of the owner is not revealed.[304]

### (j) Jurisdictional issues

Two issues must be distinguished. First, jurisdiction on the merits in respect of actions under the 1996 HNS. Second, jurisdiction in respect of the management and the distribution of the shipowner's limitation fund.

The jurisdiction on the merits of the courts is closely linked with the jurisdictional zone where the damage was suffered. Two situations need to be distinguished here depending on whether the damage was suffered within the territorial waters or the EEZ of one or more contracting States or elsewhere.

Where damage covered by the 1996 HNS is suffered in the territorial waters or the EEZ or equivalent 200 miles zone of one or more contracting States, then only[305] these States have jurisdiction to hear the claims. However, as can be seen in Table 3 (see page 280) the 1996 HNS covers[306] damages in the High Seas and the EEZs of non-contracting States, in particular loss of life inside and outside the ship and damages to property outside the ship. Thus there are situations where liability under the 1996 HNS is established but no damage has been suffered in the territorial sea or the EEZ (or equivalent zone) of any contracting State. In such circumstances Article 38.2 provides for alternative jurisdiction in either the courts of the State where the ship is registered,[307] or where the owner has his habitual residence or a principal place of business, provided that these are in a contracting State or the State party where the required limitation fund is established.[308]

The shipowner can establish the limitation fund in any competent court in which an action is brought or if an action has not been brought (yet) he can establish the fund in any of the competent courts. However, the courts of the State party where the limitation fund is established retain exclusive jurisdiction in relation to the distribution of the fund[309] irrespective of whether it also has jurisdiction on the merits in respect of all claims or no claim at all.

Under the 1996 HNS, Article 40, judgments by a competent court[310] which are final, that is, not subject to any formal appeal or review, are to be recognised by all State Parties to the 1996 HNS[311] and must be directly enforceable as soon as the formalities for recognition[312] at each State party are fulfilled.[313] Only where the judgment was obtained by fraud or the defendant was not given reasonable

303. Where there is a series of occurrences, the date of the last occurrence is the starting point for the ten-year period (Art. 37.4).
304. 1996 HNS, Art. 37.3.
305. *Ibid.*, Art. 38.1.
306. Provided the ship is registered, or is entitled to fly the flag of a contracting State.
307. 1996 HNS, Art. 38.2(a). If unregistered then the flag State.
308. 1996 HNS, Art. 38.2.
309. *Ibid.*, Art. 38.5.
310. Under 1996 HNS, Art. 38.
311. 1996 HNS, Art. 40.1.
312. It is expressly prohibited to reopen the merits of the case within the context of the required formalities (Art. 40.2).
313. 1996 HNS, Art. 40.2.

notice and a fair chance to defend the claim may such a judgment not be recognised by other States party.[314]

Because of Council Regulation 44/2001 enforcement arrangements under Article 40 of the 1996 HNS should be excluded from an EU application to the extent they fall under the Council Regulation 44/2001. However, because the recognition and enforcement of judgments[315] is, under Regulation 44/2001, automatic,[316] the courts cannot re-open the merits of the case;[317] and only in a few situations can the decision be avoided;[318] the difference appears to be small.

It is also worth noting that as the 1996 HNS does not include provisions for parallel proceedings, the EC Regulation 44/ 2001 provisions in this respect will remain operational[319] where EU Member States' courts are concerned.

## 7. THE 1996 HNS FUND

The 1996 HNS Convention provides for the establishment[320] of a Fund (HNS Fund) which will provide compensation in cases covered by the convention and where:

- either the damages exceed the owner's limit of liability;[321]
- the owner and his insurer are financially incapable of covering their part of liability;[322] or
- the owner is exempted from liability under the 1996 HNS.[323]

The HNS Fund is only exempted from liability where the damage was caused by war, hostilities insurrections, etc, or where the damage was caused by ships excluded from the application of the 1996 HNS.[324]

In addition, the HNS Fund will not pay where the claimant cannot demonstrate that the damage involved one or more ships.[325] Thus if the damage is caused by a drum of chemicals which was floating but could not be linked with a ship then the liability of the HNS Fund is exempted. In all other cases the claimants will be compensated to the same extent whether the shipowner or his insurer covers the first tier or not.

Whole or partial exoneration of the HNS Fund, to the same extent as that of the owner,[326] is also possible where the damage was caused by the claimant's negligence or intentional act.[327]

314. 1996 HNS, Art. 40.1.
315. Art. 32 of EC Regulation 44/2001 defines as judgment any decision of the court "... including a decree, order, decision or writ of execution, as well as the determination of costs or expenses by an officer of the court".
316. Art. 33.1 states that "A judgment given in a Member State shall be recognised in the other Member States without any special procedure being required".
317. Art. 36 of EC Regulation 44/ 2001.
318. Art. 34 of EC Regulation 44/ 2001.
319. *The Maciej Rataj* (C 406/92), see fn. 195.
320. 1996 HNS, Art. 13.
321. *Ibid.*, Art. 14.1(c).
322. *Ibid.*, Art. 14.1(b).
323. *Ibid.*, Art. 14.1(a).
324. *Ibid.*, Art. 14.3(a). However, the 1996 HNS Fund has the burden of proving the exemption.
325. *Ibid.*, Art. 14.3(b).
326. Under 1996 HNS, Art. 7.3.
327. 1996 HNS, Art. 14.4. The burden of proving the negligence or the intentional acts is on the HNS Fund.

The HNS Fund provides compensation up to 250,000,000 SDRs[328] inclusive of any compensation provided by the owner under the 1996 HNS. Owner's expenses and sacrifices for pollution minimisation and prevention during an incident can be claimed against the HNS Fund.[329]

Personal injury claims are paid out first up to 2/3rds of the total amount of the HNS Fund (166.667 million SDR).[330] The remaining personal injury claims together with any other property or loss claims are paid out in proportion up to the limit of liability. When making payments the HNS Fund acquires by subrogation any rights any claimant may have against the owner.[331]

### (a) Time bar

As with actions against the owner or his insurer a three-year time bar is applicable in respect of claims against the HNS Fund.[332] The starting point for the calculation of the three-year period is the time at which the claimant "knew or ought to have known of the damage".[333] The time bar is protected either by the initiation of a claim against the HNS Fund or, more simply, by serving a notification to the HNS Fund of proceedings that have started against the owner.[334] The formalities to which the notification applies depend on the court that has jurisdiction to hear the claim.

The additional time bar of 10 years from the date of the incident[335] applicable to claims against the owner and his insurer is also applicable to claims against the HNS Fund.

### (b) Jurisdictional issues

The jurisdiction on the merits for legal actions against the HNS Fund is closely linked with the jurisdiction on the merits against the owner and his insurer. Thus claims against the HNS Fund are only permitted where a court of a contracting State is a competent court for an action against the shipowner.[336] Where the shipowner's liability is exempted or the ship that caused the damage is not identified there are no actions against the shipowner and thus no competent courts. In such a case the competent courts for actions against the HNS Fund are identifiable as those which would have jurisdiction had the owner been liable.[337]

There is no choice of jurisdiction in respect of actions against the HNS Fund if there is already an action pending against the shipowner in front of a competent

328. 1996 HNS, Art. 14.5.
329. *Ibid.*, Art. 14.2. However, interest accrued on the owner's fund is not used in calculating the limits of liability for the HNS Fund (Art. 14.5(c)).
330. 1996 HNS, Art. 14.6.
331. *Ibid.*, Art. 41. The rights of recourse acquired include those against the shippers of dangerous goods (Art. 41.2).
332. 1996 HNS, Art. 37.2.
333. *Ibid.*, Art. 37.2.
334. *Ibid.* and Art. 39.7.
335. Where there is a series of occurrences the date of the last occurrence is the starting point for the ten-year period (Art. 37.4).
336. 1996 HNS, Art. 39.1.
337. *Ibid.* and 39.2.

court. In such a case the same court has exclusive jurisdiction for claims against the HNS Fund for the same damage.[338]

Where there is no action pending against the owner in any competent court then the courts that have jurisdiction in respect of a claim against the owner or his insurer also have jurisdiction to hear claims against the HNS Fund.[339]

Judgments in proceedings against the owner or his insurer are binding against the HNS Fund only where the HNS Fund has been notified about the claims brought in such a manner that it permits the HNS Fund to intervene in the proceedings.[340]

It is also worth noting that as the 1996 HNS does not include provisions for parallel proceedings, the EC Regulation 44/2001 provisions in this respect will remain operational[341] where courts of EU Member States are concerned.

## 8. THE OBSTACLES TO THE RATIFICATION OF THE 1996 HNS

From the point of view of a claimant the HNS Fund operates exactly as the 1992 IOPC Fund, that is, it provides the second tier of liability. However, from the point of view of financial contributions to the HNS Fund, the 1996 HNS is much more complicated than the 1992 IOPC Fund.

### (a) The HNS accounts[342]

The 1996 HNS provides for the creation of a general account divided into sectors[343] and, in addition, an oil account,[344] an LNG account,[345] and LPG account.[346] The reason for the various separate accounts appears to be the unwillingness of the various sectors to cross-subsidise damages. Thus, relatively safe sectors, like the LNG lobbied and achieved the creation of separate accounts. However, for the system to work each account needs to be viable, that is, there should be enough contributors for the account to be capable of compensating accidents arising from contributing cargo. Contributions to the various accounts are due by importers of hazardous and noxious substances.[347]

However, contributions to the LNG account are due from any person holding title to an LNG cargo discharged in a port or terminal of a contracting State. This is in fact one of the obstacles in moving towards the ratification of the 1996 HNS. There is no way of guaranteeing that the person holding title is subject to the

338. 1996 HNS, Art. 38.4.
339. *Ibid.*, Art. 39.1.
340. *Ibid.*, Art. 39.5.
341. *The Maciej Rataj*, see fn. 195.
342. In the UK the contributions to the various accounts as well as the compulsory insurance provisions are set out in the relevant Draft Order.
343. Art. 16.1.
344. Art. 16.2(a) with oil as defined in Art. 1.5(a)(1).
345. Art. 16.2(b), liquefied natural gases of light hydrocarbons with methane as the main constituent.
346. Art. 16.2(c), liquefied petroleum gases of light hydrocarbons with propane and butane as the main components.
347. See Art. 19 for the minimum amounts that incur contributions,

jurisdiction of a contracting State and thus can be made to pay.[348] The situation is made more difficult by the fact that the LNG trade is based on long-term sale contracts, which makes it difficult for parties to existing contracts to shift the costs down the line as they are contractually bound for, in some cases for 10 years or more.

### (b) The definition of "receiver"

The second obstacle with the 1996 HNS concerns the definition of receiver under Article 4.1.[349] This definition contains two alternatives. The first is the physical receiver of the cargo at the port of a contracting State. The 1996 HNS gives further the option to the physical receiver where it acts as an agent to disclose its principal to the HNS Fund and if this disclosure is made and the principal is subject to the jurisdiction of any contracting State then the principal becomes the receiver. However, the operation of this article depends on the definition of agency under national law[350] and may lead to conflicts between the agent and the principal in respect of the liability for the contributions. The problem is acute in respect of packed or containerised hazardous and noxious goods because there the agency relationship is not clear and there could be many parties including freight forwarders and logistics companies as well as inland carriers. Disentangling the contractual relationship in order to identify the person acting as principal is not something that can practically be done if a simple reporting system is to be created.[351]

Another difficulty relates to the issue of multimodal carriage of HNS between contracting and non-contracting States. The 1996 HNS excludes from the reporting and contribution HNS cargo which is transhipped. However, if HNS cargo is discharged and then carried on to a non-contracting State by rail or road this would be deemed to be contributing cargo with the receiving facility either being made liable for contributions or trying to pass the liability to the rail or road carrier.

Article 4.1(b) provides as an alternative that the receiver could be the person deemed to be so under national law, provided that the contributing cargo received is substantially the same under Article 4.1(a). However, it appears that the first part of the definition is the preferred one by most countries subject to their objections in respect of the passing of liability from the agent to his principal.[352]

### (c) Reporting obligations

The third obstacle in bringing the 1996 HNS into force refers to the reporting requirements under Article 43. According to this provision, every country that ratifies the 1996 HNS and until the convention is in force for that State, is obliged

348. See E Rosaeg, (2007), "Non-collectable contributions to the separate LNG account of the HNS Convention" [2007] 13 JML 94 *et seq*.
349. 92FUND/A.ES.12/9 and 92FUND/A/ES.12/9/2 and 92FUND/A.12/28.
350. 92FUND/A/ES.12/9/2.
351. *Ibid.*
352. *Ibid.*

to submit reports on the relevant quantities of the HNS goods received or discharged (for LNG). Apparently from the 10 countries that have so far ratified the 1996 HNS, only two have done so while two others have sought help from the IOPC Fund as they have found it difficult to produce such reports.[353]

The 1996 HNS will enter into force when two conditions are satisfied. First, when at least 12 States, including four States each with not less than 2 million units of gross tonnage, have expressed their consent to be bound by it. Second, when the IMO Secretary-General has received information in accordance with Article 43, that the person in these States who would be liable to contribute to the general account have received, during the preceding calendar year, a total quantity of at least 40 million tonnes of contributing cargo.[354] Clearly if no reports are received the second condition cannot be fulfilled. However, the difficulties faced by States that have opted for early ratification of the 1996 HNS indicate that developing an easy to manage reporting system with such variable cargoes and so many traders involved is far from an easy task.

### (d) The draft Protocol to the 1996 HNS Convention

Because of these difficulties a focus group was formed in Autumn 2007 with the view of producing a Protocol to the 1996 HNS in order to avoid the problems discussed above.[355] The Draft Protocol[356] consists of 26 Articles of which 11 are identical to the final Clauses of the 1996 HNS Convention. However, the other 15 articles significantly amend the Convention in various respects. In particular, a distinction is introduced between packaged HNS[357] and bulk HNS.[358] Only bulk HNS is considered as contributing cargo under the amended Article 1.10.[359] This means that importers of packaged HNS will not be contributing to the HNS Fund. This partly resolves the problem of tracing numerous small quantities of packaged HNS cargoes for contributions and would presumably simplify the implementation procedures for the 1996 HNS Convention. The 1996 HNS Fund will continue covering the damages arising from packaged HNS cargoes. However, the liability of shipowner in respect of packaged HNS will be increased above that prescribed for bulk HNS.[360] However, the Draft Protocol does not specify the amount of increased liability and presumably this will be left for negotiation at a later stage.

The problem of the LNG contributions will be solved by replacing the liability of the title holder with that of the receiver of the cargo[361] in line with all other HNS contributions.

353. 92FUND/A.12/28.
354 1996 HNS, Art. 46.
355. IMO LEG 93/13, 2 November, 2007, s. 6.4.
356. IOPCF 1992 92/FUND/WGR.5/6, 14 February 2008. Draft Protocol to amend the International Convention on Liability and Compensation for Damage in Connection with the Carriage of Hazardous and Noxious Substances by Sea, 1996 (submitted for consideration and further approval as this volume went to press).
357. Art. 3 of the Draft Protocol adding paragraph 5*ter* to Art. 1 of the 1996 HNS.
358. Art. 3 of the Draft Protocol adding paragraph 5*bis* to Art. 1 of the 1996 HNS.
359. Art. 3.2 of the Draft Protocol.
360. Art. 5 of the Draft Protocol replacing Art. 9(1) of the Convention and introducing a new Art. 9(1)(b).
361. Art. 7 of the Draft Protocol replacing Art. 19.1(b) of the 1996 HNS. The same holds for the LNG contributions under Art. 20(1) amended by Art. 8 of the Draft Protocol and under Art. 21.5(5) amended by Art. 9 of the same.

The problem of non-reporting of the importers of HNS and the quantities in respect of which contributions are due is dealt with by a number of measures. First, the Draft Protocol repeats the liability on the State Party to compensate the HNS Fund where the HNS Fund has suffered damage because of breach of the reporting obligations under Article 21(2).[362] Second, it permits the HNS Fund to refrain from paying damages in respect of a State Party who hasn't paid contributions due for the years before an incident for which contributions are due. Where this State Party is notified of its failure to fulfil such obligations and does not remedy the situation within a year, then compensation is to be denied permanently.[363] However, the non-payment option is only available in respect of pollution and property damage but does not apply to loss of life or personal injury losses.[364]

This Protocol appears to be a practical way of solving the most pressing problems, but as with all compromises it remains to be seen how quickly the proposed amendments will be agreed in order to speed up the process of bringing the amended 1996 HNS into force.

## 9. POLLUTION FROM RADIOACTIVE SUBSTANCES

The 1960 Paris Convention and the 1963 Brussels Convention as well as the 1997 Protocol to Amend the Vienna Convention on Civil Liability for Nuclear Damage and the Joint Protocol Relating to the Application of the Vienna Convention and the Paris Convention compose the international liability framework which channels liability exclusively to the operator of a nuclear installation on the basis of strict liability. They also provide for limitation of liability for the operator.

The International Convention relating to Civil Liability in the field of Maritime Carriage of Nuclear Material (NUCLEAR), 1971, also relates to the issue of liability of sea carriers of nuclear materials. Where these international instruments or other national instruments are applicable there is no limitation of liability for the shipowner of a ship carrying nuclear substances by virtue of the exclusion under Article 3(c) of the 1976 LLMC. However, this would only be relevant where the operator of a nuclear site is also the shipowner, charterer, manager or operator of the ship as otherwise by virtue of the aforementioned conventions there is no liability on the legal persons owning or running the ship.

In the UK this framework as provided by the 1960 Paris Convention and the 1963 Brussels Convention as enacted in the Nuclear Installations Act 1965. The enactment of the 1976/1996 LLMC in the UK clarifies that the claims under this section are those under sections 7–11 of the Nuclear Installations Act 1965.

The abovementioned conventions related to the carriage of radioactive materials are applicable to nuclear installations and do not cover liability in respect of nuclear powered ships. The liability of the shipowner of a nuclear ship is excluded from limitation under Article 3(d) of the 1996 LLMC.

362. Art. 21*bis* introduced by Art. 10 of the Draft Protocol. Art. 21(4) has been moved to Art. 21*bis*(1). Art. 21(4) is amended by a provision by which a contracting State is obliged to report that there are no contributions due by anyone in the country for years where this is the case.
363. Art. 21*bis*(2) and (3) introduced by Art. 10 of the Draft Protocol.
364. Art. 21*bis*(5) introduced by Art. 10 of the Draft Protocol.

## 10. LIABILITY ARISING FROM CARRIAGE OF HAZARDOUS WASTES

Dumping of substances at sea is generally prohibited under the Convention on the Prevention of Marine Pollution by Dumping of Wastes and Other Matter, 1972 (London Convention 1972) as amended by its 1996 Protocol. However, in this section we will be concerned with the influence of the international legal framework for hazardous wastes on shipping. This influence is important in two respects. First, in relation to the liability of the carrier, and second, and perhaps more surprising, in relation to scrapping of ships.

### (a) General legal framework

The export of hazardous wastes is regulated by the 1989 Basel Convention on the Control of the Transboundary Movements of Hazardous Wastes and Their Disposal (Basel Convention).[365] In the UK any export of hazardous wastes to a non-OECD[366] country is completely banned, by virtue of the EU adoption of the 1995 amendment to the Basel Convention.[367]

The 1989 Basel Convention applies to hazardous wastes[368] which are subject to transboundary movement,[369] (hereinafter "transport"). Such wastes are hazardous if they fall within the rather involved Convention definition[370] or if they are deemed hazardous under the domestic legislation of a party to the Convention that is involved in the transport of the waste. Radioactive wastes and wastes which are derived from the normal operations of a ship[371] are excluded from the Basel Convention, provided they are subject to an international regulatory system.[372] The Basel Convention applies to all international carriage of hazardous wastes whether by land, air or sea but not to national carriage.

Parties to the Basel Convention are under a general obligation to minimise the generation of hazardous wastes[373] and to ensure that there are adequate disposal facilities within the generating State.[374] Five natural or legal persons[375] that could be involved in the transport of hazardous wastes are identified: the producer of the wastes is termed the "Generator";[376] the "Exporter"[377] is any person under the jurisdiction of the State of export[378] who arranges for the export of hazardous wastes;

365. The Convention has 170 parties and entered into force in 5 May 1992. The UK ratified the Basel Convention in February 1994.
366. Organisation for Economic Cooperation and Development.
367. Ban Amendment to the Basel Convention on the Control of Transboundary Movements of Hazardous Wastes and their Disposal, Geneva, 22 September 1995. The Ban Amendment must be ratified by three-fourths of the Parties who accepted it in order to enter into force. At the moment 63 States have ratified the Protocol.
368. Article 2.1 of the Basel Convention defines "wastes" as "substances or objects which are disposed of or are intended to be disposed of or are required to be disposed of by the provisions of national law".
369. Article 2.3 of the Basel Convention.
370. Under Article 1.1(a) of the Basel Convention hazardous wastes are those listed in Annex I of the Convention, unless they are devoid of the characteristics that are contained in Annex III.
371. *Ibid.*, Art. 1.4.
372. Basel Convention 1989, Art. 1.3.
373. *Ibid.*, Art. 4.2(a), "taking into account social, technological and economic aspects".
374. *Ibid.*, Art. 4.2(b).
375. *Ibid.*, Art. 2.14.
376. *Ibid.*, Art. 2.18.
377. *Ibid.*, Art. 2.15.
378. Article 2.10 of the Basel Convention defines a "State of export" as one "from which a transboundary movement of hazardous wastes or other wastes is planned to be initiated or is initiated".

the "Importer"[379] is any person under the jurisdiction of the State of import[380] who arranges for the import of hazardous wastes; the "Carrier" is the performing carrier[381]; finally, the "Disposer" is any person who receives and disposes of cargo deemed hazardous wastes.[382] Another role, taken either by the "Generator" or the "Exporter" under the Basel Convention is that of the notifier, the person responsible to inform and seek permission from the relevant authority for the export of the hazardous wastes.[383]

States party to the Basel Convention can only transport hazardous wastes to other States party to the Convention, whilst transport from and to non-party States is precluded.[384] Transports are authorised and monitored through the dual requirements of the "movement document"[385] and the "notification document".[386] Compulsory insurance is provided for under the Convention.[387] The State of export, at the end of the transport, has to be informed by the Disposer of the receipt and of the disposal of the wastes.[388]

Failure to comply with the procedures of the Basel Convention renders the transport "illegal traffic".[389] This term includes cases where documentation was obtained fraudulently or by misrepresentation[390] or, notwithstanding the absence of fraud or misrepresentation, where the transport fails to comply with the documentation.[391] The transport of wastes for dumping in breach of the Basel Convention is also classed as illegal traffic.[392]

Illegal traffic is deemed a criminal offence.[393] If the Generator or Exporter is the person liable for the illegal traffic, then the State of export is under an obligation to dispose of the wastes rendered illegal traffic.[394] Likewise for the State of import if the Importer or Disposer is the person liable.[395]

### (b) Carrier's liability

In December 1999, the fifth Conference of the Parties to the Basel Convention agreed on a Liability Protocol which will enter into force 90 days after 20 States

379. Basel Convention 1989, Art. 2.16.
380. Article 2.11 of the Basel Convention 1989 defines a "State of import" as one "to which a transboundary movement of hazardous wastes or other wastes is planned or takes place for the purpose of disposal therein or for the purpose of loading prior to disposal in an area not under the national jurisdiction of any State".
381. Basel Convention 1989, Art. 2.17.
382. *Ibid.*, Art. 2.19. See Art. 2.4 for the definition of disposal.
383. Arts 4 and 6 of the Basel Convention 1989.
384. Basel Convention 1989, Art. 4.5.
385. A requirement by virtue of Art. 4.7(c) of the Basel Convention. The information that is required under the document is set out in Annex V, Part B, of the Convention.
386. A requirement by virtue of Art. 6.1 of the Basel Convention. The information that is required under the document is set out in Annex V, Part A, of the Convention.
387. *Ibid.*, Art. 6.11 states that "any transboundary movement of hazardous wastes or other wastes shall be covered by insurance, bond or other guarantee as may be required by the State of import or any State of transit which is a Party".
388. *Ibid.*, Art. 6.9.
389. Failure to comply with procedures for notification or consent is covered in Arts. 9.1(a) and 9.1(b) of the Basel Convention, respectively.
390. *Ibid.*, Art. 9.1(c).
391. *Ibid.*, Art. 9.1(d).
392. *Ibid.*, Art. 9.1(e), which states: "That results in deliberate disposal (e.g. dumping) of hazardous wastes or other wastes in contravention of this Convention and of general principles of international law."
393. *Ibid.*, Art. 4.3.
394. *Ibid.*, Art. 9.2. The State of export must either take the wastes back or arrange for its disposal elsewhere, in accordance with the Convention provisions.
395. *Ibid.*, Art. 9.3.

have ratified it.[396] The 1999 Basel Liability Protocol deals with liability and compensation arising from hazardous wastes in transboundary transport, whether this transport is in compliance with the provisions of the Basel Convention or considered as illegal traffic.

The Basel Liability Protocol ensures that there should be compensation available for damage caused during the transport of hazardous wastes by providing both for strict liability[397] of one of the designated persons[398] and, in addition, provides for fault-based[399] liability. The strict liability fails to attach where the damage is caused by extreme political events or natural disasters;[400] or where the damage is a result of compliance with State regulations,[401] or sabotage.[402] No strict or fault based-liability attaches to a person if he controls and/or possesses hazardous wastes solely for the purpose of preventing pollution.[403]

Persons who are strictly liable are not excluded from fault-based liability. However, if their liability is not fault-based, then limits of liability can be introduced under national law. Minimum amounts for such limits are prescribed under Annex B of the Liability Protocol.[404]

A carrier will, in general, face unlimited, fault-based, liability under the Liability Protocol. If he is also one of the designated persons then his liability will be strict but probably limited. The Liability Protocol arguably permits[405] the application of other liability regimes. Thus, for example, where the carrier is also liable for damage under the 1996 HNS then the 1996 HNS will prevail, thus limiting the carrier's liability.

### (c) Scrapping of ships

The second way by which the 1989 Basel Convention affects shipping is in respect of dismantling, scrapping or, to be politically correct, "recycling" of ships. When a ship is sent off for scrapping it may be considered as a hazardous waste within the meaning of the Basel Convention. The majority of ships that are at the end of their lives contain hazardous chemical constituents within their structural make-up, if not in their cargo residues.[406] State-owned ships and war ships are

396. In February 2008, eight States have accepted the Liability Protocol. The UK signed the Liability Protocol in 2000 but has not yet ratified it.
397. Basel Protocol, Art. 4.
398. I.e. the Exporter, the Importer and the Disposer.
399. Basel Protocol, Art. 5.
400. I.e. resulting from an act of "armed conflict, hostilities, civil war, insurrection" (Basel Protocol, Art. 4.5.a) or resulting from natural phenomena of "exceptional, inevitable, unforeseeable and irresistible character" (Basel Protocol, Art. 4.5.b). The strict liability attaches, presumably, even if the causes described in Art. 4.5 are foreseeable.
401. This holds only if the compulsory measures are of the State in which the damage occurred (Basel Protocol, Art. 4.5.c).
402. "wrongful intentional conduct of a third party" (Basel Protocol, Art. 4.5.d).
403. Basel Protocol, Art. 6.2. Provided that the measures this person takes are reasonable and lawful.
404. These increase with the size of the cargo. Thus every participant in the transport is liable for damage arising from its own faults and, in addition, the responsible person (i.e. the exporter or the importer or the disposer) is also strictly liable for all the damage. The minimum limit of (maximum) liability that can be imposed for cargoes larger than 10,000 tons is 30,000,000 SDR.
405. Art. 11, but the wording is ambiguous.
406. The literal reading of the Convention indicates that ships were not considered when the Convention was agreed and they fall uneasily within the scope of the Basel Convention (M N Tsimplis (2001) "Liability and Compensation in international transport of hazardous wastes by sea: The 1999 Protocol to the Basel Convention", *International Journal of Coastal and Marine Law*, 16(2), 295–347). However, the parties to the Convention have taken a different view.

not excluded from the scope of the 1989 Basel Convention. Thus the procedure applicable for all hazardous wastes and the restrictions in exports are also applicable to ships destined for recycling. The Basel Convention also prohibits the exportation of hazardous wastes if a State of export believes that the wastes will not be managed in an environmentally sound manner.[407] There is a reciprocal obligation upon the State of import as well.[408] Environmentally sound management is defined as meaning: "taking all practicable steps to ensure that hazardous wastes or other wastes are managed in a manner which will protect human health and the environment against the adverse effects which may result from such wastes."[409] It is well documented that shipbreaking operations in non-OECD countries, such as India, Pakistan and Bangladesh, do not always constitute environmentally sound management as defined in the Convention.[410] Consequently, transboundary movement of ships destined for shipbreaking are prohibited under the Convention since it does not constitute environmentally sound management, as well as falling within other prohibition measures which were outlined above. As a result, transport of such ships is illegal traffic, thus rendering the persons involved liable to criminal sanctions.[411]

This results in a major problem not only for commercial ships but also for older war ships which are then sold to governments of developing States for further use. It is questionable whether the 1989 Basel Convention permits such transactions because if it does indeed permit them then sham sales of ships or other wastes would also be able to circumvent the convention's restrictions. In addition the 1995 Basel Convention Ban Amendment completely prohibits exports of hazardous wastes for final disposal and recycling from OECD countries to non-OECD countries. Although not yet in force, the European Union has implemented its provisions in the form of a Regulation in 1993.[412]

The Conference of the Parties to the Basel Convention has passed the problem to the IMO. As a response the IMO has developed Guidelines on Ship Recycling[413] and a draft Ship Recycling Convention which is presently under discussion. The draft Recycling Convention as it stands avoids the question of whether the ship is waste or not, which may be a complication when and if the 1995 Amendment to the Basel Convention comes into force. The draft Recycling Convention will on the one hand ensure that the use of hazardous materials in the construction of ships will be minimised, and on the other hand the dismantling of ships will be carried out in a manner which protects human health and the environment.

### (d) The fate of old ships and pollution issues

Removing hazardous materials from the ship before recycling it is expected to be an expensive operation in some cases exceeding the value of the ship as scrap.

407. *Ibid.*, Art. 4(2)(e).
408. *Ibid.*, Art.4(2)(g).
409. *Ibid.*, Art. 2(8).
410. See, for example, *www.greenpeaceweb.org/shipbreak.*
411. Basel Convention 1989, Art. 4.3 and 4.4.
412. Council Reg. 259/93/EEC on the Supervision and Control of Shipments of Waste within, into and out of the European Community (OJ 1993 L30/1). This has been transposed into English law by the Transfrontier Shipment of Waste Regulations 1994.
413. Resolution A.962(23), adopted on 5 December 2003.

This financial reality may lead to the abandonment of ships in ports or scuttling of ships on the high seas.

Abandonment of ships in ports or within the territorial seas is a matter of national law. Scuttling of ships is considered as "dumping" and is prohibited under the Convention on the Prevention of Marine Pollution by Dumping of Wastes and Other Matter, 1972 (London Convention 1972) as amended by its 1996 Protocol.

When the Nairobi International Convention on the Removal of Wrecks 2007 comes into force, ships scuttled in the EEZ of signatory parties will be wrecks and thus covered by the Convention. As a result where such ships pose dangers to the environment or to navigation the coastal State will obtain rights for wreck removal with strict liability for the removal costs on the shipowner who should be covered by compulsory insurance.[414]

An alternative option is scuttling the ship either as a cheap and effective way of disposing of it after a shipping incident or for using it as an artificial reef for the enjoyment of divers or for enhancing particular species. The short-term effects of such actions to the marine environment depend on the amount and type of pollutants on the ship. Such options are based on short-term financial efficiency and are defined on an assessment of the scrap value of the ship against the costs of decontaminating it and transporting it to a dismantling place. Arguably the total environmental costs of extracting minerals, carrying them to a location and processing them in order to construct a new ship cannot be as high as reusing already processed materials. Thus, it is doubtful whether the practice of scuttling the ships at sea can be considered sustainable in the long term.

414. For details on the Wreck Removal Convention, see Chapter 6, p. 190.

CHAPTER 9

# Public International Law Aspects of Shipping Regulation

*ANDREW SERDY*

## 1. INTRODUCTION

As in most fields of human endeavour, it is not possible to escape the influence of public international law, nor wise to overlook it.[1] This is the system of law that governs relations between States[2] and other actors whose personality is recognised on the international plane, in other words international organisations established by States.[3] Natural and legal persons, i.e. human beings and companies or other entities that the law of a given country endows with personality, were until quite recently not subjects of international law, and their role in it today remains marginal.

Every State is a single legal person in international law, even if it is federal in character like the United States, Canada, Mexico, Germany, Switzerland, India, Australia or Nigeria. International organisations are established by treaties between States, which usually provide that the organisation is to have independent legal personality. The oldest international organisations such as the Universal Postal Union appeared in the late nineteenth century, but it is since the Second World War that the growth in their number has been most rapid. Examples include the United Nations (UN) and its specialised agencies like the International Maritime Organisation (IMO) discussed below,[4] as well as regional organisations such as the European Community (EC) or the North Atlantic Treaty Organisation (NATO).[5]

With the exception of ships owned by governments, shipping interests as natural or more frequently legal persons were not subjects of international law under the traditional view. While treaties might be entered into by States for their benefit,

1. A fine recent general introduction to public international law is V Lowe, *International Law* (Oxford: Oxford University Press, 2007). For an even briefer introduction from a law of the sea perspective, see Chapter 1 of R R Churchill and A V Lowe, *The Law of the Sea* (3rd ed) (Manchester: Manchester University Press, 1999) (hereinafter "*Churchill & Lowe*"), esp at pp. 1–13 and 22–25.
2. "State" is the term preferred to "country" or "nation". The former has a much looser meaning, e.g. Hong Kong may for most purposes be thought of as a country, but formally it is a Special Administrative Region of the People's Republic of China, the State ultimately responsible for its international relations. The latter, though part of an older name by which public international law was once known (the law of nations) too easily risks confusion with the people(s) inhabiting a given State.
3. Non-governmental organisations are thus excluded.
4. See pp. 312–323.
5. International organisations are not always as large or as well known as these. Those with specialised functions such as managing world supply and demand of a commodity, e.g. the International Coffee Organisation or regulating international fisheries, such as the North-East Atlantic Fisheries Commission, have a staff small enough in the cases of these examples to be able to share between them a modest office building in central London.

they did not confer rights on those persons under international law – rather, they conferred rights on their States of nationality to insist that all other States party to the treaty comply with its provisions. Although some modern treaties confer rights directly on individuals (usually in the field of human rights) and companies (usually in the field of investment protection), it does not automatically follow – unless that is, the treaty specifically provides such a mechanism for it – that they will have some means of enforcing these rights on the international law plane. For example, if a company's rights are violated by a foreign State, it must rely on its own State of nationality (incorporation) to espouse a diplomatic claim on its behalf against the delinquent State. Thus, while today it is accepted that such persons can have certain rights and obligations under international law, these are far more limited in extent than those of States.[6]

## 2. SOURCES OF INTERNATIONAL LAW

One of the crucial differences between the international legal system and its national counterparts is that there is no international legislature which can enact laws binding on all States. Four sources of international law are listed in Article 38 of the Statute of the International Court of Justice (ICJ):[7]

"Article 38.(1) The Court, whose function is to decide in accordance with international law such disputes as are submitted to it, shall apply:

(a) international conventions, whether general or particular, establishing rules expressly recognized by the contesting states;
(b) international custom, as evidence of a general practice accepted as law;
(c) the general principles of law recognized by civilized nations;
(d) subject to the provisions of Article 59, judicial decisions and the teachings of the most highly qualified publicists of the various nations, as subsidiary means for the determination of rules of law."

This provision does not purport to lay down the sources of international law as such, but merely to guide the court as to where to find the law to apply to decide disputes that it hears. We now proceed to examine each of these sources in turn, though in a slightly different order.[8]

6. Underscoring its exceptional nature, the most prominent direct application of public international law to natural persons in recent years has been by way of prosecutions before the International Criminal Court and the tribunals established by UN Security Council resolutions after the Yugoslavia and Rwanda conflicts for war crimes, crimes against humanity and genocide under the instruments by which they were established.
7. The ICJ at The Hague is a permanent judicial body for the settlement of disputes between States. As its Statute is annexed to the UN Charter, all members of the UN are automatically parties to it. The Court has 15 judges representative of the "main forms of civilization" and principal legal systems of the world. Some multilateral treaties contain special dispute procedure clauses, notably the United Nations Convention on the Law of the Sea (UNCLOS), *infra*, fn. 11, contains in Part XV (Articles 279–299) an elaborate compulsory dispute settlement mechanism. Other permanent bodies besides the ICJ exist for settling international disputes, for example UNCLOS is also the vehicle by which the International Tribunal for the Law of the Sea (ITLOS) was established. The Statute of ITLOS forms Annex VI to UNCLOS.
8. Some commentators believe that the order of listing is significant and that the court should look for sources in that order. While to some degree this makes sense, for explanatory purposes it is more convenient to begin with custom. From time to time suggestions are made that modern developments have rendered this list incomplete, but the additional avenues not mentioned in Article 38 (acts of international organisations and so-called non-binding "soft law") always, when they produce results recognisable as law, do so directly or indirectly by way of one or other of custom and treaties. Some international organisations are authorised by the treaties that establish them to adopt resolutions

### (a) "international custom, as evidence of a general practice accepted as law"

This refers to the body of international law rules having their source in the customary practice of States. Not all practices which States customarily observe, however, are required by international law – the reason for them may be no more than courtesy, or the relevant State's own self-interest. To be a rule of customary international law, the practice of States must meet two requirements:

- constant and uniform usage practised by States (State practice for short); and
- recognition by them that this practice is the result of a rule of law or legal obligation. This psychological element is called *opinio juris sive necessitatis*, usually abbreviated simply to *opinio juris*.[9]

Some rules of custom have evolved over centuries of practice, such as those regulating diplomatic immunity. It is, however, possible for a permissive rule (i.e. a State may do X) to be established by the practice of just a few States over a short period if other States acquiesce in it, as occurred at the beginning of the space age when States began to send satellites into orbit passing over other States' territories. Until then a State's sovereignty had been thought to extend indefinitely upwards from the earth above its territory, but henceforth it was confined to airspace only. On the other hand, a mandatory rule (i.e. a State must (not) do Y) requires the widespread practice of States acknowledging its existence, especially by those States particularly affected – though it need not be completely uniform (since States do after all sometimes breach international law).

One of the obscurities about rules of customary international law is that it is often difficult to know whether, and if so when, they have been modified by the subsequent practice of States. A new customary rule often begins life by way of an apparent breach of the old one that goes largely unchallenged. Thus, the various claims made by States from the 1960s onwards to extended fisheries and pollution jurisdiction beyond the territorial sea were, on their face, contrary to the customary rule codified in the 1958 Convention on the High Seas, that "[t]he high seas being open to all nations, no State may validly purport to subject any part of them to its sovereignty".[10] Since not all States accepted the validity of such

automatically binding on all members, for example certain decisions of the UN Security Council under Article 25 of the UN Charter. Resolutions of international organisations can also be evidence of rules of customary international law if supported by most States with few or none voting against. This is so especially where the resolution itself asserts the existence of a particular rule of international law, e.g. the UN General Assembly's Declaration on Principles of International Law Concerning Friendly Relations and Co-operation Among States (UN General Assembly Resolution 2625/XXV of 24 October 1970). Similarly, soft-law instruments, typically phrased in the form "States should ..." rather than "States shall ..." to avoid being binding as treaties, may harden into custom.

9. State practice and expressions of *opinio juris* can take many forms, e.g. national legislation, parliamentary or other policy statements, press releases, official government publications, diplomatic correspondence and protests, statements in international organisations and arguments before international courts and tribunals, comments by governments on draft international treaties, decisions by States' domestic courts. See D J Harris, *Cases and Materials on International Law* (5th ed) (London: Sweet & Maxwell, 2004) at p. 23 and sources there cited.
10. Convention on the High Seas (Geneva, 29 April 1958); 450 United Nations Treaty Series (hereinafter UNTS) 11, Article 2. Most treaties are registered with the UN Secretariat under Article 102 of the UN Charter and are then published in the UNTS, whose online version is available, with some time lag, on the UN Treaty Section website *http://untreaty.un.org*.

claims, there ensued a period of chaos in the law of the sea, putting an end to which was one of the aims of the Third United Nations Conference on the Law of the Sea. This conference produced the 1982 United Nations Convention on the Law of the Sea (UNCLOS),[11] the central instrument of the modern law of the sea since its entry into force on 16 November 1994.

### (b) Treaties

UNCLOS is a treaty. Treaties come under a variety of formal titles (apart from "treaty" itself, "convention" as in UNCLOS, "protocol", "covenant", "agreement", "exchange of letters" are often encountered), but their essence is that they are agreements between States or international organisations intended by their parties to be binding in international law. They are a versatile instrument. Bilateral treaties (those concluded between two States) serve some of the same functions as contracts under national law, particularly where they are for a specific purpose. By contrast, multilateral treaties – those laying down general rules of conduct for all States parties – are to some degree comparable to legislation in national law, for instance the 1944 Chicago Convention on International Civil Aviation,[12] and the many shipping-related conventions negotiated under the aegis of the IMO.[13] The most important distinction from legislation, however, is that a treaty is only ever binding on those States which are parties to it.[14]

The last sentence does, however, require a qualification, for treaties can themselves be a source of customary international law. If many States are parties to a multilateral treaty containing a certain rule, and there is no practice of other States inconsistent with that rule, then the treaty may be evidence of a rule of custom. Thus over time treaties exert what Mendelson has called a "gravitational pull" on the pre-existing custom, so that even non-parties become bound – not by the treaty as such, but by some or all of the substantive rules within it.[15] Some multilateral treaties are expressed to codify existing rules of international law in a given field, the 1958 Convention on the High Seas being a prominent example.[16]

As between parties to a treaty, its provisions prevail over rules of customary international law. Thus, by entering into treaties, States modify their mutual rights and obligations under custom. Because of the relative certainty and ease of reference they offer as a source of law by comparison with custom, treaties have

11. United Nations Convention on the Law of the Sea (Montego Bay, 10 December 1982); 1833 UNTS 3.
12. 15 UNTS 295.
13. An incomplete list of these is given *infra* at pp. 318–319.
14. This rule, sometimes called the *pacta tertiis* principle after the Latin maxim *Pacta tertiis nec nocent nec prosunt* (treaties neither harm nor favour third parties) is found in Article 34 of the 1969 Vienna Convention on the Law of Treaties, 1155 UNTS 331, and, like most of that Convention, represents a codification of the pre-existing customary law regarding treaties.
15. M H Mendelson, "Fragmentation of the law of the sea" (1988) 12 *Marine Policy* 192 at p. 199. Some treaty provisions, such as those relating to the settlement of disputes arising under the treaty, can never enter the realm of custom. The general rule as expressed by the ICJ in the *North Sea Continental Shelf* case (*Federal Republic of Germany/Denmark; Federal Republic of Germany/Netherlands*), ICJ Reports 1969, p. 3 at pp. 41–42 (paragraph 72) is that only those provisions can do so which are "of fundamentally norm-creating character" capable of forming the basis of a general rule of law.
16. *Supra*, fn. 10; see both paragraphs of the preamble.

become the major vehicle for international cooperation. Developed States are commonly party to hundreds of treaties affecting all areas of governmental activity.

### (c) General principles of law recognised by civilised nations

Cases can highlight gaps in the existing customary and conventional (treaty) law. These can be filled by using general principles of law common to most or all major legal systems, in order to avoid the undesirable situation of the court being unable to decide a case; some of them, such as good faith, have long histories dating back to Roman law.

### (d) Judicial decisions and academic writings

As there is no doctrine of precedent in international law,[17] decisions of international courts and tribunals are binding only on the parties to the actual dispute. (Nor does international law impose judicial settlement and arbitration *a priori* as methods of settling disputes – the basic obligation is no more than that they be settled peacefully.[18]) Even so, they are influential as a subsidiary means for determination of rules of international law, especially ICJ judgments.

Academic writings can also be evidence of a rule of international law, if the writer is eminent, and the study is based on a comprehensive and impartial examination of State practice. Also significant in this regard, and frequently cited by the ICJ in its judgments, are reports of the International Law Commission (ILC), a body of eminent international lawyers established by the UN General Assembly in 1947 to promote the codification and progressive development of international law.[19]

## 3. MARITIME ZONES RELEVANT TO SHIPPING

In this work, concentrating as it does on navigation, it is not necessary to consider the full panoply of maritime zones known to the contemporary law of the sea, as most of the modern ones were created in order to deal with problems of the exploitation of oceanic resources. The following introduction is based on the two "traditional" zones only, expanded where appropriate to take into account developments in the twentieth century.

17. This is the effect of the provision in Article 59 of the ICJ Statute, to which this subparagraph 38(1)(d) is expressed to be subject, that "The decision of the court has no binding force except between the parties and in respect of that particular case".
18. UN Charter, Article 2(3). Judicial settlement and arbitration are merely two of a non-exhaustive list of means offered by Article 33(1) of the UN Charter. The jurisdiction of international courts and tribunals is therefore ultimately always based on the consent of the disputing parties – there is no way of compelling a non-consenting State to appear. So-called "compulsory" jurisdiction can only be based on a treaty into which there is no compulsion to enter, so that the obligation to submit to a particular body's jurisdiction is itself always ultimately voluntarily undertaken.
19. See Article 13(1) of the UN Charter, which gave this role to the General Assembly itself, and General Assembly Resolution 174/II of 21 November 1947, by which the ILC was created and to which its Statute is annexed.

### (a) The two "traditional" maritime zones

The traditional zones are (i) a narrow belt of water running along the coast, known as the territorial sea, beyond which are (ii) the high seas. The territorial sea is in places supplemented by internal waters (under the full sovereignty of the coastal State, and treated as equivalent to land) lying landward of the baselines from which the breadth of the territorial sea is measured. The territorial sea is also under the coastal State's sovereignty, but subject to the right of innocent passage for foreign ships, a concept considered further below. The high seas were defined negatively as an area beyond the territorial sea, in which no claim to sovereignty or jurisdiction by any State was permitted.[20] Freedom of navigation was thus guaranteed on the high seas, as well as certain other well recognised freedoms such as fishing. This is not to say that States could act as they pleased on the high seas, for that would have been anarchy; rather, States had to exercise their freedoms with reasonable regard for the like exercise of freedoms by other States.[21] Since the advent of the EEZ the high seas are much reduced in area, and the seabed is subject to changed rules, but the outlines of the regime affecting the surface and water column – which is all we are interested in for shipping purposes – are largely left unaltered by UNCLOS. Instead of the four freedoms in the 1958 Convention (navigation, fishing, laying of cables and pipelines, and overflight) there are now six; but this does not mean the high seas are becoming freer, the two new ones were implicit before but are expressly gratified (construction of artificial islands and other installations permitted under international law, subject to Part VI, and scientific research, subject to Parts VI and XIII). The EEZ, as explained below, can by virtue of Article 58 also be treated as equivalent to the high seas for navigational purposes.

In the pre-UNCLOS era the major controversies were over the maximum permissible breadth of the territorial sea and the use of straight baselines from which that breadth is measured to enclose areas of ocean as internal waters. The major maritime powers of the day – the United Kingdom (UK), United States (US), Germany, Japan, France – maintained that the territorial sea was three nautical miles (nm),[22] but even then there were widely tolerated regional departures from this practice, such as 4 nm in Scandinavia and 6 nm in many parts of the Mediterranean. The twentieth century saw the making of claims by increasingly numerous States to a territorial sea of 12 nm, mainly because of security and fisheries concerns, and in the 1940s and 1950s a number of mostly Latin American States made claims to a territorial sea of 200 nm. Reaching agreement on the maximum breadth was one of the aims of the 1930 League of Nations Conference on the Codification of International Law, but this effort ended in failure. Attempts to reach a compromise of a six-mile territorial sea plus a further six miles of exclusive coastal State fishery jurisdiction came close to success at the First (1958) and Second (1960) UN Conferences on the Law of the Sea, but agreement remained elusive. All that the ILC could conclude in the commentary to its draft articles prepared for the 1958 conference was that the limit was certainly no more than 12 nm, but might be less.[23]

20. *Supra*, fn. 10. This provision is now reproduced in Article 89 of UNCLOS.
21. The "reasonable regard" standard was codified in Article 2(2) of the High Seas Convention, *supra*, fn. 10, but replaced by the slightly more rigorous "due regard" in UNCLOS, Article 87(2).
22. A nautical mile equals exactly 1852 metres and is a close approximation to one minute of latitude anywhere on the earth's surface and one minute of longitude at the equator.
23. *Report of the International Law Commission covering the work of its eighth session, 23 April–4 July 1956* (UN doc A/3159), reprinted in *Yearbook of the International Law Commission 1956*, Vol. II (New York: United Nations, 1957), 253 at p. 265.

UNCLOS, Article 3, has now settled the maximum breadth of the territorial sea at 12 nm. The rules on straight baselines and bay-closing lines, however (Articles 7–10), though admittedly putting some discipline on the drawing of baselines as a way of expanding the area under a coastal State's sovereignty, still leave quite some leeway for their manipulation to this end. Only the US through its Freedom of Navigation programme dating from the 1970s systematically challenges baselines it believes to have been improperly drawn, by a combination of diplomatic protest and directing the US Navy to exercise navigational rights in the area concerned without seeking prior permission from the relevant coastal State. By contrast, other States tend to protest at only those baselines that directly affect the extent of their own maritime zones, i.e. those of their near neighbours, and take interest in the baselines of more distant States only if they impinge on some specific navigational interest.[24]

Why was the breadth of the territorial sea so controversial? The long insistence by maritime States on 3 nm was fuelled by the fear that certain narrow straits essential for military and commercial communication would lose the high seas corridor down their middle if a broader territorial sea were to become the norm. Innocent passage was not an acceptable substitute because it could be suspended by the coastal State.[25] Ultimately they accepted 12 nm as the maximum only in return for new a regime of transit passage through straits used for international navigation that forms Part III (Articles 34–45) of UNCLOS.[26] This regime incorporates freedom of navigation (subject to the requirement that the transit be "continuous and expeditious") into a new concept of non-suspendable transit passage in those straits, which the littoral State may not hamper, superimposed on the territorial sea status of the strait.[27]

### (b) New maritime zones in the modern law of the sea

Several more zones now exist, but other than the first in the list below are of limited relevance to shipping:

(1) *Archipelagic waters*, added by Part IV (Articles 46–54) of UNCLOS. This concept recognises the special interest of States such as Indonesia and the Philippines, whose territory consists of many islands, in the waters within the archipelago previously regarded as high seas. They wished to be permitted to draw baselines around the archipelago, but this would have transformed the waters within into internal waters. The compromise solution is for archipelagic

24. See J R V Prescott, "Straight Baselines: Theory and Practice", in E D Brown & R R Churchill (eds), *The UN Convention on the Law of the Sea: Impact and Implementation* (Honolulu: Law of the Sea Institute, 1987), p. 288, for a pessimistic account of this state of affairs, concluding that inaction by other States has amounted to their acquiescence in the capture of large areas of ocean to which UNCLOS does not entitle the state concerned. Seafarers would certainly be well advised to proceed on the presumption that baselines are valid or have become validated in this way, absent an assurance from the flag State of the ship that it has protested against the baseline in timely fashion – and even this is no guarantee against an incident occurring that will result in at best delay and at worst the ship's arrest.
25. Convention on the Territorial Sea and Contiguous Zone (Geneva, 29 April 1958), 516 UNTS 205, Article 16(3); see now UNCLOS, Article 25(3).
26. In the late 1960s the US circulated to other States a list of 116 straits between 6 nm and 24 nm wide at their narrowest point, which would thus become completely overlapped by territorial sea. Many of these are of little or no navigational importance, but several are crucial for international commerce: the Straits of Dover, Gibraltar, Malacca, Singapore, Bab-el-Mandab at the southern end of the Red Sea and Hormuz at the mouth of the Persian Gulf.
27. UNCLOS, Article 38(1) and (2).

States (defined in Article 46) to have such baselines,[28] but within them the waters – known as archipelagic waters – have a status more akin to the territorial sea, including the rules on innocent passage, while the routes hitherto used for transit through the archipelago now have a special regime of archipelagic sea lanes passage (Article 53) modelled on transit passage through international straits.[29]

(2) *The contiguous zone.* From the early twentieth century many States claimed not full territorial sea rights but jurisdiction over certain matters in a zone adjacent to and seaward of the territorial sea. Article 24 of the 1958 Convention on the Territorial Sea and Contiguous Zone permitted any State claiming a territorial sea of less than 12 nm to exercise out to 12 nm jurisdiction to prevent and punish infringements of its customs, fiscal, immigration and sanitary (i.e. animal and plant quarantine) laws in its territorial sea or any land or water landward of it.[30] Article 33 of UNCLOS retains the 1958 regime but extends the outer limit of the contiguous zone to 24 nm from the baselines.

(3) *The exclusive economic zone (EEZ).* This is another of the compromises in UNCLOS, added by Part V (Articles 55–75). Beyond the territorial sea, up to a maximum of 200 nm from the baselines from which the breadth of the territorial sea is measured,[31] the coastal State may claim sovereign rights over the exploration and exploitation, conservation and management of the living and non-living resources, jurisdiction over artificial islands, protection of the marine environment (including against pollution) and certain other matters.[32] In this zone the coastal State in exercising its rights and duties must have "due regard to the rights and duties of other States" (Article 56(2)), which by Article 58(1) include the freedoms of navigation and overflight as well as laying cables and pipelines and "other internationally lawful uses of the sea related to these freedoms, such as those associated with the operation of ships ...". Article 58(2) imports into the EEZ the high seas rules (other than on resources) "in so far as they are not incompatible with this Part". The net result is that for almost all navigational purposes, although the EEZ is no longer part of the high seas,[33] it can still be treated as though it were. Hence the frequency of reference in navigational circles to "international waters", a term unknown to the law of the sea, but useful nonetheless, as it refers to the area seaward of the territorial sea (i.e. an amalgam of the EEZ and the high seas).

(4) *The continental shelf.* Dating from the mid-twentieth century,[34] this zone, in which the coastal State has sovereign rights over mineral resources and sedentary

28. The UK as well as other island States such as Japan and New Zealand, though they meet the definition of archipelagic States in Article 46 of UNCLOS, are not permitted to draw archipelagic baselines because they do not satisfy one of the conditions in Article 47 for doing so: that between 10% and 50% of the area enclosed by baselines be land. In other words, they have too much land.
29. For the IMO's role in approving the axis lines to these sea lanes, see pp. 321–322.
30. Note that this is enforcement rather than legislative jurisdiction, so making this a buffer zone in which the laws themselves do not apply, in the sense that acts within the contiguous zone as opposed to the territorial sea cannot themselves attract punishment.
31. Thus if the State has a 12 nm territorial sea, the maximum breadth of its EEZ is 188 nm, not 200 nm.
32. See UNCLOS, Article 56(1).
33. UNCLOS, Articles 55 and 86.
34. See the Treaty between His Britannic Majesty and the President of Venezuela relating to the Submarine Areas of the Gulf of Paria (Caracas, 26 February 1942), 205 League of Nations Treaty Series (hereinafter LNTS) 122, and the Truman Proclamation (Proclamation No 2667, *Concerning the Policy of the United States with respect to the Natural Resources of the Subsoil and Sea Bed of the Continental Shelf*, (1945) 10 *Federal Register* 12303).

living species (those which at the harvestable stage of their life cycle are unable to move except in constant physical contact with the seabed or subsoil), for the first time introduced a vertical separation into the law of the sea, as the waters above retained their high seas status, as confirmed by Article 3 of the 1958 Continental Shelf Convention.[35] The seaward extent of the continental shelf was originally based on the 200-metre isobath (an imaginary line joining points of equal water depth) or beyond to the maximum exploitable water depth, but this provoked fears that the progress of technology would eventually result in the whole ocean becoming exploitable and thus, inequitably, falling under the jurisdiction of the nearest coastal State. In UNCLOS Article 76 the outer limit has therefore been changed to an approximation of the geologically inexact boundary between continental crust and oceanic crust[36] but, reflecting the introduction meanwhile of the EEZ, in any event to a minimum of 200 nm from the baselines.[37]

(5) *The seabed beyond national jurisdiction (i.e. beyond the continental shelf).* An internationalised deep seabed mining regime exists here under Part XI of UNCLOS (Articles 133–191), administered by the International Seabed Authority.[38]

The main remaining task is for States to delimit their overlapping entitlements to maritime zones and establish the outer limit of the continental shelf where it extends beyond 200 nm, both matters being beyond the scope of this chapter.

## 4. COASTAL AND FLAG STATE RIGHTS OVER SHIPPING IN THE MAIN MARITIME ZONES

The main tension in the shipping world is between coastal or port States on the one hand and flag States on the other, particularly as regards pollution. The measures favoured by coastal States to minimise the risk of pollution to their coastlines may well have adverse economic consequences for shipping. Let us now examine the principal zones in turn.

### (a) Internal waters (including ports)

A State's ports are part of its internal waters, since Article 11 of UNCLOS provides that "[f]or the purposes of delimiting the territorial sea, the outermost permanent harbour works which form an integral part of the harbour system are regarded as forming part of the coast". The clear position is that foreign ships

35. Convention on the Continental Shelf (Geneva, 29 April 1958), 499 UNTS 311, Article 3. See now UNCLOS, Article 78.
36. Despite this zone in fact thereby coming to encompass the entire continental margin (shelf, slope and rise) rather than just the shelf, it is still known by its old name.
37. Notwithstanding the general irrelevance of this zone to shipping – after all, it is only to be expected that shipping interests would actively seek to avoid coming into contact with the seabed – it is curious that the new rules in the Nairobi International Convention on the Removal of Wrecks (Nairobi, 18 May 2007; IMO doc LEG/CONF.16/19 (23 May 2007)) that apply to the EEZ have not been extended to the continental shelf, inasmuch as wrecks settle on the seabed rather than remaining suspended in the water column.
38. Contrary to the expectations held at the time UNCLOS was under negotiation, deep seabed mining looks set to remain uneconomic for some time, whereas genetic resources, from which valuable chemical compounds usable in pharmaceuticals may be extracted, have a ready market. Controversy is therefore building over whether non-mineral resources are, as Articles 133(a), 136 and 137 of UNCLOS together imply, excluded from the regime and thus still subject to the high seas rules.

have no general right to enter internal waters,[39] although there is a customary exception for ships in distress, preserved by the preambular paragraph of UNCLOS "affirming that matters not regulated by this Convention continue to be governed by the rules and principles of general international law". This gives the port (coastal) State the upper hand, since if it can withhold permission to enter, then *a fortiori* it can grant permission on whatever conditions it chooses. This, however, is only the default position in the law of the sea. A right of ships flagged to State A to enter the ports of State B may be contained in a treaty between those States. Such provisions were typically included in the many bilateral "friendship commerce and navigation" treaties common in the late nineteenth and early twentieth centuries, and some multilateral treaties also accord a right to parties to enter each other's ports, such as the 1923 Statute on the International Regime of Maritime Ports,[40] of which Article 2 requires, *inter alia*, that each party must allow all other parties' ships into its ports on the same terms as its own ships. Note also that in the General Agreement on Tariffs and Trade,[41] by which all members of the World Trade Organization are bound, Article V:2 on freedom of transit may prevent closure of ports to a ship wanting to unload goods destined for a third State. A claim of breach of this provision was brought by the European Community against Chile in the WTO in 2000, but proceedings have been suspended since 2001.[42]

A ship voluntarily in port subjects itself to the jurisdiction of the port State. Because its presence is only temporary, often there will be practical reasons for the port State to refrain from exercising this jurisdiction, but it retains the right to do so.[43]

### (b) The territorial sea

The principal qualification of a coastal State's sovereignty over the territorial sea is that foreign ships have a right of innocent passage.[44] UNCLOS, Article 18, defines this as "continuous and expeditious" navigation through the territorial sea to or from the internal waters or a port of a coastal State, or a traverse without entering its internal waters. Stopping and anchoring are not allowed, except as incidental to ordinary navigation or necessary due to *force majeure*, distress or in order to render assistance to persons, ships or aircraft in danger or distress.

39. A V Lowe, "The Right of Entry into Maritime Ports in International Law" (1977) 14 *San Diego Law Review* 597 at p. 621; L de La Fayette, "Access to Ports in International Law" (1996) 11 *International Journal of Marine and Coastal Law* 1 at p. 12.
40. Part of the 1923 Convention and Statute on the International Régime of Maritime Ports (Geneva, 9 December 1923), 58 LNTS 285.
41. Since 1995 GATT has been maintained in force among Members of the World Trade Organization pursuant to the Agreement Establishing the World Trade Organization (Marrakesh, 15 April 1994), 1867 UNTS 3, Article II (2) and (4).
42. See WTO doc WT/DS193/3 (6 April 2001), "Chile – Measures Affecting the Transit and Importation of Swordfish: Arrangement between the European Communities and Chile" and A Serdy, "See You in Port: Australia and New Zealand as Third Parties in the Dispute between Chile and the European Community over Chile's Denial of Port Access to Spanish Vessels Fishing for Swordfish on the High Seas" (2002) 3 *Melbourne Journal of International Law* 79 at p. 87.
43. D J Harris, *Cases and Materials on International Law* (5th ed) at p. 432 indicates that this position is taken by States having a common law heritage, while those with civil law systems tend to treat the non-exercise of jurisdiction as *opinio juris* in support of the proposition, contrary to what is maintained here, that no such jurisdiction in fact exists.
44. UNCLOS, *supra*, fn. 11, Article 17.

In the territorial sea the main duties of the coastal State are not to hamper innocent passage and to publicise any danger to navigation of which it knows.[45] It may not levy any toll for passage,[46] but may suspend innocent passage for weapons exercises or other essential security reason on due advance publicity.[47]

UNCLOS, Article 19, elaborates to a much greater degree than the equivalent 1958 Convention[48] the activities which render passage no longer innocent if the ship engages in them. These comprise the threat or use of force against the coastal State's sovereignty or territorial integrity,[49] exercise or practice of weapons of any kind,[50] collection of information prejudicial to the security of the coastal State,[51] any act of propaganda aimed at the coastal State's defence or security,[52] the launching or taking on board of any aircraft or military device,[53] the loading or unloading of any commodity, currency or person contrary to the coastal State's laws,[54] any act of wilful and serious pollution,[55] fishing activity,[56] research or survey activities,[57] interference with communications,[58] or any other activity not directly related to passage.[59] The coastal State may prevent passage which is not innocent.[60]

The only other significant qualification is that coastal States may not prescribe their own conditions for the construction, design, manning and equipment of ships in the territorial sea, but can instead only enact and enforce the regulations in "generally accepted international rules or standards".[61] It will readily be seen that this is necessary if the right of innocent passage is to be at all meaningful, since otherwise ships would be subject to several different and possibly contradictory design rules in the course of a single voyage and would not be in a position to comply with all of them.

In a judgment due to be delivered in 2008 but not yet available when this book went to press,[62] the European Court of Justice will rule whether Directive 2005/35/EC of the European Parliament and Council on Ship-Source Pollution, by which pollution caused by "serious negligence" must attract criminal sanctions, is contrary to UNCLOS. Such a possibility arises since by Article 19(2)(h) only an act of "serious and wilful" pollution would deprive a passage of its innocence, hence pollution caused by serious negligence, yet not wilful, remains innocent. The industry coalition's case is that the mere presence of these laws on Member

45. UNCLOS, Article 24(1) and (2) respectively.
46. *Ibid.*, Article 26(1).
47. *Ibid.*, Article 25(3).
48. *Supra*, fn. 25.
49. UNCLOS, *supra*, fn. 11, Article 19(2)(a).
50. *Ibid.*, Article 19(2)(b).
51. *Ibid.*, Article 19(2)(c).
52. *Ibid.*, Article 19(2)(d).
53. *Ibid.*, Article 19(2)(e) and (f).
54. *Ibid.*, Article 19(2)(g).
55. *Ibid.*, Article 19(2)(h).
56. *Ibid.*, Article 19(2)(i).
57. *Ibid.*, Article 19(2)(j).
58. *Ibid.*, Article 19(2)(k).
59. *Ibid.*, Article 19(2)(l). Although the aim of this list is sometimes said to have been to enhance legal certainty by enumerating exhaustively what makes passage non-innocent, this last catch-all provision has the effect of undermining that aim.
60. *Ibid.*, Article 25(1).
61. *Ibid.*, Article 21(2).
62. Case C-308/06, *R (INTERTANKO and Ors) v Secretary of State for Transport.*

States' statute books, whether or not they are enforced, has the effect of hampering innocent passage contrary to UNCLOS Article 24(1) (though note that this provision speaks of the "application" of coastal State regulations). The prior opinion of Advocate-General Kokott took the view that, because this as a directive did not govern shipping of its own force but needed to be transposed into the national law of the Member States, it would be for the Member States to ensure that the transposed laws remained in conformity with UNCLOS. She also suggested, somewhat curiously, that in order to bring this about, "serious negligence" might need to be equated with recklessness outside the territorial sea (as well as in international straits) but could be given a broader interpretation within it.[63] If the Court adopts this reasoning, the issue will thus not have been definitively disposed of, but may resurface through challenges to the implementing laws of one or more Member States.

### (c) The high seas and the nationality of ships

The most important regulatory matter on the high seas pertains to the nationality of ships. The basic rule is set out in Article 92 of UNCLOS, identical (but for a cross-reference) to Article 6 of the 1958 High Seas Convention:

> "Article 92 – Status of ships
> 1. Ships shall sail under the flag of one State only and, save in exceptional cases expressly provided for in international treaties or in this Convention, shall be subject to its exclusive jurisdiction on the high seas. A ship may not change its flag during a voyage or while in a port of call, save in the case of a real transfer of ownership or change of registry.
> 2. A ship which sails under the flags of two or more States, using them according to convenience, may not claim any of the nationalities in question with respect to any other State, and may be assimilated to a ship without nationality."

There are two frequently encountered misconceptions as to the high seas regime. The first is that high seas freedoms and exclusivity of flag State jurisdiction are absolute. This is not so – and not merely because there are several exceptions to exclusivity considered below, so that primacy rather than exclusivity for the flag State gives a truer picture of the actual position. Flag State jurisdiction should rather be seen as a way of preventing a legal vacuum on the high seas, given that no State has the competence to regulate activities there on a spatial basis. Seen in this light, allocating primacy of jurisdiction to the flag State, irrespective of the States of nationality of the owners and the various other interests connected with the ship – crew, cargo, insurers – ensures that the ship presents a single legal "face" to the outside world.

Secondly, the provision that ships must "sail under the flag of one State only" does not mean that ships can have only a single nationality at any given time.[64] The possibility of multiple nationality is a direct consequence of UNCLOS, Article 91:

63. Opinion of Advocate-General Kokott delivered on 20 November 2007 in Case C-308/06 (see previous fn.), available at *http://curia.europa.eu*, at paras 102–138 and 144.
64. *Contra* the otherwise highly recommended D Anderson, "Freedoms of the High Seas in the Modern Law of the Sea" in D Freestone, R Barnes and D Ong (eds), *The Law of the Sea: Progress and Prospects* (Oxford: OUP, 2006), 327 at p. 333 ("dual nationality is permissible in the case of individuals but not ships").

"Article 91 – Nationality of ships

1. Every State shall fix the conditions for the grant of its nationality to ships, for the registration of ships in its territory, and for the right to fly its flag. Ships have the nationality of the State whose flag they are entitled to fly. There must exist a genuine link between the State and the ship.

2. Every State shall issue to ships to which it has granted the right to fly its flag documents to that effect."

Since States are free to grant their nationality or the right to fly their flag on whatever basis they choose, provided there is a genuine link (often not observed) between ship and State, it follows that inevitably States will do so on different bases and that there will thus be instances in which a ship satisfies distinct nationality criteria of two or more States simultaneously.[65] While from a policy prospective there is much to be said for the practice of many States that refuse to register a ship without proof that the previous flag State has deleted it from its own registry, there is no legal requirement underpinning this.

The "genuine link" wording is taken from Article 5 of the High Seas Convention,[66] which in turn was inspired by the ICJ decision in the *Nottebohm Case*,[67] where the facts concerned an individual with, at least on one view, multiple nationalities. Just as such an individual can only present one passport when entering a State, and thereafter that State can insist on treating him or her as a national of the issuing State and no other, a ship must elect one of its nationalities under which to undertake any given voyage; the penalty for using more than one flag is that it cannot claim any of the relevant nationalities and may be treated as though it were stateless.[68]

The "genuine link" requirement is often ignored, assisted by the 1960 Advisory Opinion[69] sought by IMCO (as it then was, see *infra*, fn. 89) on the meaning of the "largest ship-owning nations" in Article 28(a) of the 1948 Convention, which interpreted it to mean those with the largest registered tonnage, irrespective of the presence or absence of such a link. This has favoured the growth of flags of convenience or open registers, maintained by States which require little or no such link and often lack the personnel and administrative infrastructure necessary in order to enforce labour and safety standards on board the ships. Precisely for this reason, however, they are popular among shipowners anxious to minimise their costs, and it is generally these interests which shape the positions taken by their States of nationality at the IMO. This is no doubt also the reason why the 1986

65. The only way of avoiding this consequence would be if the granting of nationality to a ship by one State automatically extinguished any other nationality, but this would reduce the Article 91 right to near-worthlessness, and is contradicted by the practice of some registries in allowing ships under demise charter to temporarily take a second flag and thus a second nationality that eclipses its first (which revives automatically at the end of the charter period, indicating that it has not been extinguished). See Chapter 2, p. 45.
66. *Supra*, fn. 10.
67. *Nottebohm Case* (*Liechtenstein v Guatemala*), Second Phase, ICJ Reports 1955, p.4 at 23 ("genuine connection").
68. *Churchill & Lowe*, *supra*, fn. 1, point out at p. 214 that, even where there is no flag State to complain of the exercise of jurisdiction over the ship on the high seas by any other State, the persons on board, and the owners of its cargo, still have legitimate interests that their States of nationality, which would normally have been eclipsed by the flag State, are able to protect. This passage should not, however, be read as implying that some other State, e.g. the State of nationality of the owner of the (deemed) stateless ship, then steps into the shoes of the flag State.
69. *Constitution of the Maritime Safety Committee of the Inter-Governmental Maritime Consultative Organisation*, ICJ Reports 1960, p.150.

United Nations Convention on Conditions for the Registration of Ships[70] fails to specify what constitutes a genuine link,[71] yet even so has received only 14 of the 40 ratifications and accessions accounting for 25% of world shipping tonnage it needs to enter into force,[72] and is now widely regarded as unlikely ever to do so. Note also that this Convention lays down the rule that a ship can only be on one State's register at a time.[73] This would not have been necessary had this been the position anyway under Article 5 of the 1958 High Seas Convention and its successor, Article 91 of UNCLOS.

### (d) Exceptions to exclusivity of flag State jurisdiction on the high seas

Article 110 of UNCLOS, little changed from Article 22 of the 1958 High Seas Convention, sets out a number of bases on which a warship of one State has a right of "visit" (boarding and inspection) over a ship flagged to another State.

"Article 110 – Right of visit

1. Except where acts of interference derive from powers conferred by treaty, a warship which encounters on the high seas a foreign ship, other than a ship entitled to complete immunity in accordance with articles 95 and 96, is not justified in boarding it unless there is reasonable ground for suspecting that:
   (a) the ship is engaged in piracy;
   (b) the ship is engaged in the slave trade;
   (c) the ship is engaged in unauthorized broadcasting and the flag State of the warship has jurisdiction under article 109;
   (d) the ship is without nationality; or
   (e) though flying a foreign flag or refusing to show its flag, the ship is, in reality, of the same nationality as the warship.
2. In the cases provided for in paragraph 1, the warship may proceed to verify the ship's right to fly its flag. To this end, it may send a boat under the command of an officer to the suspected ship. If suspicion remains after the documents have been checked, it may proceed to a further examination on board the ship, which must be carried out with all possible consideration.
3. If the suspicions prove to be unfounded, and provided that the ship boarded has not committed any act justifying them, it shall be compensated for any loss or damage that may have been sustained.
4. These provisions apply *mutatis mutandis* to military aircraft.
5. These provisions also apply to any other duly authorized ships or aircraft clearly marked and identifiable as being on government service."

As is seen from the foregoing, the bases fall into two classes:

(i) where there is reasonable ground for suspecting the ship is engaged in a specified unlawful activity (piracy, slave trading or unauthorised broadcasting);

(ii) the ship is either stateless or actually of the same nationality as the warship, despite either failing to fly or refusing to show its flag. If the suspicions

70. Geneva, 7 February 1986; UN doc TD/RS/CONF/23 (13 March 1986).
71. By Article 7, a flag State need only either require in its laws and regulations for the ownership of ships flying its flag such level of participation by itself or its nationals as is sufficient to permit it to exercise effectively its jurisdiction and control over those ships (see Article 8(1) and (2)), or require a "satisfactory part" of the officers and crew of ships flying its flag to be nationals or persons domiciled or lawfully in permanent residence in that State (Article 9(1)), or both.
72. *Ibid.*, Article 19(1); the tonnage is to be calculated in accordance with the figures given in Annex III.
73. *Ibid.*, Article 4(4), which provides also for certain exceptions.

prove unfounded, however, and the ship boarded did nothing to justify them, it must be compensated for any loss or damage sustained.

A second exception is "hot pursuit" of a fleeing ship from one of the coastal State's maritime zones where it is suspected of having committed a relevant offence. That is, fisheries offences and others falling under the jurisdiction of the coastal State in the EEZ may be commenced from that zone; offences against customs, fiscal, immigration and sanitary laws may be commenced in the contiguous zone (though the offences must have taken place within or landward of the territorial sea[74]); pursuit for any other offences must be commenced in the territorial sea. The conditions for valid commencement and maintenance of such a pursuit are to be found in Article 111 of UNCLOS, also little changed from Article 23 of the High Seas Convention.

Note also that the opening words of UNCLOS Article 110(1) above preserve the right of visit where a separate treaty basis for it exists. The US under the Proliferation Security Initiative has concluded a number of treaties with prominent flag States such as Panama and Liberia by which such visits may occur.[75] The most prominent example of such a treaty provision is Article 21 of the 1995 UN Fish Stocks Agreement,[76] which has the effect of advance consent by its parties to boarding and inspection of their fishing vessels by any State that is a member of a regional fisheries management organisation or arrangement, whether or not the flag State is itself a member.

More recently, the IMO has adopted a 2005 Protocol[77] (not yet in force) amending its 1988 Convention for the Suppression of Unlawful Acts against the Safety of Navigation[78] to cover carriage of weapons of mass destruction at sea. This inserts new Article 8*bis* on cooperation and procedures where a State Party desires to board a ship flying the flag of another party on reasonable suspicion that the ship or a person on board is, has been or is about to be involved in committing any of the offences in the revised Article 3[79] and new Articles 3*bis*,[80] 3*ter*[81] and 3*quater*.[82] Article 3*bis* prohibits a person from using against or on a ship or discharging from a ship any explosive, radioactive material or biological, chemical or nuclear weapon, using a ship in a manner that causes death or serious injury, transporting any explosive or radioactive material knowing that it is intended to cause death or serious injury, or committing any of a number of ancillary offences with intent to intimidate a population or to compel a government or international organisation to do or refrain from doing any act.

74. See *supra*, fn. 30.
75. S Kaye, "Freedom of Navigation in a Post 9/11 World: Security and Creeping Jurisdiction", in Freestone *et al.*, *supra*, fn. 64, at p. 358 lists six flag States (Belize, Croatia, Cyprus, Liberia, the Marshall Islands and Panama) with which the US has such agreements, that with Liberia being reciprocal.
76. Agreement for the Implementation of the Provisions of the United Nations Convention on the Law of the Sea of 10 December 1982 Relating to the Conservation and Management of Straddling Fish Stocks and Highly Migratory Fish Stocks (New York, 4 December 1995), 2167 UNTS 3.
77. IMO doc LEG/CONF.15/21 (1 November 2005), Protocol of 2005 to the Convention for the Suppression of Unlawful Acts against the Safety of Maritime Navigation (London, 14 October 2005).
78. Rome, 10 March 1988, 1678 UNTS 221. This is the IMO's anti-terrorism Convention.
79. Amended by Article 4(1)–(4) of the 2005 Protocol.
80. Inserted by Article 4(5) of the 2005 Protocol.
81. Inserted by Article 4(6) of the 2005 Protocol.
82. Inserted by Article 4(7) of the 2005 Protocol.

The flag State's authorisation and cooperation are required before a boarding may take place. The Protocol offers two ways for a State Party to give this authorisation in advance, by making either of the following notifications to the IMO Secretary-General in his capacity as depositary of the 1988 Convention, who then circulates them to the other parties. One is a general authorisation to board and search a ship flying its flag, its cargo and persons on board, and to question those persons to determine whether a relevant offence, set forth in Article 3, 3*bis*, 3*ter* or 3*quater* has been, is being or is about to be, committed.[83] The second way is that the flag State's permission must still be sought through the usual channels, but is deemed to have been given if no response to the request to confirm nationality is received from the flag State within four hours of the request being made.[84] No use of force is allowed, unless either it becomes necessary to ensure the safety of the inspecting officials and other persons on board, or the officials are obstructed in the execution of authorised actions, provided it does not exceed the minimum degree of force which is necessary and reasonable in the circumstances.[85]

Despite the publicity given to the adoption of this Protocol as an anti-terrorism measure, however, States are evidently not treating becoming party to it with any priority. Although it requires only 12 ratifications or accessions to enter into force,[86] as at 31 March 2008, over two years after its adoption, a mere two States had taken this step according to the IMO's website.[87]

## 5. THE IMO AND ITS CONVENTIONS

### (a) Role of the IMO

The IMO is one of the 17 Specialised Agencies of the UN,[88] and is the only one whose headquarters are in the UK. Because both the UN and the IMO are created by treaties (the UN Charter and the Convention on the Intergovernmental Maritime Consultative Organization[89] respectively), and treaties are all of the same status, the IMO, like the other specialised agencies, is not formally subordinated to the UN, but rather has been "brought into relationship" with the UN by an agreement with it under Articles 57 and 63 of the UN Charter, and reports each year to the UN's Economic and Social Council on its activities.

As at 31 March 2008 the IMO had 167 Member States. The EC is not among them, because the 1948 Convention is only open to States.[90] The EC has none-

83. New Article 8*bis*(5)(e) of the 1988 Convention.
84. New Article 8*bis*(5)(d) of the 1988 Convention. This procedure may prove most useful to the inspecting State when it is night in the flag State, or on weekends and public holidays when the decision-makers are not at their desks.
85. New Article 8*bis*(9) of the 1988 Convention.
86. Article 18(1) of the 2005 Protocol.
87. See *www.imo.org/Conventions/mainframe.asp?topic_id=247* (accessed on 24 April 2008). The same website has equivalent information on the status of all other treaties negotiated in the IMO.
88. Some of the best known of the others are UNESCO, the World Health Organization, the Food and Agriculture Organization and the International Labour Organization. Another that is relevant to shipping is the World Meteorological Organization.
89. Geneva, 6 March 1948, 289 UNTS 3. As this name suggests, the IMO was originally known as IMCO. The change of name to IMO was included in one of the several subsequent amendments to this Convention, namely those adopted in 1975 (by Resolution A.358(IX)) (1276 UNTS 468), which entered into force in 1982.

theless expressed the view that the Convention should be amended to allow it to accede, but some of its Member States are thought to be unenthusiastic about such a proposal.[91]

Under its Convention, the IMO is responsible for both shipping and, since a 1977 amendment,[92] its effect on the marine environment. Its purposes and functions are enumerated in Articles 1 and 2 (originally 3) respectively, *viz*:

"Article 1
The purposes of the Organization are:

(a) To provide machinery for co-operation among Governments in the field of governmental regulation and practices relating to technical matters of all kinds affecting shipping engaged in international trade; to encourage and facilitate the general adoption of the highest practicable standards in matters concerning the maritime safety, efficiency of navigation and prevention and control of marine pollution from ships; and to deal with administrative and legal matters related to the purposes set out in this Article;
(b) To encourage the removal of discriminatory action and unnecessary restrictions by Governments affecting shipping engaged in international trade so as to promote the availability of shipping services to the commerce of the world without discrimination; assistance and encouragement given by a Government for the development of its national shipping and for purposes of security does not in itself constitute discrimination, provided that such assistance and encouragement is not based on measures designed to restrict the freedom of shipping of all flags to take part in international trade;
(c) To provide for the consideration by the Organization of matters concerning unfair restrictive practices by shipping concerns in accordance with Part II;
(d) To provide for the consideration by the Organization of any matters concerning shipping and the effect of shipping on the marine environment that may be referred to it by any organ or specialized agency of the United Nations;
(e) To provide for the exchange of information among Governments on matters under consideration by the Organization.

Article 2
In order to achieve the purposes set out in Part I [*i.e. Article 1*] the Organization shall:

(a) Subject to the provisions of Article 3, consider and make recommendations upon matters arising under Article 1 (a), (b) and (c) that may be remitted to it by Members, by any organ or specialized agency of the United Nations or by any other intergovernmental organization or upon matters referred to it under Article 1 (d);
(b) Provide for the drafting of conventions, agreements, or other suitable instruments, and recommend these to Governments and to intergovernmental organizations, and convene such conferences as may be necessary;

90. Articles 4 and 76. Article numbers here and henceforth are cited as those of the text of the Convention as it stands after entry into force of the last outstanding amendments in late 2008 (see *infra*, fn. 127), except where otherwise indicated.
91. See the 2001 White Paper, *European Transport Policy for 2010: time to decide*, COM(2001) 370 final, p. 98; and the 2006 Green Paper, *Towards a Future Maritime Policy for the Union: A European vision for the oceans and seas*, COM(2006) 275 final, p. 5. The UK's opposition was expressed in the Department for Transport's response to the 2006 Green Paper, *www.dft.gov.uk/pgr/shippingports/shipping/govresponseeeumaritimegreen* (accessed on 14 February 2008): "[T]he UK believes that the current arrangements for co-ordination and Community involvement are working and that an attempt to seek a wider Community role is likely to be counterproductive as it carries the risk that non-EU IMO actors will perceive the EU bloc as a threat to IMO's tradition of honest, open technical debate." Perhaps bowing to this sentiment, in the recent "Blue Paper", *An Integrated Maritime Policy for the European Union,* COM(2007) 575 final (10 October 2007) the only mention (at p. 13) is an anodyne one to "promot[ing] coordination of European interests in key international fora".
92. The amendments were adopted by Assembly Resolution A.400(X) of 17 November 1977, which entered into force in 1984: see 1380 UNTS 268, in particular the new text of Article 64 as compared with the original Article 45 of 1948.

(c) Provide machinery for consultation among Members and the exchange of information among Governments;
(d) Perform functions arising in connexion with paragraphs (a), (b) and (c) of the Article, in particular those assigned to it by or under international instruments relating to maritime matters and the effect of shipping on the marine environment;
(e) Facilitate as necessary, and in accordance with Part X, technical co-operation within the scope of the Organization."

Initially, the focus of the IMO's activity was on safety of navigation, but more recently it has also engaged in related matters such as prevention of pollution. In both capacities IMO is given a variety of roles in UNCLOS, where it is mentioned not by name but as the "competent international organization".

### (b) Structure of the IMO

By Article 12 of the 1948 Convention, the IMO consisted at first of an Assembly, a Council, a Maritime Safety Committee, such subsidiary organs as it "may at any time consider necessary" and a Secretariat. The 1975 amendments that included the name change also entrenched the Legal and Marine Environment Protection Committees in the structure, as did the 1977 amendments for the Technical Co-operation Committee.[93]

The Assembly consists of all the Member States[94] and meets in regular session every two years, with provision for extraordinary sessions to be convened on 60 days' notice.[95] Among its functions are to elect the Members to be represented on the Council,[96] to determine the budget and financial arrangements of the IMO and approve its accounts[97] and to recommend to Members for adoption regulations and guidelines (or amendments to these) concerning maritime safety, the prevention and control of marine pollution from ships and other matters concerning the effect of shipping on the marine environment which have been referred to it.[98]

The Council consists of 40 Members as follows: (a) 10 States with the largest interest in providing international shipping services; (b) 10 other States with the largest interest in international seaborne trade; (c) 20 further States having special interests in maritime transport and navigation elected so as to ensure the representation of all major geographic areas of the world.[99] It meets on a month's notice as often as necessary on the summons of its Chairman or on request by not less than four of its members, but in recent years there has been a pattern of meeting twice yearly.[100] It receives the recommendations and reports of the

93. *Supra*, fns 89 and 92 respectively; see the latest text in Article 11 as substituted by the latter.
94. IMO Convention, *supra*, fn. 89, Article 12.
95. *Ibid.*, Article 13.
96. *Ibid.*, Article 15(d).
97. *Ibid.*, Article 15(g) and (h).
98. *Ibid.*, Article 15(j).
99. *Ibid.*, Articles 16 and 17, as amended by Assembly Resolution A.735(18) adopted on 4 November 1993, which entered into force in 2002: see 2199 UNTS 122. The original Article 17 of 1948 had a Council of 16 and it has undergone three expansions to reach its present size and composition. By Article 18 of the original 1948 Convention the Council itself determined which Members had the largest or a substantial interest in providing international shipping services, and the Members with the largest interest in international seaborne trade, but this was removed with the first of the expansions and the Convention is now silent on the matter; presumably by default the calculation is left to the Secretariat to perform.
100. *Ibid.*, Article 19(c).

various Committees and transmits them to the Assembly together with its own comments and recommendations.[101]

The Council, with the approval of the Assembly, also appoints the Secretary-General.[102] It reports to the Assembly at each regular session on the IMO's work since the previous regular session,[103] and submits to the Assembly budget estimates and financial statements together with its comments and recommendations.[104] Between sessions of the Assembly, the Council performs all the functions of the IMO other than making recommendations for the adoption of regulations.[105]

The Maritime Safety Committee now consists of all IMO Members,[106] as do all other IMO Committees.[107] It meets once a year and at other times upon request of any five of its members.[108] The Committee's main duty is to consider matters concerned with aids to navigation, construction and equipment of vessels, manning from a safety standpoint, rules for the prevention of collisions, handling of dangerous cargoes, maritime safety procedures and requirements, hydrographic information, log-books and navigational records, marine casualty investigation, salvage and rescue, and any other matters directly affecting maritime safety.[109] It submits to the Council proposals for new safety regulations or amendments to existing ones, as well as recommendations and guidelines,[110] and reports to the Council on its work since the previous session of the latter.[111]

The Marine Environment Protection Committee, first established by the Assembly in 1973 as a subsidiary body of the Assembly,[112] was made permanent by the 1975 amendments to the IMO Convention.[113] Its remit is to consider any matter concerned with prevention and control of pollution from ships, in particular the adoption and amendment of relevant conventions and other regulations and measures for their enforcement.[114] Meeting at least once a year,[115] it submits to the Council proposals for regulations on prevention and control of marine pollution from ships or amendments to existing ones, as well as recommendations and guidelines,[116] and reports to the Council on its work since the previous session of the latter.[117]

101. *Ibid.*, Article 21(b).
102. *Ibid.*, Article 22.
103. *Ibid.*, Article 23.
104. *Ibid.*, Article 24.
105. *Ibid.*, Article 26.
106. *Ibid.*, Article 27. Article 28(a) of the original 1948 Convention provided for only 14 Members, elected by the Assembly, of which not less than eight had to be the "largest ship-owning nations"; it was this phrase that fell to be interpreted in the ICJ advisory opinion of 1960, *supra*, fn. 69.
107. See, e.g., *ibid.*, Articles 32 (Marine Environment Protection Committee) and 37 (Legal Committee).
108. *Ibid.*, Article 30.
109. *Ibid.*, Article 28(a). Note that the International Hydrographic Organisation, based in Monaco, is the international organisation mandated to deal with matters of hydrography (though it is not *stricto sensu* a UN specialised agency).
110. *Ibid.*, Article 29(a) and (b).
111. *Ibid.*, Article 29(c). Under the original Article 30 of the 1948 Convention, the Committee reported to the Assembly rather than the Council.
112. See Resolution A.297(VIII).
113. *Supra*, fn. 89.
114. *Ibid.*, Article 38(a) and (b).
115. *Ibid.*, Article 40. In more recent practice, as can be seen from the number of meetings held since its inception (56 by the end of 2007), it usually meets twice a year – accord S Mankabady, *International Shipping Law* (London: Euromoney, 1991), vol. 1, p. 5.
116. *Ibid.*, Article 39(a) and (b).
117. *Ibid.*, Article 39(c).

Reporting to both the Maritime Safety Committee and the Marine Environment Protection Committee are nine subcommittees that are open to all Member States.[118]

The Legal Committee traces its history to 1967 when it was established as a subsidiary body of the Council to deal with legal issues arising from the sinking of the *Torrey Canyon*.[119] Meeting twice a year, usually in April and October (though it is only required to do so annually[120]), it now oversees all the IMO's legal work, including the negotiation of IMO Conventions, which are submitted in draft to the Council,[121] and reports to the Council on its work since the previous session of the latter.[122] The detailed drafting of conventions is largely delegated to correspondence groups working intersessionally, usually under the supervision of an appointed "lead delegation". Occasionally instruments are adopted without reference to the Legal Committee, such as the Ballast Water Convention.[123]

There are also two committees of lesser importance: the Technical Co-operation Committee is concerned with the implementation of technical cooperation projects in which the IMO participates and any other matters related to its activities in this field. It was first established in 1969 as a subsidiary body of the Council,[124] but since 1984 has had a permanent existence by virtue of an amendment to the 1948 Convention.[125] The Facilitation Committee was created in 1972[126] as a focal point for IMO's work in eliminating unnecessary formalities and bureaucracy in international shipping. It remains a subsidiary body of the Council pending the entry into force in late 2008 of the 1991 amendments to the IMO Convention[127] that will elevate it to the same status as the other Committees.

The IMO's Secretariat with its headquarters in London[128] consists of the Secretary-General and nearly 300 staff who service the meetings of the various organs and committees[129] as well as the diplomatic conferences at which IMO convention texts are finalised for adoption. The Secretary-General serves as the depositary of these Conventions.

118. These are the Subcommittees on (i) Bulk Liquids and Gases; (ii) Carriage of Dangerous Goods, Solid Cargoes and Containers; (iii) Fire Protection; (iv) Flag State Implementation; (v) Radio-Communications and Search and Rescue; (vi) Safety of Navigation; (vii) Ship Design and Equipment; (viii) Stability and Load Lines and Fishing Vessels Safety; and (ix) Standards of Training and Watchkeeping.
119. See R P Balkin, "The Establishment and Work of the IMO Legal Committee", in M H Nordquist and J Norton Moore (eds), *Current Maritime Issues and the International Maritime Organisation* (The Hague: Martinus Nijhoff, 1999), 291 at pp. 293–297.
120. IMO Convention, *supra*, fn. 89, Article 36.
121. *Ibid.*, Articles 33(a) and 34(a). For a fascinating view of the Committee's *modus operandi*, see also N J J Gaskell, "Decision Making and the Legal Committee of the IMO", (2003) 18 IJMCL 155. The Maritime Safety Committee and the Marine Environment Protection Committee are also asked for their views on amendments to the public law regulatory conventions: *ibid.*, at p. 166.
122. IMO Convention, *supra*, fn. 89, Article 34(b).
123. International Convention for the Control and Management of Ships' Ballast Water and Sediments (London, 13 February 2004); IMO doc BWM/CONF/36 (16 February 2004).
124. By Council Resolution C.49 (ES.IV) of 13 March 1969.
125. See now Articles 42–46 of the IMO Convention, inserted by the 1977 amendments, *supra*, fn. 92.
126. By Council Resolution C.54 (XXVIII) of 24 May 1972.
127. The amendments were adopted by Assembly Resolution A.724(17) of 7 November 1991 and the 112th acceptance, triggering their entry into force a year later, was deposited by Yemen on 7 December 2007: see *www.imo.org/Newsroom/mainframe.asp?topic_id=1472&doc_id=8825* (accessed on 14 February 2008).
128. IMO Convention, *supra*, fn. 89, Article 63(a).
129. *Ibid.*, Article 52.

### (c) IMO Conventions as multilateral treaties

Although the law of treaties applies equally to bilateral and multilateral treaties, the latter are a relatively new phenomenon.[130] The dynamics of multilateral negotiations with many States taking part means that in the drafting of the treaties clarity often has to be sacrificed.[131] The IMO is somewhat unusual among international organisations in that it first works through its own Legal Committee to develop and draft its conventions, and then convenes diplomatic conferences at which the draft texts will be refined and ultimately adopted.

The IMO has the reputation of being among the least politicised of the UN specialised agencies and political considerations rarely interfere with the negotiations in the Legal Committee of conventions or have a disproportionate impact on their largely technical content. Once the Legal Committee has developed a text as far as it can, it reports to that effect to the Council, which then calls a diplomatic conference, at which the final remaining points of disagreement – usually the more political ones such as the precise figures for liability limits – are resolved and the treaty is formally adopted.[132] Although the Rules of Procedure at international conferences may provide for the resulting treaty to be adopted by a vote,[133] in multilateral negotiations it is generally preferable to adopt by consensus where possible, usually defined as the absence of a formal objection, since that maximises the chances of States going on to become party to the treaty, albeit at the cost of dilution of many of its provisions.

### (d) Becoming party to IMO Conventions – "final clauses"

A special set of provisions in multilateral treaties known as final clauses governs such mechanical matters as the requirements for entry into force.[134] Under customary international law, as codified in the Vienna Convention on the Law

130. The idea of one instrument reflecting the will of a large number of States began only with the Vienna Congress of 1815. This was the origin of the Final Act (see *infra*, fn. 134) and was the first time a single instrument had been signed by multiple parties. In fact the Final Act was the only document that all parties at the Congress of Vienna signed, uniting the traditional range of bilateral treaties under it into a coherent whole.

131. As to how this affects the IMO, see Gaskell, *supra*, fn. 121, particularly at pp. 181–182 and 207–211.

132. Negotiations tend to involve a combination of formal and informal mechanisms. Often the informal side is more productive, with many decisions being made through "corridor chat" outside the main meeting hall, where more genuine debate is possible than in the series of usually prepared statements that tends to characterise the formal proceedings: see *ibid.*, at pp. 188–189. Nonetheless, it is what happens in the main forum that counts in terms of the final text of a treaty – the informal substantive discussions are merged with the formal process, creating the instrument to be formally adopted.

133. Article 9(2) of the Vienna Convention on the Law of Treaties, *supra*, fn. 14, provides that, for treaties negotiated at international conferences, adoption of the text requires a two-thirds majority of States present and voting, unless by the same majority they decide to adopt a different procedure. The Rules of Procedure at IMO diplomatic conferences seldom if ever depart from this default rule.

134. These should not be confused with the Final Act of the conference, to which the text of a multilateral treaty negotiated at the conference is normally annexed. The Final Act is a record of the proceedings of the conference and includes, besides the text of the treaty, such matters as the way in which the conference's work was organised, a list of the States represented, the delegates' names and any resolutions adopted by the conference. Nowadays the Final Act also plays a formal role of authenticating the text: Article 10(b) of the Vienna Convention on the Law of Treaties, *supra*, fn. 14. By signing the Final Act of a conference, a State is not expressing any view on the treaty and its signature neither binds the State nor commits it eventually to become party to the treaty.

of Treaties, there are two basic modes for expressing consent to be bound, one involving a single step and the other two steps. The two-step procedure is more common for multilateral treaties and is used in the IMO. It consists of signature, followed by ratification.[135] The second step, ratification, is the one by which the State establishes on the international plane its consent to be bound *vis-à-vis* all other ratifying States. Usually some time elapses between signature and ratification, to permit States to decide whether they wish to or can enact internal laws so as to put the treaty into operation domestically, or consult their legislature where the internal constitutional arrangements require this.

Treaties are typically left open for signature for a year or two, though the period can be shorter. By Article 18 of the Vienna Convention, which is considered to be a codification of the pre-existing customary rule, the effect of signature subject to ratification is that the State is obliged to refrain from acts which would defeat the object and purpose of the treaty, unless it makes clear that it will not ratify it. This obligation continues after ratification if the treaty is not yet in force, until it does actually enter into force. Signature not subject to ratification, sometimes known as definitive signature, is the one-step process, but this is more common for bilateral treaties.[136]

After the treaty closes for signature, the process reverts to a single step, in this case called accession: this allows States to become party to the treaty even if they did not take part in its original negotiation.

In multilateral treaties a certain number of ratifications or accessions is required before a treaty comes into force for any party. IMO final clauses often say these must in addition account for a given proportion of world shipping tonnage. Alternatively, entry into force may also be on a particular date as stipulated in the treaty.

The IMO Conventions adopted by this process, most of which have been amended or supplemented by Protocols (some of them many times) not separately listed, are as follows:

- 1965 Convention on Facilitation of International Maritime Traffic;[137]
- 1966 International Convention on Load Lines;[138]
- 1969 International Convention on Tonnage Measurement of Ships;[139]
- 1969 International Convention Relating to Intervention on the High Seas in the case of Oil Pollution Casualties;[140]
- 1969 International Convention on Civil Liability for Oil Pollution Damage;[141]
- 1971 Special Trade Passenger Ships Agreement;[142]

135. *Ibid.*, Article 14. The heading is "Consent to be bound by a treaty expressed by ratification, acceptance or approval", but as paragraph 2 of this Article makes clear, the terms *acceptance* and *approval* are functionally equivalent to ratification, which will be the sole term used from this point.
136. Note that, since signature can either (in the one-step process) be sufficient to bind a State or (in the two-step process) not, to describe a State as a "signatory" of a treaty without further explanation is ambiguous as to whether it is bound by the treaty or merely obliged not to defeat its object and purpose, so that a more precise term will always be preferable.
137. 591 UNTS 265. The purpose of this Convention is to simplify governmental formalities and documentary requirements.
138. 640 UNTS 133.
139. 1291 UNTS 3. See further, section on *Limitation of Liability* in Chapter 6.
140. 970 UNTS 211. See further, Chapter 8.
141. 973 UNTS 3. See further, Chapter 8.
142. 910 UNTS 61.

- 1971 Convention relating to Civil Liability in the Field of Maritime Carriage of Nuclear Materials;[143]
- 1971 International Convention on the Establishment of an International Fund for Compensation for Oil Pollution Damage;[144]
- 1972 International Convention for Safe Containers;[145]
- 1972 Convention on the International Regulations for Preventing Collisions at Sea (COLREG);[146]
- 1973 International Convention for the Prevention of Pollution from Ships (MARPOL);[147]
- 1974 International Convention for the Safety of Life at Sea (SOLAS);[148]
- 1974 Convention relating to the Carriage of Passengers and their Luggage by Sea;[149]
- 1976 Convention on the International Maritime Satellite Organisation;[150]
- 1976 Convention on Limitation of Liability for Maritime Claims;[151]
- 1978 International Convention on Standards of Training, Certification and Watchkeeping for Seafarers;[152]
- 1979 International Convention on Maritime Search and Rescue;[153]
- 1988 Convention for the Suppression of Unlawful Acts Against the Safety of Maritime Navigation;[154]
- 1989 International Convention on Salvage;[155]
- 1990 International Convention on Oil Pollution Preparedness, Response and Cooperation;[156]
- 1993 International Convention on Maritime Liens and Mortgages.[157]

143. 974 UNTS 255. See further, Chapter 8.
144. 1110 UNTS 57. See further, Chapter 8.
145. 1064 UNTS 3.
146. 1050 UNTS 16. This Convention makes the IMO responsible for traffic separation schemes (a role reserved in UNCLOS, Articles 22(3)(a) and 41(4) and (5), for the unnamed "competent international organization" regarding the territorial sea and in particular in straits used for international navigation). Independently of the Convention, the IMO has a role as the competent international organisation for archipelagic sea lanes and any traffic separation schemes within them under UNCLOS Article 53(9). See further, section on *Collisions* in Chapter 6.
147. 1340 UNTS 61. Originally this Convention's six annexes (on oil, bulk noxious liquids, harmful packaged substances, sewage, garbage, air pollution) were all compulsory, but when it appeared that this was delaying its entry into force, an amendment negotiated in 1978 changed this so that only Annexes I and II remained compulsory and the remainder became optional. For this reason the Convention is often referred to as MARPOL 73/78. This enabled the Convention to enter into force in 1983. All the other Annexes are also now in force. See further, Chapter 8.
148. 1184 UNTS 3. This is a frequently amended Convention, e.g. in 1983 to incorporate the previously non-binding Code for the Construction and Equipment of Ships carrying Dangerous Chemicals in Bulk. See further, Chapter 7.
149. 1463 UNTS 19. See further, Chapter 5.
150. 1143 UNTS 105.
151. 1456 UNTS 221. See further, section on *Limitation of Liability* in Chapter 6.
152. 1361 UNTS 2. See further, Chapter 7: The International Convention on Standards of Training; Certification and Watch-Keeping as amended in 1995 (STCW95).
153. 1405 UNTS 97.
154. *Supra*, fn. 78.
155. 1953 UNTS 165. This Convention replaces the traditional "no cure–no pay" rule with a system of reward to the salvor for preventing a major pollution incident, even if the ship itself is not saved. See further, section on *Salvage* in Chapter 6
156. 1891 UNTS 51.
157. Geneva, 12 March 1993. UN doc A/CONF.162/7 (6 May 1993). The aim of this Convention is to promote uniformity in private law but few of its 12 parties are common law jurisdictions. See further, Chapter 11.

In addition, the IMO serves as the secretariat to the 1972 Convention on the Prevention of Marine Pollution by Dumping of Wastes and Other Matter[158] and its 1996 Protocol.

The texts of these Conventions are available (for a fee) from the IMO, which also as the depositary maintains status lists indicating which States are party to which Conventions. Since, under Article 102(1) of the Charter of the United Nations, treaties are supposed to be registered with the Secretariat and published by it, they also appear, once they have entered into force, in the United Nations Treaty Series, which can be accessed online free of charge.[159]

Two IMO Conventions are due to enter into force during 2008: the 2001 International Convention on Civil Liability for Bunker Oil Pollution Damage[160] and the 2001 International Convention on the Control of Harmful Anti-fouling Systems on Ships.[161] As a result, there are relatively few IMO Conventions still not in force: the 1996 International Convention on Liability and Compensation for Damage in Connection with the Carriage of Hazardous and Noxious Substances,[162] the 1999 Convention on the Arrest of Ships,[163] the 2004 International Convention for the Control and Management of Ships' Ballast Water and Sediments[164] and the 2007 Nairobi International Convention on the Removal of Wrecks.[165] A convention on the recycling of ships is currently being negotiated in the Marine Environment Protection Committee and a diplomatic conference to finalise and adopt its text is expected to be called in 2008 or 2009.[166]

Relevant conventions negotiated elsewhere than in the IMO include the 1974 Convention on a Code of Conduct for Liner Conferences,[167] the 1978 United Nations Convention on the Carriage of Goods by Sea[168] and the 1986 United Nations Convention on the Conditions for Registration of Ships,[169] all negotiated in

158. London, Mexico City, Moscow and Washington, 29 December 1972; 1046 UNTS 120. See further, Chapter 8.
159. At *http://untreaty.un.org/English/access.asp*. Regrettably, however, it is not particularly user-friendly. Another way of circumventing the IMO charge is to find the treaty on the treaties website of one of the parties, an especially easy-to-use one being that maintained by the Australian Legal Information Institute at *www.austlii.edu.au/au/other/dfat/*. (Note: If Australia has signed but not yet ratified the Convention, it will be found under Australian Treaties Not in Force rather than in the Australian Treaty Series.)
160. London, 23 March 2001; IMO doc LEG/CONF.12/19 (27 March 2001). See further, Chapter 8.
161. London, 5 October 2001; IMO doc AFS/CONF/26 (18 October 2001). See further, Chapter 8.
162. London, 3 May 1996, IMO doc LEG/CONF.10/8/2 (9 May 1996). By Article 46(1), it requires 12 States including four each with 2,000,000 units of gross tonnage to consent to be bound by it in order to enter into force. As at 31 March 2008 10 had done so according to the IMO's Status of Conventions webpage, *supra*, fn. 87. See further, Chapter 8.
163. Geneva, 12 March 1999. The Final Act of the diplomatic conference including the text of the Convention as an annex is in UN doc A/CONF.188/6 (19 March 1999). By Article 14(1), it requires 10 States to consent to be bound by it in order to enter into force. As at 31 March 2008 seven had done so according to the IMO's Status of Conventions webpage, *http://untreaty.un.org/English/bible/englishinternetbible/partI/chapterXII/treaty17.asp*. See further, Chapters 1 and 11.
164. *Supra*, fn. 123. By Article 18(1), it requires 30 States representing 35% of gross registered tonnage to consent to be bound by it in order to enter into force. As at 31 March 2008, 13 had done so (3.62%) according to the IMO's Status of Conventions webpage, *supra*, fn. 87. See further, Chapter 8.
165. *Supra*, fn. 37. By Article 18(1), it requires 10 States to consent to be bound by it in order to enter into force. As at 31 March 2008 none had yet done so according to the IMO's Status of Conventions webpage, *supra*, fn. 87. See further, section on *Wreck Removal* in Chapter 6.
166. See *www.imo.org/Environment/mainframe.asp?topic_id=818* (accessed on 14 February 2008).
167. Geneva, 6 April 1974; 1334 UNTS 15.
168. Hamburg, 31 March 1978; 1695 UNTS 3.
169. *Supra*, fn. 70, not in force.

UNCTAD. The 1993 International Convention on Maritime Liens and Mortgages[170] and the 1999 Convention on the Arrest of Ships[171] were negotiated under the joint auspices of IMO and UNCTAD.

Amendment of treaties is often a problem for international law because it is normally more difficult to gain governments' attention and legislative time for them than for the original treaty negotiations, with the result that amendments typically take a very long time to enter into force, and even then bind only the parties to them,[172] while as between a State party to the amendment and a State only party to the original treaty, it is the latter that remains in force. The IMO has, however, pioneered a "tacit acceptance" procedure for technical amendments, which allows such amendments to come into force after a specified period for all parties other than those that specifically object to them. This is why it has been possible to amend some of the IMO Conventions many times, notably those on safety of life at sea and the collision regulations. Substantive amendments are still subject to the Vienna Convention rules, however, the 2002 Protocol to the 1974 Athens Convention relating to the Carriage of Passengers and their Luggage by Sea[173] being an example.

### (e) IMO as the "competent international organization" in UNCLOS

Being in some respects a framework convention, UNCLOS in many of its provisions does not itself set out binding rules but instead incorporates by reference those made by what it refers to as the "competent international organization(s)" in various fields, which it never names. In the field of navigation and pollution from ships, IMO is universally regarded as the body meant by this phrase.[174] In the territorial sea in general, the coastal State is free to prescribe sea lanes and traffic separation schemes as it sees fit, and need only take into account the IMO's recommendations.[175] In waters where the interests of unimpeded navigation have required special regimes, by contrast – that is, straits used for international navigation and archipelagic sea lanes – the coastal or archipelagic State must refer its proposals to the IMO for adoption, which in turn may adopt only such sea lanes and traffic separation schemes as are agreed with that State.[176] The Assembly in 1997 delegated the Maritime Safety Committee to act on the IMO's behalf in these matters.[177] Traffic separation schemes, of which there are many, are notified to the shipping community by means of Circulars in the COLREG.2 series available on the IMO website.[178] The only instance to date of archipelagic

170. *Supra*, fn. 157.
171. *Supra*, fn. 164.
172. See Vienna Convention on the Law of Treaties, *supra*, fn. 14, Article 40(4).
173. IMO doc LEG/CONF.13/20 (19 November 2002).
174. See the papers by R Wolfrum, S Rosenne and A Blanco-Bazán all entitled "IMO Interface with the Law of the Sea Convention" in Nordquist and Norton Moore (eds), *supra*, fn. 119, at pp. 223, 251 and 269 respectively, especially that of Rosenne at p. 254.
175. UNCLOS, *supra*, fn. 11, Article 22(3)(a).
176. *Ibid.*, Articles 41(4) (straits) and 53(9) (archipelagic sea lanes).
177. Assembly Resolution A.858(20) (undated), paragraph 1. Independently of UNCLOS, the IMO has power to adopt such schemes: see Rule 1(d) of the International Regulations for Preventing Collisions at Sea 1972 annexed to the COLREG Convention, *supra*, fn. 146.
178. See *www.imo.org/Circulars/mainframe.asp?topic_id=328.*

sea lanes is the partial designation by Indonesia,[179] although the Philippines is also understood to have been working for some years on a bringing a designation to the IMO.

The "generally accepted international regulations" emanating from IMO's work are given indirect legal force by UNCLOS where mentioned in the context of rules to be complied with, including, it would seem, by non-parties to the relevant IMO Conventions.[180] Thus the rules on safety of navigation are incorporated by reference on such matters as traffic separation schemes in straits and archipelagic sea lanes,[181] as well as the rules on the construction, design, equipment and manning of ships and the prevention of collisions at sea.[182] Of the numerous provisions of this type in Part XII on protection of the marine environment, Article 211 on pollution from ships is particularly significant – the essence of the scheme established by this article is that the coastal State may make and enforce pollution regulations in its EEZ in order to implement the rules formulated through the IMO, but may not ordinarily have more stringent ones.[183] For any defined area within its EEZ where the coastal State nevertheless has reasonable grounds for believing that these rules are inadequate for the special circumstances of that area, and that special mandatory measures (other than design, construction, manning and equipment standards) for preventing pollution are necessary because of oceanographic or ecological conditions, the coastal State may submit scientific and technical information to the IMO, which within 12 months of the receipt of the communication must determine whether the conditions do in fact warrant such measures. If so, the coastal State may adopt the special regulations proposed, though they become binding on foreign ships no earlier than 15 months from the original communication.[184] The IMO has grouped this provision procedurally with similar ones in other instruments within its process for establishing what it calls Particularly Sensitive Sea Areas, not necessarily confined to EEZs, in which special rules apply (each set of rules being unique to each such area).[185] The IMO's website lists several such areas including the Great Barrier Reef off Australia, the Florida Keys, Western European Waters, the Canary Islands, the Galapagos Archipelago and the Baltic Sea.[186]

179. IMO doc SN/Circ.200 (26 May 1998) annexing Maritime Safety Committee Resolution MSC.72(69) (adopted on 19 May 1998), Adoption, Designation and Substitution of Archipelagic Sea Lanes, para. 1.
180. Blanco-Bazán, *supra*, fn. 174, cautions at pp. 281–282 against taking this too far – the failure by non-parties to ensure compliance by their ships with the more technical provisions of these IMO Conventions does not automatically place them in breach of UNCLOS.
181. UNCLOS, *supra*, fn. 11, Articles 41(3) (straits) and 53(8) (archipelagic sea lanes).
182. *Ibid.*, Article 21(2) and (4) respectively. An example of the former is the requirement for new oil tankers to be fitted with double hulls separated by a space of at least 2 metres (on tankers of 5,000 dwt or above) or of at least 0.76 metres (tankers below 5,000 dwt), contained in Regulation 13F of Annex I to MARPOL 73/78, inserted by Resolution MEPC.52(32) adopted on 6 March 1992 and in force since 6 July 1993, reproduced at 1733 UNTS 385. A very long list of such requirements, though only up to November 1998, is in IMO doc MSC/Circ.815 (13 November 1998). The latter may be taken as a reference to the COLREG Convention, *supra*, fn. 146.
183. See in particular paragraphs (1) and (5) of Article 211. In the territorial sea the coastal State is given more latitude: by paragraph (4), echoing Article 24(1), its rules on prevention of pollution from ships must merely "not hamper innocent passage of foreign vessels".
184. *Ibid.*, Article 211(6).
185. See IMO doc A.24/Res.982 (6 February 2006), "[Assembly] Resolution A.982(24) Adopted on 1 December 2005 (Agenda item 11), Revised Guidelines for the Identification and Designation of Particularly Sensitive Sea Areas", available at *www.imo.org/includes/blastDataOnly.asp/data_id %3D14373/982.pdf* (accessed on 10 March 2008).
186. See *www.imo.org/Environment/mainframe.asp?topic_id=1357* (accessed on 10 March 2008).

Finally, the IMO is uniquely mentioned by name in Annex VIII to UNCLOS as responsible for drawing up and maintaining a list of experts in the field of navigation including pollution from vessels by dumping, who are available to serve on special *ad hoc* arbitral panels that States Parties may constitute to decide disputes in this field if they so elect.[187]

## 6. THE UNCLOS ARTICLE 292 PROMPT RELEASE PROCEDURES

Under Article 220 of UNCLOS, a coastal State may detain and prosecute a foreign ship voluntarily in one of its ports for violating pollution laws in its territorial sea or EEZ, or may inspect ships in the territorial sea for such violation there and, where the evidence so warrants, institute legal proceedings against the ship, which may include its detention.[188] Detention may also occur in the EEZ in the case of "clear objective evidence" that the ship has "committed a violation ... resulting in a discharge causing major damage or threat of major damage to the coastline or related interests of the coastal State, or to any resources of its territorial sea or exclusive economic zone".[189] This is subject to Article 226(1)(b), which requires that, if the investigation indicates a violation of international environmental rules, "release shall be made promptly subject to reasonable procedures such as bonding or other appropriate financial security".[190]

This in turn is subject to Article 292, whose paragraph 1 provides that, if the detaining State is alleged not to have complied with any provision in UNCLOS for the prompt release of a ship and its crew,[191] the question may be submitted to any court or tribunal agreed on by the parties or, failing such agreement within 10 days from the detention, to ITLOS. Paragraph 2 adds that the application may be made only by or on behalf of the flag State, in other words the flag State need not take part in the proceedings, but must give its consent to them if they are to be admissible. By paragraph 3, the court or tribunal must deal without delay with the application for release – but only with the question of release, without prejudice to the merits of the case before any domestic forum against the ship, its owner or its crew.

There have been several such prompt release cases taken to ITLOS under this procedure, which make up the bulk of its judicial activity to date.[192] Although they all concern fishing vessels,[193] the principles enunciated apply equally to

187. UNCLOS, *supra*, fn. 11, Article 287(1)(d) and Annex VIII, Article 2(2).
188. UNCLOS, *supra*, fn. 11, Article 220(1) and (2).
189. *Ibid.*, Article 220(6).
190. See also *ibid.*, Article 226(1)(c), by which the release of an unseaworthy ship presenting an unreasonable threat of damage to the marine environment may be refused or made conditional on proceeding to the nearest appropriate repair yard. In that event, the flag State must be promptly notified.
191. The only provisions relevant are those cited above and Article 73 on the enforcement of resources laws in the EEZ. For reasons that are not entirely clear, shipping interests have not used this procedure, and all the cases on it have been in respect either of fishing vessels or of ships servicing fishing vessels.
192. For a survey of the prompt release cases up to 2004 by the first President of ITLOS, see T A Mensah, "The Tribunal and the Prompt Release of Vessels" (2007) 22 *International Journal of Marine and Coastal Law* 425.
193. Other than the first, *The M/V Saiga (No 1) (Saint Vincent and the Grenadines v Guinea)*, ITLOS Reports 1997, p.16, where the offence which led to the detention was the supply of bunkers to a fishing vessel in the EEZ, which ITLOS elected to treat as a fisheries offence attracting Article 292 rather than as a customs offence for which Article 292 would not have been available. The judgments,

detentions arising from pollution incidents. In the first of the fishing vessel prompt release applications, *The Camouco*, ITLOS set out the criteria by which the reasonableness of any bond such as that required under Article 226(1)(b) would be judged:

> "[F]actors...relevant in an assessment of the reasonableness of bonds or other financial security...include the gravity of the alleged offences, the penalties imposed or imposable under the laws of the detaining State, the value of the detained vessel and of the cargo seized, the amount of the bond imposed by the detaining State and its form."[194]

In the next case, *The Monte Confurco*, the majority judgment noted that under UNCLOS Article 292, ITLOS "is not an appellate forum against a decision of the national court", but added that "nevertheless ... the Tribunal is not precluded from examining the facts and circumstances of the case to the extent necessary for a proper appreciation of the reasonableness of the bond".[195] In doing so, it criticised the French Court of First Instance's assumption that half the catch seized by the French authorities was taken illegally in the EEZ, stating that the information before it "does not give an adequate basis to assume" this. The majority thus found that the bond fixed by the French court (FF56.4 million) was not reasonable, and substituted a total of FF18 million.

It is submitted, however, that this reasoning is questionable, and the dissenting opinions were more persuasive. Judge Anderson, who dissented on all substantive points, was of the view that the assumption that the seized fish were taken in French waters was not unreasonable.[196] Judge Jesus thought that ITLOS had intervened in the merits contrary to Article 292(3).[197] Judge Mensah, though not dissenting, agreed that the majority had "come perilously close" to trespassing upon the merits, and criticised the direct approach taken by ITLOS in assessing the facts, forming a view on the merits different from that of the French court and so finding its bond unreasonable, overlooking the possibility that the bond the latter had imposed could be "reasonable" within the meaning of Article 73 of UNCLOS without necessarily being the exact amount that ITLOS itself would have imposed:

> "The Tribunal is, of course, entitled to disagree with the actual figure chosen by the court of first instance. This is because there is no single correct figure in the circumstances of the case ... [This] does not mean that the basis of computation adopted by the court of first instance is "inconsistent" with the facts."[198]

Although the outcome in *The Monte Confurco* might appear to suggest that, in effect if not in name, belying the passage quoted above, an appeal to ITLOS is

---

orders and written and oral pleadings in this and all other ITLOS cases are available on its website, *http://www.itlos.org/start2_en.html.*

194. *The Camouco (Panama v France)*, ITLOS Reports 2000, Chapter 10 at p. 31 (para. 67). For a useful case note see B H Oxman and V P Bantz, (2000) 94 *American Journal of International Law* 713.

195. *The Monte Confurco (Seychelles v France)*, ITLOS Reports 2000, 86 at p. 109 (para. 74). For criticism of this case see A Serdy and M Bliss, "Prompt Release of Fishing Vessels: State Practice in the Light of the Cases before the International Tribunal for the Law of the Sea" in A G Oude Elferink and D R Rothwell (eds), *Oceans Management in the 21st Century: Institutional Frameworks and Responses* (Leiden/Boston: Martinus Nijhoff, 2004), 273 at pp. 280–290.

196. *The Monte Confurco (Seychelles v France)*, Dissenting Opinion of Judge Anderson, ITLOS Reports 2000, 127 at pp. 128–131.

197. *The Monte Confurco (Seychelles v France)*, Dissenting Opinion of Judge Jesus, ITLOS Reports 2000, 139 at pp. 142–143 (paras 24–30).

198. *The Monte Confurco (Seychelles v France)*, Declaration of Judge Mensah, ITLOS Reports 2000, 118 at pp. 118–119.

indeed possible from a decision of a domestic court as to bond, a salutary lesson to litigants tempted to do just that is given by the 2001 case of *The Grand Prince*. The facts here were that Belize, notified by France of its ship's arrest for illegal fishing, cancelled its registration and sent a diplomatic note to France to that effect. Later, however, the Belizean registry stated in a letter to France's Honorary Consul in Belize that:

> "...while we were in the process of cancelling ex-officio the vessel's status, the owners requested an opportunity to defend themselves of the accusations by submitting an appeal to [ITLOS]. Under this context and Belize being a [party to UNCLOS] we considered fair to allow the affected party to file its petition ... Depending on the result of this court proceeding we will decide whether or not to enforce our decision to delete the vessel from our records."[199]

Treating the earlier note as conclusive, a narrow majority found the ship as at the date of application did not in fact have Belizean nationality, so that ITLOS lacked jurisdiction to hear the application.[200] Nine judges dissented jointly, arguing that the official documents issued by Belize subsequent to the Note indicated that the deregistration was not definitive, and had been suspended.[201]

Overall, however, the subsequent prompt release decisions indicate that ITLOS and Article 292 are still a very worthwhile avenue for owners to pursue should the occasion arise. In *The Volga*, ITLOS by majority found unreasonable the bond set by Australia for release of a Russian-flagged fishing vessel because it included an amount of A$1 million as a bond securing compliance with a condition of release, being the installation and operation of a satellite-based vessel monitoring system (VMS) to allow for tracking of the *Volga*. This was based on its interpretation of Article 73 of UNCLOS as not allowing for the imposition of non-financial conditions for releasing a ship such as the VMS bond and disclosure of its beneficial ownership which the Australian authorities had also demanded.[202] Nonetheless, in this case for the first time ITLOS was prepared to set a bond equal to the full value of the ship,[203] disregarding an argument on behalf of the shipowner that its own case law dictated a going rate for bonds of about 25% of the ship's value.

Although forfeiture of the ship involved is more commonly a penalty for fisheries than for pollution offences, ITLOS has shown itself prepared to go behind the wording of the coastal State's forfeiture law. In *The Juno Trader*[204] ITLOS treated the ostensibly definitive forfeiture of a ship under the law of Guinea-Bissau as reversible as long as proceedings of some kind to overturn it were on foot. On the other hand, in *The Tomimaru*,[205] the flag State (Japan) and owner

199. *The Grand Prince (Belize v France)*, ITLOS Reports 2001, 17 at p. 40 (para. 74).
200. *Ibid.*, at p. 44 (paras 93 and 95). See also the case note by B H Oxman & V P Bantz, (2002) 96 *American Journal of International Law* 219.
201. *The Grand Prince (Belize v France)*, Dissenting Opinion of Judges Caminos, Marotta Rangel, Yankov, Yamamoto, Akl, Vukas, Marsit, Eiriksson and Jesus, ITLOS Reports 2001, 66.
202. *The Volga (Russian Federation v Australia)*, ITLOS Reports 2002, 10 at pp. 34–36 (paras 75–80) and p. 37 (para. 88).
203. *Ibid.*, at p. 34 (para. 73).
204. *The Juno Trader (St Vincent and the Grenadines v Guinea-Bissau)*, ITLOS Reports 2004, 17. See further V P Bantz, "Views from Hamburg – The Juno Trader or how to make sense of the coastal state's rights in light of its duty of prompt release" (2005) 24 *University of Queensland Law Journal* 415.
205. *The Tomimaru (Japan v Russian Federation)*, 6 August 2007, available online at *www.itlos.org/case_documents/2007document_en_296.pdf* (accessed on 13 November 2007).

delayed too long before invoking Article 292, by when the last possible window of remedial opportunity in the Russian courts had closed, and the application was as a consequence declared without object.

Since detention of the ship rather than of the crew is the necessary condition for its invocation, the Article 292 procedure was not available to assist the Master of the *Prestige*, controversially detained by the Spanish authorities after her sinking in 2002. Even so, this seems insufficient to account for the forbearance of shipping interests from using this procedure. Since the prompt release procedure has lived up to its name and the reputation of ITLOS as an international court capable of applying and developing the public international law of the sea now appears increasingly well established, it is quite possible that the imbalance will begin to be redressed in the coming years.

CHAPTER 10

# Marine Insurance

*PROFESSOR ROBERT MERKIN, RICHARD SHAW, RICHARD PILLEY AND JOHANNA HJALMARSSON*

## 1. INTRODUCTION[1]

This chapter provides a general picture of marine insurance, with particular focus on what is unique to that part of the insurance market. The chapter commences with an introduction to marine insurance, followed by an overview of contemporary hull and cargo policy cover. It then goes on to look at some of the particular forms of insurance available in the marine market, namely General Average and the various forms of insurance provided by P&I Clubs to conclude with a brief overview of letters of undertaking.

## 2. INTRODUCTION TO MARINE INSURANCE LAW

### (a) Background

English marine insurance law was codified in the Marine Insurance Act 1906. The Act brought together all of the marine insurance decisions of the courts to date: there was no attempt to change the law or to clarify uncertainties. The provisions of the 1906 Act thus afford the starting point for the resolution of any dispute in respect of a marine policy,[2] but two very important qualifications should be noted. The first is that much of the Act is subject to contract, and in practice the standard clauses adopted in the London Market – the Institute Clauses[3] – oust or modify many of the provisions of the legislation. The second is that the practice of marine insurance is not static and accordingly there are numerous modern decisions on the meaning of the 1906 Act and on its application to new scenarios.

### (b) Policies within the 1906 Act

Marine risks are written in London by insurance companies, by Lloyd's Syndicates and by mutual associations (Protection & Indemnity (P&I) Clubs).[4] The 1906 Act applies to the insurance of losses incident to a marine adventure

1. Sections 1 to 3 have been written by Professor Robert Merkin, Section 4 by Richard Shaw, Section 5 by Richard Pilley and Section 6 by Johanna Hjalmarsson.
2. Some parts of the Act apply to non-marine risks, in particular ss 17–20 (utmost good faith).
3. Issued by the body known since 1998 as the International Underwriting Association. Clauses exist for virtually all forms of marine cover, and there are separate clauses for war risks.
4. See below.

(section 1). Marine risks include risks on inland waterways, construction risks and land risks ancillary to a marine voyage (section 2). The most important classes of policy are: hull and machinery; cargo; freight; and liability to third parties (section 3). In practice, most classes of liability cover are written by P&I Clubs rather than by conventional insurers.

Marine policies may be written on a voyage basis (from place to place) or on a time basis (for a specified period of time) (section 25). Hull and machinery policies may be on either basis, but the majority of cargo insurances cover the cargo on a voyage basis, from its origin to place of delivery.

### (c) Formation of marine policies

A contract of marine insurance must be embodied in a policy (section 22)[5] signed by the insurers (section 24) and specifying the name of the assured (section 23). The subject matter must be designated with reasonable certainty (section 26), although it is possible to have a declaration policy under which risks falling within the scope of the insuring words may be declared from time to time and the insurers are bound to accept such declarations.[6] The policy may be "valued" or "unvalued": a valued policy is one under which the assured is entitled to recover the insured sum in the event of a loss, even though the subject matter is actually worth more or less than that sum; by contrast, an unvalued policy is one under which the assured must prove the amount of its loss, and the sum insured simply represents the maximum that can be recovered (sections 27–28). The premium for cover is fixed at the outset, although if for one or other reason there is no agreement then a reasonable premium must be paid (section 31).[7] In marine insurance, unlike all other forms of insurance, it is the duty of the broker to pay the premium to the insurers whether or not the broker has first been paid by the assured (sections 53–54), payment of the premium being a condition concurrent with the issue of the policy itself (section 52).

Unless the assured possesses an "insurable interest" in the insured subject matter or has an expectation of acquiring such an interest, a policy taken out by him is regarded as by way of gaming or wagering and is void (section 4).[8] Insurable interest is possessed by a person who stands in a legal or equitable relation to the marine adventure or to any insured property at risk (section 5) and in recent times the courts have recognised that insurable interest is potentially a wide concept.[9] The Act provides a specific illustrative list of insurable interests[10]

5. The form of the old Lloyd's SG Policy is appended to the 1906 Act, although that wording fell into disuse in the London Market in 1982 on the adoption of new policy forms.
6. The only form of declaration policy referred to in the 1906 Act is the "floating policy" (s. 29), which specifies a maximum sum insured and each declaration goes to reduce that figure.
7. In the event that the policy is avoided or otherwise is treated as non-existent, the assured is entitled to a full return of his premium. By contrast, once the risk has started but is then terminated, none of the premium is repayable (ss 82–84), These rules are of course subject to contrary agreement.
8. The prohibition dates back to the Marine Insurance Act 1745. There is some dispute as to whether this provision has been affected by the legalisation of gambling contracts by the Gambling Act 2005, s. 335, although the view of most commentators is that the 1906 Act is unaffected. Taking out or issuing marine insurance without interest is also a criminal offence under the Marine Insurance (Gambling Policies) Act 1909, although that Act has lain dormant since the day it was passed.
9. *Feasey v Sun Alliance Life Assurance Corporation* [2003] Lloyd's Rep IR 640.
10. Sections 7–14.

although those illustrations are for the most part outmoded and the key interests recognised by the modern law are ownership, possession coupled with a right of enjoyment[11] or a duty with respect to the subject matter[12] and security interests of various classes. Unsecured creditors, including company shareholders, do not have any insurable interest in their debtors' property.[13] Marine policies are contracts of indemnity, so that an assured who has no interest in the subject matter at the date of the occurrence of the insured peril, e.g. because he has sold the subject matter, simply has no claim (section 6). Equally, an assured who has taken out more than one policy on the subject matter cannot recover more than his actual loss, although he is free to decide exactly how that loss is to be allocated between the various insurers (section 32).[14] A marine policy, unlike other forms of first party cover, is capable of being assigned to a third party (section 50), although any such assignment must be accompanied by an express transfer to the third party of the insured subject matter (section 51).[15]

Marine policies are contracts of utmost good faith (section 17). The practical consequences of that principle are that: (a) the assured must disclose every material circumstance known to him (section 18); (b) the assured must not misrepresent any material fact (section 20); and (c) any person placing insurance on behalf of the assured must disclose material facts known to him whether or not they were known to the assured (section 19). If the assured fails to do so, the policy may be avoided[16] and the premium is to be returned. The duty of disclosure comes to an end when the contract between the parties is concluded (section 21).[17] A fact is material if it "would influence the judgment of a prudent insurer in fixing the premium, or determining whether he will take the risk", a phrase which has been construed as meaning that a fact has to be disclosed or not misrepresented if it would be of interest to a prudent insurer writing risks in the market at the time whether or not the fact would ultimately have caused a prudent insurer to reach a different conclusion.[18] This wide-ranging objective test is, however, tempered by a requirement on the insurers in question to prove that they were induced to enter into the contract by the manner in which the risk was presented by the assured, and the mere fact that there is proof that a prudent insurer would have been interested in the fact in question does not automatically lead to the conclusion that the insurers themselves would have acted differently had the fact been disclosed.[19]

11. *Sharp v Sphere Drake Insurance Insurance Co, The Moonacre* [1992] 2 Lloyd's Rep 501.
12. *O'Kane v Jones, The Martin P* [2005] Lloyd's Rep IR 174 (ship managers).
13. *Moran, Galloway & Co v Uzielli* [1905] 2 KB 555.
14. A paying insurer is, however, entitled to seek payment – contribution – from the other insurers so that each ultimately bears no more than its own proportion of the risk: see s. 80 and *O'Kane v Jones, The Martin P* [2005] Lloyd's Rep IR 174.
15. Sale of the subject matter does not automatically operate to transfer the policy to the purchaser: s. 15.
16. *HIH Casualty and General Insurance Co v Chase Manhattan Bank* [2003] Lloyd's Rep IR 230.
17. There may be a residual post-contractual duty of utmost good faith owed by the assured, but the duty has no practical significance and post contractual matters are dealt with by the contract itself: *Manifest Shipping Co Ltd v Uni-Polaris Insurance Co Ltd, The Star Sea* [2001] Lloyd's Rep IR 247; *K/S Merc-Skandia XXXXII v Lloyd's Underwriters, The Mercandian Continent* [2001] Lloyd's Rep IR 802. Similarly, post-contractual duties owed by insurers are based on express or implied terms in the contract.
18. *Pan Atlantic Insurance Co Ltd v Pine Top Insurance Co Ltd* [1994] 3 All ER 581.
19. *Assicurazioni Generali v Arab Insurance Group* [2003] Lloyd's Rep IR 131.

### (d) Content of the policy

A marine policy typically consists of the insuring clause (setting out the risks covered), exclusions (setting out the excepted perils) and the various obligations of the parties.

As far as coverage is concerned, the most important terms used to delimit the risk run (or excluded from cover) are defined in the schedule to the 1906 Act (section 30). In general terms what is covered is a matter for the policy, although there are certain default rules set out in section 55 of the Act: the insurers are liable for losses proximately caused by an insured peril,[20] or for losses which are caused by the operation of an insured peril and some other peril which is not specifically excluded under the policy;[21] the insurers are liable for loss from an insured peril which would not have arisen but for the negligence of the Master or crew; the insurers are not liable for loss attributable to the wilful misconduct of the assured (a principle which reflects the common law and is not capable of being ousted by agreement); and the insurers are not liable for inevitable losses, e.g. wear and tear, inherent vice, rats or vermin, or leakage and breakage.

The 1906 Act says nothing about the post-contractual obligations of the insurers, and relatively little about the post-contractual obligations of the assured. Traditionally marine policies have contained warranties, which are terms relating to the risk run by the insurers, although the modern tendency of insurers is to replace warranties with other terms of less draconian effect if broken. Where the assured fails to comply with a warranty, the risk terminates automatically and any remedial action taken by the assured does not operate to reinstate the risk (sections 33–34).[22] Express marine warranties must be included in the policy itself (section 35). The 1906 Act sets out various rules for the construction of particular warranties,[23] confirms that there are no warranties of nationality (section 37) or the seaworthiness of goods (section 40) and sets out the two warranties which are to be implied into a marine policy, namely, the seaworthiness of a ship insured under a voyage policy (section 39)[24] and the legality of the voyage (section 41).

The 1906 Act goes on to imply into voyage policies (but not time policies) a series of restrictions on the cover provided by insurers. All of these are designed to ensure that the risk actually run by the insurers is that specified in the policy. First, if the hull or cargo is insured "at and from" a particular place, there is an implied obligation that the adventure is to be commenced within a reasonable time, failing which the policy may be avoided (section 42). In the same way, if the place of departure is specified by the policy and the ship sails from any other place, the risk does not attach (section 43). Thirdly, if the ship sails for a different destination to that specified in the policy, the risk never attaches (section 44).[25]

20. See *Leyland Shipping v Norwich Union Fire Insurance Society* [1918] AC 350.
21. *Lloyd Instruments Ltd v Northern Star Insurance Co Ltd, The Miss Jay Jay* [1987] 1 Lloyd's Rep 32.
22. As construed by the House of Lords in *Bank of Nova Scotia v Hellenic War Risks Association Ltd (Bermuda) Ltd, The Good Luck* [1991] 3 All ER 1.
23. Neutrality (s. 36); good safety (s. 38).
24. There is no warranty of seaworthiness set out in s. 39 in respect of a time policy, although the assured is unable to recover under a time policy if the loss is caused by unseaworthiness of which the assured is aware.
25. Or unattached if it had earlier attached, as in the case of cargo which is insured from the time when it leaves the warehouse as well as for the later voyage: *Nima SARL v Deves Insurance plc* [2002] Lloyd's Rep IR 752.

Fourthly, if the ship deviates from its agreed route, or delays, in either case without proper excuse, then the insurers are automatically discharged (sections 45–49).

### (e) Marine insurance losses and claims

Marine insurance losses are of three classes (section 56). The most severe form of loss is actual total loss, which arises where the subject matter is destroyed or the assured has been irretrievably deprived of it (section 57): a ship which is missing after the lapse of a reasonable time is presumed to have been the victim of an actual total loss. The least severe form of loss is a partial loss, which arises where the subject matter has been damaged (section 56). The third form, which is intermediate, is the constructive total loss. There are various forms of constructive total loss (section 60), the common theme being that the subject matter has as a result of an insured peril ceased to be economically viable for the assured to continue to operate. The most important forms are damage which is more costly to repair than the repaired value of the subject matter, and seizure of the subject matter in circumstances where it is unlikely to be restored to the assured within a reasonable time. The significance of a constructive total loss is that the assured may, if he so wishes (and he almost always will so wish), require the insurers to treat the loss as an actual total loss for the purpose of measuring the amount of indemnity. The assured can do this by serving a notice of abandonment on the insurers (sections 61 and 62). Where a notice of abandonment is served so that a constructive total loss is to be treated as an actual total loss, or in the case of a pure actual total loss, the insurers are entitled to take over whatever is left of the insured subject matter (section 63).

In addition to covering loss caused by the insured peril, a marine policy will also cover general average losses (sections 64–66, discussed below), and also any sums reasonably expended by the assured in fulfilling his duty to prevent or mitigate any loss arising from an insured peril (section 78).

The amount recoverable depends upon whether the policy is valued or unvalued. In the case of a valued policy the general rule is that the assured is entitled to recover the agreed value. In the case of an unvalued policy the assured is only entitled to recover his actual loss, measured by the difference between the value of the subject matter at the date of the policy[26] and the value of the subject matter immediately after the casualty. There are nevertheless special rules which apply to the measure of indemnity in respect of partial losses (sections 67–76). It is also the case that marine policies are "subject to average", so that if the assured suffers a partial loss and is underinsured, the assured can recover only the amount of that loss proportionate to the sum insured (section 81). Insurers are liable for successive partial losses even if they in aggregate exceed the sum insured for a total loss, and they will also be liable for a total loss even though there have been previous paid claims for partial losses (section 77). Once the insurers have paid for a total loss, they are entitled, by way of subrogation, to exercise any legal

26. Section 16. In practice, however, modern policies follow the non-marine rule and look to the value of the subject matter immediately before the loss and not to its value at the inception of the policy: *Thor Navigation Inc v Ingosstrakh Insurance* [2005] Lloyd's Rep IR 490.

rights possessed by the assured against third parties who may have been fully or partly responsible for the loss (section 79).

## 3. HULL AND MACHINERY INSURANCE

The Institute Hulls Clauses are of some antiquity. They were revised in 1982, and again in 1995. Most recently, in 2003,[27] a new version of the Clauses – the International Hull Clauses – was published. All three sets of Clauses remain in use, and somewhat surprisingly the market continues to adhere primarily to the 1982 Clauses,[28] although the later Clauses are used in the minority of cases. It suffices here to outline the coverage provisions of the 2003 Clauses.

The 2003 Clauses provide four classes of cover for hull and machinery owned or leased by the assured, and parts taken off the vessel. The insured perils are as follows:

(1) Losses from marine perils for which the insurers are liable whether or not the assured has exercised due diligence. The perils are: perils of the seas, rivers, lakes or other navigable waters; fire, explosion; violent theft by persons from outside the vessel; jettison; piracy; contact with land conveyance, dock or harbour equipment or installation; earthquake, volcanic eruption or lightning; accidents in loading, discharging or shifting cargo, fuel, stores or parts; and contact with satellites, aircraft, helicopters or similar objects, or objects falling therefrom.

(2) Losses from marine perils for which the insurers are liable only if the assured has acted with due diligence. The perils are: bursting of boilers or breakage of shafts but does not cover any of the costs of repairing or replacing the boiler which bursts or the shaft which breaks; any latent defect in the machinery or hull, but only to the extent that the cost of repairing the loss or damage caused thereby exceeds the cost that would have been incurred to correct the latent defect; negligence of Master, Officers, Crew or Pilots; negligence of repairers or charterers provided such repairers or charterers are not an Assured under this insurance; barratry[29] of Master, Officers or Crew. This is known as the *Inchmaree* clause, reversing the common law rule[30] that insurers are not liable for damage caused by mechanical breakdown.[31]

(3) Loss of or damage to the vessel caused by any governmental authority acting under the powers vested in it to prevent or mitigate a pollution hazard or damage to the environment or threat thereof, subject to the assured having exercised due diligence.

27. Replacing an earlier version published in 2002.
28. The International Hull Clauses 2003 are more clearly drafted than their predecessors and set out in detail the obligations of both parties as regards claims and other matters, and the time for the payment of premium. Also, the 2003 Clauses have eliminated virtually all warranties and have replaced them with suspensory provisions under which cover is simply suspended in circumstances where previously the risk would have terminated once and for all.
29. Fraud on the assured.
30. *Thames & Mersey Marine Insurance Co Ltd v Hamilton, Fraser & Co, The Inchmaree* (1887) 12 App Cas 484.
31. The insurance also covers "one half of the costs common to the repair of the burst boiler or the broken shaft and to the repair of the loss or damage caused thereby", and the assured may also take out additional cover. Further, the assured may for an additional premium insure against damage to the boiler or shaft itself.

(4) Three-fourths cover in respect of legal liability by way of damages arising out of collisions. If both vessels are to blame then the sum recoverable is calculated by reference to cross-liabilities. The three-fourths cover may be topped up for additional premium, or it may in the alternative be insured with a P&I Club.

## 4. CARGO INSURANCE

Cargo insurance is placed in the London Market on the terms of the Institute Cargo Clauses. There are three classes of cover:

(1) ICC(A), which is all risks.
(2) ICC(B), which are for a specified list of risks: fire or explosion; vessel or craft being stranded, grounded, sunk or capsized; overturning or derailment of land conveyance; collision or contact of vessel, craft or conveyance with any external object other than water; discharge of cargo at a port of distress; earthquake, volcanic eruption or lightning; general average sacrifice; jettison or washing overboard; and entry of sea, lake or river water into vessel, craft, hold, conveyance, container, liftvan or place of storage.
(3) ICC(C); which are for a narrower range of risks: fire or explosion; vessel or craft being stranded, grounded, sunk or capsized; overturning or derailment of land conveyance; collision or contact of vessel, craft or conveyance with any external object other than water; discharge of cargo at a port of distress; earthquake, volcanic eruption or lightning; general average sacrifice; and jettison.

## 5. GENERAL AVERAGE

### (a) What is general average?

"There is a general average act when, and only when, any extraordinary sacrifice or expenditure is intentionally and reasonably made or incurred for the common safety for the purpose of preserving from peril the property involved in the common maritime adventure."[32]

General average ("GA") is the sharing the financial consequences of an unexpected casualty between the commercial parties which have a financial interest in seeing the "adventure" completed. The expenses which fall within this definition are borne by those parties in proportion to the value of their respective interests at the time when and place where the adventure ends.

The concept is of very ancient origin, and references can be traced to the "Lex Rhodia de Iactu" probably in the fourth century BC.[33] It has, however, been the subject of development over time and still applies to modern seaborne trade. Insurance policies on hull, cargo and freight all provide that the insurers will pay

32. York-Antwerp Rules, Rule A.1.
33. "What is given for everyone should be contributed to by everyone." Justinian Digest: "TITLE II. Concerning the Rhodian Law of Jettison". 1. Paulus, *Sentences*, Book II: "It is provided by the Rhodian Law that where merchandise is thrown overboard for the purpose of lightening a ship, what has been lost for the benefit of all must be made up by the contribution of all". See *www.admiraltylawguide.com/documents/digestxiv.html*

the contribution in GA due from the assured,[34] and GA is therefore closely related to marine insurance.[35]

GA now forms part of the maritime law of every State with maritime jurisdiction. It arises by *operation of law*, independently of contract or statute. It is one of the class of obligations usually classified as "quasi contract", but a reference to GA and the York-Antwerp Rules is also expressly incorporated into most contracts of carriage.[36]

### (b) Typical examples of general average sacrifices or expenditure

The many laws, national and international, for the protection of the marine environment mean that the classic example of a general average sacrifice, namely the jettisoning of cargo to lighten a ship in danger of foundering, takes place extremely rarely today. However, the injection of compressed air into the cargo tanks of a grounded tanker, as part of a salvage operation to refloat her, may cause increased cargo leakage through the damaged bottom, and this will be treated as a general average loss, since the benefits of saving the ship and cargo will be mutual.[37]

More common now are claims based on hull and engine damage caused by efforts to refloat a grounded ship, and the cost of tugs engaged to assist refloating. These expenses must be distinguished from the cost of repairing damage caused by the grounding itself, which is treated as *particular average* and covered by the ship's hull insurance. Other examples of GA expenses are hull and cargo damage, typically water damage, caused by fire fighting operations, discharge and reloading of cargo at a port of refuge, and expenses incurred at a port of refuge. Expenses incurred, either by the ship or cargo owners, to forward cargo to its destination in another ship where the damage to the original carrying ship renders the continuation of her voyage physically or financially impracticable, will not usually be treated as GA, in the absence of an express agreement between the parties.[38]

### (c) The York-Antwerp Rules

The principle of GA was adopted in the medieval maritime codes,[39] but its application varied widely from port to port. Following a series of conferences promoted by marine insurers between 1865 and 1890, a set of Rules codifying the generally accepted practices of average adjusters was adopted in 1890 as the York-Antwerp Rules ("YAR"). These have been updated in 1924, 1950, 1974, 1990, 1994 and 2004.

The YAR have no statutory or legislative force, but are generally incorporated into contracts of carriage, so are contractually binding on the parties. The contract of carriage may also provide:

- *where* the adjustment shall be drawn up;
- the *currency* to be used for the adjustment; and
- the *security* which may be required.

34. Institute Time Clauses Hulls 1/10/83, clause 11; ITC (H) 1/11/95, clause 10; International Hull Clauses 1/11/03, clause 8; Institute Cargo Clauses A, B and C (1/1/82), clause 2.
35. Marine Insurance Act 1906, s. 66.
36. E.g. New Jason Clause in Congenbill, and in charterparties; clause 20(b)(iii) of ASBATANKVOY.
37. A modern example of this took place during the salvage of the *Sea Empress* off Milford Haven in 1996, and was recognised as legitimate in Lord Donaldson's Report, 17 May 1994, Cm. 2560.
38. Subject to Rule G(3) of the York-Antwerp Rules 1994 and 2004.
39. E.g. Consolado del Mare (1494), Laws of Oleron (13th Cent), Ordonnance de la Marine (1681).

The modern YAR are divided into *lettered* rules A to G, and *numbered* rules 1 to 23. The lettered rules are statements of general principle, while the numbered rules are specific applications of those principles. The Rule of Interpretation provides that the numbered rules prevail over the lettered rules, and that the YAR shall prevail over any contrary law or practice.

Revision of the YAR is now in the hands of the Comité Maritime International (CMI), which most recently adopted new Rules at its conference in June 2004. These came into effect in January 2005, but it should be noted that in March 2005 the Baltic and International Maritime Council (BIMCO) recommended that its members continue to use the 1994 Rules, which contain provisions, particularly those relating to port of refuge expenses, which are more favourable to shipowners.

## (d) General average on an unseaworthy ship

It is of the essence of general average that it operates independently of the cause of the GA act: see YAR Rule D which provides:

> "Rights to contribution in general average shall not be affected, though the event which gave rise to the sacrifice or expenditure may have been due to the fault of one of the parties to the adventure, but this shall not prejudice any remedies or defences which may be open against or to that party in respect of such fault."

If therefore the casualty giving rise to the need for extraordinary sacrifice or expenditure was the result of the ship having been unseaworthy at the commencement of the relevant voyage, this will probably be a breach of the relevant contract of carriage. However, the need for extraordinary measures is not diminished, and the underlying philosophy of GA is that such measures should be undertaken promptly, and the liability aspects dealt with afterwards; hence Rule D.

However, in *Goulandris Bros v Goldman*[40] it was held that where the general average act was brought about by the shipowner's *actionable fault* (e.g. failure to exercise due diligence to make the ship seaworthy before and at the commencement of the voyage[41]), the shipowner's claim against cargo for contribution in GA failed. In those circumstances, cargo's contribution would usually be reimbursed by the P&I Club in which the ship was entered, provided that there was no breach of the terms of the club cover.[42]

Any attempt by a carrier to include provisions in its contracts of carriage which purport to permit it to recover general average contributions notwithstanding its actionable fault will usually be neutralised by the repugnancy provisions in Article III.8 of the Hague and Hague-Visby Rules.

## (e) How general average works

Following a marine casualty a "Declaration of General Average" may be made by the Master of the ship, although this is not necessary in most legal systems – GA operates as a matter of law. It is, however, customary for the Master to put a statement to this effect in the ship's log.

40. [1957] 2 Lloyd's Rep 207.
41. Hague and Hague-Visby Rules, Article III.1.
42. E.g. failure to comply with the ISM Code – see Chapter 7.

The *average adjuster* is usually appointed by the shipowner. He is an independent professional – in some countries he is treated as a judge or arbitrator. He will usually, though not necessarily, be a member of the Association of Average Adjusters, the international body based in London. He will coordinate the collection of documents and information and prepare the *average adjustment*. If a cargo interest is not happy with the appointed adjuster, he may appoint a *co-adjuster* to supervise the process at his expense.

The adjuster will distribute a *valuation form* to all parties together with a *GA Bond* and *GA Guarantee* which must be completed and returned, usually by the cargo receivers and their insurers:

- The Valuation form sets out the value of each cargo interest and the amount of any deductions claimed in respect of damage found at destination.
- The GA Bond identifies the cargo receiver, who undertakes to pay the proportion of GA due from the cargo in question: this has limited legal effect.
- The GA Guarantee is signed by the cargo insurer creating a direct liability to pay the contribution due from the cargo in question.

Collecting these documents is the most time-consuming part of average adjusting.

The terms of YAR Rule E(3) are important. They allow the adjuster to *estimate* the allowance or contributory value if the party in question fails to supply the necessary information.

Where there are difficult questions of apportionment e.g. between damage caused by grounding (Particular Average) and damage caused by efforts to refloat (General Average), the adjuster will often appoint a consultant surveyor to advise him. The cost of the consultant's advice will be included in the adjustment. Likewise a professional ship valuer will usually be engaged to fix the sound market value of the ship, from which the cost of repairing any damage (actual or estimated) will be deducted in order to arrive at the ship's contributory value.

On completion the Average Adjuster will publish his adjustment, often a large volume, with details of all general average sacrifices and allowances which he has admitted (and those which he has not), the contributory values of ship and cargo interests, and the apportionment between those interests. An extract will be sent to each contributing interest setting out the amount due from or to them. The adjuster will usually act as the clearing house for the payments.

### (f) Recent developments

*1990*

Following the adoption by the 1989 Diplomatic Conference of the 1989 Salvage Convention including provisions for the assessment of Special Compensation for measures preventing pollution, an amended version of Rule VI was adopted which makes clear that Special Compensation payments will not be treated as GA.[43]

*1994*

Following the decision in *The Alpha*,[44] the Rule Paramount was added to the YAR. Amendments were also made to exclude any expense or sacrifice in connection with pollution save for the exceptional circumstances specified in Rule XI(d).

43. As requested by the Special Resolution annexed to the Salvage Convention 1989.
44. [1991] 2 Lloyd's Rep 515.

*2004*

After the 1994 CMI Conference underwriting interests began a concerted campaign to circumscribe the extent of admissible GA expenditure. An International Sub-Committee of the CMI prepared a detailed report[45] with recommendations which was presented to the CMI Conference at Vancouver. A revised set of York-Antwerp Rules 2004 was adopted which (i) exclude salvage from GA (Rule VI); (ii) limit admissible Port of Refuge expenses to those of putting into a port of refuge excluding crew's wages; (iii) clarify the position relating to temporary repairs in the light of the *Bijela* decision;[46] (iv) abolish the allowance of commission; and (v) adopt a variable rate of interest fixed annually.

These changes have not been popular with shipowners, and pressure has been brought to bear on BIMCO to retain references to the 1994 YAR in charterparties and bills of lading published by them.

### (g) The future?

Many writers have suggested that GA is archaic and should be abolished. However, it forms part of maritime codes and laws throughout so many States that it would require a special international convention (which would have to be ratified world-wide) to achieve this. There is no prospect of such a convention. Meanwhile we shall no doubt see a contest between the insurers (led by their association The International Association of Marine Insurance (IUMI)) who seek to reduce its importance, and the shipping interests such as BIMCO who will seek to retain it.

## 6. PROTECTION AND INDEMNITY INSURANCE: P&I CLUBS

### (a) Introduction

P&I Clubs provide third party liability insurance for shipowners. The modern Protection and Indemnity Associations (P&I Clubs) are the descendants of the mutual protection clubs and indemnity clubs which were founded by British shipowners in the nineteenth century in reaction to changes in the legislation affecting their third party liabilities and to the perceived failure of marine insurance companies and marine underwriters satisfactorily to respond to their needs. The distinction between protection and indemnity risks is today largely academic but originally, protection covered liabilities to personnel and for damage to property, while indemnity covered liabilities to cargo owners under a contract of carriage. Today most shipowners still obtain their third party insurance cover from P&I Clubs although it is possible to insure with other underwriters, usually for a fixed premium and with generally lower limits of cover than those offered by the clubs. Two of the features which distinguish P&I Clubs from other insurers are that they are controlled or governed by their shipowner members, which ensures their members a measure of flexibility, and that they are run on a non-profit making or mutual basis, making them economically attractive.

45. Which can be found at *www.comitemaritime.org*
46. [1994] 2 Lloyd's Rep 1.

### (b) The risks covered

The risks covered by protection and indemnity insurance are set out in detail within the rules of each club: these also include conditions, exceptions and limitations and other provisions, including the bye-laws relevant to the operation of the club.

P&I risks include:

- claims for loss or damage to cargo;
- unrecoverable general average contributions;
- liabilities to passengers, crew or others, including personal injury and death claims;
- medical treatment and the repatriation of sick, injured or deceased crew members;
- crew unemployment indemnity following a casualty;
- stowaways;
- collisions – 25% of damages payable to the colliding ship;
- damage to fixed and floating objects;
- liabilities under approved towage contracts;
- wreck removal;
- expenses of marine inquiries;
- expenses incidental to the operation of ships – subject to the discretion of the club directors;
- special compensation under the 1989 Salvage Convention;
- fines, including those for pollution;
- civil liability for pollution.

Readers who require a more detailed understanding of the cover provided are recommended to refer to the rulebook of any one of the Group clubs most of whom make these available on their websites.

In any given period, the greatest numbers of claims experienced by a P&I Club are cargo claims and those related to personal injuries; among the most expensive claims are the costs of wreck removal. Under the Lloyd's Hull form, the running-down clause covers 75% of the collision liabilities and the P&I Clubs cover the remaining 25% or one-fourth. Often, this may mean that the club is the largest underwriter sharing this risk. Under other Hull forms, notably the Norwegian form and the French form, these costs are met 100% by the hull underwriter. If a member chooses, clubs are able, in any case, to offer 100% cover for collision liabilities. It is interesting to note that the stated aim of the first Protection Club to be formed in 1865 was to "protect shipowners against their liabilities for loss of life and personal injury under the Merchant Shipping Act of 1854 *and also the risk of running down other vessels, not covered by their ordinary Marine Policies*".[47] This refers not to one-fourth of the collision liability but to the fact that it was then not legally possible for hull insurance to provide cover in excess of the insured value of the ship.

### (c) Structure of the clubs

The clubs have a long tradition of caring for the needs of their members and have responded over the years to changes and developments in the legislation affecting

47. Preface to the Deed of the Shipowners' Mutual Protection Society.

the responsibilities and liabilities of shipowners and the scope of the cover provided has obviously expanded considerably. The essence of the modern club remains that it is a group of shipowners who pool or share their risks. The corporate entity which accepts the risks and which pays the claims is nowadays often located offshore, as is the management company appointed by the club to handle its affairs. Most of the English clubs originally operated within the United Kingdom using the pound sterling as their currency but following the devaluation of the pound in 1967 many clubs moved offshore to such locations as Bermuda or Luxembourg, where they were able to hold their funds in US dollars and to enjoy some protection from UK exchange control. The visible presence of the club, whether in the United Kingdom or elsewhere, is likely to be the agent for the managers, who employs the underwriters and the claims handlers who are responsible for the day-to-day running of the club. Particular arrangements however, vary from one club to another.

Any person who has an interest in a ship may be a club member including not only shipowners but also, for example, charterers and third party ship managers: typically a club may include several hundred members. From their number, the Board of Directors is elected, usually holding office for three years. The Board generally meets three or four times each year. Its principal responsibilities are to determine the liabilities which are to be covered, to decide the level of calls or premium required each financial year, the coordination of club policy in general, the planning of financial strategy, particularly regarding the holding of reserve funds, the supervision of the club managers, including the handling of claims and the exercise of their discretion regarding the application of the club rules.

### (d) Conditions and exceptions

It is noteworthy that in all cases, subject to the discretion of the club directors, cover is conditional on the entered ship's classification being maintained and upon compliance with statutory obligations including for example, SOLAS[48] and the ISM (International Safety Management) Code, the STCW (Standards of Training, Certification and Watch-keeping) Convention 1995 and the ISPS (International Ship and Port Security) Code.

Since most of the claims covered by P&I are liability claims, the club rules also require that members take the benefit of any available regime of limitation of liability. Where a member loses the right to limit, this does not deprive him necessarily of the right to claim reimbursement from the club. Under the 1976 Limitation Convention, the test for the loss of the right to limit is stricter than under the 1957 Limitation Convention: the claimant must prove that the loss resulted from the owner's personal act or omission, committed with intent to cause such loss, or recklessly and with the knowledge that such loss would probably result. If this is proved, then it is likely that the owner would fall foul of subsections 39(5) and 55(2) of the Marine Insurance Act of 1906,[49] which applies to all club cover governed by English law.[50]

48. See Chapter 7 for more information on SOLAS.
49. See *Compania Maritima San Basilio SA v Oceanus Mutual Underwriting Association (Bermuda) Ltd (The Eurysthenes)* [1976] 2 Lloyd's Rep 171 (CA).
50. See, e.g., the 2007 North of England P&I Club rules: Rule 26(4) at *www.nepia.com/pdf/PandI_Rules_2007.pdf*

### (e) The International Group of P&I Clubs

The International Group of P&I Clubs is an association of the largest P&I Clubs, most of them originally based in the United Kingdom, with others in Scandinavia, Japan and the USA. Other clubs exist outside the International Group, often established in order to serve a particular sector of the market. The China P&I Club is an example of this, having been established in the 1980s in order to insure Chinese-owned ships not trading outside Chinese waters. The main purpose of the International Group is the pooling of the cost of large claims, currently those in excess of $7 million up to $50 million and the purchase of $2,000 million of reinsurance for the excess over that limit, bringing the total funds available at this point to $2,050 million. The cost of any claim beyond this amount, were such a situation to arise, would be met by overspill funds collected by each club in the Group: it is the essence of mutual insurance that each club member is the reinsurer of last resort. In 2007, the Group for the first time purchased overspill reinsurance on behalf of each club for all categories of claim up to $1,000 million in excess of the limit of the Group's reinsurance.

Traditionally the clubs offered unlimited cover for any one claim, with the exception of oil pollution claims[51] which have been limited for some time and which are currently restricted to $1 billion. In the 1990s it was decided, after a prolonged debate, to impose a ceiling on the cover provided, albeit at a very high level. This was in response to mounting concerns that any overspill claim in excess of the Group reinsurance limit would fall back on the clubs and thus on their members, in amounts which might not realistically be collectable. There was also a fear that in some cases, some shipowners would be unable to pay the call or might default, leaving the burden to fall on other, more prosperous members. Most shipowners felt that while they did not object in principle to paying overspill calls, it was preferable that the amount of the call should at least be quantified. The limit of any overspill call for any ship entered in a Group club was eventually fixed at 2.5% of the 1976 limitation fund for that ship. For a 10,000 gt ship, for example, the maximum overspill call would be about $65,000. It is reckoned that this gives an effective limit for club cover for any one claim of $4.25 billion, comprised of $2.05 billion provided by the club, the Group pool and reinsurance and the balance from overspill funds.

In addition to the limit on pollution, which is mentioned above, the Group in 2007 imposed a further limit on cover, whereby a maximum of $3,000 million applies to claims in respect of liability to passengers and seamen with a sub-limit on passenger claims of $2,000 million.

The International Group Agreement (IGA) has been under the scrutiny of the European Commission as being in possible restraint of free competition in insurance matters. A 10 years' exemption was granted in 1986; its renewal in 1996 became the subject of intense debate and it was not until 1999 that it was conceded that the Group Agreement was not in breach of EC principles.

The International Group also represents the interests of P&I Clubs and their members at the IMO (International Maritime Organization) and at other international organisations, where treaties and international conventions on maritime private law are under discussion. The Group also maintains contact with the

51. See Chapter 8 on Marine Pollution.

classification societies through the medium of IACS (International Association of Classification Societies.) Another example of the Group's wider role is the Code of Practice relating to SCOPIC agreed between the Group and the International Salvage Union.[52]

### (f) The managers' agents: Underwriting and claims handling; Calls

The role of the managers' agent or of those who deal with the everyday business of the club involves three important functions: underwriting, claims handling and the prudent investment of the club's financial reserves. The board of directors decide at the start of each financial year on the total amount of premium likely to be required to fund claims anticipated in that period. It is the role of the P&I underwriters to see that individual members pay the appropriate call in order to achieve that target. There is no standard tariff for P&I calls – the amount paid by each member depends entirely upon the member's loss record. Those who have a good claims record pay less: those who have a poor record pay more. Charges are levied usually in US dollars in dollars and cents per entered ton. Generally the entered tonnage nowadays is likely to be the gross tonnage. Thus it is perfectly possible for two physically identical ships to be charged different rates for P&I cover – depending upon loss record. It is worth mentioning that the P&I financial year runs from noon on 20 February each year – a relic from the days of the original hull clubs, when ships were laid up during the winter months in the northern hemisphere and were re-commissioned in mid-February.

When the financial year opens members are sent an invoice for the payment of an advance call, which may be settled by one payment or more usually paid in instalments. At some point later, generally six months or so after the end of the financial year, the directors customarily review the claims position and establish whether sufficient money has been generated by the advance call to pay claims incurred during that year. If more funds are required, they may make a supplementary call in order to balance the account. Members who elect to leave the club before the supplementary call is made are likely to be required to pay a release call in lieu or to provide an undertaking which is satisfactory to the club managers that the eventual supplementary call will be settled.

One significant difference between market insurance and club insurance is possibly that the clubs are able to assume control when a situation arises on a member's ship, which is likely to lead to a claim. The shipmaster and shipowner are encouraged, when facing a potential liability, immediately to contact the club for assistance. They are also able in overseas ports to contact the local club correspondent, who will provide further support and advice. Surveyors can be appointed and, if necessary, lawyers in order to protect the owners' interests from the outset, with the club meeting the costs. The clubs have correspondents in most ports worldwide, numbering several hundreds. Many of these are commercial correspondents and may have other shipping interests, operating as Customs or ships' agents for example. Others are legal correspondents. They all, however, possess wide local knowledge and contacts and are able to provide valuable support to the shipmaster. They are also able to assist where required, with the provision of security if the ship is arrested or threatened with arrest.

52. See Kennedy and Rose, *Law of Salvage* (6th ed, 2002), p. 760.

### (g) Technical advice and support

Another function filled by the managers or their agents includes the provision at all times of advice and support to members in any matters related to their business. Many clubs regularly publish materials giving topical advice on the safe and efficient operation of ships. This may include technical advice on such matters as the carriage of certain cargo products, the wording of charterparty clauses and valuable loss prevention advice. Some clubs also run a ship inspection programme, whereby the club is able to offer guidance on the management, operation or manning of members' ships, aimed at reducing their exposure to claims.

### (h) "Pay to be paid" rule: Direct action

All Group club rules provide that the member in order to claim reimbursement from the club must first have been held liable for and have paid a claim. Where the member has been wound up or adjudged bankrupt before the claim is finally assessed, the member is clearly not in a position to pay the claim. The question then arises whether the claimant can sue the club directly. Two test cases were brought against two clubs in the International Group, concerning two ships, the *Fanti* and the *Padre Island*.[53] In these cases, the claimants sought to rely on the provisions of the Third Parties (Rights against Insurers) Act of 1930 whereby any rights which a defendant may have to be indemnified by insurers, are transferred, on the defendant's bankruptcy or winding up, to the claimant. The claimant may then stand in the shoes of the insured party. Subsection 1(3) of the Act also states that any provision in the insurance policy intended to defeat this transfer of rights, is deemed void. The House of Lords held that the "pay to be paid" rule was an integral part of P&I cover and that subsection 1(3) did not apply.[54]

Similar provisions apply to the rules of those Group clubs, which are governed by a law other than English law. It is also worth noting that in the event of an owner being bankrupt and unable to pay a claim, it is highly likely that the owner might also have failed to pay P&I calls, in which case membership of the club would have been terminated.

On occasion the clubs, entirely without prejudice to their right to invoke the "pay to be paid" rule, may be prepared to advance funds before the member has settled a claim. This procedure is likely to be considered in personal injury cases and obviously applies where a club guarantee has been given. When particularly large sums of money are involved in a settlement it may make practical sense for the club to provide funds rather than requiring the member to do so.

It should also be borne in mind that some recent legislation including the US Oil Pollution Act (1990) and the revised Athens Convention[55] call for direct action against insurers. As already mentioned, English law governs the rules of most of the group clubs. From 11 May 2000 all such contracts are subject to the Contracts (Rights of Third Parties) Act 1999. Under this Act, persons who are not a party to

53. See *Firma C-Trade v Newcastle Protection and Indemnity Association (The Fanti); Socony Mobil Oil Co Inc and Others v West of England Ship Owners Mutual Insurance Association Ltd (London) (The Padre Island) (No 2)* [1990] 2 Lloyd's Rep 191 (HL).

54. See Bennett, *The Law of Marine Insurance* (2nd ed), pp. 611–616.

55. 2002 Protocol to the Athens Convention, which has not yet entered into force. See Chapter 5 on Carriage of Passengers.

an insurance contract may in their own right enforce a term of the contract if the contract expressly allows them to do so, or if the term in question "purports to confer a benefit on him".[56] However, the Act also allows the parties, if they wish, to make it clear in the wording of the contract, that it is not their intention to confer benefits on third parties. The clubs in the International Group have accordingly amended their rules to this effect.

### (i) Claims settlement: Disputes

P&I Clubs in the course of a year handle many thousands of claims. Many of the claims involved are cargo claims or personal injury claims, the great majority of which are settled by negotiation and without the involvement of lawyers or any legal process. Clearly, however, there are likely to be a substantial number of claims, which cannot be amicably settled and which are resolved either in the courts or by arbitration. In such cases, the club managers appoint lawyers in London or elsewhere, in the appropriate jurisdiction. Occasionally, disputes may arise between member and club over the conduct of a case or circumstances may arise where the managers may wish to reserve the club's position. This might be, for example, because of a suspected breach of the club rules (such as a failure to maintain the ship in compliance with classification society rules). In such cases, it may be appropriate for the member and the club to have separate legal representation. In the event of such a dispute not being resolved by the managers, members have the right to have their case presented to their fellow members, the directors of the club, with the request that they establish whether there has been a breach of the rules or, if they deem it suitable, that they exercise their discretion in favour of the member. Should the member not be satisfied by the directors' decision, there is an appeal procedure whereby in the first instance the case is again put before the directors as adjudicators or thereafter it may be submitted to independent arbitrators in London.

### (j) Freight, demurrage and defence cover

All clubs offer freight, demurrage and defence (FD&D) or "defence" cover as an adjunct to P&I cover. Usually, the defence cover is insured in a separate club, with a separate board of directors, but under the same managers. In other cases the insurance is provided by the P&I Club and is defined as a separate "class" of cover. Defence clubs provide a claims-handling service and insurance of legal costs and fees for those claims not covered by P&I. These might include disputes with shipbuilders, post-fixture disputes with charterers, disputes with suppliers including ship-chandlers or disputes with crew. The insurance provided is always discretionary and covers only the legal costs, not the principal amounts in dispute.

### (k) Conclusion

It is interesting to reflect whether shipowners in the twenty-first century, faced with the need to find insurance cover for their third party claims, would still opt for the club system as did their predecessors in the nineteenth century. It may

56. Section 1(1) of the 1999 Act.

seem likely that they would, bearing in mind the success that the clubs have enjoyed over the past 150 years and the attractions of self-governing, mutual, non-profit making insurance, provided at cost.

## 7. LETTERS OF UNDERTAKING

### (a) Purpose of a letter of undertaking

The purpose of a letter of undertaking or guarantee is to ensure that a ship is not arrested in port by a creditor, or to allow an arrested ship to sail. Whether the owners or managers are unwilling or unable to pay the underlying debt, their interest will be that the ship is enabled to continue trading and earning freight. A speedy release of the ship is also in the interests of the creditor, as it will help a shipowner or manager in financial straits to pay the debt. By the letter of undertaking, the P&I Club provides security for the debt of the shipowner or manager by undertaking to settle the debt and to accept service of *in rem* proceedings in a competent court.[57] A letter of undertaking is also a means of allowing the parties the time to discuss the precise amount of the liability and acceptable ways of paying it, while avoiding resorting to court or arbitration proceedings for as long as possible.

Most P&I Clubs make it clear in their rules that the club is under no obligation to provide bail or security on behalf of a member.[58] However, when, following an incident likely to give rise to a claim, a ship is arrested, or where there is a threat of arrest by the claimant, the P&I Club will generally agree to issue a letter of undertaking in order to release the ship and allow the voyage to continue, thereby avoiding further possible delays and financial loss. The letter will state that the club undertakes to pay the addressee on demand such sum or sums, in respect of the particular claim, as may be agreed by negotiation or awarded to the addressee by final judgment or arbitration award no longer subject to appeal. This creates a collateral contract between the claimant and the club. It is always expressed to be in consideration of the creditor releasing the ship from arrest or refraining from arrest.

Such letters are issued on condition that the claim is covered by the club rules and is included in the ship's terms of entry; the member's calls are paid up to date and there are no calls outstanding on that ship or any other ship in that entry; the ship is arrested or there is an imminent threat of arrest; the ship is not in breach of club rules, for example with respect to classification; and that the wording of the letter is approved by the club managers or their agents.

The P&I Clubs, particularly those in the International Group, are scrupulous in ensuring that such letters of undertaking are always honoured according to their terms. Any default would reduce the confidence of claimants and thus the whole system of club letters of undertaking.

The alternative to a club letter for the shipowner may be the issue of a bank undertaking. In certain jurisdictions, claimants may insist on such guarantees.

57. As in, e.g., *The Juntha Rajprueck* [2003] 2 Lloyd's Rep 107.
58. See, e.g., 2007 Gard P&I Statutes and Rules: Rule 88, at *www.gard.no/gard/Publications/statutesandrules/rules/p6_chapter2.html*

The disadvantage of these is firstly that they may take a considerable time to arrange while club letters can be issued very quickly. Also bank guarantees can be costly whereas club letters are provided free of charge to members. Some P&I Clubs are prepared, in some circumstances, to issue non-club bail, that is, club letters covering non-club matters, but this is usually on a short-term or interim basis, until owners are able themselves to provide suitable security.[59]

### (b) Construction of a letter of undertaking

General contract law is applicable to letters of undertaking, and so is the law on surety or guarantees. It has been confirmed in several cases[60] that *Investors Compensation Scheme v West Bromwich Building Society*[61] applies to letters of undertaking, so that the factual matrix must be taken into account in their interpretation. The factual matrix in the case of P&I Club letters of undertaking has a specific characteristic compared to other forms of surety and compared to most other forms of contract: they are not lengthy and precise documents negotiated over a period of time to precisely match other documents involved in the transaction, like, for instance, the letters of undertaking provided as part of a credit trans-action. They are one-page documents, more often than not negotiated on the basis of standard forms between parties who do not necessarily do business together on a regular basis and across more than one continent. There is usually a strong element of time pressure involved – many letters of undertaking are negotiated in a period not much longer than a day or two. All this is part of the factual matrix surrounding P&I Club letters of undertaking and must affect their interpretation.

The tendency is, nevertheless, to interpret letters of undertaking quite literally. Although they are often negotiated in emergency or urgent situations, courts usually hold the parties to the wording of the document, unless there is cause for rectification or otherwise some obvious mistake. There are various reasons for this. The explanation provided by Gloster J in *The Rays*[62] was that the negotiations in that case had taken place over two weeks between two experienced solicitors who were each partners of their respective firms, and that the Club's solicitors had had sufficient time to review the final version of the one-page document. In *The Tutova*,[63] the judge declined to imply a term into a letter of undertaking, considering that "the LOU is a common form of document which, despite being governed by English law and subject to the jurisdiction of this court, is widely used across the world often, as here, by those whose first language is not English". As a result, the court should be "more cautious about assuming a chorus of 'yes of course'[64] than it might be in a domestic case unaffected by these considerations or the effect of different legal systems and professional assumptions". The inter-

59. See Hazelwood, *P&I Clubs – Law and Practice* (3rd ed) (Informa, 2000).
60. Most recently in *Canmer International Inc v UK Mutual Steamship Assurance Association (Bermuda) Ltd* [2005] 2 Lloyd's Rep 479.
61. [1998] 1 All ER 98.
62. *Canmer International Inc v UK Mutual Steamship Assurance Association (Bermuda) Ltd* [2005] 2 Lloyd's Rep 479.
63. *Almatrans SA v Steamship Mutual Underwriting Association* [2007] 1 Lloyd's Rep 104, at para. 23.
64. In response to the officious bystander pointing out the need for an additional clause.

national nature and the commercial purpose of the letter of undertaking were the most important considerations in its interpretation. There are exceptions to the rule of strictly literal interpretation: in *The Rio Assu*,[65] the Court of Appeal held that a reference to the demise charterers (a corporate body) included a reference to their successors.

Case law provides few final conclusions and it is probably fair to say that the outcome will depend on the wording of the letter of undertaking at issue in the individual case.

For instance, the question whether the letter of undertaking provided for a primary or secondary liability is a matter of construction. In *The Rays* (*supra*), a letter of undertaking on the standard form was contrasted with performance bonds and held to entail a secondary liability, whereas the Privy Council in *The Potoi Chau*[66] held that a letter of undertaking from a cargo insurer in respect of general average contributions constituted a primary liability.

### (c) The effect of a letter of undertaking

Letters of undertaking usually also contain provisions specifying how the claim should be pursued, such as a choice of law and jurisdiction (or arbitration) clause. These are important provisions, as they render the claim capable of being pursued, since the security is a private contractual matter between the parties to the letter of undertaking and only involves the court for the purpose of the arrest itself. The chosen law or jurisdiction may be different from those in the underlying claim.

Although courts are technically not involved in the letter of undertaking, they are keen to help enforce this type of security; in *The Oakwell*,[67] a ship had been arrested and released upon the provision of a letter of undertaking by the shipowner's P&I Club. There followed a period of negotiations between the parties. Before the litigation started, shipowners had sold the ship. As a result, the Club's solicitors refused to accept service of a writ *in rem*. The judge held that in spite of the sale, the Club would be in breach of the letter of undertaking if it did not participate in the proceedings. The Club must accept service, because it would be unacceptable in the market if claimants were to find themselves in a worse position as a result of having accepted a club undertaking than if they had gone ahead and arrested. Emphasis was placed on the commercial purpose of the letter of undertaking and its role in the shipping trade.

Once security in the form of a letter of undertaking has been provided, the ship is protected from being arrested again. This presumes that sufficient security has been provided, which may not always prove the case – the provider of the security may for instance have become insolvent. In *The Ruta*,[68] the relevant issue for decision was on what terms as to priority a claimant who had obtained security could proceed against the proceeds from a forced sale of the ship, following arrest. The claim had arisen from a collision between several ships caused by a small

65. *C Itoh & Co v Companhia de Navegaçao Lloyd Brasileiro (No 2)* [1999] 1 Lloyd's Rep 115.
66. *Castle Insurance Co Ltd v Hong Kong Islands Shipping Co Ltd* [1983] 2 Lloyd's Rep 376.
67. *Galaxy Energy International Ltd v Assuranceforeningen Skuld (Gjensidig)* [1999] 1 Lloyd's Rep 249.
68. [2000] 1 Lloyd's Rep 359.

cargo ship, the *Ruta*. The P&I Club of the *Ruta*, which was not a member of the International Group of P&I Clubs, had provided security to the owners of the *Lutra II*, but not to the other two yachts involved in the collision, in the form of a letter of undertaking in order to secure the release of the ship. The *Ruta* was released but re-arrested and sold. The P&I Club later became insolvent, rendering the letter of undertaking worthless. Following the judicial sale of the *Ruta*, the creditors who had not taken out a letter of undertaking had a priority interest in the proceeds of sale, and the question was whether the holders of the letter of undertaking, who were essentially unsecured creditors, should be granted the same priority. The judge, exercising his admiralty discretion, held that they should. The fact that the ship could technically have been re-arrested for the debt contributed to the conclusion that the priority should be the same.

CHAPTER 11

# Procedures for Enforcement

*DR MICHAEL TSIMPLIS*

## 1. ENFORCEMENT OF MARITIME CLAIMS

### (a) Introduction

The enforcement procedures for maritime claims differ in many aspects from those related to non-maritime claims. There are simple practical reasons for these differences. A ship travelling the world's oceans is likely to get involved in legal disputes arising either by the way of its operation or its trade. Thus it is not unusual for ships to get involved in collisions, salvage, towage or pollution claims as well as contractual claims by cargo or passengers and insurance disputes. Historically, where a claimant had a claim against a ship his claim would have very small chances of recovery if the ship was permitted to leave the jurisdiction because usually the defendant shipowner would have been in a foreign jurisdiction and the only asset in the claimant's jurisdiction would be the ship. However, proceeding against the property of the defendant shipowner without due notice and a right to defend would have also been very difficult.[1]

Thus a special legal regime of actions against the ship, coupled with the notion that the ship itself was the defendant in such an action, provided for a practical solution to the problem. Such actions were historically subject to the Admiralty Court which was the only one that had the jurisdiction to proceed against the ship and only in respect of particular claims. Following several statutory interventions nationally and through international conventions what is left of this special regime can presently be found in the Admiralty Jurisdiction of the High Court.[2]

This chapter explains the Admiralty jurisdiction of the High Court, the Admiralty procedure for the arrest of a ship under an action *in rem* and links these procedures with those of limitation of liability. In addition, another form of security available both for maritime and non-maritime claims, the freezing injunction, is also discussed.

The International Convention Relating to the Arrest of Sea-Going Ships, Brussels, 1 May 1952 (Arrest Convention 1952) to which the UK is a signatory defines "arrest" in Article 1(2) as "the detention of a ship by judicial process to secure a maritime claim, but does not include the seizure of a ship in execution or satisfaction of a judgment". The incorporation of the Arrest Convention 1952 into

1. See, for example, the difficulties in the development of the freezing injunction in *Lister v Stubbs* (1890) 45 ChD 1; *Mareva Compania Naviera SA v International Bulkcarriers SA (The Mareva)* [1975] 2 Lloyd's Rep 509 (CA) and *Nippon Yusen v Karageorgis* [1975] 2 Lloyd's Rep 137; [1975] 1 WLR 1093 (CA).
2. See D C Jackson on *Enforcement of Maritime Claims* (Informa, 2005) (hereinafter "*Jackson*") for a detailed analysis of the Admiralty jurisdiction.

English Law has not been made by direct inclusion of the text of the Convention but by rewriting the Convention as part of, what is today, the Admiralty Jurisdiction of the High Court under the Supreme Court Act 1981 which provides for rights for an action in rem and the Civil Procedure Rules for Admiralty Part 61.5 (CPR 61.5) which provides for the right to arrest. Thus no definition of arrest is available under English law.[3]

### (b) The Admiralty Jurisdiction of the High Court

The basis of the Admiralty jurisdiction of the High Court can be found in the Supreme Court Act 1981 ("SCA 1981"), sections 20–24. The wording of section 20 includes in the Admiralty jurisdiction of the High Court not only the heads of jurisdiction described within the SCA 1981 but in addition any previous[4] and any future Admiralty jurisdiction assigned to the High Court. The Arrest Convention 1952 and the International Convention on Certain Rules Concerning Civil Jurisdiction in Matters of Collision, Brussels, 10 May 1952 (Collision Jurisdiction Convention 1952) are enacted into English Law as part of the SCA 1981.

The Admiralty Jurisdiction of the High Court applies in respect of all vessels, British or not, in relation to all claims wherever they occur[5] and to all ship mortgages.[6] The Civil Procedure Rules for Admiralty[7] Part 61 (CPR 61) and the accompanying Practice Directions Part 61 (PD 61) must be considered together with the SCA 1981 in order to understand the Admiralty jurisdiction and procedures.

The Admiralty jurisdiction encompasses jurisdiction for a list of claims[8] which are, in essence, the claims covered by the Arrest Convention 1952[9] as well as all claims under the MSA 1995. Thus most shipping claims, like collision damage, salvage,[10] towage, claims arising from charterparties or bills of lading,[11] provisions to a ship, wreck removal, ownership and mortgage disputes for ships, are subject to the Admiralty jurisdiction.[12] In addition claims for oil pollution from

3. See *The Anna H* [1995] 1 Lloyd's Rep 11 (CA) for the difference between the definition and the purpose of arrest under English law.
4. Section 20(1)(b) of the SCA 1981.
5. For cargo and wreck even if the cargo or wreck are found on land: SCA 1981, s. 20(7)(b).
6. SCA 1981, s. 21(7).
7. The civil procedure system in England and Wales has undergone major reform with the development of the Civil Procedure Rules (CPR). A reform aiming, amongst other things, to make the process of litigation more understandable to the public. For this reason many Latin terms were replaced with English terms. The CPR for Admiralty entered into force on 25 March 2002 replacing Part 49f, primarily by CPR Part 61 and Practice Direction 61 (PD 61), but also partly by CPR Part 58 and PD 58 in relation to actions against a defendant; the *in personam* act under the previous procedural rules. The term *in personam* is still retained under the SCA 1981. On 25 March 2002 a new *Admiralty and Commercial Court Guide* was also issued, replacing the 5th edition of the *Commercial Court Guide*. The new title reflects the fact that the two courts have for some time been administered by a single Registry and Listing Office, with many common procedures. The new *Guide* contains the same basic structure as the previous *Guide*, but with a new Section N to cover Admiralty matters.
8. Included in s. 20(2).
9. Art. 1. However, pre-existing Admiralty jurisdiction not expressly included in the Supreme Court Act 1981 is expressly incorporated by s. 20. Note that a new Arrest Convention 1999 has been agreed but has not come into force. Small changes are to be introduced into English law if the UK becomes a party to the Arrest Convention 1999 and this convention comes into force. Richard Shaw and Nicholas Gaskell, "The Arrest Convention 1999", (1999) LMCLQ 4 (November), pp. 470–490.
10. SCA 1981, s. 20(6).
11. Whether contractually or otherwise. See *Samick Lines Co Ltd v Owners of the Ship "Antonis P Lemos" (The Antonis P Lemos)* [1985] AC 711; [1985] 1 Lloyd's Rep 283 (HL).
12. SCA 1981, s. 20(2) and s. 20(3).

ships,[13] and limitation of liability issues[14] are also subject to the Admiralty jurisdiction of the High Court. Some actions, in particular those including limitation of liability actions, can only be started at the Admiralty Court.[15] However, this does not apply to other actions for which the Admiralty Court does not have exclusive jurisdiction.[16]

### (c) Enforcement

Two procedures of enforcement are available under the Admiralty jurisdiction of the High Court. The first, the action *in personam*, is the ordinary action against a named defendant.[17] The second, the action *in rem*, is a special action only available under the Admiralty Jurisdiction of the High Court and it is an action against the ship or ships of named or unnamed defendants.

The nature of the action *in rem* has been considered an action against the ship itself as if the ship was the defendant, or as a device to put pressure on the shipowner to defend. The point that matters in practice is whether the ship and the shipowner can be considered as distinct parties in a claim *in rem* and a claim *in personam* concerning the same cause of action. This question has been answered in the negative in two occasions.

First, the European Court of Justice held that for the application of the provisions on multiple proceedings of the EC Jurisdiction Convention, actions *in rem* and actions *in personam* are between the same parties.[18]

More importantly, in a case where there was a judgment in the Indian Courts, and an action *in rem* in respect of the same cause of action was later initiated before the English Courts, the House of Lords held that for the purpose of section 34 of the Civil Jurisdiction and Judgments Act 1982, the action *in rem* and the action *in personam* was between the same parties. Thus, because of the foreign judgment *in personam* section 34 was a bar to the action *in rem*.[19] The decision on *The Indian Grace (No 2)* did not decide cases where a maritime lien is the basis of the action *in rem* thus the issue remains open in this respect.[20]

The action *in personam* is in general available in all cases where the High Court has jurisdiction on the merits except in cases where the jurisdiction is constraint under section 22 of the Supreme Court Act 1981 (SCA 1981) in respect of collision cases[21] and where an international convention and its implementation in the 1995 MSA restricts such an action.

13. SCA 1981, s. 20(5).
14. Section 20(3)(c), interpreting s. 20(1)(b).
15. CPR 61.2(1)(c) includes all actions *in rem*, all actions under the Merchant Shipping Act 1995, ship collision, pilotage and towage disputes, ownership disputes, loss of life and personal injury under SCA 1981, s. 20(2)(f), Master and crew member claims for wages, limitation, and salvage claims.
16. CPR 61.2. Such claims include charterparty and bill of lading claims.
17. The CPR have removed the reference to the action *in personam* from the court procedure. But as the term "action *in personam*" still exists within the Supreme Court Act 1981 the deletion of the definition is not very helpful.
18. *Owners of Cargo Lately Laden on Board the Tatry v Owners of the Maciej Rataj (The Maciej Rataj)* ECJ (C-406/92) [1995] 1 Lloyd's Rep 302; [1994] ECR I-5439.
19. *Republic of India and the Government of the Republic of India (Ministry of Defence) v India Steamship Co Ltd (The Indian Grace) (No 2)* [1998] 1 Lloyd's Rep 1; [1997] 4 All ER 380.
20. See the discussion in *Jackson*. For a different view see *Comandate Marine Corporation v Pan Australia Pty Ltd (The Comandate)* [2006] FCAFC 192; [2008] 1 Lloyd's Rep 119.
21. In collision cases, s. 22 of the SCA 1981 permits an action (or a counterclaim) *in personam* only where the defendant is resident or has a place of business in England or Wales; or where the colli-

The action *in rem* can best be described nowadays as a procedural tool with which a claimant can force the defendant shipowner to appear in front of an English court or risk losing its ship.[22] This is because the action *in rem* carries with it, in the general case, a right to apply to the court for the arrest of the vessel under CPR 61.5. Thus, arrest of a ship as security for a civil claim is only available under the Admiralty jurisdiction of the High Court.

However, the reverse is not true and not all claims subject to the Admiralty jurisdiction carry with them a right to arrest the ship of the defendant. From the claims listed under section 20(2) of the SCA 1981 all but section 20(2)(d) can lead to the arrest of some property of the defendant.[23]

The SCA 1981 specifies, under section 21, three categories of claims that can be enforced by an action *in rem*.

### *(i) Action* in rem *in respect of claims to the possession or ownership of a ship*

The first category of claims[24] includes claims related to ownership and possession of the ship or the shares related to the ship; disputes between co-owners related to possession, employment or earning of the ship; claims on mortgages or charges on a ship; and claims related to the forfeiture or condemnation of the ship or its cargo and the restoration of goods or cargo.[25] We will refer to these claims as "ownership" claims. In respect of ownership claims the action *in rem* can be against the ship or other property involved in the ownership dispute.

### *(ii) Action* in rem *arising from maritime liens*

Section 21(3) of the SCA 1981 permits an action *in rem* against the relevant ship, cargo or freight[26] when a maritime lien is in existence. The claims that carry maritime liens are neither defined nor listed within the SCA 1981. However, it is well established under English law that maritime liens arise only in respect of collision claims, salvage claims, crew and Master's wages, Master's disbursements, bottomry and respondentia.[27] Maritime liens will be discussed further below.

---

sion took place in inland waters or in a port of England or Wales or there are already proceedings (or proceedings have already been determined) by the High Court. Otherwise, there is no jurisdiction for an *in personam* action in collision cases whether such an action is started under the Admiralty jurisdiction of the High Court or otherwise (s. 22(7) of the SCA 1981).

22. This was not always so. Historically the action *in rem* was considered to be against the ship itself. Thus the ship was the person sued. However, gradually the position changed to one recognising that from the time/moment the defendant appears in court, the case proceeds both *in rem* and *in personam* (see *The Dictator* [1892] P 304). Later in *The Indian Grace* (see fn. 19) it was decided that, from the start, a claim *in rem* is against the shipowner. There are significant doubts in the effect of this last decision where maritime liens are concerned; however, it appears that the procedural character of the action *in rem* where no maritime lien has been created is firmly established.
23. See *Owners of Cargo Lately Laden on Board the MV Erkowit v Owners of the Eschersheim (The Eschersheim, the Jade and the Erkowit)* [1976] 1 WLR 430; [1976] 1 All ER 920; [1976] 2 Lloyd's Rep 1; (1976) 120 SJ 315; 1976 WL 46782 (HL).
24. SCA 1981, s. 21(2).
25. SCA 1981, s. 21(2), referring to s. 20(a), 20(b), 20(c) and 20(s).
26. Only freight at risk is subject to the lien.
27. *The Bold Buccleugh* (1851) 7 Moo PC 267. Bottomry bonds were a form of loan signed by the Master and secured on the ship. These were used to obtain supplies or services for the ship without undue delay (see, for example, *Douglas v Owners of Yacht St George (The St George)* (1926) 25 Ll L Rep 482, one of the last cases on a bottomry claim). These bonds were considered to give rights against the ship, protected by a maritime lien. Respondentia concerned similar rights in respect of loans against the value of the cargo. Both bottomry and respondentia were methods by which the difficulties of transferring information and funds were dealt with and they are both presently obsolete.

*(iii) Action* in rem *in respect of other claims*

The third category of claims for which an action *in rem* is permitted is the widest one and involves a variety of shipping claims except "ownership" claims. These are listed in section 20(2)(e)–(r) of the SCA 1981. Thus, claims for collision and pollution damages; claims for loss of life and personal injury caused by a ship; claims arising out of a charterparty or a contract of carriage of cargo; cargo damage; salvage claims under the 1989 Salvage Convention or otherwise; towage claims; pilotage claims; claims in respect of supplies to the ship; ship repair and construction claims; dock charges and dues; claims related to the crew and Master's wages, claims in relation to Master's, agent's and charterer's disbursements and general average claims are all entitled to an action *in rem* under section 21(4) of the SCA 1981.

However, for this category of claims, the action *in rem* is based on different criteria from those of the ownership[28] and the maritime liens[29] categories described above and includes the possibility of an action *in rem* against the ship involved in the incident as well as other ships under the same ownership, namely, sister ships.[30] In particular, to arrest the ship in respect of which the claim has arisen, two requirements need to be fulfilled. First, the claim must be linked to a ship, this will be called the relevant ship, and the person who would be personally liable (the *relevant person*)[31] under the claim is either the owner or charterer[32] or in possession or in control of the *relevant ship* at the time of the actions that created the claim. The second requirement is that at the time the action *in rem* is initiated the relevant person is either the owner in respect of all shares or the demise-charterer of the *relevant ship*.[33]

In respect of the arrest of another ship under the same ownership as the relevant ship (*sister ship*) the first requirement remains the same, namely, that the person who would be personally liable (the *relevant person*) under the claim is either the owner or charterer[34] or the person in possession or in control of the *relevant ship* at the time of the actions that created the claim. However, in this case the second requirement is that at the time the action *in rem* is initiated the *relevant person* is the owner in respect of all shares of the *sister ship*.

Although this section only mentions the arrest of the ship, the interpretation of the word "ship" has been held to include all property on board the ship including bunkers and cargo if owned by the defendant shipowner.[35] The wording of section 21(4) permits the shipowner to arrest ships owned by its charterer. This is a

28. SCA 1981, s. 21(2).
29. *Ibid.*, s. 21(3).
30. *Ibid.*, s. 21(4).
31. The terminology used by s. 21(4) of the Supreme Court Act 1981 is "the person who would be liable on the claim in an action *in personam* ('the relevant person')". The "relevant person" is only used to establish the link between the property against which the action *in rem* is undertaken and the owner of that property and does not require first to show that the relevant person is in fact liable for the complaint. Of course if the relevant person is not in fact liable, the property arrested will be released.
32. The term charterer includes demise, time and voyage charterers as well as slot charterers. See *The Span-Terza* [1982] 1 Lloyd's Rep 225 and *The Mediterranean Shipping Co SA v Polish Ocean Lines (The Tychy) (No 2)* [1999] 2 Lloyd's Rep 11.
33. SCA 1981, s. 21(4)(b)(i) and (ii).
34. The term charterer includes demise, time and voyage charterers as well as slot charterers. See *The Span-Terza*, fn. 32, and *The Tychy (No 2)*, fn. 32.
35. *The Silia* [1981] 2 Lloyd's Rep 534; [1981] Com LR 256; 1981 WL 186630. Difficulties arise where the charterer owns the bunkers (see *Stellar Chartering and Brokerage Inc v Efibanca-Ente Finanziario Intercambiario SpA (The Span-Terza No 2)* [1984] 1 Lloyd's Rep 119 (HL), at p. 120;

significant extension of the scope of arrest and a significant advantage for the shipowner.

It is evident that claims supported by maritime liens are also within the list of claims covered by section 21(4) which permits arrest of the relevant ship or a sister ship. For example, where there is a claim for a salvage reward the salvors can either arrest the ship they have assisted, under section 21(3), in which case they can rely upon the priority of the maritime lien or they can proceed against a ship under the same ownership as provided in section 21(4). However, although more than one ship can be named in the claim form, only one can be arrested in respect of each claim.[36]

The choice made on whether to arrest the particular ship and exercise the maritime lien or a sister ship will determine the priority of the claim, the time at which the rights in Admiralty attach to the ship and the security available as the value of the ships may be significantly different.

Note that only claims which strictly fall within the wording of section 20(2), except (d), can be enforced by means of an action *in rem*. If the wording of the relevant subsection of section 20(2) does not include the claim then enforcement can only be made by an action *in personam* even if the character of the claim is arguably maritime in nature.[37]

In addition, the ownership requirements described under section 21(4) need also to be strictly applicable. Thus, where a Soviet State company was privatised as a Russian company, arrest of the ship belonging originally to the Soviet company and then to its Russian successor was not permitted as it was a change of legal personality under the applicable Russian law.[38] By contrast where the shipowning company goes into voluntary liquidation, beneficial ownership arguably does not change.[39]

Where a bareboat charter is terminated because the vessel sinks and the owner then incurs expenses for wreck removal for which he would normally be indemnified under the charter, the first requirement of the wording of section 21(4) is not satisfied and a ship of the charterer cannot be arrested.[40]

In a case where judicial proceedings including arrest were avoided through a P&I letter of undertaking and the ship was later sold, the shipowner sought to claim that the wording of Article 21(4) of the SCA 1981 was not fulfilled as the owner at the time of issuance of the claim form *in rem* was different from the owner at the time of the incident. The High Court rejected this claim and obliged the defending shipowner who was in breach of the undertakings agreement to accept service of the *in rem* claim form.[41]

---

see also *The Yuta Bondarovskaya* [1998] 2 Lloyd's Rep 357) or where the ship is under arrest and cargo is not (CPR r. 61.8(8)), and where goods and materials not directly for the use of the ship but for the passengers have been supplied to the ship (*The Edinburgh Castle* [1999] 2 Lloyd's Rep 362).

36. SCA 1981, s. 21(8), and *The Tjaskemolen Now Named Visvliet (No 2)* [1997] 2 Lloyd's Rep 476.
37. See *Gatoil International Inc v Arkwright-Boston Manufacturers Mutual Insurance Co and Others (The Sandrina)* [1985] 1 Lloyd's Rep 181 (HL) relating to unpaid insurance premiums, *Petrofina SA v AOT Ltd (The Maersk Nimrod)* [1991] 1 Lloyd's Rep 269 for a demurrage provision in a c.i.f. contract, and *The River Rima* [1987] 2 Lloyd's Rep 106; [1988] 2 All ER 641 related to an agreement of container leasing to ships. In all cases there was no action *in rem* available.
38. *Centro Latino Americano de Commercio Exterior SA v Owners of the Ship "Kommunar" (The Kommunar) (No 2)* [1997] 1 Lloyd's Rep 8.
39. *International Transportation Service Inc v Owners and/or Demise Charterers of the Ship or Vessel Convenience Container* [2006] 2 Lloyd's Rep 556.
40. *Aluflet SA v Vinave Empresa de Navegaçao Maritima LDA (The Faial)* [2000] 1 Lloyd's Rep 473. Novation will also have the same effect, see *The Tychy (No 2)* [2001] 2 Lloyd's Rep 403 (CA).
41. *Galaxy Energy International Ltd and Corona Trading Associates SA v Assuranceforeningen Skuld (Ejensidie) (The Oakwell)* [1999] 1 Lloyd's Rep 249.

The organisation of a fleet of ships in a number of one-ship companies poses the problem on whether one can arrest the ship of one company for claims against a ship belonging to another company. The Court of Appeal in *The Evpo Agnic*[42] where the same shipowner held the shares of several one-ship owning companies interpreted the term "owner" in section 21(4) as referring to the registered owner alone. Thus, actions *in rem* against the other companies owned by the same shipowner was not permitted and the corporate structure chosen by the shipowner is respected. Only where the corporate structure is changed for the purpose of avoiding the satisfaction of a claim will the English court exercise their inherent discretion to "lift the corporate veil" and identify the beneficial owner.

### (d) Procedure for claims *in rem*

The procedure relating to actions *in rem* is governed by the Civil Procedure Rules ("CPR") 61 and the Practice Direction ("PD") 61. The claimant simply issues a claim on a special *in rem* claim form.[43] The period for service of an *in rem* form is 12 months.[44] The methods of service of an *in rem* claim form include:[45] service on the *res* itself as it was done traditionally, but it can also be effected in some new ways. For example, if the property to be served is in the custody of a person who will not permit access to it, service may be effected by leaving a copy of the *in rem* claim form with that person.[46] Where the parties agree, for example in a jurisdiction agreement, that service may be effected upon a named person, for example, a firm of solicitors, service can be effected on this named person. Provided that the ship or property is within the jurisdiction, service may also be effected in any other manner directed under CPR 6.8.[47] This means that the court in appropriate circumstances may make an order permitting service in any manner not specifically authorised by the rule, for example serving the claim form on a vessel equipped with a fax machine, as the ship is sailing within territorial waters.[48]

The particulars of claims must be contained within the claim form or, otherwise must be served on the defendant within 75 days from the day they are issued.[49] This period is longer than the relevant period for a claim *in personam*, i.e. 14 days, and ought to be sufficient time to allow a claimant to collect, and its lawyers to collate and review properly, the necessary information to particularise the claim.[50] The particulars of claim must be verified by a "*Statement of Truth*".[51] The Practice Direction provides that an acknowledgement of service must be filed

42. *The Evpo Agnic* [1988] 2 Lloyd's Rep 411 (CA).
43. PD 61.3.2 and PD 61.3.1–61.3.3 made no changes to this practice.
44. See PD 49f. 2.1(6). There is no change in CPR 61.3(5). The form can then be renewed.
45. See PD 49f. 2.2 and PD 61 3.6.
46. See PD 49f. 2.2 and PD 61 3.6(2).
47. Apart from replacing the term "*res*" with the word "property", this now appears in PD 61.3.6(7)).
48. Where the vessel is passing through the territorial waters without using or without any intention to use any coastal facilities it may not be possible to arrest it as a matter under/in accordance with s. 3 of UNCLOS 1982 defining the right of innocent passage.
49. CPR 7.4.
50. This variation of the general CPR regime appeared in PD 49f. 2.1(2). This is one of the areas where the Admiralty Practice Direction differed from the Commercial Court Guide – because whilst both allowed a longer period than that set out in the general provisions of the CPR, the basic period allowed by the Commercial Court was only 28 days (see para. C 2.4 of the *Commercial Court Guide 1998*).
51. This applies to all Admiralty claims but it could give rise to practical problems in circumstances where the claimant no longer has any commercial interest in the action because, for example, he has been paid out by his insurer.

in every action *in rem*.[52] After filing an acknowledgement of service the claim continues to be a claim *in rem*. However, the procedure relating to the claim becomes the same as the procedure relating to a claim *in personam*.[53] Under CPR 24.3 it is not possible for a claimant to obtain summary judgment in an action *in rem*. The issue of default judgments in actions *in rem* is dealt with in CPR 61.9 and PD 61.9, where the different conditions applying for a judgment in default in collision cases (CPR 61.9(2)) and in other cases (CPR 61.9(1)) are spelt out. All references to judgments in default for actions *in personam* have been removed and therefore CPR 58.8 will be applicable.

### (e) Action *in rem* in respect of collisions

A collision action is commenced by issuing a claim form.[54] An acknowledgement of service is compulsory whether the claim is *in rem* or *in personam*.[55] The acknowledgement of service triggers the lodging of a Collision Statement.[56] Briefly, unless the defendant contests the jurisdiction of the court, the parties are obliged to file their Collision Statements within two months as from the date when the acknowledgement of service is filed.[57] The Collision Statement has to be supported by a statement of truth.[58] The requirement of lodging Collision Statements by the parties to a collision action makes the serving of Particulars of Claim unnecessary.

### (f) Arrest

Claims *in rem* can easily lead to the arrest of the vessel. Provided that an action *in rem* is available under section 21 of the SCA 1981 the right to arrest the defendant's ship arises.[59] When an appropriate application is made then the Admiralty Court will issue a warrant of arrest and arrest the ship.[60] In order to effect an arrest it is only necessary to prepare an application for arrest, which includes an undertaking to pay the Admiralty Marshal's expenses[61] and to make a sworn declaration of facts.[62]

52. This is now split between CPR 61.4(3) and PD 61 3.4 and PD 61 3.5, but no change of/in the substance is made.
53. This remains the case (PD 61.3.10) although there is no express statement, as there was before, that the claim remains a claim *in rem*. This is unlikely to cause any difficulty as the reference is to the procedure applicable rather than to the character of the claim.
54. CPR 61.4 and PD 61.4.
55. *In personam* claims are dealt with in/by CPR 58, subject to the provisions of CPR 61 and PD 61 relating to collision and limitation claims (see PD 61.12.1). This arrangement does not appear to alter the existing practice.
56. Previously called Preliminary Act.
57. See CPR 61.4(5). PD 61.4.5 provides that the law relating to Preliminary Acts continues to apply to Collision Statements.
58. See CPR 61.4(6)(b).
59. See CPR 61.5 which extends the right to arrest to judgment creditors.
60. PD 61.5(5.2).
61. See PD 61.5(1).
62. See CPR 61.5(3) and PD 61.5.3. The declaration must be accompanied with a statement of truth stating, the nature of the claim or counterclaim, that the claim has not been satisfied, that it arises in connection with a ship as well as the name of that ship. In addition the nature of the property and, where the property is a ship, the name of the ship, her port of registry, as well as the amount of the security sought. In addition, if the action *in rem* is brought under s. 21(4) of the SCA 1981, all the relevant details that satisfy that the claims are under s. 21(4) will need to be contained in the statement, and if it is a foreign vessel and where appropriate under intergovernmental agreements, it will be added that notice has been filed with the consul of the flag State. Also in a claim for oil pollution under s. 153 of the Merchant Shipping Act 1995, the facts relied on as establishing that the court is not prevented from considering the claim by reason of s.166(2) of the MSA 1995.

An arrest may only be effected by the Admiralty Marshal or his nominated substitute. An arrest may be effected by service of the arrest warrant on the vessel itself, by fixing the warrant on the outside of the property; or by serving notice of the issue of the warrant on the vessel itself; or by just giving notice to those in charge of the property.[63] The Master is usually the person in charge of the ship thus service of the warrant of arrest to the ship's owner or managers would not be an effective service of the warrant or notice of its issuance.

Normally ships are arrested when in an English port. If the vessel is under innocent passage,[64] most likely a warrant of arrest cannot be served. However, if the vessel is not under innocent passage because it has called or is planning to call at an English port, it is arguably subject to arrest even if it is underway. Very rarely arrest has been effected when the ship is underway within English territorial waters.[65] Such arrests were only effected where the Admiralty Marshal had the support of the vessel's crew as otherwise there were physical risks to the Marshal or his nominated substitute.

### *(i) Consequences of the arrest of the ship*

Where the ship is arrested under an action *in rem* a number of important consequences arise. The ship comes under the custody of the Admiralty Court. It cannot be moved without the Court's permission and may also be immobilised or prevented from sailing.[66] Thus, it follows that the vessel cannot trade even if it were to trade only within English territorial waters.[67] The person that moves a ship under arrest is in contempt of court and liable for fines or imprisonment.[68] Another consequence is that arrest by itself establishes English jurisdiction on the merits.[69] This arises from the practical need to be able to satisfy a claimant at the state where it obtained security. Otherwise the situation may arise where the security obtained would not be transferable between the State that has jurisdiction on the merits and the English jurisdiction, thus rendering the security obtained ineffective. Under arrest, the ship becomes the financial security for the claimant *in rem*. This means that unless the shipowner puts up security in order to have the ship released from arrest, the ship will be sold and the claimants will be paid out of the proceeds of sale.

Difficulties may arise where a ship is under arrest but its cargo is not or vice versa. The Admiralty Marshal has in such circumstances authority to apply to the Court for the discharge of the cargo and the release of the property not arrested.[70]

63. PD 61.5(5).
64. UNCLOS 1982, Art. 28.
65. See *Chorley & Giles' Shipping Law*, R S T Chorley, and O C Giles, N J J Gaskell, C Debattista and R J Swatton (8th ed) (Pitman Publishing, 1987) (hereinafter "*Chorley & Giles*"), Parts 1 and 2, on the relationship between arrest and the Law of the Sea rules on innocent passage.
66. CPR 61.5(9).
67. *Greenmar Navigation v Owners of Ships Bazias 3 and Bazias 4 and Sally Line (The Bazias 3 and The Bazias 4)* [1993] QB 673; [1993] 2 WLR 854; [1993] 2 All ER 964; [1993] 1 Lloyd's Rep 101; *The Independent* (16 November 1992); 1993 WL 963319 (CA).
68. *The Merdeka* [1982] 1 Lloyd's Rep 401 and CPR 49.6.4(3).
69. *The Anna H*: see fn. 3.
70. CPR 61.8(9). Problems related to liability for the expenses incurred may arise, see, for example, *The Jogoo* [1981] 1 Lloyd's Rep 513, where the cargo owners had to pay for own removal and sue the shipowner for breach of contract.

### *(ii) Release of the ship under arrest*

The procedure for releasing the ship from arrest is described in CPR 61.8. The shipowner can have its ship released by providing security. In England the security amount required to release the vessel is based on the claimant's best arguable case plus interests and costs, usually a subject of negotiation. Where there is no agreement, the court may decide on the type and amount of security.[71] The security cannot be more than the value of the ship.[72]

The ship will also be released if a limitation fund is constituted in accordance with the 1996 Limitation Convention,[73] or, if the claim is under the 1992 CLC as enacted,[74] when an appropriate fund will be established whether this limitation fund is in England or in another contracting State.

### *(iii) Judicial sale*

The arrested ship or property will also be released from arrest after judicial sale. Judicial sale is a crucial component in the enforcement mechanism ensuring that where the shipowner does not turn up to submit to the jurisdiction of the court or does not provide security either because it does not want to or cannot do so, the claimant will be paid out of the sale proceeds of the property arrested. Judicial sale can be effected at any stage of the proceedings even if the merits of the case have not been decided. The rationale for this discretion is that there could be circumstances in which keeping the ship under arrest would mean increasing expenses which will diminish any subsequent amount recovered by the judicial sale of the ship.[75] In such a case the ship is sold and the amount obtained replaces the ship. However, payment out of the proceeds of the sale are only made to claimants who have obtained favourable judgments and subject to priorities as determined by the court.[76] In this way the claimant's position is optimised. If adequate security is provided, it is unlikely that the court will proceed to the judicial sale of the vessel.

The court has authority to sell the ship if any party to the litigation applies for the ship's sale.[77] The shipowner as well as any claimant can apply to the court for the ship to be sold.[78] However, the shipowner cannot sell the ship itself as it may become in contempt of the arrest order.[79] The most important consequence of a judicial sale is that it releases the ship from all claims against it.[80]

### *(iv) Caution against arrest and caution against the release of the ship*

If it is foreseeable that a ship will be arrested then the shipowner or the P&I Club can enter in the Admiralty and Commercial Registry a caution against arrest.

71. *The Moschanthy* [1971] Lloyd's Rep 37. See also CPR 61.6 and *Global Marine Drilling v Triton Holdings (The Sovereign Explorer) (No 2)* [2001] 1 Lloyd's Rep 60).
72. CPR 61.6(3).
73. 1995 MSA, Sch. 7, Art. 13. See Chapter 6, p. 219.
74. 1995 MSA, ss 159 and 160. See Chapter 8, p. 262.
75. *The Myrto* [1978] 1 Lloyd's Rep 11; 1978 WL 57210 (CA).
76. CPR 61.10(5).
77. CPR 61.10(1).
78. The application for the sale must be served to all parties to the litigation: CPR 61.10(4).
79. *The Cerro Colorado* [1993] 1 Lloyd's Rep 58.
80. *Ibid*. See also *The Acrux (No 2)* [1962] 1 Lloyd's Rep 405.

The person filing the caution against arrest undertakes to acknowledge service of the claim form and provides security for the claim, interests and costs or, if that person has already established a limitation fund under the 1996 LLMC to confirm this fact and acknowledge service against the limitation fund.[81] However, the filing of a caution against arrest does not stop the claimant from arresting the ship, for example for the purpose of establishing English jurisdiction on the merits,[82] although in such a case the court may order the discharge of the arrest and may make the claimant pay any damages caused by the arrest.[83]

If the ship is already under arrest by one claimant it is of little use to the other claimants to arrest the vessel too.[84] After all, payment depends on the priority of claims that have obtained judgment and not on which of the claimants have arrested first or at all. However, if the claimant who has arrested the vessel obtains security, then the vessel will be released and the claims of all other claimants may be jeopardised. To avoid such a situation an entry in the Admiralty and Commercial Registry of a caution against release is available to all other claimants with claims *in rem*.[85] As a result of the caveat against release the claimant will be notified when the ship is to be released in order to take action and arrest the ship if necessary and the ship will not be released without this party's consent.[86] However, entry of a caution against release may entitle the shipowner to damages for delay.[87]

The court has discretion to permit the re-arrest of a ship where it is fair and appropriate.[88] Thus where the security provided would turn out to be worthless or insufficient re-arrest may be permitted. However, only one ship can be arrested for each claim, and multiple arrests for the same claim are not permissible.[89]

### *(v) Damages for wrongful arrest*

Unless the arrest is done with bad faith or gross negligence there is no remedy for damages where the ship has been wrongfully arrested.[90] This makes arrest a very powerful weapon in the hands of a claimant because without consideration of the monetary value of the claim advanced and without examining the strength of the claim on the merits, the defendant's ship can be stopped from trading with only a remote possibility of an obligation of the claimant to pay damages.[91] Thus, in general it is very difficult to obtain a remedy if the claim that lead to arrest simply fails or is abandoned unless bad faith or gross negligence is shown.

81. CPR 61.7(2).
82. *The Anna H*, see fn. 3.
83. CPR 61.7(5).
84. However, arresting a ship which is under arrest by another claimant is expressly permitted under CPR 61.8(1).
85. CPR 61.8(2).
86. CPR 61.8(4).
87. *Ibid.*
88. *Owners of the Carbonnade v Owners of the Ruta (The Ruta)* [2000] 1 WLR 2068; [2001] 1 All ER 450; [2000] 1 All ER (Comm) 847; [2000] 1 Lloyd's Rep 359; [2000] CLC 784; [2000] ICR 1024; (2000) 97(12) LSG 39 (2000) 144.
89. SCA 1981, s. 21(8).
90. *Xenos v Aldersley (The Evangelismos)* (1858) 14 ER 945; (1858) 12 Moo PC 352. See also *The Kommunar (No 2)*, fn. 38.
91. The test only applies where there is no caution against arrest or release. Where such cautions have been entered and the ship is subsequently arrested or not released it is arguable that recovery of damages would be easier.

### (g) Priority of claims

The court that has arrested the ship must have in hand the ship itself, or the proceeds of the ship's sale if the ship has been sold, or the security provided if the ship has been permitted to sail. Where the claims against the ship exceed the amount available for the compensation of the various claims, disputes arise as to which claim will be satisfied first. Five categories of claims can be identified: the Admiralty Court's expenses related to the ship's arrest and management while the ship was under arrest, maritime liens, mortgages, other claims enforceable by an action *in rem* under section 21 of the SCA 1981 and other claims *in personam* not carrying an action *in rem*. Maritime liens cover claims arising from the absolutely essential elements of shipping, namely the Master's and crew's wages and disbursements of the Master; salvage claims and damage claims caused by the ship. They also include bottomry and respondentia which were emergency funding mechanisms for the shipping adventure.[92] However, the most extensive liability would probably be that incurred against the financier of the shipping adventure, the mortgagee. In practice if the mortgage of a damaged ship were to be paid first, little would be left for other claimants. If crew members knew that unpaid wages would probably not be recoverable they would be reluctant to go to sea. Similarly, salvors would hesitate to get involved with the salvage of a stricken vessel if they could lose their claim to mortgagees. And one can easily imagine the outcry that would be caused if, after a collision, loss of life and personal injury claimants remained unpaid in order for the bank which financed the negligent shipowner to be repaid. It is therefore not surprising that priority is given to claims that correspond to maritime liens and these claims will be paid before the mortgagees will be paid. Of course not every claim *in rem* can be considered superior to the mortgagees' claim. If that were the case financing of shipping would be even riskier than it is now. Involvement with the ship under bills of lading, charterparty, supplies, repairs, towage contracts, etc, are all contractual arrangements like mortgages are, and in each case there is a choice made to interact with the defendant shipowner. Within this group of contractual claims, mortgages[93] are considered as having priority over later actions *in rem* which do not carry a maritime lien.[94]

Thus the distribution of the proceeds of the judicial sale or the security after judgment is as follows: the claims of the court and harbour authorities[95] are paid first, followed by maritime liens, followed by mortgages and the other *in rem*

92. See fn. 29.
93. See *The Shizelle* [1992] 2 Lloyd's Rep 444 for a discussion on the position of unregistered mortgages on unregistered ships.
94. See, for example, *The Two Ellens* (1869–72) LR 3 A&E 345; *Donald Johnson and Others v John Alexander Black (The Two Ellens)* (1871–73) LR 4 PC 161; 17 ER 361; (1872) 8 Moo PCNS 398; 1871 WL 13751 (Judicial Committee). In this case the right of the mortgagee to possession and sale of the vessel under the mortgage were considered to be superior to claims of repair costs which, as it was decided in this case, did not carry the status of maritime liens. See also *The Leoborg (No 2)* [1964] 1 Lloyd's Rep 380.
95. These are usually based on specific statutes. *British Transport Docks Board v Owners of the Proceeds of Sale of the Charger, Probe, Vigia, Dideki, Surveyor, Constellation, Errol and Regency (The Charger) (No 1)* [1966] 1 Lloyd's Rep 670; [1966] 3 All ER 117, *The Blitz* [1992] 2 Lloyd's Rep 441. If the claim of the Authority is not in the capacity of being an Authority but one equivalent to that of a civil claimant, then it is strongly arguable that the priority will be determined on the basis of the civil claim and not under the statute.

claims after them. Any other claims not enforceable by an action *in rem* would then follow.

Priority of claims and in particular between maritime liens is subject to the court's discretion.[96] Extensive case law can be found determining the relevant priority in particular circumstances. For example, between competing maritime liens salvage generally comes first[97] on the basis that the availability of the ship as security for arrest would not exist without the salvage operation. Following the same argument between two salvage claims the latest has priority. However, older cases must be read subject to the prevailing court's discretion as expressed in *The Ruta*.[98] A registered mortgagee has priority over all mortgages registered after and all unregistered mortgages created before.[99]

Claims *in rem* which are not maritime liens are subordinated to maritime liens, whenever created, and to mortgages created before them. Statutory rights *in rem* between themselves probably rank *pari passu*.[100]

A possessory lien[101] ranks before all later claims, but is dependent on possession being retained. There may also be a statutory right *in rem* available to persons such as ship repairers.

### (h) Limitation actions

Under English law there are three ways under which one may seek limitation of liability. The first way is where a party raises limitation as a defence.[102] This is the case where this party is sued for damages and, as a defence, relies on the right to limit liability. The second way in which limitation of liability can be claimed is by commencing a limitation claim by way of counterclaim in an existing action. In such a case one uses the counterclaim to obtain a general declaration of one's right to limit against all potential claims arising out of a particular incident. Thus, in this case the declaration sought is not simply a declaration that one is entitled to limit one's liability as against the person who has brought the action in question as in the first case, but a general limitation declaration.[103] Finally, the more general situation is where a party seeks a general limitation decree under a limitation action. These are proceedings whereby a claimant (for example,

96. *The Ruta*, fn. 88,where priority was linked to public policy not only in the UK but in other countries too.
97. *The Lyrma (No 2)* [1978] 2 Lloyd's Rep 30.
98. See fn. 88.
99. Merchant Shipping Act 1995, Sched. 1, ss 7–14, and 1993 Registration Regulations. Questions arise in respect of the priority of mortgages on unregistered ships as well as foreign registered and unregistered mortgages. See *Jackson*, n. 2, for a detailed discussion.
100. *Festival Holidays Limited v The Demise Charterers of the Ship Ocean Glory 1 (The Ocean Glory 1)* [2002] 1 Lloyd's Rep 679; 2001 WL 1560842.
101. The exercise of a possessory lien is a form of self-help. The person who has possession of the property of another in respect of which he has a claim, usually of unpaid services, retains possession of the property until paid by the property's owner. This right of possession is recognised in common law. See, for example, *The Gaupen* (1925) 22 Ll L Rep 57; [1925]; *The Ally* [1952] 2 Lloyd's Rep 427 and *The Tergeste* [1903] P 26.
102. PD 61.11(10.18) states that "Nothing in Rule 61.11 prevents limitation being relied on by way of defence".
103. A "restricted decree", where one or more defendants admit the rights to limit, may be brought by counterclaim under CPR 61.11(22)(a). A "general decree", where limitation is not admitted, may be brought by counterclaim, but only with permission of the courts (see CPR 61.11(22)).

a shipowner) may seek an order confirming that its total liability arising out of a particular incident is limited to a certain figure pursuant to the relevant legislation. The practice and procedure relating to limitation actions appear in PD 61, section 11. A limitation fund can be established before or after a limitation claim has been started[104] either by the initiative of the claimant who may pay the limitation amount into court[105] or by order of the court following the granting of a limitation decree.[106] The establishment of the limitation fund does not transfer the rights to these amounts to those claiming against the fund and payments from the limitation fund can only be made when ordered by the court.[107] The claimant must give notice to all named defendants including the date of payment, the amount of limitation and the interest paid into court together with the value of the monetary unit used in the calculation of the limitation fund.[108]

## 2. MARITIME LIENS[109]

Maritime liens are not required to be registered, therefore they act as "hidden" interests. It is easier to describe how a maritime lien operates rather than define it precisely. Maritime liens are rights created at the time of the incident[110] which attach to the ship.[111] If the ship is sold[112] before the claimant has arrested it, the maritime lien is not destroyed but remains attached to the ship. As a consequence when a maritime lien is in existence the ship can be arrested after its sale even if the new owner, who would have to put up security or lose the ship, has nothing to do with the incident which gave rise to the maritime lien.

This should be contrasted with the statutory action *in rem* under which the rights arise at the time of the issuance of the claim form. Thus, if the ship is sold before the issuance of the relevant claim form, the claimant will be deprived of the right to arrest the ship. However, an action against a sister ship may be available, an option not available with a maritime lien.

Maritime liens are enforceable by an action *in rem* to which they are entitled under section 21(3) of the 1981 SCA. Their differences and distinction from the other claims *in rem* do not arise under the 1981 SCA or any earlier statutory provision nor under the CPR but directly from case law.[113] Notably this statement raises the question whether the modification of the categories of claims with time

104. CPR 61.11.19.
105. CPR 61.11.18.
106. CPR 61.11.13. However, under this section the court also enjoys the right to order "other arrangements for payment against the claims subject to limitation".
107. CPR 61.11.21.
108. PD 61.11.10.13.
109. There are several international conventions dealing with Maritime Liens and Morgtgages. However, the only one in force is The International Convention on Maritime Liens and Mortgages 1993, Geneva, April 1993. This entered into force on 5/9/2004. The UK is not a Party to the Convention. However, the priority structure of The Convention on Maritime Liens and Mortgages (1926), which was signed but not ratified by Great Britain, the Maritime Liens and Mortgages Convention of 1967 and Maritime Liens and Mortgages Convention of 1993 was taken into account in *The Ruta*, fn. 88.
110. *The Bold Buccleugh*, fn. 27.
111. Also cargo or freight.
112. Maritime liens cannot be exercised against ships of /belonging to a government.
113. *C & C J Northcote v the Owners of the Heinrich BJ RN (The Heinrich Bjorn)* (1886) 11 App Cas 270 at p. 278 (HL); *The Two Ellens*, fn. 94. Although historically the view changed repeatedly until settled to the present one.

would also modify the claims which attract maritime liens. In particular, the statutory action *in rem* in relation to salvage[114] includes any claim under the 1989 Salvage Convention including claims for Special Compensation under Article 14. Whether this can be taken to mean that a claim in salvage under Article 14 is secured by a maritime lien as would any ordinary claim for salvage now under Article 13 of the 1989 Salvage Convention is questionable. It would arguably depend on whether *The Bold Buccleugh*[115] is authority for defining the broad categories of claims attracting maritime liens, or authority restricting the claims attracting maritime liens only to the particular claims as defined at the time of the decision. Strong policy arguments suggest that the first interpretation is preferable although this would mean that maritime liens are created by statute indirectly through the expansion of the relevant definitions.

Maritime liens are probably not transferable rights. Thus, for example, where an agent pays off outstanding crew wages which arose before the arrest, he does not then become entitled to the maritime lien which the crew wages normally attract but only a claimant with a statutory right *in rem*.[116] It is unclear whether a maritime lien can be assigned, with the exception of bottomry which apparently can be assigned.[117]

The maritime lien for wages arises without the personal liability of the shipowner[118] and irrespective of the contract of employment; the damage lien requires the personal liability of the owner.[119] For other liens the issue is not decided.

Maritime liens rank above mortgages and statutory rights arising from section 21(4) thus exercising a maritime lien would give higher priority than mortgages or other actions *in rem* created by the SCA 1981 under section 21(2) or 21(4).

It is probably worth mentioning again that the decision of the House of Lords in *The Indian Grace*,[120] by which an action *in rem* against a ship is to be treated as an action against the shipowners, did not resolve the issue in respect of maritime liens.

However, it is submitted that, in spite of the important differences between maritime liens and other actions enforceable *in rem* the position adopted should be the same.

An interesting and difficult issue is whether maritime liens recognised under foreign law are to be recognised as such in English proceedings thus taking priority over other claims. For example, where the repairs on a ship are effected in a foreign country and under foreign law, a maritime lien supports the claim of the ship repairers. The question was asked whether the claim continued to be supported by a maritime lien even where the arrest was effected in a forum in which these

114. SCA 1981, s. 20(2)(j).
115. See fn. 27.
116. *The Petone* [1917] P 198; *The Leoborg (No 2)*, fn. 94.
117. *The Petone, ibid.* Subrogation of rights under a statute, for example, the Marine Insurance Act 1906, would arguably include rights of recovery. It is also arguable that priority and other advantages of the maritime lien may also be subrogated by statute.
118. For a recent case see *Crew Members of the Ever Success v Owners of the Ever Success (The Ever Success)* [1999] 1 Lloyd's Rep 824; 1998 WL 1045100.
119. See, as examples: *The Tasmania* (1888) LR 13 PD 110. However, where the vessel is in the hands of a third party under a demise charter the maritime lien attaches: *The Father Thames* [1979] 2 Lloyd's Rep 364.
120. *The Indian Grace (No 2)*, fn. 19.

claims were not supported by a maritime lien. The answer given by the Privy Council was[121] that the maritime lien is procedural in character and therefore a matter for the law of the forum. In other words foreign maritime liens would not be recognised as such unless they also have the same character under English law.

## 3. FREEZING INJUNCTIONS[122]

A freezing injunction, which was called "Mareva injunction" before the development of the Civil Procedure Rules, is an interlocutory order aimed at securing funds for the satisfaction of a legal right. It is not restricted to maritime claims but it is granted in support of claims *in personam*. The purpose of the freezing injunction is "... to prevent a defendant from taking action designed to frustrate subsequent orders of the court".[123] However, it has also been described as used to protect the satisfaction of a legal right.[124] A freezing injunction can be granted before or after judgment and can concern all or part of the assets of the defendant within the English jurisdiction or worldwide. It is routinely assisted by an order for disclosure of assets.[125]

Freezing injunctions are not pre-trial attachments and they do not give rise to a lien or give priority to the applicant's claim.[126] To that extent they are not pre-trial security for the claim in the way the arrest of the ship is.

An action to restrict a defendant from dealing with its property before judgment was considered up to 1975 as not available to a claimant.[127] However, in two cases[128] in 1975 the Court of Appeal had to deal with *ex parte* applications by shipowners complaining that foreign time charterers whose only assets within the jurisdiction were bank accounts in London, had not paid hire. The shipowners feared that the money would be removed from the jurisdiction thus leaving them empty-handed. In both cases the Court of Appeal issued injunctions restraining the defendants from dealing with the money in the bank. The issuance of the injunction succeeded in making the time charterers pay. Both cases concerned foreign defendants who were abroad and had bank accounts within the jurisdiction. The absence of the defendant from the jurisdiction was the basis of distinguishing

121. *Bankers Trust International Ltd v Todd Shipyards Corporation (The Halcyon Isle)* [1980] 2 Lloyd's Rep 325; [1981] AC 221.
122. A full account of freezing injunctions is beyond the scope of this book. Several books have treated this topic, e.g. S Gee on *Mareva Injunctions and Anton Piller Relief*, and A Briggs and P Rees on *Civil Jurisdiction and Judgments*.
123. *Derby & Co Ltd and Others v Weldon and Others (Nos 3 and 4)* [1990] Ch 65 (CA).
124. *C Inc plc v Mrs L and Mr L* [2001] 2 Lloyd's Rep 459; [2001] 151 NLJ 535.
125. The court has discretion under CPR Part 25.1(1)(g) to order disclosure of information related to property or assets which "... are or may be the subject of an application of a freezing injunction". Nevertheless, this does not create a free standing option for the court, that is, one cannot apply for disclosure and then on the basis of the information collected apply for a freezing injunction (*Andrew Frederick Parker v CS Structured Credit Fund Limited, Elegant Hotels Limited* [2003] EWHC 391).
126. *Cretanor Maritime Co Ltd v Irish Marine Management Ltd (The Cretan Harmony)* [1978] 1 Lloyd's Rep 425; *Gangway Ltd v Caledonian Park Investments (Jersey) Ltd* [2001] 2 Lloyd's Rep 715. See also *Kastner v Jason* [2005] 1 Lloyd's Rep 397; [2004] EWHC (CA).
127. *Lister v Stubbs* [1890] 45 ChD 1.
128. *Nippon Yusen Kaisha v G and J Karageorgis* [1975] 2 Lloyd's Rep 137; [1975] 1 WLR 1093 and *Mareva Compania Naviera SA v International Bulkcarriers SA* [1975] 2 Lloyd's Rep 509 (CA).

*Lister v Stubbs* which concerned an application for restricting a defendant within the jurisdiction from disposing of his property.

### (a) When can the English courts issue a freezing injunction?

Since 1975 the use and the scope of the freezing injunction has increased and aided by significant statutory changes and judicial improvisation it has presently become a "nuclear weapon" of the law.[129] Today this type of injunction is available against any defendant whether within the jurisdiction or not and for any type of asset whether the asset is in England or not. Presently the High Court[130] has discretion to grant freezing orders in support of a wide variety of proceedings. Thus, there is jurisdiction to grant a freezing order in respect of cases where the English court has jurisdiction on the merits or in relation to the enforcement of English judgments.[131] In addition there is jurisdiction to grant a freezing injunction in support of proceedings in a Member State for proceedings under EC Regulation 44/2001[132] or in relation to any other proceedings to be heard by any other foreign court whether in a Member State or not.[133] Freezing injunctions are also available for arbitration proceedings.[134]

Within EC Regulation 44/2001 freezing injunctions are covered as provisional measures under Article 37. In addition, in respect of enforcement of judgments from other Member States' courts, Article 47(2) and (3) permit the granting of a freezing injunction in respect of the defendant's property linked with the English jurisdiction but not in respect of property abroad.[135]

Procedural issues are presently dealt with in CPR 25. No standard forms are needed but an example is provided in CPR 25(6). Applications can, in urgent cases, be made over the phone.[136]

### (b) When will the English courts issue a freezing injunction?

The granting of a freezing injunction is discretionary and is normally granted without notice to the defendant. Because the freezing injunction is for the purpose of assisting the substantive proceedings if there is no accrued legal right

129. *Bank Mellat v Nikpour* [1985] FSR 87 at p. 92 (CA) (Lord Donaldson).
130. But not the county courts: see *Schmidt v Wong* [2005] EWCA Civ 1506; [2006] 1 WLR 561 (CA).
131. SCA 1981, s. 37(3). The High Court has jurisdiction whether the defendant is within or outside the English jurisdiction.
132. Section 25 of the Civil Jurisdiction and Judgments Act 1982 extends the jurisdiction to grant interim relief for proceedings that have or were to be commenced before one of the European Union courts (and if the proceedings fall within the Regulations' substantive scope of application).
133. In addition the CJJA 1982 (Interim Relief) Order 1997 extends the application of s. 25(1) to all proceedings commenced, started or to be commenced in a non-contracting State to the Jurisdiction conventions and for all proceedings commenced or to be commenced before a court in a Convention/contracting State for subject matters outside the Jurisdiction conventions.
134. Section 44 of the Arbitration Act 1996 gives jurisdiction to grant freezing orders in support of arbitrations within or outside the jurisdiction. For the position before the Arbitration Act 1996 see *Channel Tunnel Group Ltd v Balfour Beatty Construction Ltd* [1993] 1 Lloyd's Rep 291; [1993] AC 334 (HL). Under s. 49(1) of the Arbitration Act 1996 the parties may agree to give power to arbitrators to issue freezing orders (*Kastner v Jason*, fn. 126).
135. *Banco Nacional de Comercio Exterior SNC v Empresa de Telecommunicaciones de Cuba SA, British Telecommunications plc (intervening)* [2007] 2 Lloyd's Rep 484 (CA).
136. CPR 25(4.5). See also CPR (Part 6) 6.20(4) for leave to serve out of the jurisdiction.

there can be no injunction.[137] For example, a freezing injunction will not be granted for a breach of contract which has not yet materialised.[138]

Provided that the court has jurisdiction under one of the various heads and there is a legal right to be protected then the court will have discretion to grant the injunction. The burden of persuading the court to grant the injunction is on the applicant, as the defendant is in most cases unaware of the application for a freezing injunction, simply because otherwise it could remove any of its assets from the English jurisdiction.

The applicant for a freezing injunction must first have a "good arguable case" that is one "... which is more than barely capable of serious argument, but not necessarily one which the judge considers would have a better than fifty per cent chance of success".[139]

In addition the applicant must demonstrate that there is a real risk that the judgment will go unsatisfied without the injunction.[140] However, the mere existence of the defendant's assets within the jurisdiction is not enough to persuade the court to grant an injunction.[141] In demonstrating the risk of dissipation of the defendant's assets the previous conduct and the financial standing of the defendant is relevant as well as the type of assets. For example, where the defendant is a foreign company, the country in which it is incorporated, the difficulty of enforcing judgments and the availability of financial information in that country are all factors to be considered by the court.[142] The fact that the defendant is short of funds is not enough to demonstrate a risk of dissipation of assets.[143]

A freezing injunction can also be issued in respect of a third party holding the assets of the defendant under an agency, trust or any other legal arrangement including the appointment of a receiver. In such cases the risk of dissipation has to be shown in respect of the third party.[144]

In attempting to persuade the court to issue the freezing injunction the applicant has a duty to make full and frank disclosure of all the matters relevant to the application including any possible defences and its financial ability to pay damages to the defendant and to third parties.[145] Breach of the obligation of full and frank disclosure will generally result in the discharge of the freezing injunction. Nevertheless, the court retains its jurisdiction to issue a new freezing injunction but will only do so when the breach of the obligation was not of a serious nature.[146]

137. The only alternative available is a *quia timet* injunction. This is different from a freezing injunction and is only available where the anticipated act is wrongful. In a freezing injunction removal of the assets from the jurisdiction is not necessarily wrongful (*Mercedes Benz AG v Herbert Heinz Horst Leiduck* [1995] 2 Lloyd's Rep 417; [1996] AC 284 (PC)).
138. *Veracruz Transportation Inc v VC Shipping Co Inc and den Norske Bank A/S (The Veracruz I)* [1992] 1 Lloyd's Rep 353 (CA) and see also *Swift-Fortune Ltd v Magnifica Marine SA (The Capaz Duckling)* [2008] 1 Lloyd's Rep 54; [2007] EWHC 1630 (Comm) (QBD (Comm)).
139. *Ninemia Maritime Corporation v Trave Schiffahrtsgesellschaft MBH und Co KG (The Niedersachsen)* [1983] 2 Lloyd's Rep 600 at p. 605 (CA).
140. *Ketchum International plc v Group Public Relations Holdings Ltd and Others* [1997] 1 WLR 4 (CA).
141. *Third Chandris Shipping Corporation Western Sealane and Aggelikai Ptera Compania Maritima SA v Unimarine SA (The Genie, Pythia and Angelic Wings)* [1979] 2 Lloyd's Rep 184.
142. *Ibid.* See also *The Niedersachsen*, fn. 139.
143. *Midas Merchant Bank plc v Senator Musa Bello, Aisha Musa Bello* [2002] EWCA Civ 1496.
144. *Gill & Others v Flightwise Travel Service Ltd & Another* [2003] EWHC 3082.
145. *The Genie, Pythia and Angelic Wings*, fn. 141, and *Thane Investments Ltd v Tomlinson (No 1)* [2003] EWCA Civ 1272 (CA).
146. For example, see *The Arena Corporation Limited (In provisional Liquidation) v Peter Schroeder* [2003] EWHC 108.

In addition to the above criteria the court will also assess whether it is just and convenient to grant the freezing injunction and, where the freezing injunction is in support of foreign proceedings, whether it is expedient to grant the injunction.[147] In respect of a case which is or will be heard by the court of another Member State because Article 31 of EC Regulation 44/2001 permits the use of provisional remedies under all European courts to assist cases before the court of any Member State it is more likely that freezing injunctions would be considered expedient.[148] However, the granting of the freezing injunction in such a case would be subject amongst others to the existence of a real connecting link between the subject matter of the freezing injunction and the territorial jurisdiction of the English court.[149] When such a link is not present, for example in respect of a worldwide freezing order, the freezing injunction may be considered inexpedient.[150] Where the case in support of which the freezing injunction is sought is heard by the court of a non-Member State two factors would affect the decision: where the defendant is resident or domiciled and the reaction of the court seized of the dispute.[151] In general the English court will not normally issue orders which are unlikely to be followed.[152]

### (c) Consequences of the freezing injunction on the defendant

Freezing orders can be destructive for the defendant long before the case on the merits is heard. When the freezing order is granted, it is up to the applicant to inform the defendant and any third parties. From that point on, the defendant can apply to the court to modify the order. However, if the defendant does not obey the injunction it is in contempt of court and can be imprisoned.[153] If the defendant violates the freezing order then it is liable for the consequences even if the court later decides that it did not have jurisdiction to grant the injunction in the first place.[154]

Thus, the defendant cannot use any frozen assets to the extent set out in the freezing order. However, the injunction may not be used as a means of putting undue pressure on the defendant. Thus, the court would permit the defendant to carry on in business in the ordinary way and, for individuals, it usually allows, *inter alia*, reasonable living expenses, legal costs, hospital bills Business payments scheduled before the issuance of the freezing order may also be allowed if they are genuine.[155]

147. Civil Jurisdiction and Judgments Act 1982, s. 25(3).
148. *Republic of Haiti and Others v Jean-Cluade Duvalier and Others* [1989] 1 Lloyd's Rep 111; [1990] 1 QB 202 (CA).
149. See *Banco Nacional de Comercio Exterior SNC v Empresa de Telecommunicaciones de Cuba SA British Telecommunications plc (intervening)*, fn. 135, applying *Van Uden Maritime BV (t/a Van Uden Africa Line) v Kommanditgesellschaft in Firma Deco-Line* (C391/95), [1999] QB 1225; [1999] 2 WLR 1181; [1999] All ER (EC) 258; [1999] 1 All ER (Comm) 385; [1998] ECR I-7091; [1999] ILPr 73; *The Times* (1 December 1998) (ECJ).
150. *Banco Nacional de Comercio Exterior SNC v Empresa de Telecommunicaciones de Cuba SA British Telecommunications plc (intervening)*, fn. 135.
151. *Credit Suisse Fides Trust v Cuoghi* [1998] QB 818 (CA).
152. *Motorola Credit Corporation v Cem Gengiz Uzan, Aysegul Akay* [2003] EWCA Civ 752; [2004] EWHC 3169 (Comm).
153. *Angelo Perotti v Kenneth Corbett and Others* [2002] EWCA Civ 1993 (CA) reported on Westlaw [2001] WL 1560759.
154. *Motorola Credit Corporation v Cem Gengiz Uzan, Aysegul Akay*, fn. 152.
155. *TDK Tape Distributor (UK) Ltd v Videochoice Ltd and Others* [1986] 1 WLR 141.

The defendant may be entitled to damages if the injunction is wrongfully obtained. Thus, where a company was being driven into administrative receivership after the claimant wrongfully obtained the injunction the company was able to recover damages based on the value of the company immediately before the injunction.[156] The award of damages depends on whether the freezing injunction was wrongfully issued, not on whether the claim was successful. The question to be asked is whether the defendant was stopped, by the freezing injunction, from doing something that he was entitled to do. Thus, damages can be awarded even where the claim is successful as this only proves that the claim was "a good arguable" one. The award is subject to the court's discretion which may take into account the conduct of the defendant and relying on that may decline to award damages. In all cases causation of damages by the injunction is needed.[157]

### (d) Consequences of the freezing injunction on third parties

Third parties who have been notified about the freezing injunction will be in contempt of court if they fail to obey it. If they are unhappy with the terms of the injunction because they may suffer damage or are unclear on its effect they are entitled to seek clarification or modification by the issuing court.

In general, pre-existing commercial transactions against the defendant's assets will be permitted. Thus banks can exercise any pre-existing rights of set-off.[158] A bank can also realise securities with the only obligation that this is done "in good faith in the ordinary course of business". The claimant does not have any interest in the assets and therefore cannot control the way the securities are realized.[159]

The effects the freezing injunction have on innocent third parties are taken into account by the courts. If the interference with the activities of the third party is not too great, the undertaking in damages by the applicant is considered sufficient. However, the award of damages is not automatic but it depends on the court's discretion.[160] Where an injunction interferes unreasonably with the third party's activities, the court may refrain from granting it.[161]

If notice of a freezing injunction is given to a bank but the bank negligently pays money out of these particular accounts, is the bank then liable in negligence to the applicant? The House of Lords, reversing the Court of Appeal decision, was satisfied that a court order is not capable of creating a duty of care and the only remedy for the breach of compliance was contempt of court.[162]

156. *Johnson Control Systems Ltd v Techni-Track Europa Ltd (In Administrative Receivership)* [2003] EWCA Civ 1126 (CA). The company was forced into receivership by its creditors who called for payments of debts as soon as they found out about the freezing injunction.
157. For example, see *Panos Eliades, Panix Promotions Limited, Panix of the US Inc v Lennox Lewis* [2005] EWHC 2966.
158. *Z Ltd v A-Z and AA-LL* [1982] Lloyd's Rep 240; [1982] QB 558 (CA).
159. *Gangway Ltd v Caledonian Park Investments*, fn. 126.
160. *Yukong Line Limited of Korea v Rendsburg Investments Corp of Liberia* [2000] WL 1881248; [2001] 2 Lloyd's Rep 113 (CA).
161. *Galaxia Maritime SA v Mineralimportexport (The Eleftherios)* [1982] 1 WLR 539; [1982] 1 Lloyd's Rep 351. A case where an injunction was granted against cargo owners to the effect that the cargo was not to be removed from the jurisdiction. The shipowners were given notice of the injunction. Consequently, if they sailed they would have been in contempt of court. The shipowners applied for the injunction to be discharged and the Court of Appeal accepted their appeal in spite of the undertaking of damages given by the claimant.
162. *Commissioners of Customs & Excise v Barclays Bank plc* [2004] EWHC 122; [2005] 1 Lloyd's Rep 165 (CA), reversed by HL judgment [2006] 2 Lloyd's Rep 327; [2006] EWCA Civ 1155.

### (e) Worldwide freezing injunctions

A freezing injunction concerned with assets outside the English jurisdiction can only be effective if recognised by the court of the country where the assets exist. In order to assess whether the granting of such an order is appropriate the court will assess whether the claimant should be permitted to attempt the enforcement of its claim in the foreign court where the assets exist. In order to make this assessment the English courts require to be informed about the law of the foreign court in order to ensure that the freezing order will not have an excessive effect. Such orders are usually granted in the presence of the defendant and with an undertaking that the applicant will not try to enforce it in the foreign court without the permission of the English court.[163] The burden of proof is on the claimant in respect of the existence of the defendant's assets abroad although the claimant only needs to show "a real prospect that the assets are in the country where enforcement is sought".[164]

The position of third parties in cases where a worldwide freezing injunction is concerned poses additional difficulties. Banks, for example, that can be served with the freezing injunction in England but also have branches abroad can be put in difficult positions. If they ignore the freezing injunction they may well be held in contempt of court. On the other hand if they comply with the freezing injunction both in their English branch and abroad they could be in breach of their contract with the defendant and this contract may be subject to foreign jurisdiction and/or law. In addition the courts of the State where they are situated may issue conflicting orders and then the bank will have to act in breach of the orders of one of the two courts. Damages are not considered by the English courts as an adequate remedy in such circumstances because damage to reputation and regulatory consequences as well as criminal liability may be involved.

These difficulties are resolved by the inclusion of a proviso in the freezing injunction by which the parties affected outside the jurisdiction are expressly protected. The form of the proviso has developed in case law. Thus, unless the injunction is declared enforceable by the court of the country concerned, only entities subject to the jurisdiction of English court and the defendant are subject to a worldwide freezing order.[165] Another proviso available in the standard form of a freezing injunction, is to the effect that the injunction does not prevent the third party from complying with what it reasonably believes are its contractual or other obligations in the country where the assets exist or under the law of the contract or court decisions. These provisos include criminal and civil obligations.[166]

### (f) Assets subject to the freezing injunction

Any property or other asset with monetary values either owned by the defendant or held on behalf of the defendant by a third party can be used to satisfy the

163. *Dadourian Group Int Inc & Others v Paul Francis Simms and Others* [2005] 2 All ER 651.
164. *Ibid.*, [2006] EWCA Civ 399; [2006] 2 Lloyd's Rep 327 (CA). See also the guidelines developed there.
165. *Babanaft Co International SA v Bassatne* [1990] Ch 13; [1988] 2 Lloyd's Rep 435 (CA) and *Derby & Co. and Others v Weldon and Others (Nos 3 and 4)* [1990] Ch 65 (CA).
166. *Bank of China v NBM LLC and Others* [2002] 1 Lloyd's Rep 1; [2002] 1 Lloyd's Rep 506 (CA) and now in the example of the freezing injunction in PD 25: Interim Injunction.

judgment. The property can be situated anywhere in the world.[167] Thus a ship can be subject to a freezing injunction as part of an *in personam* action against the shipowner.[168] Such an action would be a useful device if the particular claim does not fall within the Admiralty jurisdiction so as to authorise arrest.[169] However, as a matter of the court's discretion such orders would rarely be granted because they are likely to interfere with the rights of innocent third parties, such as charterers or cargo owners.[170]

167. *Babanaft Co International v Bassatne*, fn. 165.
168. *The Rena K* [1978] 1 Lloyd's Rep 545; [1979] QB 377, but most probably not in support of an action *in rem*: *The Stolt Filia* [1980] LMLN 15.
169. *The Irina Zharkikh, and The Ksenia Zharkikh* [2001] 2 Lloyd's Rep 319; 2001 WL 949854.
170. *Cf. The Rena K*, fn. 168.

CHAPTER 12

# The Application of the EC Competition Rules to the Maritime Sector

*ANDREA LISTA*

## 1. THE MEANING OF COMPETITION LAW – THE GENERAL PICTURE

Competition law is a constantly developing legal field. Although it is characterised by an idiosyncratic and technical nature, competition law has a great deal of influence on every area of law and on rules of politics and economic policy.

Its principal function is to safeguard and promote the competitive process, with the aim of ensuring an optimum allocation of resources in a market and to maximise consumer welfare. In other words, competition law regulates market activities in order to preserve a free market system. In a market without any form of control, undertakings would be naturally inclined to collude to fix prices, those in a dominant position to abuse their market strength and mergers might inevitably lead to excessive concentrations of economic power. Such practices can hinder or inhibit the competitive process.

The aim of competition law is therefore to regulate the relationships between undertakings selling goods or providing services of the same kind at the same time to an identifiable group of customers within the same geographical market.

The creation of the European Economic Community in 1957 started a process of economic integration in which competition law has played a principal role. Within this process, for more than 50 years the Commission and the Community Courts have built a complex and wide-ranging framework of competition law principles, with which Member States are required to comply.[1] EC competition law is a unique legislative framework: it has been structured on the basis of the different historical and legal experiences that have shaped national competition laws of the various Member States and has been superimposed on them.

EC Competition law includes four main policy areas arising from the Treaty rules:

(i) The control of any type of cartels, or control of collusion and other anti-competitive practices which have an effect on the EU (Article 81 of the Treaty);
(ii) The prohibition of monopolies, or of any abuse of dominant market positions (governed by Article 82);
(iii) The control of direct and indirect aid given by EU Member States to companies (State aid, covered under Article 87); and
(iv) The control of proposed mergers, acquisitions and joint ventures involving companies having a defined amount of turnover in the EU/EEA

1. EC competition law is destined to prevail in case of contrast with national law of Member States by virtue of the principle of primacy of EC Law established by the European Court of Justice (ECJ) in the case *Costa v ENEL* (Case 6/64 [1964] ECR 585).

(governed by Article 82 and by Council Regulation 139/2004 EC, the Merger Regulation).

This chapter will consider these policy areas in turn below in conjunction with their application to the maritime sector.

## 2. ARTICLE 81 OF THE TREATY AND THE CONTROL OF COLLUSIVE BEHAVIOURS

Article 81 of the Treaty prohibits all agreements between undertakings, decisions by associations of undertakings and concerted practices which may affect trade between Member States and which have as their object or effect the prevention, restriction or distortion of competition within the common market.

Article 81 is structured into three paragraphs. The first paragraph of Article 81 lays down a general prohibition of any collusive behaviour between undertakings having as its object or effect the restriction, prevention or distortion of competition in the market. This prohibition has a vast area of application which includes both informal agreements (gentlemen's agreements) and concerted practices, i.e. forms of practical collusion where undertakings adopt the same behaviour raising or lowering prices at the same time in absence of a formal agreement (i.e. without having physically agreed to do so). Further, Article 81 covers both horizontal agreements (agreements between undertakings occupying the same position in the production or distribution chain, e.g. agreements between retailers) and vertical agreements (between undertakings having a different position in the production or distribution chain, e.g. agreements between retailers and suppliers), effectively outlawing the operation of cartels within the EU.

Horizontal agreements represent the most serious threat to competition, and include the so-called "hard core" restrictions, i.e. price-fixing, establishment of quotas, and market sharing. Information exchange agreements are another very controversial form of horizontal agreement due to their capability of facilitating collusive conduct among competing firms, as such agreements are likely to enhance the possibility of monitoring competitors' conduct. Vertical agreements are also seen as a possible danger to the competition as they tend to lead to the so-called "market foreclosure", i.e. the side effect of exclusive agreements between a producer and certain distributors to sell only its brand of a specific product.

The second paragraph of Article 81 provides that any arrangement prohibited by Article 81(1) is prohibited and automatically void.

Finally, the third paragraph of Article 81 lays down an "exemption" mechanism permitting an arrangement within the meaning of Article 81(1) which would otherwise be prohibited by Article 81(2).

In practice, Article 81(3) provides for an exemption of any collusive practice capable of impairing competition insofar as it creates efficiencies that outweigh the restriction of competition, consumers obtain a fair share of those benefits, there are no less restrictive means of achieving the efficiencies, and competition is not eliminated altogether.[2]

2. Price fixing agreements cannot, nevertheless, be exempted. The only example of price-fixing agreements exempted was the block exemption for freight-rate fixing by liner conferences in the EU maritime transport sector under Regulation 4056/86 which was repealed, as we will see, in 2006.

Article 81(3) constitutes the basis for the so-called "Block Exemption Regulations" that have been introduced by the Commission over the years in order to grant exemption on a large scale to specific kinds of agreements.

### (a) The application of Article 81 EC to the shipping industry

There is no reason in theory why Article 81 should not apply to the maritime transport. However, for many years the competition law system created by Articles 81 and 82 of the EC Treaty did not find application in the field of maritime transport. One feasible reason for this was the fact that, before the accession of the UK, Ireland and Denmark in 1973 and Greece in 1981, most transport between the Member States was landbound.

Another reason may be the long tradition of self-regulation characterising the international shipping industry. Its self-regulatory system was based partly on agreements among carriers, concluded in order to provide stability to the maritime transport sector (conferences), and partly on a particular form of alliance among carriers, the aim of which was to share the high costs involved in managing container fleets and to improve the quality of the service (consortia).

The first attempt at regulating competition in the maritime transport sector at EU level was the simultaneous promulgation in 1986 of four regulations. Council Regulation (EEC) Nos 4055/86 and 4058/86 ensured the application of the principle of freedom of services to the maritime transport sector. Council Regulation (EEC) No 4057/86 aimed to eliminate distortion of competition coming from third country carriers. Finally, the cardinal piece of legislation relating to the maritime sector was the controversial Council Regulation (EEC) No 4056/86, which entered into force on 1 July 1986 and was repealed in 2006. The Regulation contained both substantive and procedural rules relating to the application of competition law to international maritime transport services from or to one or more Community ports, other than tramp vessel services.[3]

Before considering the current situation and possible future scenarios, the analysis will briefly focus on Regulation 4056/86 and the past regime.

### (b) The past regime: Regulation 4056/86 and the block exemption for liner conferences

Regulation 4056/86 used to lay down detailed rules for the application of Article 81 EC to international maritime transport services, empowering the European Commission to investigate alleged infringements. Most importantly, the Regulation provided for an automatic open-ended block exemption for liner conferences (i.e. associations of shipowners operating the transport of cargo, chiefly by container on the same route, served by a secretariat) and for agreements between

3. Art. 1(3)(a) of Reg.4056/86 defined "tramp vessel services" as "the transport of goods in bulk or in break-bulk in a vessel chartered wholly or partly to one or more shippers on the basis of a voyage or time charter or any other form of contract for non-regularly scheduled or non-advertised sailings where the freight rates are freely negotiated case by case in accordance with the conditions of supply and demand". The fourth recital to Reg. 4056/86 provided that tramp vessel services were excluded because the rates for these services are negotiated on an *ad hoc* basis in accordance with the level of supply and demand patterns prevailing in the market. Tramp vessel services are subject to the transitional provisions of EC competition rules (i.e. Arts. 84 and 85 of the EC Treaty).

transport users and the latter concerning the use of the conference services. The Regulation applied only to certain types of maritime transport services. For instance, it did not apply to any activity not intended as a "transport" service; consequently, ancillary services or transport related activity (e.g. travel agency, shipping agency, ship broking) did not fall within the scope of the Regulation. Further, the definition of liner conference only embraced the carriage of cargo and not the carriage of passengers

The block exemption was enshrined in Article 3 of the Regulation which provided an exemption of agreements, decisions and concerted practices of all or part of the members of one or more liner conferences of container vessels. The block exemption contained in Article 3 of Regulation 4056/86 had some singular features compared to the norm. Unlike other block exemptions, it was not subject to renewal but unlimited in time. It also permitted the use of joint price-fixing and capacity regulation – practices not permitted by any other block exemption. As a result, it allowed any type of cooperation between carriers, provided that it fulfilled the terms and conditions set out by Article 4 of the Regulation (i.e. subject to the condition that the agreement, decision or concerted practice shall not, within the common market, cause detriment to certain ports, transport users or carriers by applying for the carriage of the same goods and in the area covered by the agreement, decision or concerted practice, rates and conditions of carriage which differ according to the country of origin or destination or port of loading or discharge, unless such rates or conditions can be economically justified).

The rationale behind the introduction of the block exemption was that, at the time of the adoption of Regulation 4056/86, the Council and the Commission believed that liner conferences were necessary to enhance productivity and capacity utilisation, reduce costs, improve the quality of services, and grant stability to the maritime sector. While originally seen as a useful tool, Regulation 4056/86 and the block exemption for price-fixing became increasingly controversial.

Opponents of the block exemption claimed that liner conferences were effectively able to act as a monopoly, representing a threat to competition within the meaning of Article 81.

The economics of the situation are straightforward – within a market, any sort of agreement to fix prices constitutes an impediment to competition, in that it removes the possibility of offering the same service at different prices. As might be expected, the legal aspect is more complex. The ruling of the European Court of Justice (ECJ) in *Pronuptia de Paris GmbH v Irmgard Schillgalis*[4] determined that restrictions to competition do not represent a distortion to competition within the meaning of Article 81, as long as they are objectively necessary in order to provide for the successful functioning of an economic system. In other words, the Court is willing to weigh up the advantages and disadvantages of an agreement related to competition.

Applying this precedent to the maritime transport sector, the argument was that liner conferences were necessary in order to provide stability in the sector.

4. Case C-161/84 *Pronuptia de Paris GmbH v Irmgard Schillgalis* [1986] ECR 353.

### (c) The repeal of Regulation 4056/86

The decision to undertake a review of the block exemption regulation for liner conferences was triggered by different, concurring factors. Firstly, the block exemption for liner conferences was in many ways exceptional. As previously mentioned, the peculiarity of Regulation 4056/86 was that it granted an exemption for a hardcore restriction of competition such as horizontal forms of price-fixing. In addition to that, unlike almost all other block exemptions, it was not subject to time-limits and had never been reviewed. Another incentive for the review process was the publication in April 2002 of a *Report on Competition Policy in Liner Shipping* by the Secretariat of the OECD. The Report raised serious doubts on the validity of the assumption that collective rate setting by members of a liner conference was an indispensable pre-requisite for efficient liner shipping services.

According to the *Report*, there was no evidence of a positive influence from the antitrust exemptions for price-fixing granted by Regulation 4056/86. In particular, the *Report* outlined the possibility of enhancing the efficiency of the sector by other means than liner conferences, by adopting agreements aimed at reducing costs. The *Report* also emphasised the exclusion from the maritime transport market of new independent operators, willing to provide liner services but not in the position due to the block exemption to compete with the liner conferences.

In October 2004 the Commission published its *White Paper on the review of Regulation (EEC) No 4056/86, applying the EC competition rules to maritime transport* (COM/2004/0675). The purpose of the *White Paper* was to assess whether to modify or repeal the provisions of Regulation 4056/86, based on an analysis of the current situation in the maritime transport sector.

The *White Paper* discussed whether, in the current market situation, there remained any justification under Article 81(3) of the Treaty for the block exemption for freight rate-fixing by liner conferences. The *White Paper* emphasised the extent to which the liner shipping market had changed in the two decades since the adoption of Regulation 4056/86. In particular, the role of independent carriers offering liner shipping services outside a conference framework had become considerably more important. Furthermore, the Commission recognised how forms of cooperation between carriers not involving price-fixing practices (such as consortia and alliances) had increased considerably. The *White Paper* also highlighted the significant growth of individual confidential contracting between carriers and shippers, by means of individual service contracts. The analysis resulted in serious doubts about the compatibility of the block exemption for liner conferences with the EU competition law system.

### (d) The current scenario for liner conferences

As a direct result of the Commission *White Paper*, Council Regulation 1419/2006[5] was adopted in September 2006. Regulation 1419/2006, subject to a transitional period of two years for existing liner conferences, repealed Regulation 4056/86 and its block exemption for liner conferences agreements.

5. Council Regulation 1419/2006, OJ L269/1, repealing Regulation (EEC) No 4056/86 laying down detailed rules for the application of Arts. 85 and 86 of the Treaty to maritime transport, and amending Regulation (EC) No 1/2003 as regards the extension of its scope to include cabotage and international tramp services.

The repeal of Regulation 4056/86 leaves the liner shipping sector exposed to the application of Article 81 of the EC Treaty directly under the European Commission's jurisdiction.[6] This means that starting from October 2008 (the end of the transitional period of Regulation 1419/2006) agreements between carriers having the object or effect of preventing, restricting or distorting the competition and capable of affecting trade between Member States will be prohibited, void and unenforceable in respect of their restrictions.

As from October 2008, shipping pools (either in the classic form of administration-controlled pools managed by a separate company, or member-controlled pools under the operational management of one or more members of the pool) will be unlawful under EC law. In other words, agreements between carriers related to the operation of scheduled maritime transport services, whose object or effect is to fix the rates and conditions of carriage, will fall within the meaning of Article 81.

On a general level, examples of agreements which will be caught by Article 81 are, *inter alia*: agreements fixing purchase/selling prices or other trading conditions; agreements limiting or controlling production, markets, technical development or investment; market sharing agreements; and agreements on information sharing of sensitive information such as pricing, capacity, joint purchasing/selling agreements.

Consequentely, any EU or non-EU carrier currently a member of liner conferences operating on trade routes to or from EU ports, which will continue to fix prices and regulate capacity on those routes as from October 2008 would be subject to substantial fines being imposed on the parties to the agreement if discovered by the European Commission.

### *Possibility of individual exemption under Article 81(3)*

Starting from 18 October 2008, without the shield of protection offered by the block exemption, shipping pools will be considered as forms of price fixing practices having as their object and effect the co-ordination of their capacity and customers sharing, in light of the restriction of each member's commercial freedom to freely operate in the shipping market in a competitive manner. All this is clearly against Article 81 EC.

Where does this new scenario leave shipping pools then? The only possibility for their survival would be through an individual exemption under Article 81(3). The repeal of the block exemption granted by Regulation 4056/86 does not preclude the possibility of an individual exemption. A block exemption is merely an exemption granted on a large scale to specific kinds of agreement. In its absence, maritime undertakings are still in the position to obtain an individual *ad hoc* exemption, insofar as they will be in the position to prove that their agreements satisfies the four conditions listed by Article 81(3). Such agreements will need therefore in first place to create efficiencies (in terms of improving the provision of the service or promoting economic or technical progress). Secondly, consumers must be allowed to share the benefits of those efficiencies. Thirdly, the agreements should not contain restrictions on competition beyond the strictly indispensable restraints. Finally, they must not eliminate competition altogether.

6. The European Commission is the relevant Community institution which enforces the EC competition rules.

If the above conditions are satisfied, the shipping pools will be in the position to benefit from an individual exemption. The prerogative of granting individual exemption under Article 81(3) EC used to be in the power of the Commission. Since 1 May 2004 (after the entry into force of Regulation 1/2003[7]), the Commission has lost this prerogative and henceforth individual exemptions are considered a legal requirement to be automatically granted by national courts and competition authorities if the conditions are met.

As a consequence, the process of evaluation of the existence of the conditions for an exemption laid down by Article 81(3) is now known as a "self assessment" exercise to be carried out by the parties involved with the support of economists and legal advisers prior to the official evaluation of the competent national authorities. The burden of proof lies on the party involved who will need to support their claim to exemption with strong arguments.

In practice, the starting point for the assessment of the maritime pools will be their impact (actual or potential) on competition.

This means that if the impact on competition is appreciable and trade between Member States is affected, in order to obtain individual exemption, shipping pools will have to prove that their agreements are necessary in order to provide their services. This can be an uneasy task to prove, especially in presence of the so-called hardcore restrictions of competition, i.e. price fixing, limitation of output (hence capacity regulation) and customer or market sharing. Under such circumstances the burden of proof for the fulfilment of the conditions enshrined in Article 81(3) is particularly high.

According to the *Commission Guidelines on the Application of Article 81 to Maritime Transport Services*,[8] the Commission in assessing whether or not to exempt cooperation agreements in the maritime transport market will take into account, *inter alia*, the impact of such agreements on the shipping market, prices, costs, quality, frequency and differentiation of the service provided, in conjunction with innovation, marketing and commercialisation of the service,

A good argument in support of the claim for an exemption might be unquestionable evidence of the creation of remarkable efficiencies in conjunction with a considerable reduction in the costs of the services.

If, by contrast, the effects (actual or potential) of the pool on competition are not appreciable, the scenario changes radically. Agreements between small and medium-sized maritime undertakings, or agreements between undertakings having very small market shares fall outside the scope of application of Article 81 EC, as explained by the Commission in its *De Minimis Notice*.[9]

Agreements between undertakings occupying the same position in the production/distribution chain (horizontal agreements) having a joint market share below 10% will be allowed without the need for an individual exemption insofar as they do not involve price fixing, output limitation or forms of customers and market sharing, for instance, a shipping pool involving maritime undertakings with a joint

7. Council Regulation (EC) No 1/2003 of 16 December 2002 on the implementation of the rules on competition laid down in Articles 81 and 82 of the Treaty, OJ 2003, L1/1.
8. Commission Draft Guidelines on the Application of Art. 81 to Maritime Transport Services OJ C 215, 14.9.2007, pp. 3–15.
9. Commission Notice on agreements of minor importance which do not appreciably restrict competition under Art. 81(1) of the Treaty establishing the European Community (*de minimis*), OJ C 368, 22.12.2001.

share of the market below 10%. Agreements between undertakings having a different position in the market (vertical agreements) will be considered lawful insofar as they will not involve more than 15% of the market share (e.g. an agreement between an owner and a shipper covering no more than 15% of the market).

### (e) Article 81 and the tramp shipping and cabotage sectors

Regulation 1419/2006 assimilates the tramp shipping (the non-regular maritime transport of bulk cargo not containerised – oil, agricultural and chemical products) and cabotage (unscheduled maritime transport services taking place exclusively between ports in one EU Member State) sectors to all the other sectors of the economy. This means that Article 81 EC now fully applies also to these two sectors of the maritime industry.

The transitional period covering liner conferences does not apply to tramp shipping and cabotage which have therefore been subject to the application of Article 81 since October 2006. As a result, the Commission has already initiated investigations related to agreements concerning the parcel tankers market.

The impact of the application of Article 81 to the tramp shipping and cabotage sectors will affect first and foremost any form of horizontal agreements between maritime undertakings. Pools or other forms of co-operation between actual or potential competitors involving the direct or indirect determination of rates, limitations on output, markets or customers sharing, information exchange and any other anti-competitive practices will be subject to an intense scrutiny.

Such pools *prima facie* represent a blatant price fixing practice capable of limiting output and considerably restricting competition. More specifically, competition concerns arise because in a typical tramp shipping or cabotage pool, the pool manager is usually empowered to negotiate contracts and rates with customers on the behalf of all the other members or ships belonging to the pool (the pool manager usually also takes sole responsibility for fleet scheduling, the determination of voyage and time charters, as well as for other influential management operations).

In order to obtain an individual exemption under Article 81(3), such forms of hardcore restrictions will be subject to a severe burden of proof falling on the parties to the agreement.

As for line conferences, the application of the Commission's *De Minimis Notice* will result in the automatic exemption of horizontal agreements between undertakings whose combined market share is below 10% only insofar as they do not involve price fixing, output limitation or forms of customers and market sharing. Since pools in the tramp shipping and cabotage sectors usually involve such practices, the *De Minimis Notice* cannot in this case be considered a useful tool.

The most recurrent form of horizontal cooperation in the tramp and cabotage shipping sectors are shipping pools. There is no universal model for a pool. Some features do, however, appear to be common to all pools in the different market segments as follows. Similarly to the line conferences agreements, standard tramp and cabotage shipping pools bring together a number of similar vessels under different ownership and operated under a single administration. A pool manager is normally responsible for the commercial management (for instance, joint marketing), negotiation of freight rates and centralisation of incomes and voyage costs and commercial operations (planning vessel movements and instructing vessels, nominating agents in ports, keeping customers updated, issuing freight invoices, ordering bunkers, collecting the vessels' earnings and distributing them under a pre-arranged weighting system, etc). The pool manager often acts under the supervision of a general executive committee representing the vessel owners. The technical operation of vessels remains the responsibility of each owner (safety, crew, repairs, maintenance, etc). Although they market their services jointly, the pool members perform the services individually.

It follows from this description that the key feature of standard tramp and cabotage shipping pools is joint selling, coupled with some features of joint production. The guidance on both joint selling, as a variant of a joint commercialisation agreement, and joint production in the *Commission Guidelines on the applicability of Article 81 of the EC Treaty to horizontal cooperation agreements*[10] is therefore relevant. However, given the variation in pools' characteristics, each pool must be analysed on a case-by-case basis. Insofar as tramp and cabotage pools have as their object or effect the coordination of the competitive behaviour of their parents, the coordination shall be appraised in accordance with the criteria of Article 81(1) EC with a view to establishing whether or not the operation is compatible with the common market and to determine whether it fulfils the four cumulative conditions of Article 81(3) of the Treaty.

Pool agreements in the tramp shipping and cabotage sectors often also involve the provision of membership rules such as the prohibition on operating vessels outside the pool, or long notice requirements in case of withdrawal of vessels from the pool, which are indeed capable of hindering competition. These provisions will inevitably be caught by Article 81 EC. Yet again, the only possibility of escape is represented by an individual exemption under Article 81(3), but this will require a careful self-assessment by the parties involved in the pool. In these circumstances the situation is very delicate and the chances of obtaining an exemption reduced to the minimum, as we need to bear in mind that under Article 81(3) EC individual exemption can be granted only in presence of the creation of economic efficiencies in the market and not only for the benefit of the owners pooling their vessels. Since such membership rules do not provide any benefits to consumers, the possibilities of an exemption are minimal.

Further, pools cannot reduce competition in the sector preventing the access to the market by external players or effectively reducing their possibility to compete with the pool.

By contrast, the impact of Regulation 1419/2006 on vertical agreements related to the tramp shipping and cabotage sectors is not particularly severe. Agreements between parties occupying a different position in the supply chain, e.g. requirements contracts, bareboat, management agreements, time or voyage charters, should be safe insofar as they will not contain anti-competitive clauses. Thus, agreements providing exclusivity of supply or purchase, long terms commitment obligations or long notice periods will require an individual exemption.

### (f) General consequences in case of non compliance with Article 81 EC

The consequences for non-compliance can be extremely severe. The competition authorities (the Commission together with the relevant anti-trust national

10. OIC3, 06.01.2001.

authorities, e.g. the Office of Fair Trading in the UK) have a wide range of powers in order to ensure the compliance of agreements and pools with Article 81 EC. Firstly, they are endowed with large investigative powers which allow them to require information on agreements, carry out dawn raids on private and business premises in order to collect evidence related to potential anti-competitive behaviours. Furthermore, in case of violation of Article 81 they are allowed to impose fines of up to 10% of the worldwide group annual turnover of any party involved in the infringement, issue cease and desist orders and other interim relief measures.

## 3. ARTICLE 82 EC: ABUSES OF DOMINANT POSITION BY ONE OR MORE UNDERTAKINGS: MEANING AND ISSUES

Article 82 of the Treaty prohibits the abuse of dominant position by one or more undertakings within the common market or in a substantial part as incompatible with the common market insofar as it may affect trade between Member States.

Such abuse may, in particular, consist in directly or indirectly imposing unfair purchase or selling prices or other unfair trading conditions; limiting production, markets or technical development to the prejudice of consumers; applying dissimilar conditions to equivalent transactions with other trading parties, thereby placing them at a competitive disadvantage; or making the conclusion of contracts subject to acceptance by the other parties of supplementary obligations which, by their nature or according to commercial usage, have no connection with the subject of such contracts.

The essence of Article 82 is to control market power. The prohibition on abuses of dominant position provided by Article 82 incorporates three cumulative elements.

Firstly, one or more undertakings need to acquire a dominant position within the Common Market or in a substantial part thereof. The concept of dominance does not exist in the abstract, but only in relation to a particular market,[11] meaning a clearly defined geographical area where a product is marketed and where the conditions of competition are sufficiently homogeneous for the effect of the economic power of the undertaking to be evaluated.[12] The relevant market thus needs to be identified in its geographical and product dimensions prior to the assessment of dominance which is mainly based on the analysis of the share of the market occupied by a specific undertaking in conjunction with the assessment of the market share of its nearest competitor.

Nevertheless, it needs to be emphasised that a dominant position within a market is not illicit in itself; it is the abuse of that position which is illegitimate. Accordingly, in order to trigger the application of Article 82 EC the undertaking or undertakings concerned must have abused that position of dominance.[13]

Lastly, the abuse of that position must affect trade between Member States. If the abuse of a dominant position does not affect the trade between the Member States, Article 82 EC will not be relevant.

11. See Case 6/72 *Europeanballage Corporation and Continental Can Co Inc v Commission* [1973] ECR 215.
12. See Case 27/76 *United Brands v Commission* [1978] ECR 207, and the Commission's Notice on Market Definition – OJ [1997] C 372/5.
13. Abusive practices undertaken by non-dominant companies do not fall within the aim of the Article here being considered.

These requirements all need to be satisfied and are considered below in the context of the shipping trade.

### (a) The application of Article 82 EC to the shipping sector

Contrary to Article 81 which will be fully applied to shipping undertakings before October 2008, Article 82 has always applied to the maritime industry. Article 8(1) of Regulation 4056/86 provided that an abuse of dominance within the meaning of Article 82 EC was prohibited without the need for a prior decision to that effect, whereas Article 8(2) provided that the Commission may withdraw the block exemption for liner conferences where the conduct of the conference had effects which were incompatible with Article 82.

The entry into force of Regulation 1419/2006 did not change the previous scenario: Article 82 currently fully applies to the maritime sector. The application of Article 82 has been particularly relevant in the context of ports.

*The identification of the relevant geographic market in the maritime sector*

As previously established, the definition of the relevant market is a core element for the application of Article 82. The reason is obvious: the abuse of dominant position needs to be identified in relation to a particular market. For example, two dominant stevedores in the port of Southampton refusing to supply their services would not have any material impact on stevedoring services in Genoa because they operate in two separate markets.

We have seen that the geographical market may be defined as the space comprising the geographical area in which the conditions of competition are sufficiently homogeneous and which can on this basis be distinguished from neighbouring areas in which the conditions of competition are appreciably different.

In the maritime sector the geographical market may involve, for instance, a single port or a cluster of ports, or a service between two ports or two countries. For example, in a case relating to ferry services across the Baltic Sea, the geographical market may involve a single port (e.g. Stockholm) at one end of the journey. By contrast, in relation to liner traffic between the UK and Italy, the relevant geographical market may involve a range of ports (e.g. Southampton, Marseille, Genova).

The importance of the relevant geographical market definition derives from the fact that under one market definition, a port could be dominant in a substantial part of the common market and, therefore, subject to Article 82 but the same port might not be in a dominant position under a different geographical market definition. An interesting example is *Irish Continental Group plc v Chambre de Commerce et Industries de Morlaix*.[14] In this case the object of dispute was the access to the port of Roscoff, a ferryport in Brittany in France. Brittany Ferries was the only company to operate a ferry service from Roscoff to Ireland carrying around 100,000 passengers annually.

14. *Irish Continental Group plc v Chambre de Commerce et Industries de Morlaix* [1995] 5 CMLR 177 (not published in the *Official Journal*).

In November 1994, an Irish ferry company, Irish Ferries, sought access to the port of Roscoff by application to CCI de Morlaix. The parties negotiated, but CCI de Morlaix denied that there was an agreement for the access of Irish Ferries to the port of Roscoff. The scenario of this case changed radically in relation to the identification of the relevant geographic market. If the geographical market were Ireland–Brittany, then Roscoff was in a dominant position in a substantial part of the common market and subject to Article 82 EC. By contrast, if the relevant geographical market was considered to be Ireland and the range of northern French ports generally considered (including Brittany and Normandy) then Roscoff did not occupy a dominant position. The reason for this was that Roscoff had a very high share of the market Ireland–Brittany, but a considerably lower percentage of the geographical market identified in Ireland and the range of northern French generally considered.

The geographical market can indeed be a limited market especially in case of passenger car ferry services where passengers are usually inclined to choose short sea journeys. For instance, in the *Holyhead* cases[15] Stena Sealink Ports and Stena Sealink Line which owned the port of Holyhead were accused of abuse of dominant position for their refusal to allow Sea Containers Limited to operate a fast ferry service through the central corridor between Holyhead (located in Anglesey, North Wales) and Dun Laoghaire (in Ireland). Sea Containers argued that Stena Sealink Line had a dominant position in the market for the provision of passenger and car-ferry services on the "central corridor" route between Britain and Ireland.

In order to identify the relevant geographical market, the Commission had defined three corridors: the northern, central and southern corridors. The Commission maintained that the substitutability of the three corridors across the Irish Sea for any traveller depended on the traveller's point of origin and his or her intended destination for the journey in question, and that the relevant geographical market in this case was represented by the central corridor. The northern and southern corridors, with service routes between Scotland and Northern Ireland and South Wales and Ireland respectively, were in fact not considered viable alternatives to the central corridor for the majority of leisure users, with or without cars. The reason for this was that almost one-third of Ireland's population resides in the Greater Dublin area and Holyhead is easily reached by inhabitants of Birmingham, Manchester and Liverpool. The Irish ports on the northern and southern corridors are far from Dublin which is the single most important destination on the Irish side. The roads from Dublin to all the rest of Ireland are faster, and the public transport more satisfactory, than the roads or public transport from Larne, Belfast or Rosslare.

### *The identification of the relevant product market in the maritime sector*

The identification of the relevant product market is essential in order to assess the dominance of a maritime undertaking. The definition of the relevant product market offered by the Commission and the European Courts focuses upon the

15. *B&I Line plc v Sealink Harbours Ltd and Sealink Stena Ltd* [1992] 5 CMLR 255, and *Sea Containers Ltd v Stena Sealink Ports and Stena Sealink Ltd*, OJL 15/8, 18/01/94; [1995] 4 CMLR 84.

notion of *interchangeability*, i.e. the extent to which the goods or services under scrutiny are interchangeable with other products. The notion of *interchangeability* entails the analysis of "cross-elasticities" of one specific product. The existence of high cross-elasticity indicates that the products are interchangeable. The more products tend to be interchangeable, the greater are the probabilities that, in practice, they belong to the same relevant market.

In the maritime sector, on a general level there is a difference in terms of product market definition in cases relating to *passenger* traffic rather than *commercial/ cargo* traffic. The reason for this is mainly due to the fact that passengers generally are inclined to prefer short sea journeys and equally do not want to travel too far by road from either their home or destination. Conversely, the logistic allocation of the resources and ships in case of commercial/cargo traffic is usually accommodated in a different way as to reserve the shortest and most convenient routing to *passenger* traffic.

Nevertheless, we need to bear in mind that the identification of the relevant product market is focused on the concept of interchangeability or substitutability of services. The more services are interchangeable, the more is it likely that they belong to the same relevant product market. The identification of the relevant product market can be a rather easy exercise in case a port provides its services in several different product markets (e.g. the passenger liner trade, the oil tanker trade and the passenger car ferry trade). In this case, each of the services above will clearly represent the relevant product market; for instance the oil tanker trade is not interchangeable with the passenger car ferry trade. This identification can be more complicated in case of shipping companies operating through car and passenger carriers due to the high level of interchangeability characterising car and passenger vessels. It is essential to emphasise that the correct identification of the relevant product market is crucial in order to assess the dominance of a specific undertakings. Dominance is very much a market-specific concept, and for instance a port may be in a dominant position for one specific service market (e.g. the oil tanker trade) but not in the case of another product market (e.g. for passenger car ferry trade).

### *The assessment of dominance in the maritime sector*

Having identified the relevant market considered both under its product and geographical dimensions, the next step is the assessment of the dominance of a specific undertaking. The concept of "dominant position" is not defined in Article 82 EC but it is generally considered in case law as a position of economic strength enjoyed by a specific undertaking which enables it to undermine, restrain and hinder competition within the relevant market. Dominance may be either individual or collective.

In order to assess whether a particular undertaking has a dominant position we need to refer in the first place to its market share. If we are dealing with a firm having a market share of around 40% or more, it is highly likely that we are dealing with a dominant undertaking. Nevertheless, even lower thresholds could hide a position of dominance, especially within very fragmented markets. The relevant element is the market share of the nearest competitor. If, for instance, we are dealing with an undertaking having 25% of the market and its nearest competitor has a share of 7% of the same market, the former will be considered to be in a dominant position.

Other elements to be taken into account in conjunction with the market share are the financial or technical resources of the undertaking concerned, or the possibility that it eventually has to control both production and distribution within the relevant market.

All these factors will have to be taken into account in order to assess the dominance of a shipping undertaking.

In liner shipping, volume and/or capacity data have been identified as the basis for calculating market shares in several Commission decisions and Court judgments. The Court of First Instance held in *Cewal I*[16] that in the absence of exceptional circumstances extremely large market shares (market share of between 70% and 80%) are in themselves evidence of the existence of a dominant position. Lower market shares (market share of 60% on the trade in question) are capable of giving rise to a strong presumption of a dominant position.[17]

In tramp shipping markets, service providers compete for the award of transport contracts, that is to say, they sell voyages. Depending on the specific services in question, various data may be used in order to calculate the annual market shares, for instance: (a) the number of voyages; (b) the parties' volume or value share in the overall transport of a specific cargo; (c) the parties' share in the market for time charter contracts; (d) data in relation to the parties' contract negotiations; (e) the parties' capacity shares in the relevant fleet (by vessel type and size).[18]

### *Examples of abuse of dominant position in the maritime industry*

As previously mentioned, the abuse of dominant position can assume different forms, e.g. charging excessive prices, refusal to supply existing customers and so on.

In the *Cewal* case, members of a liner conference were found to infringe Article 82 for abusing a collective dominant position by taking collective action designed to eliminate their principal competitor. Specifically, their abuse consisted in predatory prices by offering lower freight rates than their competitors and through the offer of loyalty rebates.

Another example of abuse arose from *Corsica Ferries Italia Srl v Corpo dei Piloti del Porto di Genova.*[19] Corsica Ferries Italia SRL (hereinafter "Corsica Ferries") considered that it was the victim of an abuse of dominant position contrary to Article 82 of the Treaty by the Corpo dei Piloti del Porto di Genova (Corporation of Pilots of the Port of Genoa).

In Italy, piloting services were made compulsory in almost all ports, including Genoa, by decrees of the President of the Republic. Failure by the captain of a vessel to use the piloting service is a criminal offence.

16. Joined Cases T-24/93 to T-26/93 and T-28/93 *Compagnie Maritime Belge Transports and Others v Commission* [1996] ECR II-1201 (CEWAL I).
17. See the Court of First Instance judgment in Joined Cases T-191/98, T-212/98 to 214/98, *Atlantic Container Line AB and Others v Commission* [2003] ECR II-3275 (TACA), at para. 908.
18. See *Commission Draft Guidelines on the Application of Art. 81 to Maritime Transport Services*, above, at para. 32.
19. Case C-18/93 *Corsica Ferries Italia Srl v Corpo dei Piloti del Porto di Genova* [1994] ECR I-1783.

At the material time, piloting services in the port of Genova were offered at discount to vessels permitted to carry on maritime cabotage, in other words traffic between two Italian ports. Only vessels flying the Italian flag could obtain permission to engage in maritime cabotage.

Such discounts were denied to Corsica Ferries, a company established under Italian law, which operated a liner service between the port of Genoa and various Corsican ports, using two ferries registered in Panama and flying the Panamanian flag.

The ECJ found the Corpo dei Piloti del Porto di Genova in a dominant position and considered the refusal to offer the above discounts to Corsica ferries as a discriminatory practice (i.e. an abuse of dominant position within the meaning of Article. 82 EC). Furthermore, the ECJ took the view that EC law prevents Member State from applying different tariffs for identical piloting services, depending on whether or not an undertaking operates a vessel entitled to operate cabotage services.

Another case quite illustrative of abuses of dominance in the maritime sector is *B&I Line plc v Sealink Harbours Ltd and Sealink Stena Ltd.*[20] Yet again, the case involved the port of Holyhead. Stena Sealink Ltd owned, through a subsidiary company, the port of Holyhead. Stena Sealink was also providing a ferry service from Holyhead to Dun Laoghaire (located in Dublin Bay). B&I Line (a competitor of Stena Sealink), was also a provider of ferry service from Holyhead to Dublin.

In order to limit its competition, Sealink Stena scheduled its ferry timetable in such a way which turned to be prejudicial to B&I's operations. B&I complained to the Commission for an alleged abuse of dominant position by Sealink Stena.

This case brought to light the application of the so-called "essential facilities" doctrine to the maritime industry. The concept of "essential facilities" entails the existence of two markets, an "upstream market" and a "downstream market", together with a dominant undertaking operating in both the upstream and the downstream market. If the dominant undertaking owns an input (the essential facility), and uses that input to compete in the downstream market, it is, as a consequence, extremely difficult for a competitor to seek access to the downstream market. Two elements are therefore necessary: the ownership or control over a "facility" by a dominant undertaking and the "essentiality" of a facility.

In EC competition law, the "essential facilities doctrine" is dealt with in conjunction with Article 82 of the EC Treaty. It is generally applied to exclusionary practices (e.g. such as refusals to supply), having the effect of abuse of a dominant position in the relevant market.[21] Whenever an essential facility is identified, the refusal of access to that facility automatically constitutes anticompetitive behaviour by the dominant undertaking.

In *B&I Line plc v Sealink Harbours Ltd and Sealink Stena Ltd*, the Commission laid down the principles that a dominant undertaking which both owns or controls and itself uses an essential facility, i.e. a facility or infrastructure without access to which competitors cannot provide services to their cus-

20. *B&I Line plc v Sealink Harbours Ltd and Sealink Stena Ltd*, Case IV/34.174.
21. The first EU law case relating to the concepts of essential facilities and refusal to deal is *ICI v Commission*, Case C-48/69 [1972] ECR 619. In this case the ECJ defined the concept of "essential facility" as a "facility or infrastructure without access to which competitors cannot provide services to their customers".

tomers, and which refuses its competitors access to that facility or grants access to competitors only on terms less favourable than those which it gives its own services, thereby placing the competitors at a competitive disadvantage, infringes Article 82, if the other conditions of that Article are met.

In first place, the European Commission emphasised that a port, an airport or any other facility, even if it is not itself a substantial part of the common market, may be considered as such in so far as reasonable access to the facility is indispensable for the exploitation of a transport route which is substantial for the purposes of the application of Article 82 of the EC Treaty.

Secondly, the European Commission considered that a company which both owns and uses an essential facility – in this case a port – should not grant its competitors access on terms less favourable than those which it gives its own services.

Therefore, a company in a dominant position may not discriminate in favour of its own activities in a related market. The owner of an essential facility which uses its power in one market in order to strengthen its position in another related market, in particular, by granting its competitor access to that related market on less favourable terms than those of its own services, infringes Article 82 where a competitive disadvantage is imposed upon its competitor without objective justification.

Furthermore, the Commission emphasised also that the owner of the essential facility, which also uses the essential facility, may not impose a competitive disadvantage on its competitor, also a user of the essential facility, by altering its own schedule to the detriment of the competitor's service, whereas in this case, the construction or the features of the facility are such that it is not possible to alter one competitor's service in the way chosen without harming the other's. Specifically, where, as in this case, the competitor is already subject to a certain level of disruption from the dominant undertaking's activities, there is a duty on the dominant undertaking not to take any action which will result in further disruption. That is so even if the latter's actions make, or are primarily intended to make, its operations more efficient. Subject to any objective elements outside its control, such an undertaking is under a duty not to impose a competitive disadvantage upon its competitor in the use of the shared facility without objective justification.

*Impact on trade between Member States*

Lastly, in order to claim the application of Article 82 EC it is necessary to prove that the abuse of dominant position taking place in the relevant market is capable of affecting trade between Member States. According to Article 82 EC, once the relevant product market and the relevant geographic market are identified, it is necessary to prohibit the abuse of a dominant position of one or more undertakings that may affect the Common Market or a substantial part of it. It is important to emphasise that it is not necessary for the abuse of dominant position to extend over the territory of two or more Member States in order to affect Community trade within the meaning of Article 82. Even an abuse of dominant position which remains confined within the territory of a single Member State will be caught by Article 82 insofar as it is capable, actually or potentially, directly or indirectly to affect trade between Member States.[22]

22. See Case T-219/99 *British Airways v Commission* [2003] ECR II-5917.

In *Merci Convenzionali Porto di Genova SpA v Siderurgica Gabrielli SpA*,[23] a number of dock companies in Italy had a monopoly in the provision of stevedoring services. The reason for this was that in Italy the loading, unloading, transhipment, storage and general movement of goods or material of any kind within the port are reserved by law to dock-work companies whose workers, who are also members of these companies, must be of Italian nationality.

Siderurgica Gabrielli, under the Italian rules, was obliged to apply to Merci Convenzionali Porto di Genova SpA, an undertaking enjoying the exclusive right to organise dock work in the Port of Genoa for ordinary goods, for the unloading of a consignment of steel imported from the Federal Republic of Germany, although the ship's crew could have performed the unloading direct. As often happens in Italy, the employees of Merci Convenzionali Porto di Genova SpA and consequently the cargo was unloaded three months late. Siderurgica Gabrielli instituted proceedings in an Italian court for damages, questioning the monopolistic scenario characterising the loading and discharging of cargo in the port of Genoa, and claiming, *inter alia*, an abuse of dominant position under Article 82 EC.

The question was referred to the ECJ,[24] which found that Merci Convenzionali Porto di Genova SpA had abused its dominant position. Interestingly, although the abuse was confined within one port (the port of Genoa), the situation, according to the ECJ was indeed capable of affecting trade between Member States and having an impact on the internal market.

Specifically, the ECJ emphasised that the port of Genoa is a substantial part of the common market and the abuse of dominant position was indeed capable of affecting trade between Member States because of: (i) the extent of the activity at the port of Genoa; (ii) the fact that Genoa is one of the most important ports within the Community; (iii) the fact that Genoa is the most important port in Italy; and (iv) users frequently do not have a choice about using the port of Genoa because of that port's infrastructure.

In light of *Merci Convenzionali Porto di Genova SpA v Siderurgica Gabrielli SpA*, it is easy to realise that the element of the impact of the abuse of dominant position on the internal market or a substantial part thereof and its possibility of affecting trade between Member States will easily be fulfilled whenever the abuse takes place in an important port, or a port equipped with specific infrastructures not easily available elsewhere.

## 4. STATE AID

State aid is a *sui generis* element of the EU competition policy regime. As the EU comprises independent Member States, competition policy could be rendered in practice ineffective if Member States were allowed to indiscriminately provide financial support to national companies.

23. *Merci Convenzionali Porto di Genova SpA v Siderurgica Gabrielli SpA*, OJ 1997 L301/27, [1998] 4 CMLR 91 (on appeal Case C-179/90, *Merci Convenzionali Porto di Genova SpA v Siderurgica Gabrielli SpA* [1991] ECR I-5889, [1994] 4 CMLR 422).
24. National courts are compelled to enforce Community law; nevertheless they cannot decide its validity nor are allowed to interpret it. In case of doubts related to the interpretation, validity or application of EC law, under Art. 234 of the Treaty, national courts can initiate preliminary ruling proceedings and refer a question to the ECJ.

Article 87(1) EC provides that any aid granted by a Member State or through State resources in any form whatsoever which distorts or threatens to distort competition by favouring certain undertakings or the production of certain goods shall, in so far as it affects trade between Member States, be incompatible with the common market.

The objective of State aid control, as laid down in the Treaty, is to ensure that government interventions do not distort competition and intra-community trade. The EC Treaty does not define the concept of "aid". The absence of a definition has assisted the Commission and the ECJ by allowing them a considerable degree of discretion. The aid may take the form of any financial support, whether in the form of capital lending, reduction in the tax levied, or a shareholding or stake by a Member State in a company so as artificially to assist that company. In essence, any aid granted by a Member State or through State resources in any form whatsoever capable of distorting competition by favouring certain undertakings or the production of certain goods is, in so far as it affects trade between Member States, deemed to be incompatible with the common market.

The Treaty, nevertheless, provides that in some circumstances, government interventions are necessary for a well-functioning and equitable economy. Therefore, the Treaty leaves room for a number of policy objectives with which State aid can be considered compatible with the common market and thus not illegal *vis-à-vis* the EC Treaty.

Article 87(2) EC states that aid having a social character, granted to individual consumers is allowed (provided that such aid is granted without discrimination related to the origin of the products concerned); similarly aid to make good the damage caused by natural disasters or exceptional occurrences will not be caught by Article 87 EC.

In addition, Article 87(3) EC provides a mechanism whereby aid may be authorised under specific circumstances.[25]

By complementing the fundamental rules through a series of legislative acts that provide for a number of exemptions, the European Commission has established a globally unique system of rules under which State aid is monitored and assessed in the European Union.

While new legislation is adopted in close cooperation with the Member States, the application of exemptions to the general prohibition of State aid rests exclusively with the European Commission, which possesses strong investigative and decision-

25. According to Art. 87(3) EC, the following may be considered to be compatible with the Common Market:
    (a) aid to promote the economic development of areas where the standard of living is abnormally low or where there is serious underemployment;
    (b) aid to promote the execution of an important project of common European interest or to remedy a serious disturbance in the economy of a Member State;
    (c) aid to facilitate the development of certain economic activities or of certain economic areas, where such aid does not adversely affect trading conditions to an extent contrary to the common interest. However, the aids granted to shipbuilding as of 1 January 1957 shall, in so far as they serve only to compensate for the absence of customs protection, be progressively reduced under the same conditions as apply to the elimination of customs duties, subject to the provisions of this Treaty concerning common commercial policy towards third countries;
    (d) aid to promote culture and heritage conservation where such aid does not affect trading conditions and competition in the Community to an extent that is contrary to the common interest;
    (e) such other categories of aid as may be specified by decision of the Council acting by a qualified majority on a proposal from the Commission.

making powers. At the heart of these powers lies the notification procedure which – except in certain instances – the Member States have to follow. It is only after the approval by the Commission that an aid measure can be implemented. Moreover, the Commission has the power to recover incompatible State aid.

The Commission aims to ensure that all European companies operate on a level playing field, where competitive companies succeed. It ascertains that government interventions do not interfere with the smooth functioning of the internal market or harm the competitiveness of EU companies.

### (a) State aid and the shipping sector

In the maritime industry, State aid has been particularly controversial in the ports sector. The reason for this is that ports often receive State aid and therefore need to ensure that the support which they receive is compatible with Article 86 EC. The situation is particularly delicate if considered within the context of the internal market. The port of Genoa in Italy, may for instance be in competition with the port of Southampton. If the port of Genoa received some form of financial support from the Italian Authorities, this competition would inevitably become unbalanced and unfair. The problem here is that in reality State aid is very common in the case of ports. This is mainly due to the nature of quasi "public service" characterising port activities and the enormous financial effort necessary to render ports operative.

The situation is also very complex due to the very low level of disclosure of State financial support to ports which very often deny being in receipt of any form of State aid. In 1997, the Commission ordered a high-level review of State aid and ports, and currently it is possible for ports to complain to the Commission about others receiving illegal forms of State financial support. Remarkably, the number of complaint procedures is quite low.

Overall, Article 87(3)(a) appears to be of vast application when it comes to ports. As previously mentioned, Article 87(3)(a) provides that forms of aid aiming to promote the economic development of areas where the standard of living is abnormally low or where there is serious underemployment may be compatible with the common market. This provision is very important for ports located in areas of economic deprivation.

In 1999, the Commission adopted a Decision related to the 1999 French Port Sector Scheme aiming at supporting the French port sector.[26] The French port sector benefited from substantial public financial support particularly in relation to the heavy port facilities (cranes, etc).

The Commission considered the aim of the proposed aid scheme as to render the provision of cargo handling services more efficient and productive. A scheme notified to the Commission provided for a proposed reduction of the tax base for the French "*taxe professionnelle*" for the private cargo handling in view of obtaining a modernisation and more rational organisation of these services.

The Commission considered such aid compatible with EC law provided it was linked to the investment(s) in that aid may only be granted for the fiscal year(s) when the investments in such equipment were made and during the subsequent amortisation of this equipment until the expiry of the scheme.

26. OJL 155/52, 28/06/2000.

The aid was also subject to the condition that the French authorities provide the Commission with appropriate annual reports about the implementation of the aid scheme, notably any public tenders, investments, the amount of aid granted and its intensity.

If the Commission was prepared to consider the State aid provided by the French Government to ports compatible with the Treaty, subject to the above conditions, the same did not happen in *Bretagne Angleterre Irlande*. The State aid at issue in this case was related to the package purchase of travel vouchers by the Basque authorities on the Bilbao-Portsmouth route.

The intervener Ferries Golfo de Vizcaya contended that the Basque authorities' undertaking to purchase in advance certain quantities of travel vouchers to be used within a certain period was a commercial transaction completely normal in the business of shipping companies. The intervener refered to reservation agreements with operators known as "ITX", who also purchased in advance large numbers of tourist tickets and consequently received volume discounts. The discounts granted to these commercial operators varied between 5 and 30% of the published tariff, depending on the volume and duration of their commitment. The reduction of approximately 15% laid down in the agreement with the Provincial Council is appropriate and conforms with normal practice in agreements of that kind.

Even though, according to the Spanish Government, the payment to Ferries Golfo de Vizcaya represented the *quid pro quo* for the travel vouchers purchased by the regional authorities, the Commission took the view that the 1992 agreement incorporated elements of State aid because the agreed conditions of the transaction did not conform with those of a normal commercial transaction. The Court found the package State aid in contrast with Article 87 of the EC Treaty.

On a general level, it is crucial that ports determine whether or not any assistance which they expect to receive, represents State aid within the meaning of Article 87 EC. Any form of aid should in fact be notified to, and approved by the European Commission before the aid is effectively provided. In case a specific form of assistance qualified as State aid, then the relevant Member State is under the obligation to notify the European Commission the proposed form of financial support.

## 5. THE EC MERGER REGULATION FRAMEWORK

Council Regulation (EC) No 139/2004[27] represents the EC mergers regulatory framework. The foremost aim of the EC Merger Regulation is to monitor and regulate mergers and concentrations having "Community dimensions"[28] capable of hindering competition in the internal market.

The two foremost concepts enshrined in the Merger Regulation are the concept of concentration and the notion of "Community dimension".

27. Council Regulation (EC) No 139/2004 of 20 January 2004 on the control of concentrations between undertakings (the EC Merger Regulation), which repealed Council Regulation (EEC) N 4064/89, the previous EC regulative framework of mergers and acquisitions.
28. See Council Regulation (EC) No 139/2004, above, Art. 1.

A concentration is defined as a change of control on a lasting basis resulting from: (i) the merger of two or more previously independent undertakings, or (ii) the acquisition of one or more persons already controlling at least one undertaking, or by one or more undertakings, whether by purchase of securities or assets, by contract or by any other means, of direct or indirect control of the whole or parts of one or more other undertakings.

The creation of a joint venture performing on a lasting basis all the functions of an autonomous economic entity also constitutes a concentration.[29]

The concept of "Community dimension" is delineated by world-wide and EU-wide turnover [30] of the undertakings concerned.[31]

Concentrations having Community dimensions must be notified to the Commission without delay,[32] and the Commission has the power to approve or deny a concentration. Under the Merger Regulation, the main task of the Commission is in fact to assess the eventual creation or enhancement of a dominant position within the internal market.[33]

The criteria by virtue of which the Commission approve or prohibit a concentration are laid down by Article 2 of Regulation 139/2004, and are basically structured on the basis of Article 82 of the Treaty. Adopting the phraseology of Article 82 EC, the Regulation prohibits a concentration in case it "would significantly impede effective competition, in the common market or in a substantial part of it, in particular as a result of the creation or strengthening of a dominant position ...".[34]

In assessing the impact of the concentration on the market, the Commission may also consider the market position of the undertakings concerned and their economic and financial power, the alternatives available to suppliers and users, their access to supplies or markets, any legal or other barriers to entry, supply and

29. *Ibid.*, Art. 3.
30. *Ibid.*, Art. 1. Turnover is defined by the Regulation as "the amounts derived by the undertakings concerned in the preceding financial year from the sale of products and the provision of services falling within the undertakings' ordinary activities after deduction of sales rebates and of value added tax and other taxes directly related to turnover" (Art. 5). Where parts only of an undertaking are to be acquired, then only the turnover attributable to the parts being acquired will be taken into account in order to determine whether the thresholds are met (Art. 5(2)).
31. Concentrations are of a "Community dimension" where the merging parties' (the "undertakings concerned"):
    "(i) combined world-wide turnover is superior to €5 billion and each of at least two of the merging parties realised superior to €250 million turnover in the EU, unless each of the merging parties obtains more than 2/3 of its EU turnover in one and the same Member State, or;
    (ii) combined world-wide turnover is superior to €2.5 billion; in each of at least three Member States, the combined turnover of the merging parties is superior to €100 million; in each of those three Member States, the turnover of each of at least two of the merging parties is superior to €25 million; the Community wide turnover of each of at least two of the merging parties is superior to €100 million; unless each of the merging parties obtains more than 2/3 of its EU turnover."
32. *Ibid.*, Art. 7(2a).
33. The assessment of concentrations having a Community dimension is the exclusive competence of the Commission. Nevertheless, the Commission may by means of a decision refer a notified concentration to the competent authorities of the Member State concerned in case "(a) a concentration threatens to affect significantly competition in a market within that Member State, which presents all the characteristics of a distinct market, or (b) a concentration affects competition in a market within that Member State, which presents all the characteristics of a distinct market and which does not constitute a substantial part of the common market". See Council Regulation (EC) No 139/2004, above, Art. 9(2).
34. See Council Regulation (EC) No 139/2004, above, Art. 2(3).

demand trends for the relevant goods and services, the interests of the intermediate and ultimate consumers, and the development of technical and economic progress provided that it is to consumers' advantage and does not form an obstacle to competition."[35]

### (a) The application of the Merger Regulation to the shipping industry

The assessment of the creation or extension of a dominant position in the shipping trade is the result of an economic analysis considering three elements which will be dealt with in the following.

The first element to be considered is the geographical dimension of the market (relevant geographical market); secondly, the product dimension of the market (relevant product market) is taken into consideration; finally, the market shares of the undertakings concerned is the last factor analysed. When it comes to the shipping industry, these elements have been characterised by the Commission through a series of decisions analysed below.

The first important merger in the shipping sector was the creation of the P&O/Nedlloyd Container Line Ltd.[36] Through this merger, the UK Peninsular and Oriental Steam Navigation Co ("P&O") and the Dutch Royal Nedlloyd NV acquired joint control of P&O Nedlloyd Container Line Ltd ("P&O Nedlloyd").

P&O engaged in a broad range of activities, including passenger and cargo shipping, and integrated transportation and warehousing, whereas Nedlloyd was an international logistics services company whose core activities are container logistics through a network of global shipping links; and transport, forwarding, stock management and distribution, primarily in Europe. The activities of both P&O and Nedlloyd included ocean container shipping and related landside activities.

The Commission defined the relevant geographic market as a service supplied between a range of ports on either the northern European or the Mediterranean coast and a range of ports in another continent or region.

Interestingly, the Commission emphasised that, on a general level, transport to and from northern Europe constitutes a relevant service market for liner shipping services. However, "P&O" and Royal Nedlloyd NV contended that on certain trades the geographical scope of the liner shipping service was indistinguishable between northern Europe and the Mediterranean, due to improved land transport links with the rest of the continent, Mediterranean ports having become substitutable with those of northern Europe. The Commission rejected this claim indicating that the possibility of inland transport or maritime transhipment between northern Europe and the Mediterranean does not lead to facility of substitution to any considerable extent. According to the Commission, this distinction is reinforced by, for example, northern European ports, such as Antwerp being cheaper to use than their Mediterranean counterparts, for example, La Spezia. Furthermore, the Commission specified that there is only limited substitution between ports in these regions and it can therefore be concluded that northern Europe and the Mediterranean do not belong to the same relevant market.

35. *Ibid.*, Art. 2(1).
36. Case No IV/M.831, *P&O/Nedlloyd*, 19/12/1996.

This definition of the relevant geographical market for liner shipping services was reiterated by the Commission in *Maersk/Safmarine*,[37] *TACA*[38] and in the largest ever merger in the liner shipping sector, *MAERSK/SEA-LAND*,[39] where the Commission found that container shipping to and from Northern Europe constitutes a distinct market from transport to and from the Mediterranean.

As for the relevant product market, the Commission in *P&O/Nedlloyd* emphasised that non-liner shipping services, either in the form of chartering the whole or part of vessels by individual customers, "tramp" operations, being unscheduled sea transport, and specialized transport, i.e. ships developed for transporting specific goods, do not compete with liner shipping services.

Liner shipping services according to the Commission may be distinguished from these other modes of transport in three ways: firstly customers demand scheduled transport in order to meet production runs and delivery deadlines. Secondly, the vast majority of customers require flexibility in available space – something unavailable when whole or parts of ships are to be chartered. Finally, specialised transport constitutes a reasonable alternative only for a few shippers who have large quantities of only a few categories of goods to transport for which such ships have to be available.

Nevertheless, in its recent decision in *Maersk/PONL*,[40] the Commission has considered transport for refrigerated goods a possibly narrower product market in the market for containerised liner shipping services. This consideration is based on the fact that the transport of refrigerated goods, could be limited to reefer (refrigerated) containers only or could include transport in conventional reefer (refrigerated) vessels. Moreover, according to the Commission, from a demand side perspective, certain goods such as fruit, meat and dairy products must be shipped under refrigerated conditions. For this reason, non-reefer containers are not considered as a substitute for reefer containers.

Finally, in relation to the concrete evaluation of the impact of mergers on the shipping market, the assessment of the Commission in this final stage aims at identifying possible concentrations having Community dimensions and leading to the eventual creation or enhancement of a dominant position within the internal market. In order to perform this delicate test, the Commission has carefully evaluated the possible coordinated effects and synergies in shipping markets where the merging shipping undertakings were parties to co-operative arrangements such as liner conferences, consortia or pools.

Under such circumstances, the analysis of the Commission focuses on the possible synergies between competitors arising as a consequence of a possible merger, which may increase the risk of co-ordinated or parallel behaviours.

In relation to past case law, in *Maersk/Safmarine* the Commission has considered, for instance, whether the parties' increased vertical integration in the liner shipping services, resulting from the combination of their respective terminal operations, could strengthen their position in the container shipping market. Similarly, in *Maersk/PONL*[41] the Commission analysed the effects that the merger between Maersk

37. Case No IV/M.1474, *Maersk/Safmarine*.
38. Case No IV/35.134, *TACA*.
39. Case No IV/M.165, *MAERSK/SEA-LAND*.
40. Case No. Comp/M.3829 – *Maersk/PONL*, decision of 29 July 2005.
41. *Ibid.*

(an international group with activities in container shipping, container terminal services, harbour towage, operation of tankers, logistics, oil and gas exploration, air transport, shipbuilding and supermarkets) and PONL (a container liner shipping company, also involved in container terminal services, logistics and air transport) might have on conferences and consortia depending on the parties' membership.

The Commission identified two general scenarios that may give rise to concern: the first scenario arose in cases where the merging parties are currently in the same conference or consortium and remain members after the merger, the concentration would not change the total market share of the conference or consortium. Depending on the structure of the conference or consortium (see below), however, this could lead to a strengthening of the internal cohesion and eventually lead to the merged entity controlling the conference.

The second scenario arose due to the fact that in some instances Maersk was in a conference or consortium, but PONL was not, even though it was active on the same trade. If Maersk maintained its membership, PONL could be expected to be integrated into the conference or consortium. The market share of the conference or consortium would rise. If only PONL was in a conference or consortium, the merger would create a link between Maersk and the conference and/or the consortium. This link would enable Maersk to take part in the exchange of information within the conference and/or the consortium.

Maersk could use the commercially sensitive information exchanged therein to adapt over time its conduct on the market, thus increasing the risk of market sharing or lessening of competition between itself and the other members of the conference or the consortium. Even without integrating itself into the conference or the consortium, Maersk would no longer be an independent competitor because it controlled a member of the conference or the consortium.

Based on the above considerations, the Commission carried out its analysis of coordinated effects in as many as 22 different trades.

The decision in *Maersk/PONL* clearly shows that the assessment of mergers and acquisitions in the shipping sector is subject to an intense and very strict scrutiny by the Commission.[42]

## 6. CONCLUDING REMARKS

This chapter has emphasised the need for the shipping industry to comply with EC competition law. As we have seen, the four areas of the EC anti-trust regulatory framework (i.e. Articles 81–82 EC, Article 87, and the Merger Regulation) currently find full application to the maritime industry.

### (a) Compliance with Article 81 EC

Article 81 EC prohibits any collusive behaviour between shipping companies whose aim or effect is the restriction, prevention or distortion of the competition in the maritime industry.

42. A similar level of analysis aiming at identifying possible Concentrations having Community dimensions and leading to the eventual creation or enhancement of a dominant position within the internal market, does not emerge in Commission decisions related to different sectors, e.g. the insurance market.

Starting from October 2008, the end of the transitional period of Regulation 1419/2006, liner conferences, shipping pools (either in the classic form of administration-controlled pools managed by a separate company, or member-controlled pools under the operational management of one or more members of the pool) capable of affecting trade between Member States will be prohibited, void and unenforceable in respect of their restrictions.

This means that liner conference agreements between carriers related to the operation of scheduled maritime transport services, whose object or effect is to fix the rates and conditions of carriage, will fall within the meaning of Article 81.

In the tramp shipping and cabotage sectors, the impact of the application of Article 81 affects pools or other forms of co-operation between actual or potential competitors involving the direct or indirect determination of rates, limitations on output, the sharing of markets or customers, information exchange and any other anti-competitive practices.

In the light of their characteristics, liner conferences (subject to the transitional period), tramp shipping or cabotage pools *prima facie* represent a blatant price fixing practice capable of limiting output and considerably restricting competition. In practice, the starting point for the assessment of their legality is represented by their impact (actual or potential) on competition. If the impact on competition is minimal and remains confined within the limits as per the Commission's *De Minimis Notice* (10% of the market share in the case of horizontal agreements, 15% for vertical agreements), pools will be automatically allowed insofar as they do not involve price fixing, output limitation or forms of sharing of markets or customers.

While the theory is clear, it is often uncertain where the line must be drawn in practice as liner conferences, tramp shipping or cabotage pools always involve elements capable of limiting output and hindering competition.

The best option is therefore an individual exemption under Article 81(3). We have seen that under this Article, maritime pools might obtain an individual *ad hoc* exemption, insofar as their agreements satisfy the four conditions listed by Article 81(3). Such agreements will need therefore to in first place create efficiencies (in terms of improving the provision of the service or promoting economic or technical progress). Secondly, consumers must be allowed to share the benefits of those efficiencies. Thirdly, the agreements should not contain restrictions on competition beyond the strictly indispensable restraints. Finally, they must not eliminate competition altogether.

If the above conditions are fulfilled, shipping pools may benefit from an individual exemption to be automatically granted by national courts and competition authorities.

It has been emphasised that the burden of proof in support of the exemption claim for shipping pools lies on the party involved who will need to support their claim with strong evidence in order to overcome the incompatibility with Article 81 EC. For instance, proving that shipping pools increase the efficiencies of the service is not enough to obtain an exemption, if consumers will not share some of the benefits, or the conditions of the pools go beyond what can be considered as strictly indispensable restrictions.

Scrutiny is very strict and will take into account, *inter alia*, the impact of such agreements on the shipping market, prices, costs, quality, frequency and differentiation of the service provided, in conjunction with innovation, marketing and commercialisation of the service.

A good starting argument in support of the claim for an exemption could be the provision of unquestionable evidence of the creation of remarkable efficiencies in conjunction with a considerable decrease of the costs of the services.

Consequently, pool membership rules such as the prohibition on operating vessels outside the pool, or long notice requirements in case of withdrawal of vessels from the pool will be very difficult to justify as they do not seem to give rise to any evident benefit for consumers.

### (b) Compliance with Article 82 EC

The application of Article 82 EC has been particularly relevant in the context of ports.

Article 82 EC is triggered only in presence of an abuse of dominant position capable of affecting trade between Member States. This abuse of dominance needs to be identified within the context of a market considered in its geographical and product dimensions.

In the maritime sector the geographical market may involve, for instance, a single port or a cluster of ports, or a service between two ports or two countries. Most importantly, the geographical market can indeed be a limited market, especially in case of passenger car ferry services where passengers are usually inclined to choose short sea journeys. This element can in practice be of crucial importance as the narrower the geographical market, the higher the possibilities that a maritime undertaking occupies a dominant position.

The identification of the relevant product market is another essential element in order to assess the dominance of a maritime undertaking. The relevant product market is focused on the concept of interchangeability or substitutability of services. The more services are interchangeable, the more likely it is that they belong to the same relevant product market.

On a general level, there is a difference in terms of product market definition in cases relating to *passenger* traffic as opposed to *commercial/cargo* traffic. In case a port provides its services in several different product markets (e.g. the passenger liner trade, the oil tanker trade and the passenger car ferry trade), each service will represent a different product market, as for instance the oil tanker trade is not interchangeable with the passenger car ferry trade.

This identification of the relevant product market can be more complicated in the case of shipping companies operating car and passenger carriers, due to the high level of interchangeability characterising car and passenger vessels.

As for the assessment of dominance, in the absence of exceptional circumstances extremely large market shares (between 70% and 80%) are in themselves evidence of the existence of a dominant position. Lower market shares (60% on the trade in question) are capable of giving rise to a strong presumption of a dominant position.

The maritime undertaking in a dominant position may not discriminate in favour of its own activities in a related market. Especially the owner of an essential facility (e.g. a port without access to which competitors cannot provide services to their customers),which uses its power in one market in order to strengthen its position in another related market, in particular, by granting its competitor access to that related market on less favourable terms than those of its own services, infringes Article 82 where a competitive disadvantage is imposed upon its competitor without objective justification.

Finally, although an abuse remains confined within one port, the situation is still capable of affecting trade between Member States and having an impact on the internal market if the port in question operates on a large scale and it is equipped with specific infrastructures not readily available elsewhere.

### (c) State aid

In the maritime industry, State aid prevents ports from receiving financial support by Member States. As previously mentioned, Article 87(3)(a) provides that forms of aid aiming to promote the economic development of areas where the standard of living is abnormally low or where there is serious underemployment may be compatible with the common market. This provision is very important for ports located in areas of economic deprivation.

On a general level, it is crucial that ports determine whether or not any assistance which they expect to receive, represents State aid within the meaning of Article 87 EC (with the exemption as per Article 87(3)(a) above, any form of direct or indirect financial subsidy qualifies as State aid).

In case a specific form of assistance qualifies as State aid, then the relevant Member State is under the obligation to notify the European Commission the proposed form of financial support.

### (d) Merger Regulation of the shipping industry

As previously mentioned, the EC mergers regulatory framework fully applies to the maritime industry, and aims at avoiding the creation or extension of a dominant position capable of affecting competition within the shipping sector in the internal market.

The assessment of the creation or extension of a dominant position in the shipping industry is the result of an economic analysis considering three elements: the geographical dimension of the market (relevant geographic market); the product dimension of the market; and finally, the market shares of the undertakings concerned.

The geographical dimension of shipping mergers has been considered by the Commission with a rather narrow approach. For instance, in the liner shipping services due to the limited substitution between ports in northern Europe and the Mediterranean, transport to and from northern Europe is deemed to represent the relevant geographical market. Yet again, this is a crucial aspect to be taken into account by shipping undertakings planning a merger, as the narrower the geographic dimension of the merger, the higher the possibilities that the merger will be considered capable of hindering competition.

As for the relevant product market, non-liner shipping services, either in the form of chartering the whole or part of vessels by individual customers, "tramp" operations, being unscheduled sea transport, and specialised transport do not compete with liner shipping services. Non-liner shipping services and liner shipping services therefore represents two separate product markets (within the market for containerised liner shipping services, transport for refrigerated goods can represent a possible narrower product market).

Finally, in relation to the concrete evaluation of the impact of mergers in the shipping market, the assessment of the merger aims at identifying possible concentrations having Community dimensions and leading to the eventual creation or enhancement of a dominant position within the internal market. In order to evaluate shipping mergers, the Commission will be considering not only the merger itself, but also the possible synergies between competitors arising as a consequence of a merger, which may increase the risk of co-ordinated or parallel behaviours.

The analysis of coordinated effects is subject to an intense and very strict scrutiny by the Commission especially in shipping markets where the merging shipping undertakings are parties to co-operative arrangements such as liner conferences, consortia or pools. In such cases, the concentration would not change the total market share of the conference or consortium. Nevertheless, in conjunction with the structure of the conference or consortium, this could lead to a strengthening of the internal cohesion and eventually lead to the merged entity controlling the conference.

Shipping companies operating in consortia or pools need therefore to carefully evaluate any possible side-effects post-merger if they intend to avoid the censure of the Commission. Maritime undertakings operating individually may also be subject to an intense scrutiny in relation to the creation of possible synergies, co-ordinated or parallel behaviours arising as a result of a merger.

# Bibliography


Aikens, R., Lord and Bools M., *Bills of Lading* (2006, Informa)

Balkin, R. P., "The Establishment and Work of the IMO Legal Committee", in Nordquist, M. H. and Norton Moore, J. (eds), *Current Maritime Issues and the International Maritime Organization* (1999, Martinus Nijhoff)

Baughen, S., *Shipping Law*, 3rd edn. (2004, Cavendish Publishing Ltd)

Beale (ed), *Chitty on Contracts*, 29th edn. (2004, Sweet & Maxwell)

Bennett, H., *Law of Marine Insurance*, 2nd edn. (2006, Oxford University Press)

Boyd QC, S., Eden, B., Burrows, A., Foxton, D., Berry, S., and Smith, C., *Scrutton on Charterparties*, 21st edn. (2008, Sweet & Maxwell)

Brice, G., *Maritime Law of Salvage*, 4th edn. (2002, Sweet & Maxwell)

Briggs, A. and Rees, P., *Civil Jurisdiction and Judgments*, 4th edn. (2005, LLP)

Brown, E.D., *The International Law of the Sea* (1994, Ashgate Publishing)

Churchill, R.R. and Lowe, A.V., *The Law of the Sea*, 3rd edn. (1999, Manchester University Press)

Churchill (ed.), *The UN Convention on the Law of the Sea: Impact and Implementation* (1987, Law of the Sea Institute)

Clarkson, C. M. V. and Hill, J., *Jaffey on the Conflict of Laws*, 2nd edn. (2002, Butterworths)

Collins, L. A. *et al.*, *Dicey and Morris on the Conflict of Laws*, 14th edn. (2000, Sweet & Maxwell)

Cooke, J. *et al.*, *Voyage Charters*, 3rd edn. (2007, Informa)

Davies, D., *Commencement of Laytime*, 4th edn. (2006, Informa)

Davies, M. (gen. ed.), "Jurisdiction and Forum Selection in International Maritime Law Essays in Honor of Robert Force", *Jurisdiction and Forum Selection in International Maritime Law* (2005, Kluwer Law International)

De la Rue, C., Anderson, C. B., and Marion, M., *Shipping and the Environment* (1998, LLP)

Debattista, C., *The Sale of Goods Carried by Sea*, 2nd edn. (1998, Tottel)

Dromgoole, S. and Gaskell, N. J. J., *Interests in Wrecks*, 2nd edn. (1998, LLP)

Falkanger, T., Bull, H. J. and Brautaset, L., *Scandinavian Maritime Law: the Norwegian Perspective*, 2nd edn. (2004, Universitetsforlag AS)

Gaskell, N. J. J., *Current Law Statutes, Merchant Shipping Act 1995*, Chapter 21

Gaskell, N. J. J., *Merchant Shipping Act and Maritime Security Act 1997, Current Law Statutes*

Gaskell, N. J. J., Debattista, C. and Swatton, R. J., *Chorley and Giles' Shipping Law*, 8th edn. (1987, Pitman Publishing)

Gaskell, N., Assariotis, R. and Baatz, Y., *Bills of Lading: Law and Contracts* (2000, LLP)

Gilman, J. and Merkin, R. (eds.), *Arnould's Law on Marine Insurance*, 17th edn. (2008, Sweet & Maxwell)

Girvin, S., *Carriage of Goods by Sea* (2007, OUP)

Goode, R., *Commercial Law*, 3rd edn. (2004, LexisNexis Butterworths)

Guest, A. (ed.), *Benjamin's Sale of Goods*, 7th edn. (2006, Sweet & Maxwell)

*Guidelines on the application of the ISM Code* (Marisec)

*Halsbury's Laws of England, Volume 41, Sale of goods and supply of services*, 4th edn. (2005)

Harris, D.J., *Cases and Materials on International Law*, 5th edn. (2004, Sweet & Maxwell)

Hazelwood, *P&I Clubs: Law and Practice*, 3rd edn. (2000, LLP)

Hill, J., *International Commercial Disputes in English Courts*, 3rd edn. (2005, Hart Publishing)

ICC Uniform Customs and Practice for Documentary Credits, 2007 Revision, ICC Publication No. 600

*Incoterms 200: ICC official rules for the interpretation of trade terms* (1999), ICC publication no. 560

*International convention for the safety of life at sea* (2001, IMO)

Jackson, D. C., *Enforcement of Maritime Claims*, 4th edn. (2005, Informa)

Lowe, V., *International Law* (2007, Oxford University Press)

Mankabady, S., *International Shipping Law* (1991, Euromoney)

McClean, D. and Beevers, K., *The Conflict of Laws*, 6th edn. (2005, Sweet & Maxwell)

Macdonald, C. and Karia, C. (gen. eds.), *Butterworths Commercial Court and Arbitration Pleadings* (2005, Tottel Publishing)

*Maritime Security: Guidance for Ship Operators* (Marisec)

Marsden, R. G., *Marsden on Collisions at Sea*, 13th edn. (2003, Sweet & Maxwell)

Merkin, R, *Annotated Marine Insurance Legislation*, 3rd edn. (2005, Informa)

Nordquist, M. H. and Norton Moore, J. (eds), *Current Maritime Issues and the International Maritime Organization* (1999, Martinus Nijhoff)

Palmer, N. and McKendrick, E., *Interests in Goods*, 2nd edn. (1998, Informa)

Plender, R. and Wilderspin, M., *The European Contracts Convention: the Rome Convention on the Choice of Law for Contracts*, 2nd edn. (2001, Sweet & Maxwell)

Rainey, S., *The Law of Tug and Tow*, 2nd edn. (2002, Informa)

Rose, F. D., *Marine Insurance Law and Practice* (2004, Informa)

Rose, F. D., *Kennedy's Law of Salvage*, 6th edn. (2002, Sweet & Maxwell)

Sassoon, *CIF and FOB contracts*, 4th edn. (1995, Sweet & Maxwell)

Schofield, J., *Laytime and Demurrage*, 5th edn. (2005, Informa)

Serdy, A. and Bliss, M., "Prompt Release of Fishing Vessels: State Practice in the Light of the Cases before the International Tribunal for the Law of the Sea" in A. G. Oude Elferink and D. R. Rothwell (eds.), *Oceans Management in the 21st Century: Institutional Frameworks and Responses* (2004, Martinus Nijhoff)

*The STCW Convention, 2nd edition* (2007, Marisec)

Tetley, W., *Marine Cargo Claims*, 3rd edn. (1988)

Thomas, R. D (gen. ed.), *Liability Regimes in Contemporary Maritime Law* (2007, Informa)

Thomas, R. D., *Modern Law of Marine Insurance*, Volumes 1 and 2 (2002, Informa)

Treitel, G. and Reynolds, F. (eds.), *Carver on Bills of Lading*, 2nd edn. (2005, Sweet & Maxwell)

Wilford, M., Coghlin, T. and Kimball, J. D., *Time Charters*, 5th edn. (2003, Informa)

Wilson, J., *Carriage of Goods by Sea*, 6th edn. (2007, Trans-Atlantic Publications)

Wolfrum, R., Rosenne, S. and Blanco-Bazán, A., "IMO Interface with the Law of the Sea Convention" in Nordquist, M. H. and Norton Moore, J. (eds), *Current Maritime Issues and the International Maritime Organization* (1999, Martinus Nijhoff)

Yates, D. (gen. ed.), *Contracts for the Carriage of Goods* (looseleaf, 1993 updated, LLP)

# Index


Abandonment of ships, 295
Abuse of a dominant position
assessment of dominance, 383–384, 396
block exemptions, 381
effect on trade requirement, 380, 386–387, 396, 397
essential facilities doctrine, 385–386, 396–397
examples, 384–386
geographic market, identification of relevant, 381–382, 392–393, 396–397
interchangeability, 383
liner conferences, 381, 384
market definition, 381, 396
market power, control of, 380
market share, 383–384
Merger Regulation, 392, 397
one or more undertakings, 380, 386
passenger market, 383, 396
predatory pricing, 384
product market, identification of relevant, 382–383, 393, 396–397
refusal to offer discounts, 385
relevant market, identification of, 381–383, 392–393, 396–397
substitutability, 383
types of abuse, 380
Academic writings, 301
Actual fault and privity, 121
Actual total loss, 331
Admiralty Court, jurisdiction of, 349–362
Admiralty Marshal's expenses, 356–357
arrest, 349–361
Arrest Convention 1952, 350
Civil Procedure Rules 350, 352, 355–356
collisions, 160–161, 350, 351, 356
default judgments, 356
EC Jurisdiction Regulation, 351
enforcement of maritime claims, 349–362
*in personam* claims, 351, 354–356
*in rem* claims, 351–356
limitation of liability, 351, 361–362
maritime liens, actions *in rem* arising from, 352–354
oil pollution, 351
particulars of claim, 355–356
Admiralty Court, jurisdiction of—*continued*
possession or ownership of ships, actions *in rem* in respect of, 352, 353, 354
practice directions, 355
service of claim forms, 355
statements of truth, 355–356
Advance hire, 66, 73
Agents
Civil Liability Convention (CLC)/Fund Convention, 260
EC Jurisdiction Regulation, 14, 19
masters, 73
P&I insurance, 339, 341, 342
Rome Convention 1980, 35
shipbrokers, 46–47
Air, carriage of passengers by, 214
Alter ego companies, 213, 262
Anti-suit injunctions
abuse of process, 30
arbitration clauses, 4
conflict of laws, 30–31
EC Jurisdiction Regulation, 31
indemnity costs, 32
jurisdiction agreements, 27, 30
Rome Convention 1980, 34
seised, court first, 30
Apparent order and condition, 109–13
Arbitration
advantages, 3
anti-suit injunctions, 4
arbitration clauses, 3–4, 34–38
arrest, 4
awards, publication of, 3
bills of lading, 38
breach, 4
charterparties, 3–4
confidentiality, 3
conflict of laws, 3–4
freezing injunctions, 365
incorporation, 3–4, 38
Lloyd's Standard and Arbitration Clauses (LASA), 172
London, 3, 4
New York Convention on Recognition and Enforcement of Arbitral Awards 1958, 3
Rome Convention 1980, 34–38

Arbitration—*continued*
  stay of proceedings, 4
Archipelagic waters, 303–304
Arrest of ships, 2, 356–361
  acknowledgment of service, 356
  Admiralty jurisdiction, 349–361
  Admiralty Marshal's expenses, 356–357
  applications, 356–357
  arbitration clauses, 4
  Arrest Convention 1952, 21–22, 349, 350
  bareboat charters, 354
  cargo, 357–358
  cautions against arrest and release, 358–359
  charterers, 353–354
  Civil Procedure Rules, 350, 358
  consequences, 357
  contempt of court, 357, 358
  damages,
    delay in release, 359
    wrongful arrest, 359
  definition, 349–250
  EC Jurisdiction Regulation, 21–22
  freezing injunctions, 370
  immobilisation, 357
  *in rem* actions, 349–361
  innocent passage, right of, 357
  judicial sale, 358, 360–361
  jurisdiction on merits, establishing, 359
  letters of undertaking, P&I clubs and, 344, 346–347
  limitation of liability, 203, 222
    commencement of claims, 361
    declarations of right to limit, 361
    limitation funds, 362
    Limitation of Liability Convention 1976, 361
    Protocol 1996 to 1976 Convention, 359
  limitation funds, 358
  maritime liens, 354, 361, 363–364
  mortgages, 360–361
  multiple arrests, 359
  one ship companies, 355
  P&I letters of undertaking, 354
  possessory liens, 361
  priority, 359, 360–361
  re-arrest, 359
  release of ship under arrest, 358–359
  salvage, 161, 360, 361
  security, 357, 358, 359
  service, 357
  ships, definition of, 353–354
  sister ships, 353
  substitution, 357
  territorial waters, 357
  towage, 185
  warrants, 356, 357
  wrongful arrest, damages for, 359
Arrived ship
  anchorage, 81
  berth, arrival in, 81–82
  congestion in port, 81
Arrived ship—*continued*
  delay, 81, 82
  notice of readiness, 81, 82, 84
  reachable on arrival, 81–82
  safe port, 80
  waiting place, 80–81
  whether in berth or not, 82
Asbatankvoy, 46
Athens Convention relating to Carriage of Passengers and their Luggage by Sea 1974, 147–149
  amendment, 321
  basis of liability, 148
  compulsory liability insurance, 149
  death or injury, 148, 149–150
  entry into force, 152–153
  fault or liability, 148
  insurance, 149
  limit of liability, 147, 148–150, 208, 217–218
    1976 Convention, 149–150
    1996 Protocol to 1976 Convention, 150
    loss of right, 148
    non-sea-going vessels, 150
    special drawing rights, 148–150
    time bar, 148
  non-sea-going vessels, 150
  Package Travel Directive, 152
  Protocol 1990, 147, 148
  Protocol 2002, 147, 148–149
  special drawing rights, 148–150
  time limits, 148, 153
Average. *See* General average

Bail, 344
Bailment, 95, 114, 120, 188
Ballast bonus, 79
Banks
  freezing injunctions, 368
  letters of credit, 124, 139–142
  letters of undertaking, guarantees as alternative to, 344–345
Bareboat charters, 45, 106, 170, 202–203, 354
Basel Convention on Control of Trans-boundary Movement of Hazardous Wastes 1989, 291–293
Baselines, 302–304
Bearer bills, 98–99, 100
Bills of lading
  apparent order and condition, 109–13
  arbitration clauses, incorporation of, 38
  bearer bulls, 98–99, 100
  cargo claims, 93–124
  cash against documents, 138–139
  charterparties, 89, 117–118
  choice of law clauses, 37
  c.i.f. contracts, 128–129
  clausing, 111–112
  clean bills, 112, 137
  constructive possession of goods, 138
  documentary duties of sellers, 138–143
  entitlement to payment, 138–143

Bills of lading—*continued*
  evidence of contract of carriage, as, 138
  functions of bill, 138
  Hague Rules, 48–49
  Hague-Visby Rules, 48–49, 108, 119
  Hamburg Rules, 41, 48–49
  identity of carrier, 104–107
  incorporation of charterparty terms, 116–117
  jurisdiction clauses, 7–8
  letters of credit, 141–142
  letters of indemnity, 112–113
  liens, 89
  negotiable instrument, as, 142
  proof of loss, 109–113
  receipt, bill as, 138, 142
  Rome Convention 1980, 33–38
  signing, 106
  straight or non-transferable bills of lading, 100–101
  third party holders, 7–8
  title to sue, 93, 95–104, 142
  Uniform Customs and Practices 600, 141–142
Block exemptions, 373–375, 381
Boarding and inspection of ships, 310–312
Both to blame collision clauses, 160
Bottomry, 363
*Brandt v Liverpool* contract, 102–103, 104
Branches, agents or other establishments, 14, 19
Breach of jurisdiction agreements, 31–32
Brokers. *See* Shipbrokers
Brussels Convention 1968, 5, 7, 22–23
Brussels Regulation. *See* EC Jurisdiction Regulation
Bulk goods, 289
Bunker Oil Pollution Convention 2001, 255, 268–273
  Civil Liability Convention/Fund Convention, 269, 272
  compensation, 269
  contributory negligence, 270–271
  direct actions against insurer, 272
  EC Jurisdiction Regulation, 273
  entry into force, 320
  Exclusive Economic Zones, 270, 273
  government vessels, 271
  insurance, 268–269, 272
  jurisdiction, 272–273
  liability, 270–271
  limitation of liability, 255, 271–272
    Civil Liability Convention, 272
    insurers, 272
    Limitation of Liability Convention 1957, 272
    loss of right to limit, 272
    Protocol 1996 to Limitation of Liability Convention 1976, 269, 272
  pollution damage, definition of, 269–270
  preventive measures, 270
  recognition and enforcement of judgments, 273
Bunker Oil Pollution Convention 2001—*continued*
  scope and definitions, 269–270
  service of claim forms, time limits for, 273
  ships, definition of, 270
  strict liability, 268–269, 272
  territorial sea, 270
  time limits, 271, 273
Bunkers, 207
Buoys, 193

Cabotage, 378–379, 395
Canals, owners of, 204
Cancellation of charterparties, 56–58, 69
Cargo. *See also* Cargo claims
  arrest, 357–358
  collisions, 159–160
  expected ready to load, 67
  Hamburg Rules, 48
  Institute Cargo Clauses, 333
  insurance, 333
  liens, 88–90
  load and stow cargo, duty to, 136
  loading marks, 109–110
Cargo claims, 93–124. *See also* Title to sue, cargo claims and
  actual fault or privity, 121
  bailment, 120
  banks, letters of credit and, 124
  bills of lading, 93–124
  breach, proof of, 94, 114–120
  carriers, claims by, 123–124
  charterparties, 123
  damages, 93
  deviation, 123
  exclusion of liability, 94, 120–123
  Hague-Visby Rules, 93–94, 107–108, 120–123
  identity of carrier, 93, 104–107
  International Safety Management (ISM) Code, 230
  letters of credit, 124
  liability towards carrier, claimant's potential, 123–124
  limitation of liability, 94, 120–123, 205, 209
  package or unit limitation, 120, 122
  parties, 93
  proof of loss, 94, 109–114
  quantification of loss, 121–123
  seaworthiness, 54–55, 230
  special drawing rights, 122
  terms of carriage contract, 94
  time limits, 120–121
  title to sue, 93, 95–104
  transfer of bills, 123–124
Carriage of passengers, 147–153
  abuse of a dominant position, 383, 396
  brochures, contents of, 152
  death and injury, quantum of damages for, 150–151
  domestic carriage, 147
  forum shopping, 151

Carriage of passengers—*continued*
international carriage, 147
International Ship & Port Facility Security (ISPS) Code, 232
limitation of liability, 208, 217–218
Mid-Atlantic Settlements, 151
Package Travel Directive, 151–153
P&I insurance, 150
punitive damages, 151
special drawing rights (SDRs), 217–218
United States, forum shopping and, 151
Cartels, 371
Cautions against arrest and release, 358–359
Certificates of financial responsibility, wreck removal and, 192
Cesser clauses, 91
CFR documents, 138
Charterparties, 45–91. *See also* Time charterparties; Voyage charterparties
affirmation, 55, 59
arbitration clauses, 3–4
arrest, 353–354
bills of lading, 89, 117–118
cancellation, 56–58, 67–68
cargo claims and bills of lading, 123
conditions, 56–57, 59
damages, 55
delay, 66–67
delivery, 66
deviation, 60–61
election to terminate, 58–59
expected ready to load, 67
express terms, 45
foreign legislation, incorporating, 50–51
frustration, 63–66
fundamental breach, 56, 59
Gencon 87–88
Hague Rules, 47–51
Hague-Visby Rules, 40, 47–51
Hamburg Rules, 47–51
identity of carrier, 105–106
implied terms, 45
incorporation of terms, 116–117
innominate terms, 57–59
laycan, 67
liens, 88–91
limitation of liability, 203, 205, 207, 213
misrepresentation, 55–56
negligence, 56
reasonable despatch, 59, 68
remedies for breach, 55–58
repudiatory breach, 68
Rome Convention 1980, 36–37, 40, 41–42
safe ports, 61–63
seaworthiness, 51–55
shipbrokers, role of, 45, 46–47
shipowners, 55–59
standard forms, 45, 46
timing at beginning of charterparties, 66–68
title to sue, cargo claims and, 96–97
warranties, 59
China P&I Club, 340
Choice of law, 1, 4, 39–41
bills of lading, 37
collisions, 155, 157–158
conflict of laws, 1
country, choice of law of a, 38–39
Hague-Visby Rules, 107–108
Hamburg Rules, 23
implied choice, 37
letters of undertakings, P&I clubs and, 346
limits on party choice, 39–41
mandatory rules, 39–40
Rome Convention 1980, 35–41
Sharia law, 38–39
validity of, 37–38
C.i.f. contracts
bills of lading, 128–129
carriage arrangements, 127–129
documentary duties of sellers, 137–138
f.o.b. contracts, 127–128
insurance, 137–138
market fluctuations, risk of, 128
parties to contracts, 128–129
passing of risk and property in goods, 130
rejection, 143
Civil Liability Convention (CLC)/Fund Convention, 254–264
additional compensation, 254–255
agents, 260
alter egos, 262
Bunker Oil Pollution Convention 2001, 269, 272
classification societies, 260
compensation, 254–255, 267–268
conflict of laws, 267
crew or servants, 260
economic loss, 258–259
Exclusive Economic Zones (EEZs), 256, 263–264
exclusion of liability, 259
fishermen, loss of earnings of, 258
floating production, storage and offloading units (FPSOs), 257
floating storage units (FSU), 257
government or other authority, exclusion of liability of, 259
Hazardous and Noxious Substances Convention (HNS) 1996, 277
incidents, definition of, 257–258
insurers,
exclusion of liability of, 259
limitation of liability, 261
IOPC Fund, 255, 266
joint and several liability, 257
jurisdiction, 263–264, 267
liability, imposition of, 257–260
liens, 263
limitation of liability, 210, 260–264, 267–269
liquefied natural gas (LNG) and liquefied petroleum gas (LPG), 256
loss of earnings, 258

C.i.f. contracts—*continued*
loss of profits, 258
maritime liens, 263
negligence, 259
Oil/Bulk/Ore (OBOs) ships, 257
oil, definition of, 256
oil tankers, 257
persistent oils, 256
pollution damage, definition of, 258
preventive measures, 256, 258, 260, 263–264
salvage, 260
security, 260
shipbuilders, 260
shipowners, definition of, 257
ships, definition of, 257
Small Tanker Oil Pollution Indemnification Agreement (STOPIA), 268
special drawing rights, 261
strict liability, 257–258, 260
Supplementary Fund, 255, 267–268
Tanker Oil Pollution Indemnification Agreement (TOPIA), 268
territorial seas, 255–256, 263–264
third party limits, 260
time limits, 259–260, 263
vessels, types of, 257
wildlife, beaches and ecosystems, effect of oil on, 256
Classification societies, 245–249
certificates, 246
Civil Liability Convention (CLC)/Fund Convention, 260
damages, 248
definition, 245–246
domicile, 248–249
EC Jurisdiction Regulation, 249
EC law, 247–249
jurisdiction, 248–249
limitation of liability, 204
Model Agreements with national administrations, 247
negligence, 247–248
P&I insurance, 339, 340–341
pollution, 248
quality monitoring systems, 247
statutory work, 246–248
surveys, 246–249
Clause paramount, 49–51
Close connection, 41–43
Coastal states
internal waters, 305–306
maritime zones, 305–312
pollution, 252
salvage, 175–176
territorial sea, 302, 303, 306–308
Codes. *See* International Safety Management (ISM) Code; International Ship & Port Facility Security (ISPS) Code
Collisions, 155–161
Admiralty Court, litigation on, 160–161, 350, 351, 356
Collisions—*continued*
both to blame, 160, 219
cargo claims, 159–160
causation, 160
choice of jurisdiction, 155, 157–158
Collision Convention 1910, 158–160
Collision Convention 1952, 21, 22
Collision Regulations, 158–159
Collision Statement of Case, 161, 356
contractual claims, 160
contributory negligence, 158
counterclaims, 219
damages, 161
Defence (FD&D) clubs, 156
division of blame, 158
EC Jurisdiction Regulation, 21, 22
Elder Brethren of Trinity House, 161
evidence, independence of, 157
*forum non conveniens*, 158
Hague Rules, 160
Hague-Visby Rules, 160
hull underwriters, 156
innocent cargo rule in United States, 160
insurance, 155–156, 333
investigations, 157
joint and several liability, 158–159, 189
letters of guarantee, 156–157
liability,
damages, decided separately to, 161
principles of, 158–160
lights and shapes, 159
limitation of liability, 202–203, 208, 214–216, 219, 222
negligence, 155, 160
P&I clubs, 156–157
radar, video recordings of, 157
remoteness, 160
security, 156–157
shipowners, 156
Statement of Case, 161
surveys, 156
Traffic Separation Schemes, 159–160, 215–216
United States, 160
visibility is restricted, where, 159
Collusive behaviours, control of, 371, 372–380, 394–396
block exemptions, 373–375
cabotage sector, 378–379, 395
Community ports, international transport from one or more, 373
dawn raids, 380
*De Minimis* Notice, 378
exemptions, 372–379, 395–396
fines, 380
freedom of services, 373
hard-core restrictions, 372, 375, 377, 378
horizontal agreements, 372, 377–379
investigative powers, 380
joint selling, 379
liner conferences, 373–380
block exemptions, 373–375

Collusive behaviours, control of—*continued*
liner conferences—*continued*
individual exemptions, 376–378, 395–396
price-fixing, 374, 375, 376, 395
Regulation 4056/86, 373–375
Regulation 1419/2006, 375–378, 395
service contracts, 375
shipping pools, 376–380, 395
market foreclosure, 372
market share, 395
membership rules, 379
non-compliance, consequences of, 379–380
price-fixing, 374, 375, 376, 378, 395
Regulation 4055/86, 373
Regulation 4056/86, 373–375
Regulation 4057/86, 373
Regulation 4058/86, 373
Regulation 1419/2006, 375–378, 395
restriction, distortion or prevention of competition, conduct amounting to, 372, 376, 394
self-regulation of maritime industry, 373
service contracts, 375
shipping pools, 376–380, 395
third country carriers, 373
towage, 178, 188–189
tramp shipping, 378–379, 395
vertical agreements, 372
Commission, shipbrokers and, 47
Common law
conflict of laws, 23–30
*forum non conveniens*, 24–25
jurisdiction agreements, 25–28
Compensation. *See also* Damages
Bunker Oil Pollution Convention 2001, 269
Civil Liability Convention (CLC)/Fund Convention, 254–255, 267–268
Hazardous and Noxious Substances Convention (HNS) 1996, 276–279, 284–287, 289–290
IOPC Fund, 254–255, 264–266
oil pollution, 254–255, 275–276
salvage, 166–168, 170, 172–175
SCOPIC (Special Compensation P&I Clubs) Clause, 172–175
Ship Source Pollution Directive, 275–276
Competition. *See* Abuse of a dominant position; Collusive behaviours, control of; Merger Regulation; State aid
Concentrations, 390–392, 397–398
Conditions
breach, 56–57, 59, 133
charterparties, breach of, 56–57, 59,
contract, conditions by, 133–134
definition, 133–134
descriptions, 134, 135
law, conditions by, 134–135
rejection, 135
samples, 134–135
satisfactory quality, 134
Confirmation notes, 126, 137, 138
Conflict of laws, 1–43. *See also* Choice of law; Governing law
anti-suit injunctions, 30–31
arbitration, 3–4
Civil Liability Convention (CLC)/Fund Convention, 267
common law, 23–30
court jurisdiction, 4–32
EC Jurisdiction Regulation, 5–23
*forum non conveniens*, 24–25
IOPC Fund, 267
jurisdiction clauses, 25–28, 31–32
tonnage limitation, 28–30
Consortium, 394, 398
Construction standards, 252–254, 307
Constructive total loss, 331
Containers of toxic substances, making safe, 209
Contempt of court, 357, 358, 367–9
Contiguous zones, 304
Continental shelf, 304–305
Contracts (Rights of Third Parties) Act 1999, 97–98, 107–108, 342–343
Contributory negligence, 158, 215, 270–271
Conventions. *See* Treaties and conventions
Corporate liability, 211–213
Costs, 31
Counterclaims, 219
Court jurisdiction, 4–32
anti-suit injunctions, 30–31
choice of law, 4
Civil Procedure Rules, 23
common law, 23–30
damages for breach of jurisdiction clauses, 31–32
EC Jurisdiction Regulation, 5 23
EC member state, domicile in, 4, 5–6, 13–14
exclusive jurisdiction clauses, 4
grounds of jurisdiction, 23–24
*in personam* rules, 23
jurisdiction clauses, 4, 31–32
service outside the jurisdiction, 23–24
Crew. *See also* STCW Convention 1975
Civil Liability Convention (CLC)/Fund Convention, 260
limitation of liability, 203–204, 211–213
Maritime Labour Convention 2006 (ILO), 240–242
masters, 53, 171, 173, 211
pollution, 252–254
seaworthiness, 53
standards, 252–254
training, 52
wages, liens for, 363
Criminal offences
environmental damage, 176
hazardous wastes, liability arising from, 292
International Safety Management (ISM) Code, 231
pollution, 253–254
Ship Source Pollution Directive, 253–254

Criminal offences—*continued*
SOLAS, 253
salvage, 176
Custom, 299–301

D terms, 125
Damages. *See also* Compensation
arrest, 359
cargo claims and bills of lading, 93
charterparties, breach of, 55–56
classification societies, 248
collisions, 161
demurrage, 86, 87
freezing injunctions, wrongfully obtained, 368
jurisdiction agreements, breach of, 31–32
limitation of liability, 207, 211–212
misrepresentation, 55
negligence, 196–197, 198
passengers, 151
pilotage, 196–197, 198
punitive damages in United States, 151
time charterparties, 70–72
towage, 182
warranties, 133
Dangerous substances. *See also* Hazardous and Noxious Substances Convention (HNS) 1996
containers, 209
explosive or radioactive material, carriage of, 311
IMDG Code, 278
radioactive substances, 290–291, 311
Death or personal injury
Athens Convention 1974, 148, 149–150
damages, quantum of, 152
Hazardous and Noxious Substances Convention (HNS) 1996, 279, 280, 283, 284
limitation of liability, 207, 208, 211, 216–218, 221, 283, 284
Default judgments, 356
Defence (FD&D) clubs, 156, 343
Delay
arrived ship, 81, 82
damages for delay in release of ship, 359
delivery, 131
demurrage, 86
frustration of charterparties, 64–66
multiple proceedings, 11–12
towage, 185
voyage charterparties, 79
Delivery
delay in, 131
freight, 79–80
passing of risk and property in goods, 131
performance, 132, 135–136
rejection, 143–144
ship's delivery orders, 101–102
voyage charterparties, 79–80
Demurrage
charterparties, 88–89, 91
damages for detention, 86, 87
Demurrage—*continued*
delay by shipowner's fault, 86
exceptions, 86
Gencon, 87–88
liens, 88–89, 91
"once on demurrage, always on demurrage", 86
termination for non-payment, 87–88
time limits, 87
voyage charterparties, 79, 86–88, 91
Descriptions, 134, 135
Deviation, 60–1, 123, 331
Disaster reaction syndrome, pollution and, 252
Docks, limitation of liability of owners of, 204
Documentary credits. *See* Letters of credit
Documentary duties of sellers
bills of lading, 137–143
cash against documents, 138–139
clean, 137
constructive possession of goods, 138
entitlement to payment, 138–143
evidence of contract of carriage, as, 138
functions of, 138
receipt, as, 138
Uniform Customs and Practices 600, 141–142
cash against documents, 138–139
CFR documents, 138
c.i.f. contracts, 137–138
commercial invoices, 137
confirmation notes, 137, 138
f.o.b. contracts, 138
Incoterms 2000, 138
insurance policies, 137–138
international trade, 137–143
letters of credit, 138, 139–143
standard forms, 137–138
tender documents, duty to, 137
time of presentation, 139, 143
usual shipping documents, meaning of, 138–139
Documents, rejection of, 143–145
Domicile, 5–6, 13–14, 20, 348–349
Drilling ships, 206
Due diligence
general average, 335
marine insurance, 332
safe ports, 61–62
seaworthiness, 52–53, 119
towage, 185
Dumping at sea, 291, 292, 295, 320

E terms, 125
EC competition rules, 371–398. *See also* Abuse of a dominant position; Collusive behaviours, control of; Merger Regulation; State aid
Admiralty Court, jurisdiction of, 351
cartels, 371
general rules, 371–372
meaning of competition law, 371–372
monopolies, 371

EC competition rules—*continued*
policy areas, 371
EC Jurisdiction Regulation, 5–23
agency, 14, 19
aims, 5
anti-suit injunctions, 31
Arrest Convention 1952, 21–22
branches, agencies or other establishments, 14, 19
Brussels Convention 1968, 5, 7, 22–23
Bunker Oil Pollution Convention 2001, 320
civil and commercial matters, 5
classification societies, 249
Collision Convention 1952, 21, 22
conflict of laws, 5–23
contract claims, 14–17, 20
delays, 11–12
domicile, 5–6, 13–14, 20
exclusive jurisdiction clauses, 10–11
first seised, court, 8–12
freezing injunctions, 365, 367
governing law, 32
grounds of jurisdiction, 24
Hague-Visby Rules, 23
Hamburg Rules, 21, 23
Hazardous and Noxious Substances Convention (HNS) 1996, 285
identical parties, 12
irreconcilable judgments, 8–9
Italian torpedo, 11
jurisdiction, 5–23
jurisdiction clauses, 6–8, 11–14, 20, 25, 27
limitation of liability, 21, 225
Lugano Convention 1988, 5
multiple defendants, 19–20
multiple proceedings, 7, 8–12, 22
place of harmful event, 16–19
place of performance, 14–17
Rome Convention 1980, 33–34
related actions, 12–13
salvage, 14, 19
same causes of action, 9–10
same parties, 12
stay of proceedings, 5–6, 9, 10–12
third party proceedings, 20–21
tort, delict or quasi-delict, 14, 16–19, 20
treaties and conventions 21–23
EC law. *See also* EC competition rules; EC Jurisdiction Regulation
classification societies, 247–249
European Maritime Safety Agency (EMSA), 243
International Maritime Organization (IMO), 312–313
International Safety Management (ISM) Code, 228
oil pollution, 176, 275–276
Package Travel Directive, 151–153
P&I insurance, 340
places of refuge, 176
salvage, 176
EC law—*continued*
Ship Source Pollution Directive, 176, 253–254, 275–276, 307–308
Waste Framework Directive, 276
Economic loss, 258–259
EEZs. *See* Exclusive Economic Zones (EEZs)
Elder Brethren of Trinity House, 161
EMSA (European Maritime Safety Agency), 243–245
Enforcement of maritime claims. *See also* Arrest of ships
Admiralty Court, jurisdiction of, 349–362
freezing injunctions, 364–370
maritime liens, 362–364
Environment. *See also* Marine pollution from shipping activities; Oil pollution
places of refuge, 196
savage, 162, 164, 166–168, 170, 171–176
special compensation, 166–168, 170, 172–175
Essential facilities doctrine, 383–386, 396–397
Estoppel, 111, 144, 145, 226
European Maritime Safety Agency (EMSA), 243–245
Administrative Board, 244–245
aims, 243
Commission, 244–245
European Union, 243
Executive Director, 245
function, 243–244
oil pollution, 243–245
*Ex works* contracts, 129–130
Exclusion of liability
cargo claims and bills of lading, 94, 120–123
Civil Liability Convention (CLC)/Fund Convention, 259
government or other authority, 259
Hazardous and Noxious Substances Convention (HNS) 1996, 281, 285
insurers, 259
oil pollution, 273, 274
towage, 179, 182
Exclusive jurisdiction agreements, 4, 10–11, 26–28, 31
Exclusive Economic Zones (EEZs)
baselines, 304
Bunker Oil Pollution Convention 2001, 270, 273
Civil Liability Convention (CLC)/Fund Convention, 256, 263–264
detention and prosecution, 323
Hazardous and Noxious Substances Convention (HNS) 1996, 279, 284
high seas, 302, 304
International Maritime Organization (IMO), 322
Law of the Sea Convention 1982, 304
Particularly Sensitive Sea Areas (PSSAs), 322
pollution, 251, 253–254
prompt release procedures, 323
state sovereignty, 304

Exclusive Economic Zones (EEZs)—*continued*
wreck removal, 190–191
Exemptions
abuse of a dominant position, 381
block exemptions, 373–375, 381
collusive behaviours, control of, 372–379, 395–396
Expected ready to load, 67
Expected time of arrival, 8
Explosive or radioactive material, carriage of, 311

Fisheries
boarding and inspection, 311
fish Stocks Agreement, 311
loss of earnings of, 258
prompt release procedures, 324–325
Flag state jurisdiction
high seas, 308–312
maritime zones, 306, 308–312
STCW Convention 1975, 237, 239–240
Floating production, storage and offloading units (FPSOs), 257
Floating storage units (FSU), 257
F.o.b. contracts
bills of lading, 128–129
carriage arrangements, 127–129
c.i.f. terms, 127–128
documentary duties of sellers, 138
market fluctuations, risk of, 128
parties to contracts, 128–129
passing of risk and property in goods, 130
performance, 136
rejection, 143
title to sue, cargo claims and, 103–104
variations, 127
Forfeiture, 74–75, 325–326
*Forum non conveniens*, 24–25, 158, 225
Forum shopping, 1–2, 28, 151
Fraudulent misrepresentation, 55–56
Freedom of services, 373
Freezing injunctions, 364–370
arbitration, 365
arrest, 370
assets subject to injunctions, 369–370
banks, negligence of, 368
consequences of injunctions, 367–368
contempt of court, 367, 368, 369
damages for wrongfully obtained injunctions, 368
definition, 364
disclosure, 366
EC Jurisdiction Regulation, 365, 367
enforcement of maritime claims, 364–370
foreign proceedings, support of, 367
good arguable case, 366, 368
*in personam* claims, 364, 370
issue injunctions, when courts will issue, 365–367
jurisdiction, 365–366
just and convenient test, 367
Freezing injunctions—*continued*
limitation of liability, 223
priority, 364
third parties, 366, 368, 369–370
time for issuing injunctions, 365
urgent cases, 365
worldwide injunctions, 369
wrongfully obtained injunctions, damages for, 368
Freight
ballast bonus, 79
calculation, 79–80
charterparties, 78–80, 88, 90–91
deductions, 80
delivery, 79–80
liens, 88, 90–91
limitation of liability, 208
sub-freight, 90–91
Friendship and navigation treaties, 306
Frustration
advance hire, 66
charterparties, 63–66, 79
consideration, 66
delay, 64–65
Law Reform (Frustrated Contracts) Act 1943, 66
self-induced frustration, 65
supervening events, 65
towage, 179
war, 64
Fund Convention. *See* Civil Liability Convention (CLC)/Fund Convention
Fundamental breach, 56, 59

GATT, 306
Gencon, 87–88
General average
abolition, proposal for, 337
apportionment, 336
average adjusters, role of, 336
Declaration of General Average, 335
definition, 333–334
due diligence, 335
estimates, 336
examples of sacrifices or expenditure, 334
Hague Rules, 335
Hague-Visby Rules, 335
jettison, 334
limitation of liability, 208
marine insurance, 331, 333–337
particular average, 334, 336
recent developments, 336–337
Rule Paramount, 336–337
Salvage Convention 1989, Special Compensation for, 336
subject to average, 331
unseaworthiness, 335
valuation forms, 336
York-Antwerp Rules, 334–335, 337
General principles of international law, 301

Geographic market, identification of relevant, 381–382, 392–393, 396–397
Governing law, 1, 32–43
causes of action, 1
defence, 1
EC Jurisdiction Regulation, 32
Rome Convention on Law Applicable to Contractual Obligations 1980, 32–43
variation, 39
Government vessels
Bunker Oil Pollution Convention 2001, 271
Hazardous and Noxious Substances Convention (HNS) 1996, 278
IOPC Fund, 265
Guarantees, 156–157, 221, 344–345

Habitual residence, 37
Hague Rules
bills of lading, 48–49
charterparties, 47–51
clause paramount, 50–51
collisions, 160
deviation, 60–61
foreign legislation, charterparties incorporating, 50–51
general average, 335
International Safety Management (ISM) Code, 230
proof of loss, 111
seaworthiness, 52–54, 230
time limits, 54, 61
US Carriage of Goods by Sea Act 1936, 48–49
Hague-Visby Rules
actual faulty or privity, 121
bills of lading, 48–49, 93–94, 107–108
charterparties, 40, 47–51
choice of law clauses, 107–108
clause paramount, 51
collisions, 160
Contracts (Rights of Third Parties) Act 1999, 107–108
deviation, 60–61, 123
EC Jurisdiction Regulation, 23
general average, 335
International Safety Management (ISM) Code, 230
jurisdiction agreements, 28
limits of liability, 48, 120–123
mandatory rules, as, 39–41
package limitation, 96, 107
proof of breach, 118, 119
proof of loss, 109, 110–114
Rome Convention on the Law Applicable to Contractual Obligations 1980, 39–41, 107–108
seaworthiness, 52–54, 119–120, 230
time limits, 2, 54, 61, 107, 120–121
title to sue, cargo claims and, 96
Hamburg Rules
bills of lading, 41, 48–49
Hamburg Rules—*continued*
cargo interests, 48
charterparties, 47–51
choice of law, 23
EC Jurisdiction Regulation, 23
International Safety Management (ISM) Code, 230
jurisdiction agreements, 26
mandatory application, 41
Rome Convention 1980, 41
seaworthiness, 54, 230
Harbours. *See* Ports and harbours
Hazardous and Noxious Substances Convention (HNS) 1996, 276–290
accounts, 287–288
bulk goods, 289
carriage by sea, definition of, 280
Civil Liability Convention/Fund Convention, 277
compensation, 276–279, 284–287, 289–290
compulsory insurance, 281
damage to property, 279, 280
entry into force, 277
EC Jurisdiction Regulation, 285
exclusion of liability, 281, 285
exclusions, 278
Exclusive Economic Zones, 279, 284
government ships, 278
HNS Fund, 277, 285–287
compensation, 285–287
exclusion from liability, 285
jurisdiction, 286–287
limitation of liability, 286
negligence, 285
parallel proceedings, 287
personal liability, 286
time limits, 286
IMDG Code, 278
implementation, 277
insurance, 281
joint and several liability, 280
jurisdiction, 279, 284–287
limitation of liability, 273, 281–286
applicable limits, 281–282
HNS Fund, 286
jurisdiction, 284
limitation fund, establishment and distribution of, 283, 284
loss of life and personal injury, 283, 284
loss of right to limit, 282
security, 273
LNG accounts, 287–288
loss of life, 279, 280, 283, 284
multimodal carriage, 288
natural phenomenons, damage caused by, 281
navigational aids, liability of public authorities for damage caused by, 281
negligence, 285
oil accounts, 287–288
oil pollution, 276, 277, 279

Hazardous and Noxious Substances Convention (HNS) 1996—*continued*
packaging, 278, 288, 289
parallel proceedings, 287
persistent and non-persistent oils, 279
personal injury, 279, 280, 283, 284, 286
preventive measures, 279, 280
Protocol (draft), 289–290
receivers, definition of, 288
recognition and enforcement of judgments, 284–285
reporting obligations, 288–289
scope of application, 277–278
security, 283
shipowners, liability of, 280
ships, definition of, 278
small ships, exclusion of 278
strict liability, 276–277, 280–281
territorial sea, 279
time limits, 283–284
war, hostilities, civil war, insurrections, 281
Hazardous goods. *See* Hazardous and Noxious Substances Convention (HNS) 1996; Hazardous wastes, liability arising from
Hazardous wastes, liability arising from, 291–295
abandonment of ships, 295
Basel Convention on Control of Transboundary Movement of Hazardous Wastes 1989, 291–293
Liability Protocol 1999, 292–293
carriers' liability, 292–293
criminal offences, 292
documentation, 292
dumping at sea, 291, 292, 295
fault, 293
general legal framework, 291–292
illegal traffic, 292
import and export, 291–292
London Convention on Dumping of Wastes at Sea 1972, 291
Nairobi International Convention on Removal of Wrecks 2007, 295
old ships, fate of, 293–295
radioactive wastes, 291
recycling ships, 293–295
scrapping, 293–295
scuttling, 295
strict liability, 293
wreck removal, 295
High seas
boarding and inspection of ships, 310–312
definition, 302
Exclusive Economic Zones, 302, 304
explosive or radioactive material, carriage of, 311
Fish Stocks Agreement, 311
flag state jurisdiction, 308–312
freedoms, 302
hot pursuit, 311
High seas—*continued*
Law of the Sea Convention 1982, 308, 310–311
multiple nationality of ships, 308–309
nationality of ships, 308–310
navigation, freedom of, 302
open registries, 309–310
ship registration, 309–310
Suppression of Unlawful Acts against Safety of Navigation Convention 1988, protocol to, 311–312
visit, right to, 310–311
weapons of mass destruction, carriage of, 311
Hire
advance hire, 66, 73
anti-technicality clause, 74
cash, payment in, 73–74
deductions, 77–78
off hire, 70, 76–77
standard forms, 76
time charterparties, 69, 70, 73–78
time for payment, 73–74
withdrawal for non-payment, 75–76, 78
Historic wrecks, 192–193
HNS. *See* Hazardous and Noxious Substances Convention (HNS) 1996
Hot pursuit, 311
Hull and machinery insurance, 156, 332–333

Identical parties, 12
Identity of carrier, cargo claims and, 104–107
actual carrier, claiming against the, 106–107
bills of lading, 93, 104–107
charterers,
not charterers, where claimants are, 105–106
where claimants are, 105
contract, 104–107
demise charters, 106
signatures on bills of lading, 106
Uniform Customs and Practice for Document Credit (UCP) 600, 105–106
Illegitimate last voyage, 63, 72
ILO Maritime Labour Convention 2006, 240–242
IMDG Code, 278
*In personam* claims, 23, 351–356, 364, 370
*In rem* claims
Admiralty Court, jurisdiction of, 351–356
arrest, 349–361
maritime liens, 362–363
salvage, 363
Incoterms
documentary duties of sellers, 138
incorporation, 126–127
performance, 137
standard forms, 126
Indemnity costs, 32
Independent contractors, limitation of liability of, 204

Injunctions, 223. *See also* Anti-suit injunctions; Freezing injunctions
Inland waters. *See* Internal waters
Innocent passage, right of, 302, 303, 304, 307–308, 357
Inspection of ships, 310–312
Institute Cargo Clauses, 333
Institute Hull Clauses, 332
Insurance. *See also* Marine insurance; P&I insurance
  Athens Convention 1974, 149
  Bunker Oil Pollution Convention 2001, 268–269, 272
  c.i.f. contracts, 137–138
  Civil Liability Convention (CLC)/Fund Convention, 259, 261
  documentary duties of sellers, 137–138
  exclusion of liability, 259
  Hazardous and Noxious Substances Convention (HNS) 1996, 281
  International Ship & Port Facility Security (ISPS) Code, 235–236
  limitation of liability, 261
  oil pollution, 274
  Rome Convention 1980, 35
  seaworthiness, 231
  wreck removal, 189–190
Interchangeability, 383
Interest, 220
Intermediate or innominate terms, 57–59, 133
Internal waters including ports, 305–306
  coastal waters, 305–306
  foreign ships, 305–306
  friendship and navigation treaties, 306
  GATT, 306
  Law of the Sea Convention 1982, 306
  port state, submission to jurisdiction of, 306
  salvage, 163
  territorial sea, 302
International Convention on Standards of Training, Certification and Watchkeeping for Seafarers (STCW) 1995. *See* STCW Convention 1975
International Labour Organization (ILO) Maritime Labour Convention 2006, 240–242
International law. *See* Conflict of laws; Public international law
International Maritime Organization (IMO) and conventions, 312–323
  amendment of treaties, 321
  Assembly, 314–315
  competent international organization, as, 321–323
  Council, 314–315
  depositary, IMO as, 320
  entry into force of treaties, 320, 321
  European Union, 312–313
  Exclusive Economic Zones (EEZs), 322
  experts, maintenance of list of, 323
  Facilitation Committee, 316
International Maritime Organization (IMO) and conventions—*continued*
  final clauses, 317–321
  International Ship & Port Facility Security (ISPS) Code, 232
  Law of the Sea Convention 1982, 321–323
  Legal and Marine Environment Protection Committee, 314
  Legal Committee, 316, 317
  London Convention on Dumping of Wastes at Sea 1972, 320
  Marine Environment Protection Committee, 315–316
  Maritime Safety Committee, 315–316
  meetings and sessions, 314–315
  navigation, rules on safety of, 321–322
  multilateral treaties, 317–321
  Particularly Sensitive Sea Areas (PSSAs), 322
  party to IMO Conventions, becoming, 317–321
  places of refuge, 195–196
  political considerations, 317
  pollution, 322
  protocols, 318–319
  ratification, 318
  role of, 312–314
  sea lanes, 321–322
  Secretariat, 316
  signature, 318
  SOLAS, 227–228
  specialised agencies, 312–313
  STCW Convention 1975, 236, 239
  structure, 314–315
  Technical Co-operation Committee, 314, 216
  traffic separation schemes, 321–322
  United Nations, 312–313
  Vienna Convention on the Law of Treaties, 317–318, 321
  websites, 322
International organizations, 297
International Seabed Authority, 305
International Safety Management (ISM) Code, 228–232
  cargo claims and unseaworthiness, 230
  certification, 228–229
  contents, 228
  control, 228–229
  criminal proceedings 231
  designated persons, 229
  disclosure of documents, 229–230, 231
  Documents of Compliance (DOC), 229, 232
  European Union, 228
  Hague Rules, 230
  Hague-Visby Rules, 230
  Hamburg Rules, 230
  insurance cover, 231
  limitation of liability, 212–213, 230–231
  litigation, impact on, 229–231
  pollution, 253
  ro ro ferries, 228

International Safety Management (ISM) Code —*continued*
Safety Management Certificates (SMC), 229
SOLAS, 228
STCW Convention 1975, 237, 240
Tanker Management Self Assessment (TMSA), 232
unseaworthiness, 230, 231
verification, 228–229
International Ship & Port Facility Security (ISPS) Code, 232–236
commercial implications, 235–236
contents, 232–233
Continuous Synopsis Record, contents of, 233–234
control measures, 234
coverage, 232
Declarations of Security, 234
entering port, ships, 234
governments, obligations of contracting, 235
insurance implications, 235–236
International Maritime Organization (IMO), 232
International Ship Safety Certificate (ISSC), 232–233
levels of security, 233
limitation of liability, 212–213
modifications to ships, 232
P&I Clubs, 237
passenger ships, 232
pollution, 253
ports, requirements for, 235
security officers, appointment of, 232–233
ship security assessment, 233
SOLAS, 232, 234–235
stowaways, 235
terrorism, 232, 236
time charter standard forms, 235
United States, 232
International Ship Safety Certificate (ISSC), 232–233
International trade
documentary duties of sellers, 137–143
performance, 132–143
shipping industry, purpose of, 123
International Tribunal for the Law of the Sea, 324–325
IOPC Fund, 254–255, 264–268
additional compensation, 254–255
Civil Liability Convention, 255, 266
compensation, 254–255, 264–266
conflict of laws, 267
financing of Fund, 266
government or other authority, negligence of, 264–265
government ships, 265
jurisdiction, 267
limitation of liability, 264, 266
mystery spills, 265
preventive spills, 265
recognition of judgments, 267
IOPC Fund—*continued*
role, 254–255, 264–267
time limits, 265–266
war, hostilities, civil war and insurrection, 265
Irreconcilable judgments, 8–9, 20–21
ISM Code. *See* International Safety Management (ISM) Code
ISPS Code. *See* International Ship & Port Facility Security (ISPS) Code
Italian torpedo, 11

Jettison, 209, 334
Joint ventures, 391
Judgments
default, 356
Hazardous and Noxious Substances Convention (HNS) 1996, 284–285
irreconcilable judgments, 8–9, 20–21
recognition and enforcement, 267, 284–285
Judicial decisions, 301
Judicial sale, 2, 358, 360–361
Jurisdiction. *See also* Admiralty Court, jurisdiction of; EC Jurisdiction Regulation; Jurisdiction agreements
arrest, 359
Bunker Oil Pollution Convention 2001, 272–273
classification societies, 248–249
conflict of laws, 4–32
court jurisdiction, 4–32
forum shopping, 1–2
freezing injunctions, 365–366
Hazardous and Noxious Substances Convention (HNS) 1996, 279, 284–287
IOPC Fund, 267
limitation of liability, 224–226, 264
time limits, 2
tonnage limitation, 1–2
treaties and conventions, 1–2
Jurisdiction agreements
anti-suit injunctions, 27, 30
bills of lading, third party holders of, 7–8
breach, 31–32
common law, 25–28
conflict of laws, 25–28, 31–32
costs, 31, 32
damages, 31–32
domicile, 20
EC Jurisdiction Regulation, 6–8, 13–14, 20, 25, 27
exclusive jurisdiction clauses, 4, 26–28, 31
first seised, court, 31
foreign jurisdiction clause, 27–28
formalities, 7–8
Hague-Visby Rules, 28
Hamburg Rules, 26
indemnity costs, 32
letters of undertaking, P&I clubs and, 346
multiple parties, 26
multiple proceedings, 11–12, 26

Jurisdiction agreements—*continued*
no clause, where there is no, 13–14
proper law, 26–27
Rome Convention 1980, 34
stay of proceedings, 25–26
third party proceedings, 21
tonnage limitation, 29
validity, 7–8
wreck removal, 190–191, 193

Lashing equipment, 119–120
Law of the Sea Convention
continental shelf, 305
custom, 300
Exclusive Economic Zones (EEZs), 304
high seas, 308, 310–311
internal waters, 306
International Maritime Organization (IMO), 321–323
maritime zones, 302–308, 310–311
pollution, 251, 254
prompt release procedures under Article 292 of Law of the Sea Convention, 323–326
Ship Source Pollution Directive, 254
territorial sea, 302, 303, 306–308
Laytime
calculation of laytime, 85–86
commencement of laytime, 80–82
notice of readiness, 82–85
voyage charterparties, 79, 80–86
weather working days, 85
working days, 85
Letters of credit
banks, 139–142
bills of lading, 124, 141–142
decision to pay or not to pay, 142–143
definition, 139
disclaimers, 141
operation of letters of credit, 139–141
performance, 136–137
presentation, 139–142
rejection, 145–146
reserve, paying under, 145
sellers, duties of, 138, 139–143
strict compliance, 141
time for presentation, 143
Uniform Customs and Practices (UCP) 600, 136, 140–142, 145–146
waiver of discrepancies, 145
Letters of indemnity, 112–113
Letters of undertaking, P&I clubs and
arrest, 344, 346–347
bail, 344
bank guarantees as alternative, 344–345
choice of law, 346
construction, 345–346
court, involvement of the, 346–347
effect, 346–347
factual matrix, 345
jurisdiction clauses, 346
primary or secondary liability, 346

Letters of undertaking, P&I clubs and—*continued*
purpose, 344–345
release, 344, 347
security, 344, 346–347
Liberty to deviate clause, 60
Liens. *See also* Maritime liens
bills of lading, 89
cargo, 88–90
cesser clauses, 91
charterparties, 88–91
Civil Liability Convention (CLC)/Fund Convention, 263
demurrage, 88–89, 91
freight, 88, 90–91
notice of exercise of lien, 89–90
possessory liens, 88–89
salvage, 161, 169
standard forms, 88
sub-freight, 90–91
time charterparties, 88, 90
towage, 184
voyage charterparties, 88, 91
Lights and shapes, collisions and, 159
Lights, lighthouses and buoys, 193
Limitation of liability, 201–226
act, neglect or default of persons whom shipowner is responsible for, 203–204
Admiralty Court, jurisdiction of, 351, 361–362
alter egos companies, 213, 262
arrest, 203, 222, 359, 361, 362
Athens Convention 1984, 147, 148–150, 208, 217
attribution, rules of, 212–213
avert or minimise loss, steps taken to, 209
bills of lading, 94, 120–123
board of directors, 212
bunkers, 207, 255, 271–272
cargo claims, 205, 209
charterers, 203, 205, 207, 213
Civil Liability Convention (CLC)/Fund Convention, 260–263, 272
claims against other shipowners, 204–205
claims subject to limitation, 206–210
classification societies, 204
clean-up, 207
collisions, 202–203, 208, 214–216, 219, 222
commencement of claims, 361
conflict of laws, 28–30
consequential damage, 208
containers of toxic substances, rendering safe, 209
contract, 204–206, 208–211
contributory negligence, 215
corporate liability, 211–213
counterclaims, 219
crew, 203–204, 211–213
damage to property, 207–208, 216
damages, 207, 211–212
death, 207, 208, 211, 216–218, 221, 283, 284
declarations of right to limit, 361

Limitation of liability—*continued*
demise charters, 202–203
deviation, 123
direct connection with operation of ship, 207
directing mind and will of company, 212
docks and canals, owners of, 204
drilling, ships engaged in, 206
EC Jurisdiction Regulation, 21, 225
estoppel, 226
exclusions, 210–211
*forum non conveniens*, 225
forum shopping, 28
freezing injunctions, 223
freight, 208
general average, 208
guarantees, 221
Hague-Visby Rules, 96, 107, 120–123
Hazardous and Noxious Substances Convention (HNS) 1996, 281–283
independent contractors, 204
injunctions, 223
insurance, 262, 272
interest, 220
International Ship Management Code (ISM), 212–213, 230–231
IOPC Fund, 264, 266
ISPS Code, 212–213
jettison, confiscation or rendering safe of cargo, 209
jurisdiction, 29, 224–226, 264, 284
knowledge, 214–216
limitation fund,
arrest, 222–224, 362
Civil Liability Convention (CLC)/Fund Convention, 262–264
constitution, 219–224
guarantees, 221
Hazardous and Noxious Substances Convention (HNS) 1996, 283, 284
interest, 220
legal proceedings, 219–220
maritime liens, 221–222
payments made out of fund, 221–224
priority, 221–222
purpose, 219
special drawing rights, 220–221
Limitation of Liability Convention 1924, 202
Limitation of Liability Convention 1957, 28–29, 202, 225–226, 230, 272
Limitation of Liability Convention 1976, 202, 204, 206, 213–214, 219–220, 224
arrest, 362
Athens Convention 1974, 149–150
exclusions, 206
International Safety Management (ISM) Code, 230
oil pollution, 275–276
tonnage limitation, 28, 30
limits, 216–218
loss of life, 122–123, 207, 208, 211, 216–218, 221, 262, 272, 282–284

Limitation of liability—*continued*
loss of privilege to limit, 148, 211–216
luggage, 208
maritime liens, 221–222, 263
masters, 211
multiple parties, 29, 218
navigation, vessel used in, 206
non-sea-going and sea-going ships, 150, 205–206
nuclear damage, 210–211
oil pollution, 210, 254, 255, 275–276
one ship companies, 202
package or unit limitation, 96, 107, 120, 122
P&I insurance, 339, 340
passengers, 208, 217–218
personal injury, 207, 208, 211, 216–218, 221, 283, 284
pilots, 200, 204
pollution, 207, 210
ports and harbours, 194, 204
priority, 221–222
Protocol 1996 to Limitation of Liability Convention 1976, 202, 205–208, 211, 216, 219–226
arrest, 359
Athens Convention 1974, 150
Bunker Oil Pollution Convention 2001, 269, 272
radioactive substances, 290
remuneration under contracts, 210
rule of attribution, 231
salvage, 170, 207, 208, 209–211, 213
sea-going ships, 205–206
security, 222–224
service, people employed under contracts of, 211
ship managers and operators, 203, 213, 230–231
Ship Source Pollution Directive, 275–276
shipowners, 202–205, 211–213
ship's agents, 204
ships subject to limitation, 205–206
size of ships, 206
Small Tanker Oil Pollution Indemnification Agreement (STOPIA), 268
special compensation, 210
special drawing rights, 122, 216–218, 220–221, 261
special liability regimes, 202
stay of proceedings, 29, 225
stevedores, 204
Tanker Oil Pollution Indemnification Agreement (STOPIA), 268
time charterers, 203, 213
Tonnage Convention, 216
tonnage limitation, 1–2, 28–30, 216–217
tort, claims in, 207
towage, 188
voyage charterers, 203, 213
Warsaw Convention 1929, 214
who is entitled to limit liability, 202–204

Limitation of liability—*continued*
  wrecks, 209
Liner conferences,
  abuse of a dominant position, 381, 384
  block exemptions, 373–375, 381
  collusive behaviours, control of, 383–380, 395–396
  individual exemptions, 376–378, 395–396
  market share, 384
  Merger Regulation, 392–394, 397–398
  predatory pricing, 384
  price-fixing, 374, 375, 376, 395
  Regulation 4056/86, 373–375
  Regulation 1419/2006, 375–378, 395
  service contracts, 375
  shipping pools, 376–380, 395
Liquefied natural gas (LNG), 256, 287–288
Liquefied petroleum gas (LPG), 256
Lloyd's Open Form (LOF), 162, 172–175
  Lloyd's Standard and Arbitration Clauses (LASA), 172
  no cure no pay principle, 162, 172–175
  retrospectivity, 173
  rewards, 173–175
  SCOPIC (Special Compensation P&I Clubs) Clause, 172–175
  towage, 186
Lloyd's syndicates, 327
Load and stow cargo, duty to, 136
Loading marks, 109–110
LOF. *See* Lloyd's Open Form (LOF)
London arbitration, 3, 4
London Convention on Dumping of Wastes at Sea 1972, 291, 320
Loss of earnings and loss of profits, oil pollution and, 258
Loss of life. *See* Death and personal injury
Lugano Convention 1988, 5
Luggage, limitation of liability and, 208

Maintenance of ships, 53, 252–253
Management. *See* International Safety Management (ISM) Code
Manning standards, 252–254
Mareva injunctions. *See* Freezing injunctions
Marine insurance, 327–347. *See also* P&I insurance
  actual total loss, 331
  background, 327
  cargo insurance, 333
  claims, 331–332
  collisions, 155–156, 333
  constructive total loss, 331
  contents of the policy, 330–331
  deviation, 61, 331
  disclosure, 329
  due diligence, 332
  formation of policies, 328–329
  general average, 331, 333–337
  hull and machinery insurance, 156, 332–333
  Institute Cargo Clauses, 333

Marine insurance—*continued*
  Institute Hull Clauses, 332
  losses, 331–332
  implied restrictions, 330–331
  insurable interest, 328–329
  International Safety Management (ISM) Code, 230
  Lloyd's syndicates, 327
  Marine Insurance Act 1906, 327–330
  marine risks, 327–328
  misrepresentation, 329
  mitigation, 331, 332
  negligence, 330
  partial loss, 331–332
  perils of the sea, 332
  post-contractual obligations, 330
  premiums, 328
  proximate cause, 330
  seaworthiness, 330
  subject to average, 331
  time basis, 328
  utmost good faith, 329
  valued or unvalued policies, 328, 331–332
  voyage basis, 328, 330–331
  warranties, 330
Marine pollution from shipping activities, 251–295. *See also* Oil pollution
  coastal states, 252
  construction standards, 252–254
  crew, standards of, 252–254
  criminal liability, 253–254
  disaster reaction syndrome, 252
  exclusive economic zones, 251, 253–254
  flag state control, 253
  International Maritime Organization (IMO), 315–316, 322
  Intervention Convention 1969, 252
  ISM Code, 253
  ISPS Code, 253
  Law of the Sea Convention 1982, 251, 254
  limitation of liability, 207, 210
  maintenance of ships, 252–253
  manning standards, 252–254
  MARPOL, 253–254
  operation standards, 252–254
  port state control, 252, 253
  salvage, 162, 164, 166–168, 170, 171–176
  Ship Source Pollution Directive, 253–254
  SOLAS, 253
  territorial waters, 253–254
  towage, 177, 187, 188
Maritime liens
  Admiralty Court, jurisdiction of, 352–354
  arrest, 361, 363–364
  attachment, 363
  bottomry, 363
  Civil Liability Convention (CLC)/Fund Convention, 263
  crew wages, 363
  definition, 362
  enforcement, 362–364

Maritime liens—*continued*
foreign law, priority of liens recognised under, 363–364
*in rem* actions, 352–354, 362–363
limitation of liability, 221–222, 263
mortgages, 363
priority, 361, 363–364
salvage, 169, 363
transfer, 363
types, 352
Maritime Labour Convention 2006 (ILO), 240–242
aims, 240–241
employment and social rights, 241–242
entry into force, 241
fundamental rights and principles, 241
Maritime zones, 301–312. *See also* Exclusive Economic Zones (EEZs); High seas; Territorial sea
archipelagic waters, 303–304
coastal state rights, 305–312
contiguous zones, 304
continental shelf, 304–305
flag state rights, 306, 308–312
innocent passage, right of, 302, 303, 304, 307–308
internal waters including ports, 305–306
Law of the Sea Convention 1982, 302–308, 310–311
mining, 305
seabed, 302, 305
navigation, freedom of, 303
traditional zones, 302–303
Market definition, 381, 396
Market share, 383–384, 392, 395, 397
MARPOL, 253–254
Masters
agents, as, 173
binding authority to sign contracts of, 171
limitation of liability, 211
salvage, 171, 173
seaworthiness, 53
Merchant Shipping Act 1995, section 154, liability for oil pollution under
exclusion of liability, 273–274
insurance, 274
navigational lights or aids, public authority liability for, 274
preventive measures, 274
recognition and enforcement of judgments, 274–275
registered shipowners, 274
third parties, 274
time limits, 274
war, hostilities, civil war, 284
Merger Regulation, 371–372, 390–394, 397–398
abuse of a dominant position, 392, 397
aims, 390
Community dimension, concept of, 390, 391, 398
Merger Regulation—*continued*
concentration,
approval or prohibition, 391,
concept of, 390–392, 397–398
consortium, 394, 398
co-ordinated or parallel behaviours, 393, 398
geographic market, relevant, 392–393, 397
joint ventures, 391
liner shipping, 392–394, 397–398
market share, 392, 397
notification, 391
product market, relevant, 393, 397
relevant market, 392–393, 397
substitutability, 392, 397
tramp shipping, 397–398
vertical integration, 393–394
Mid-Atlantic Settlements, 151
Military wrecks, 192
Mining, 305
Misrepresentation, 47, 55–56, 179, 329
Monopolies, 371
Mortgages, 360–361, 363–364
Multimodal carriage, 288
Multiple parties, 19–20, 26, 29, 218
Multiple proceedings, EC Judgments Convention and, 7–12
Arrest Convention, 22
delays, 11–12
exclusive jurisdiction proceedings, 10–11
first seised, court, 8–12
identical parties, 12
irreconcilable judgments, 8–9
Italian torpedo, 11
jurisdiction agreements, 11–12, 26
same causes of action, 9–10
same parties, 12
stay of proceedings, 9, 10–12

Nairobi International Convention on Removal of Wrecks 2007, 295
Nationality of ships, 308–310
Navigation
aids, liability of public authorities for damage caused by navigational, 274, 281
friendship and navigation treaties, 306
high seas, freedom of navigation on the, 302
International Maritime Organization (IMO), 321–322
maritime zones, 303
negligence, 53–54
oil pollution, 274
ports and harbours, 193
rules on safety of navigation, 321–322
seaworthiness, 53–54
vessels used in navigation, 206
Negligence
banks, freezing injunctions and, 368
charterparties, breach of, 56
Civil Liability Convention (CLC)/Fund Convention, 259
classification societies, 247–248

Negligence—*continued*
collisions, 155, 160
damages, 196–197, 198
government or other public authorities, 264–265
Hazardous and Noxious Substances Convention (HNS) 1996, 285
IOPC Fund, 264–265
marine insurance, 330
navigation, 53–54
pilotage, 196–197, 198–199
seaworthiness, 53–54
towage, 182, 183
No cure no pay, 162, 166, 172–175
Notice of readiness
accurate statements, notice must contain, 83–84
arrival of ship, 81, 82, 84
cancellation, 83
early commencement of laytime, 82–83
expected time of arrival, 82
form of notice, 83
laytime, 82–85
validity, 84
Noxious substances. *See* Hazardous and Noxious Substances Convention (HNS) 1996
Nuclear damage
limitation of liability, 210–211
Paris Convention, 210
radioactive substances, liability for, 290
Vienna Convention, 210
NYPE, 46

Off hire, 70, 76–77
Oil/Bulk/Ore (OBOS) ships, oil pollution and, 257
Oil pollution, 254–268. *See also* Civil Liability Convention (CLC)/Fund Convention; IOPC Fund
Admiralty Court, jurisdiction of, 351
Bunker Oil Pollution Convention 2001, 255, 268–274
compensation, 254–255, 275–276
definition, 274
EC law, 176, 275–276
European Maritime Safety Agency (EMSA), 243–245
exclusion of liability, 273–274
Hazardous and Noxious Substances Convention 1996, 276, 277, 279
insurance, 274
limited liability, 210, 254, 255, 275–276
Limitation of Liability Convention 1976, 276
Merchant Shipping Act 1995, section 154, liability under, 273–275, 284
navigational lights or aids, public authority liability for, 274
non-persistent oils, 276
P&I insurance, 340
polluter pays, 275
preventive measures, 274
recognition and enforcement of judgments, 274–275
registered shipowners, 274
Ship Source Pollution Directive, 176, 275–276
shipowners, 274
strict liability, 254
third parties, 274
time limits, 274
war, hostilities, civil war, 284
Waste Framework Directive, 276
wreck removal, 190–191
Old ships, fate of, 293–295
One ship companies, 202, 355
Open registries, 309–10
Operation standards, 252–254
Out turn clauses, 131

Package or unit limitation, 96, 107, 120, 122
Package Travel Directive, 151–153
Packaging, 278, 288, 289
P&I insurance, 327–328, 337–347
advance calls, 341
agents, 339, 341, 342
arrest, 354
Board of Directors, 339
China P&I Club, 340
claims handling, 341–342
claims settlement, 343
classification societies, 339, 340–341
collisions, 156–157
competition, 340
conditions and exceptions, 339–340
Contracts (Rights of Third Parties) Act 1999, 342–343
correspondents, 341
direct actions, 342–343
disputes, 343
EC law, 340
freight, demurrage and defence (FD&D) cover, 156, 343
International Group, 340–341
classification societies, 340–341
competition, 340
limits, 340
oil pollution, 340
overspill calls, 340
reinsurance, 340
International Ship & Port Facility Security (ISPS) Code, 237
legal representation, 343–347
letters of guarantee, 156–157
letters of undertaking, 344–347, 354
limitation of liability, 339, 340
managers' agents, 339, 341, 342
members, 339
oil pollution, 340
overspill calls, 340
P&I Clubs, 337
passengers, 150
pay to be paid, 342–343
reinsurance, 340

P&I insurance—*continued*
risks covered, 338
salvage, 170
SCOPIC (Special Compensation P&I Clubs) Clause, 172–175
statutory obligations, compliance with, 339
technical advice and support, 342
underwriting, 341–342
wreck removal, 189–190
Paramount clause, 49–51
Partial loss, 331–332
Particular average, 334, 336
Particularly Sensitive Sea Areas (PSSAs), 322
Particulars of claim 355–356
Passengers. *See* Athens Convention relating to Carriage of Passengers and their Luggage by Sea 1974; Carriage of passengers
Passing of risk and property in goods
c.i.f. contracts, 130
contractual exceptions, 131
D terms, 130
delivery, delay in, 131
exceptions to rule, 131–132
*ex works* contracts, 129–130
f.o.b. contracts, 130
intention, 132
international trade, 129–132
legal exceptions, 131–132
out turn clauses, 131
performance, 136–137
quality or condition, 131
shipment, risk passes on or as from, 129–130
shipment terms, 130
title to sue, 130
Passengers. *See* Carriage of passengers
Pay to be paid, 340
Performance of the contract
breach, 133
conditions, 133
conditions,
breach, 133
contract, conditions by, 133–134
definition, 133–134
descriptions, 134, 135
law, conditions by, 134–135
rejection, 135
samples, 134–135
satisfactory quality, 134
contractual goods, definition of, 133–135
delivery, 132, 135–136
documentary duties, 132, 137–143
f.o.b. contracts, 136
Incoterms, 137
intermediate or innominate terms, 133
international trade, 132–143
letters of credit, 136–137
load and stow cargo, duty to, 136
passing of risk, 136–137
physical delivery, 132, 135–136
reasonableness of contract of carriage, 136–137
Performance of the contract—*continued*
rejection, 146
sellers,
documentary duties, 137–143
physical duties, 133–137
technical rejections, 135
tender of documents, 132
terms, 133–135
transport arrangements, duty to make, 136–137
warranties, 133, 135
Perils of the sea, 332
Personal injury. *See* Death and personal injury
Pilotage, 196–201
charges, 197
coastal pilotage, 196
compulsory pilotage, 196–197, 199, 201
contract, 198
damages for negligence, 196–197, 198
deep sea pilotage, 196
definition of pilot, 196
directions, 197
harbour authorities, 197, 198–200
liability for faults of ships, 198–201
licensing, 197, 199
limitation of liability, 200, 204
negligence, 196–197, 198–199
pilots, liability of, 198
Port Maritime Safety Code, 197
shipowners' vicarious liability, 200–201
training, 197
vicarious liability, 198–201
voluntary pilotage, 196, 198–199
Place of harmful event, 16–19
Place of performance, 14–17
Places of refuge
CMI Working Group, 196
environmental damage, 196
European Union, 196
IMO Guidelines, 195–196
ports and harbours, 195–196
salvage, 176
wreck removal, 192
Pollution. *See* Marine pollution from shipping activities; Oil pollution
Ports and harbours, 193–196. *See also* International Ship & Port Facility Security (ISPS) Code
claims by port authorities, 194
coastal waters, 305–306
foreign ships, 305–306
friendship and navigation treaties, 306
GATT, 306
General Lighthouse Authorities, 193
Law of the Sea Convention 1982, 306
lights, lighthouses and buoys, 193
limitation of liability, 194, 204
navigation, safety of, 193
nomination of ports, 79
pilotage, 197, 198–200
places of refuge, 195–196

Ports and harbours—*continued*
pollution, port state control and, 252, 253
Port Safety Code, 193
port safety management, 193–194
port state control, 194–195, 240, 252, 253
safe ports, 61–63
state aid, 389–390, 397
wrecks, raising, 194
Possessory liens, 88–89, 175, 361
Predatory pricing, 384
Price-fixing, 374, 375, 376, 378, 384, 395
Priority, 221–222, 359, 360–364
Privity of contract, 97–98, 102
Product market, identification of relevant, 382–383, 393, 396–397
Prompt release procedures under Article 292 of Law of the Sea Convention
applications for release, 323–324
detention, 323–326
Exclusive Economic Zones, 323
fishing vessels, 324–325
forfeiture of ships, 325–326
International Tribunal for the Law of the Sea, 324–325
prosecutions, 323
security for release, 323
territorial sea, 323
Proof of carriers' breach, cargo claims and
bailment, 114
bills of lading, 115–119
charterparties, terms in, 116–117
charterparty bills of lading, 117–118
Hague-Visby Rules, 118, 119
terms of carriage contracts, 114–20
third parties, transfer to, 118
Proof of loss, cargo claims and
apparent order and condition, 109–113
bills of lading, 109–113
clausing, 111
estoppel, 111
evidence, 110–111, 122
Hague Rules, 111
Hague-Visby Rules, 109, 110–114
letters of indemnity, 112–113
loading marks, 109–110
notice of loss at discharge, 109
presumption, 109–110
third party claims, 110–111
weight and quantity unknown clauses, 111–114
Proper law, 35, 41
Protection and indemnity. *See* P&I insurance
Proximate cause, 330
PSSAs (Particularly Sensitive Sea Areas), 322
Public international law, 297–326
academic writings, 301
custom, 299–300
general principles of international law, 301
International Maritime Organization (IMO) and conventions, 312–323
Public international law—*continued*
international organisations,
examples, 297
legal personality of, 297
judicial decisions, 301
Law of the Sea Convention Article 292 prompt release procedures, 323–326
maritime zones, 301–312
sources of international law, 298–301
states, legal personality of, 297
subjects of international law, shipping interests as, 297–298
treaties and conventions, 297–298, 300–301, 312–323

Radar, collision and, 157
Radioactive substances
Brussels Convention 1963, 290
high seas, 311
International Convention on Civil Liability in the field of Maritime Carriage of Nuclear Materials (NUCLEAR) 1971, 290
Joint Protocol to Vienna and Paris Convention, 290
limitation of liability, 290
nuclear ships, liability for, 290
Paris Convention 1960, 290
Vienna Convention, Protocol to, 290
waste, 291
Reachable on arrival, 81–82
Reasonable despatch, charterparties and, 59
Receivers, definition of, 288
Recognition and enforcement of judgments, 267, 273–275, 284–285
Recycling ships, 293–295
Refuge, places of. *See* Places of refuge
Registration of ships
high seas, 309–10
open registries, 309–310
oil pollution, 274
Reinsurance, 33, 35, 43, 240
Rejection, 143–146
bank, rejection of documents by, 145–146
buyers' remedies, 143–146
c.i.f. contracts, 143
cure a defective tender, sellers' right to, 146
delivery,
documentary, 143
evidence of physical performance, 144
physical, 143
documents, acceptance of, 144–145
documents, rejection of, 143–145
documentary tender in cash against documents transactions, curing, 146
estoppel, 144, 145
evidence,
physical performance, of, 144
physical repudiatory breach, as evidence of, 144–145
f.o.b. contracts, 143

Rejection—*continued*
goods, rejection of, 144–145
letters of credit, rejection by bank of, 145–146
physical delivery and documentary duties, independence of, 143–144
physical performance, curing, 146
repudiatory breach, 144–145
sellers' physical duties, 144
termination of contracts, 143
Related actions, 12–13
Relevant market, identification of, 381–383, 393–393, 396–397
Remedies for breach of charterparties
affirmation, 55, 59
cancellation, 56–58
conditions, 56–57, 59
damages, 55–56
election to terminate, 58–59
fraudulent misrepresentation, 55–56
fundamental breach, 56, 59
innominate terms, 57–59
misrepresentation, 55–56
negligence, 56
shipowners, 55–59
time charterparties, 58
warranties, 59
Repairs, 53
Repudiatory breach, 70–71, 144–145
Risk. *See* Passing of risk and property in goods
Ro ro ferries, 228
Rome Convention on Law Applicable to Contractual Obligations 1980, 32–43
agents, 35
anti-suit injunctions, 34
arbitration agreements, 34–38
bills of lading, 33–34, 35, 36–38, 41
characteristic performance, 42–43
charterparties, 36–37, 40, 41–42
choice of law, 35–41
close connection, 41–43
Contracts (Applicable Law) Act 1990, 33
EC Jurisdiction Regulation, 33–34
exclusions, 34
freedom of choice, 35–39
Giuliano and Lagarde Report, 33
governing law, 32–43
habitual residence, 37
Hague-Visby Rules, 39–41, 107–108
Hamburg Rules, mandatory application of, 41
implied choice of law, 37
insurance contracts, 35
interpretation, 33
jurisdiction agreements, 34
limits on party choice, 39–41
mandatory rules, 39–41
negotiable instruments, 34
principal place of business, 42
proper law, 35, 41
reinsurance contracts, 33, 35, 43
Rome Convention on Law Applicable to Contractual Obligations 1980—*continued*
Rome II Regulation 864/2007, 32, 33
scope, 33–35
Sharia law, 38–39
treaties as mandatory law, 41
variation of governing law, 39

Safe ports
arrived ship, 80
charterparties, 61–63
due diligence, 61–62
illegitimate last voyage, 63
time charterparties, 62–63
voyage charterparties, 63
warranties, 62–63
weather, 61–62
Safety at sea. *See* SOLAS
Safety Management Certificates (SMC), 229
Salvage, 161–176
apportionment of rewards, 170
arrest, 161, 360, 361
best endeavours, 173
breach of contract, 172
Civil Liability Convention (CLC)/Fund Convention, 260
coastal state, control of operation by, 175–176
contracts, 162, 171–175
criminal liability for environmental damage, 176
danger,
deliberate creation of, 168
meaning of, 163–164
towage, 186
demise charters, 170
dismissal of salvors, 172
EC Jurisdiction Regulation, 14, 19
EC law,
places of refuge, provision of, 176
Ship Source Pollution Directive, 176
environment, damage to, 162, 164, 166–168, 170, 171–176
financial security, 169–170
general average, 336
government or public services, 168–169
*in rem* claims, 363
inland waters, 163
International Group of P&I Clubs and International Salvage Union, code of practice on security between, 170
liens, 161, 169
limitation of liability, 170, 207, 208, 209–211, 213
Lloyd's Open Form (LOF), 162, 172–175
Lloyd's Standard and Arbitration Clauses (LASA), 172
no cure no pay principle, 162, 172–175
retrospectivity, 173
rewards, 173–175

Salvage—*continued*
Lloyd's Open Form (LOF)—*continued*
SCOPIC (Special Compensation P&I Clubs) Clause, 172–175
towage, 186
marine pollution, 162, 164, 166–168, 170, 171–176
maritime liens, 169, 363
masters,
agents, as, 173
binding authority to sign contracts of, 171
no cure no pay principle, 162, 166, 172–175
nuclear ships, 211
objects of salvage, 163
possessory liens, 169
public law issues, 175
public policy, 161, 168
redelivery obligation when property is at place of safety, 165, 173, 187
refuge, places of, 176
responder immunity, 176
rewards, 161–162, 165–171, 173–175, 185–187, 210
Salvage Convention 1989, 162–172, 175–176, 186–187, 363
saving lives, rewards for, 165–166
Ship Source Pollution Directive, 176
shipowners, 162
SOSREP (Secretary of State's Representative), 176
special compensation for environmental damage, 166–175, 187, 210, 336, 363
time charters, 170
time limit, 170
towage, 177, 179, 182, 185–188
Samples, 134–135
Satisfactory quality, 134
SCOPIC (Special Compensation P&I Clubs) Clause, 172–175
Scrapping, 293–295
Scuttling, 295
Seabed, 302, 305
Sea-going ships, limitation of liability and, 205–206
Sea lanes, 321–322
Sea waybills, 100–101
Seaworthiness
act, neglect or fault of master, mariner, pilot or servants, 53
burden of proof, 53
cargo claims, 54–55
charterparties, 51–55
crew, training of, 52
deviation, 60
due diligence, 52–53, 119
exceptions, 53–54
general average, 335
Hague Rules, 52–54, 230
Hague-Visby Rules, 52–54, 119–120, 230
Hamburg Rules, 54, 230
implied obligation, 51–52
Seaworthiness—*continued*
insurance, 231, 330
International Safety Management (ISM) Code, 230, 231
lashing equipment, 119–120
maintenance, 53
navigation or management of vessel, neglect in, 53–54
repairs, 53
standard form charterparties, 51, 53–55
subjective test, 52
time limits, 54
towage, 183, 184
Self-regulation of maritime industry, 373
Sellers. *See* Documentary duties of sellers
Service
arrest, 357
Bunker Oil Pollution Convention 2001, 273
Civil Procedure Rules, 23
claim forms, 273, 355
contract claims, 23
jurisdiction, 23–25
outside the jurisdiction, 24–25
permission, 23–24
Sharia law, 38–39
Ship Source Pollution Directive, 176, 253–254, 275–276, 307–308
Shipbrokers, 45, 46–47
Shipbuilders, oil pollution and, 260
Shipment terms, international commercial sales on, 125–129
confirmation notes, 126
conflict between clauses, 126
D terms (destination/arrival or delivered contracts), 125
E terms or ex works contracts, 125
formation of contracts, 126
hierarchy clauses in contracts, 126
Incoterms, incorporation of, 126–127
intention, 126
negotiated terms prevailing over standard terms, 126
standard forms, terms in, 126–127
trade associations, 126–127
Shipowners
charterparties, breach of, 55–59
Civil Liability Convention (CLC)/Fund Convention, 257
definition, 257
Hazardous and Noxious Substances Convention (HNS), liability under, 280
limitation of liability, 202–205, 211–213
oil pollution, 274
pilotage, 200–201
salvage, 162
STCW Convention 1975, 239
vicarious liability, 200–201
Shipper's orders bills, 99
Shipping pools, 376–380, 395
Ship's agents, 204

Ships, definition of
arrest, 353–354
Bunker Oil Pollution Convention 2001, 270
Civil Liability Convention (CLC)/Fund Convention, 257
Hazardous and Noxious Substances Convention (HNS), 278
Ship's delivery orders, 101–102
Sister ships, arrest of, 353
SOLAS, 227–228
amendments, 227–228
criminal liability, 253
International Maritime Organization (IMO), 227–228
International Safety Management (ISM) Code, 228
International Ship & Port Facility Security (ISPS) Code, 232, 234–235
pollution, 253
ship surveys, 227
SOSREP (Secretary of State's Representative), 176
Sources of international law, 298–301
Sovereignty. *See* State sovereignty
Special compensation
limitation of liability, 210
salvage, 166–175, 187, 210, 336
towage, 187
Special drawing rights (SDRs)
Athens Convention 1974, 148–150
cargo claims and bills of lading, 122
Civil Liability Convention (CLC)/Fund Convention, 261
limitation of liability, 122, 216–218, 220–221, 261
passengers, 148–150, 217–218
Standard forms
charterparties, 45–46, 51, 53–55, 88
conflict between clauses, 126
documentary duties of sellers, 137–138
hire, 76
Incoterms, 127
liens, 88
negotiated terms prevailing over standard terms, 126
seaworthiness, 51, 53–55
shipbrokers, 46
shipment terms, international commercial sales on, 126–127
time charterparties, 76, 235
towage, 177, 179–185
trade associations, 126
wreck removal, 190
Standing. *See* Title to sue, cargo claims and
State aid, 371, 387–390, 397
distortion of competition and intra-community trade, 388
exemptions, 388–389
forms of aid, 388
ports sector, 389–390, 397
social character, aid having a, 388, 397
State sovereignty
coastal states, 302, 303, 306–308
continental shelf, 304–305
custom, 299–300
Exclusive Economic Zones (EEZs), 306, 308–312
Statements of truth, 355–356
States, legal personality of, 297
Stay of proceedings
arbitration clauses, 4
EC Jurisdiction Regulation, 5–6
exclusive jurisdiction agreements, 9, 10–12
*forum non conveniens*, 24–25
jurisdiction agreements, 25–26
limitation of liability, 225
multiple proceedings, 9, 10–12
related actions, 12
tonnage limitation, 28
STCW Convention 1975, 236–240
aims, 236–237
certification, 237–239
crew coordination, 238
documentation, 237, 239
evidence of compliance, 239
familiarisation with ship and safety matters, 238
flag administration, duties of, 237, 239–240
International Maritime Organization (IMO), 236, 239
ISM Code, 237, 240
language, 238
manning, 238
medical examinations, 238
non-compliance and legal consequences, 240
port state control, 240
quality standards system, 239–240
record-keeping, 238
rest periods, 238
safety training, 239
shipowners, duties of, 237–239
third parties, delegation to, 239
white list, 239
Stevedores, limitation of liability of, 204
Stowaways, 235
Strict liability
Bunker Oil Pollution Convention 2001, 268–269, 272
Civil Liability Convention (CLC)/Fund Convention, 257–258, 269
Hazardous and Noxious Substances Convention (HNS), 276–277, 280–281
hazardous wastes, liability arising from, 293
oil pollution, 254
Sub-freight, 90–91
Subject to average, 331
Subjects of international law, shipping interests as, 297–298
Substitutability, 383, 392, 397
Suppression of Unlawful Acts against Safety of Navigation Convention 1988, protocol to, 311–312
Surveys, 156, 227, 246–249

Tanker Management Self Assessment (TMSA), 232
Terms
  cargo claims and bills of lading, 120–121
  conditions, 56–57, 59, 133–134
  charterparties, 45
  intermediate or innominate terms, 57–59, 133
  shipment terms, international commercial sales on, 125–129
  towage, 178–179
  warranties, 62–63, 133, 135, 189, 330
Territorial sea
  arrest, 357
  baselines, 302–303
  breadth, 302–303
  Bunker Oil Pollution Convention 2001, 270
  Civil Liability Convention (CLC)/Fund Convention, 255–256, 263–264
  coastal state sovereignty, 302, 303, 306–308
  construction, design, manning and equipment of ships, rules on, 307
  definition, 302
  foreign ships, 306–307
  Hazardous and Noxious Substances Convention (HNS), 279
  innocent passage, right of, 302, 303, 306–308
  internal waters, 302
  Law of the Sea Convention 1982, 302–303, 306–308
  non-innocent passage, examples of, 307
  pollution, 253–256, 263–264, 270
  prompt release procedures, 323
  Ship Source Pollution Directive, 307–308
  stopping and anchoring, 306
Terrorism, 232, 236, 312
Third party proceedings, EC Judgments Convention and, 20–21
Time charterparties, 69–78
  advance hire, 73
  breach, 58
  cancellation, 58, 69
  clause paramount, 50
  damages, measure of, 70–72
  definition, 45
  demise charters, definition of, 45
  deviation, 60
  duration of charter, 69–73
  early redelivery, 70–71
  forfeiture, relief from, 74–75
  frustration, 66
  hire, 69, 73–78
  illegitimate last voyage, 72
  instructions, 69, 72
  International Ship & Port Facility Security (ISPS) Code, 235
  late redelivery, 71–73
  legitimate last voyage, 73
  liens, 88, 90
  limitation of liability, 203, 213
  off hire, 70, 76–77
Time charterparties—*continued*
  redelivery, 69–73
  repudiatory breach, 70–71
  safe ports, 62–63
  salvage, 170
  standard forms, 76, 235
  sub-freight, 90
  use of ship, duration of, 69–73
  war, 70–71
  withdrawal for non–payment, 75–76, 78
Timing at beginning of charterparties, 66–68
Title to sue, cargo claims and
  bailment, 95
  bearer bills, 98–99, 100
  benefit of another, claiming for the, 103
  bills of lading, 93, 95–104, 142
  *Brandt v Liverpool* contract, 102–103, 104
  Carriage of Goods by Sea Act 1992, 98–102
  charterers, 96–97
  consignee who is not shipowner, bills of lading made out to named, 99
  contract, 95–98
  Contracts (Rights of Third Parties) Act 1999, 97–98
  f.o.b. contracts, 103–104
  Hague-Visby Rules, 96
  lawful holders of transferable bills, 98
  package limitation, 96
  passing of risk and property in goods, 130
  privity of contract, 97–98, 102
  sea waybills, 100–101
  shippers, 96–97
  shipper's order bills, 99
  ship's delivery orders, 101–102
  straight or non-transferable bills of lading, 100–101
  tort, 95–96
  transfer of bills, 99–101
Tonnage limitation, 28–30, 216–217
  conflict of laws, 28–30
  forum shopping, 28
  jurisdiction, 1–2, 29
  Limitation of Liability Convention 1957, 28–29
  Limitation of Liability Convention 1976, 28, 30
  multiple parties, 29
  stay of proceedings, 29
  Tonnage Convention, 216
  treaties and conventions, 1–2, 216
Tort, delict or quasi-delict, 14, 16–19, 20, 46, 95–96, 207
Towage, 177–189
  arrest, 185
  bailment, 188
  best endeavours, 178
  care and skill, 178, 188
  carriage of goods by sea, 188
  collisions, 178, 188–189
  contract, 177–187
  damages, 182

Towage—*continued*
danger, existence of, 186
definition, 177, 181
delay payments, 185
due diligence, 185
exclusions of liability, 179, 182
fitness of tugs, 178
frustration, 179
identity of parties, 179
implied duties, 178–179
implied terms and conditions, 178
indemnity clauses, 179–180, 182, 183
joint and several liability, 189
knock for knock liability, 183–184
liens, 184
limitation of liability, 188
Lloyd's Open Form, 186
misrepresentation, 179
negligence, 182, 183
pollution, 177, 187, 188
redelivery at place of safety, 187
remedies, 179
remuneration, 177
salvage, 177, 179, 182, 185–188
seaworthiness, 183, 184
special compensation, environmental damage and, 187
standard forms, 177, 179–185
third parties, liability to, 177
TOWCON, 183, 184, 185
TOWHIRE 1985, 182–184, 185
tow-worthiness, 183, 184
UK Standing Towing Conditions 1986 (UKSTC), 180–183
usage, 177
warranty of authority clause, 180
Trade associations, 126–127
Traffic Separation Schemes, 159–160, 321–322
Tramp shipping, 378–379, 395, 397–398
Treaties and conventions. *See also* International Maritime Organization (IMO) and conventions; Particular conventions (e.g. Rome Convention on Law Applicable to Contractual Obligations 1980)
customary law, 300–301
definition, 300
EC Jurisdiction Regulation, 21–23
friendship and navigation treaties, 306
mandatory law, as, 41
public international law, 297–298, 300–301, 312–323
Ship Source Pollution Directive, 275
tonnage limitation, 1–2
Vienna Convention on the Law of Treaties, 317–318, 321
wreck removal, 190–193

UK Standing Towing Conditions 1986 (UKSTC), 180–183
UNCLOS. *See* Law of the Sea Convention
Uniform Customs and Practice for Document Credit (UCP) 600 105–106, 136–147,
United States
Carriage of Goods by Sea Act 1936, 48–50
collisions, 160
clause paramount, 49–50
Hague Rules, 48–49
innocent cargo rule, 160
Mid-Atlantic Settlement, 151
passengers, 151
punitive damages, 151
Unseaworthiness. *See* Seaworthiness
Utmost good faith, marine insurance and, 329

Vicarious liability, 198–201
Vienna Convention on the Law of Treaties, 317–318, 321
Visit ships, right to, 310–311
Voyage charterparties, 78–88
Asbatankvoy, 46
cesser clauses, 91
deductions from freight, 80
definition, 45
delay, 79
delivery, 79–80
demurrage, 79, 86–88, 91
freight, 78–80
frustration, 79
laytime, 79, 80–86
liens, 88, 91
limitation of liability, 203, 213
nomination of ports, 79
safe ports, 63

War, hostilities or civil war
charterparties, breach of, 58
frustration of charterparties, 64
Hazardous and Noxious Substances Convention (HNS), 281
IOPC Fund, 265
oil pollution, 284
time charterparties, 75–76, 78
Warranties
damages, 133
insurance, 330
performance, 133, 135
safe ports, 62–63
towage, 189
Warsaw Convention 1929, 214
Waste, 276. *See also* Hazardous wastes, liability arising from
Weapons of mass destruction, carriage of, 311
Weather working days, 85
Weight and quantity unknown clauses, 111–114
Whether in berth or not, 82
Wildlife, beaches and ecosystems, effect of oil on, 256
Working days, 85
Wreck removal, 189–193
certificates of financial responsibility, 192
designated wrecks, 192

Wreck removal—*continued*
Exclusive Economic Zones (EEZs), 190–191
expenses, reimbursement of, 191–192
hazardous wastes, liability arising from, 295
historic wrecks, 192–193
insurance, 189–190
Law of the Sea Convention 1982, 190–191, 193
limitation of liability, 209
military wrecks, 192
Nairobi Wreck Removal Convention 2007, 190–192
oil pollution, 190–191
P&I insurance, 189–190

Wreck removal—*continued*
Places of Refuge, 192
ports and harbours, 194
sale of ships, 189–190
standard forms, 190
title to wrecks, 192
treaties and conventions, 190–193
UNESCO Convention on the Protection of Underwater Cultural Heritage 2001, 193
Wreck Removal Orders, 190
Wrongful arrest, damages for, 359

York-Antwerp Rules, 334–335, 337